Springer Texts in Business and Economics

Springer Texts in Business and Economics (STBE) delivers high-quality instructional content for undergraduates and graduates in all areas of Business/Management Science and Economics. The series is comprised of self-contained books with a broad and comprehensive coverage that are suitable for class as well as for individual self-study. All texts are authored by established experts in their fields and offer a solid methodological background, often accompanied by problems and exercises.

Yuxing Yan

Introduction to FinTech using Excel

In an R-assisted Learning Environment

Springer

Yuxing Yan
Sinica Education
Los Angeles, NY, USA

ISSN 2192-4333 ISSN 2192-4341 (electronic)
Springer Texts in Business and Economics
ISBN 978-3-031-89778-8 ISBN 978-3-031-89779-5 (eBook)
https://doi.org/10.1007/978-3-031-89779-5

This Springer imprint is published by the registered company Springer Nature Switzerland AG
The registered company address is: Gewerbestrasse 11, 6330 Cham, Switzerland

To Hofstra University

Preface

FinTech (Financial Technology) has disrupted our financial system in many ways. In other words, FinTech has contributed heavily in many areas once dominated by traditional finance, such as borrowing and lending, payment systems, auditing, distributed ledgers, seamless transfer of money, and a system that does not need trust. For a FinTech major, the related topics (courses) could be Introduction to Blockchain and its Applications, Cryptocurrency, Machine Learning in Finance, and Robo-advising. Readers and students must learn one programming language to understand those more advanced topics (courses).

On the other hand, traditional finance covers Corporate Finance, Portfolio Theory, Financial Modeling using Excel, and Options and Futures. For those courses, Excel is used as a computational tool. There is no doubt that a considerable barrier exists between those two distinct areas: FinTech and traditional finance. In a sense, students and readers need a course to help them cross this barrier. In other words, they need a bridge to link those two distinct areas. This book serves this very need.

Like taking our traditional finance courses, the computational tool for this book (course) is Excel. Thus, most finance, accounting, and other business school students will feel confident since they know Excel well; it has frequently been used in their traditional finance courses. For example, students can use Excel's "Random Number Generations" to generate distributed ledgers. They can use Excel to code and decode a given phrase for encryption by applying the letter-shifting scheme. For basic blockchain concepts, students can use Excel to form their blockchains using only numbers, numbers and letters, and ASCII. The Excel `mod ()` function could be used to verify whether a given pair of (`x, y`) values is on the Elliptic Curve (used for Cryptography).

However, Excel is insufficient since hands-on experience is vital to understanding many FinTech concepts. For example, Excel could not handle big numbers of `x`, `y`, and `p`(prime numbers). When discussing public and private keys, it is a good idea for students to generate them themselves. In addition, readers and students would understand those concepts better after using a private key to develop a public key. Another example is the application of the Merkle Tree to combine 100 transactions into a block by generating and merging their hashes. Students who can develop a QR code for a website or public key will appreciate this method better. To help students do those operations easily, we have generated nearly 100 hidden functions written in R. All functions are self-explanatory, i.e., typing a function's name will show its usage and a few examples. In the following sections, we will explain how the combination of Excel and R will help students immensely in understanding FinTech.

R Installation

Readers and students must install R before using it. Since R is open-source software, it is free, and anyone can download and install it. After going to https://r-project.org, click "CRAN" on the left-hand side, choose a near mirror (server location), and download the appropriate software (for Mac or PC). Users can generate a desktop shortcut to make launching R a little easier. To help new users, we have one optional chapter: Chapter 16: *R Installation and Basics*, which will be discussed later in this preface.

Just Two Lines of R Code to Remember or Copy

For this book (course), readers only need to know two lines of R commands. After launching R, issue the following line to access the first week's materials.

```
source("http://datayyy.com/i2ft/week1.txt")
```

This is the first line that students and potential instructors who adopt this book should know. For Week 2, `week1.txt` will be replaced by `week2.txt`. Later in this preface, the contents will be shown after issuing the above line. The second command line is related to R package installation.

```
install.packages("qrcode").
```

The R package `qrcode` will be installed using the above code after choosing a nearby location (server). For other packages, `qrcode` will be replaced with an appropriate name. Readers and students can save those two lines on their computers. Later, they copy and paste those lines to their R Console.

In an R-assisted Learning Environment

Students and readers can use this book *In an R-assisted Learning Environment* to learn FinTech more efficiently. In simple words, there are many more interesting materials beyond this book. After launching R, issue one of the following lines of

R code for a 15-week course. Again, readers and students can use the copy-and-paste method.

```
source("http://datayyy.com/i2ft/week1.txt")
source("http://datayyy.com/i2ft/week2.txt")
...
source("http://datayyy.com/i2ft/week14.txt")
source("http://datayyy.com/i2ft/week15.txt")
```

For example, the following menu would appear after issuing the first line above.

```
*-------------------------------------------------------------------*
* Introduction to FinTech using Excel                        2025   *
*        (in an R-assisted learning environment)                    *
*-------------------------------------------------------------------*
*  .c1 Introduction & Excel Basics          .c16 R basics(optional) *
*-------------------------------------------------------------------*
* >.c1       # go to chapter 1                                      *
* >.uu       # go to utility submenu                                *
* >.ft       # same as .fintech                                     *
*-------------------------------------------------------------------*
```

Fig. 1 The menu for Week 1

We will get the following menu for the first chapter after typing `.chapter1`.

```
> .chapter1
function(i=0){
" i  Chapter 1: Introduction/Excel  i  Excel Basics                    i  Excel Basics
  -  ----------------------------- --  ------------------------------ --  ---------------------
  1  Self-introduction             21  Excel:2-dimensional spreadsheet 41  formulatext()
  2  Syllabus                      22  =A1 What does it mean?          42  Copy: as values
  3     : Description of the course 23 +, -, /, and *                  43      : as formula
  4     : textbook                 24  Format our cell                 44      : better way to copy formula
  5     : about this book          25  count() vs. counta() functions  45      : note
  6     : Excel is the main tool   26  name a set of data              46  mod() function
  7     : R-assisted environment   27  isnumber()                      47  vlookup()
  8     : Time and location        28  true or false                   48  vlookup(): example #2
  9     : Hands-on approach        29  if()                            49  relative vs. absolute addresses
 10  R  : no R knowledge is needed 30  String: variable                50            : example PVIF
 11     : R installation           31         : istext()               51  SUBSTITUTE() function
 12     : (alternatively) RStudio  32         : len()                  52  rename your spreadsheet
 13     : Launch and quit R        33         : left()                 53  copy your spreadsheet
 14     : R is case-sensitive      34         : right()                54  Macro: why copy others' macro/VBA?
 15     : One line for this course 35         : right(left())          55       : how
 16     : Chapter 16 (optional)    36         : concatenate()          56       : Example of VBA
 17  FinTech vs. programming       37         : text to columns        57       : Example of Macro
 18  After this course (book)      38         : text to number         58       : How to record your own micro?
 19  Videos                        39         : alignment              59       : more on macro
 20  Links                         40         : number to text         60       : more on VBA

 Example #1:>.c1    # see the above list
 Example #2:>.c1()  # the same as the above
 Example #3:>.c1(1) # see the first explanation
```

Fig. 2 The contents of Chapter 1

Many Utility Functions

The main menu has a `.uu` entry used for utility functions. After typing `.uu`, we get the following result for the first week. Over the semester, more utility functions might be added to the menu.

```
> .uu
function(){
"
 *-----------------------------------------*
 * Utilities              -- short-cut -   *
 *-----------------------------------------*
 * .allChapters             .all           *
 * .calendar                .cal           *
 * .dictionary              .dict          *
 * .getdata                . gd            *
 * .inClassEx               .ice           *
 * .macUsers                .mac           *
 * .searchExcelFiles        .sef           *
 * .searchFigures           .fig           *
 * .searchHiddenFunctions   .sf            *
 * .watchVideos             .v2            *
 * .videos                  .v             *
 *-----------------------------------------*
 * >.ice               # see a list of ice *
 * >.uu                # back to utilities *
 * >.ft                # back to main menu *
 *-----------------------------------------*
```

Fig. 3 The utility submenu

The first item from the above menu is `.allChapter`, abbreviated as `.all`. After typing `.all`, we will see the following menu.

```
> .all
function(i=0){
"
 *------------------------------------------------------------*
 * Introduction to FinTech using Excel        by Dr. Yan 2025 *
 *     [in an R-assisted Learning Environment]                *
 *------------------------------------------------------------*
 *   .c1  Introduction and Excel Basics                       *
 *   .c2  Blockchain       1: (Numbers & alphanumeric cases)  *
 *   .c3                   2: (ASCII and Sha256)              *
 *   .c4  Ledger and distributed ledger                       *
 *   .c5  Cryptography     1: and public/private keys         *
 *   .c6                   2: Advanced                        *
 *   .c7  Cryptocurrency and Ganache                          *
 *   .c8                   2: crypto markets, risk, and tradeoff *
 *   .c9  Blockchain applications with Monte Carlo Simulations *
 * -----------------------------------------------------------*
 *        Machine Learning in finance                         *
 * .c10                 1: Unsupervised Learning              *
 * .c11                 2: Supervised Learning: classification etc. *
 * .c12                                     : regressions     *
 * .c13                 3: Neural Network and deep learning   *
 * .c14   Smart Contracts (optional)                          *
 * -----------------------------------------------------------*
 * .c15   Term projects                                       *
 * .c16   R basics     (optional)                             *
 * .c17   Excel Macro (optional)                              *
 * .c18   Excel VBA    (optional)                             *
 * -----------------------------------------------------------*
```

Fig. 4 The titles of all chapters

`.searchWebs()` function

We have collected over several hundred websites students and instructors can use. To make searching and loading websites more efficient, we have designed a utility function, `.searchWebs()`, abbreviated as `.sw()`. Assuming that we are interested in the website that generates a hash using the Sha256 method, we use "`sha256`" as our keyword, shown below.

```
> .searchWebs('sha256')
  ID            NAME                                                    WEBSITE
 611 hashing website https://passwordsgenerator.net/sha256-hash-generator/
```

Fig. 5 The .searchWebs function with 'sha256' as an input

Since the website's ID is `611`, we call the function the second time by entering `611`. The underlying software will launch that website conveniently. Readers can use the upper arrow key to recall the previous command and the left and right arrow keys to move the cursor within the command line to modify it.

Many Hidden Functions

We have written many hidden functions to help readers and students understand basic concepts such as public and private keys, sha256, and cryptography. The word "hidden" indicates that those functions start with a dot (.). Thus, they are hidden from us. We can use the `.searchHiddenFunctions()` function to search for related functions. There are two ways to use this function: by chapter or keywords. We input an integer to find all the functions for a given chapter. Assume that we are interested in functions related to Chapter 5.

```
> .searchHiddenFunctions(5)
  CHAPTER                              NAME                        SHORTCUT
        5 install.packages('openssl')
        5 .encode_6letters              .en6
        5 .decode_6letters              .de6
        5 .positionKeyword              .pkw
        5 .keywordEncode                .en2
        5 .keywordDecode                .de2
        5  install.packages('openssl')
        5 .generatePublicPrivateKeys    .ppkeys   # need 'openssl'
        5 .encodeWithPublicKey          .en7      # need 'openssl'
        5 .decodeWithPriateKey          .de7      # need 'openssl'
        5 .listOfPublicPrivateKeys      .listpp
        5 .letterFrequency              .lf
>
```

Fig. 6 The hidden functions related to Chapter 5

The second way is to use a keyword, as shown below. The `.sf()` is a short-cut name.

```
> .sf("public")
  CHAPTER                        NAME                       SHORTCUT
        5 .generatePublicPrivateKeys  .ppkeys  # need 'openssl'
        5 .encodeWithPublicKey        .en7     # need 'openssl'
        5 .listOfPublicPrivateKeys    .listpp
        5 .generatePublicPrivateKeys  .ppkeys  # need 'openssl'
        6 .encodeWithPublicKey        .en7     # need 'openssl'
        7 .secondWayPublicPrivateKeys .ppkeys2 # need 'openssl'
```

Fig. 7 The search function with "public" as an input

The following sections will give more details about a few hidden functions.

.generatePublicPrivateKeys() function

A deep understanding of public and private key concepts will give readers and students a good start. If students can generate a few pairs of public and private keys themselves, they will have first-hand experience. The shortcut to the above-hidden function is `.ppkeys()`. One example is shown below.

```
> .ppkeys()
Linking to: OpenSSL 3.3.0 9 Apr 2024
Public key in PEM format:
 -----BEGIN PUBLIC KEY-----
MIIBIjANBgkqhkiG9w0BAQEFAAOCAQ8AMIIBCgKCAQEA1ZTrkyFt41We/rdpPwyQ
7MZz7qAfACZ2DRqgomwMQbYYOza1DG0UbNuj49rqT14+4dFjs7u7cZxuBQ9DlyrR
anImbz5EmdhtY8Z6/jcmKUB4h9esDFVKWYLPVLEV9XN6hzOqVHfo3VQ38+AEipns
F/a9oUd5wV9N+QzV4fsrwIF9CLGw8y3KdxI6Yb9lXlitARFk+iir4XHA1Eso3+7k
bA57kEYhflIjmVXNMlVswzVDaj87nxCZm4FiUip2lX3RzaPhOMXqZkeoZlZSs1fN
cLaIk2990jHkJPyjWzDPudfoW+r60DPh6I22eUkZ0D+3LCvWIeglZTdhepIskLnP
aQIDAQAB
-----END PUBLIC KEY-----
```

Fig. 8 One example of a public key (from the.ppkeys function)

The corresponding private key is shown below.

```
Private key in PEM format:
 -----BEGIN PRIVATE KEY-----
MIIEvwIBADANBgkqhkiG9w0BAQEFAASCBKkwggSlAgEAAoIBAQDVlOuTIW3jVZ7+
t2k/DJDsxnPuoB8AJnYNGqCibAxBthg7NrUMbRRs26Pj2upPXj7hOWOzu7txnG4F
DOOXKtFqciZvPkSZ2G1jxnr+NyYpQHiH16wMVUpZgs9UsRX1c3qHM6pUd+jdVDfz
4ASKmewX9r2hR3nBX035DNXh+yvAgX0IsbDzLcp3Ejphv2VeWKOBEWT6KKvhcCDU
Syjf7uRsDnuQRiF+UiOZVc0yVWzDNUNqPzufEJmbgWJSKnaVfdHNo+E4xepmR6hm
VlKzV81wtoiTb33SMeQk/KNbMM+51+hb6vrQM+HojbZ5SRnQP7csK9Yh6CVlN2F6
kiyQuc9pAgMBAAECggEAKBEwYmEeksvAsIsq2NOcKncOT6FFP4t3kPzCTsYTRI6L
HCymqUabUtKfe8LZOvt0s3tLB3A7+VO9xgA3j1fOgngYorzdNLlHyDR3ZVJmO83m
7qD0mzmy4XjrOTmhY3L+9PcpyH/YNREOD/GiGHhItLQqneNhQXgGEicoxqSOcCXi
nS/rEGbJWuQR6HDYl5Z4kIXq3u48kW9T0Z/nJoP+saH5XpXYk8DpLF6D78SuVPpY
j3iiUPu7esxStYFp2JHE3adT23NgVHDZBgLl9/yHXnYSCnAJ8itgSVpkmbXQkgK8
cdMpiGLa4ndtAmgU1Zsi49Id8OyWILMpWwkVJwagWwKBgQD7pgB6y8yjfWaCQfYI
D6wpMTL8v2K86MoccSoLlNElcWjHAbVNJKMVGSf9xdBuHJKQfSC/MTaj7dOWvQIb
k6vaWENDU4dQVFCnjQVH1NmP29SST4e1+6zzGtojKQ+tfZN4UsPtpUJ7tr1nB8ow
sEmXsWOpRrYcuqPJDuYH7HBc+wKBgQDZRmeJdQ9uAcWwWMhKnDmtN6Bz2gJ2yAQe
gtj4QztfLvBlGQJEH1mvyNhMCiGw5aaM3eospVzZfAA9tp3WjoOiaU6NnfcCRNSA
YMxyQ8XfUbNh5UmAjw+RKzplNTvVH6QDVOGPVmQdN1CTiSs4gYu7PesMEhUe+LIj
/Q4eXzlP6wKBgQDAByqyibX8xAJnP6JZAGylek+oIvtboGAqWAh3kfYPFn2X7qvE
1EJGJU4pDrxAajlFXNaSTyGc8izWCCEFnigzk8qwI5tMJyrs0GXJLJlgd6w8iEfN
DOIrGMCAuCKohvzzgmTUgZk8AnSBnKYjhUKDKPAeCkGJprq5AE90mG4d5QKBgQDG
SBn0t399RODELkGa1TdNfJZRI4NcIuyfa4nWBoUIOC3qFQicYn/Wi9PYkOZuKSX1
KA+s7rvtPdx6dU1VoHlAnhmx45an22iSP8RUAsVxJ34suLJ7QBNUx75i3lHcDSQA
ZlXyGUUD5JcEDQoEZzS9i6QVP+tGeG8ZqLZZwUzsQQKBgQDazXeuiQqQS1HsT6es
ciciWQisc3ZPOcLpgz4oIGYkbnCrVBSA7MFa3q7rGTP97/ZpzESKhISxpbJ/nxsu
7VC5sXu5rcJZPl4gF7yWK9di2L94VAqvYfXD/bJgXLvT79qTKWfk1OcY6uhKiFAL
QkFp+RXygX6WgpKnjOsSFEdUBQ==
-----END PRIVATE KEY-----

   Launch your text editor and paste two keys there.
```

Fig. 9 One example of a private key (from the.ppkeys function)

The last line in the above image tells us we can paste both keys into a text editor, such as MS Word or Notepad. Public and private keys in binary format are more convenient for many follow-up operations, such as encrypting a message with a public key and decrypting a cipher text with a private key. However, viewing public and private keys in text helps new learners greatly.

Encrypt and Decrypt Using Public and Private Keys

After readers and students generate their public and private keys, they can encode text using their public key and decode the secret message using their corresponding private key. Thus, they will understand those concepts better than just a general statement. The related functions are `.encodeWithPublicKey()` and `.decodeWithPrivateKey()`. The keyword `code` can be used in `.searchHiddenFunctions()`, as shown below.

```
> .searchHiddenFunctions("code")
 CHAPTER                        NAME                        SHORTCUT
       5 .encode_6letters          .en6
       5 .decode_6letters          .de6
       5 .keywordEncode            .en2
       5 .keywordDecode            .de2
       5 .encodeWithPublicKey      .en7      # need 'openssl'
       5 .decodeWithPriateKey      .de7      # need 'openssl'
       6 install.packages('qrcode')
       6 .enigmaEncode             .enigma
       6 .encodeWithPublicKey      .en7      # need 'openssl'
       6 .decodeWithPriateKey      .de7      # need 'openssl'
       6 .qrcode                             # need 'qrcode'
       6 .deQRcode               .qrcode2 # need 'opencv'
>
```

Fig. 10 The hidden functions associated with "code"

`.sha256` function

At https://passwordsgenerator.net/sha256-hash-generator/, readers can generate a hash based on the sha256 methodology, as shown below. The phrase "`Introduction to FinTech using Excel.`" is used as an illustration. Note that we added a dot at the end of the sentence on purpose. Without this dot, we will get a completely different hash.

Fig. 11 The image of a public website generating sha256

```
SHA256 Hash of your string: [ Copy to clipboard ]

E7760065250E283697A19BEDF65713F04DEBDC051479E5246DB0AD94F2E9AC53
```

Fig. 12 One example of sha256

Our.`sha256()` function will achieve the same objective: generate a hash based on an input text, as shown below.

```
> .sha256("Introduction to FinTech using Excel.")
SHA-256 hash: E7760065250E283697A19BEDF65713F04DEBDC051479E5246DB0AD94F2E9AC53
   Launch your text editor and paste it there.
```

Fig. 13 The same output from the hidden .sha256 function

Generating Our QR code

Assume that we plan to generate a QR code for https://passwordsgenerator.net/sha256-hash-generator/. After issuing `.qrcode()`, we enter the link below.

```
> .qrcode()

 * ------------------------------------------------------------ *
 * Objective: Generate a QR code for a given account address    *
 *            public, private key or a website                  *
 *            if the R package 'qrcode' is not installed,       *
 *            install.packages('qrcode')                        *
 * ------------------------------------------------------------ *
 *   Hit the Enter Key to continue                              *

 * ------------------------------------------------------------ *
 *     A few examples are given below                           *
 * ------------------------------------------------------------ *
 *   0x997145749ff2CCA393493a9548fd8FbC37226CBd                 *
 *   https://blockstream.info                                   *
 *   https://www.r-project.org                                  *
 *   https://passwordsgenerator.net/sha256-hash-generator/      *
 *   It is a great idea to learn FinTech.                       *
 * ------------------------------------------------------------ *
 *   Copy an address, website, a key, or something below.       *
 *   Then hit the Enter Key to continue
```

Fig. 14 The hidden qrcode function

The related QR code is shown below.

Fig. 15 The QR code output from the qrcode function

Merkle Tree Method

The Merkle Tree method generates a block's hash by continuously merging ntransactions via repeating a two-to-one option. With just four transactions corresponding to four hashes, Nakamoto (2008) shows the methodology in the image below.

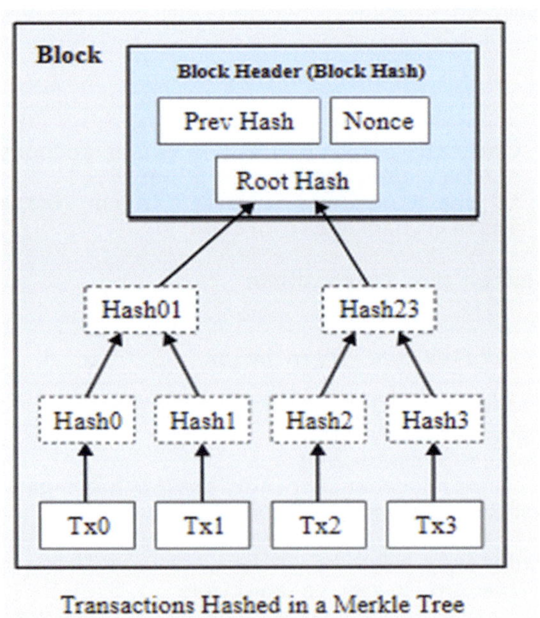

Fig. 16 The illustration of a Merkle Tree (Nakamoto, 2008)

At https://passwordsgenerator.net/sha256-hash-generator/, users can generate a Root Hash (Merkle Root) for just a few transactions. However, achieving a more significant number of transactions, such as 100, is practically impossible. Our `.merkleTree()` method will help in this regard. Typing the function's name, usage, and an example will show the following image.

```
> .merkleTree
function(){
"Objective: show how a Merkle tree works
            install.packages('digest')

Example > .mtree()   # copy the following three lines

TX4: 2024-02-06 20:34:02   Dan receives 0.0621 ETH from Emma.
TX5: 2024-02-07 21:23:15   Alice receives 0.0794 BTC from Diana.
TX6: 2024-02-08 01:26:57   Sue sends 0.0391 BTC to Bob.

 * ------------------------------------------------------------ *
 *  Objective: generate a Merkle Tree (Root)                    *
 *             Copy your transactions, then hit the Enter key   *
 * ------------------------------------------------------------ *
 * Launch a text editor/Excel and paste your hashes there       *
 *     Then hit the Enter Key to continue                       *

 Round #: 1  and n= 4
6023AF59B812567CE947DADEDFCEF8911756EFE0B4AA4398A753817C22BE085E
37DA70ED821E51983BA4E27FBC273872A47F494CB8230EEAB8E598DCEF676DF4
1BF67BE5169BA0520B8BDA39211D95DA66592FF742CC0C04727361D4F6BCFED3
1BF67BE5169BA0520B8BDA39211D95DA66592FF742CC0C04727361D4F6BCFED3

 Round #: 2  and n= 2
130121DED8EA9F85FE4B4F69C4835B3DF2DF3FABD7491DE44E2AE8155A48DD99
1CAD444C55684555299631D378E2DFE5CCAFF2CF4D8F9BFCE39314264A764767

 * ------------------------------------------------------------ *
 * Your merkle root:                                            *
C1E4331C466373E87949AAF3E09F9A5475CAE625C10C2B1218A8E366AE48D0ED
 * ------------------------------------------------------------ *
```

Fig. 17 The illustration using the hidden.merkleTree function

In addition to the above function, we have two other similar functions.

```
> .searchHiddenFunctions('merkle')
 CHAPTER                      NAME                    SHORTCUT
       9 .merkleTree              .mtree    # need 'digest'
       9 .merkleTreeBothCases     .mtree2   # need 'digest'
       9 .merkleTreeHashAsInput   .mtree3   # need 'digest'
```

Fig. 18 The hidden functions associated with "merkle"

Many In-Class Exercises

The best way to learn difficult concepts is via hands-on learning. For this reason, we have developed close to 100 in-class exercises. For each lecture, students will do at least two in-class exercises. To access a list of in-class exercises, type `.inClassEx` or `.ice`. Over a 15-week semester, the number of in-class exercises will increase from 5 to 98. For the first week, we have just 5, shown below.

```
> .inClassEx
function(i=0){
"i  class  Description
 -  ----   -------------------------------
 1    1   Watch two videos (R installation)
 2    1   How to launch and quit R?
 3    1   One-line for this course
 4    1   Watch videos related to FinTech
 5    1   Excel left(), right(), isnumber(), mode() functions

Example 1:>.ice        # show all the exercises
Example 2:>.ice()      # the same as the above
Example 3:>.ice(1)     # see the first one
```

Fig. 19 The hidden in-class exercises function (.ice)

We have the first-in-class exercise to help students download and install R.

```
> .ice(1)
Watch two videos on R installation
///////////////////////////
Video to install R

How to download and install R  [for Windows)
    (6m39s)
    https://www.youtube.com/watch?v=ZoPJGmpYJzw

Programming in R - Getting Started - Installing R and RStudio on a Mac
    (5m59s)
    https://www.youtube.com/watch?v=Ywj6yNfc5nM

///////////////////////////
```

Fig. 20 The in-class exercise #1

.dictionary() for searching definitions

To help readers and students search for various definitions of blockchain, cryptocurrency, cryptography, public and private keys, and related concepts, we have designed the `.dictionary()` function, abbreviated as `.dict()`. For example, to get related information for sha256, we issue the command `.dict("sha256")`. The result is shown below.

```
----------------------------------------------------------
Keyword:         sha256
----------------------------------------------------------
 SHA-256 (Secure Hash Algorithm 256-bit) is a cryptographic hash function that
takes an input (or "message") and produces a fixed-size, 256-bit (32-byte) hash
value, which is typically represented as a 64-character hexadecimal number. It
is designed to be a one-way function, meaning that it is computationally
infeasible to reverse the process or find two different inputs that produce the
same hash output. SHA-256 is commonly used in security protocols and blockchain
technology to ensure data integrity and secure digital signatures.
----------------------------------------------------------
----------------------------------------------------------
Keyword:         Sha256 properties
----------------------------------------------------------
 1) deterministic: always produce the same hash from the same input;2) 'one-way
ticket': nobody can find the original data or information from the hash; 3)
"avalanche effect": a small change leads to a completely different hash; 4)
collision resistant: it is impossible for two data sets with the same hash.
----------------------------------------------------------
```

Fig. 21 One example of using the hidden dictionary function

Our dictionary file has two columns: a keyword and a short explanation. By design, the default format is that the function will search both columns. Users can limit output by searching for the first column with the second input as `1` if they see too many output entries. One example is `.dict('private',1)` .

```
----------------------------------------------------------
Keyword:         private key
----------------------------------------------------------
 Only the corresponding private key can decrypt the message encrypted by its
corresponding public key.
----------------------------------------------------------
----------------------------------------------------------
Keyword:         Private Key
----------------------------------------------------------
 A secret key that is used to sign transactions and prove ownership of a
blockchain address.
----------------------------------------------------------
```

Fig. 22 The.dictinary function with "private" as an input

Big Number Function

When discussing cryptography, readers and students might see big numbers. A typical example is the operation of `y^2 mod (p)` and `x^3 + 7 mod (p)`, where `mod()` is a modulus function. When `x`, `y`, and `p` (a prime number) are pretty big, Excel could not handle them. To solve this dilemma, readers can use a function called `.bigNumberCalculation()`, abbreviated as `.bigN()`. After typing its name, we will see the following examples.

```
> .bigN
function(){
"Objective: solve the issue with big nubmers


Example 1># x^3 +7 (mod p)
        x=55066263022277343669578718895168534326250603453777594175500187360389116729240
        p=115792089237316195423570985008687907853269984665640564039457584007908834671663
        -----  result ----------------------------------------
        32748224938747404814623910738487752935528512903530129802856995983256684603122

Example 2># y^2 (mod p)
          y=32670510020758816978083085130507043184471273380659243275938904335757337482424
          p=115792089237316195423570985008687907853269984665640564039457584007908834671663
         -----  result ----------------------------------------
         32748224938747404814623910738487752935528512903530129802856995983256684603122
```

Fig. 23 The hidden function related to big numbers (.bigN)

Videos to Watch Outside the Classroom

There are many excellent YouTube videos on topics related to FinTech. Certain students learn better by watching these videos rather than sitting in a classroom listening to dry lectures. For those students, we have a list of related videos.

```
> .videos
function(i){
" i      Class                                                n
 --   ----------------------------------------               --
  1   Introduction and Excel Basics                           4
  2   Blockchain 1: Numbers & alphanumeric cases              5
  3              2: ASCII and Sha256                          5
  4   Ledger and distributed ledger                           4
  5   Cryptography    1: and public/private keys              4
  6                   2: Advanced                             4
  7 Cryptocurrency and Ganache                                5
  8 Cryptocurrency Market, Investment, and Risks              3
  9 Blockchain Applications and Simulations                   4
 10   Machine Learning 1: Supervised Learning                 5
 11                    2: Unsupervised Learning               4
 12                    3: Neural Network                      3
 13   Robo-Advisor and automated trading                      4
 14   Smart Contracts                                         5
 15   Term projects                                           4
 16   R basics     (optional)                                 4
 17   Excel Macro (optional)                                  4
 18   Excel VBA    (optional)                                 4

 Example #1> .videos      # get the above list
 Example #2> .v           # same as .videos
 Example #3> .v(1)        # see the first explanation
```

Fig. 24 The.videos function

Watching Videos When Teaching

Instructors can watch short videos with students and add their comments or explanations afterward. The related hidden function is `.watchVideos()`. Typing the function's name will reveal the following instructions.

```
> .watchVideos
function(i=0){
"Videos for various courses
 i  chapter  Description    [ ! watched already ]
---  ---------------------------------
 1  1  R installation [for Windows]    (t6:39,2010)    https://www.youtube.com/watch?v=ZoPJGmpYJzw
 2  1  R installation [on a Mac]       (t5:59,2014)    https://www.youtube.com/watch?v=Ywj6yNfc5nM
 3  1  Installing R/RStudio on a Mac   (t5:59,2014)    https://www.youtube.com/watch?v=Ywj6yNfc5nM
 4  1  What is FinTech                 (t1:01,2023)    https://www.youtube.com/watch?v=XMTevrgV0pE
 5  1  FinTech: How it works           (t3:34,2018)    https://www.youtube.com/watch?v=PuAbqwTDeh0
 6  5  Public and Private Key Work     (t3:31,2023)    https://www.youtube.com/watch?v=bvSJm7fHXto
 7  5  Encryption and public keys      (t6:39,2019)    https://www.youtube.com/watch?v=6-JjHa-qLPk
 8  5  Asymmetric Encryption           (t4:40,2018)    https://www.youtube.com/watch?v=AQDCe585Lnc
 9  6  QR code                         (t4:18,2022)    https://www.youtube.com/watch?v=t0xsuYiqO9w
10  7  Download Ganache for windows 11 (t2:21,2022)    https://www.youtube.com/watch?v=bJriXCtGrLY
11  7  Install Ganache for Mac         (t2:05,2023)    https://www.youtube.com/watch?v=5bf4UzzXvXM
12  11 Getting Started with Orange 01  (t2:15,2016)    https://www.youtube.com/watch?v=HXjnDIgGDuI
13  11 Orange 02: Data Workflows       (t2:34,2016)    https://www.youtube.com/watch?v=lb-x36xqJ-E
14  11 Machine Learning With Orange    (t5:20,2018)    https://www.youtube.com/watch?v=nNNl7Jws5Mk
15  8  Cryptocurrency Tether (USDT)    (t2:30,2018)    https://www.youtube.com/watch?v=ecLDO7LpN8k
16  8  What is Tether?                 (t9:36,2021)    https://www.youtube.com/watch?v=cK8bAA6H5PY&t=48s
17  9  Basic Attention Token (BAT)?    (t6:21,2021)    https://www.youtube.com/watch?v=Cs7FEQgaVpo
18  9  Basic Attention Token?          (t3:03,2019)    https://www.youtube.com/watch?v=7p5cxCaUwm4
19  9  What is Augur?                  (t1:35,2018)    https://www.youtube.com/watch?v=1-GReJCeAIw
20  9  Augur (REP) Crypto Special?     (t3:06,2022)    https://www.youtube.com/watch?v=dO11Ek1g0sk
21  9  Merkle Tree | Merkle Root       (t2:30,2019)    https://www.youtube.com/watch?v=fB41w3JcR7U
22  12 Smart contracts- Explained      (t4:16,2018)    https://www.youtube.com/watch?v=ZE2HxTmxfrI
23  12 What are ERC Tokens? ERC20      (t3:33,2023)    https://www.youtube.com/watch?v=mh1ouonPl5o&t=2s

  Example #1:> .videos2      # see this list
  Example #2:> .v2           # see this list (a short-cut)
  Example #3:> .v2(1)        # show the first video
               Note: you can issue the following line
                    rm(.videoData)
```

Fig. 25 The.watchVideos function

The duration of those videos is relatively short, just a few minutes. In addition, by entering the ID of a given video, the underlying function will launch the video automatically.

Term Projects

Doing a good term project at the end of the semester is a great idea. After typing `.chapter15` or `.c15`, the following list will pop up.

```
> .chapter15
function(i=0){
"i  Chapter 15: Term Projects        i  Projects
 -  ---------------------------     --  ---------------------------
 1  Requirements                    21  Unsupervised learning 1
 2  'Data analysis' not available   22     :2
 3  'VBA' is not available          23     :3
 4  Blockchain: template 1          24     :4
 5            : template 2          25     :5
 6     :3 transaction data          26 Supervised learning
 7     :4                           27     : Retirement calculator
 8     :5                           28     : CAPM, FF3, FFC4, or FF5?
 9     :6                           29     : Test of the January Effect
10     :7                           30     : Bankruptcy prediction: Z-score
11  Public/private keys             31  Neural Network 1
12     :2                           32     :2
13     :3                           33     :3
14     :4                           34     :4
15  Signature 1                     35     :5
16     :2                           36 Smart contract 1
17     :3                           37     :2
18     :4                           38     :3
19  Videos                          39     :4
20  Links                           40  Topics taken already (updated on mm/dd/yyyy)

 Example 1:>.c15     # see the above list
 Example 2:>.c15()   # see the above list
 Example 3:>.c15(1)  # see the first explanation
```

Fig. 26 The contents of Chapter 15: Term Projects

To save space, Chapter 15: *Term Projects*, Chapter 16: *R Installation and Basics*, Chapter 17: *Excel Macros*, and Chapter 18: *Excel VBA* are not included in the printed book. However, all of them will be available online.

What This Book Covers

Chapter 1: *Introduction and Excel Basics* explains the basic concepts of FinTech, such as its usage, why it interrupts current financial systems, and potential applications of FinTech. After that, we review many essential Excel functions that will be used in this book, such as the `mod()`, `left()`, `right()`, `vlookup()`, `code()`, and `concat()` functions. Since we will generate some simulated distributed ledgers, the Excel 'Random Number Generations" will also be reviewed.

Chapter 2: *Blockchain 1: Numbers and Alphanumeric* explains the basic concept of blockchains. Since this concept is fundamental to many potential applications, such as cryptocurrency, we use a four-stage approach. This chapter covers the first two stages, while the next covers the last two. The first stage is for numbers, while the second is for letters and numbers.

Chapter 3: *Blockchain 2: Hash, ASCII, and Sha256* first discusses how to build a blockchain using Excel `code()` functions to deal with ASCII characters. Then, students learn how to form a blockchain using sha256. This chapter is for Stages 3 and 4.

Chapter 4: *Ledger and Distributed Ledger* explains traditional ledgers first. Then, students learn how to use Excel to generate simulated ledgers. After that, students learn how to link those distributed ledgers using sha256.

Chapter 5: *Cryptography, Mnemonic, Public and Private Keys* discusses several simple methods to encrypt and decrypt a text, such as the letter-shifting scheme, keyword approach, and Enigma. Since public and private keys are vital in FinTech, our hidden functions can generate a pair of public and private keys at will. In addition, our hidden functions can encrypt a text message using a private key and encode it with the corresponding public key.

Chapter 6: *Cryptography (2): Advanced* discusses more advanced concepts related to prime numbers, big number calculation, Elliptic Curve Cryptography, and how to conduct tests such as whether a given point (x, y) is on an ECC curve from a private key to create a public key and an account number. Readers and students can skip this chapter when learning for the first time since its concepts are pretty advanced. They can come to this chapter at a later time.

Chapter 7: *Cryptocurrency and Ganache* discusses why cryptocurrencies are one of the major applications of Blockchain. After the basic concepts of cryptocurrencies, Ganache will be used to explain mnemonic, HTTPS, public and private keys. Our hidden functions can be used to check Ganache's account address and balance, transfer WEI (the smallest unit of Ethereum), and check transactions and blocks.

Chapter 8: *Crypto Markets, Risk, Risk-Return Tradeoff* will discuss the cryptocurrency market and its associated risks. Students will learn how to compare the risks of cryptos with those of stocks and bonds. Several ratios, such as Sharpe, Treynor Ratio, and Sortino Ratios, will be discussed and calculated for cryptocurrency, individual stocks, and the S&P500.

Chapter 9: *Blockchain Applications and Simulations* discusses various applications of Blockchain, such as in finance, supply chain, healthcare records, voting systems, and real estate transactions. In the second part, students learn to use Excel random number generation to generate simulated transactions, distributed ledgers, and other activities.

Chapter 10: *Unsupervised Learning Using Excel* deals with unlabeled data and aims to discover patterns, relationships, or structures within the data without explicit guidance on the desired output. The K-means methodology will group a given data set into various categories. In addition, PCA (Principal Component Analysis) will be discussed to reduce the dimensions of complex data sets.

Chapter 11: *Supervised Learning (I) Using Excel: Classifications* first introduces the basic concepts. Then, the differences and similarities between this chapter and the previous one are explained in more detail. After that, the focus is on the `kNN` (K-Nearest Neighbor) method. Logistic regression will also be discussed to deal with the binary dependent variable.

Chapter 12: *Supervised Learning (II): Regressions* will first discuss linear regression and multicollinearity, how to detect and deal with it, how to set up a dummy variable, and how to use linear regression for non-linear variables.

Chapter 13: *Neural Networks Using Excel and Our Hidden Functions* first explains a neural network's basic concepts and graphs. Then, Excel will be used to build the most straightforward neural network (one layer and one neuron) using the famous Iris data set. After understanding the basic operations using Excel, our hidden functions such as `.showNN()`, `.showNN_iris()`, `.showNN_iris2()`, and `.nn()` will be used. In those function names, `NN` (`nn`) stands for Neural Network.

Chapter 14: *Smart Contracts* explains the importance of understanding the concepts of smart contracts since many dApp (Deep Applications) in finance are carried out by various smart contracts. To have a good grasp of smart contracts, hands-on experience is vital. Unfortunately, readers must understand a programming language called Solidity when writing a smart contract (in terms of the Ethereum blockchain). Teaching a programming language is beyond the scope of this book. To have a tradeoff, the second half of this chapter optional will be since it will discuss a few smart contracts written in Solidity. Even this part is quite essential.

The following four chapters are optional and are not included in the book's printed version. However, they are accessible online or by using R. To access the following chapters, just type the following line.

```
source("http://datayyy.com/i2ft/week15.txt")
```

Chapter 15: *Term Projects* will discuss several types of projects students could do as a final term project. After learners/students understand the requirements, they can choose from a list of potential topics.

Chapter 16: *R Installation and Basics* teaches R's basic concepts and code. First, students learn how to install R and RStudio and some basic concepts, such as assigning values to a new variable, whether R is case-sensitive, using embedded R functions, and finding help.

Chapter 17: *Excel Macros* shows many Excel Macros where students/readers can use the copy-and-paste method. In total, we have close to 50 macro programs available.

Chapter 18: *Excel VBA* show many VBA examples, and students/readers can use the copy-and-paste method to choose appropriate VBAs. There are close to 50 VBAs students can use.

Los Angeles, USA Yuxing Yan

Reference

Nakamoto, Satoshi, 2008, Bitcoin: A Peer-to-Peer Electronic Cash System, https://nakamotoinstitute.org/library/bitcoin/

Acknowledgments First, I thank Edward J. Zychowicz, Na Wang, and John Lynch for allowing me to teach the first part of the course titled "Introduction to FinTech" at Hofstra University to their undergraduate and graduate students. In addition, I thank Rocio Torregrosa (Senior Editor Business & Finance), Gayathri Sampath Kumar (Production Editor) from Springer for their help. I thank Dr. Mark Lennon and Dr. Shaojun Zhang for serving as professional evaluators for the publisher.

I want to thank Ben Amoako-Adu, Brian Smith (who taught me the first two finance courses and offered unstinting support for many years after my graduation), George Athanassakos (one of his assignments "forced" me to learn C), and Jin-Chun Duan. I would also like to thank Wei-Hung Mao, Jerome Detemple, Bill Sealey, Chris Jacobs, Mo Chaudhury, Summon Mazumdar (my former professors at McGill), and Lawrence Kryzanowski (his wonderful teaching inspired me to concentrate on empirical finance and he edited my doctoral thesis word by word even though he was not my supervisor!); Mark Lennon, Frank P. D'Souza, Kee Chung, Cristian Tiu, Sudhir Suchak, Yoon Shin, Lisa Fairchild, Karyl Leggio, Shuo Chen, Lei Gao, Ken Pan, Rafiqul Bhuyan, James Early, Qian Sun, Shaujun Zhang, Paul Sauer, Edward J. Garrity, James Goldstein, Mark P. Zaporrowski, Jinsook Lee, K. G. Viswanathan, Lian Hsu, Vadim S. Balashov, Xiaodi Zhu, and Christopher Armstrong. In addition, I'd like to thank Anthony Gu, Shaobo Ji, Tong Yu, Shaoming Huang, and Xing Zhang. I thank Eric Ulm, Premal Vora, Ronald Crowe, Dehong Wang, Andreas Chouliaras, Andy Kim, Sheng Xiao, Cong Xie, Mesu Ozdag, Lulu Zeng, Daniel Folkins, and James Nordlund for adopting my R o Python books ass their textbooks.

Undoubtedly, my experience at Wharton has shaped my thinking and enhanced my skill sets. I thank Chris Schull and Michael Boldin for offering me the job; Mark Keintz, Dong Xu, Steven Crispi, and Dave Robinson, my former colleagues, who helped me greatly during my first two years at Wharton; and Eric Zhu, Paul Ratnaraj, Premal Vora, Shuguang Zhang, Michelle Duan, Nicholle Mcniece, Russ Ney, Robin Nussbaum-Gold, and Mireia Gine for all their help.

In particular, I would like to thank my wife for her strong support and James Yan for proofreading the whole manuscript and checking the code.

Competing Interests The author has no competing interests to declare that are relevant to the content of this manuscript.

Contents

About the Author

Yuxing Yan graduated from McGill University with a PhD in finance. Over the years, he has taught various finance, statistics, and programming courses at eight universities: McGill University and Wilfrid Laurier University (in Canada), Nanyang Technological University (in Singapore), Loyola University of Maryland, Hofstra University, University at Buffalo, Canisius College, and Geneseo (in the US).

His research areas include FinTech, Financial Data Analytics, and Market Microstructure. He has 27 publications, including papers in the *Journal of Banking and Finance*, *Journal of Empirical Finance*, *Pacific Basin Finance Journal*, *Applied Financial Economics*, and *Annals of Operations Research.*

He is good at programming languages like Python, R, SAS, Matlab, and C. He has published a few books applying Python and R to finance: *Learning R and Python for Business School Students* (2023), *Financial Analysis and Modeling using R* (in Chinese, 2021), *Python for Finance* (2nd edition, 2017), *Python for Finance* (Chinese and Korean versions, 2017), and *Financial Modeling Using R* (2016). In addition, he is an expert on data, especially on financial databases. From 2003 to 2010, he worked at Wharton School as a consultant, helping researchers with their programs and data issues. In 2007, he published a book titled *Financial Databases* (with S.W. Zhu, in Chinese).

Introduction and Excel Basics 1

This chapter briefly introduces FinTech, including its basic definition, evolution, benefits, challenges, and future. After that, we offer a list of potential courses after this course. Since Excel will be the computational tool, we will discuss some basic techniques related to Excel, such as `len ()`, `left ()`, `right ()`, `if ()`, `formulatext ()`, and `vlookup ()` functions. Since a few prewritten Excel VBAs and Macros will be used in future chapters, we explain how to copy and paste others' VBA or Macro. In this chapter, the following topics will be covered:

- Introduction
- What is DeFi?
- What kinds of skills are involved?
- What kind of languages are used in FinTech?
- The Excel `mod ()` function for calculating the remainder
- The Excel `vlookup ()` and `hlookup ()` functions to search a table
- Text: `len ()`, `left ()`, `right ()`, `concat()`, and the `&` operation
- How to download and launch R
- An R-assisted learning environment

Supplementary Information The online version contains supplementary material available at https://doi.org/10.1007/978-3-031-89779-5_1.

Y. Yan, *Introduction to FinTech using Excel*, Springer Texts in Business and Economics, https://doi.org/10.1007/978-3-031-89779-5_1

1.1 What is Fintech?

FinTech, short for Financial Technology, refers to the integration of technology into offerings by financial services companies to improve their use and delivery to consumers. It encompasses various applications, including online banking, mobile payments, investment management, and blockchain technologies. FinTech aims to streamline financial operations and provide innovative solutions that are faster, more efficient, and more accessible compared to traditional financial services.

In recent years, FinTech has transformed the financial landscape by making services more user-friendly and accessible to a broader audience. For example, digital wallets like PayPal and mobile payment systems like Apple Pay have revolutionized how people conduct transactions, making them faster and more secure. The rise of peer-to-peer (P2P) lending platforms has also changed how individuals and businesses access loans, bypassing traditional banking intermediaries.

Advancements in technology and changes in consumer behavior drive the rapid growth of FinTech. People are increasingly comfortable with digital interactions and personalized financial services that we demand seamless. As a result, FinTech companies are pushing the boundaries of what is possible, constantly innovating to meet the evolving needs of the modern consumer.

1.2 The Evolution of Fintech

FinTech is not entirely new; its roots can be traced back to the introduction of the first credit cards in the 1950s, which simplified how people made purchases. However, the term "FinTech" became widely recognized in the twenty-first century, coinciding with the explosion of internet usage and mobile technology. The digital revolution laid the groundwork for developing online banking, e-commerce, and payment systems that we see today.

The 2008 global financial crisis was a pivotal moment for FinTech. It exposed the vulnerabilities of traditional financial institutions and led to a surge in demand for more transparent and efficient financial services. Startups and tech giants began exploring leveraging technology to create more reliable and user-friendly financial products. This period marked the beginning of an era where technology-driven financial solutions gained significant traction.

Today, FinTech is a dynamic and rapidly growing industry that constantly evolves to adapt to new technologies and consumer expectations. From cryptocurrencies to robo-advisors, the landscape is continuously changing. The industry's evolution is characterized by its ability to disrupt traditional financial systems, making it an exciting and challenging field for innovation.

1.3 The Areas of Fintech

FinTech covers a broad spectrum of areas, each focused on improving a specific aspect of financial services. One of the most prominent areas is payment processing, which includes digital wallets, mobile payments, and online transaction platforms. Companies like Square, PayPal, and Stripe have made it easier for businesses and individuals to send and receive money with minimal hassle.

Another critical area is personal finance and investment, which involves tools and platforms that help users manage their finances, invest, and plan for the future. Robo-advisors, such as Betterment and Wealthfront, use algorithms to provide automated investment advice, making financial planning more accessible and affordable for the average person. Budgeting apps like Mint help users track their spending and savings goals, clearly showing their financial health.

Blockchain and cryptocurrencies represent another revolutionary area of FinTech. Blockchain technology enables secure, transparent, and tamper-proof transactions, the foundation for cryptocurrencies like Bitcoin and Ethereum. These digital currencies challenge traditional notions of money and finance, offering new ways to store and transfer value without relying on centralized financial institutions.

1.4 The Benefits of Fintech

FinTech offers numerous benefits to both consumers and businesses. One of the primary advantages is increased accessibility. FinTech solutions break down geographical barriers, allowing people from all over the world to access financial services. Mobile banking apps and online lending platforms enable users to perform transactions and apply for loans from the comfort of their homes, which is particularly beneficial in underserved or remote areas.

Another significant benefit is efficiency. By automating processes and reducing the need for manual intervention, FinTech can lower costs and speed up transactions. This efficiency translates into consumer savings as services become cheaper and more competitive. For businesses, FinTech solutions can streamline operations, reduce overhead costs, and improve customer service by providing faster and more accurate responses.

FinTech also enhances transparency and security. Advanced encryption methods and blockchain technology ensure that transactions are secure and traceable, reducing the risk of fraud and errors. By providing clear and accessible information, FinTech tools help users make more informed financial decisions, fostering trust and confidence in the economic system.

1.5 The Challenges and Future of Fintech

While FinTech brings many benefits, it also faces several challenges. Regulation is one of the primary obstacles. FinTech companies operate at the intersection of technology and finance, so they must navigate complex regulatory environments that vary by region. Ensuring compliance while fostering innovation is a delicate balance that requires cooperation between regulators and industry players.

Another challenge is cybersecurity. FinTech relies heavily on digital infrastructure, making it a prime target for cyberattacks. Protecting sensitive financial data and maintaining user trust are critical issues that require constant attention and investment in security measures. Data privacy is also a concern, as the increasing use of data analytics and AI raises questions about how personal information is used and protected.

Despite these challenges, the future of FinTech is bright. Emerging technologies like artificial intelligence, machine learning, and blockchain continue to drive innovation, opening up new possibilities for financial services. The ongoing digital transformation of the financial industry is expected to create a more inclusive, efficient, and transparent financial ecosystem. As FinTech evolves, it will play a crucial role in shaping the future of finance, offering exciting opportunities for consumers, businesses, and investors.

1.6 A Programming Language

Learning one or two programming languages is essential for students and learners who wish to delve deeper into FinTech beyond this course. Programming skills provide the tools necessary to understand, analyze, and innovate within the FinTech landscape. Languages like Python and R, for example, are widely used in data analysis, algorithm development, and automation, all of which are critical components of FinTech. By mastering these languages, students can not only manipulate and analyze financial data but also develop trading algorithms, create financial modeling applications, and implement automated solutions for payment processing.

Moreover, as FinTech continues to evolve, the ability to code becomes increasingly important for understanding new technologies such as blockchain, smart contracts, and machine learning. These technologies are at the forefront of FinTech innovation, driving the development of decentralized finance (DeFi) systems, AI-driven investment platforms, and secure transaction methods. By learning to program, students gain the skills to participate in and contribute to these cutting-edge developments, positioning themselves as valuable players in the rapidly growing FinTech industry. Thus, programming enhances their technical proficiency and expands their career opportunities and potential impact in finance.

Table 1.1 Courses could be taken after this one

#	Name	Main contents
1	Introduction to Python	Teach students fundamental concepts, such as assignments, while and for loops, logic conditions, and Python modules
2	Python for Finance	Help students apply Python to Finance, such as downloading and processing stock data using the `yfinance` module, running CAPM, and optimizing portfolios by maximizing the Sharpe Ratio
3	Technical Analyses/ Machine Learning using Python	First, review basic Python concepts. Then, teach students Financial Analytics: Technical Analysis and Text Analysis. Then, students will learn Unsupervised/Supervised Reinforcement Learning and Neural Networks
4	Blockchain & Cryptocurrency using Python	Introduce Blockchain, Smart contracts, DeFi related concepts and programs. In addition to Python, the Solidity language will be used to write smart contracts
5	Robo-advising using Python	Introduce Machine Learning and apply it to Robo-advising. In addition to Markowitz portfolio optimization, the Black-Litterman Model (1991) and Parametric Portfolio Policies by Brandt, Santa-Clara, and Valkanov (2009) will be introduced and programmed

1.7 Suggested Courses After This

Five-course suggestions could be helpful, and their contents are summarized in the following table. Python was chosen as the computation tool (Table 1.1).

A few books are listed in the references.

1.8 Excel: Relative Addresses

What is the meaning of = `A1`? The following image shows our logic and explanation.

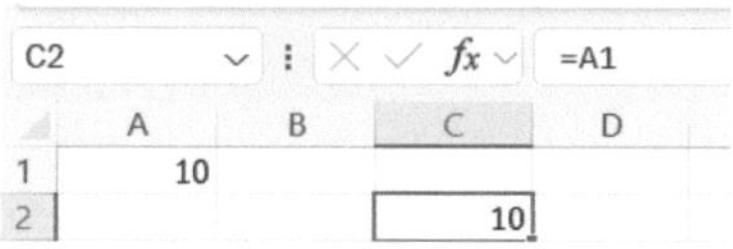

Fig. 1.1 The formula in cell C2

Assume that we type 10 in A1. Then, in C2, we type = A1. We will see a value of 10 in B2. However, ' = A1' does not mean taking the value in Cell A1. This means we could use the value in the cell, one row above and two columns to the left. Assume we copy the formula in C2 to C5 using the formula (third image from the left) below.

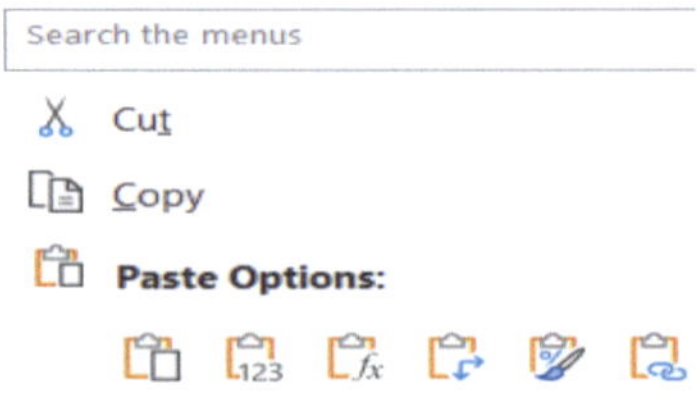

Fig. 1.2 To paste as a formula

We will get a zero; the formula is = A3, precisely one cell up and two cells left.

C4 | fx | =A3

	A	B	C	D
1	10			
2			10	
3				
4			0	=A3

Fig. 1.3 The result is cell C4

1.9 Absolute Addresses

The following formula calculates a future value for a given present value, a compounding rate, and the number of periods.

$$fv = pv(1 + R)^n \tag{1.1}$$

Assume that we want to examine the return on the future value. One solution is to fix the present value and the number of periods by changing R only. Cells B1 and B2 show the present value and the number of periods, as shown below.

Q21 | fx

	A	B	C	D	E
1	pv	100			
2	n	5			
3		r	fv		
4		0.01	105.101	=$B$1*(1+B4)^$B$2	
5		0.02	110.4081	=$B$1*(1+B5)^$B$2	
6		0.03	115.9274	=$B$1*(1+B6)^$B$2	
7		0.04	121.6653	=$B$1*(1+B7)^$B$2	
8		0.05	127.6282	=$B$1*(1+B8)^$B$2	
9		0.06	133.8226	=$B$1*(1+B9)^$B$2	
10		0.07	140.2552	=$B$1*(1+B10)^$B$2	

Fig. 1.4 Coping with the future value function

We have different rates for cells C4 to C10. Since we fix B1 and B2, we use $B$1 and $B$2 to fix their locations.

1.10 Excel: Semi-Absolute Address

In finance, we use the following formula to calculate the present value for a given future value, a discount rate, and the number of periods.

$$pv = \frac{fv}{(1+R)^n} \tag{1.2}$$

For some tests, financial calculators and Excel are prohibited. Instead, students are usually given a piece of paper containing a table called PFIF (Present Value Interest Factor), defined below.

$$pv = \frac{fv}{(1+R)^n} = \text{PFIF} * \text{FV} \tag{1.3}$$

$$PVIF = \frac{1}{(1+R)^n} \tag{1.4}$$

PFIF depends on both R and n. To generate such a table, we have the following design. For column B, we have the numbers of periods from 1 to 19. For Row 2, we have different discount rates.

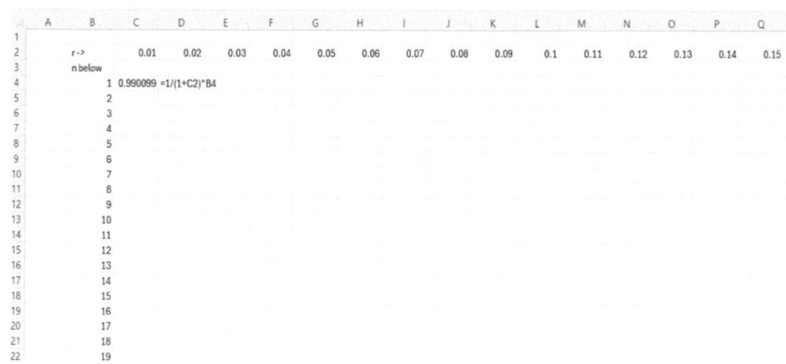

	A	B	C	D	E	F	G	H	I	J	K	L	M	N	O	P	Q
1																	
2		r->	0.01	0.02	0.03	0.04	0.05	0.06	0.07	0.08	0.09	0.1	0.11	0.12	0.13	0.14	0.15
3		n below															
4		1	0.990099	=1/(1+C2)^B4													
5		2															
6		3															
7		4															
8		5															
9		6															
10		7															
11		8															
12		9															
13		10															
14		11															
15		12															
16		13															
17		14															
18		15															
19		16															
20		17															
21		18															
22		19															

Fig. 1.5 The formula in cell C4

In cell D4, we enter the formula = 1/(1 + C2)^B4 and get the correct result. Before copying the formula to the rest of the table, we must make certain adjustments. Since Column B will be used for all the cells, which is true for Row 2, we have to fix those two, as shown below.

	A	B	C	D	E	F
1						
2		r->	0.01	0.02	0.03	0.04
3		n below				
4		1	0.990099	=1/(1+C$2)^$B4		
5		2				

Fig. 1.6 Adding two $ signs

1.11 Excel: Copy as Formula vs. as Values

In the above example, we pasted our cell as a formula. However, if we choose the second image of 123, we will paste the result as values.

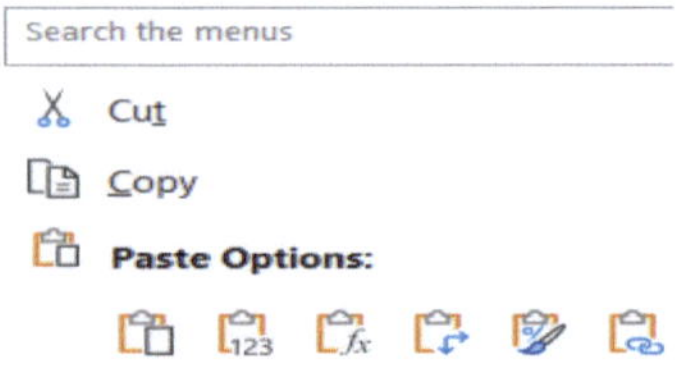

Fig. 1.7 10 To paste as a value [123]

For example, we want to generate ten random numbers between 0 and 1. The Excel rand() function can be used, as shown below.

A1 =RAND()

	A	B	C	D
1	0.813304			
2	0.836327			
3	0.739944			
4	0.95197			
5	0.598929			
6	0.36808			
7	0.300784			
8	0.573098			
9	0.692836			
10	0.509923			

Fig. 1.8 The Excel RAND function

One issue is that those random values will constantly change when we try other operations. One solution is to copy them to another column as values, shown below.

C1 fx 0.226489313773332

	A	B	C	D	E
1	0.737805		0.226489		
2	0.261428		0.994628		
3	0.619202		0.740373		
4	0.143732		0.054197		
5	0.157523		0.774379		
6	0.86413		0.827461		
7	0.561847		0.436071		
8	0.349805		0.257597		
9	0.174823		0.87318		
10	0.378338		0.066962		

Fig. 1.9 Coping as values

1.12 Excel COUNT () and COUNTA () Functions

The Excel `count()` function calculates the number of numbers, while the `counta ()` function calculates both numbers and text. One example is shown below.

	A	B	C	D
1	type			
2	1			
3	2		4	=COUNT(A2:A9)
4	3			
5	4		8	=COUNTA(A2:A9)
6	a			
7	b			
8	c			
9	d			

Fig. 1.10 The Excel count vs. Counta functions

1.13 Excel: FORMULATEXT () Function

The Excel formula function can show the formula in a cell. We know that for a given present value, compounding rate, and the number of periods, the function value is defined as fv = pv(1 + R)^n. In cells B1, B2, and B3, we have 10, 0.1, and 4. In B5, we enter the formula = B1*(1 + B2)^B3. To show this formula, we apply the `formulatext ()` function in C5 below.

C5 fx =FORMULATEXT(B5)

	A	B	C	D	E
1	pv	100			
2	r	0.1			
3	n	4			
4					
5	fv=	146.41	=B1*(1+B2)^B3		

Fig. 1.11 The Excel FORMULATEXT function

1.14 Excel: `LEN ()`, `LEFT ()`, and `RIGHT ()`

The `len ()` function shows the number character of a string.

C2 fx =FORMULATEXT(B2)

	A	B	C	D	E
1		Hofstra			
2		7	=LEN(B1)		

Fig. 1.12 The Excel LEN function

The `left ()` function shows the substring.

N21 fx

	A	B	C	D	E	F
1		Hofstra			left	
2		7	=LEN(B1)	1	H	=LEFT($B$1,D2)
3				2	Ho	=LEFT($B$1,D3)
4				3	Hof	=LEFT($B$1,D4)
5				4	Hofs	=LEFT($B$1,D5)
6				5	Hofst	=LEFT($B$1,D6)
7				6	Hofstr	=LEFT($B$1,D7)
8				7	Hofstra	=LEFT($B$1,D8)

Fig. 1.13 The Excel LEFT function

The right function works identically to the `left ()` function. Assuming that we only care about the last character, we could pick up each character of the phrase.

	A	B	C	D	E	F	G	H
1		Hofstra			left		right 1	
2		7	=LEN(B1)	1	H	=LEFT($B$1,D2)	H	=RIGHT(E2,1)
3				2	Ho		o	
4				3	Hof		f	
5				4	Hofs		s	
6				5	Hofst		t	
7				6	Hofstr		r	
8				7	Hofstra		a	

Fig. 1.14 The Excel RIGHT function

Note that we use the `left ()` and right () functions separately in the above example. In this case, we can combine them. In cell F2, we can enter = `right(left($B$1,D2),1)`.

1.15 Excel Text to Columns

One issue is that we might end up with just one column when copying a multi-column data set from a text editor and pasting it to Excel. Assume that we have the following data set.

```
5.1,3.5,1.4,0.2,Iris-setosa
4.9,3.0,1.4,0.2,Iris-setosa
4.7,3.2,1.3,0.2,Iris-setosa
4.6,3.1,1.5,0.2,Iris-setosa
5.0,3.6,1.4,0.2,Iris-setosa
5.4,3.9,1.7,0.4,Iris-setosa
4.6,3.4,1.4,0.3,Iris-setosa
```

The data should have five columns with a comma as a delimiter based on its structure. However, copying and pasting it into Excel might result in just one column, as shown below.

	A	B
1	5.1,3.5,1.4,0.2,Iris-setosa	
2	4.9,3.0,1.4,0.2,Iris-setosa	
3	4.7,3.2,1.3,0.2,Iris-setosa	
4	4.6,3.1,1.5,0.2,Iris-setosa	
5	5.0,3.6,1.4,0.2,Iris-setosa	
6	5.4,3.9,1.7,0.4,Iris-setosa	
7	4.6,3.4,1.4,0.3,Iris-setosa	

Fig. 1.15 The Iris data in one column

If this is the case, we highlight the column. Choose 'Data' on the menu bar, 'Text to Columns', 'Delimited', choose an appropriate delimiter—a comma in this case—and then 'Finish'. The final result is shown below.

	A	B	C	D	E
1	5.1	3.5	1.4	0.2	Iris-setosa
2	4.9	3	1.4	0.2	Iris-setosa
3	4.7	3.2	1.3	0.2	Iris-setosa
4	4.6	3.1	1.5	0.2	Iris-setosa
5	5	3.6	1.4	0.2	Iris-setosa
6	5.4	3.9	1.7	0.4	Iris-setosa
7	4.6	3.4	1.4	0.3	Iris-setosa

Fig. 1.16 The Iris data in 5 columns

1.16 Excel `HIDE` and `UNHIDE`

When we have a relatively big data set, hiding some rows or columns is a good idea. In other situations, we can adopt this technique to improve our illustration by hiding some less critical parts.

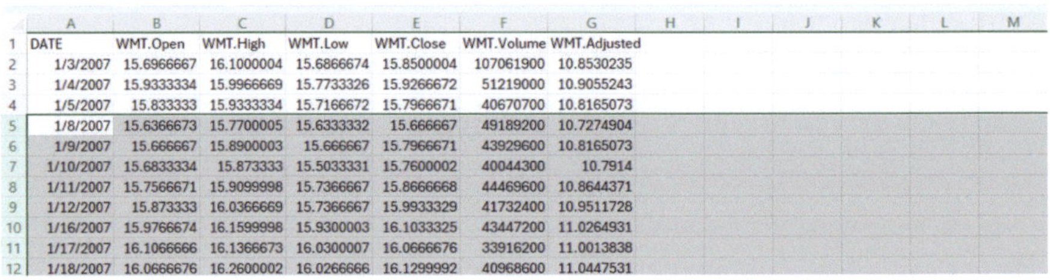

	A	B	C	D	E	F	G
1	DATE	WMT.Open	WMT.High	WMT.Low	WMT.Close	WMT.Volume	WMT.Adjusted
2	1/3/2007	15.6966667	16.1000004	15.6866674	15.8500004	107061900	10.8530235
3	1/4/2007	15.9333334	15.9966669	15.7733326	15.9266672	51219000	10.9055243
4	1/5/2007	15.833333	15.9333334	15.7166672	15.7966671	40670700	10.8165073
5	1/8/2007	15.6366673	15.7700005	15.6333332	15.666667	49189200	10.7274904
6	1/9/2007	15.666667	15.8900003	15.666667	15.7966671	43929600	10.8165073
7	1/10/2007	15.6833334	15.873333	15.5033331	15.7600002	40044300	10.7914
8	1/11/2007	15.7566671	15.9099998	15.7366667	15.8666668	44469600	10.8644371
9	1/12/2007	15.873333	16.0366669	15.7366667	15.9933329	41732400	10.9511728
10	1/16/2007	15.9766674	16.1599998	15.9300003	16.1033325	43447200	11.0264931
11	1/17/2007	16.1066666	16.1366673	16.0300007	16.0666676	33916200	11.0013838
12	1/18/2007	16.0666676	16.2600002	16.0266666	16.1299992	40968600	11.0447531

Fig. 1.17 Highlighting several rows

When choosing rows to hide, it is not just your data set. It should be all rows, as shown above. After that, right-click your mouse and choose "`Hide`", as shown below.

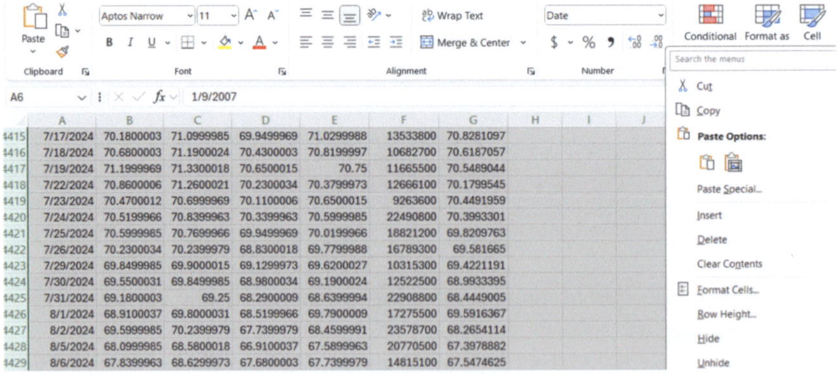

	A	B	C	D	E	F	G
4415	7/17/2024	70.1800003	71.0999985	69.9499969	71.0299988	13533800	70.8281097
4416	7/18/2024	70.6800003	71.1900024	70.4300003	70.8199997	10682700	70.6187057
4417	7/19/2024	71.1999969	71.3300018	70.6500015	70.75	11665500	70.5489044
4418	7/22/2024	70.8600006	71.2600021	70.2300034	70.3799973	12666100	70.1799545
4419	7/23/2024	70.4700012	70.6999969	70.1100006	70.6500015	9263600	70.4491959
4420	7/24/2024	70.5199966	70.8399963	70.3399963	70.5999985	22490800	70.3993301
4421	7/25/2024	70.5999985	70.7699966	69.9499969	70.0199966	18821200	69.8209763
4422	7/26/2024	70.2300034	70.2399979	68.8300018	69.7799988	16789300	69.581665
4423	7/29/2024	69.8499985	69.9000015	69.1299973	69.6200027	10315300	69.4221191
4424	7/30/2024	69.5500031	69.8499985	68.9800034	69.1900024	12522500	68.9933395
4425	7/31/2024	69.1800003	69.25	68.2900009	68.6399994	22908800	68.4449005
4426	8/1/2024	68.9100037	69.8000031	68.5199966	69.7900009	17275500	69.5916367
4427	8/2/2024	69.5999985	70.2399979	67.7399979	68.4599991	23578700	68.2654114
4428	8/5/2024	68.0999985	68.5800018	66.9100037	67.5899963	20770500	67.3978882
4429	8/6/2024	67.8399963	68.6299973	67.6800003	67.7399979	14815100	67.5474625

Fig. 1.18 The Excel HIDE functionality

The result is shown below. You can use the `count ()` function to show the number of data rows.

	A	B	C	D	E	F	G	H	I	J	K
1	DATE	WMT.Open	WMT.High	WMT.Low	WMT.Close	WMT.Volume	WMT.Adjusted				
2	1/3/2007	15.6966667	16.1000004	15.6866674	15.8500004	107061900	10.8530235				
3	1/4/2007	15.9333334	15.9966669	15.7733326	15.9266672	51219000	10.9055243				
4	1/5/2007	15.833333	15.9333334	15.7166672	15.7966671	40670700	10.8165073				
5	1/8/2007	15.6366673	15.7700005	15.6333332	15.666667	49189200	10.7274904				
1436	8/15/2024	74.1200027	74.4400024	72.7799988	73.1800003	49567500	72.9720001				
1437	8/16/2024	72.6999969	73.6100006	72.5199966	73.4499969	19872100	73.4499969				
1438	8/19/2024	73.3899994	73.9800034	73.3399963	73.7200012	13709300	73.7200012				
1439	8/20/2024	73.75	74.75	73.7200012	74.5400009	14434000	74.5400009				
1440	8/21/2024	75.3000031	75.5800018	74.5899963	75.2399979	14832000	75.2399979				
1441	8/22/2024	75.3700027	76.2200012	75.1500015	75.5800018	16511100	75.5800018				
1442											
1443					4440	=COUNT(E1:E4441)					

Fig. 1.19 The result after a few rows were hidden

One word of caution: when working with some hidden rows, be careful with the locations of your calculation. Assume you are working on the right of your data set, such as columns I, J, and K. After unhiding, you suddenly find that your calculations mysteriously "disappeared". To unhide a few rows, choose rows across both unhidden and hidden rows, right-click your mouse, and choose "`unhide`."

1.17 Excel: Sorting Your Data

Sometimes, we need to sort our data set before further processing. For example, today's return is defined as the difference between today's price and yesterday's price divided by yesterday's price, as shown below.

$$R_t = \frac{R_t - R_{t-1}}{R_{t-1}} \tag{1.5}$$

Alternatively, we can use today's price divided by yesterday's price, then minus 1.

$$R_t = \frac{R_t}{R_{t-1}} - 1 \tag{1.6}$$

Although we would get the same results, the second method of calculating returns is less likely to make a mistake than the first one when using Excel. Another issue is how your data was sorted. If the data was sorted from oldest to newest, the return on the first day is missing.

	A	G	H	I	J
1	DATE	WMT.Adjusted		return	
2	1/3/2007	10.8530235			
3	1/4/2007	10.9055243		0.004837	=G3/G2-1
4	1/5/2007	10.8165073		-0.00816	
5	1/8/2007	10.7274904		-0.00823	
6	1/9/2007	10.8165073		0.008298	
4436	8/15/2024	72.9720001		0.065832	
4437	8/16/2024	73.4499969		0.00655	
4438	8/19/2024	73.7200012		0.003676	
4439	8/20/2024	74.5400009		0.011123	
4440	8/21/2024	75.2399979		0.009391	
4441	8/22/2024	75.5800018		0.004519	
4442					
4443		n of returns		4439	

Fig. 1.20 Return calculation (G3/G2-1)

To sort a data set, we highlight the whole set, then right-click our mouse and choose the column based on how we would like to sort our data and the order. In this case, we chose "Newest to Oldest," as shown below.

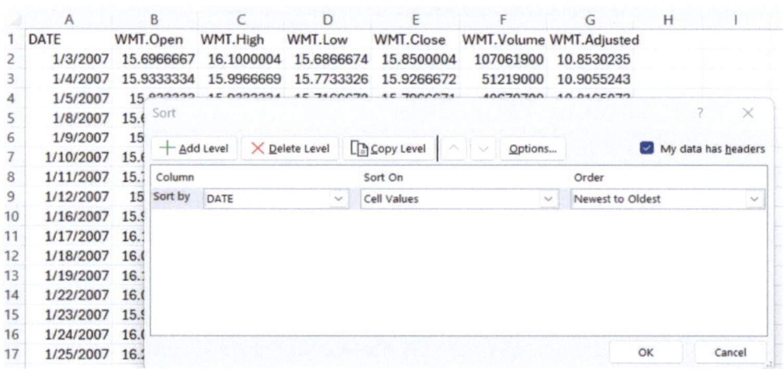

Fig. 1.21 When the data is sorted differently

On the other hand, if the data is sorted with the latest first, then the last return should be missing, as shown below.

	A	G	H	I	J	K
1	DATE	WMT.Adjusted		return		
2	8/22/2024	75.5800018		0.00451893	=G2/G3-1	
3	8/21/2024	75.2399979		0.00939089		
4	8/20/2024	74.5400009		0.01112316		
4436	1/10/2007	10.7914		-0.0023212		
4437	1/9/2007	10.8165073		0.00829802		
4438	1/8/2007	10.7274904		-0.0082297		
4439	1/5/2007	10.8165073		-0.0081626		
4440	1/4/2007	10.9055243		0.00483743		
4441	1/3/2007	10.8530235		#DIV/0!	=G4441/G4442-1	
4442						
4443		number of returns		4439		

Fig. 1.22 Different way to calculate returns (G2/G3-1)

For the last date (1/3/2007), we got an error message. The reason is that there is no data before 1/3/2007. How do we avoid such an error message? See one of the end-of-chapter problems.

1.18 Excel: `IF ()` Function

The format of the `if ()` function is `if (logical_test, value_if_true, value_if_false)`. The NPV criteria is to take the project if its NPV is positive and reject it otherwise; see below.

	A	B	C	D	E	F	G
1		npv	100				
2		Accept the project	=IF(C1>0, "Accept the project", "Reject")				

Fig. 1.23 The Excel IF function

1.19 Excel: Rename/Copy Your Spreadsheet

To rename our spreadsheet, choose an appropriate one, right-click your mouse, and choose "`rename`" from the following menu.

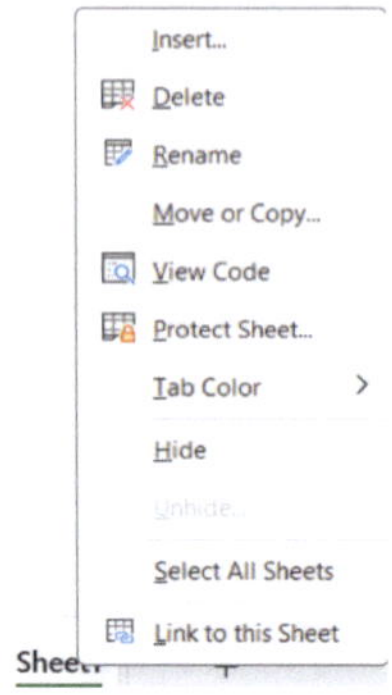

Fig. 1.24 Renaming a spreadsheet

After retrieving data into Excel, keeping the original data set intact is a good idea. If our original data is not 'touched' or modified, we can remove any doubt that our initial data caused the issues later found. One way is to make a copy of our spreadsheet.

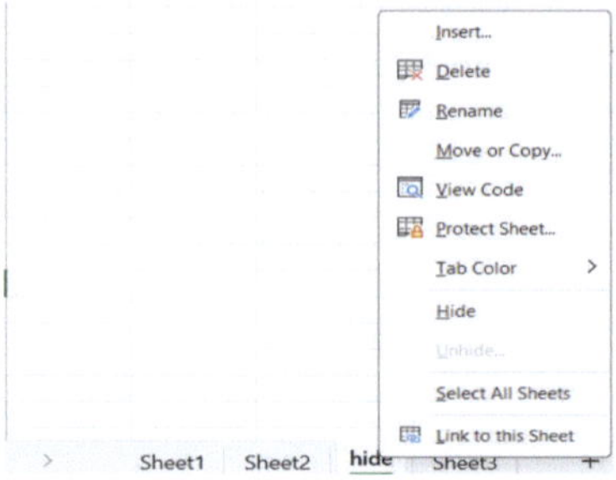

Fig. 1.25 Copying a spreadsheet

After clicking "`Move or Copy...`", choose a spreadsheet from your multiple sheets, check "`Create a Copy`," and click `OK`.

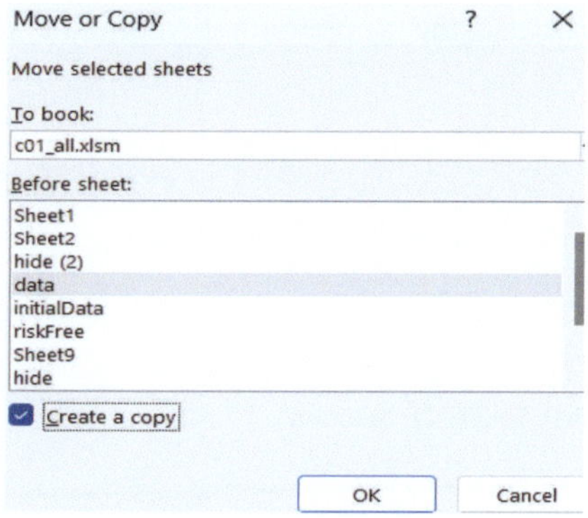

Fig. 1.26 Creating a copy

1.20 Excel: `SUBSTITUTE ()` Function

With this function, we can replace one word with another one. The format of this function is = `substitute(text,old_text,new_text, [instance_num])`. One example is shown below.

	A	B	C	D	E	F
1	This is a great idea.					
2						
3		This is a bad idea.		=SUBSTITUTE(A1,"great","bad")		

Fig. 1.27 The Excel SUBSTITUTE function

1.21 Excel: `CONCATENATE()` and the $ Operator

The Excel `concatenate ()` or `concat()` functions will combine text or numbers together. The following two examples show its usage.

	A	B	C	D	E
1		H			
2		o	Hofstra	=CONCAT(B1:B7)	
3		f			
4		s	2024		
5		t	year2024	=CONCAT("year",C4)	
6		r			
7		a			

Fig. 1.28 The Excel CONCATENATE function

Alternatively, we can use the & operator to combine two strings, as shown below.

C3 fx =FORMULATEXT(B3)

	A	B	C	D	E
1	2024				
2	year				
3		2024year	=A1&A2		

Fig. 1.29 The Excel FORMULATEXT function

1.22 ISNUMBER (), ISTEXT (), Numbers to Text

The Excel `isnumber ()` and `istext ()` functions can be used to check the data type of a given cell. We can use the `text()` function to convert a number to a text, as shown below.

	A	B	C	D	E	F
1	number	check			to text	
2	234	FALSE	=ISTEXT(A2)		234	=TEXT(A2,"0")
3	20222	TRUE	=ISNUMBER(A3)		20222	
4	123	FALSE	=ISNUMBER(A4)		123	

Fig. 1.30 The ISTEXT and ISNUMBER functions

1.23 Excel: NA () and ISNA () Functions

In the following example, `Data1` is divided by `Data2`. When `Data2` is zero, we will have an error message. One solution is to check whether the divisor is zero or not. If it is a zero, we generate a #N/A; the missing code for Excel means "Not Available." In addition, we can use the ISNA () function to check this missing code.

	A	B	C	D	E	F	G	H	I	J	K
1	Data1	Data2	result1			result2			result3		
2	1	4	0.25	=A2/B2		0.25	=IF(B2<>0,A2/B2,NA())		0.25	=IF(ISNA(F2),"",F2)	
3	2	5	0.4	=A3/B3		0.4	=IF(B3<>0,A3/B3,NA())		0.4	=IF(ISNA(F3),"",F3)	
4	3	0	#DIV/0!	=A4/B4		#N/A	=IF(B4<>0,A4/B4,NA())			=IF(ISNA(F4),"",F4)	

Fig. 1.31 The Excel ISNA function

In the above example, we can jump from result1 to `result3` without going through `result2`.

1.24 Random Numbers and Random Seed

It is worth mentioning Method 4. Assume that we have 100 letters. The basic design is to generate 199 integers randomly from (1,2,3,…,24, and 25). Chapter 1 discussed generating a set of random numbers using a random seed. One example is shown below. We click "Data" on the menu bar, then "Data Analysis" and "Random Number Generations," and fill in the values shown below.

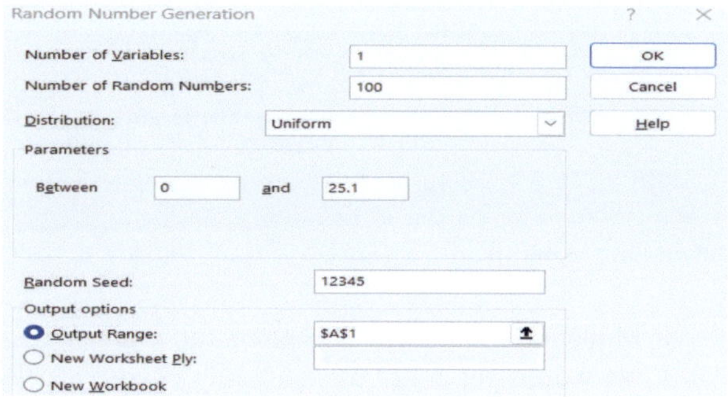

Fig. 1.32 Random number generation

In the above image, we generate 1 column with 100 random numbers drawn from a uniform distribution between 0 and 25.1. The random seed is 12345. The output is shown below.

	A	B	C
1	5.809455	5	=INT(A1)
2	14.6799	14	
3	19.75935	19	
4	16.94807	16	
5	4.464333	4	
6	17.92857	17	
7	21.04778	21	
8	4.146437	4	
9	22.26958	22	

Fig. 1.33 The Excel INT function

Column A contains real numbers, not integers. Column B includes all integers applied using the Excel `int()` function. The first letter moves to the right by 5 positions, and the second letter moves to the right by 14 positions. Now, the key is remembering that the random seed is 12345.

1.25 Excel VLOOKUP () Function

The Excel `vlookup ()` function can search a table by matching the ID. The function format is `vlookup(lookup_value,table_array,col_index_num)`. Let's use a simple example. Assume we have the following table with four columns: ID, Name, Price, and Unit.

	A	B	C	D
1	ID	Name	Price	Unit
2		1 Candy	10.2	bag
3		2 Bread	2.34	loaf
4		3 Milk	3.12	bag
5		4 Apple	10	bag
6		5 Banada	2.34	box
7		6 Wine #1	33	bottle
8		7 Eggs	3.55	box

Fig. 1.34 The data set for VLOOPUP

Assume that our objective is to show the price for a given ID. For example, for a given ID of 3, we would get 3.12. We randomly choose a cell, e.g., E5, and enter a value of 3. For cell F5, we want its price to appear. The formula is = `vlookup(E5,A1:D8,3)`. The last input of 3 indicates the function will report the corresponding value in column 3. For a value of 2, the product's name will appear instead.

	A	B	C	D	E	F	G	H
1	ID	Name	Price	Unit				
2		1 Candy	10.2	bag				
3		2 Bread	2.34	loaf				
4		3 Milk	3.12	bag	ID	price		
5		4 Apple	10	bag	3	3.12	=VLOOKUP(E5,A1:D8,3)	
6		5 Banada	2.34	box				
7		6 Wine #1	33	bottle				
8		7 Eggs	3.55	box				

Fig. 1.35 The Excel VLOOKUP function

Assume we have 16 characters: all digits from 0 to 9, plus a, b, c, d, e, and f. If we assume values from 1, 2, 3.., up to 16 to them, we have the following table on the left.

Two column table

	A	B
1	character	value
2	0	1
3	1	2
4	2	3
5	3	4
6	4	5
7	5	6
8	6	7
9	7	8
10	8	9
11	9	10
12	a	11
13	b	12
14	c	13
15	d	14
16	e	15
17	f	16

Usage of the vlookup() function

	A	B	C	D	E
1	character	value			
2	0	1			
3	1	2	given character	a	
4	2	3	value	11	
5	3	4		=VLOOKUP(D3,A1:B17,2)	
6	4	5			
7	5	6			
8	6	7			
9	7	8			
10	8	9			
11	9	10			
12	a	11			
13	b	12			
14	c	13			
15	d	14			
16	e	15			
17	f	16			

Fig. 1.36 Two-column tables

For cell D4, we have a value of "a." In cell D4, we enter the function: = `vlookup(D3,A1:B12,2)`. The first input is a given ID, the second input is the table to search for, and the last input indicates which column's value will be reported.

1.26 Excel `HLOOKUP ()` Function

Excel `hlookup ()` function is identical to `vlookup ()` with just one exception: now the table is designed horizontally instead of vertically.

	A	B	C	D	E	F	G	H	I	J	K	L	M	N	O	P	Q	R	S	T	U	V	W	X	Y	Z	AA	AB
1			1	2	3	4	5	6	7	8	9	10	11	12	13	14	15	16	17	18	19	20	21	22	23	24	25	26
2		rotor1->	B	C	D	E	F	G	H	I	J	K	L	M	N	O	P	Q	R	S	T	U	V	W	X	Y	Z	A

Fig. 1.37 The data for the HLOOKUP function

1.27 Excel: Name a Cell or Set of Data

Assume that we enter 0.1 for a risk-free rate in cell B1. For the rest of the spreadsheet, we can use \$B\$1 whenever we need this interest rate.

	A	B	C	D	E	F
1	risk-free	0.05				
2	freq	2				
3		the risk-free rate is		0.05 =B1		
4		effective annual rate is		0.050625 =EFFECT(B1,B2)		

Fig. 1.38 The risk-free in cell B1

On the other hand, we can name B1 as `risk-free and B2 as free`, as shown below.

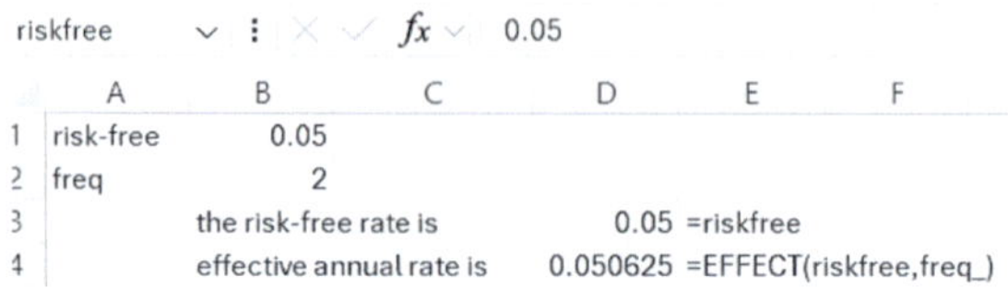

Fig. 1.39 To name a cell

There are at least two advantages to naming a cell. First, it is easy to design the rest of our spreadsheet since we can simply enter 'risk-free' instead of a specific cell address. Second, our formula is more meaningful; just compare = `effect(B1,B2)` with = `effect(riskfree, freq_)`. Note that we name B2 as `freq_` instead of `freq`, as shown below. The reason is that `freq` is one of the reserved words by Excel.

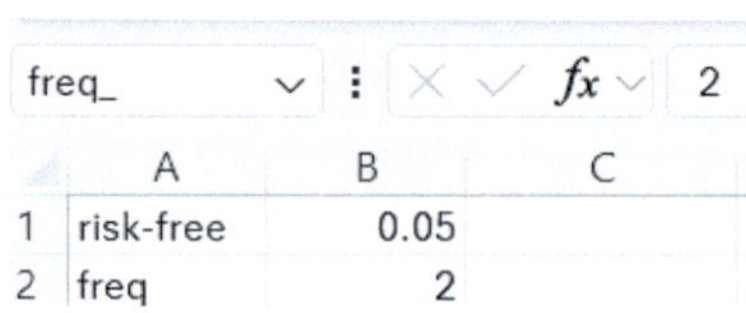

Fig. 1.40 To name the freq cell

To delete those name cells, we click "formulas" on the menu bar and then "Name Manager."

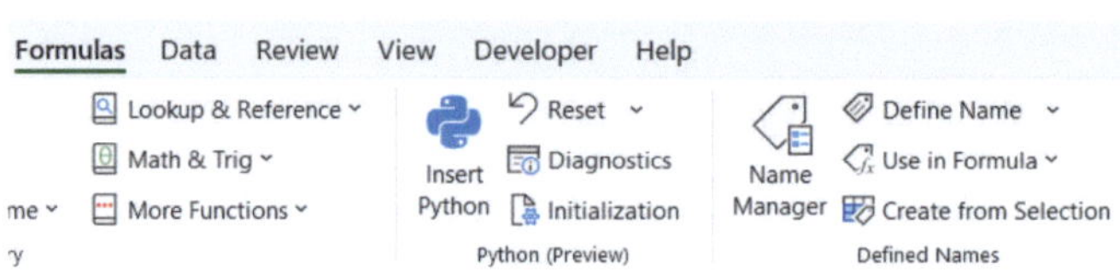

Fig. 1.41 Excel "Formulas" on the menu bar

From the above short menu, we know that we can use this method to define a name by clicking "Define Name." After clicking "Name Manager," we will see the following menu. We can edit and delete those two existing Names.

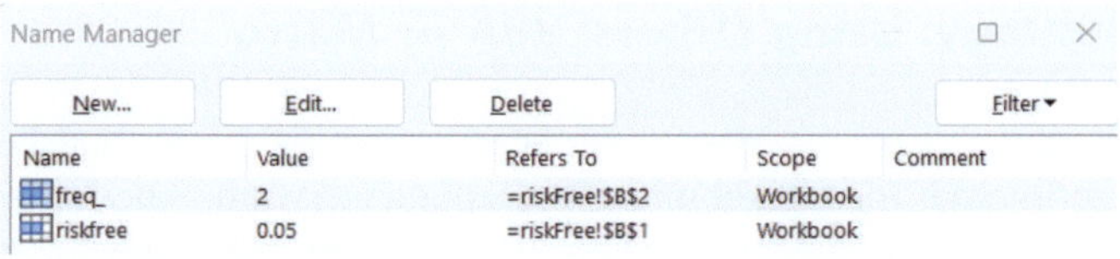

Name	Value	Refers To	Scope	Comment
freq_	2	=riskFree!$B$2	Workbook	
riskfree	0.05	=riskFree!$B$1	Workbook	

Fig. 1.42 Two cells defined

Instead of naming just one cell, we can name a data set.

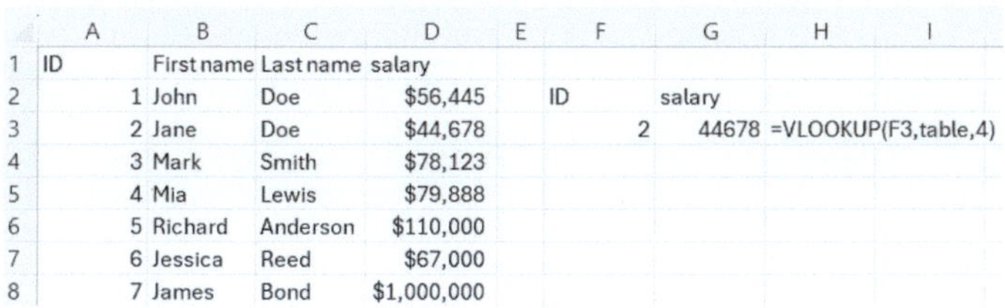

	A	B	C	D	E	F	G	H	I
1	ID	First name	Last name	salary					
2	1	John	Doe	$56,445	ID		salary		
3	2	Jane	Doe	$44,678		2	44678	=VLOOKUP(F3,table,4)	
4	3	Mark	Smith	$78,123					
5	4	Mia	Lewis	$79,888					
6	5	Richard	Anderson	$110,000					
7	6	Jessica	Reed	$67,000					
8	7	James	Bond	$1,000,000					

Fig. 1.43 To name a data set

In the above example, we name A1:D8 as `table`. Thus, in cell G3, we use a `table` instead of A1:D8 as our second input variable. This substitution simplifies our notation and makes us much less likely to make mistakes.

1.28 Why Excel Macro and VBA Are Useful

Excel VBA (Visual Basic for Applications) and Macros are potential tools that greatly enhance the functionality and efficiency of Excel. Using VBA and Macros, users can automate repetitive tasks, such as data entry, report generation, and complex calculations, saving time and reducing the likelihood of human error. This automation capability makes Excel an invaluable tool for professionals who deal with large datasets and must perform consistent and accurate operations regularly. Moreover, VBA enables users to create custom functions and interfaces that extend the default capabilities of Excel, allowing for a more tailored and user-friendly experience that can adapt to specific business needs.

Additionally, VBA and Macros are accessible even to those with limited programming experience, making it possible for many users to develop custom solutions without requiring extensive training. This ease of use and robust functionality means businesses can quickly implement and deploy automated processes that enhance productivity and efficiency. Empowering users to handle more sophisticated tasks directly within Excel, VBA, and Macros contributes to a more agile and responsive workflow, ultimately improving overall business performance and decision-making.

1.29 Strategy: Using Others' VBA or Macro

When using others' VBA or Macro, the best strategy is "Copy and Paste." First, we search the Internet for a good macro utilizing a keyword. Alternatively, we can ask ChatGPT to give us a Macro. Then, we copy and paste others' macros into our Excel. If it works, that will be great. However, if it is not good, don't try to debug it. Just delete it and try to find another one.

1.30 If Data Analysis is Not Available

When using others' VBA or Macro, we need to click "Data" on the menu bar and then "Data Analysis" on the right, as shown below.

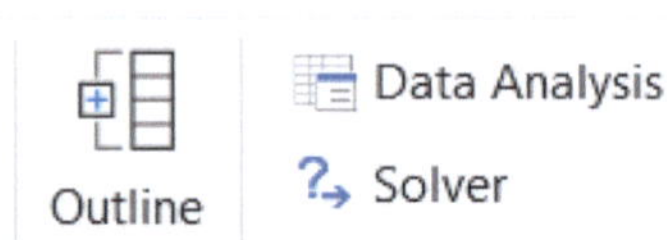

Fig. 1.44 Data Analysis on the menu bar

If "Developer" is not available on your menu bar, click 'File' on the menu bar, click 'Options', 'Customize Ribbon', Activate 'developer', and click 'OK'. After this operation, "Data Analysis" will appear on your menu bar.

1.31 Excel VBA Example: `EFFECTYAN ()`

To calculate an effect rate, Excel offers the `effect()` function to calculate an effective annual rate. For example, if the annual percentage rate (APR) is 10%, compounded semi-annually, what is its equivalent effective annual rate? Its value is calculated below.

	A	B	C	D
1	ARP	0.1		
2	n	2		
3				
4	effective annual rate	0.1025	=EFFECT(B1,B2)	

Fig. 1.45 The Excel EFFECT function

However, there is no Excel function to calculate the equivalent quarterly rate. For this purpose, we designed a VBA called `EffectYan ()` to calculate effective annual, monthly, quarterly, or daily rates. We have a help function called `effectYanHelp()` for this function.

	A	B	C	D	E	F
1						
2		usage: =effectYan(APR1,n1,n2)			=effectYanHelp()	
3						
4		APR1	0.1			
5		n1	2			
6		n2	4			
7		effect	0.024695		=effectYan(C4,C5,C6)	

Fig. 1.46 The EFFECTYAN VBA function

1.32 Excel Macro: Rotate a Set of Cells

In Chapter 4, we will discuss encryption. One of them is Enigma, used by the Nazis in World II. By design, Rotor 1 will rotate by one letter after one operation. Manually doing this is not feasible. Because of this, we have designed a Macro to rotate `Rotor1`. Below is the original position for Rotor1.

	A	B	C	D	E	F	G	H	I	J	K	L	M	N	O	P	Q	R	S	T	U	V	W	X	Y	Z	AA	AB
1			1	2	3	4	5	6	7	8	9	10	11	12	13	14	15	16	17	18	19	20	21	22	23	24	25	26
2		rotor1->	B	C	D	E	F	G	H	I	J	K	L	M	N	O	P	Q	R	S	T	U	V	W	X	Y	Z	A
3																												
4																												
5																												
6																												
7																						Click to rotate Rotor #1						
8																												

Fig. 1.47 The image of Rotor1

After one click, we will see the following result: every letter moves to the left, and the first, "B," moves to the end of the original one.

	A	B	C	D	E	F	G	H	I	J	K	L	M	N	O	P	Q	R	S	T	U	V	W	X	Y	Z	AA	AB
1			1	2	3	4	5	6	7	8	9	10	11	12	13	14	15	16	17	18	19	20	21	22	23	24	25	26
2		rotor1->	C	D	E	F	G	H	I	J	K	L	M	N	O	P	Q	R	S	T	U	V	W	X	Y	Z	A	B

Fig. 1.48 After one click, move one letter to the right

The macro is in Appendix C.

1.33 Excel: Retrieving a Text or CSV File

We downloaded the Apple historical daily data set from Yahoo! Finance. If the data set has a CSV extension, clicking the file might open it automatically. Another way to use Excel to read a given file is to highlight it and right-click your mouse to choose a software program to open it.

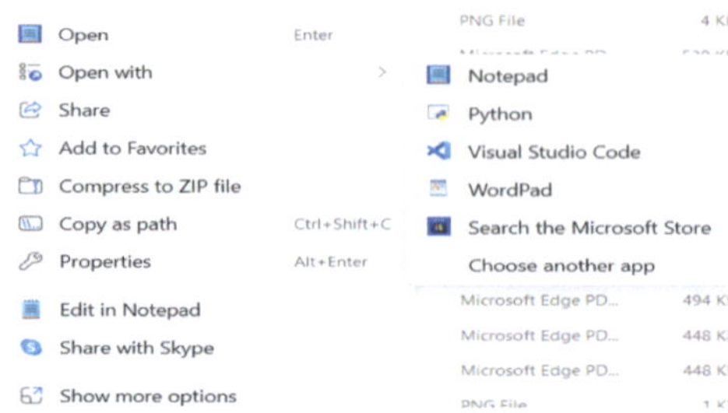

Fig. 1.49 Retrieving an external file (a text or CSV file)

Another way is to use Excel to open your file directly. After launching Excel, click "Data" on the menu bar, choose "From Text/CSV," and find your file to retrieve.

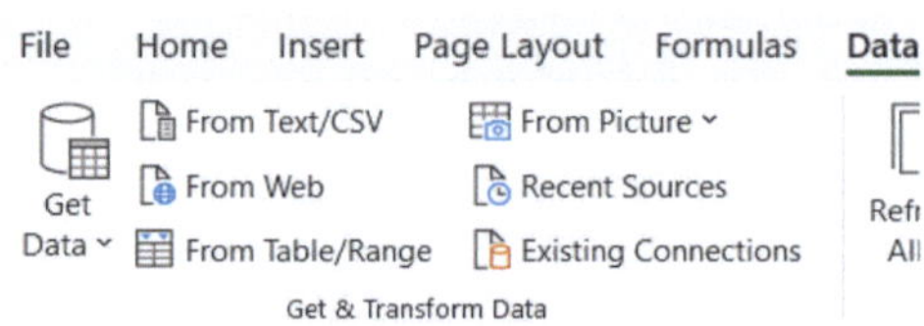

Fig. 1.50 From Text/CSV

1.34 Ctrl-End, Ctrl-Shift, and Down Arrow

We should check the last observation when retrieving a relatively big data set. In this case, we can use Ctrl-End to reach the end of the data set. One example is shown below. After hitting Ctrl-End, we have 4,441 observations; the last trading day is 8/22/2024.

4437	8/16/2024	72.6999969	73.6100006	72.5199966	73.4499969	19872100	73.4499969
4438	8/19/2024	73.3899994	73.9800034	73.3399963	73.7200012	13709300	73.7200012
4439	8/20/2024	73.75	74.75	73.7200012	74.5400009	14434000	74.5400009
4440	8/21/2024	75.3000031	75.5800018	74.5899963	75.2399979	14832000	75.2399979
4441	8/22/2024	75.3700027	76.2200012	75.1500015	75.5800018	16511100	75.5800018
4442							

Fig. 1.51 Ctrl-End to the end of your data set

Assume that we want to keep the first and last several lines. An efficient way is to highlight a few lines, as shown below.

	A	B	C	D	E	F	G	H
1	DATE	WMT.Open	WMT.High	WMT.Low	WMT.Close	WMT.Volume	WMT.Adjusted	
2	1/3/2007	15.6966667	16.1000004	15.6866674	15.8500004	107061900	10.8530235	
3	1/4/2007	15.9333334	15.9966669	15.7733326	15.9266672	51219000	10.9055243	
4	1/5/2007	15.833333	15.9333334	15.7166672	15.7966671	40670700	10.8165073	
5	1/8/2007	15.6366673	15.7700005	15.6333332	15.666667	49189200	10.7274904	
6	1/9/2007	15.666667	15.8900003	15.666667	15.7966671	43929600	10.8165073	
7	1/10/2007	15.6833334	15.873333	15.5033331	15.7600002	40044300	10.7914	
8	1/11/2007	15.7566671	15.9099998	15.7366667	15.8666668	44469600	10.8644371	

Fig. 1.52 Highlighting rows

After hitting the Ctrl-Shift keys plus the Down arrow key to reach the bottom of our data set, we move back a few lines and then delete.

1.35 An Efficient Way to Copy a Formula

Assume using the adjusted closing price to calculate returns. In cell H3, we enter a correct formula. Assume we plan to copy it to the rest of the column.

	A	B	C	D	E	F	G	H	I
1	DATE	WMT.Open	WMT.High	WMT.Low	WMT.Close	WMT.Volume	WMT.Adjusted	ret	
2	1/3/2007	15.6966667	16.1000004	15.6866674	15.8500004	107061900	10.85302353		
3	1/4/2007	15.9333334	15.9966669	15.7733326	15.9266672	51219000	10.90552425	0.004837	=G3/G2-1
4	1/5/2007	15.833333	15.9333334	15.7166672	15.7966671	40670700	10.81650734		
5	1/8/2007	15.6366673	15.7700005	15.6333332	15.666667	49189200	10.72749043		
6	1/9/2007	15.666667	15.8900003	15.666667	15.7966671	43929600	10.81650734		
7	1/10/2007	15.6833334	15.873333	15.5033331	15.7600002	40044300	10.79139996		

Fig. 1.53 An efficient way to copy a formula

We can see a dot at the right-down corner of cell H3 (cell with a formula). If we double-click this dot, the formula will be populated for the whole H column. This method would not work if there is a blank row or the H column is not adjacent to the G column.

1.36 An R-Assisted Learning Environment

Over the years, we have developed an excellent teaching method called an R-assisted learning environment. With the assistance of R, we could benefit greatly from many prewritten programs. The beauty of the process is that students and potential instructors don't need any prior knowledge related to R. Students need to download R and issue one for the following 15 lines for 15 weeks' lectures.

```
source("http://datayyy.com/fin136/week1.txt")
source("http://datayyy.com/fin136/week2.txt")
```

Note that only the first six weeks' materials are available so far.

In the next few sections, we will briefly discuss some benefits. For a more detailed discussion, please read the book's preface.

1.37 BENEFIT #1:.inClassEx ()

Doing hands-on exercises will benefit students immensely. We have a list of in-class exercises. For example, for Week 1, we have the following in-class exercises.

```
> .ice
function(i=0){
"i  class  Description
 -  ----   ------------------------------
 1   1     Watch two videos (R installation)
 2   1     How to launch and quit R?
 3   1     One-line for this course
 4   1     Watch videos related to FinTech
 5   1     Excel left(), right(), isnumber(), mode() functions

Example 1:>.ice        # show all the exercises
Example 2:>.ice()      # the same as the above
Example 3:>.ice(1)     # see the first one
```

Fig. 1.54 In-Class Exercise function:.ice

1.38 BENEFIT #2:.searchWebs ()

We have designed a function called `.searchWebs ()`, with a shortcut `.sw()`, to search a few hundred web links. This function serves two purposes: it searches for ID numbers using a keyword and goes to the website for a given ID number. For example, we are interested in Ganache, a personal Crypto transaction simulation platform. The keyword is "Ganache," as shown below.

```
> .searchWebs("ganache")
 ID                                        NAME                                                    WEBSITE
709 Ganache 1                              https://www.trufflesuite.com/ganache
711 smart contract video2 Remix Ganache and MetaMask https://youtu.be/iOCgjsqfF_w
680 yan's code crypto                      https://github.com/paulyxy/Python-Ganache-and-Crypto-transactions
>
```

Fig. 1.55 The hidden.searchWebs function

If using `.sw(709)`, we will go to that website.

Fig. 1.56 To download Ganache

1.39 Benefit #3:.`anyDailyData()`

In Chapter 6, we will discuss the risk of cryptocurrencies and compare it with trading stocks and market indexes. One risk measure is the total risk, defined as the standard deviation of returns. To download Walmart's historical daily data, go to https://finance.yahoo.com, enter WMT, choose "Historical Data" on the left, select the period and daily frequency, and download, as shown below.

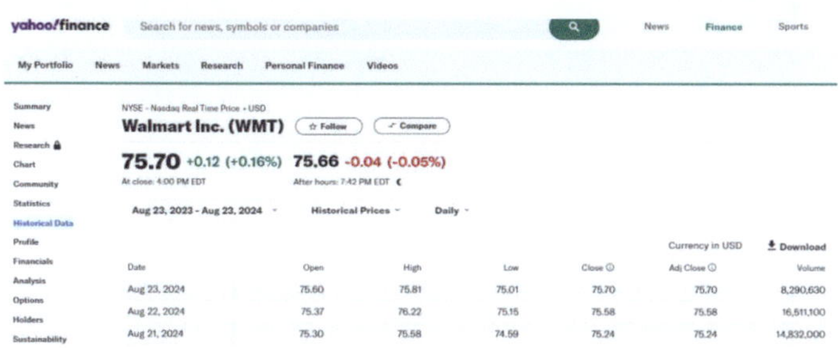

Fig. 1.57 The Yahoo Finance website

Alternatively, we can use the `.anyStockDataDailyData()` function, shown below.

```
> .anyStockDailyData ()
   Input your ticker here:
wmt
Launch Excel and paste the data there
```

```
Note that if you see just one column
        highlight it, click on 'Data' ->'Text to Columns'
        choose 'Delimiter'-> Comma -> Finish
```

It is pretty easy and takes a few seconds to download the data to Excel. This makes it less likely that students will have issues with their downloaded data for an in-class exercise.

1.40 Benefit #4:`.dictionary()`

We designed a function called `.dictionary ()` with a shortcut `.dist()`. We can use a keyword to search for its explanation.

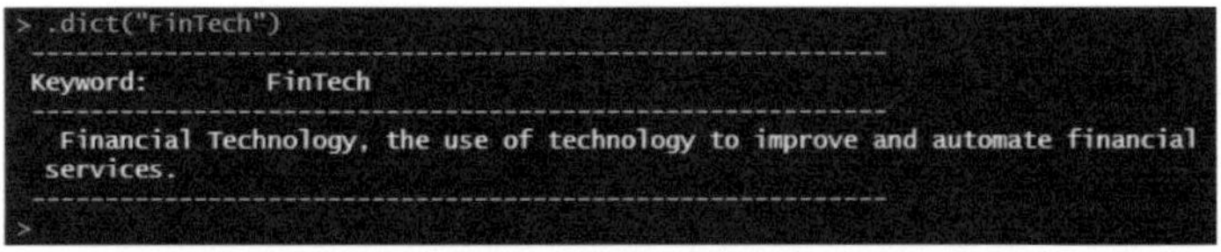

```
> .dict("FinTech")
-----------------------------------------------------------
Keyword:          FinTech
-----------------------------------------------------------
  Financial Technology, the use of technology to improve and automate financial
 services.
-----------------------------------------------------------
>
```

Fig. 1.58 The hidden.dictionary function

If using the keyword "`encryption`", we will have the following result.

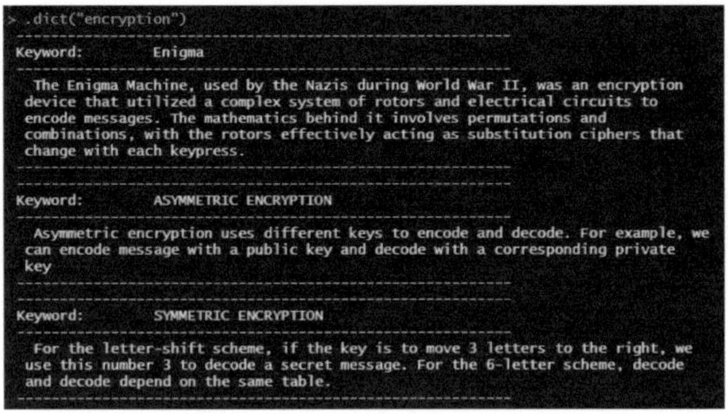

```
> .dict("encryption")
-----------------------------------------------------------
Keyword:          Enigma
-----------------------------------------------------------
  The Enigma Machine, used by the Nazis during World War II, was an encryption
 device that utilized a complex system of rotors and electrical circuits to
 encode messages. The mathematics behind it involves permutations and
 combinations, with the rotors effectively acting as substitution ciphers that
 change with each keypress.
-----------------------------------------------------------
-----------------------------------------------------------
Keyword:          ASYMMETRIC ENCRYPTION
-----------------------------------------------------------
  Asymmetric encryption uses different keys to encode and decode. For example, we
 can encode message with a public key and decode with a corresponding private
 key
-----------------------------------------------------------
-----------------------------------------------------------
Keyword:          SYMMETRIC ENCRYPTION
-----------------------------------------------------------
  For the letter-shift scheme, if the key is to move 3 letters to the right, we
 use this number 3 to decode a secret message. For the 6-letter scheme, decode
 and decode depend on the same table.
-----------------------------------------------------------
```

Fig. 1.59 The hidden.dict function using "encryption" as an input

Note that this dictionary is constantly modified.

1.41 Benefit #4:`.watchVideos ()`

Many students prefer watching short videos to understand some concepts that are difficult to explain. By typing `.watchVideos`, we would get the following list.

```
> .watchVideos
function(i=0){
"Videos for various courses
 i   Description    [ ! watched already ]
---  -----------------------------------
 1  R installation [for Windows]      (t6:39,2010)     https://www.youtube.com/watch?v=ZoPJGmpYJzw
 2  R installation [on a Mac]         (t5:59,2014)     https://www.youtube.com/watch?v=Ywj6yNfc5nM
 3  Installing R/RStudio on a Mac     (t5:59,2014)     https://www.youtube.com/watch?v=Ywj6yNfc5nM
 4  What is FinTech                   (t1:01,2023)     https://www.youtube.com/watch?v=XMTevrgV0pE
 5  FinTech: How it works             (t3:34,2018)     https://www.youtube.com/watch?v=PuAbqwTDeh0
 6  Download Ganache for windows 11 (t2:21,2022)     https://www.youtube.com/watch?v=bJriXCtGrLY
 7  Install Ganache for Mac           (t2:05,2023)     https://www.youtube.com/watch?v=5bf4UzzXvXM
 8  Getting Started with Orange 01    (t2:15,2016)     https://www.youtube.com/watch?v=HXjnDIgGDuI
 9  Orange 02: Data Workflows         (t2:34,2016)     https://www.youtube.com/watch?v=lb-x36xqJ-E
10  Machine Learning With Orange      (t5:20,2018)     https://www.youtube.com/watch?v=nNNl7Jws5Mk
11  Cryptocurrency Tether (USDT)      (t2:30,2018)     https://www.youtube.com/watch?v=ecLD07LpN8k
12  What is Tether?                   (t9:36,2021)     https://www.youtube.com/watch?v=cK8bAA6H5PY&t=48s
13  Basic Attention Token (BAT)?      (t6:21,2021)     https://www.youtube.com/watch?v=Cs7FEQgaVpo
14  Basic Attention Token?            (t3:03,2019)     https://www.youtube.com/watch?v=7p5cxCaUwm4
15  Augur (REP) Crypto Special?       (t3:06,2022)     https://www.youtube.com/watch?v=d011Eklg0sk
16  Smart contracts- Explained        (t4:16,2018)     https://www.youtube.com/watch?v=ZE2HxTmxfrI

 Example #1:> .videos2       # see this list
 Example #2:> .v2            # see this list (a short-cut)
 Example #3:> .v2(1)         # show the first video
            Note: you can issue the following line
                        rm(.videos2)
```

Fig. 1.60 The hidden.watchVideos function

To watch the first one, use its ID, i.e.,`.watcVideos(1)`.

1.42 How to Install R

To install R, we have the following five steps.

Step 1: Go to http://www.r-project.org/
Step 2: Click "CRAN" under "Download, Packages" (left-hand side)
Step 3: Choose a mirror address
Step 4: Choose appropriate software (PC, Mac)
Step 5: Click "base"

After you have finished the installation, an R icon will appear on your desktop. Alternatively, users can download RStudio (see related sections at the end of this chapter). For this course/book, either R Console or RStudio will be fine. The advantages and disadvantages of those two will be discussed at the end of this chapter.

1.43 How to Launch and Quit R

To start R, double-click the R icon on your desktop. To quit, just type `q()` from the R prompt (>).

```
> q() # first way to quit
```

Anything after # is a comment.

```
# anything after # is a comment
# the larger than sign > is the R prompt
```

When quitting, the program will ask you whether to "Save the workspace image," which means keeping all your variables or functions for future usage. At this stage, answer No.

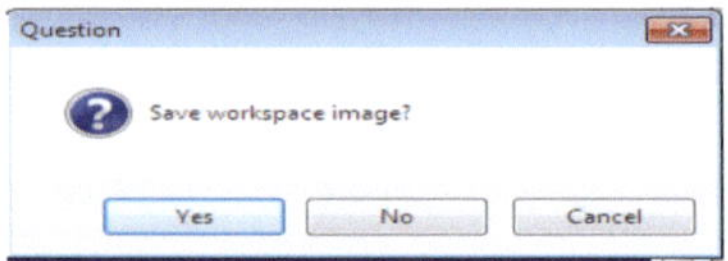

Fig. 1.61 The image of "Save workspace image?"

See below for another way to quit.

```
# [click] "file" on the menu bar - - > "exit"
```

We also could use the `q("no")` command to quit R without saving.

```
> q("no") # quit R without saving variables and functions
> q("yes") # quit R and keep variables and functions.
```

1.44 The Related Figures and Excel Files

We have made figures and Excel files available to help readers, instructors, and students use this book more effectively. The first way is to download them at https://github.com/paulyxy/Introduction-to-FinTech-using-Excel. The second way is to use the hidden `.searchFigures` (abbreviated as `.fig`) and `.searchExcelFiles` functions. Typing a function name will see its usage. For example, when typing.fig, you will see its usage, as shown below.

```
> .fig
function(chapterOrName=-9){
"Objective: 1) searching IDs for a chapter (1, 2, ..., 18)
            2) searching IDs for a given keyword
            3) showing a figure for a given ID (input ID>18)

    Example #1> .searchFigures   # show this help
    Example #2> .fig             # show this help (short-cut name)
    Example #3> .fig()           # show this help
    Example #4> .fig(1)          # show IDs for chapter 1
                ID                                         NAME
                29 fig01_01_A1.png
                30 fig01_02_paste.png
                31 fig01_03_equal_A1.png
                         more
    Example #5> .fig('fig01')    # show IDs for chapter 1
    Example #6> .fig('private')  # keyword is 'private'
    Example #7> .fig(55)         # show a figure with ID=55
```

Fig. 1.62 The function used to search figures (.searchFigures)

For the second function, typing its name will get its usage, shown below.

```
> .sef()
function(chapterOrName=-9){
"Objective: 1) search for IDs for a chapter (input value: 1, 2, .., 18)
            2) search for IDs for a given keyword
            3) download an Excel file for a given ID (input > 18)

     Example #1> .searchExcelFiles # see the usage
     Example #2> .sef              # see the usage (.sef is the short-cut name)
     Example #3> .sef()            # see the usage
     Example #4> .sef(1)           # show IDs of the Excel files related to Chpter 1
              ID                            NAME
               1 c01_01_equal_A1.xlsx
               2 c01_02_copy_as_values.xlsx

               9 c01_09_concat.xlsx
               10 c01_10_data_effect.xlsm

     Example #5> .sef('block')   # show related IDs for the keyword
              ID                                          NAME
              20 c02_10_blockchainGame3_ASCII.xlsx
              27 c02_17_to_excel_3methods_6digits_block1.xlsx
     Example #6> .sef(55)          # download the Excel file with 55 as its ID
                                   # same as .downloadExcel(55)
     Example #7> .downloadExcel(1) # for ID <18
```

Fig. 1.63 The function used to search Excel files (.searchExcelFiles)

Appendix A: Issue the Following line of R Code for Week 1

```
source("http://datayyy.com/i2ft/week1.txt")
```

```
*---------------------------------------------------------------------*
* Introduction to FinTech using Excel                     2025        *
*       (in an R-assisted learning environment)                       *
*---------------------------------------------------------------------*
*  .c1 Introduction & Excel Basics           .c16 R basics(optional)  *
*---------------------------------------------------------------------*
* >.c1       # go to chapter 1                                        *
* >.uu       # go to utility submenu                                  *
* >.fintech  # back to this menu                                      *
* >.ft       # same as .fintech                                       *
*---------------------------------------------------------------------*
```

Fig. 1.64 The menu for Week 1

Appendix B: For Chapter 1, Type `.chapter1` or `.c1`.

```
> .chapter1
function(i=0){
" i  Chapter 1: Introduction/Excel  i  Excel Basics                   i  Excel Basics
  -  ------------------------------ -- ------------------------------ -- ---------------------
  1  Self-introduction             21  Excel:2-dimensional spreadsheet 41 formulatext()
  2  Syllabus                      22  =A1 What does it mean?         42  Copy: as values
  3    : Description of the course 23  +, -, /, and *                 43      : as formula
  4    : textbook                  24  Format our cell                44      : better way to copy formula
  5    : about this book           25  count() vs. counta() functions 45      : note
  6    : Excel is the main tool    26  name a set of data             46  mod() function
  7    : R-assisted environment    27  isnumber()                     47  vlookup()
  8    : Time and location         28  true or false                  48  vlookup(): example #2
  9    : Hands-on approach         29  if()                           49  relative vs. absolute addresses
 10  R : no R knowledge is needed  30  String: variable               50            : example PVIF
 11    : R installation            31        : istext()               51  SUBSTITUTE() function
 12    : (alternatively) RStudio   32        : len()                  52  rename your spreadsheet
 13    : Launch and quit R         33        : left()                 53  copy your spreadsheet
 14    : R is case-sensitive       34        : right()                54  Macro: why copy others' macro/VBA?
 15    : One line for this course  35        : right(left())          55       : how
 16    : Chapter 16 (optional)     36        : concatenate()          56       : Example of VBA
 17  FinTech vs. programming       37        : text to columns        57       : Example of Macro
 18  After this course (book)      38        : text to number         58       : How to record your own micro?
 19  Videos                        39        : alignment              59       : more on macro
 20  Links                         40        : number to text         60       : more on VBA

 Example #1:>.c1    # see the above list
 Example #2:>.c1()  # the same as the above
 Example #3:>.c1(1) # see the first explanation
```

Fig. 1.65 The contents of Chapter 1

Appendix C: The Excel Macro to Rotate a Rotor (for Enigma Scheme)

From C2 to AB2, we have the following 26 letters.
B,C,D,E,F,G,H,I,J,K,L,M,N,O,P,Q,R,S,T,U,V,W,X,Y,Z,A

After running the macro once, the row will become
C,D,E,F,G,H,I,J,K,L,M,N,O,P,Q,R,S,T,U,V,W,X,Y,Z,A,B

```
Sub RotateRow()
      Dim i As Integer
      Dim temp As String
      ' Store the first letter in a temporary variable
      temp = Range("C2").Value
      ' Shift all letters to the left
      For i = 3 To 27 ' C to AB
           Range(Cells(2, i), Cells(2, i)).Value = Range(Cells(2, i
+ 1), Cells(2, i + 1)).Value
      Next i
      ' Place the first letter at the end
      Range("AB2").Value = temp
End Sub
```

Appendix D: Effective Rate Conversion

```
Function EFFECTyan (APR1 As Variant, n1 As Integer, n2 As Integer)
As Variant
' author yuxing.yan
' date : 2/4/2013
      Dim i, n, roduct As String
      If n1 > 365 And n2 > 365 Then
            EFFECTyan = APR1
      ElseIf n1 > 365 And n2 < 365 Then
            EFFECTyan = Exp(APR1) ^ (1 / n2) - 1
      ElseIf n1 < 365 And n2 > 365 Then
            EFFECTyan = n1 * Log(1 + APR1 / n1)
      Else
            EFFECTyan = (1 + APR1 / n1) ^ (n1 / n2) - 1
      End If
End Function
Function effectYanHelp() As String
      effectYanHelp= "usage: =effectYan(APR1,n1,n2)"
End Function
```

Exercises

1.1 What is FinTech, and how has it transformed the traditional financial industry?
1.2 Describe three critical areas of FinTech and provide examples of companies or technologies in each region.

1.3 How did the 2008 global financial crisis influence the growth of FinTech?
1.4 Explain the role of mobile technology in the development of FinTech solutions.
1.5 What are the benefits of FinTech for consumers, and how does it improve financial accessibility?
1.6 Discuss the impact of blockchain technology on FinTech. Please provide examples of how it is being used today.
1.7 What challenges do FinTech companies face when innovating within the financial sector?
1.8 How does FinTech enhance the transparency and security of financial transactions?
1.9 Describe the peer-to-peer (P2P) lending concept and its significance in FinTech.
1.10 What is a Robo-advisor, and how does it change how individuals manage their investments?
1.11 What is the difference between the `LEFT()` and `RIGHT()` functions in Excel? Provide an example of each.
1.12 How can the `LEN()` function be proper when working with text data in Excel?
1.13 Describe a scenario where the `FORMULATEXT()` function would be useful.
1.14 Explain the difference between `VLOOKUP()` and `HLOOKUP()`. When would you use one over the other?
1.15 What is the purpose of hiding and unhiding rows and columns in Excel, and how can it be done?
1.16 How can the `TEXT TO COLUMNS` feature be used to manipulate data in Excel? Provide a practical example.
1.17 Define relative and absolute cell references in Excel and provide an example of each.
1.18 How do the `COUNT()` and `COUNTA ()` functions differ in Excel? When would you use each?
1.19 What is the purpose of the `CONCAT()` function, and how does it differ from using the `&` operator?
1.20 How can the `IF()` function be used to perform conditional calculations? Provide a basic example.
1.21 Describe how the `SUBSTITUTE()` function works and give an example of its use.
1.22 What does the `ISNA()` function do, and why is it essential when working with lookup functions like `VLOOKUP()`?
1.23 How can the `ISNUMBER ()` and `ISTEXT()` functions be used to validate data in Excel?
1.24 Explain how random number generation works in Excel. How can a random seed be used to ensure consistency in random numbers?
1.25 What is the significance of using random numbers and seeds in financial modeling?

1.26 What are some advantages of using VBA or Macros in Excel for repetitive tasks?
1.27 Describe a strategy for effectively using someone else's VBA or Macro in your Excel projects.
1.28 What are the risks and benefits associated with using Macros in Excel?
1.29 How can the `ISNUMBER()` function be combined with `IF()` to create a simple error-checking formula?
1.30 Describe a practical application where `VLOOKUP ()` can be combined with `IF()` to provide more dynamic results.
1.31 When our data set is sorted from the newest to the oldest, we get an error message for the last return.

	A	G	H	I	J	K
1	DATE	WMT.Adjusted		return		
2	8/22/2024	75.5800018		0.00451893	=G2/G3-1	
3	8/21/2024	75.2399979		0.00939089		
4	8/20/2024	74.5400009		0.01112316		
4436	1/10/2007	10.7914		-0.0023212		
4437	1/9/2007	10.8165073		0.00829802		
4438	1/8/2007	10.7274904		-0.0082297		
4439	1/5/2007	10.8165073		-0.0081626		
4440	1/4/2007	10.9055243		0.00483743		
4441	1/3/2007	10.8530235		#DIV/0!	=G4441/G4442-1	
4442						
4443		number of returns		4439		

Fig. 1.66 Several lines of WMT's daily data

Design a solution to avoid such an error message.
1.32 What happens if we choose only the Date Column to sort for a data set with multiple columns? For example, go to https://finance.yahoo.com and enter AAPL to download the historical data for Apple. Sort the data both ways: from the oldest to the newest and the other way around.

References

Damsker, A. (2024). *Understanding DeFi, the roles, tools, risks, and rewards of decentralized finance*. O'Reilly.

Dumas, A. (1844). *Count of Monte Cristo*. http://gutenberg.org/files/1184/1184-0.txt

Yan, Y. (2023). *Learning R and Python for business school students*. Cambridge Scholars Publishing. Click here for the link, the preface, and the https://github.com/paulyxy/Learning-R-and-Python-for-Business-School-Students- on GitHub.

Yan, Y. (2017). *Python for finance* (2nd ed.). Packt Publishing. Click https://www.packtpub.com/product/python-for-finance-second-edition/9781787125698 for the book link, for the code, and https://github.com/paulyxy/slides-for-Python-for-Finance-2nd-edition for the slides (15 weeks).

Yan, Yuxing's Excel home page. http://datayyy.com/excel/

Blockchain 1: Numbers and Alphanumeric

2

The concept of blockchain is quite difficult to explain and understand. Since this confusing part discourages students from exploring FinTech further, we designed an innovative way to explain those concepts in four stages: from the easiest to the most difficult. Another strategy is to use Excel to generate hypothetical blocks linking with the previous ones. This hands-on approach will help students and new learners comprehend those abstract concepts. In this chapter, the following topics will be covered:

- Definition of block and blockchain
- Our innovative 4-stage approach
- Stage #1: Numbers only with a 2-digit (and 10-digit) check number
- Stage #2: Alphabets and numbers with a 6-character Hash
- Stage #3: All ASCII characters with a 6-character Hash
- Stage #4: Sha256 with 64-character Hash
- [Note Stages # and 4 will be discussed in Chapter 4]
- Our.`sha256()`,.`sha256web ()`, and.`sha256LocalFile()` functions
- Four Blockchain-based games (one game for each stage)

Supplementary Information The online version contains supplementary material available at https://doi.org/10.1007/978-3-031-89779-5_2.

Y. Yan, *Introduction to FinTech using Excel*, Springer Texts in Business and Economics, https://doi.org/10.1007/978-3-031-89779-5_2

2.1 Introduction

First, we offer a standard definition of Block and Blockchain. In the next section, we specify our 4-stage approach. A block is a unit of data in a blockchain. It contains a list of transactions or records. Its components include data, the actual transactions or records, timestamps, when the block was created, and previous Hash, a unique identifier (hash) of the last block in the chain, ensuring the integrity of the blockchain (will be discussed much later (in this chapter). Nonce is a random number used in mining to find a hash that meets the network's difficulty criteria, and a hash is a unique identifier for the block generated based on its contents and the previous block's hash. The concept of the hash or sha256 is the most difficult one to understand.

A blockchain is a distributed ledger technology consisting of a blockchain, each containing a list of transactions. It is decentralized, transparent, and, most importantly, secure. Its key Characteristics are (1) decentralization: No central authority; it is maintained by a network of nodes (computers); (2) transparency: All transactions are publicly recorded and can be verified; (3) immutability: Once a block is added to the blockchain, it cannot be altered without changing all subsequent blocks, which is computationally infeasible. And most importantly, (4) security: It uses cryptographic hashing to ensure data integrity and security, providing a robust foundation for FinTech.

2.2 What is a Hash?

In blockchain, a hash is a fixed-size alphanumeric string generated by a cryptographic hash function that uniquely represents data of any size. Hashes are used to secure data, verify integrity, and link blocks together in the chain, ensuring that any alteration to the data will change the hash, making tampering evident. Below, let's look at a simple example.

We would get the following hash for "`John Doe`".

```
6CEA57C2FB6CBC2A40411135005760F241FFFC3E5E67AB99882726431037F908
```

Now, readers/students don't have to understand the concept thoroughly; a couple of points. The length of the actual hash is 64, as shown below.

	A	B	C	D	E	F	G	I
1	6CEA57C2FB6CBC2A40411135005760F241FFFC3E5E67AB99882726431037F908							
2								
3	n	64	=LEN(A1)					

Fig. 2.1 The length of a Hash

Table 2.1 Four stages to understand the concepts of block and blockchain

Stage	Name	Method	Check values
1	Numbers only: 2 digits	(just 0,1,…, 9)	0 to 9
	Numbers only: 10 digits		
2	Alphabetic and numbers	(0,1,2,…,9,a,b,c, …,z)	Checking characters limited to 10 digits plus a, b, c, d, e, and f
3	all ASCII characters	All ASCII characters	
4	Sha256	The Crypto True Hash	

We can manually find the unique characters as 0, 1, 2, 3, 4, 5, 6, 7, 8, 9, A, B, C, D, E, and F. The letter D is missing in the hash. The unique values consist of ten digits plus A to F. In Appendix D, we show how to get those unique values.

2.3 Our Four-Stage Approach

Many students are completely at a loss when they are taught the concepts of Sha256. They either remember it or do not understand its underlying logic, which will hurt their desire to learn more. Understanding the reasoning behind blockchain is essential. However, it is pretty challenging to explain it. To help students understand that concept better, we have designed a unique approach: our four-stage approach, from the simplest to the most complex. Those four stages are listed in the Table 2.1.

For Stage #1, using just numbers makes it easy to understand the logic. More importantly, we know how to link this block with previous ones, i.e., how to form a blockchain. After understanding this basic structure, we will move on to more advanced stages. However, the logic remains the same.

2.4 Stage #1: Numbers Only with 2 Digits

Assume that John sent Mary a set of numbers. How do we verify that Mary has received the correct set of numbers? A straightforward solution is to break those numbers into digits and add them. Mary will email John a check number with just two digits. For example, if the summation of those digits is 3451678, then tell John the check number is 38. Below, let's try a simple case with just five numbers. One example is given below. In total, we have five values.

```
12345
555
23456
123
431
```

We can break those five numbers into 24 digits and then add them. The first and the last digits will be our final result, as shown below.

```
1+2+3+4+5+ 5+5+5 + 2+3+4+5+6 + 1+2+3+4+3+1 =64
```

Our checking number is 64. No one can figure out our original five values from this value. In other words, it is computationally infeasible to reverse engineer it. In addition, it is deterministic, i.e., our simple method always produces the same hash value for a particular input.

On the other hand, this simple method is unreliable since changing the order of the digits will give us the same answer. For example, if we replace the first number, 12345, with 54123, it will end up with the same check number. Later in the chapter, we show how to improve it using ten digits instead of 2.

2.5 The Second Block

From the previous section, we have five numbers. The first and last digits of their simple summation are 64. Let's call it the first block. Now, let's show how to calculate the check digit of the second block. For a new set of values, such as 7, we calculate the sum of all the digits plus 6 and 4. In other words, we also include the check number of the first block. This time, let's assume that we have the following seven numbers.

```
4567
234
5623456
34123
731
129
37
64   <- from block 1
```

The sum will be

```
4+5+6+7+ 2+3+4+ 5+6+2+3+4+5+6 + 3+4+1+2+3 +7+3+1 +1+2+9+3+7+6+4 =
118
```

Now, the check number for the second set of numbers is 18. Block 2 is linked to block 1 since we add 64 to calculate the new sum. Another way to link Block 1 with Block 2 is to multiply the new sum with Block 1' check number (or Hash).

Table 2.2 Five methods to calculate summations

	Multiplier	Explanation
Method 1	1,1,1,1,1, ….,	A simple average
Method 2	1,2,1,2,1,2,….	Recycle 1 and 2:
Method 3	1,2,3,1,2,3,1,2,3	Recycle 1,2, and 3
Method 4	1,2,3,4,1,2,3,4	Recycle 1,2,3, and 4
Method 5	1,2,3,4,5,1,2,3,4,5,,,,	Recycle 1,2,3,4, and 5

2.6 Numbers Only with 10 Digits

For the previous method, we use simple summation, i.e., adding those digits directly. Let's design a 10-digit check number. Below is our five-way design: calculate products first, then add them together. After that, we still take the first and last digits (Table 2.2).

Those five methods are shown in the following Excel image.

	A	B	C	D	E	F	G	H	I	J	K	L	M
1				=IF(D3<2,D3+1,1)					=$B3*C3				
2	raw data	digits	factor 1	factor2	factor 3	factor 4	factor 5		product1	product2	product3	product4	product5
3	12345	1	1	1	1	1	1		1	1	1	1	1
4	555	2	1	2	2	2	2		2	4	4	4	4
5	23456	3	1	1	3	3	3		3	3	9	9	9
6	123	4	1	2	1	4	4		4	8	4	16	16
7	431	5	1	1	2	1	5		5	5	10	5	25
8		5	1	2	3	2	1		5	10	15	10	5
9		5	1	1	1	3	2		5	5	5	15	10
10		5	1	2	2	4	3		5	10	10	20	15
11		2	1	1	3	1	4		2	2	6	2	8
12		3	1	2	1	2	5		3	6	3	6	15
13		4	1	1	2	3	1		4	4	8	12	4
14		5	1	2	3	4	2		5	10	15	20	10
15		6	1	1	1	1	3		6	6	6	6	18
16		1	1	2	2	2	4		1	2	2	2	4
17		2	1	1	3	3	5		2	2	6	6	10
18		3	1	2	1	4	1		3	6	3	12	3
19		4	1	1	2	1	2		4	4	8	4	8
20		3	1	2	3	2	3		3	6	9	6	9
21		1	1	1	1	3	4		1	1	1	3	4
22													
23									64	95	125	159	178

Fig. 2.2 Five ways to calculate a summation

Colum A contains our five values. We manually break up the digits and put them in Column B. Five methods are shown in columns C to G. Cell D1 shows the formula in cell D2. After getting those sets of multipliers for five methods, we can see the products in columns I to M. Cell I1 shows the formula in cell I3. The final summations are 64, 95, 125, 159, and 178. For choosing the first and last digits, our final ten digits are 6,495,151,918. This method is also deterministic and reversible.

2.7 Remainder: Excel `MOD ()` Function

The `mod ()` Excel function offers the remainder. The function has two inputs: number and divisor. Let's use the most frequently used divisor, 10, as an example. For a value of 14, it is 10 + 4, thus the remainder is 4. For 145, its value is 14*10

+ 5; so its remainder is 5 (see below). In C2, we enter = `formulatext(B2)` since we want to know the formula in cell B2. This is also true for cells C3 and C4.

	A	B	C
1	value	mod() function	
2	14	4	=MOD(A2,10)
3	145	5	=MOD(A3,10)
4	2345	5	=MOD(A4,10)

Fig. 2.3 The Excel MOD function with 10 as the divisor

Let's use another divisor, such as 7; see a few examples below.

	A	B	C
1	value	mod() function	
2	10	3	=MOD(A2,7)
3	14	0	=MOD(A3,7)
4	20	6	=MOD(A4,7)
5	2345	0	=MOD(A5,7)

Fig. 2.4 The MOD function with 7 as the divisor

Since the logic remains the same, we explain two values. For 10, we know its value is 7 + 3. Thus, the remainder is 3. For 14, we know that its value is 2*7. Then, the remainder is zero. Next, we will use a unique divisor: 16. A few examples are shown below. Again, the underlying logic is the same.

	A	B	C
1	value	mod() function	
2	14	14	=MOD(A2,16)
3	145	1	=MOD(A3,16)
4	2345	9	=MOD(A4,16)

Fig. 2.5 The Excel MOD function with 16 as the divisor

The last divisor of 16 will be used in our calculation in the rest of the chapter.

2.8 Stage #2: Numbers and Letters

We keep the first and last digits for Stage 1 (with numbers only). Thus, there are two digits for each way to summarize our values. For this stage (Stage 2), we modify the old design of getting the first and last digit of the sum. Now, we get a remainder by dividing a summation by 16. For example, a remainder of 1 will be "0" while a remainder of 15 will be "e". Thus, unlike Stage #1, five methods will only give us five final characters. We generate two tables before we explain this stage. Both tables have two columns,

Table #1:

The first column has ten digits plus 26 letters, i.e., 0,1,2,…,9, a,b,…,z
The second column has a set of assigned values such as 1,2, …, 36

One example of Table 1 is shown below on the left (Columns A and B). Later, we search this table for its corresponding value for a given letter or digit. For example, the letter 'a' will get a value of 11, and a digit of 9 will get a value of 10. We hide a few rows (rows 15 to 36) for an easy illustration.

	A	B
1	Table #1	
2	character	assigned value
3	0	1
4	1	2
5	2	3
6	3	4
7	4	5
8	5	6
9	6	7
10	7	8
11	8	9
12	9	10
13	a	11
14	b	12
37	y	35
38	z	36
39		
40		

	D	E
1	Table #2	
2	remainder	character
3	1	0
4	2	1
5	3	2
6	4	3
7	5	4
8	6	5
9	7	6
10	8	7
11	9	8
12	10	9
13	11	a
14	12	b
15	13	c
16	14	d
17	15	e
18	16	f

Figs. 2.6 and 2.7 Table #1 and Table #2

Table 2 (one example shown above on the right):

Column D is named "Remainder" with values from 1 to 16.
Column E has 10 digits and 6 letters from A to F.

With those tables ready, we have the following procedure (for this Stage).

- Step 1: Input a sentence
- Step 2: Extract numbers and letters
- Step 3: Convert those characters to a column
- Step 4: Based on this column, search Table 1 to generate a column with corresponding values
- Step 5: Calculate the summation and divide 16 to get the remainder.
- Step 6: Search Table 2 to get our first check value.

To make our explanation easy to understand, we highlight the range of Table 1 and enter the name of 'table1' on the top left. Along the same logic, we highlight the range of Table 2 and enter the name of 'Table' on the top left. Later in our formulae, we use 'table1' instead of A1:A38 or \$A\$1:\$A\$38. This is true for the second table; we use "table2" instead of `$D$1:$E$18`.

Range of Table 1: A1:B38 (name box: table1)

	A	B
1	Table #1	
2	character	assigned v
3	0	1
4	1	2
5	2	3
6	3	4
7	4	5
8	5	6
9	6	7
10	7	8
11	8	9
12	9	10
13	a	11
14	b	12
33	u	31
34	v	32
35	w	33
36	x	34
37	y	35
38	z	36

Range of Table 2: D1:E18 (name box: table2)

	D	E
1	Table #2	
2	remainder	character
3	1	0
4	2	1
5	3	2
6	4	3
7	5	4
8	6	5
9	7	6
10	8	7
11	9	8
12	10	9
13	11	a
14	12	b
15	13	c
16	14	d
17	15	e
18	16	f

Figs. 2.8 and 2.9 The ranges of two tables

2.9 Example for Alphabets and Numbers

Let's use a simple sentence to illustrate: `John Doe borrowed $100 from Mary.` We entered this sentence in cell G2. For Column H, we manually enter those letters or numbers. The result is shown below.

	G	H
1	sentence	column
2	John Doe borrowed $100 from Mary.	J
3		o
4	the number of characters of G2	h
5	33	n
6	=LEN(G2)	d
7		o
8	the number of characters of Column H	e
9	26	b
10	=COUNTA(H2:H27)	o
11		r
12		r
13		o
14		w
15		e
16		d
17		1
18		0
19		0
20		f
21		r

Fig. 2.10 Sentence to symbols

To double-check, we can calculate the length of the original sentence, 33, and the count of column H starting from cell H2. Manually, we found seven characters. We will remove five spaces, a dollar sign, and a period (33–7 = 26). The following image shows the operation. Based on Column H, we generate Column I by applying the Excel `vlookup ()` for Table 1. After dividing 514 (total summation) by 16, we have a remainder of 2. From Table 2, we find our result is 1.

	H	I	J	K	L	M
1	column	search Table 1				
2	J	20	=VLOOKUP(H2,table1,2)			
3	o	25				
4	h	18	sum ->	514	=SUM(I2:I27)	
5	n	24	remainder ->	2	=MOD(K4,16)	
6	d	14	search Table2 ->	1	=VLOOKUP(K5,table2,2)	
7	o	25				
8	e	15	our final result ->	1		
9	b	12				
10	o	25				
11	r	28				
12	r	28				
13	o	25				
14	w	33				
15	e	15				
16	d	14				
17	1	2				
18	0	1				
19	0	1				

Fig. 2.11 Searching Table 1 using Excel vlookup

The above operation applies the simple summation. Like Stage 1 (for numbers only), we can use different ways to calculate other summations. In the next section, we show five ways to calculate summations.

2.10 Example 2: Alphabets and Numbers

The underlying logic will be the same as the example for "Number-Only" with ten digits. Since we use the remainder from each method, six methods will give us six characters chosen from (0, 1, 2,.., 9, a, b, …, f). The following table shows the five ways to generate factors used to create products from the original values of our sentence (Table 2.3).

We use the same sentence, "`John Doe borrowed $100 from Mary`", as shown below.

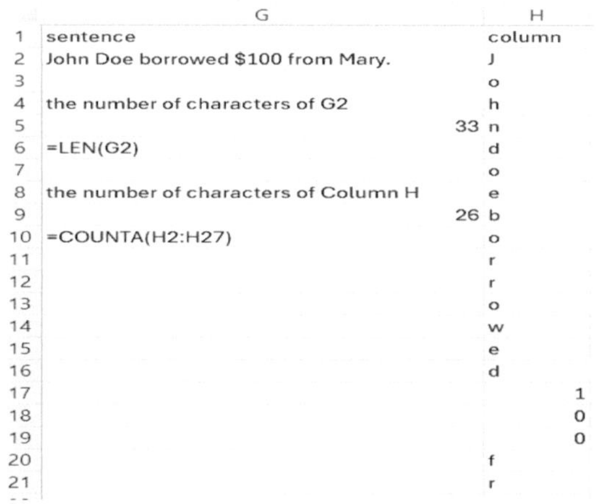

	G	H	
1	sentence	column	
2	John Doe borrowed $100 from Mary.	J	
3		o	
4	the number of characters of G2	h	
5	33	n	
6	=LEN(G2)	d	
7		o	
8	the number of characters of Column H	e	
9	26	b	
10	=COUNTA(H2:H27)	o	
11		r	
12		r	
13		o	
14		w	
15		e	
16		d	
17			1
18			0
19			0
20		f	
21		r	

Fig. 2.12 Sentence to symbols

Below, Columns K to O contains five different ways to generate factors, while Columns Q to V shows the products. For example, S2 has a value of 40, the product of 20 (J's value) and 2 (the first factor for Method 3). The formula in cell V2 is = `$I2*O2`, shown in Cell Y2.

Table 2.3 Five methods to calculate summations (this is the same as Table 2.2 but applied to both Alphabets and numbers)

	Multiplier	Explanation
Method 1	1,1,1,1,1, …..,	A simple average
Method 2	1,2,3,4, ….	Starting from 1, then add one for the next value
Method 3	2,3,4,5…,	Same as the above except starting from 2
Method 4	3,4,5,6,,…	Same as the above except starting from 3
Method 5	4,5,6,7,…	Same as the above except starting from 4

	H	I	J	K	L	M	N	O	P	Q	R	S	T	U	V	W	X	Y	Z	AA	AB
1	column	value	factor1	factor2	factor3	factor4	factor5	factor6		prod1	prod2	prod3	prod4	prod5	prod6						
2	J	20	1	1	2	3	4	5		20	20	40	60	80	100	<- =$I2*O2					
3	o	25	1	2	3	4	5	6		25	50	75	100	125	150						
4	h	18	1	3	4	5	6	7		18	54	72	90	108	126						
5	n	24	1	4	5	6	7	8		24	96	120	144	168	192						
6	d	14	1	5	6	7	8	9		14	70	84	98	112	126						
7	o	25	1	6	7	8	9	10		25	150	175	200	225	250						
8	e	15	1	7	8	9	10	11		15	105	120	135	150	165						
9	b	12	1	8	9	10	11	12		12	96	108	120	132	144						
10	o	25	1	9	10	11	12	13		25	225	250	275	300	325						
11	r	28	1	10	11	12	13	14		28	280	308	336	364	392						
25	a	11	1	24	25	26	27	28		11	264	275	286	297	308						
26	r	28	1	25	26	27	28	29		28	700	728	756	784	812						
27	y	35	1	26	27	28	29	30		35	910	945	980	1015	1050						
28																					
29									sum->	514	6968	7482	7996	8510	9024						
30									remainder->	2	8	10	12	14	16	<- =IF(MOD(V29,16)=0,16,MOD(V29,16))					
31										1	7	9	b	d	f						
32									final hash	179bdf		<- =CONCAT(Q31:V31)									

Fig. 2.13 Generating a 6-symbol Hash

Method 1's final summation is 514, and the remainder is 2 after being divided by 16. Based on Table 2, a value of 2 (reminder) will give us a result of 1. For the last method, the remainder of 9024 will be zero. However, there is no zero in Column D Table 2. Thus, we add an `if()` function, i.e., when a remainder is 0, we assign 16 to it; see the formula in cell V30.

2.11 Decimal System Illustration

This section serves the next section, the hexadecimal system, since we are all used to the decimal system. The following procedure is given.

Step 1: Use 10 digits from 0, 1, …, 9 to form a Lego (Lego1)
Step 2: Pick up the first digit, 0, and repeat it 10 times (Lego2)
Step 3: Put Lego2 and Lego1 side-by-side with Lego2 on the left
Step 4: Repeat Steps 3 and 2 with a digit 1
Step 5: Repeat Step 4 with other digits, such as 2,3,…,

Those four steps are shown in the following table.

Step 1	Step 2	Step 3		Step 4	
Lego1	Lego2	Lego2&Lego1		Lego3	Legos3&1
0	0	00	0	1	10
1	0	01	1	1	11
2	0	02	2	1	12
3	0	03	3	1	13
4	0	04	4	1	14
5	0	05	5	1	15
6	0	06	6	1	16
7	0	07	7	1	17
8	0	08	8	1	18
9	0	09	9	1	19

Fig. 2.14 Lego 1

For Step 4, shown above, the Lego3 is for 1. We can use 2, 3, or other values for this step.

2.12 Hexadecimal System Illustration

Similarly, for a hexadecimal system, we have the following steps.

Step 1: Use 10 digits (0, 1, …, 9) and 6 letters (a, b, c, d, e, f) to form a Lego (Lego1)
Step 2: Pick up the first digit, 0, and repeat it 16 times (Lego2)
Step 3: Put Lego2 and Lego1 side-by-side with Lego2 on the left
Step 4: Repeat Steps 3 and 2 with a digit 1
Step 5: Repeat Step 4 with other digits, such as 2,3,…,

Those four steps are shown in the following table.

Step 1	Step 2	Step 3		Step 4	
Lego1	Lego2	Legos2&1		Lego3	Legos3&1
0	0	00	0	1	10
1	0	01	1	1	11
2	0	02	2	1	12
3	0	03	3	1	13
4	0	04	4	1	14
5	0	05	5	1	15
6	0	06	6	1	16
7	0	07	7	1	17
8	0	08	8	1	18
9	0	09	9	1	19
a	0	0a	a	1	1a
b	0	0b	b	1	1b
c	0	0c	c	1	1c
d	0	0d	d	1	1d
e	0	0e	e	1	1e
f	0	0f	f	1	1f

Fig. 2.15 Lego 2

For Step 4, shown above, the Lego3 is for 1. We can use 2, 3, or other values for this step.

2.13 Searching Our Hidden Functionsc

For this chapter, we have written some R functions. As mentioned in the preface and Chapter 1, readers are not required to have any prior knowledge related to R. Our functions are self-explanatory. Typing a function's name will give learners instructions on how to use the function. Later, we will show a few concrete examples. To get those hidden functions, readers can use the `.searchHiddenFunctions ()` or `.sf ()`, as shown below.

```
> .searchHiddenFunctions(2)
CHAPTER                                      NAME SHORTCUT
      2 .keyboard2excel_numbers2digits         .k2e
      2 .excel2excel_numbers2digits            .e2e
      2 .remainderDividedBy16                  .re16
      2 .centence2ASCII_keyboard2excel         .c2e
      2 .copyCentence2ASCII_2excel             .cc2
      2 .breakSentence                         .bs
      2 .blockchainGame1numbersOnly            .g1
      2 .blockChainGame2lettersAndNumbers      .g2
      2 .isHexadecimal                         .isHex
      2 .decimal2hex                           .d2h
      2 .hex2decimal                           .h2d
>
```

Fig. 2.16 The hidden function related to Chapter 2

2.14 Blockchain Game #1

The first game is called `.blockchainGame1numbers2digits`. with a shortcut of `.g1`. This is the most straightforward game we can think of. The design follows our Stage 1: player 1 enters a set of numbers, and the Game will break them down into digits. Then, we calculate a simple sum by adding up those digits. The first player's check number of Hash will be this sum's first digit and last digits. For example, for a summation of 178, the check number of the Hash value will be 18. For the second player, everything will be the same except his/her Hash, which will be linked to the previous check number or Hash. There are two ways to link: addition or multiplication. For example, the last check number is 18, and the sum of the numbers of the second player is 245.

Method I: we add 1 and 9. Now, the new sum will be the following:

```
> .g1()

 *----------------------------------------------------------------*
 *  This is a Blockchain-based game with numbers only             *
 *----------------------------------------------------------------*
 *  Objeective: calculate each player's check number (hash)       *
 *     Choice var: add or multiply the previous player's hash     *
 *  For each player:                                              *
 *     enter a number, then hit the Enter Key                     *
 *     hit the Enter Key twice to finish entering numbers         *
 *----------------------------------------------------------------*
 *     1)  break those numbers into digits                        *
 *     2)  calculate a simple summation of those digits           *
 *     3)  show the result and an explanation                     *
 *----------------------------------------------------------------*
 *     4)  go to the next player                                  *
 *----------------------------------------------------------------*

Do you want to add the previous Hash to your current sum,
    or mulplify your sum by the previous Hash?
 1     for plus
 2     for multiplication
```

Fig. 2.17 Blockchain Game #1

Assume we choose 1, shown below.

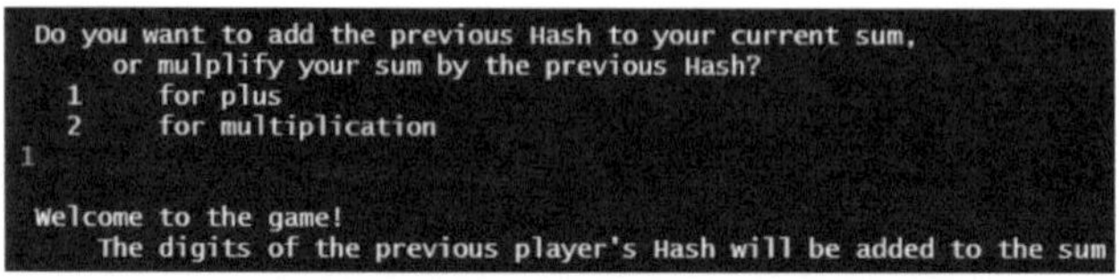

Fig. 2.18 Choosing 1 for adding the previous Hash

This method indicates that we will add the previous Hash to the sum of the next player. For the first player, we enter a set of numbers. The Game breaks those numbers into digits, calculates the summation, and chooses the first and last one as his/her Hash.

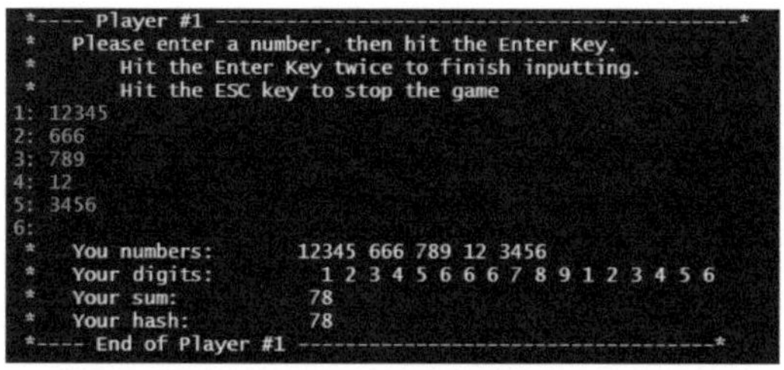

Fig. 2.19 Paler 1 using five numbers

You can verify it by comping those digits to Excel.

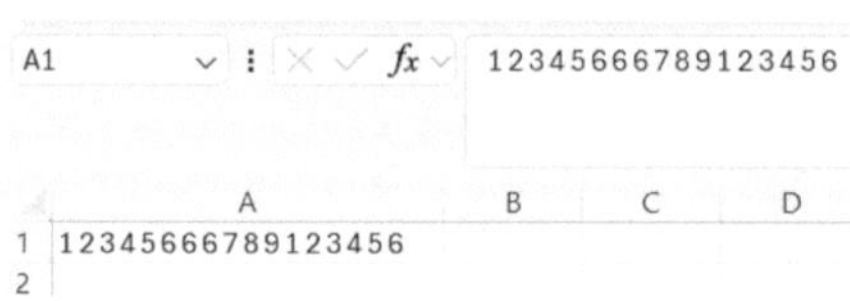

Fig. 2.20 Copying digits to Excel

Choose this cell, click on "Data" on the menu bar, "Text to Columns", "Delimited", Choose "Space", shown below.

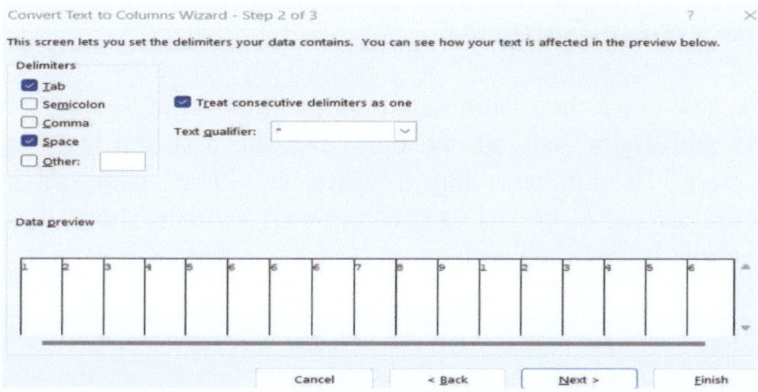

Fig. 2.21 Breaking one column into multiple columns

The summation is indeed 78, shown below.

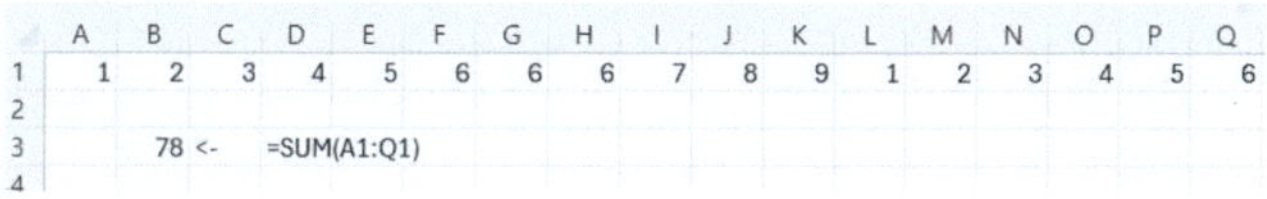

Fig. 2.22 Calculating the sum

Now, let's look at the second player.

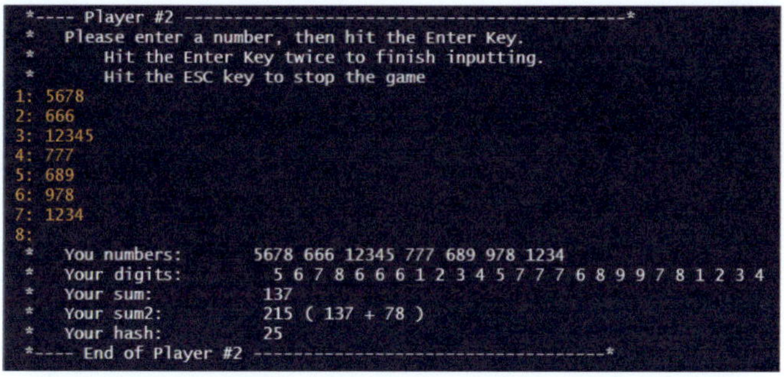

Fig. 2.23 Player 2 using seven numbers

We can add more players. The beauty of this game is its simplicity since we can explain it using a few sentences. More importantly, we can use Excel to reproduce the same results for just a few players. It is a good in-class exercise to produce the above results (for just two players).

2.15 Blockchain Game #2

For Game 2, we have two significant extensions from Game #1. First, we choose letters and digits. Second, we don't use the first and last digits. Instead, we choose from 16 numbers and a letter set. The name of the function is `.blockChainGame2lettersAndNumbers`, with a shortcut of `.g2`. Let's play the game just for two players.

```
> .g2()

*------------------------------------------------------------------------*
*  Blockchain Game #2 (with letters and numbers)                         *
*------------------------------------------------------------------------*
*  Game will                                                             *
*    1) choose only letters and numbers for an inputted phrase           *
*    2) search values for each letter/digit by the following table      *
*       letter/digit -> 0, 1, 2, 3, ...., 9,  a, b , ...., z             *
*             value  -> 1, 2, 3, 4, ....,10, 11, 12, ...., 36            *
*    3) calculate 6 summations with the following methods                *
*       method 1 multiplier 1, 1, 1, 1, 1, 1, ... (simple summation)     *
*              2 multiplier 1, 2, 1, 2, 1, 2, ...  (repeat 1,2)          *
*              3 multiplier 1, 2, 3, 1, 2, 3, ...  (repeat 1,2,3)        *
*              4 multiplier 1, 2, 3, 4, 1, 2,3,4 ..(repeat 1,2,3,4)      *
*              5 multiplier 1, 2, 3, 4, 5, 1,2,3,  (repeat 1,2,3,4,5)    *
*              6 multiplier 1, 2, 3, 4, 5, 6, ....,(repeat 1,2,3,4,5,6)  *
*    4) Get 6 reminders dividing sums  by 16                             *
*    5) Check the following table for a Hash value                       *
*        remainder  -> 1, 2, 3, ..., 11, 12, 13, 14, 15, 0               *
*             hash  -> 0, 1, 2, ...,  a, b,   c,  d,  e, f               *
*      choice variable: add the previous Hash belfore or after           *
*------------------------------------------------------------------------*
```

Fig. 2.24 Blockchain Game #2

Since we can add a previous hash before or after our current digits by adding it, it is a choice variable.

```
When adding the previous Hash, do you want add it
   1      before your current digits
   2      after  your current digits
```

Fig. 2.25 Choice variable: adding the previous Hash before or after

Let's look at the first player's result.

```
*---- Player #1 ---------------------------------------------------------*
*   Enter a phrase below (hit the Esc Key to exit):
Hello World 2024!
*   Your phrase:          helloworld2024
*   Your digits:           h e l l o w o r l d 2 0 2 4
*   Your values:           18 15 22 22 25 33 25 28 22 14 3 1 3 5
*                       Method 1: Sum = 236, Remainder = 12, Hash Code = c
*                       Method 2: Sum = 354, Remainder = 2, Hash Code = 2
*                       Method 3: Sum = 468, Remainder = 4, Hash Code = 4
*                       Method 4: Sum = 556, Remainder = 12, Hash Code = c
*                       Method 5: Sum = 686, Remainder = 14, Hash Code = e
*                       Method 6: Sum = 762, Remainder = 10, Hash Code = a
*   Final stand alone Hash: c24cea
*---- End of Player #1 --------------------------------------------------*
```

Fig. 2.26 Player #1

The phrase entered is "Hello World!". The Game shows 'digits' by keeping only letters and digits. After searching for appropriate values of those digits, the Game reports them. This is to produce the same values using Excel. Then, six summations are reported plus their remainder (after being divided by 16). Then the Game matches those remainders with the 16-element set (0,1,..,9, a,b,c,d,e,f). The Hash for the first player is `c24cea`.

Next, let's enter the sentence from Player #2. The results are shown below.

```
*---- Player #2 ---------------------------------------------------------*
*   Enter a phrase below (hit the Esc Key to exit):
John borrowed $5000 from Mary on 8/26/2024.
*   Your phrase:        johnborrowed5000frommaryon8262024
*   Your digits:        j o h n b o r r o w e d 5 0 0 0 f r o m m a r y o n 8 2 6 2 0 2 4
*   Your values:        20 25 18 24 12 25 28 28 25 33 15 14 6 1 1 1 16 28 25 23 23 11 28 35 25 24 9 3 7 3 1 3 5
*                    Method 1: Sum = 545, Remainder = 1, Hash Code = 1
*                    Method 2: Sum = 826, Remainder = 10, Hash Code = a
*                    Method 3: Sum = 1099, Remainder = 11, Hash Code = b
*                    Method 4: Sum = 1338, Remainder = 10, Hash Code = a
*                    Method 5: Sum = 1622, Remainder = 6, Hash Code = 6
*                    Method 6: Sum = 1864, Remainder = 8, Hash Code = 8
*   Final stand alone Hash: 1aba68
*-----------------------------------------------
*   Previous hash  :    c24cea
*   Your new digits:    c 2 4 c e a j o h n b o r r o w e d 5 0 0 0 f r o m m a r y o n 8 2 6 2 0 2 4
*   Your values:        13 3 5 13 15 11 20 25 18 24 12 25 28 28 25 33 15 14 6 1 1 1 16 28 25 23 23 11 28 35 25 24 9 3 7 3 1 3 5
*                    Method 1: Sum = 605, Remainder = 13, Hash Code = d
*                    Method 2: Sum = 913, Remainder = 1, Hash Code = 1
*                    Method 3: Sum = 1209, Remainder = 9, Hash Code = 9
*                    Method 4: Sum = 1527, Remainder = 7, Hash Code = 7
*                    Method 5: Sum = 1854, Remainder = 14, Hash Code = e
*                    Method 6: Sum = 2091, Remainder = 11, Hash Code = b
*   Final true Hash: d197eb
*---- End of Player #2 -------------------------------------------------*
```

Fig. 2.27 Player #2

As before, the Game breaks down letters and digits. In addition, the previous Hash was added to accommodate the new set of digits. The Hash value without adding the previous Hash is `1aba68`. On the other hand, the Hash linked to the previous Hash value is `d197eb`.

Appendix A: Issue the Following Line of R Code for Week 2

```
source("http://datayyy.com/i2ft/week2.txt")
```

```
*--------------------------------------------------------------------*
* Introduction to FinTech using Excel                by Dr. Yan 2025   *
*        (in an R-assisted learning environment)                      *
*--------------------------------------------------------------------*
*  .c1 Introduction & Excel Basics               .c16 R basics(optional) *
*  .c2 Blockchain (I) : Numbers/alphanumeric cases                    *
*--------------------------------------------------------------------*
* >.c2       # go to chapter 3                                        *
* >.uu       # go to utility submenu                                  *
* >.ft       # back to this menu                                      *
*--------------------------------------------------------------------*
```

Fig. 2.28 The menu for Week 2

Appendix B: Issue the Following Line of R Code for Chapter 2

```
> .chapter2
function(i=0){
"i Chapter 2: Blockchain (I)              i   Explanations
 - -------------------------------        --  --------------------------
 1  Block vs. Blockchain                  21  CUSIP: Excel example
 2  our 4-stage explanation               22        : Excel macro
 3  Excel: left()                         23        : our .cusip()
 4       : right()                        24        : .keep_digit_word
 5       : right(left()) combination      25  Blockchain: concepts
 6       : mod()                          26     : explain_blockchain_numbers_only
 7       : vlookup()                      27     : our design with just two digits
 8  1) numbers only 2-digit               28     : our design with six digits
 9             : keep numbers             29  Blockchain Game #1
10             : 4-digit                  30     : play
11             : 6 or more digits         31  Blockchain Game #2
12             : our functions            32     : play
13      :Fin Statement 2 Excel            33  .digit16() function
14 2) numbers and letters only            34  .cd1()
15      CUSIP: what is it                 35  our function
16          : an explanation              36        : .remainderDividedBy16
17          : formula 4 check digit       37        : .keyboard2excel_numbers2digits
18          : online check digit          38  placeholder 10 letters plus six letters
19  Videos                                39  placeholder
20  Links                                 40  RPC API Reference  [optional]

Example #1:> .c2     # get the above list
Example #2:> .c2()   # the same as the above
Example #3:> .c2(1)  # see the first explanation
```

Fig. 2.29 The contents of Chapter 2

Exercises

2.1 What is a cryptographic hash, and why is it crucial in blockchain technology?

2.2 What does it mean to say a hash function is "deterministic"? Why is this property important?

2.3 Why is the immutability of a hash output crucial in preventing data tampering in a blockchain?

2.4 What is a "hash collision," and why is it undesirable in blockchain systems?

2.5 Discuss the concept of a "hash pointer" and its significance in blockchain structure.

2.6 Explain how blockchain systems use hashes to maintain a distributed ledger without relying on a central authority.

2.7 How does the computational effort to find a specific hash output contribute to blockchain security?

2.8 Why can't hash outputs be reversed to obtain the original input? How does this one-way characteristic enhance blockchain security?

2.9 How does the difficulty adjustment mechanism in Bitcoin's blockchain depend on hashing?

2.10 Describe the process of mining in blockchain and the role of hash functions in this process.

2.11 Explain how hashes are used to verify transactions without revealing the actual data in blockchain systems.

2.12 Discuss how a change in any transaction in a block would affect the hash of that block and subsequent blocks.

2.13 What is a "hash rate," and why is it a critical metric in blockchain networks?
2.14 At http://datayyy.com/data_txt/list.txt, you can find a list of text files. Download five of them and try our `.sha256LocalFile ()` function to generate five Sha246 Hashes.
2.15 Reproduce the same result in the chapter using numbers only for the two sets of numbers below.
   Data set #1: `12345 666 789 12 3456`
   Data set #2: 5678 45678 12345 777 689 978 1234
2.16 What are the advantages and disadvantages of the so-called 4-stage approach?
2.17 Play Blockchain-based Game #1. What are the Hash values for three players with the following inputs:
   Player 1: 12345 66 77 90 1234
   Player 2: 456 783 7890 22 9
   Player 3: 56 78 90 123 45
   Player 4: 766 890 777 888 999
2.18 Play Blockchain-based Game #2. What are the Hash values for three players with the following inputs:
   Input 1: Hello Hofstra!
   Input 2: John Doe borrowed $5,000 from Mary Smith on 1/5/2024.
   Input 3: Mary Smith received a $550 repayment from John on 8/12/2024.
   Input 4: 766 890 777 888 999
2.19 What is the Excel function offering ASCII values for a given sentence? Generate a set of values for this question: What Excel function offers ASCII values for a given sentence?

References

ASCII Table. https://www.ascii-code.com/characters
Belyh, A. (2019). *The definitive guide to Fama-French three-factor model*. https://www.cleverism.com/fama-french-three-factor-model-guide/
CFI Team, Capital Asset Pricing Model (CAPM). https://corporatefinanceinstitute.com/resources/valuation/what-is-capm-formula/
Dumas, A. (1844). *Count of Monte Cristo*. http://gutenberg.org/files/1184/1184-0.txt
Lepcha, M. (2023). *What is SHA-256?* https://www.techopedia.com/definition/sha-256
Sha256 website. https://passwordsgenerator.net/sha256-hash-generator/

Blockchain 2: Hash, ASCII, and Sha256

3

This chapter continues "Chapter 2: Blockchain 1: Numbers and Alphanumeric". We will discuss ASCII, how to find the hash for ASCII characters, and our general target of Sha256: what is it, how to get sha256 hash from a webpage, and our three functions:`.sha256()`,`.sha256web ()`,`.sha256LocalFile ()`, and`.sha256add()`. In addition, we will show you how to play games #3 and #4. In this chapter, the following topics will be covered:

- Our innovative 4-stage approach
- Stage #3: All ASCII characters with a 6-character Hash
- Stage #4: Sha256 with 64-character Hash
- Our`.sha256()`, `.sha256web ()`, and`.sha256LocalFile ()` functions
- Four Blockchain-based games (one game for each stage)

3.1 Our Four-Stage Approach

We will present the Table 3.1 again.

The previous chapter discussed Stages 1 and 2, and this chapter will focus on Stages 3 and 4.

Supplementary Information The online version contains supplementary material available at https://doi.org/10.1007/978-3-031-89779-5_3.

Y. Yan, *Introduction to FinTech using Excel*, Springer Texts in Business and Economics, https://doi.org/10.1007/978-3-031-89779-5_3

Table 3.1 Four stages to understand the concepts of block and blockchain

Stage	Name	Method	Check values
1	Numbers only: 2 digits	(just 0,1,..., 9)	0 to 9
2	Alphabetic and numbers	(0,1,2,...,9,a,b,c, ...,z)	Checking characters limited to 10 digits plus a, b, c, d, e, and f
3	all ASCII characters	All ASCII characters	
4	Sha256	The Crypto True Hash	

3.2 What is a Hash?

In blockchain, a hash is a fixed-size alphanumeric string generated by a cryptographic hash function that uniquely represents data of any size. Hashes are used to secure data, verify integrity, and link blocks together in the chain, ensuring that any alteration to the data will change the hash, making tampering evident. Below, let's look at a simple example.

We would get the following hash for "`John Doe`".

```
6CEA57C2FB6CBC2A40411135005760F241FFFC3E5E67AB9988272643l037F908
```

Now, readers/students don't have to understand the concept thoroughly; a couple of points. The length of the true hash is 64, as shown below.

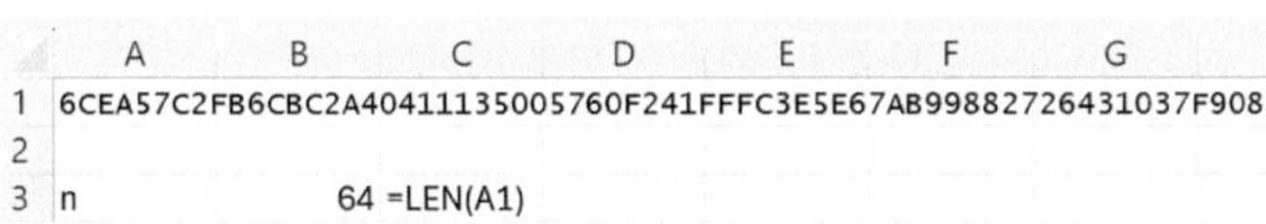

	A	B	C	D	E	F	G	I
1	6CEA57C2FB6CBC2A40411135005760F241FFFC3E5E67AB9988272643l037F908							
2								
3	n		64 =LEN(A1)					

Fig. 3.1 The length of a Hash

We can manually find the unique characters as 0, 1, 2, 3, 4, 5, 6, 7, 8, 9, A, B, C, D, E, and F. The letter D is missing in the hash. The unique values consist of ten digits plus A to F. In Appendix D, we show how to get those unique values.

3.3 Clipboard

There is an intermediate step when we copy a text file from one location to another, such as from a webpage to Notepad. Most users do not realize this. After we highlight a text and copy it (before pasting it), we copy the text to a Clipboard. When pasting it to our new destination, we copy it from the Clipboard and paste it to our new location. For R, we can read data from Clipboard and write data to Clipboard. When entering text data, we can enter it with our keyboard, copy and paste it when asked, or copy it to the clipboard. When the underlying function copies from the Clipboard, it is less likely to have an error happen. Another advantage is that the output (pasted to the Clipboard) from one function can be used as input (copied from the Clipboard) by the second function.

3.4 Stage #3: ASCII with a 6-Character Hash

ASCII printable characters are the 95 characters in the ASCII character set that can be displayed on screen or printed on paper. They include letters, numbers, symbols, and punctuation marks, represented by codes 32 to 126. These characters are used to create written text and other visual content. The Excel `char()` function can print those ASCII characters, as shown below.

	A	B	C	D	E	F	G	H	I	J	K	L	M	N	O	P	Q	R	S	T
1	ASCII printable characters 33-127																			
2																				
3	n	33	34	35	36	37	38	39	40	41	42	43	44	45	46	47	48	49	50	
4	ASCII	!	"	#	$	%	&	'	(	)	*	+	,	-	.	/	0	1	2	
5		51	52	53	54	55	56	57	58	59	60	61	62	63	64	65	66	67	68	
6		3	4	5	6	7	8	9	:	;	<	=	>	?	@	A	B	C	D	=CHAR(S5)
7		69	70	71	72	73	74	75	76	77	78	79	80	81	82	83	84	85	86	
8		E	F	G	H	I	J	K	L	M	N	O	P	Q	R	S	T	U	V	
9		87	88	89	90	91	92	93	94	95	96	97	98	99	100	101	102	103	104	
10		W	X	Y	Z	[	\	]	^	_	`	a	b	c	d	e	f	g	h	
11		105	106	107	108	109	110	111	112	113	114	115	116	117	118	119	120	121	122	
12		i	j	k	l	m	n	o	p	q	r	s	t	u	v	w	x	y	z	
13		123	124	125	126	127														
14		{	|	}	~	▯														

Fig. 3.2 The ASCII characters

Here is the basic design.

Step 1: for a given phrase, we keep the ASCII characters.
Step 2: Get the value of each ASCII character, as shown in the example below.

	A	B	C
1	H	72	=CODE(A1)

Fig. 3.3 The Excel CODE function

Step 3: Based on the one of 6 methods, we calculate the sum (more details)

$$sum = \sum_{i=1}^{n} v_i * m_i, \tag{3.3}$$

where m_i is the multiplier. For a simple summation, $m_1 = m_2 = \ldots, = m_n = 1$.

Step 4: Calculate the remainder =mod(sum,16).
Step 5: Hash will be one of (0,1,2,3,4,5,6,7,8,9,a,b,c,d,e,f).

For example, if the remainder is 10, then Hash=”9”. On the other hand, if the remainder is zero, then Hash will be “f”.

The six methods are specified below.

Method 1’s multiplier: 1, 1, 1, 1, 1, …, (a simple summation)
Method 2’s multiplier: 1, 2, 1, 2, 1,2 …, repeat (1,2)
Method 3’s multiplier: 1, 2, 3, 1, 2, 3, …, repeat (1,2,3)
Method 4’s multiplier: 1, 2, 3, 4, 1, 2, 3, 4, …, repeat (1,2,3,4)
Method 5’s multiplier: 1, 2, 3, 4, 5, 1, 2, 3, 4,5,…, repeat (1,2,3,4,5)
Method 5’s multiplier: 1, 2, 3, 4, 5, 6,, 2, 3, 4,5,6, …, repeat (1,2,3,4,5,6)

Below, we use the phrase “Welcome World 2024!” as an example.

	A	B	C	D
1	Welcome World 2024!			
2				ASCII value
3	19	1	W	87
4		2	e	101
5		3	l	108
6		4	c	99
7		5	o	111
8		6	m	109
9		7	e	101
10		8		32
11		9	W	87
12		10	o	111
13		11	r	114
14		12	l	108
15		13	d	100
16		14		32
17		15	2	50
18		16	0	48
19		17	2	50
20		18	4	52
21		19	!	33

Fig. 3.4 The ASCII characters for “Welcome World 2024!”

In the above image, the phrase is broken down into individual characters. Then, the Excel code() function calculates their values. We then have six types of multipliers, as shown below.

F4 | fx | =IF(F3<F$2,F3+1,1)

	E	F	G	H	I	J
1			multiplier			
2	1	2	3	4	5	6
3	1	1	1	1	1	1
4	1	2	2	2	2	2
5	1	1	3	3	3	3
6	1	2	1	4	4	4
7	1	1	2	1	5	5
8	1	2	3	2	1	6
9	1	1	1	3	2	1
10	1	2	2	4	3	2
11	1	1	3	1	4	3
12	1	2	1	2	5	4
13	1	1	2	3	1	5
14	1	2	3	4	2	6
15	1	1	1	1	3	1
16	1	2	2	2	4	2
17	1	1	3	3	5	3
18	1	2	1	4	1	4
19	1	1	2	1	2	5
20	1	2	3	2	3	6
21	1	1	1	3	4	1

Fig. 3.5 Multipliers for 6 ways to calculate a sum

Please pay attention to the formula in cell F4, = `if(F3 < F$2,F3 + 1,1)`. After entering the correct formula, copy it to the rest of the areas. For the two steps, we calculate the products for each item and then summarize them. After that, we calculate the remainder.

	K	L	M	N	O	P	Q	R
1		products						
2		1	2	3	4	5	6	
3		87	87	87	87	87	87	
4		101	202	202	202	202	202	
5		108	108	324	324	324	324	
6		99	198	99	396	396	396	
7		111	111	222	111	555	555	
8		109	218	327	218	109	654	
9		101	101	101	303	202	101	
10		32	64	64	128	96	64	
11		87	87	261	87	348	261	
12		111	222	111	222	555	444	
13		114	114	228	342	114	570	
14		108	216	324	432	216	648	
15		100	100	100	100	300	100	
16		32	64	64	64	128	64	
17		50	50	150	150	250	150	
18		48	96	48	192	48	192	
19		50	50	100	50	100	250	
20		52	104	156	104	156	312	
21		33	33	33	99	132	33	
22								
23		1533	2225	3001	3611	4318	5407	=SUM(Q3:Q21)
24	remainderr	13	1	9	11	14	15	=MOD(Q23,16)

Fig. 3.6 The Excel MOD function with a divisor of 16

For example, Method I sums all 21 ASCII values. Since its value is 1533, thus its remainder is 13, i.e., `mod(1533,16)` = 13. As the last step, we search for the hash value based on columns T and U, as shown below.

	S	T	U	V	W	X	Y	Z	AA	AB
2		1	0							
3		2	1							
4		3	2							
5		4	3							
6		5	4							
7		6	5							
8		7	6							
9		8	7							
10		9	8							
11		10	9							
12		11	a							
13		12	b							
14		13	c							
15		14	d							
16		15	e							
17		16	f							
18										
19	remainder ->	13	1	9	11	14	15			
20		c	0	8	a	d	e	=VLOOKUP(Y19,$T$1:$U$17,2		
21	Hash ->	c08ade	=CONCAT(T20:Y20)							

Fig. 3.7 Calculating a 6-character Hash

The Hash value for "Welcome World 2024" is `c08ade`. Later in the chapter, we show that we can use a hidden function to obtain this Hash quickly.

3.5 Our `.make64()` Function

This section can be optional.

We only generate a few characters in the above exercises, such as 5 to 10. This is far away from 64 characters. On the other hand, it is not practical or manageable to have 64 methods to calculate our summations. We have designed a function to extend our current Hash to generate a 64-character hash and save readers' time. Our intention is traceable, i.e., for any given character in a 64-character long Hash, we can manually verify its value. We have three methods for a given Hash:

Method I: Moving the complete Hash to the right by 1, 2, …, 16 position
Method II: Moving each character by 1, 2, …., 16 positions
Method III: A random set of values

Let's illustrate a hypothetical Hash value, 'abc12'. We deliberately choose such a Hash for an easy explanation.

Method I: all original Hashes will move to the right by 1, 2, …, 16 positions. First, we have the following two tables. The first table is used to search for value for a given character. For example, the value of 'a' is 11. By adding 1 to its value, it leads to 12. By searching Table 2, we find its value 'b'.

	A	B	C	D	E	F	G	H
8								
9	character	text format	value			value	character	
10	0	0	1			1	0	
11	1	1	2			2	1	
12	2	2	3			3	2	
13	3	3	4			4	3	
14	4	4	5			5	4	
15	5	5	6			6	5	
16	6	6	7			7	6	
17	7	7	8			8	7	
18	8	8	9			9	8	
19	9	9	10			10	9	
20	a	a	11			11	a	
21	b	b	12			12	b	
22	c	c	13			13	c	
23	d	d	14			14	d	
24	e	e	15			15	e	
25	f	f	16			16	f	

Fig. 3.8 Character to value vs. value to character

3.6 Stage #4: Sha256 Hash

Secure Hash Algorithm 256-bit, or SHA-256, is a cryptographic hash function that converts text of any length to an almost unique alphanumeric string of 256 bits. The output is known as a hash value or hash. At https://passwordsgenerator.net/sha256-hash-generator/, we can input our text, "`John Doe`".

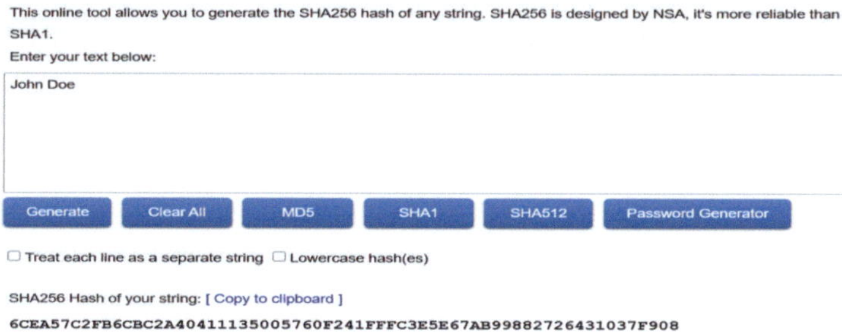

Fig. 3.9 The website for generating a Sha256 Hash

The hash is shown below.

```
6CEA57C2FB6CBC2A40411135005760F241FFFC3E5E67AB99882726431037F908
```

On the other hand, adding another space between John and Doe shows an entirely different Hash.

Table 3.2 Three properties of Sha256

Properties	Explanation
Uniqueness	The SHA-256 hash function guarantees that different inputs will generate unique hash values. Even a slight change in the input will cause a drastically different hash value, a phenomenon known as the 'avalanche effect.' Additionally, the resulting hash will consistently be 2 Fifty-six bits in length, regardless of the input size
Irreversibility	Hash values generated by SHA-256 cannot be reverse-engineered, making retrieving the original data from the hash computationally unfeasible. This characteristic ensures the security of the data, even if the hash is made public, allowing for safe file sharing without the risk of decryption by malicious actors
Deterministic	SHA-256 consistently produces the same hash value for a given input. This property guarantees uniformity in the hashing process, enabling reliable data verification across different systems

```
07EC77F973070EC6F9FB370CDB9D825B5EF02BF96CD627A306FDBEA46F217B93
```

The three properties of Sha256 are listed in the Table 3.2.

Let's look at the following example.

```
John Doe borrowed $100 from Mary on 5/3/2023.
On 8/17/2024, John paid back $40 to Mary.
```

Let's treat the first sentence as Block 1. The sha256 Hash value is given below using the website at https://passwordsgenerator.net/sha256-hash-generator/.

```
D28ED2172654BE035714647696F7334C338E556D6EC51D8255AF3A8C01706445.
```

The Hash of Block 2 is the second sentence plus the hash from Block 1. The "sentence" we will paste onto that web page is below.

```
On 8/17/2024, John paid back $40 to Mary.D28ED2172654BE035714647696F7334C338E556D6EC51D8255AF3A8C01706445
```

Fig. 3.10 New sentence plus the previous Hash

The Hash linked to Block 1 is given below.

```
5B1CDA148DEA3112779AF9804A921C41BEAF11846D6FE898FADA39A185A536A6.
```

3.7 Stage #4: "digest" Package Installation

Our sha256-related functions depend on an R package called "digest." Whenever a function is called, underlying programs upload this package. The condition for successfully loading this package is that it was preinstalled on our computers. We issue the following command to install it after launching R condole or RStudio.

```
install.packages("digest").
```

The software will ask you to choose a location (server location) for the R console. In that case, find an area close to your city. Remember, R is case-sensitive. We include another way to install R packages in Appendix D.

3.8 Stage #4: Our Sha256 Related Functions

To help students understand the concept of Sha256, we have written four related functions, such as `.sha256()`,`.sha256web ()`, and `.sha256LocalFile ()`. The first is called `.sha256()`, mimicking the webpage at hashing https://passwordsgenerator.net/sha256-hash-generator/. Two examples are shown below.

Fig. 3.11 The hidden function generating sha256 Hash (.sha256)

Again, the second input has two spaces between two words. Hash is pretty different from the others. We cannot simply give a weblink or unload a local file on the above webpage. To input a link for a remote text file, we have generated a function called `.sha256web ()`. Typing its name would offer help-me instructions.

```
> .sha256web
function(){
  "Objective: generate the sha256 hash by inputting a remote text file

  Example 1> .sha256web    # see this instruction
  Example 2> .s2           # a short-cut
  Example 3> .s2()
             Copy a web page, such as https://datayyy.com/data_txt/ibmBS.csv.txt
                then hit the Enter-key

             The number of words: 313
             SHA-256 hash: E9120DBA0B88E396BFDE9AF0EE3614C9466F5CE15B06EDD6B56FDD63ECD452CF

             You can verify the result, type .combined_text, then copy-and-paste
             the text to  https://passwordsgenerator.net/sha256-hash-generator/


  Example #2: # copy the link at https://www.gutenberg.org/cache/epub/10/pg10.txt
              .s2()

              The number of words: 824538
              SHA-256 hash: B5616F60CA4201EECAAF7054815D72A21DFC6AB66630D965BBD624DB8A882C7F

              You can verify the result, type .combined_text, then copy-and-paste
                  the text to  https://passwordsgenerator.net/sha256-hash-generator/

   Note: This program uses an R package 'digest'. If you haven't installed it,
            copy and paste the following line to your R console to install it.
            install.packages('digest')
```

Fig. 3.12 The hidden.sha256web function

We use the same sentences shown below to test our `.sha256()` function.

```
John Doe borrowed $100 from Mary on 5/3/2023.
On 8/17/2024, John paid back $40 to Mary.
```

```
> .sha256()
Copy a string then hit the Enter-key: John Doe borrowed $100 from Mary on 5/3/2023.
SHA-256 hash: D28ED2172654BE035714647696F7334C338E556D6EC51D8255AF3A8C01706445
```

Fig. 3.13 Output from the.sha256 function

For Block 2's Hash, we have the following result.

```
> .sha256()
Copy a string then hit the Enter-key: On 8/17/2024, John paid back $40 to
Mary.D28ED2172654BE035714647696F7334C338E556D6EC51D8255AF3A8C01706445
SHA-256 hash: 5B1CDA148DEA3112779AF9804A921C41BEAF11846D6FE898FADA39A185A536A6
```

Fig. 3.14 The output from the.sha256 function

They are both the same as on the website. For a sentence or small paragraph, the website is good enough.

3.9 Our.`Sha256web ()` Function

Our.`sha256()` function discussed in the previous section helps enter a short string or sentence. The function mimics the website at https://passwordsgenerator.net/sha256-hash-generator/. However, we cannot use the website to store a remote file. For this purpose, we have written a function called.`sha256web()`. Let's use Count of Monte Cristo (Dumas, 1844) as an example. The text is located at http://gutenberg.org/files/1184/1184-0.txt. We type.`sha256web ()` to start.

```
> .sha256web ()
Copy a web page, such as
https://datayyy.com/data_txt/ibmBS.csv.txt
      then hit the Enter key
The number of words: 461000
SHA-256 hash:
333A28997F02156E2DABA7BB5A475C033D499D082501DD7B3A8ACB48896A2599
```

You can verify the result by typing `.combined_text` and copy-and-paste to https://passwordsgenerator.net/sha256-hash-generator/. The number of words is 461,000, and the related Hash value is:

```
333A28997F02156E2DABA7BB5A475C033D499D082501DD7B3A8ACB48896A2599
```

In addition, if a reader wants to verify, they should refrain from copying directly from the website. Instead, they would use the `.combined_text` file. Since this file is too big, we will use a small one. Using the http://datayyy.com/data_txt/list.txt file, we can find a list of text files.

https://datayyy.com/data_txt/list.txt

```
aaplBS.txt
aaplCF.txt
aaplIS.txt
allRpackages.txt
anaconda_c10_07_abalone_data_set.txt
anaconda_c10_15_octave_logistic_gd.m.txt
anaconda_c10_16_summarize_by_date.txt
anaconda_c10_18_annual_ret_sp500.txt
anaconda_c10_29_catwalk_info.txt
anaconda_c12_09_pwordfreq.txt
anaconda_c12_18_taskview.txt
anaconda_c12_20_parallelpi.txt
anaconda_c12_22_pidigits.txt
```

Fig. 3.15 The list of data files

For example, we can use the first one, http://datayyy.com/data_txt/aaplBS.txt.

```
    .sha256web ()
Copy a web page, such as
https://datayyy.com/data_txt/ibmBS.csv.txt
     then hit the Enter key
The number of words: 99
SHA-256 hash:
12891134DD9B199094FD2DE1338696E93D5CE3EAC84DC16DC2738B9806002A6C
```

You can verify the result, type `.combined_text`, then copy-and-paste to the following website: https://passwordsgenerator.net/sha256-hash-generator/

3.10 Our.Sha256LocalFile () Function

The name.`sha256LoclFile()` suggests using a local file as our input. For example, we download http://datayyy.com/data_txt/aaplBS.txt and save it under c://temp/.

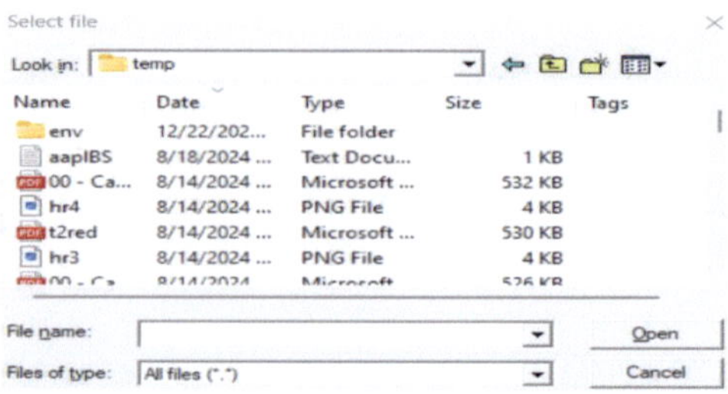

Fig. 3.16 Locating a local file for the.sha256LocalFile function

```
> .sha256LocalFile ()
The number of words: 99
SHA-256 hash:
12891134DD9B199094FD2DE1338696E93D5CE3EAC84DC16DC2738B9806002A6C
```

You can verify the result, type.`combined_text`, then copy-and-paste to https://passwordsgenerator.net/sha256-hash-generator/

3.11 Blockchain Games

The Table 3.3 shows our four games associated with our four-stage approach to explaining the concept of Blockchain.

We use the simple summation for the previous method, i.e., adding those digits directly.

Table 3.3 Four Blockchain-based Game

Games	Full name	Short-cut	
1	.blockchainGame1numbers2digits	.bcg1	.g1
2	.blockchainGame2alphfhaNumbers	.bcg2	.g2
3	.blockchainGame3ACII	.bcg3	.g3
4	.blockchainGame4Sha256	.bcg4	.g4

3.12 Blockchain Game #3

This Game is almost identical to Game 2, except we accept all ASCII characters. The function is called.`blockChainGame3ASCII` and has a shortcut of.`g3`. Let's look at the result of running this Game.

```
> .g3()

*--------------------------------------------------------------------------*
*  Blockchain Game #3 (with all ASCII characters)                          *
*--------------------------------------------------------------------------*
*  Game will                                                               *
*    1) Accept all ASCII symbols for an inputted phrase                    *
*    2) Get ASCII values for each character                                *
*    3) Calculate 6 summations with the following methods                  *
*       method 1 multiplier 1, 1, 1, 1, 1, 1, ... (simple summation)       *
*              2 multiplier 1, 2, 1, 2, 1, 2, ...  (repeat 1,2)            *
*              3 multiplier 1, 2, 3, 1, 2, 3, ...  (repeat 1,2,3)          *
*              4 multiplier 1, 2, 3, 4, 1, 2,3,4 ..(repeat 1,2,3,4)        *
*              5 multiplier 1, 2, 3, 4, 5, 1,2,3,  (repeat 1,2,3,4,5)      *
*              6 multiplier 1, 2, 3, 4, 5, 6, ...,(repeat 1,2,3,4,5,6)     *
*    4) Get 6 remainders by dividing sums by 16                            *
*    5) Check the following table for a Hash value                         *
*         remainder  -> 0, 1, 2, ..., 15                                   *
*             hash   -> 0, 1, 2, ..., 9, a, b, c, d, e, f                  *
*      choice variable: add the previous Hash before or after              *
*--------------------------------------------------------------------------*
```

Fig. 3.17 Blockchain Game #3

We have a choice variable to decide whether we add the previous Hash before or after our ASCII characters. Assume that we choose 2, as shown below.

```
When adding the previous Hash, do you want add it
   1     before your current ASCII characters
   2     after  your current ASCII characters
2
```

Fig. 3.18 Decision: adding the previous Hash before or after the current one

For Player #1, we enter "Hello World 2424!".

```
*---- Player #1 -------------------------------------------------------*
*   Enter a phrase below (hit the Esc Key to exit):
Hello World 2024!
*   Your phrase:         Hello World 2024!
*   Your characters:      H e l l o   W o r l d   2 0 2 4 !
*   Your values:          72 101 108 108 111 32 87 111 114 108 100 32 50 48 50 52 33
*                      Method 1: Sum = 1317, Remainder = 5, Hash Code = 4
*                      Method 2: Sum = 1909, Remainder = 5, Hash Code = 4
*                      Method 3: Sum = 2493, Remainder = 13, Hash Code = c
*                      Method 4: Sum = 3205, Remainder = 5, Hash Code = 4
*                      Method 5: Sum = 3994, Remainder = 10, Hash Code = 9
*                      Method 6: Sum = 4221, Remainder = 13, Hash Code = c
*   Final stand alone Hash: 44c49c
*---- End of Player #1 ------------------------------------------------*
```

Fig. 3.19 Game #3: Player #1

The Game finds their corresponding ASCII values. Based on the Excel `code()` function, we can easily verify that set of SCII values, as shown below.

	A	B	C	D	E	F	G
1	Hello World 2024!						
2				ASCII		value	
3		17	=LEN(A1) 1	H	=RIGHT(LEFT($A$1,C3),1)	72	=CODE(D3)
4			2	e		101	
5			3	l		108	
6			4	l		108	
7			5	o		111	
8			6			32	
9			7	W		87	
10			8	o		111	
11			9	r		114	
12			10	l		108	
13			11	d		100	
14			12			32	
15			13	2		50	
16			14	0		48	
17			15	2		50	
18			16	4		52	
19			17	!		33	

Fig. 3.20 Sentence to characters, then to values

Let's look at Player #2.

```
*---- Player #2 -------------------------------------------------------*
*   Enter a phrase below (hit the Esc Key to exit):
John Doe is happy today.
*   Your phrase:         John Doe is happy today.
*   Your characters:     J o h n   D o e   i s   h a p p y   t o d a y .
*   Your values:         74 111 104 110 32 68 111 101 32 105 115 32 104 97 112 112 121 32 116 111 100 97 121 46
*                   Method 1: Sum = 2164, Remainder = 4, Hash Code = 3
*                   Method 2: Sum = 3186, Remainder = 2, Hash Code = 1
*                   Method 3: Sum = 4025, Remainder = 9, Hash Code = 8
*                   Method 4: Sum = 5568, Remainder = 16, Hash Code = f
*                   Method 5: Sum = 6203, Remainder = 11, Hash Code = a
*                   Method 6: Sum = 6998, Remainder = 6, Hash Code = 5
*   Final stand alone Hash: 318fa5
*-----------------------------------------------
*   Previous hash  :     44c49c
*   Your new characters:        J o h n   D o e   i s   h a p p y   t o d a y . 4 4 c 4 9 c
*   Your values:         74 111 104 110 32 68 111 101 32 105 115 32 104 97 112 112 121 32 116 111 100 97 121 46 52 52 99 52 57 99
*                   Method 1: Sum = 2575, Remainder = 15, Hash Code = e
*                   Method 2: Sum = 3800, Remainder = 8, Hash Code = 7
*                   Method 3: Sum = 4941, Remainder = 13, Hash Code = c
*                   Method 4: Sum = 6484, Remainder = 4, Hash Code = 3
*                   Method 5: Sum = 7592, Remainder = 8, Hash Code = 7
*                   Method 6: Sum = 8538, Remainder = 10, Hash Code = 9
*   Final true Hash: e7c379
*---- End of Player #2 ------------------------------------------------*
```

Fig. 3.21 Game #3 player #2

Since our choice is 2, i.e., attach the previous Hash to the end of the ASCII characters, `44c49c` appears at the end of your new ASCII characters.

3.13 Blockchain Game #4

For this game, players enter anything to generate a sha256 Hash. In addition, the next player's Hash is linked to the previous one. In other words, we form a blockchain. When adding the last player's Hash, we can add it in front of new information or after. Because of this, we report three Hashes: stand-alone, i.e., not linked with the previous one, the previous Hash added before and added after (new information). The beauty of this game is that everything can be checked at https://passwordsgenerator.net/sha256-hash-generator/. To start the game, we type `.g4 ()`, shown below.

```
> .g4()

 *------------------------------------------------------------*
 * This is a Blockchain-based Game using Sha256 Hash          *
 *------------------------------------------------------------*
 * Objective   : Generate a Hash value for a given phrase     *
 *    Choice var: add previous Hash before or after your phrase *
 *     Verify your result at the following website:          *
 *       https://passwordsgenerator.net/sha256-hash-generator/ *
 *------------------------------------------------------------*
```

Fig. 3.22 Blockchain Game #4

Assume that we enter 2 to add the previous Hash to the end of the following phrase, as shown below.

```
 Choose 1 or 2 on how to add the previous Hash:
   1     before  your new phrase
   2     after   your new phrase
2

 *--------------------------------------------------------------*
 * Welcome to the Game!                                         *
 *    The previous player's Hash will be added after the new phrase. *
 *        phrase2 =  phrase + previous Hash                     *
 *--------------------------------------------------------------*
```

Fig. 3.23 Choice: adding the previous Hash before or after the current one

Users can add their name or pseudo name or remain anonymous, as shown below.

```
 * Enter your name or hit the Enter Key to remain anonymous: *
 *         [Hit the Esc Key to exit the game.]
John
```

Fig. 3.24 Entering a name or remaining anonymous

We entered 'John' as the first player. The game will ask the first phrase: `John Doe borrowed $5000 from Mary on 1/2/2024.`

```
*---- Player #1:John ------------------------------------------------*
*        Please enter a phrase below (for example):
*        John borrowed $5,000 from Mary on 1/2/2024.
*       You can paste the above sentence since it is on clipboard.
John borrowed $5,000 from Mary on 1/2/2024.
* Your input:   John borrowed $5,000 from Mary on 1/2/2024.
* Your phrase2: John borrowed $5,000 from Mary on 1/2/2024.
* Your hash: E8A82FB08DCCE47C7B5FE0F1ED23DE9046658908DE85E7CCBD39C061908C0960
* You can copy your phrase or modified phrase to a text editor
*   or to https://passwordsgenerator.net/sha256-hash-generator/
*---- End of Player #1:John -----------------------------------------*
```

Fig. 3.25 Game #4 player #1

At https://passwordsgenerator.net/sha256-hash-generator/, we can verify the above Hash value, shown below.

Fig. 3.26 The website to generate a sha256 Hash

We got the same Hash value. Let's look at the next player. Assume her name is Mary.

```
*  Enter your name or hit the Enter Key to remain anonymous: *
*          [Hit the Esc Key to exit the game.]
Mary
```

Fig. 3.27 Entering a name or remaining anonymous

After hitting the Enter Key, we enter a sentence, as shown below.

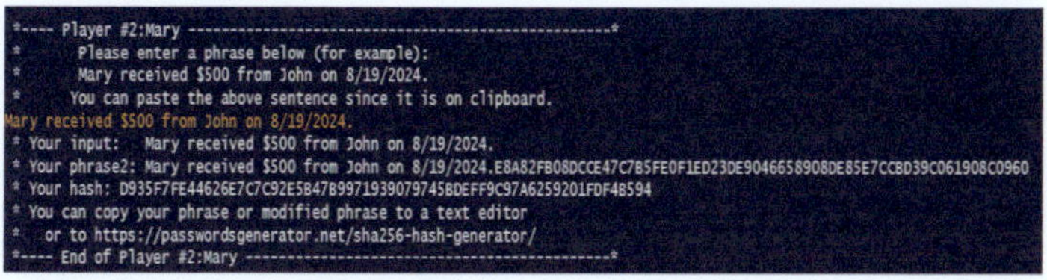

Fig. 3.28 The Hash value for Player #2

The input variable will be our original phrase, and phrase two will be the original phrase plus the previous player's hash since we have chosen Method 2 (put the last hash after our new sentence). Below, we paste phrase2 to the webpage at https://passwordsgenerator.net/sha256-hash-generator/.

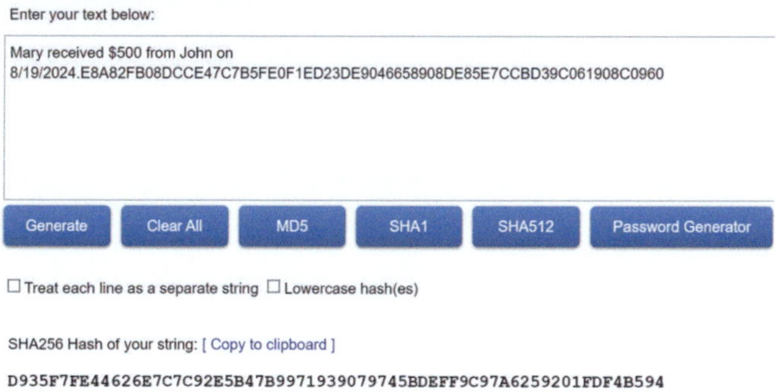

Fig. 3.29 Verification from the website

Interested readers can continue this Game by adding more players.

3.14 .QuickHash3ASCII Function

To help students verify their results, we have generated a hidden function called `.quickHash3ASCII` with a shortcut of `.quick3`. One example is shown below.

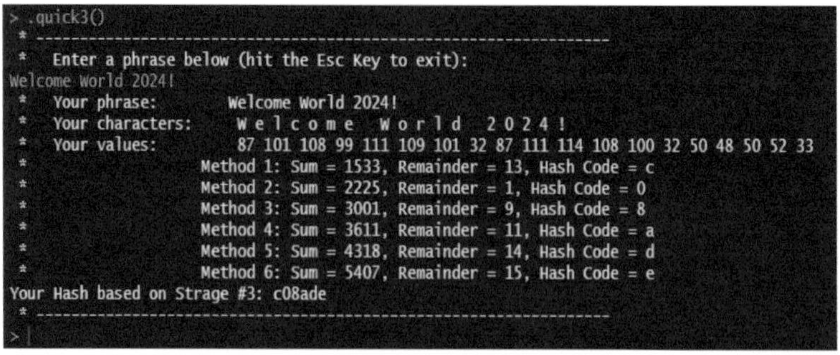

Fig. 3.30 The hidden.quickHash3ASCII function

3.15 One Fun Example of Using Sha256

When asking the audience a question, we can give our answer. However, it is not in plain language. Instead, it is in the format of a Hash value generated by Sha256. For example, we have the following questions and answers. We can give the above hash value to the audience. After they offer various questions, we input our answers to match the above hash value (Table 3.4).

The answers are given below.

- A1: John Doe
- A2: effect
- A3: No. Excel does not have a function to calculate an effective quarterly rate.
- A4: EAR = 0.1025 and the effective quarterly rate = 0. 0.02469508.

To verify our answers, we can use the website https://passwordsgenerator.net/sha256-hash-generator/. Alternatively, we can apply our function.sha256().

Table 3.4 Pairs of Q&A (Answers are Hash)

Q1	What is the name used to refer to common males?
A1	6CEA57C2FB6CBC2A40411135005760F241FFFC3E5E67AB9988272643 1037F908
Q2	What is the Excel function to calculate an Effective Annual Rate?
A2	DCB576426A17B7DF13907007CB02A1F1DFC12FC6C69F603717ABCA59D03B888E
Q3	Does Excel have a function to calculate an Effective Quarterly Rate??
A3	28E7FDDF01DF4F401E8267CF4CB127729CA40C0F5D0737AFAE49783F9B5F0CF8
Q4	The APR (annual percentage rate is 10%, compounded semi-annually. What are the corresponding EAR (Effective Annual Rate) and effective quarterly rate?
A5	9D29816DC531D80F3ACC0B6C68F1ECEE2B8FD88D02FD1A62975ABFFEA7D7684D

```
> .sha256("John Doe")
SHA-256 hash: 6CEA57C2FB6CBC2A40411135005760F241FFFC3E5E67AB99882726431037F908
   Launch your text deitor and paste it there.
>
```

Fig. 3.31 The Hash value for "John Doe"

The Hash for the phrase "`John Doe`" is given below.

```
6CEA57C2FB6CBC2A40411135005760F241FFFC3E5E67AB99882726431037F908
```

3.16 Comparing Two Hashes

Sometimes, we must compare two hashes to see whether they are equal. The first method is to use Excel, shown below.

	A	B	C	D	E	F	G	H	I
1	0x90bf279fdfc0c8aa78ce86f7a879eca5ee0b70b3ac9d0e87acea27cd098cc393								
2									
3	0x90bf279fdfc0c8aa78ce86f7a879eca5ee0b70b3ac9d0e87acea27cd098cc393								
4									
5	Yes, they are equal			=IF(hash1=hash2,"Yes, they are equal", "No they are not equal")					

Fig. 3.32 Using Excel to compare two Hashes

Interested readers can first generate a hash at https://passwordsgenerator.net/sha256-hash-generator/ and copy it to Excel. Try changing the cases of letters to see if they are still equal. Alternatively, readers and students can use our hidden function `.compareHashes ()` with a short name `.ch()`, shown below.

```
> .ch()
 * ------------------------------------------------- *
 *   compare two hashes
 * ------------------------------------------------- *
 *    Input the first hash
0x90bf279fdfc0c8aa78ce86f7a879eca5ee0b70b3ac9d0e87acea27cd098cc393
 *  Input the second hash
0x90bf279fdfc0c8aa78ce86f7a879eca5ee0b70b3ac9d0e87acea27cd098CC393
 *   yes
 * they are equal
>
```

Fig. 3.33 The hidden function to compare Hashes (.compareHashes)

3.17 Proof of Work vs. Poof of Stake

Proof of Work (PoW) and Proof of Stake (PoS) are two fundamental consensus mechanisms used in blockchain networks to validate transactions and secure the system against attacks. Both PoW and PoS have their strengths and weaknesses. PoW offers robust security at the cost of high energy usage, while PoS provides efficiency and scalability but requires careful economic design to prevent manipulation. Many modern blockchains, such as Ethereum, have transitioned from PoW to PoS to address scalability and environmental concerns while maintaining network security.

Proof of Work (PoW) is the original consensus mechanism introduced by Bitcoin. It requires participants, known as miners, to solve complex mathematical puzzles using computational power. The first miner to solve the puzzle gets the right to add a new block to the blockchain and receive a reward in cryptocurrency. PoW ensures network security by making it computationally expensive and time-consuming to alter past transactions. However, this mechanism has significant drawbacks, including high energy consumption and the risk of centralization, as large mining pools dominate the process.

Proof of Stake (PoS) is an alternative that replaces computational work with economic incentives. Instead of solving puzzles, validators are chosen based on the amount of cryptocurrency they "stake" as collateral. The more a participant stakes, the higher the chance to validate a new block and earn rewards. PoS is designed to be more energy-efficient and scalable than PoW since it eliminates the need for expensive mining equipment. However, it introduces different security considerations, such as the "nothing at stake" problem, where validators might attempt to support multiple blockchain forks without financial consequences.

Appendix A: Issue the Following line of R Code for Week 3

```
source("http://datayyy.com/i2ft/week3.txt")
```

```
*-------------------------------------------------------------------------*
* Introduction to FinTech using Excel                  by Dr. Yan 2025     *
*        (in an R-assisted learning environment)                           *
*-------------------------------------------------------------------------*
*  .c1 Introduction & Excel Basics                 .c16 R basics(optional) *
*  .c2 Blockchain (I) : Numbers/alphanumeric cases                         *
*  .c3 Blockchain (II): ASCII and Sha256                                   *
*-------------------------------------------------------------------------*
* >.c3        # go to chapter 3                                            *
* >.uu        # go to utility submenu                                      *
* >.ft        # back to this menu                                          *
*-------------------------------------------------------------------------*
```

Fig. 3.34 Menu for Week 3

Appendix B: Type `.chapter3` or `.c3` to Find the Contents Related to Chapter 3.

```
> .c3
function(i=0){
"i Chapter 3: Blockchain II          i  Explanations                   i    Explanation
 - -------------------------------- --  ------------------------       --   -------------------------
 1  Block vs. blockchain             21  our function: .sha256()       41  .isHexadecimal    .isHash
 2  our 4-stage explanation          22               : .sha256web()   42  .compareHashes    .ch
 3  Stage #3: ASCII                  23               : .sha256LocalFile()  43  sha256 -> values (numbers)
 4        : mod() function           24               : .sha256add()
 5        : 10 digits/6 letters      25               :[placeholder]
 6        : Excel vlookup()          26  Blockchain: concepts
 7        :  functions for ASCII     27       :  numbers only
 8        : .digit16() function      28       :  alphanumeric
 9        : logic 6-character hash   29       :  ASCIII
10        : .quickHash3ASCII         30       [placeholder]
11 Stage #4: sha256                  31  Blockchain Game #3
12        : hexadecimal              32       : .blockChainGame3ASCII
13        : hex table                33        [placeholder]
14        : hexadecimal converter    34  Blockchain Game #4
15        : website                  35       : .blockchainGame4
16        : unique shap256           36    [placeholder]
17        : 'digest' package         37    [placeholder]
18  [placeholder]                    38    [placeholder]
19  Videos                           39   .cdl1()
20  Links                            40   find the hash value of a software

Example #1:> .c3     # get the above list
Example #2:> .c3()   # the same as the above
Example #3:> .c3(1)  # see the first explanation
```

Fig. 3.35 The contents of Chapter 3

Appendix C: For Chapter-Related Functions, type `.searchHiddenFunctions(3)`

```
> .searchHiddenFunctions(3)
 CHAPTER                               NAME               SHORTCUT
        3  install.packages('digest')
        3 .sha256                         .s1  # need 'digest'
        3 .sha256web                      .s2  # need 'digest'
        3 .sha256LocalFile                .s3  # need 'digest'
        3 .sha256add                      .s4  # need 'digest'
        3 .make64
        3 .compareHashes                  .ch
        3 .blockChainGame3ASCII()}        .g3
        3 .blockchainGame4()}             .g4  # need 'digest'
        3 .isHexadecimal                  .isHash
        3 .compareHashes                  .ch
>
```

Fig. 3.36 The hidden functions related to Chapter 3

Appendix D: Find the Unique Characters of a hash

At https://passwordsgenerator.net/sha256-hash-generator/, after entering John Doe, we would get the following hash

```
6CEA57C2FB6CBC2A40411135005760F241FFFC3E5E67AB99882726431037F908
```

Now, readers/students don't have to understand the concept thoroughly; just two points: the length of the true hash is 64, as shown below.

	A	B	C	D	E	F	G	I
1	6CEA57C2FB6CBC2A40411135005760F241FFFC3E5E67AB99882726431037F908							
2								
3	n		64	=LEN(A1)				

Fig. 3.37 The length of a Hash

First, break up into characters. Second, sort them. Third, find unique characters, i.e., report one if it differs from the previous one.

	I	J	K	L	M	N	O	P	Q	R	S
1	1	6	=RIGHT(LEFT($A$1,I1),1)			0	0	=N1+0	0		
2	2	C				0	0			=IF(O1=O2,"",O2)	
3	3	E				0	0				
4	4	A		1		0	0				
5	5	5				0	0				
6	6	7				0	0				
7	7	C				1	1		1		
8	8	2				1	1				
9	9	F				1	1				
10	10	B				1	1				
11	11	6				1	1				
12	12	C				2	2		2		
13	13	B				2	2				
14	14	C				2	2				
15	15	2				2	2				
16	16	A				2	2				
17	17	4				3	3		3		

Fig. 3.38 The Excel RIGHT function

Exercises

3.1 What is a cryptographic hash, and why is it crucial in blockchain technology?
3.2 Explain how the SHA-256 hash function works and why it is widely used in blockchain.
3.3 How does a hash ensure the integrity of data in a blockchain?
3.4 What does it mean when we say a hash function is "deterministic"? Why is this property important?
3.5 Why is the immutability of a hash output crucial in preventing data tampering in a blockchain?

3.6 What role does the SHA-256 algorithm play in linking blocks in a blockchain?
3.7 What is a "hash collision," and why is it undesirable in blockchain systems?
3.8 Discuss the concept of a "hash pointer" and its significance in blockchain structure.
3.9 Explain how blockchain systems use hashes to maintain a distributed ledger without relying on a central authority.
3.10 How does the computational effort to find a specific hash output contribute to blockchain security?
3.11 Why can't hash outputs be reversed to obtain the original input? How does this one-way characteristic enhance blockchain security?
3.12 How does the difficulty adjustment mechanism in Bitcoin's blockchain depend on hashing?
3.13 Explain how hashes are used to verify transactions without revealing the actual data in blockchain systems.
3.14 Discuss how a change in any transaction in a block would affect the hash of that block and subsequent blocks.
3.15 How does a "nonce" relate to finding a valid hash in blockchain mining?
3.16 What is a "hash rate," and why is it a critical metric in blockchain networks?
3.17 At http://datayyy.com/data_txt/list.txt, you can find a list of text files. Download five of them and try our `.sha256LocalFile ()` function to generate five Sha246 Hashes.
3.18 Reproduce the same result in the chapter using numbers only for the two sets of numbers below.

Data set #1: `12345 666 789 12 3456`

Data set #2: `5678 45678 12345 777 689 978 1234`

3.19 Play Blockchain-based Game #3. What are the Hash values for three players with the same inputs as the previous question? Comment on your results.
3.20 Play Blockchain-based Game #4. What are the Hash values for three players with the same inputs as the previous question? Comment on your results.
3.21 What is the Excel function offering ASCII values for a given sentence? Generate a set of values for this question: `What Excel function offers ASCII values for a given sentence?`
3.22 What is the usage of a hidden function called `.quick3()`? Try a few sentences by using this function.
3.23 Explain the concepts of PoW and PoS.
3.24 Find out which blockchain networks use PoW and which use PoS.

References

ASCII Table. https://www.ascii-code.com/characters

Belyh, A. (2019). *The definitive guide to Fama-French three-factor model*. https://www.cleverism.com/fama-french-three-factor-model-guide/

CFI Team, Capital Asset Pricing Model (CAPM). https://corporatefinanceinstitute.com/resources/valuation/what-is-capm-formula/
Dumas, A. (1844). *Count of Monte Cristo*. http://gutenberg.org/files/1184/1184-0.txt
Lepcha, M. (2023). *What is SHA-256?* https://www.techopedia.com/definition/sha-256
Sha256 website. https://passwordsgenerator.net/sha256-hash-generator/

Ledger and Distributed Ledger

4

We will explain the traditional ledger, single-, double- and triple-bookkeeping, the differences between centralized, decentralized, and distributed systems, and accounting fraud with several famous cases. Simulation is used in this chapter to show a simulated ledger, Balance Sheet, and Income Statement, a centralized, decentralized, and distributed system with different nodes (players and centers). This chapter focuses on connecting a set of ledger records with Hash by using our function called `.ledger2hash ()`. In this chapter, the following topics will be covered:

- Traditional ledger system
- Single-, double- and triple-bookkeeping
- Blockchain is essentially a ledger
- Accounting fraud
- Simulated ledgers, Balance Sheet and Income Statement
- Graphic presentations of centralized, decentralized, and distributed systems with different nodes (players)
- Ledger to Hash using our `.ledger2hash ()` function

Supplementary Information The online version contains supplementary material available at https://doi.org/10.1007/978-3-031-89779-5_4.

Y. Yan, *Introduction to FinTech using Excel*, Springer Texts in Business and Economics, https://doi.org/10.1007/978-3-031-89779-5_4

4.1 Traditional Ledger Systems

Traditional ledgers, the backbone of financial accounting for centuries, are essentially records of financial transactions. Bookkeepers manually maintain these ledgers, either in large, bound books or within accounting software. Each entry in a traditional ledger, which includes details such as the date, transaction description, and debit and credit amounts, is a testament to the bookkeeper's role in ensuring a clear audit trail. These systems are widely used across industries to maintain accurate and comprehensive records of financial activities.

While traditional ledgers provide reliable record-keeping, they are not without limitations. Their manual nature makes them prone to human errors, fraud, and tampering. Moreover, updating and reconciling these records can be time-consuming, especially for large organizations with numerous transactions. These drawbacks have underscored the need for more advanced, automated, and secure methods of managing financial data, leading to the emergence of distributed ledger technologies.

4.2 Distributed Ledger Technology (DLT)

Distributed Ledger Technology (DLT) is a digital system for recording the transaction of assets in which the details are recorded in multiple places simultaneously. Unlike traditional ledgers, distributed ledgers have no central data store or administration functionality. Each node (participant) in the network maintains a copy of the ledger, ensuring that data is replicated and shared across the system. This decentralization enhances transparency, security, and efficiency, making DLT a robust alternative to conventional record-keeping methods.

The most well-known application of DLT is blockchain technology, which underpins cryptocurrencies like Bitcoin. However, DLT's use cases extend far beyond digital currencies. It can be applied in various sectors, including supply chain management, healthcare, finance, and government, to improve processes by providing a tamper-proof, immutable record of transactions. DLTs ensure that any change in the ledger is visible to all participants, fostering trust and collaboration among users.

4.3 Blockchain: A Type of Distributed Ledger

Blockchain is a distributed ledger that organizes data into blocks chained together chronologically. Each block contains a set of transactions linked to the previous block through cryptographic hashes, creating an unbreakable chain of records. This structure ensures the integrity and security of data, as altering any information within a block would require changing all subsequent blocks, which is computationally impractical.

The decentralized nature of blockchain eliminates the need for a central authority, allowing for peer-to-peer transactions without intermediaries. This feature has significant implications for industries such as banking, where it can reduce costs, increase transaction speed, and enhance security. Beyond financial applications, blockchain is being explored for use cases such as smart contracts, digital identity verification, and secure voting systems, showcasing its versatility as a distributed ledger technology.

4.4 Consensus Mechanisms in Distributed Ledgers

Consensus mechanisms are protocols that ensure all participants in a distributed ledger agree on its state. These mechanisms are critical for maintaining the ledger's integrity and reliability, especially in decentralized systems where trust is distributed among many nodes. Different types of consensus mechanisms, such as Proof of Work (PoW), Proof of Stake (PoS), and Practical Byzantine Fault Tolerance (PBFT), offer various ways to achieve agreement among network participants.

Proof of Work, used by Bitcoin, requires participants to solve complex mathematical problems to validate transactions and create new blocks. This method ensures security but can be resource-intensive. On the other hand, Proof of Stake selects validators based on the number of coins they hold and are willing to "stake" as collateral. PBFT is used in permissioned blockchains, where nodes are known and trusted to a certain extent. Each mechanism has its security, efficiency, and scalability trade-offs, influencing the choice of technology for specific use cases.

4.5 Applications and Use Cases of DLT

Distributed ledger technologies (DLT) have numerous applications across various industries. They offer solutions to traditional challenges by providing more efficient, secure, and transparent methods of managing data. In the financial sector, DLT is used for cross-border payments, reducing transaction times and costs while increasing security. In supply chain management, DLT ensures traceability and transparency, allowing all parties to track the movement of goods from production to delivery.

Healthcare is another sector benefiting from DLT, where patient records can be securely shared among authorized parties, improving data accessibility and reducing the risk of breaches. Governments are also exploring DLT for secure voting systems, property registries, and identity management. These applications demonstrate the potential of distributed ledgers to transform industries by enhancing data security, improving operational efficiencies, and fostering greater trust among stakeholders.

These sections provide a comprehensive overview of ledger systems, highlighting the shift from traditional to distributed ledgers and its implications for various industries.

4.6 Single-Entry Bookkeeping

Single-entry bookkeeping is the simplest form, where each financial transaction is recorded only once, typically in a cash book. Small businesses or individuals with straightforward financial transactions often use this method. In single-entry bookkeeping, entries are usually made for cash receipts and payments, with minimal attention to other elements like accounts payable or receivable. While this approach is easy to implement and understand, it provides limited insight into the financial health of a business, as it does not capture the complete picture of financial transactions. There is no systematic method to ensure accuracy and completeness, making it prone to errors and fraud.

4.7 Double-Entry Bookkeeping

Double-entry bookkeeping, on the other hand, is a more sophisticated method where each transaction affects at least two accounts, with a debit entry in one account and a corresponding credit entry in another. This system provides a more comprehensive view of a company's financial position by maintaining a balance between debits and credits. The double-entry system is the foundation of modern accounting, enabling the preparation of detailed financial statements such as balance sheets and income statements. It enhances accuracy and reliability because it inherently checks and balances itself, reducing the risk of errors and providing a clearer understanding of an organization's financial activities.

4.8 Triple-Entry Bookkeeping

Triple-entry bookkeeping builds upon the double-entry system by adding a third entry, which involves recording transactions on a shared, immutable ledger, such as a blockchain. This innovation provides an extra layer of transparency and security, as transactions are cryptographically sealed and can be independently verified by all participants. Triple-entry bookkeeping enhances trust between parties and reduces the risk of disputes and fraud by providing a single source of truth accessible to all relevant stakeholders. This system is particularly relevant in the digital age, where secure and transparent record-keeping is essential for managing complex, high-value transactions.

4.9 Monte Carlo Simulation

In this chapter, we plan to use Monte Carlo Simulation to generate fake ledgers and graphs to explain concepts such as centralized, decentralized, and distributed systems.

Monte Carlo Simulation is a powerful statistical technique that models the probability of different outcomes in inherently uncertain processes. Using random sampling to generate a range of possible scenarios, Monte Carlo Simulation helps understand complex systems' behavior and make informed decisions under uncertainty. In the context of centralized, decentralized, and distributed ledger systems, Monte Carlo Simulation can model various aspects, such as transaction flows, network reliability, and the impact of different consensus mechanisms. By visualizing these simulations using graphs, one can gain insights into how these systems perform under various conditions, highlighting potential bottlenecks, vulnerabilities, and efficiency metrics.

The concept of a random seed is crucial in Monte Carlo Simulations because it ensures the reproducibility of the simulation results. A random seed initializes the random number generator used in the simulation, allowing the same set of random numbers to be generated across different runs. This consistency is vital for validating results, comparing scenarios, and debugging simulation models. Researchers can replicate their findings by setting a specific random seed, enabling others to verify and build upon their work. In simulating centralized, decentralized, and distributed systems, using a random seed allows for consistent comparisons of how these different architectures respond to similar conditions, providing a clearer understanding of their advantages and drawbacks.

4.10 Centralized, Decentralized, and Distributed Systems

Centralized systems are structured with a single central point of control, where a single entity or server handles all data processing, storage, and management. This setup allows for streamlined decision-making and easier management, as all operations are controlled from a central location. However, it also presents significant vulnerabilities, such as the risk of a single point of failure—if the central server is compromised, the entire system can be disrupted. Additionally, centralized systems may face issues with scalability and bottlenecks as they grow, as all traffic and data processing are channeled through one central hub.

Decentralized systems, on the other hand, distribute control across multiple nodes or locations, reducing reliance on a single central authority. Each node in a decentralized system operates independently yet works towards a common goal, making the system more resilient to failures and attacks. While decentralized systems can improve security and reduce the risk of a single point of failure, they may face challenges in coordination and consensus among nodes.

Distributed systems extend this concept by ensuring all nodes operate independently and share and synchronize data and processing power. This structure enhances scalability and fault tolerance, as the system can continue functioning even if multiple nodes fail. Distributed systems, such as blockchain networks, are particularly effective in environments requiring high availability, reliability, and robustness.

According to https://medium.com/nakamo-to, we have the following graph describing those three systems.

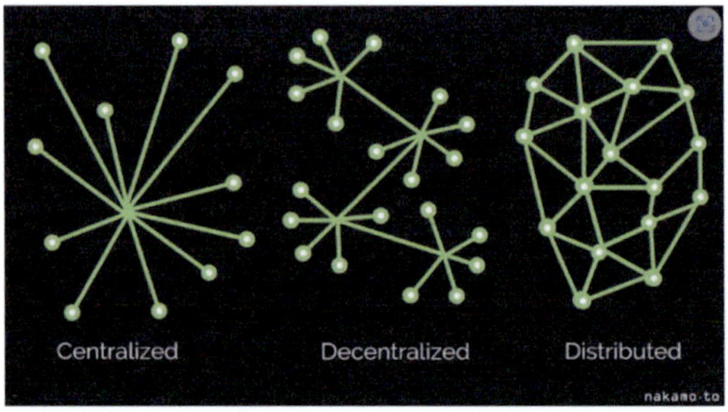

Fig. 4.1 An illustration of three types

For this chapter and for fun, we have generated three hidden functions: `.centralizedLedger ()`, `.decentralizedLedger ()`, and `.distribuedLedger ()`. For the first function, we have one input: the number of nodes.

```
> .centralizedLedger ().
Input the number of nodes
30
```

The graph is shown below.

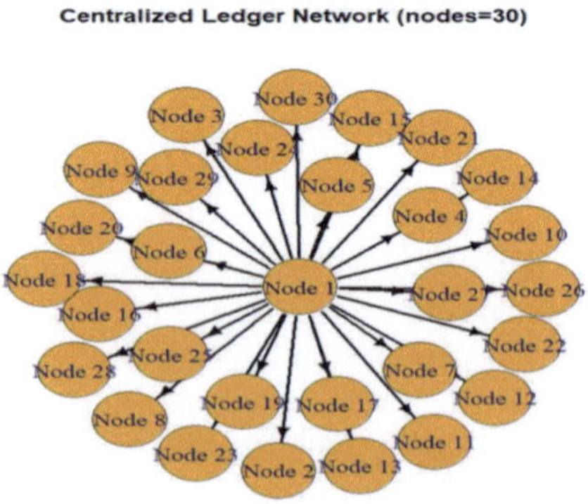

Fig. 4.2 A centralized ledger network with 30 nodes

The.`dencentralizedLedger()` function has a shortcut named.`dl ()`.

```
> .decentralizedLedger ()
Input the number of nodes:
30
 Input the number of centers:
4
>
```

The graphs are shown below.

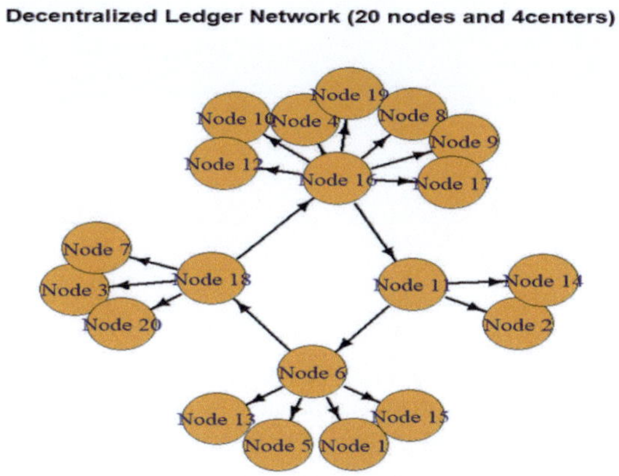

Fig. 4.3 A decentralized ledger network: 4 centers with 20 nodes

In the above graph, all nodes are around four centers. The third function is called the.`distributedLedger() function.`

```
> .distributedLedger()
Input number of nodes:
20
Enter your seed below:
123
```

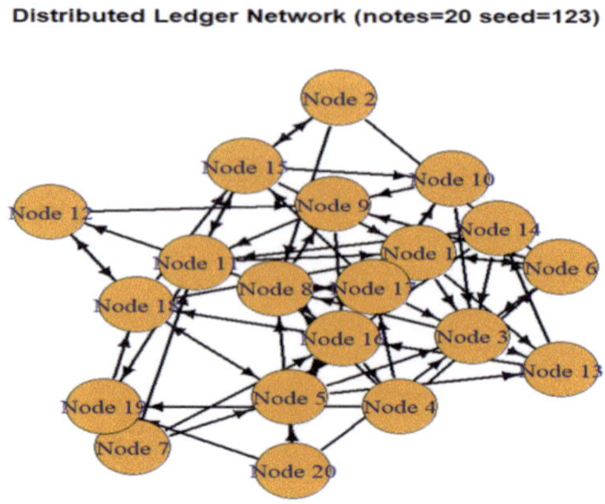

Fig. 4.4 A distributed ledger network with 20 nodes

4.11 Trilemma

The term 'trilemma' refers to a situation with three desirable attributes or factors, but achieving two simultaneously is possible. Improving or optimizing two factors will inevitably lead to a compromise or reduction in the third. This concept is commonly used in various fields, such as economics, engineering, and computer science, to describe inherent trade-offs in complex systems.

4.12 Blockchain Trilemma

One prominent example of the trilemma is the **Blockchain Trilemma** in the context of distributed ledger technology, notably blockchain systems. The three factors in this trilemma are summarized in the following Table 4.1.

According to the blockchain trilemma, optimizing all three factors simultaneously is challenging. For instance:

Table 4.1 Three Objectives of Blockchain

Decentralization	Decentralization distributes control across many nodes, ensuring no single entity has full authority over the system. Eliminating a single point of failure enhances security and trust
Scalability	The ability of the system to handle a growing number of transactions efficiently without compromising performance. A scalable system can support a large user base and high transaction volumes
Security	The robustness of the system against attacks, fraud, and tampering. A secure system ensures that the integrity of the data and the network is maintained, even in the presence of malicious actors

A highly 'decentralized' system may struggle with 'scalability' because the need for consensus among many nodes can slow down transaction processing.
A highly 'scalable' system might require some level of 'centralization' to achieve faster processing speeds, potentially compromising its decentralized nature and trust.
A system that focuses on both 'scalability' and 'security' may need to reduce 'decentralization' by having fewer, more trusted nodes, which could undermine the democratic aspect of decentralization.

Understanding the trilemma helps make informed decisions about system design, where trade-offs are inevitable, and priorities must be set based on the application's specific goals and requirements.

4.13 Accounting Fraud: Enron Case

Enron, once a major American energy company, became infamous for one of history's most prominent accounting fraud scandals. The company's executives used complex accounting loopholes, Special Purpose Entities (SPEs), and dubious financial reporting to hide massive debts and inflate profits. These deceptive practices made Enron appear more profitable than it was, artificially boosting its stock price. The seemingly solid financial statements misled investors and analysts, while the true extent of Enron's financial problems remained hidden.

The scandal came to light in late 2001, leading to Enron's bankruptcy and the loss of thousands of jobs and billions of dollars in shareholder value. The fallout from the scandal had far-reaching consequences, including the dissolution of Arthur Andersen, one of the world's largest accounting firms, which was found complicit in the fraud. The Enron case prompted significant changes in regulatory and compliance standards, leading to the passage of the Sarbanes–Oxley Act in 2002, which aimed to improve corporate governance and restore investor confidence in financial reporting.

4.14 Accounting Fraud: WorldCom

WorldCom, a telecommunications giant, was involved in a massive accounting fraud uncovered in 2002. The company inflated its assets by approximately $11 billion through improper accounting practices, including capitalizing ordinary operating expenses to enhance profitability falsely. This scheme allowed WorldCom to report inflated earnings, misrepresenting its financial health to investors, creditors, and regulators. The fraudulent activities were primarily orchestrated by the company's CEO, Bernie Ebbers, and CFO, Scott Sullivan, who sought to maintain high stock prices and personal gain.

When the fraud was exposed, WorldCom filed for bankruptcy, marking it as one of the largest bankruptcies in U.S. history. The scandal led to severe financial losses for investors, job losses for employees, and a significant shakeup in the telecommunications industry. The WorldCom case highlighted the importance of ethical corporate governance and the need for strict internal controls and auditing standards to prevent and detect fraudulent activities.

4.15 Accounting Fraud: HealthSouth

HealthSouth, a significant healthcare services provider, was involved in a massive accounting scandal in the early 2000s. The company's executives, led by CEO Richard Scrushy, inflated earnings by approximately $1.4 billion over several years. This was achieved by falsifying financial statements and overstating revenues, expenses, and assets to meet Wall Street expectations and maintain high stock prices. The fraudulent activities involved numerous employees, including top executives, who manipulated accounting entries to cover up the company's financial performance.

The HealthSouth scandal came to light when the company's whistleblowers revealed the extent of the fraud. The exposure of fraud led to significant legal consequences for HealthSouth executives, including prison sentences and fines. The scandal underscored the importance of whistleblower protections and the need for strong ethical standards and transparency in corporate financial reporting. It also led to greater scrutiny of financial practices in the healthcare industry, emphasizing the need for robust internal controls and ethical leadership.

4.16 Accounting Fraud: Tyco

Tyco International, a diversified manufacturing conglomerate, became embroiled in a major corporate scandal in the early 2000s when it was revealed that top executives, including CEO Dennis Kozlowski and CFO Mark Swartz, had engaged in massive accounting fraud and embezzlement. They looted the company for over $600 million through unauthorized bonuses, stock fraud, and fraudulent expense reimbursements. The executives disguised their activities by falsifying financial statements and misleading shareholders and regulators about Tyco's financial health.

The Tyco scandal led to a significant decline in investor confidence, with the company's stock price plummeting and numerous lawsuits filed. The exposure of the fraud resulted in criminal charges against Kozlowski and Swartz, who were eventually convicted and sentenced to prison. The Tyco case highlighted the need for robust corporate governance and accountability, particularly concerning executive compensation and the integrity of financial reporting. It also contributed to the broader push for corporate reform and more robust regulatory oversight in the wake of the early 2000s corporate scandals.

4.17 Accounting Fraud: AIG

American International Group (AIG), a multinational insurance corporation, was involved in an accounting scandal in the early 2000s centered around misleading financial reporting and manipulating accounting records to inflate profits and misstate the company's financial position. AIG engaged in complex transactions, including reinsurance deals that were essentially loans, to disguise financial losses and present a more favorable financial outlook. These deceptive practices were intended to maintain the company's credit rating and keep its stock price high.

The fraudulent activities came to light in 2005, leading to regulatory investigations and significant legal and financial repercussions for AIG. The company was forced to restate its earnings, resulting in a substantial loss of investor confidence and a sharp decline in its stock price. The AIG scandal underscored the risks associated with complex financial products and the need for transparent and accurate financial reporting. It also highlighted the importance of strong internal controls and the role of regulatory oversight in maintaining the integrity of financial markets.

4.18 Accounting Fraud and System

One significant reason for accounting fraud is the centralized nature of many corporate systems. In a centralized system, financial information and decision-making authority are concentrated in the hands of a few top executives or managers. This concentration of power can create opportunities for those in control to manipulate financial statements and records without sufficient oversight. When internal checks and balances are weak or absent, and there is a lack of independent auditing, it becomes easier for executives to engage in fraudulent activities such as inflating profits, hiding losses, or misrepresenting the company's financial health to meet market expectations and enhance personal gain.

The availability of SEC (Securities and Exchange Commission) filings as public documents can help deter accounting fraud by providing transparency and allowing investors, analysts, and regulators to scrutinize a company's financial statements. These filings include detailed reports on a company's financial performance, operations, and management activities, offering insights into its business practices. Public access to this information means that discrepancies or red flags can be identified, leading to investigations and enforcement actions by regulatory bodies. However, even with these safeguards, centralized systems can still facilitate fraud if those responsible for oversight fail to act on warning signs or if the company effectively conceals fraudulent activities through complex financial maneuvers.

4.19 Simulated Ledger

In blockchain, a hash is a fixed-size alphanumeric string generated by a cryptographic hash function that uniquely represents data of any size. Hashes are used to secure and verify data.

A1 fx Date,Description,Debit,Credit

	A	B	C	D	E	F
1	Date,Description,Debit,Credit					
2	2024-01-02,Account Receivable,806.87,					
3	2024-01-03,Expense#2,38.93,					
4	2024-01-04,RentalCost,39.83,					
5	2024-01-05,Expense#2,632.54,					
6	2024-01-08,Account Receivable,239.09,					
7	2024-01-09,Expense#1,252.53,					
8	2024-01-10,Revenue,,803.24					
9	2024-01-11,Cost of Material#1,405.69,					
10	2024-01-12,Account Receivable,798.47,					
11	2024-01-15,Account Receivable,117.46,					
12	2024-01-16,Expense#1,994.5,					

Fig. 4.5 The initial data (just one column)

Choose this column, and click "Data" on the menu bar.

	A	B	C	D
1	Date	Description	Debit	Credit
2	1/2/2024	Account Receivable	806.87	
3	1/3/2024	Expense#2	38.93	
4	1/4/2024	RentalCost	39.83	
5	1/5/2024	Expense#2	632.54	
6	1/8/2024	Account Receivable	239.09	
7	1/9/2024	Expense#1	252.53	
8	1/10/2024	Revenue		803.24
9	1/11/2024	Cost of Material#1	405.69	
10	1/12/2024	Account Receivable	798.47	
11	1/15/2024	Account Receivable	117.46	
12	1/16/2024	Expense#1	994.5	
13	1/17/2024	Cost of Material#2	649.86	
14	1/18/2024	Expense#1	655.61	
15	1/19/2024	Expense#1	747.48	
16	1/22/2024	Expense#2	514.27	
17	1/23/2024	Cost of Material#2	380.33	
18	1/24/2024	Expense#1	611.31	
19	1/25/2024	Cost of Material#2	966	
20	1/26/2024	Account Payable		188.58

Fig. 4.6 One column to multiple columns

4.20 Ledger Records to Hash

As we mentioned before, Blockchain can be viewed as a decentralized ledger. To vividly demonstrate this, we have generated a hidden function converting a set of ledger records to Hash. The function is called `.ledgerRecords2hash_ASCII`. The function will accept a set of ledger entries to produce a blockchain by combining the previous Hash (before or after our current entry). The underlying logic is the same as Blockchain Game 3 discussed in the last chapter, i.e., it accepts all ASCII characters and produces a 6-character Hash value. In the same space, we will not explain six ways to calculate the summation of ASCII values. As the first step, let's generate five fake ledger records.

```
> .fakeLedger()

  Input starting date, such as 1/1/2024
1/1/2023

  Input the number of days, such as 200
5

  Input a random seed for reproducibility.
     If you don't want a seed, hit the enter-key.
123
The first few observations are shown below.

        Date         Description  Debit Credit
1 2023-01-02     Account Payable         899.82
2 2023-01-03     Account Payable         246.09
3 2023-01-04             Revenue          42.06
4 2023-01-05  Account Receivable 572.63
5 2023-01-06           Expense#2 102.92

  Launch Excel and paste it there.
```

Fig. 4.7 The function generating fake ledgers (`.fakeLeder`).

Again, choosing the same random seed, 123, will generate the same results. Since the data is on the Clipboard, we can immediately run the .ledgerRecords2hash_ASCII() function.

```
> .ledgerRecords2hash_ASCII()
 * ------------------------------------------------------- *
 *   Copy your ledger records then hit the Enter Key       *

 * Enter your chose by adding previous Hash

 *    1          before your current ledger record
 *    2          after  your current ledger record
1


 The first several observations are shown below.
                         LedgerRecord PreviousHash                                   NewMessage   Hash
1     2023-01-02,Account Payable,,899.82                           2023-01-02,Account Payable,,899.82 4834f6
2     2023-01-03,Account Payable,,246.09       4834f6   4834f62023-01-03,Account Payable,,246.09 5e441e
3            2023-01-04,Revenue,,42.06        5e441e          5e441e2023-01-04,Revenue,,42.06 50c8f8
4 2023-01-05,Account Receivable,572.63,       50c8f8 50c8f82023-01-05,Account Receivable,572.63, cd7363
5          2023-01-06,Expense#2,102.92,       cd7363         cd73632023-01-06,Expense#2,102.92, e0262a
```

Fig. 4.8 Converting ledger records to Hash and ASCII (`.ledgerRecords2hash_ASCII`)

For Excel, the result is shown below.

	A	B	C	
1	LedgerRecord	PreviousHash	NewMessage	Hash
2	2023-01-02,Account Payable,,899.82	""	2023-01-02,Account Payable,,899.82	"4834f6"
3	2023-01-03,Account Payable,,246.09	"4834f6"	4834f62023-01-03,Account Payable,,246.09	"5e441e"
4	2023-01-04,Revenue,,42.06	"5e441e"	5e441e2023-01-04,Revenue,,42.06	"50c8f8"
5	2023-01-05,Account Receivable,572.63,	"50c8f8"	50c8f82023-01-05,Account Receivable,572.63,	"cd7363"
6	2023-01-06,Expense#2,102.92,	"cd7363"	cd73632023-01-06,Expense#2,102.92,	"e0262a"

Fig. 4.9 The result shown in Excel

4.21 Verifying the Result Using Game 3

In the previous chapter, we explained how to play Blockchain-based Game 3, which uses ASCII characters to generate a 6-character long Hash. Below, we present those five ledger entries.

```
LedgerRecord
2023-01-02,Account Payable„899.82
2023-01-03,Account Payable„246.09
2023-01-04,Revenue„42.06
2023-01-05,Account Receivable,572.63
2023-01-06,Expense#2,102.92
```

To play Game #3, remember that we have a choice variable whether to combine the previous Hash before or after our current ASCII characters. After that, we copy the above records one after another. After launching the Game, we copy the first ledger record, and the result is shown in the following image.

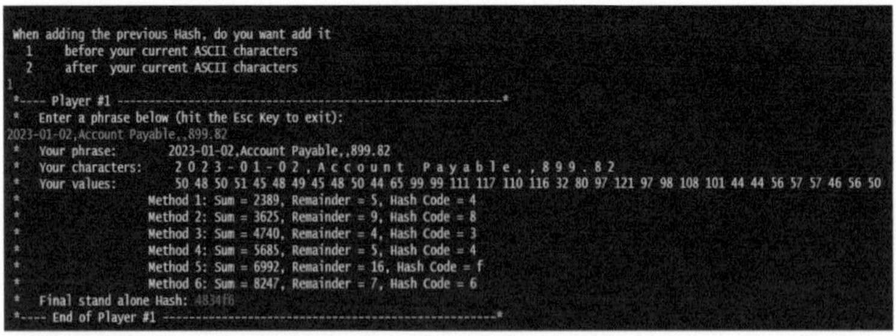

Fig. 4.10 Blockchain Game 3

The first entry is "`2023-01-02,Account Payable„899.82`". Since this is the first block, there is no previous Hash. The Hash of the record is `4834f6`, the same as the previous output. Then we enter the second ledger record:

`2023-01-03,Account Payable„246.09.`

The result is shown below.

```
*---- Player #2 ----------------------------------------------------------*
*   Enter a phrase below (hit the Esc Key to exit):
2023-01-03,Account Payable,,246.09
*   Your phrase:          2023-01-03,Account Payable,,246.09
*   Your characters:      2 0 2 3 - 0 1 - 0 3 , A c c o u n t   P a y a b l e , , 2 4 6 . 0 9
*   Your values:          50 48 50 51 45 48 49 45 48 51 44 65 99 99 111 117 110 116 32 80 97 121 97 98 108 101 44 44 50 52 54 46 48 57
*                    Method 1: Sum = 2375, Remainder = 7, Hash Code = 6
*                    Method 2: Sum = 3614, Remainder = 14, Hash Code = d
*                    Method 3: Sum = 4694, Remainder = 6, Hash Code = 5
*                    Method 4: Sum = 5668, Remainder = 4, Hash Code = 3
*                    Method 5: Sum = 6949, Remainder = 5, Hash Code = 4
*                    Method 6: Sum = 8192, Remainder = 16, Hash Code = f
*   Final stand alone Hash: 6d534f
*--------------------------------------------------
*   Previous hash  :      4834f6
*   Your new characters:         4 8 3 4 f 6 2 0 2 3 - 0 1 - 0 3 , A c c o u n t   P a y a b l e , , 2 4 6 . 0 9
*   Your values:          52 56 51 52 102 54 50 48 50 51 45 48 49 45 48 51 44 65 99 99 111 117 110 116 32 80 97 121 97 98 108 101 44 44 50 52 54 46 48 57
*                    Method 1: Sum = 2742, Remainder = 6, Hash Code = 5
*                    Method 2: Sum = 4143, Remainder = 15, Hash Code = e
*                    Method 3: Sum = 5429, Remainder = 5, Hash Code = 4
*                    Method 4: Sum = 7045, Remainder = 5, Hash Code = 4
*                    Method 5: Sum = 8178, Remainder = 2, Hash Code = 1
*                    Method 6: Sum = 9551, Remainder = 15, Hash Code = e
*   Final true Hash: 5e441e
*---- End of Player #2 ---------------------------------------------------*
```

Fig. 4.11 Player #2

The previous hash value is `4834f6`, added before the current one. The new message is.

```
4834f62023-01-03,Account Payable„246.09
```

This is the so-called `NewMessage`. The Hash value for the second ledger record is `5e441e`.

Interested readers can try the methods we have discussed in this section. Again, this is a great exercise.

4.22 Seamless Connection with Clipboard

When the first program copies the result to the clipboard, the second program receives input from the clipboard, so we can simplify our operation, i.e., after finishing the first one, launch the second one immediately. For example,`.fakeLedger ()` will generate a set of fake ledger records and copy them to the clipboard. On the other hand, our`.ledgerRecords2hash_ASCII()` receives input from the clipboard. Because of this, we can run them in sequence.

```
> .fakeLedger()

  Input starting date, such as 1/1/2024
1/2/2024

  Input the number of days, such as 200
50

  Input a random seed for reproducibility.
     If you don't want a seed, hit the enter-key.
123
The first few observations are shown below.

        Date        Description  Debit Credit
1 2024-01-02     Account Payable         10.47
2 2024-01-03     Account Payable        183.85
3 2024-01-04             Revenue        842.73
4 2024-01-05 Account Receivable 187.69
5 2024-01-08          Expense#2 782.29
6 2024-01-09          Expense#1  93.59

  Launch Excel and paste it there.
```

Fig. 4.12 The fake ledger function (`.fakeLedger`)

Immediately, run the second program.

```
> .ledgerRecords2hash_ASCII()
 * --------------------------------------------------- *
 *   Copy your ledger records then hit the Enter Key      *

 * Enter your chose by adding previous Hash

 *    1          before your current ledger record
 *    2          after  your current ledger record
1


 The first several observations are shown below.
                         LedgerRecord PreviousHash                                  NewMessage   Hash
1     2024-01-02,Account Payable,,10.47                         2024-01-02,Account Payable,,10.47 dd7107
2    2024-01-03,Account Payable,,183.85       dd7107    dd71072024-01-03,Account Payable,,183.85 268c6a
3            2024-01-04,Revenue,,842.73       268c6a           268c6a2024-01-04,Revenue,,842.73 4fc1b7
4 2024-01-05,Account Receivable,187.69,       4fc1b7 4fc1b72024-01-05,Account Receivable,187.69, e5070d
5          2024-01-08,Expense#2,782.29,       e5070d         e5070d2024-01-08,Expense#2,782.29, a4c644
6           2024-01-09,Expense#1,93.59,       a4c644          a4c6442024-01-09,Expense#1,93.59, 9a323e


 Launch Excel and paste it there.
```

Fig. 4.13 The fake ledger function (`.ledgerRecords2hash_ASCII`)

4.23 Balance-Sheet

Companies will summarize ledgers for businesses to produce balance sheets, income statements, and cash flow statements. Usually, we summarize daily ledgers to produce quarterly financial statements, then from quarterly to annual ones.

A balance sheet is a financial statement that provides a snapshot of a company's financial position at a specific time. It is structured around the fundamental accounting equation: Assets = Liabilities + Equity. This equation reflects the principle that a company's assets are financed by its liabilities (what it owes) and equity (what it owns). The balance sheet is divided into three main sections: assets, liabilities, and shareholders' equity. Assets include current assets, such as cash and accounts receivable, and non-current assets, such as property, plant, and equipment. Liabilities are categorized into current liabilities, like accounts payable, and long-term liabilities, such as bonds payable. Shareholders' equity represents the owners' residual interest in the company, typically comprising common stock, retained earnings, and additional paid-in capital.

The balance sheet is crucial for investors, creditors, and management to assess the company's financial health and stability. It helps stakeholders understand the company's ability to meet its short-term obligations, manage its operational needs, and fund future growth. By analyzing trends in the balance sheet over time, stakeholders can gain insights into how effectively a company utilizes its resources and manages its debt. Furthermore, the balance sheet provides a basis for calculating various financial ratios, such as the current and debt-to-equity ratios, which are key financial performance and risk indicators.

4.24 Income Statement

An income statement, a profit and loss statement, summarizes a company's revenues, expenses, and profits or losses over a specific period, typically a quarter or a year. This financial statement shows how well a company generates revenue from its operations, manages costs, and creates profit for its shareholders. The income statement begins with the revenue or sales, from which the cost of goods sold (COGS) is subtracted to determine the gross profit. Operating expenses, such as selling, general, and administrative expenses (SG&A), are then subtracted from the gross profit to calculate operating income. Finally, non-operating items, including interest and taxes, are factored in to determine the net income.

The income statement is critical for assessing a company's operational efficiency and profitability. It allows stakeholders to see where a company's money is coming from and where it is being spent, thus providing insights into its core business activities. By examining trends in revenues and expenses, management can make informed decisions about cost control, pricing strategies, and market expansion. Investors use the income statement to evaluate a company's financial performance, profitability, and growth potential. It also helps calculate profitability ratios, such as gross margin, operating margin, and net profit margin, which provide further insights into the company's financial health and operational efficiency.

4.25 Getting Financial Statements from Yahoo!Finance

We can use Yahoo!Finance to get many companies' financial statements, such as Balance Sheets and Income Statements. Let's use IBM as an example. Go to http://finance.yahoo.com, then enter IBM, as shown below.

Fig. 4.14 Yahoo!Finance

After clicking "`Financials`", the last entry on the left shown in the above image, you will see the following image (only the top part is shown to save space).

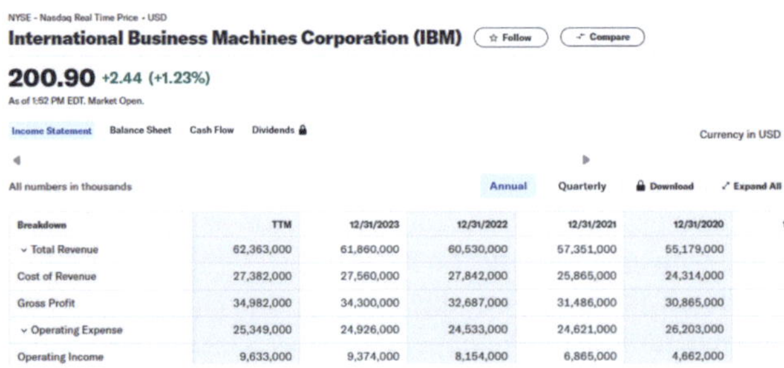

Breakdown	TTM	12/31/2023	12/31/2022	12/31/2021	12/31/2020
Total Revenue	62,363,000	61,860,000	60,530,000	57,351,000	55,179,000
Cost of Revenue	27,382,000	27,560,000	27,842,000	25,865,000	24,314,000
Gross Profit	34,982,000	34,300,000	32,687,000	31,486,000	30,865,000
Operating Expense	25,349,000	24,926,000	24,533,000	24,621,000	26,203,000
Operating Income	9,633,000	9,374,000	8,154,000	6,865,000	4,662,000

Fig. 4.15 Yahoo!Finance for IBM

The default is the Income Statement. However, you can choose a Balance Sheet, Cash Flow, or Dividends. In addition, two frequency options, Annual and Quarterly, are available.

4.26 Our `.FakeBS()` Function

Our function, `.fakeBS ()`, allows two inputs: a year and a random seed. Below is an example.

```
> .fakeBS()
 Input a year below:
2023

  Input a random seed such as 123 (for reproducibility).
     If you don't want a seed, hit the enter-key.
123
   Year                        Component    Amount
1  2023        Cash and Cash Equivalents  21503.10
2  2023              Accounts Receivable  16824.58
3  2023                        Inventory   9089.77
4  2023 Property, Plant, and Equipment 138301.74
5  2023                     Total Assets 185719.19
6  2023                 Accounts Payable  19107.01
7  2023                  Short-term Debt   5227.78
8  2023                   Long-term Debt  51686.33
9  2023                Total Liabilities  76021.12
10 2023                     Common Stock  45696.76
11 2023                Retained Earnings  64001.31
12 2023                     Total Equity 109698.07

 You can paste it into Excel (tab is the separator).
```

Fig. 4.16 The function generates fake Balance Sheet (.fakeBS)

After launching Excel, we will have the following result.

	A	B	C
1	Year	Component	Amount
2	2023	Cash and Cash Equivalents	21503.1
3	2023	Accounts Receivable	16824.58
4	2023	Inventory	9089.77
5	2023	Property, Plant, and Equipment	138301.74
6	2023	Total Assets	185719.19
7	2023	Accounts Payable	19107.01
8	2023	Short-term Debt	5227.78
9	2023	Long-term Debt	51686.33
10	2023	Total Liabilities	76021.12
11	2023	Common Stock	45696.76
12	2023	Retained Earnings	64001.31
13	2023	Total Equity	109698.07

Fig. 4.17 One result from the .fakeBS function

4.27 Our.FakeIS () Function

This function works similarly to the previous one.

```
> .fakeIS()

  Input a random seed such as 123 (for reproducibility).
     If you don't want a seed, hit the enter-key.
2023
                   Component     Amount
1                    Revenue  286645.58
2  Cost of Goods Sold (COGS) -133874.43
3               Gross Profit  152771.15
4         Operating Expenses  -61996.21
5           Operating Income   90774.94
6           Interest Expense   -7408.30
7               Other Income    3040.69
8          Income Before Tax   86407.33
9                Tax Expense  -17281.47
10                Net Income   69125.86

 You can paste it into Excel.
>
```

Fig. 4.18 The function generates fake Income Statements (.fakeIS).

Appendix A: Issue the Following Line of R Code for Week 4

```
source("http://datayyy.com/i2ft/week4.txt")
```

```
*----------------------------------------------------------------------*
* Introduction to FinTech using Excel                 by Dr. Yan 2025   *
*       (in an R-assisted learning environment)                         *
*----------------------------------------------------------------------*
*  .c1 Introduction & Excel Basics                 .c16 R basics(optional) *
*  .c2 Blockchain  1: Numbers/alphanumeric cases   .c17 Macro (optional)   *
*  .c3             2: ASCII and Sha256)            .c18 VBA  (optional)    *
*  .c4 Ledger and distributed ledger                                    *
*----------------------------------------------------------------------*
* >.c4      # go to chapter 4                                          *
* >.uu      # go to utility submenu                                    *
* >.ft      # back to this menu                                        *
*----------------------------------------------------------------------*
```

Fig. 4.19 The menu for Week 4

Appendix B: Type `.chapter4` or `.c4` for the contents of Chapter 4

```
> .c4
function(i=0){
" i  Chapter 4: Ledger/distributed ledger  i  Explanation
  -  ----------------------------------- -- ---------------------
  1 Simulation                            21  Balance Sheet
  2     : random numbers                  22      : example from Yahoo
  3     : Excel example #1                23      : .fakeBS() function
  4     : random seed                     24      : .fake2BS (two balance sheets)
  5     : data analysis is not available  25  Income Statement
  6     : Excel example #2                26      : example from Yahoo
  7     : Excel example #3                27      : our .fakeIS() function
  8 Ledger definition                     28      : more example
  9     : Ledger in Accounting            29  Clipboard effect
 10     : Rules for debit and credit      30  our .ledger2hash() function
 11     : ledger vs. statement            31      : .fakeLedger example 1
 12     : Example                         32      :                     2
 13     : decentralized ledger            33      : .fakeBS example     1
 14     : .fakeLedger() function          34      :                     2
 15     : more examples                   35      : .fakeIS example     1
 16       Plot: centralized   ledger      36      :                     2
 17            : decentralized ledger     37      :  your data example  1
 18            : distributed   ledger     38      :                     2
 19  Videos                               39      :                     3
 20  Links                                40      :                     4

 Example #1:>.c4     # find out the list
 Example #2:>.c4()   # the same as the above
 Example #3:>.c4(1)  # see the first explanation
```

Fig. 4.20 The contents of Chapter 4

Appendix C: For chapter-related functions, type `.searchHiddenFunctions(4)`

```
> .searchHiddenFunctions(4)
 CHAPTER                          NAME                SHORTCUT
       4 install.packages('dplyr')
       4 install.packages('igraph')
       4 --------------------------------
       4 .fakeLedger                        .fl    # need 'dplyr'
       4 .fakeIS                            .fi
       4 .fakeBS                            .fb
       4 .IS2ledger                         .is2l
       4 .fake2BS                           .f2b
       4 .centralizedLedger                 .cl     # need 'igraph'
       4 .decentralizedLedger               .dc     # need 'igraph'
       4 .distributedLedger                 .dl     # need 'igraph'
>
```

Fig. 4.21 The hidden functions related to Chapter 4

Exercises

Note that * indicates difficult ones.

4.1. What are the main differences between single-entry and double-entry bookkeeping? How do these differences impact the accuracy of financial records?
4.2. Explain the concept of triple-entry bookkeeping. How does it enhance security and transparency compared to traditional bookkeeping methods?
4.3. Define a centralized system. What are the main advantages and disadvantages of using a centralized system for managing ledgers?
4.4. What is a decentralized system, and how does it differ from a centralized system? Provide examples of real-world applications that benefit from decentralization.
4.5. Describe the characteristics of a distributed system. How does a distributed system improve reliability and fault tolerance?
4.6. What is a distributed ledger, and how does it differ from a traditional ledger? What are some of the key benefits of using a distributed ledger?
4.7. Discuss the role of consensus mechanisms in distributed ledger systems. Why are they important, and how do they contribute to the ledger's integrity?
4.8. What are some of the common consensus mechanisms used in distributed ledger technologies? Provide a brief explanation of at least two mechanisms.

4.9. How does the concept of a random seed contribute to the reproducibility of simulations? Why is reproducibility necessary in the context of simulating ledger systems?
4.10. Compare and contrast the use of Monte Carlo Simulation in centralized, decentralized, and distributed systems. How can simulation help understand the behavior of these systems?
4.11. How can Monte Carlo Simulation be used to model transaction flows in a centralized ledger system? What insights can this provide to businesses or organizations?
4.12. Imagine a decentralized ledger network with ten nodes. Describe a scenario where using Monte Carlo Simulation could help identify potential bottlenecks or vulnerabilities in the network.
4.13. In a distributed system with multiple centers, how can simulation help determine the optimal number of centers to balance load and ensure reliability?
4.14. What role does simulation play in generating balance sheets and income statements? How can this be useful for financial planning and analysis?
4.15. Provide an example of how a seed can be used in a simulation to ensure consistent results across different runs. Why is this important when comparing different system architectures?
4.16. Discuss how a simulated ledger can be used to test the impact of fraudulent activities in a decentralized system. What benefits does this provide for system security?
4.17. How can graphs generated through simulation help visualize the performance of centralized versus distributed systems? What key metrics might be represented in these graphs?
4.18. Describe how you would set up a simulation to compare the efficiency of a double-entry bookkeeping system with a triple-entry bookkeeping system. What outcomes would you expect to observe?
4.19. What are some potential limitations or challenges of using Monte Carlo Simulation for modeling ledger systems? How might these challenges be addressed?
4.20. In your opinion, how will the future of bookkeeping and ledger systems evolve with the adoption of distributed ledger technologies? Provide reasons to support your view.
4.21. Try the hidden function related to the centralized system with 50 nodes.
4.22. Try the hidden function related to the decentralized system with 50 nodes and 10 centers.
4.23. Try the hidden function related to the distributed system with 60 nodes.
4.24. What is trilemma?
4.25. What are the three essential factors for Blockchain?
4.26. Explain Blockchain trilemma. Why is it important to understand the concept of Blockchain technology?
4.27. What is the Blockchain Trilemma? Offer a few examples.
4.28. Plot a centralized system with 35 nodes (players).

4.29. Plot a decentralized system with 35 nodes and five centers.
4.30. Plot a distributed system with 50 nodes (players).
4.31. How do we use the clipboard to connect two hidden functions to speed up our understanding?
4.32. Use the `.fakeBS()` function to generate a set of Balance Sheets with the following inputs: 2024, 50, and 145.
4.33*. Use the output from the above question as input to the function called `.ledger2hash ()`. What are your first and last hash values?
4.34. Use the `.fakeIS ()` function to generate a set of Balance Sheets with the following inputs: 2023, 40, and 12345.
4.35*. Use the output from the above question as input to the function called `.ledger2hash ()`. What are your first and last hash values?
4.36. Use the `.fakeLedger ()` function to generate a set of ledger records with the following inputs: 2024, 50, and 145.
4.37*. Using the output from the above question as input to the function called `.ledger2hash ()`. What are your first and last hash values?

References

Merriam-webster. https://www.merriam-webster.com/dictionary/ledger
Kenton, W. (2024). *How a general ledger works with double-entry accounting along with examples.* https://www.investopedia.com/terms/g/generalledger.asp

Cryptography, Mnemonic, Public and Private Keys 5

Encryption is the foundation of blockchain. In Chapter 3: Blockchain (II): ASCII and Sha256, we know that it is impossible to use so-called brute force to find a solution to a given hash generated by Sha256. This chapter will explain basic encryption mechanisms, such as the letter-shift scheme, keyword method, and 6-letter pairs. More importantly, we will explain public and private keys and how to receive a message with a public key while sending a message or money with a private key. In this chapter, the following topics will be covered:

- Introduction
- Using the letter-shift scheme to encode "`Hello World manually!`"
- Removing or keeping space
- In-class exercise encoding "`Hello World!`"
- Excel example and our functions
- Generating your pair of public and private keys
- Encrypt and decode with public and private keys

5.1 Introduction

Cryptography or encryption is crucial in securing digital information and transforming readable data, or plaintext, into an encoded format known as ciphertext. This ensures that only authorized parties can access the information, using a specific decryption key to revert the ciphertext to its original form. Encryption techniques are widely used in various applications, from securing online communications, financial transactions, and sensitive data storage to protecting user privacy on the internet. By understanding how encryption works, you can feel more secure and confident in your online activities, knowing your privacy is protected.

Y. Yan, *Introduction to FinTech using Excel*, Springer Texts in Business and Economics, https://doi.org/10.1007/978-3-031-89779-5_5

Modern encryption relies on complex algorithms and cryptographic keys, which can be classified into two main types: (1) symmetric encryption, where the same key is used for both encryption and decryption, and (2) asymmetric encryption, which uses a pair of public and private keys. Encryption is vital in safeguarding transactions, protecting customer data, and ensuring blockchain networks' integrity in financial technology (FinTech). As cryptocurrencies and digital payment systems become more prevalent, the importance of robust encryption mechanisms cannot be overstated. By encrypting sensitive information, FinTech applications can prevent unauthorized access, mitigate the risk of fraud, and comply with regulatory requirements, thereby enhancing trust and confidence among users and stakeholders.

5.2 Removing or Keeping Spaces

All spaces will be removed for the best result when encoding a message. The logic goes this way: Assuming we find a single letter around empty spaces, decoders will try different single words, such as "a." This is also true for 2-letter words using the most frequently used words. In short, if spaces are removed, it is more difficult to decode a secret message. However, we will keep spaces for two reasons. First, we aim to teach the basic underlying logic instead of techniques. Second, maintaining spaces will make our decoding process more fun.

5.3 Letter-Shift Scheme

The letter-shift encryption scheme, also known as the Caesar cipher, is a simple and classical encryption technique where each letter in the plaintext is shifted a certain number of places down or up the alphabet. For example, with a shift value of 3, 'A' becomes 'D', 'B' becomes 'E', and so forth, wrapping around to the beginning of the alphabet when necessary. This method transforms the original message into an encoded form that appears nonsensical to anyone who does not know the shift value, thus providing a basic level of security.

To decrypt the message, the recipient shifts the letters back by the same number of places, reversing the encryption process and revealing the original plaintext. Teaching the Caesar cipher using Excel can be highly effective in an educational context. Students can create a dynamic encryption and decryption system by leveraging Excel functions such as VLOOKUP and MOD. They can construct tables to map letters to numerical positions and apply formulas to shift these positions according to a given key.

Table 5.1 26 letters and positions

Letter	Position	Letter	Position	Letter	position
A	1	J	10	S	19
B	2	K	11	T	20
C	3	L	12	U	21
D	4	M	13	V	22
E	5	N	14	W	23
F	6	O	15	X	24
G	7	P	16	Y	25
H	8	Q	17	Z	26
I	9	R	18		

5.4 Manually Encoding "`Hello World!`"

To understand the underlying logic, use the letter-shift scheme to manually encode "Hello World!". After the underlying logic, we will use Excel to encode this phrase. One advantage of using Excel to encode is using the template for other words or sentences. The following Table 5.1 shows all 26 letters and their corresponding positions.

Assume that we plan to shift our phrase three letters to the right. Encoding "Hello World!" involves three steps.

Step 1: find the locations of our phrase by searching the table.
Step 2: new location = (old location + 3) mod 26.
Step 3: find the corresponding letters using the new locations from Step 2.

By searching the table twice, we have the following results.

For Step 1: we have 8,5,12,12,15 space, 23,15,18,12,4,!
For Step 2: we have 11,8,15,15,18 spaces, 26,18,21,15,7!
For Step 3: we have k,h,o,o,r,space,z,r,u,o,g,!

Our final answer is "`khoor zruog!`". Note that when the new location value is above 26, we use the Excel mod () function with a divisor of 26.

5.5 Excel is Case-Insensitive

Excel is not case-sensitive. It suggests that lower-case letters are the same as upper-case letters. One example is shown below.

Table 5.2 Procedure using Excel for a letter-shift scheme

Step	Explanation
1	We generate two tables. From Table 1, we search for the location of a given letter (let's call it the old location). From Table 2, we search for a letter for a given location (let's call it the new location)
2	Enter a string
3	Calculate the length of the string and generate two columns. Assume the length is n from 1 to n and all characters from our string
4	For a given letter, we search Table 1 to find its location (old location)
5	Add the planned shift number, such as 3, to get the new location
6	Search Table 2 based on the new locations
7	Put those letters together

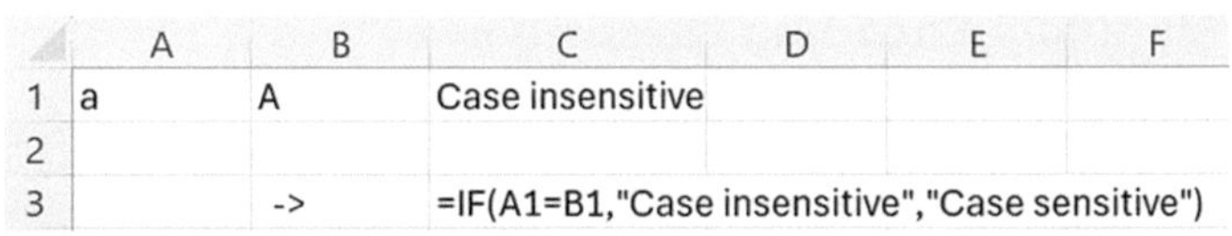

Fig. 5.1 Excel is case insensitive

For cells A1 and B1, we have one lowercase letter and one uppercase letter, A. Excel treats them as equal, suggesting that Excel is case insensitive.

5.6 Letter-Shift Scheme: Procedure

Using the letter-shift scheme, we can use Excel to encode and decode simple sentences. Based on the manually encoded example, the procedure is listed in the following Table 5.2.

In the next section, we try to code "`Hello World!`".

5.7 Encode "Hello World!" Using Excel

The sentence we will encode is "`Hello World!`" In the first step, we create three columns (A to C), shown below. We name A1:B27 "table1″ and B1:C27 " table2."

	A	B	C	D	E
1	letter	numbe	letter		
2	a	1	a	Hello World!	
3	b	2	b		
4	c	3	c	12	=LEN(D2)
5	d	4	d		
6	e	5	e	shift	3
7	f	6	f		
8	g	7	g		
9	h	8	h		
10	i	9	i		
11	j	10	j		
12	k	11	k		
13	l	12	l		
14	m	13	m		
15	n	14	n		
24	w	23	w		
25	x	24	x		
26	y	25	y		
27	z	26	z		
28					

Fig. 5.2 Two tables: letters to numbers and numbers to letters

Cell D2 contains the sentence "`Hello World!`". Assume we plan to shift three positions to the right. From "table1", the number is 8 for the first letter of H. The summation of 8 and 3 is 11. After searching `table2` (B and C columns), the coded letter is "`k`".

	D	E	F	G	H	I	J	K	L	M
1				=RIGHT(LEFT($D$2,F4),1)		=IF(ISNA(H4),"",H4+$E$6)				
2	Hello World!				=VLOOKUP(G4,table1,2)		=IF(ISNA(H4),G4,VLOOKUP(I4,table2,2))			
3			loc in the string	character	old locatioin	new location	coded letter			
4	12	=LEN(D2)	1	H	8	11	k			
5			2	e	5	8	h			
6	shift	3	3	l	12	15	o			
7			4	l	12	15	o			
8			5	o	15	18	r			
9			6		#N/A					
10			7	W	23	26	z			
11			8	o	15	18	r			
12			9	r	18	21	u			
13			10	l	12	15	o			
14			11	d	4	7	g			
15			12	!	#N/A		!			
24										
25					final coded message ->	khoor zruog!	=CONCAT(J4:J15)			

Fig. 5.3 The combination of Excel RIHGT and LEFT functions

For Column H, we generate numbers from 1, 2,.., to 12 (where n is the length of our string). Column G, we use the `vlookup ()` to search for "`table1`". The formula in Cell G4 is = `right(left($D$2,F4),1)` shown in cell G1. For Column H, we search "`table1`" for the old location. For Column I, we add 3 to the new location of the letter. Finally, we search for Table 2 to find the corresponding new letters. Finally, we apply the Excel `concat ()` function to combine those letters. For decoding, we treat it as an end-of-chapter exercise.

Table 5.3 Letter frequencies for 26 letters

Letter	Count	Frequency	Letter	Count	Frequency
E	21,912	12.02	M	4761	2.61
T	16,587	9.10	F	4200	2.30
A	14,810	8.12	Y	3853	2.11
O	14,003	7.68	W	3819	2.09
I	13,318	7.31	G	3693	2.03
N	12,666	6.95	P	3316	1.82
S	11,450	6.28	B	2715	1.49
R	10,977	6.02	V	2019	1.11
H	10,795	5.92	K	1257	0.69
D	7874	4.32	X	315	0.17
L	7253	3.98	Q	205	0.11
U	5246	2.88	J	188	0.10
C	4943	2.71	Z	128	0.07

5.8 Frequency Table for Letters

According to Cornell (2024), the frequency Table 5.3 is shown below.

For Stage, using just numbers makes it easy to understand the logic. More importantly, we know how to link this block with previous ones, i.e., how to form a blockchain. After understanding this basic structure, we will move on to more advanced stages. However, the logic remains the same.

5.9 Macro: Calculating Letter Frequency

This section is optional.

The Macro in Appendix E can generate a letter frequency table. In Chapter 1, we show how to copy others' macros. First, copy the Macro. After launching Excel, click "Developer", "Macro," then any name such as "`tt`", and create. Then, replace those several lines with your copied macro. After entering a few lines, as shown below, we can run the macro to generate a frequency table in columns B and C.

	A	B	C	D	E	F	G	H
1	this is a good idea	Letter	Frequency					
2	Hello World!	A	7					
3	Hofstra is an excellent school	B	0					
4	Good morning	C	4					
5	Introduction to FinTech	D	5					
6	aaa	E	6					
7		F	2					
8		G	3					
9		H	5					
10		I	8					
11		J	0					

Step 1: enter sentences A1 to A50
(a few lines are fine)
Step 2: click here to run the Macro

Fig. 5.4 Running a Macro to calculate letter frequency

Assume that we have text data from A1:A50. For more lines, readers can modify the following Macro accordingly. Interested readers can try it themselves.

5.10 Brute Force in Encryption

Brute force in encryption refers to systematically attempting every possible key or password until the correct one is found. This approach does not rely on sophisticated techniques or insights into the encryption algorithm; instead, it relies purely on computational power and time. In encryption, a brute force attack can involve testing millions, billions, or even more potential keys to decrypt a message. The effectiveness of a brute force attack depends on the encryption algorithm's strength and the key's length. For modern encryption standards, which use 128 bits or longer, brute-force attacks can be practically impossible due to the astronomical number of possible keys.

Brute force attacks are considered a last resort because of the sheer time and computational resources required to perform them, especially against robust encryption algorithms. The complexity of such attacks grows exponentially with each additional bit of key length, making well-designed encryption schemes highly resistant to brute force. However, with advances in computing power, including quantum computing, the feasibility of brute force attacks is a continually evolving threat, driving the need for increasingly robust encryption techniques.

5.11 One Example Using Brute Force

Let's look at a straightforward example. For the simplest letter-shift scheme, we know that we will get the result if we try a maximum of 25 trials. The first part will be the same as below. Cell H2 contains the number of letters that will be shifted for all the letters.

	A	B	C	D	E	F	G	I	J	K	L	M	N	O
1	1	a	1											
2	2	b	2		Phrase	Hello World!		<- cell H2 contains n letters hidden						
3	3	c	3								encode			
4	4	d	4		12	position	letter	7			old positi	new position	mod	coded
5	5	e	5			1	H	=RIGHT(LEFT($F$2,F5),1)			8	32	6	f
6	6	f	6			2	e				5	29	3	c
7	7	g	7			3	l				12	36	10	j
8	8	h	8			4	l	7	=MOD(I4,26)		12	36	10	j
9	9	i	9			5	o	7	=IF(I8=0,26,I8)		15	39	13	m
10	10	j	10			6					#N/A	#N/A	#N/A	
11	11	k	11			7	W				23	47	21	u
12	12	l	12			8	o				15	39	13	m
13	13	m	13			9	r				18	42	16	p
14	14	n	14			10	l				12	36	10	j
15	15	o	15			11	d				4	28	2	b
16	16	p	16			12	!				#N/A	#N/A	#N/A	!
17	17	q	17											
18	18	r	18		define B1:C26 as table1									
19	19	s	19		define A1:B26 as table2									
20	20	t	20											

Fig. 5.5 Decoding with brute force

In cell P2, we enter 1, i.e., try to shift all the letters to the right by one position. The Excel Macro in Appendix D makes our efforts more fun.

	P	Q	R	S	T	U	V	W	X	Y	Z
1				origiinal	hello world!						
2	1	<-try this value		decoded	ebiil tloia!		Not correc	=IF(T1=T2,"We find the solution!","Not correct")			
3		decode									
4		position	new pos	mod	letter	clean					
5		6	31	5	e	e	=IF(ISNA(T5),O5,T5)				
6		3	28	2	b	b					
7		10	35	9	i	i					
8		10	35	9	i	i					
9		13	38	12	l	l					
10		#N/A	#N/A	#N/A	#N/A						
11		21	46	20	t	t	Increase P2' value by 1				
12		13	38	12	l	l					
13		16	41	15	o	o					
14		10	35	9	i	i					
15		2	27	1	a	a					
16		#N/A	#N/A	#N/A	#N/A	!					
17											

Fig. 5.6 Running a Macro to add 1 to cell P2's value

5.12 Making It More Complex

In the above design, we move all letters to the right by three positions. Since we can only move by 25 possible possibilities, it is easy to decode by brute force. For example, we can try 1, 2, ..., up to 25 to decode our original message; see one of the end-of-chapter problems. To make it more complex, we can choose different positions to shift. The following Table 5.4 shows four methods.

Table 5.4 Several Methods for Letter-shift Scheme

Method	Moving by those positions
1	3,3,3,3,3,3,3.... (all letters move to the right by three positions)
2	1,2,3,1,2,3,1,2,3,,,, (move to the right by 1,2,3 positions, repeat)
3	1,2,3,4,5,6,..., (move to the right by 1,2,3,4,5,6,,..., positions)
4	A set of random values (see below)

For Method 1, all letters will be shifted to the right by 3. Method 2's first three letters will be shifted to the right by 1, 2, and 3 positions. Letters 4 to 6 will repeat, i.e., move to the right by 1, 2, and 3, respectively. This procedure will repeat itself for the rest of the remaining letters. Method 3 can be interpreted similarly.

It is worth mentioning Method 4. Assume that we have 100 letters. The basic design is to generate 199 integers randomly from (1,2,3,...,24, and 25). Chapter 1 discussed generating a set of random numbers using a random seed. One example is shown below. We click "Data" on the menu bar, then "Data Analysis" and "Random Number Generations," and fill in the values shown below.

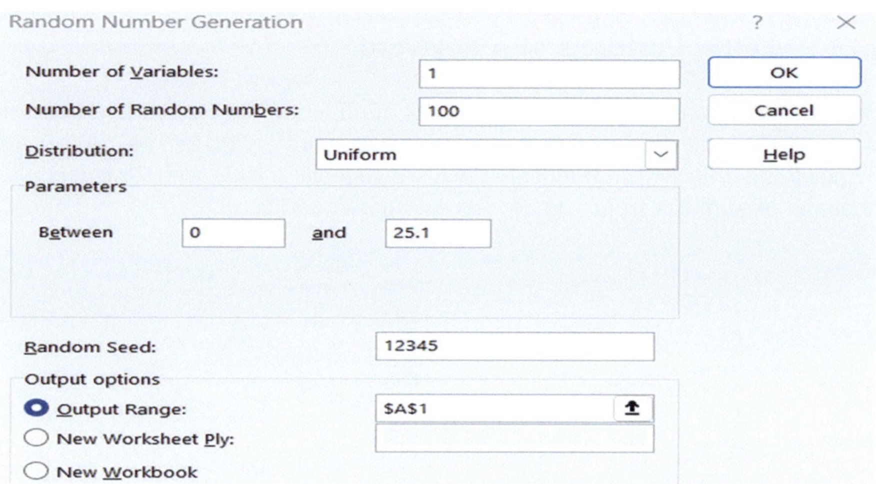

Fig. 5.7 The Excel Random Number Generation functionality

In the above image, we generate 1 column with 100 random numbers drawn from a uniform distribution between 0 and 25.1. The random seed is 12345. The output is shown below.

	A	B	C
1	5.809455	5	=INT(A1)
2	14.6799	14	
3	19.75935	19	
4	16.94807	16	
5	4.464333	4	
6	17.92857	17	
7	21.04778	21	
8	4.146437	4	
9	22.26958	22	

Fig. 5.8 The Excel INT function (integer)

Column A contains real numbers, not integers. Column B includes all integers applied using the Excel `int()` function. The first letter moves to the right by five positions, and the second letter moves to the right by 14. Now, the key is remembering that the random seed is 12345.

5.13 Letter Positions of a Keyword

This section shows how to find the positions of all letters for a given keyword and motivates the next section. For example, our keyword is "`Hofstra`". What are the positions of those seven letters? First, we generate a table with 26 letters plus a column of numbers from 1 to 26; see columns A and B.

	A	B	C	D	E	F	G	H	I
1	a	1	Hofstra						
2	b	2	7	=LEN(C1)					
3	c	3							
4	d	4		letter		position			
5	e	5	1	H	=RIGHT(LEFT($C$1,C5),1)	8	=VLOOKUP(D5,$A$1:$B$26,2)		
6	f	6	2	o		15			
7	g	7	3	f		6			
8	h	8	4	s		19			
9	i	9	5	t		20			
10	j	10	6	r		18			
11	k	11	7	a		1			
12	l	12							
13	m	13							
24	x	24							
25	y	25							
26	z	26							
27									

Fig. 5.9 A keyword and its letters' positions

Secondly, we enter our keyword, such as "`Hofstra`" in cell C1. Using the len () function, we know that the length of the given keyword is 7. Then, we generate a column from 1 to 7 (in cells C5 to C11). Next, combining the `right ()` and `left ()` functions is used to extract each letter. The formula of cell D5 is shown in cell E5. Finally, we apply the Excel `vlookup ()` function to report their positions. The formula of cell F5 is reported in G5. The final result is that the positions of those seven letters are 8, 15, 6, 19, 20, 18, and 1.

5.14 The Vigenère Cipher

The Vigenère cipher is a method of encrypting alphabetic text using a simple form of polyalphabetic substitution. Unlike a simple Caesar cipher that shifts all letters by a fixed number, the Vigenère cipher uses a keyword to vary the shift for each letter in the plaintext. Assume the keyword is "Hofstra." Based on each letter's position in the alphabet, we have numbers 8, 15, 6, 19, 20, 18, and 1, as discussed in the previous section. This set of values (8, 15, 6, 19, 20, and 18) will be the positions moving to the right.

The basic logic is that the letters of a plaintext will shift by this set of values. In the following example, our plaintext is "`It is a great idea to learn R`".

	A	B	C	D	E	F	G	H	I	J	K
1	a	1						It is a great idea to learn R			
2	b	2						29			shift n
3	c	3		Hofstra			shifting n		1	I	8
4	d	4		7	1	H	8		2	t	15
5	e	5			2	o	15		3		6
6	f	6			3	f	6		4	i	19
7	g	7			4	s	19		5	s	20
8	h	8			5	t	20		6		18
9	i	9			6	r	18		7	a	1
10	j	10			7	a	1		8		8
11	k	11							9	g	15
12	l	12							10	r	6
13	m	13							11	e	19
14	n	14							12	a	20
15	o	15							13	t	18
16	p	16							14		1

Fig. 5.10 The application of Vigenère Cipher

Since the word "Hofstra" has seven letters, the first seven letters from the phrase "It is a" will be shifted by 8, 15, 6, 19, 20, 18, and 1. Since we keep all the blanks, those shifting numbers will not impact them.

5.15 Asymmetric Encryption

So far, we have discussed symmetric encryption. For the letter-shift scheme, if the key is to move 3 letters to the right, we use this number 3 to decode a secret message. For the 6-letter scheme, encode and decode depend on the same table. Asymmetric encryption is different since the keys are different. For example, we can encode public and corresponding private keys.

5.16 Public and Private Keys

A public key is part of an asymmetric cryptographic key pair. It's a long string of characters generated using mathematical algorithms. The public key is openly shared with anyone who wants to send encrypted messages to its owner. When someone wants to send a secure message, they use the recipient's public key to encrypt it. Only the corresponding private key can decrypt this message. Imagine a journalist publishing their public key on a website. Sources can then send secret messages to the journalist using this key, ensuring confidentiality.

The private key is the other half of the key pair. It must be kept confidential and known only to its owner. When the recipient receives an encrypted message, they use their private key to decrypt it and reveal the original content. Private keys are also used to create digital signatures. For instance, a software publisher signs updates with their private key, allowing recipients to verify the authenticity of those updates using the corresponding public key. Safeguarding the private key is crucial; the entire system's security is compromised if it falls into the wrong hands.

5.17 Website to Get Public and Private Keys

At https://codehex.dev/tools/keypair-generator/, readers and students can generate their own public and private keys. The top part of the website is shown below.

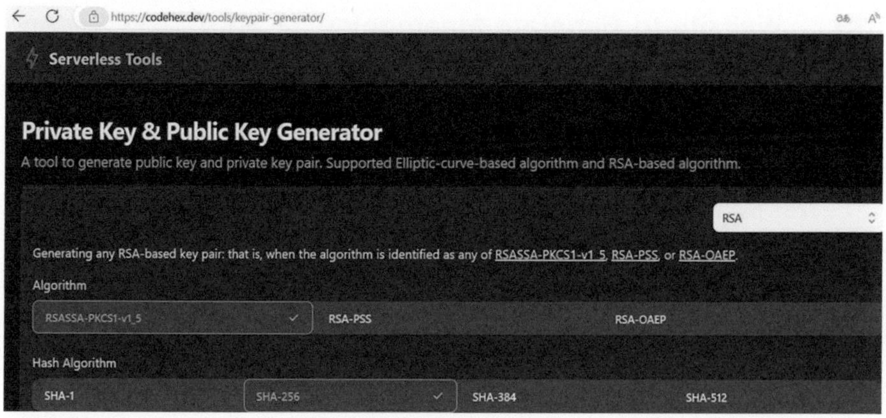

Fig. 5.11 The website to generate private and public keys

One pair of public and private keys are shown below.

Fig. 5.12 One illustration of a pair of private and public keys

By clicking the download buttons, we can download both public and private keys.

5.18 What Is a Mnemonic?

A mnemonic phrase, also known as a seed phrase or secret recovery phrase, is a series of words that can be used to access private keys and recover funds associated with a crypto wallet. Mnemonic phrases are generated using an algorithm that transforms a private key into a series of words that are easier to memorize than the private key itself. A mnemonic phrase is a list of 12–24 words used to back up a wallet. These words can be decoded to yield the seed of a wallet, which generates public and private keys for the wallet.

5.19 Website to Generate Mnemonics

At https://allprivatekeys.com/mnemonic-code-converter, we can generate our own mnemonic. Assume that we choose 18. One generated mnemonic (the top part is shown below).

```
zero hair try pyramid own photo cotton steak remember uphold
beef husband only stable afraid earth news canoe
```

Fig. 5.13 The website to generate Mnemonics

Account Extended Private Key:

```
xprv9yureGZAAM1FCAtdXKSFTfXZuj1GwKM2YHs6sg55XEcHkTqnmL8TKtpmWy
kvu4G2fWdfWvZpyXrtYpu7k2vdphTjAGBBnqHCi9PVV23owbZ
```

Account Extended Public Key:

```
xpub6CuD3n63ziZYQey6dLyFpoUJTkqmLn4suWnhg4Uh5a9GdGAwJsShsh9FNF
6wwurgSzJDS5ZArb4K2w7PNd18tm4RUFUcjXAxxa9hVrLBChB
```

In Chapter 6: Cryptocurrency and the Ganache platform, we will come back to this issue when discussing the Ganache platform.

5.20 Generating Mnemonics Using Excel

From the previous section, we know that a mnemonic would have 12 to 24 words. The word list is at raw.githubusercontent.com/bitcoin/bips/master/bip-0039/english.txt. The top part is shown in the following image.

Fig. 5.14 A word list

It is a good exercise to use this text file to generate our own mnemonic phrases. First, we download the text file. Then we retrieve it to the Excel.

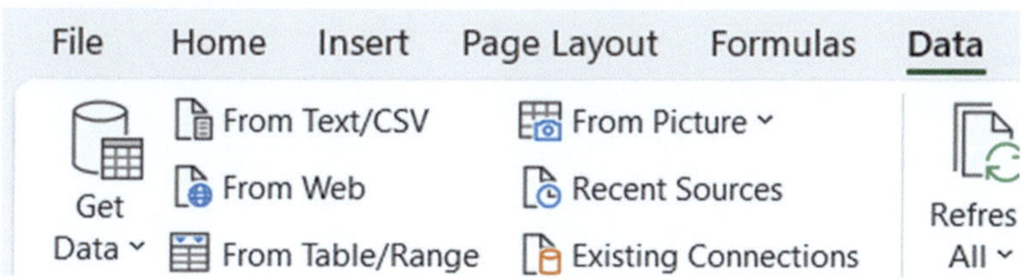

Fig. 5.15 Retrieving the word list into Excel (from Text/CSV)

The top few lines in Excel are shown below. In total, we have 2048 words.

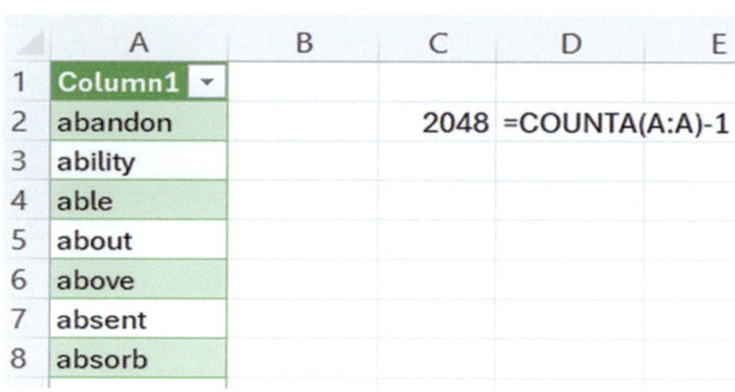

Fig. 5.16 Counting the number of words by using the Excel COUNTA function

Since we plan to randomly choose a maximum of 18 words randomly, we add a column A with values 1, 2, …, to n.

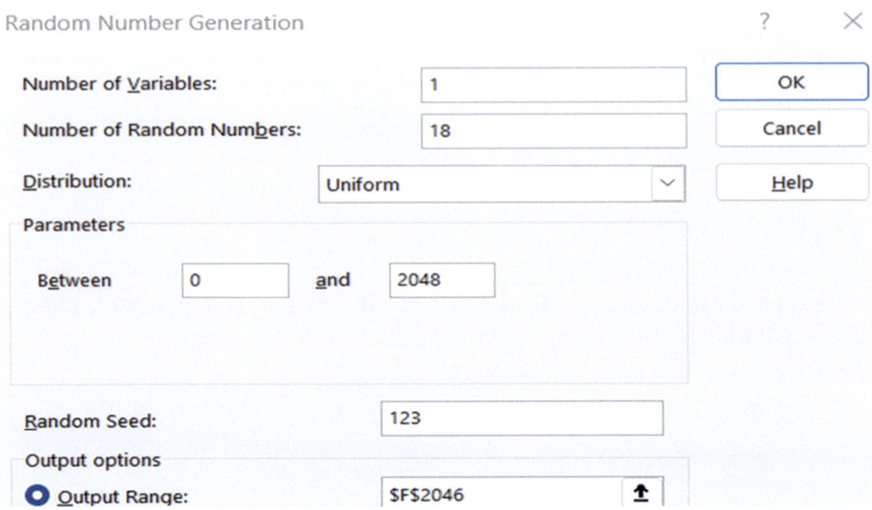

Fig. 5.17 Generating random numbers from a uniform distribution

The following image shows the process and the result.

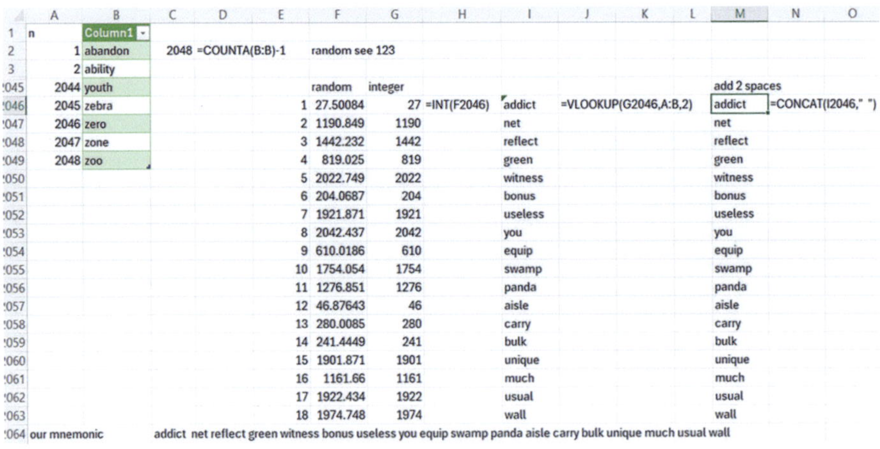

Fig. 5.18 The result of 18 random words

Again, using the link at https://allprivatekeys.com/mnemonic-code-converter, we have to double-check the validity of our mnemonic generated this way. Later in the chapter, our hidden function can be used to generate our mnemonic phrases.

5.21 Installation of `Openssl` R Package

We will generate public and private keys for the rest of the chapter. Then, we use a public key to encode our message and the corresponding private key to decode. However, our functions need an R package called `openssl`. The objective of this package is a Toolkit for Encryption, Signatures, and Certificates Based on OpenSSL. We copy and paste the following line to your R console to install it.

```
install.packages('openssl')
```

This is a one-time installation; it suggests you only need to install it once during this course.

5.22 Generating Public and Private Keys

We generate a function called `.generatePublicPrivateKeys ()` with a shortcut name `.ppkeys ()`. This function does not need any input. One result is shown below.

```
> .ppkeys ()
Public key in PEM format:
-----BEGIN PUBLIC KEY-----
MIIBIjANBgkqhkiG9w0BAQEFAAOCAQ8AMIIBCgKCAQEApFv+I7s32snaaEFE81Cl
78D9rAHNx994iDh1GXxtgB1rjLpOn/ULFNUu+d5BdtRaixM7JgF4YhkFWGE0t9L+
DSZugjk+dlpavvDA3CulTcVYnk4de7OuaBYJcD3c5uP92PrFi/sTYq20RpX1Lb1L
PJNaY2WQ+aguCOyAsVmrHobqzfxvuXrQZ0XhjueZpc8S17s911urb8SjGphZrjhl
2q1Yjvp8CQVmqTNJJWydEEhllVLgOJ5bwnXDafPvMM9KzDfn0VN5Hiqi49tiSjKD
EtYtM2z6PTgIvYSH3kkbY8889ULZHGeSiB5ec4VS++wLH2wdRy0uZK21lZp10qON
DwIDAQAB
-----END PUBLIC KEY-----

Private key in PEM format:
-----BEGIN PRIVATE KEY-----
MIIEvgIBADANBgkqhkiG9w0BAQEFAASCBKgwggSkAgEAAoIBAQCkW/4juzfaydpo
QUTzUKXvwP2sAc3H33iIOHUZfG2AHWuMuk6f9QsU1S753kF21FqLEzsmAXhiGQVY
YTS30v4NJm6COT52Wlq+8MDcK6VNxVieTh17s65oFglwPdzm4/3Y+sWL+xNirbRG
lfUtvUs8k1pjZZD5qC4I7ICxWasehurN/G+5etBnReGO55mlzxLXuz3XW6tvxKMa
mFmuOGXarViO+nwJBWapM0klbJ0QSGWVUuA4nlvCdcNp8+8wz0rMN+fRU3keKqLj
22JKMoMS1i0zbPo9OAi9hIfeSRtjzzz1QtkcZ5KIHl5zhVL77AsfbB1HLS5krbWV
mnXSo40PAgMBAAECggEAIJ+z78K7IP39EMGX3pYNAex0Tb6j6n8EjUFrmO32TD5K
uUnHzn9UvkNcijNgGianfECKdo5HJ22g/nx4+t3yGIke2VFkgRiJN6pRFcLCEpBP
+Ug3GPU+8qEhKXrWDKyHmBiauqDRJb6l8HbWjkgrFXCIOf+QicWksZfEKa/LRAkg
wQisvx8/xHcWzKq4qJ92SyCgfxW9W2qHaAVDdfjm9lxFH4Ggb0Rf1il3lAqDUy4D
zZC+fRqPVldTM78JoJ51JpShZAaCOKLeANdznIDNj6ndFc3mYpqSB8zgFwMIAg/c
q2w6yCX221/J20nK9OlkOIuoDNphUsoHl2oViMa1eQKBgQDltpVoAP2+nxbJxOtl
```

```
GCyWmPXUXzpvMEWRXH7U4d9BOhYlfL3EnkEh5nspB7/0erUF4J7fB/mIA+fPgdL9
YZHk2XrPSDe2bYeudnSXmn0R1+BAIzVk7O+PI6eKVF/3Y9I744d56KB6z7tjnNba
WYIEL93fg3f5lV3qlFjN9AhC6QKBgQC3KuBtVuX2ipmXxOrU7xW9V9CWZKwLoH0d
XMCCTdx+qljYc6pIbVaufNnrj9LAL5wcowKpjPWLI5XnA+vSiStlZXvjegu6DECf
rHmbMOBfKk2xAht1JcG3pyEIwhpbx4zbOFhPt4lbr7cJOQbOsszf0vlBlQUNWWU3
Zn5vy7WlNwKBgQC5fU33xZUgL+Z+1vwdjf+zO6CF9L+CuT/zuPTRgfJ9ASKQ8sFp
20BM14fsAc4G5G74aADhp9be9ghhjzuITxk36kU4y9/w91Dwl8ZeBOmpVuBF6ihb
bteihe/ry2YSphBFO91Rm366rLNsJGF5v301VFGdAtQGPY6wtUlgRQXGwQKBgHs4
ZPIpW1qXsuvelPvaOw29XZ1O7E6GEKUIGJmQN50ei9ZROWSv6XhIlXFat7SCUssQ
/mGBak3ICrf2c1aW4JK9yrIlEG6Af5jrNoOoRci/dLR3bnFIjSE3VYnGymSjwaZY
KVC3b7g2ZTPXITU8I4cPLo9n6JYqZWT3lmcu62vRAoGBANF6XGzDFiDUx92HRwMX
nzHj8S5QCq1E60svnLX9FzQIA/Fz23EFP2n1aV/KBkNLKuhMD8AshrGC79HqAcLR
d04GLz8aR/SggRrkHn4trb+I3gLSCN6uPr2QTsFpYisA7bINkMHcBDoXxtbwHdIF
9PY20QdW2dG6deZdf6JB+wj+
-----END PRIVATE KEY-----
```


5.23 Encoding with a Public Key

The function name is `.encodeWithPublicKey ()` with a shortcut name `.en7 ()`. Its objective is to code our message with a public key. One pair of public/private keys are given below.

https://datayyy.com/i2ft/data/public1key.pem.txt

https://datayyy.com/i2ft/data/private1key.pem.txt

For this purpose, we generate a hidden function called `.encodeWithPublicKey ()`, shown below.

```
> .encodeWithPublicKey()

 * ------------------------------------------------------------
 *  Encrypt your message with a public key
 *    One pair of keys is given below
 *    public   https://datayyy.com/i2ft/data/public1key.pem.txt
 *    private  https://datayyy.com/i2ft/data/private1key.pem.txt
 * ------------------------------------------------------------
 * Enter your secret message below:
This is a great idea!
```

Fig. 5.19 Encoding with a public key (`.encodeWithPublicKey`)

The message is, "This is a great idea!" Users have three ways to input their public key. The first is to copy and paste. The second is to give a URL such as https://datayyy.com/i2ft/data/public1key.pem.txt. The third is to find a local file that contains their public key. Assume that we choose the second method and offer a link.

```
 * ---------------------------------------------------------- *
 * 1       provide a URL                                      *
 * 2       copy and paste a public key                        *
 * 3       from a local file                                  *
 * ---------------------------------------------------------- *
1

Enter the URL for the public key:
https://datayyy.com/i2ft/data/publiclkey.pem.txt
```

Fig. 5.20 Three ways to input a public key

The result and code message are shown below.

```
Encrypted message:
 IPAiVLMo45n7LruKcL+pibjIHjz/H9BhveCkWg3WxdoLV60EXh1isB2Qz60beAhnQHtGslGIW1rVkUjU2EZppnU3m
i4+0vSbuBzQ461ehB0ZujHh3AOUhUP1H5UM5dXNGHQMKwHcvpg0PvExhVT0HOnCYGgXdrzZhk1Ob5RkvT+Pna8nust
4TaDsuptMMUe+Eu8rzFaG91QwvAUhfhf8KE4pCggsbWpSX2znpKDLRyb46wvv0seaB5FT5mp3I/DAKN1uDk98cElE+
T4cgUUBcHXpKiw0RjPrmDnTLMcKQiaMQP35NPNPPtuyYgQhRylRUGspfQCcHoWv8nEmCZUdfg==

Launch a text editor, such as Notepad, and paste it there.

 * ---------------------------------------------------
```

Fig. 5.21 The result of an encrypted message

The coded message is given below:


```
IPAiVLMo45n7LruKcL+pibjIHjz/H9BhveCkWg3WxdoLV60EXh1isB2Qz60beAhn
QHtGslGIW1rVkUjU2EZppnU3mi4+0vSbuBzQ461ehB0ZujHh3AOUhUP1H5UM5dXN
GHQMKwHcvpg0PvExhVT0HOnCYGgXdrzZhk1Ob5RkvT+Pna8nust4TaDsuptMMU
e+Eu8rzFaG91QwvAUhfhf8KE4pCggsbWpSX2znpKDLRyb46wvv0seaB5FT5mp3I/
DAKN1uDk98cElE+T4cgUUBcHXpKiw0RjPrmDnTLMcKQiaMQP35NP
NPPtuyYgQhRylRUGspfQCcHoWv8nEmCZUdfg==
```


5.24 Decoding with a Private Key

To decode a secret message (i.e., a coded message), we generated a hidden function called `.decodeWithPrivateKey ()`, as shown below.

```
> .decodeWithPrivateKey()
 * ---------------------------------------------------------- *
 * Step 1: enter a private key                                *
 * ---------------------------------------------------------- *
 * 1       provide a URL                                      *
 * 2       copy and paste it                                  *
 * 3       from a local file                                  *
 * ---------------------------------------------------------- *
```

Fig. 5.22 Three ways to input a private key

Assume that we choose method 1, as shown below.

```
> .decodeWithPrivateKey()
 * ------------------------------------------------------------ *
 * Step 1: enter a private key                                  *
 * ------------------------------------------------------------ *
 * 1      provide a URL                                         *
 * 2      copy and paste it                                     *
 * 3      from a local file                                     *
 * ------------------------------------------------------------ *
1

Enter the URL for the private key:
https://datayyy.com/i2ft/data/private1key.pem.txt
```

Fig. 5.23 Method 1 and its related private key

After that, we copy and paste our coded message to get our initial plain text.

```
 * ------------------------------------------------------- *
 * Step 2: copy and paste your coded message               *
 * ------------------------------------------------------- *
IPAiVLMo45n7LruKcL+pibjIHjz/H9BhveCkWg3WxdoLV60EXh1isB2Qz60beAhnQHtGslGIW1rVkUjU2EZppnU3mi
4+0vSbuBzQ461ehB0ZujHh3AOUhUP1H5UM5dXNGHQMKwHcvpg0PvExhVT0HOnCYGgXdrzZhk1Ob5RkvT+Pna8nust4
TaDsuptMMUe+Eu8rzFaG91QwvAUhfhf8KE4pCggsbWpSX2znpKDLRyb46wvv0seaB5FT5mp3I/DAKN1uDk98cElE+T
4cgUUBcHXpKiw0RjPrmDnTLMcKQiaMQP35NPNPPtuyYgQhRylRUGspfQCcHoWv8nEmCZUdfg==

 Original secret message is:
 This is a great idea!
>
```

Fig. 5.24 Decoding Step 2 and the result.

5.25 The Lengths of Public and Private Keys

The length of public and private keys in cryptography depends on several factors, including the type of cryptographic algorithm used, the level of security required, and the underlying mathematical principles. Shorter keys are found in systems using ECC and symmetric key algorithms (e.g., AES). They provide robust security with efficient performance, while longer keys are found in RSA and other asymmetric systems to ensure protection against brute-force attacks due to their reliance on larger mathematical constructs. Choosing between short and long keys balances security, computational resources, and speed. As technology evolves, key lengths are adjusted to protect against emerging threats.

Shorter Keys:

Symmetric keys (like AES) with 128 bits use about 16 characters; 256 bits use 32 characters.

ECC keys for 160 bits use around 40 characters; for 256 bits, about 64 characters.

Longer Keys:

RSA keys with 1024 bits use around 172–178 characters in base64.
RSA keys with 2048 bits use around 344–356 characters in base64.
RSA keys with 4096 bits use around 684–700 characters in base64.

5.26 Brute Force for Private Key?

Can hackers use brute force to decode the message ciphered by a public key? We know that the number of symbols of a private key is 64, drawn from 10 digits plus six letters. Assume that the time spent needed for one trial is 1 s. Thus, for a 64-character long private key, we need 16^64 s, as shown below.

	A	B	C	D
1	Time needed for one trial (second)	1		
2	private-key is n-chracter long	64		
3	chose from (m) such as 0,1,...,9,a,b,c,d,e, and f	16		
4	total time (in second)	1.15792E+77	=B3^B2	
5				
6	1 year = how many seconds	31536000	=1*365*24*60*60	
7	How many years needed?	3.67174E+69	=B4/B6*B1	

Fig. 5.25 Years needed by using brute force to get a private key

As shown below, we can speed up by spending just 0.01 s for one trial and a short 16-character long.

	A	B	C	D
1	Time needed for one trial (second)	0.001		
2	private-key is n-chracter long	16		
3	chose from (m) such as 0,1,...,9,a,b,c,d,e, and f	16		
4	total time (in second)	1.84467E+19	=B3^B2	
5				
6	1 year = how many seconds	31536000	=1*365*24*60*60	
7	How many years needed?	584942417.4	=B4/B6*B1	

Fig. 5.26 Years needed assuming 0.01 s per trial.

5.27 Our Hidden Functions

We have generated a few functions to help our readers/students understand those concepts better and simplify operations. As shown below, we use the `.searchHiddenFunctions ()` to find those hidden functions. In addition to hidden functions, the links of three pairs of public and private keys are included.

```
> .searchHiddenFunctions(5)
 CHAPTER                                     NAME              SHORTCUT
       5 install.packages('openssl')
       5 install.packages('openssl')
       5 --------------------------------
       5 https://datayyy.com/i2ft/data/public1key.pem.txt
       5 https://datayyy.com/i2ft/data/private1key.pem.txt
       5 https://datayyy.com/i2ft/data/public2key.pem.txt
       5 https://datayyy.com/i2ft/data/private2key.pem.txt
       5 https://datayyy.com/i2ft/data/public3key.pem.txt
       5 https://datayyy.com/i2ft/data/private3key.pem.txt
       5 --------------------------------
       5 .encode_6letters                         .en6
       5 .decode_6letters                         .de6
       5 .positionKeyword                         .pkw
       5 .keywordEncode                           .en2
       5 .keywordDecode                           .de2
       5 .generatePublicPrivateKeys               .ppkeys  # need 'openssl'
       5 .encodeWithPublicKey                     .en7     # need 'openssl'
       5 .decodeWithPriateKey                     .de7     # need 'openssl'
       5 .listOfPublicPrivateKeys                 .listpp
       5 .letterFrequency                         .lf
       5 .enigmaEncode                            .enigma
       5 .generatePublicPrivateKeys               .ppkeys  # need 'openssl'
```

Fig. 5.27 The hidden functions related to Chapter 5

Below are a few examples. To access `.enigmaEncode()`, we can use its shortcut, `.engima()`.

```
> .enigma()
 * -------------------------------------- *
 *   Input your phrase below:             *
 *         [Hit the Esc Key to exit]      *
 * -------------------------------------- *
Hello World
[1] "RPXYD MFLGZ"
```

Fig. 5.28 The.enigmaEncode function

The function `.letterFrequency()` will calculate the letter frequencies of 26 letters.

```
* ------------------------------------------------------------- *
*   calculate letter frequency for a given text file           *
* ------------------------------------------------------------- *
*     Make a choice                                              *
* ------------------------------------------------------------- *
* 1    from the clipboard                                        *
* 2    from a remote file                                        *
* 3    from a local file                                         *
* Esc    exit                                                    *
* ------------------------------------------------------------- *
```

Fig. 5.29 The function calculating letter frequency (.letterFrequency)

For example, if we choose number 2 and enter the link for The Count Of Monte Cristo by Alexandre Dumas, we will get the following result.

```
2
  Paste your web link below.
    e.g., https://gutenberg.org/files/1184/1184-0.txt
https://gutenberg.org/files/1184/1184-0.txt
[1] "https://gutenberg.org/files/1184/1184-0.txt"
   Letter Frequency percent
1       e    257205  12.735
2       t    178963   8.861
3       a    164519   8.146
4       o    155701   7.710
5       i    141185   6.991
6       n    136497   6.759
7       h    125846   6.231
8       s    125819   6.230
9       r    120151   5.949
10      d     93550   4.632
11      l     80243   3.973
12      u     59757   2.959
13      m     56788   2.812
14      c     51911   2.570
15      f     44998   2.228
16      w     43596   2.159
17      y     42302   2.095
18      g     35178   1.742
19      p     34515   1.709
20      b     27692   1.371
21      v     21372   1.058
22      k     12512   0.620
23      x      3832   0.190
24      q      2002   0.099
25      j      1950   0.097
26      z      1511   0.075
```

Fig. 5.30 The result of letter frequency

Appendix A: Issue the Following Line of R Code for Week 5

```
source("http://datayyy.com/i2ft/week5.txt")
```

```
*------------------------------------------------------------------------*
* Introduction to FinTech using Excel                by Dr. Yan 2025     *
*       (in an R-assisted learning environment)                          *
*------------------------------------------------------------------------*
*  .c1 Introduction & Excel Basics                .c16 R basics(optional) *
*  .c2 Blockchain  1: Numbers/alphanumeric cases  .c17 Macro (optional)   *
*  .c3             2: ASCII and Sha256)           .c18 VBA  (optional)    *
*  .c4 Ledger and distributed ledger                                      *
*  .c5 Encryption, public and private keys                                *
*------------------------------------------------------------------------*
* >.c5       # go to chapter 5                                            *
* >.uu       # go to utility submenu                                      *
* >.ft       # back to this menu                                          *
*------------------------------------------------------------------------*
```

Fig. 5.31 The menu for Week 5

Appendix B: Issue `.chapter5` or `.c5` to Get the Contents of Chapter 5

```
> .chapter5
function(i=0){
"i  Chapter 5: Encryption              i  Public and Private Keys
 -  -----------------------------      -- ------------------------------------
 1   Introduction                      21  Letter frequency table 26 letters
 2   symmetric/asymmetric &space issue 22       : Excel Macro for a frequency table
 3   letter-shift method               23       : website
 4     Manually encode Hello World!    24   Public/private keys: introduction
 5       : Excel is case-insensitive   25       : one pair: public key
 6       :  encode in Excel            26                 : private key
 7       :  decode in Excel            27       : links to the above pair
 8       :  one example                28       : links to several pairs
 9       :  our 2 functions            29       : website to generate public/private keys
10  Vigenère cipher using a keyword    30       : Installation of one R package
11       : function .letterPositionen  31       : Encode with a public key
12                                     32       : decode with a public key
13  Six letters: 26 letters/10 digits  33       : hidden function: generate public/private keys
14       : encode Excel                34  What is Mnemonic?
15       : our function encode         35       : how many words
16  Nazi-Enigma (simplest design)      36       : examples
17       : Excel for the 1st letter    37       : generate a random mnemonic
18       : macro to rotate rotor 1     38       : mnemonic to public/private keys
19  Videos                             39       : QR code : from the website
20  Links                              40                 : hidden function

  Example #1:>.c5    # see the above list
  Example #2:>.c5()  # the same as the above
  Example #3:>.c5(1) # see the 1st explanation
```

Fig. 5.32 The contents of Chapter 5

Appendix D: The Excel Macro for a Letter Frequency Table

Assume that you have text data from cells A1:A50. If you have more lines, modify the following Macro accordingly.

```
Sub GenerateLetterFrequencyTable()
    Dim cell As Range
    Dim letter As String
    Dim letterCounts As Object
    Dim i As Integer
    Dim text As String
    Dim key As Variant ' Declare the control variable as Variant

    Set letterCounts = CreateObject("Scripting.Dictionary")

    ' Initialize the letterCounts dictionary
    For i = 65 To 90 ' ASCII values for A to Z
        letterCounts.Add Chr(i), 0
    Next i

    ' Loop through each cell in the range A1:A50
    For Each cell In Range("A1:A50")
        text = UCase(cell.Value) ' Convert text to uppercase
        ' Loop through each character in the cell's text
        For i = 1 To Len(text)
            letter = Mid(text, i, 1)
            ' Check if the character is a letter A-Z
            If letter >= "A" And letter <= "Z" Then
                letterCounts(letter) = letterCounts(letter) + 1
            End If
        Next i
    Next cell

    ' Output the results starting at cell B1
    Range("B1").Value = "Letter"
    Range("C1").Value = "Frequency"
    i = 2
   For Each key In letterCounts.Keys ' Use 'key' as the control variable
        Range("B" & i).Value = key
        Range("C" & i).Value = letterCounts(key)
        i = i + 1
    Next key

    MsgBox "Letter frequency table generated successfully!"
    End Sub
```

Appendix E: Excel Macro: increase the value in cell H4 by 1.

```
Sub IncrementH4()
    Check if H4 contains a number
    If IsNumeric(Range("H4").Value) Then
        ' Increment the value in H4 by 1
        Range("H4").Value = Range("H4").Value + 1
    Else
        ' If H4 is not a number, show an error message
        MsgBox "H4 does not contain a number.", vbExclamation
    End If
End Sub
```

Exercises

Note that * indicates difficult ones.

5.1. Encrypt the message "It is a great idea!" using a shift cipher with a shift of 5. Use Excel to perform the encryption.
5.2. Decryption with Shift Cipher: Given the encrypted message "KHOOR ZRUOG," use Excel to decrypt it using a shift cipher with a shift of 3.
5.3. Calculate the remainder of dividing 12345 by 26 using Excel. Explain how modular arithmetic is used in encryption.
5.4. Generating Random Keys: Use Excel to generate a random 8-character key in a simple substitution cipher.
5.5. Implement the Vigenère cipher in Excel. Encrypt the message "SECURE COMMUNICATION" using the keyword "KEY".
5.6. Decryption with Vigenère Cipher: Given the encrypted message "WKGJ KLPACRVUUKVPQVR," decrypt it using the keyword "KEY" with Excel.
5.7. Frequency Analysis: Use Excel to analyze the letters in the message "ENCRYPTION IS FUN." Determine which letter occurs most frequently.
5.8. We have a coded message: "`rwpv jwzzweml nqdm bpwcaivl lwttiza nzwu uizg.`" We know that a letter-shift scheme coded it. Please decode it.
5.9. This chapter has a set of random numbers, shown below.

	A	B	C
1	5.809455	5	=INT(A1)
2	14.6799	14	
3	19.75935	19	
4	16.94807	16	
5	4.464333	4	
6	17.92857	17	
7	21.04778	21	
8	4.146437	4	
9	22.26958	22	

Fig. 5.33 What is 10's value?

5.10. Using Excel to encode the phrase "`This is a wonderful day indeed!`" via the most straightforward letter-shift scheme.
5.11. The most straightforward letter-shifting scheme is symmetric to encode or decode a message since we can use three positions to code and use the same 3 to decode. However, if we use 3 to code, we can use 23 to decode (26-3). Thus, it is also an asymmetric encryption. Is this right?
5.12. What is a mnemonic, and what are its usages?
5.13. From where can we generate a mnemonic randomly?
5.14. Why is it impossible to use brute force to decode a message coded by using a public key?
5.15. How many years are needed to use the Brute Force to decipher a coded message if we know it is coded using a public key? Assume that the number of private keys is eight characters long from just 16 characters (0, 1, 2, 3,4,5,6,7,8, 9, a, b, c, d, e, and f).
5.16.* Generate a letter frequency table for the speech "I Have a Dream" by Martin Luther King, Jr. The link to the speech is at https://www.americanrhetoric.com/speeches/mlkihaveadream.htm.
5.17. Calculate the letter frequencies of 26 letters for the Bible.
5.18.* Generate public and private keys to code the following message.
"`Jone Deo borrowed $500 from Mary on 9/6/2024`".

References

Cornell, English Letter Frequency (based on a sample of 40,000 words). https://pi.math.cornell.edu/~mec/2003-2004/cryptography/subs/frequencies.html
Dumas, A. (1844). *Count of Monte Cristo.* http://gutenberg.org/files/1184/1184-0.txt
Lepcha, M. (2023). *What Is SHA-256?* https://www.techopedia.com/definition/sha-256
Mnemonic word list, https://raw.githubusercontent.com/bitcoin/bips/master/bip-0039/english.txt
QR code generator, https://www.qr-code-generator.com/
Sha256 website. https://passwordsgenerator.net/sha256-hash-generator/.
Singh, S. (2000). *The Code Book.* Fourth Estate Limited.

Cryptography (2): Advanced

6

This chapter will discuss more advanced concepts related to cryptography, such as prime numbers, ECC (Elliptic Curve Cryptography), its formulae and graphs, how to verify whether a point is on the ECC curve, and how to generate a public key from a private key. Since many concepts, formulas, and operations are quite advanced and difficult to comprehend, readers/students could skip this chapter without negatively impacting the understanding of the rest of the book. On the other hand, readers and students can always come back to this chapter later if necessary. In this chapter, the following topics will be covered:

- Prime numbers
- Several ways to get a set of prime numbers
- ECC (Elliptic Curve Cryptography), its related formulae and graphs
- ECC: one Excel example
- Review: the Excel `mod ()` function
- Checking whether a point is on the ECC curve
- Elliptic Curve Cryptography mechanism
- Our hidden function to deal with big numbers
- QR code for a public key and an account address
- Optional: from a private key to a public key
- Optional: from a public key to an account address

Supplementary Information The online version contains supplementary material available at https://doi.org/10.1007/978-3-031-89779-5_6.

Y. Yan, *Introduction to FinTech using Excel*, Springer Texts in Business and Economics, https://doi.org/10.1007/978-3-031-89779-5_6

6.1 Prime Numbers

Prime numbers are natural numbers greater than 1 with exactly two factors: 1 and the number itself. This means they cannot be divided evenly by any other number. For example, the first several prime numbers are 2, 3, 5, 7, 11, 13, 17, and 19. Notably, 2 is the only even prime number, and all other prime numbers are odd numbers. At https://www.mathsisfun.com/numbers/prime-number-lists.html, interested readers can download several zip files for up to 1 million prime numbers. Alternatively, our hidden function called `.prime ()` can be used. To launch the program, we type `.prime ()`.

```
* ----------------------------------------------------------------- *
* Objective: generate all primes for a given n                      *
* ---------------------------------------------------------------- *
* Step 1: Enter n below, such as 100 (max 1000000000, i.e., 1e9) *
100
```

Fig. 6.1 The prime number function (.prime)

We can view the first and last ten prime numbers below.

```
 * ----------------------------------------------------------------- *
 * Step 2: do you want to print the first and last 10 numbers?     *
1    yes
2    no
 * ----------------------------------------------------------------- *
1
 * ----------------------------------------------------------------- *
 *  the first 10 prime are shown below                              *
 [1]  2  3  5  7 11 13 17 19 23 29
```

Fig. 6.2 Choice: print a few prime numbers or not

As the last step, we can copy and paste those prime numbers into Excel or a text editor such as Notepad or MS Word.

```
 * ----------------------------------------------------------------- *
 * Step 3: do you want to copy those prime numbers to Excel?       *
1    yes
2    no
 * ----------------------------------------------------------------- *
1
 *  Launch Exce and paste those prime there                         *
 * ----------------------------------------------------------------- *
>
```

Fig. 6.3 Coping those prime numbers to Excel

The above function needs two packages. Interested readers can copy and paste the following two lines to their R Console to install those two packages.

```
install.packages("gmp")
install.packages("clipr").
```

6.2 Review: The Excel `MOD ()` Function

The Excel `mod ()` function is a modulus function that shows us the remainder when we divide `x` by a base. For example, 15 divided by 10 will give us a remainder of 5. On the other hand, the remainder is 1 when 18 is divided by 17.

	x	base	mod	formulatext
1	x	base	mod	formulatext
2	15	10	5	=MOD(A2,B2)
3	16	10	6	=MOD(A3,B3)
4	18	17	1	=MOD(A4,B4)
5	266	17	11	=MOD(A5,B5)

Fig. 6.4 The Excel MOD function with different divisors

There are two rules. Rule #1: if the number is less than the base, the remainder is the value. For example, mod(16,17) will be 16. Rule #2: when `x` is more significant than a given base, we will find an `n` where the base is less than `x` and `(n + 1)*base` is more significant than `x`. Now, the remainder will be `x−n*base`. For example, `x` is 266, and `base` is 17. Since 266/17 = 15.64706, we have `n` = 15. The remainder will be 266−15*17 = 11.

6.3 Modulus of a Negative Number

What is −7 mod 5? To find −7 mod 5, we first see the most significant number that is less than or equal to −7 and divisible by 5. That number is −10. To get the remainder, subtract −10 from −7, which gives 3, which is the remainder. The Excel `mod ()` function would consider this case automatically.

A1 | fx =MOD(-7,5)

	A	B	C	D	E
1	3	=MOD(-7,5)			

Fig. 6.5 The Excel MOD function with a negative input

6.4 The Trapdoor Functions

A trapdoor function is a function that is easy to compute in one direction yet difficult to calculate in the opposite direction (finding its inverse) without particular information. Trapdoor functions are a special case of one-way functions widely used in public-key cryptography. Recall that in Chapter 3, Blockchain (I): Numbers and Alphanumeric Cases, we pick the first and last digits of the summation of all digits as our check number. This operation is one-way, i.e., it is easy to calculate this 2-digit checking number. However, figuring out the underlying number, not the digits themselves, is impossible. For example, the check number is 19. Then it could come from 1,234,569, or 133,449, or any number starting with 1 and ending with 9. Another example is the Excel `mod ()` function discussed in the previous section. For example, assume we know the reminder is 5 with a base of 10. Then, we will have unlimited numbers satisfying this set of conditions: 15, 25, 12,345, and the like.

6.5 ECC (Elliptic Curve Cryptography)

Elliptic Curve Cryptography (ECC) generates public and private keys because it relies on the mathematical properties of elliptic curves, providing a high-security level with relatively small key sizes. The key idea is that it's computationally easy to perform operations on an elliptic curve but extremely difficult to reverse these operations (like solving for the discrete logarithm). This is known as the Elliptic Curve Discrete Logarithm Problem (ECDLP), which provides the foundation for ECC's security. This chapter will start with the simplest form to explain these concepts. Excel will be used to illustrate how to calculate pairs of `x` and `y` satisfying a given ECC formula.

6.6 A Simple Formula for ECC

Let's look at one of the most straightforward ECC formulae. For a pair of `x` and `y`, we have the following formula:

$$y^2(\bmod p) = x^3 + 7(\bmod p), \tag{6.1}$$

where `mod ()` is a modulus function. For a prime number of 17, x = 12 and y = 1 will satisfy the above equation. For the left-hand side, y^2 = 1^2 = 1 and `mod(1,17) = 1`. For the right-hand side, `x^3 + 7 = 12^3 + 7 = 1735` and `mod(1735,17) = 1`.

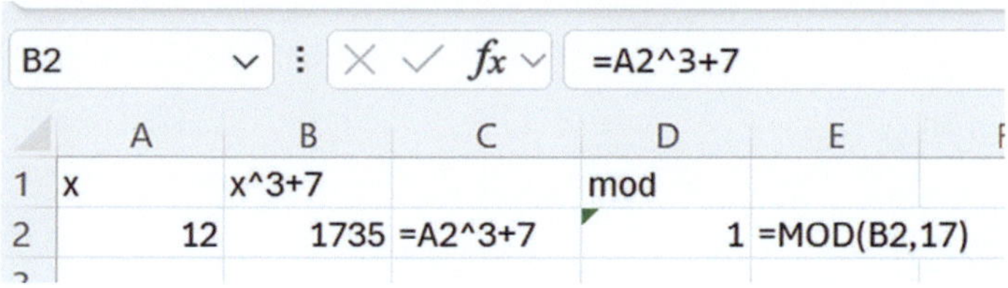

Fig. 6.6 The Excel MOD function with 17 as an advisor

For the next exercise, for a given prime of 17, we will find all x−y pairs (less than 17) satisfying the above equation. The procedure is shown below.

Step 1: Generate a column from 1 to 289 (17*17). There are two ways to do so. The first method is to enter the values 1 and 2 manually. Then, highlight them and drag the dot at the bottom right downward until 289. The second method is to use the fill function, click 'Home', and then the down arrow icon, as shown below.

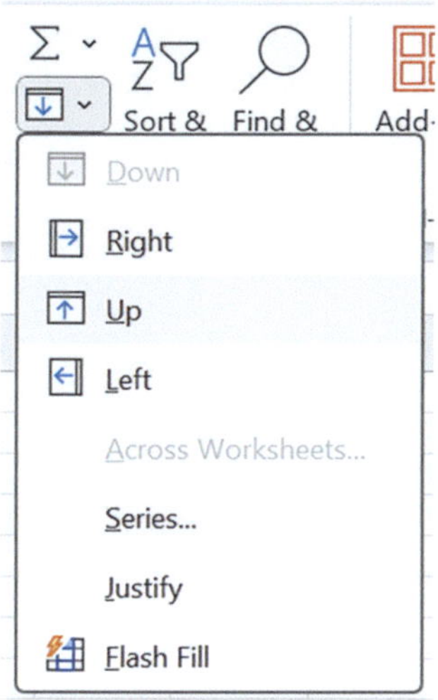

Fig. 6.7 An illustration of the Excel "fill" functionality

After clicking 'Series …', enter the following values.

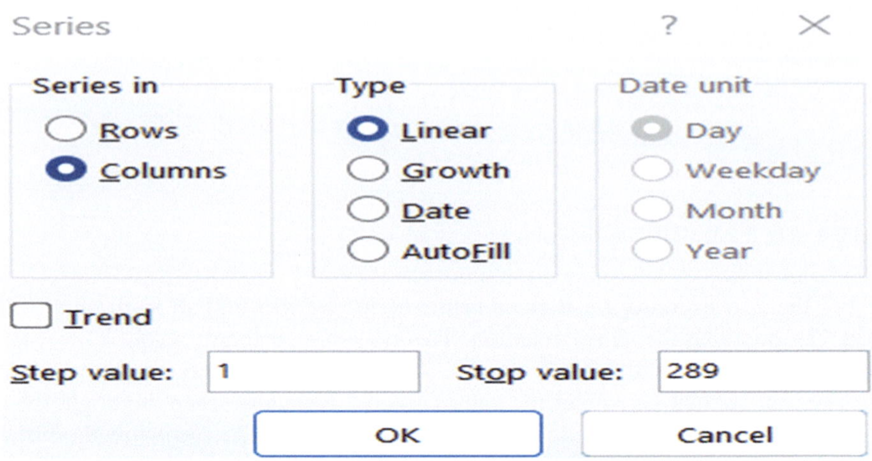

Fig. 6.8 Parameters for "Series in", Type, Step value, and Stop value

Step 2: Generate Column x: repeat 1 17 times, 2 17 times, and continue until we repeat 17 17 times. We can use a formula to achieve this: the formula in cell B2 is `=INT(A2/17−1/18)+1`.

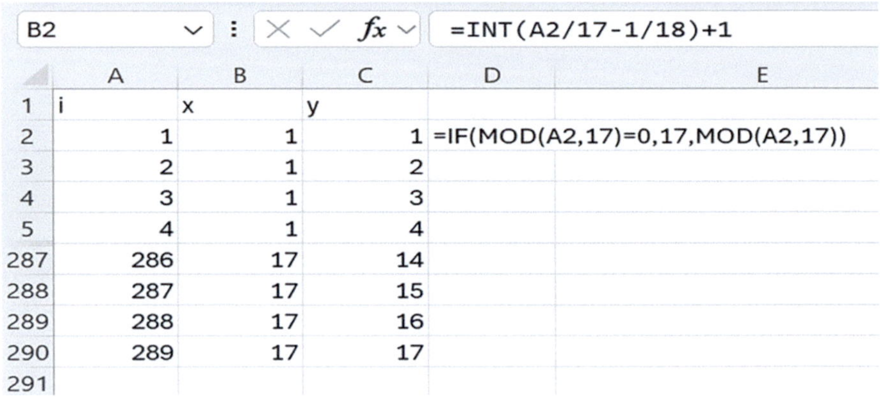

B2 | =INT(A2/17-1/18)+1

	A	B	C	D	E
1	i	x	y		
2	1	1	1	=IF(MOD(A2,17)=0,17,MOD(A2,17))	
3	2	1	2		
4	3	1	3		
5	4	1	4		
287	286	17	14		
288	287	17	15		
289	288	17	16		
290	289	17	17		
291					

Fig. 6.9 The Excel INT and MOD functions

Step 3: Generate Column `y`: enter 1, 2 up to 17; then repeat this procedure 17 times. Again, we can use a formula to achieve this: the formula in cell C2 is `=IF(MOD(A2,17)=0,17, MOD(A2,17))`; see the above image.

Step 4: Calculate the left-hand side of the above formula: `y^2 (mod p)`. The formula in D2 is `=MOD(C2^2,17)`, shown in the following image.

D2 | =MOD(C2^2,17)

	A	B	C	D	E	F
1	i	x	y	mod(y^2,17)	mod(x^3+7,17)	
2	1	1	1	1	8	=MOD(B2^3+7,17)
3	2	1	2	4	8	
4	3	1	3	9	8	
5	4	1	4	16	8	
6	5	1	5	8	8	
7	6	1	6	2	8	
8	7	1	7	15	8	
9	8	1	8	13	8	
10	9	1	9	13	8	
11	10	1	10	15	8	
12	11	1	11	2	8	
13	12	1	12	8	8	

Fig. 6.10 The Excel MOD function with 17 as the divisor

Step 5: Calculate the right-hand side of the equation: `x^3+7 (mod p).` the formula in cell E2 is `=MOD(B2^3+7,17)`, as shown in the above image. After manually checking the above result, we find two pairs, `x` and `y`, satisfying the equation (`x`=`1`,`y`=`5`) and (`x`=`1`,`y`=`12`). We have two steps to find all those pairs.

Step 6: Generate a column called '`matched`,' as shown below.

F2 | =IF(D2=E2,"yes","no")

	A	B	C	D	E	F
1	i	x	y	mod(y^2,17)	mod(x^3+7,17)	matched
2	1	1	1	1	8	no
3	2	1	2	4	8	no
4	3	1	3	9	8	no
5	4	1	4	16	8	no
6	5	1	5	8	8	yes
7	6	1	6	2	8	no

Fig. 6.11 The Excel IF function for "yes" or "no"

Step 7: Sort the data by this "`matched`" column and remove the "`no`" rows.

	A	B	C	D	E	F
1	i	x	y	mod(y^2,17)	mod(x^3+7,17)	matched
2	5	1	5	8	8	yes
3	12	1	12	8	8	yes
4	24	2	7	15	15	yes
5	27	2	10	15	15	yes
6	51	3	17	0	0	yes
7	76	5	8	13	13	yes
8	77	5	9	13	13	yes
9	91	6	6	2	2	yes
10	96	6	11	2	2	yes
11	122	8	3	9	9	yes
12	133	8	14	9	9	yes
13	155	10	2	4	4	yes
14	168	10	15	4	4	yes
15	188	12	1	1	1	yes
16	203	12	16	1	1	yes
17	242	15	4	16	16	yes
18	251	15	13	16	16	yes

Fig. 6.12 Adding a "matched" column

For the next section, we will use x and y from the above image to draw a graph.

6.7 Generating an ECC Graph

The data set used is the same one generated in the previous section. We copy and paste just two columns, x and y. After highlighting those two columns, choose 'Insert,' and "Recommended Graph," as shown below.

	A	B	C
1	i	x	y
2	5	1	5
3	12	1	12
4	24	2	7
5	27	2	10
6	51	3	17
7	76	5	8
8	77	5	9
9	91	6	6
10	96	6	11
11	122	8	3
12	133	8	14
13	155	10	2
14	168	10	15
15	188	12	1
16	203	12	16
17	242	15	4
18	251	15	13

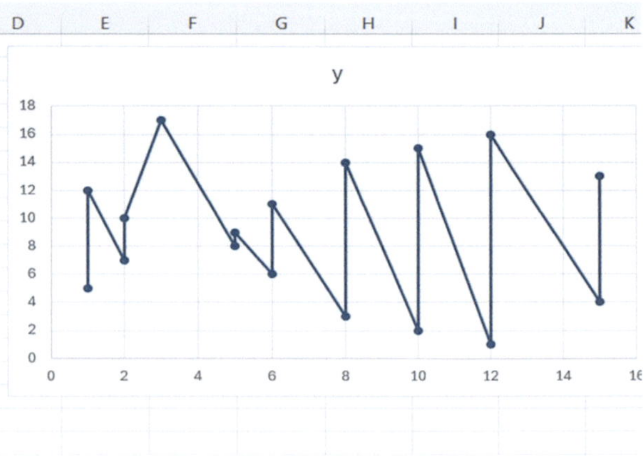

Fig. 6.13 An ECC graph

We prefer scatter graphs without the lines connecting the dots. After moving our cursor to the graph, we right-click our mouse and choose "Change Chart Type," as shown below.

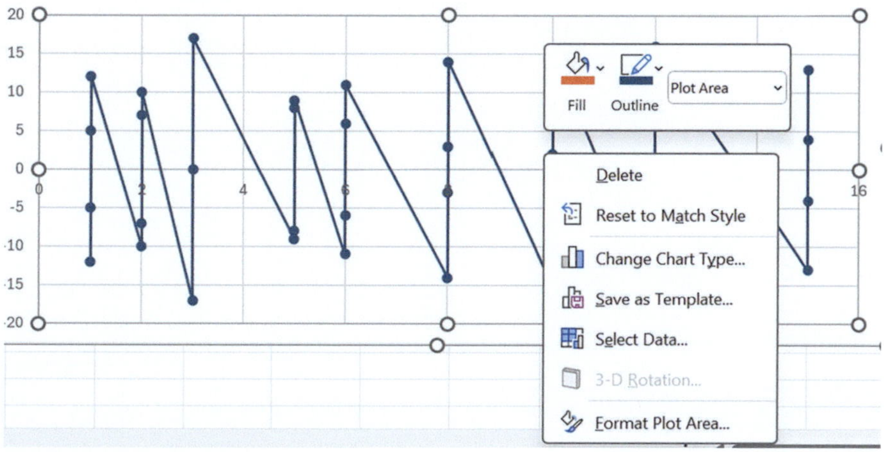

Fig. 6.14 Changing Type

The following image would pop up, and we chose the first one, an accurate scatter graph without those lines linking them.

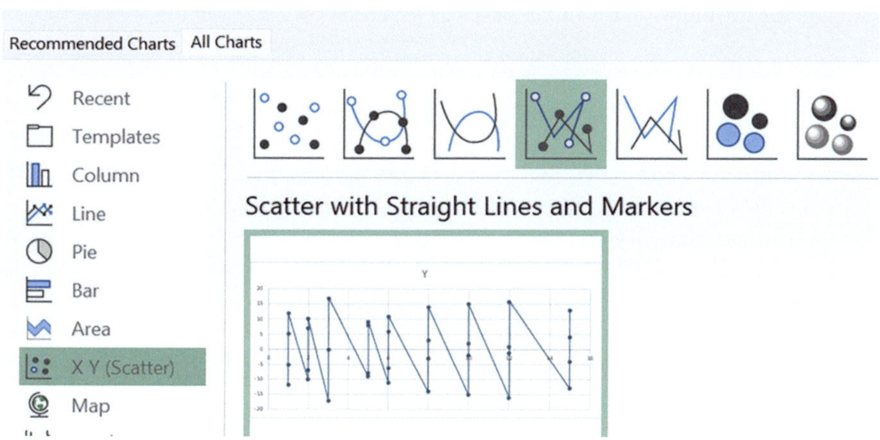

Fig. 6.15 Choosing "X Y (scatter)"

The result is shown below.

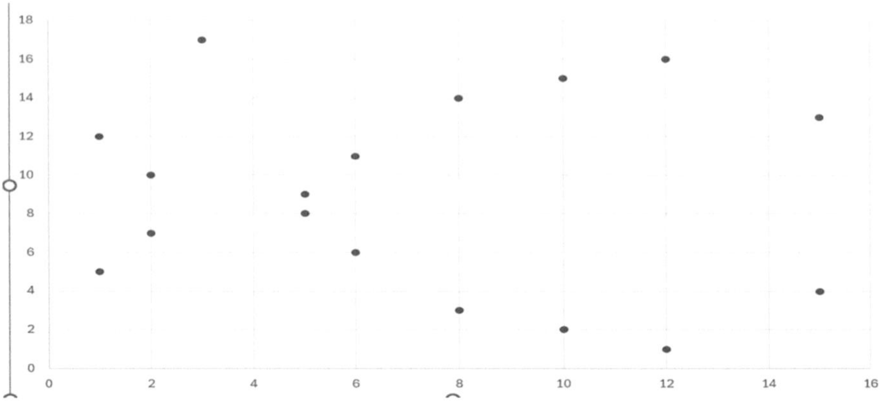

Fig. 6.16 The ECC finial graph

6.8 The ECC's General Formula

The general formula for Elliptic Curves is given below:

$$\begin{cases} y^2(modp) = x^3 + ax + b(modp) \\ \quad subjet\ to : 4a^3 + 27b^2 \neq 0 \end{cases} \tag{6.2}$$

where a and b are constants, and p is a prime number that defines the field over which the curve is defined. The curve equation must satisfy the condition $4a^3 + 27b^2 \neq 0$ ensure the curve has no singularities (sharp points or cusps). Each valid point on the curve is a pair (x, y) that satisfies the equation. Let's look at a simple one when a = −1 and b = 1, shown below.

$$y^2 = x^3 - x + 1 \tag{6.3}$$

Let's use Excel to draw the picture below. We generate three columns: x, y, and −y (negative y).

B2 fx =SQRT(A2^3-A2+1)

	A	B	C	D	E
1	x	y	-y		
2	-1.3247	0.008751	-0.00875	=-B2	
3	-1.2247	0.622724	-0.62272		
4	-1.1247	0.837861	-0.83786		

Fig. 6.17 The results of the square root of (x^3−x + 1)

Based on the above equation, we know that `x^3−x + 1` should be larger than or equal to 0. Our starting value for `x` is −1.3247 (see cell A2). By trial and error, the incremental value for the `x` column is 0.1. The formula in cell A3 is = `A2 + 0.1`. The formula in cell B2 is = `SQRT(A2^3−A2 + 1)` according to the above equation. The formula in cell C2 is = `−B2`, i.e., the negative value of B2. The reason is that the graph is symmetric along the `x`-axis. Then, we convert columns `x`, `y`, and `−y` to two columns by repeating `x` values together with `−y`, as shown below.

	A	B	C
1	x	y	
2	-1.3247	0.008751	< - a
3	-1.2247	0.622724	<- b
32	1.6753	2.006651	
33	1.7753	2.195426	
34	-1.3247	-0.00875	<- -a
35	-1.2247	-0.62272	<- -b
36	-1.1247	-0.83786	
37	-1.0247	-0.97404	
53	1.5753	-1.8259	
54	1.6753	-2.00665	
55	1.7753	-2.19543	

Fig. 6.18 An illustration of x and y columns

We have the following graph using those two columns, `x` and `y`.

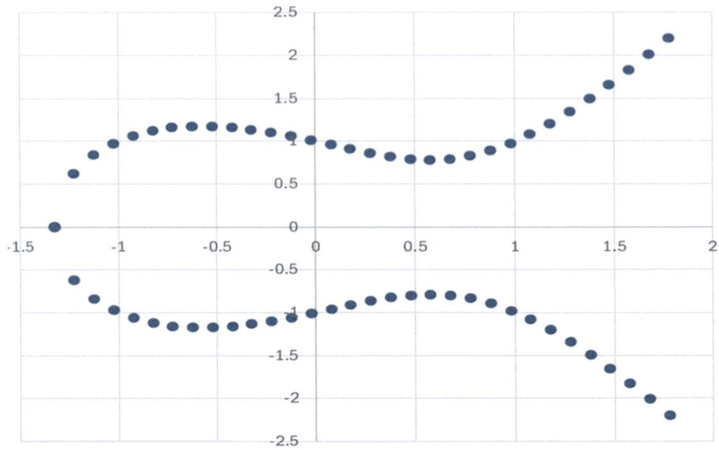

Fig. 6.19 A much nicer ECC graph

One of the end-of-chapter questions is related to the above graph.

6.9 ECC: Generating Public/Private Keys

Table 6.1 summarizes the properties of public and private keys. Again, this is a review since we discussed these properties in Chapter 5: Cryptography (I): public and private keys.

The generator point is a predefined point on the elliptic curve, and the multiplication of G by the private key k results in another point, P, on the curve, which is the public key.

$$P = k * G \tag{6.4}$$

Here, the multiplication refers to Elliptic Curve point multiplication, which involves repeatedly adding the point G to itself k times. Importantly, given P (the public key) and G, it is computationally infeasible to determine k (the private key) due to the ECDLP.

Table 6.1 Private and public keys

Key	Explanation
Private Key	The private key is a randomly chosen number, typically denoted as k. This is a large integer that is kept secret
Public Key	The public key is derived from the private key using the elliptic curve. Specifically, it multiples the private key by a generator point G on the curve

6.10 Elliptic Curve Point Multiplication

Elliptic curves point multiplication is a process that involves repeated point addition over an elliptic curve. Point multiplication means adding a point G to itself k times, where k is the private key, and G is the generator point. Let's break down how point addition works on elliptic curves and provide an R function to do this for a simple elliptic curve. The two basic operations are point addition and point doubling. Here's how the point addition works: Given two points P = (x_1,y_1) and Q = (x_2,y_2), their sum R = P + Q = (x_3,y_3) is calculated as follows: If $P \neq Q$, the slope is $\lambda = \frac{y_2 - y_1}{x_2 - x_1}$. If $P = Q$ (point doubling), the slop is $\lambda = \frac{3x_1^2 + a}{2y_1}$. The coordinates of $R = (x_3, y_3)$ are given below.

$$\begin{cases} x_3 = \lambda^2 - x_1 - x_2 \\ y_3 = \lambda(x_1 - x_3) - y_1 \end{cases} \tag{6.5}$$

Source of formula: https://www.cs.purdue.edu/homes/ssw/cs655/ec.pdf.

6.11 Modular Inverse of 7 Modulo 97

The modular inverse of a number x modulo n is a number y such that:

$$x * y \equiv 1(\text{mod } n) \tag{6.6}$$

In other words, y is the modular inverse of x if multiplying x and y gives a product of 1 modulo n. Assume that we choose 97 as our prime number. Let's find out the Modular Inverse of 7 modulo 97.

$$\lambda = \frac{1}{7}(mod\, 97)$$

Here, we are looking for a number such that the following formula holds.

$$7 * y \equiv 1(mod\, 97)$$

According to the above condition, $y = 14$ satisfies this equation, i.e., = `mod(7*14, 97)` = `mod (98,97)` = 1. The modular inverse of 7 modulo 97 is 14 because multiplying 7 by 14 yields 98, and 98 mod 97 is 1. This means 7×14 is congruent to 1 in the field $F97$, satisfying the definition of a modular inverse. In summary, the modular inverse is used to find a multiplicative "partner" for a number such that its product is congruent to 1 under a given modulo. In this case, 14 is the modular inverse of 7 modulo 97.

In modular arithmetic, division by a number (5/7 mod 97) is equivalent to multiplying by its modular inverse. 5/7 mod 97 is comparable to:

$$5 * \frac{1}{7} mod\, 97$$

Since 7^{-1} mod 97 is 14, this becomes 5*14 = 70. Now take 70 mod 97 = 70. Thus, we have the following summary.

$$\frac{5}{7} mod\, 97 \equiv 70(mod\, 97)$$

The notation F_{97} refers to a finite field with 97 elements. In this context, the elements are integers from 0 to 96. Arithmetic operations (addition, subtraction, multiplication) are performed in modulus 97.

6.12 Example #1

Assume that an Elliptic curve is defined over `Fp` using the following equation:

$$y^2(mod\, 97) = x^3 + 2x + 3(mod\, 97) \tag{6.7}$$

Consider two points: `P = (3,6), Q = (17,10).` We can easily verify that both points are on the ECC curve. The result is shown below.

E2 =B2^3+2*B2+3

	A	B	C	D	E	F	G	H
1		x	y	y^2	x^3+2x+3	mod (y^2, 97)	mod(x^3+2x+3)	
2	P	3	6	36	36	36	36	
3	Q	17	10	100	4950	3	3	

Fig. 6.20 Excel MOD applied to y^2 and (x^3 + 2x + 3)

The slope can be computed using the following result.

$$\lambda = \frac{y_2 - y_1}{x_2 - x_1} = \frac{10 - 6}{17 - 3} = \frac{4}{14} = \frac{1}{14} * 4$$

Based on the previous discussion, we know that 14* 7 = 98≡1 (mod 97). Thus, λ = 7*4 = 28. To calculate × 3 and y3, we have the following results.

$$x_3 = \lambda^2 - x_1 - x_2 = 28^2 - 3 - 17 = 764 \equiv 85(mod\, 97)$$

$$y_3 = \lambda(x_1 - x_3) - y_1* = 28(3 - 764) - 10 = -21314 \equiv 26(mod\, 97)$$

Based on the above calculation, we conclude that P(3,6) + Q(17,10) = (85, 26). The webpage https://andrea.corbellini.name/ecc/interactive/modk-add.html can be used to verify our result, as shown below.

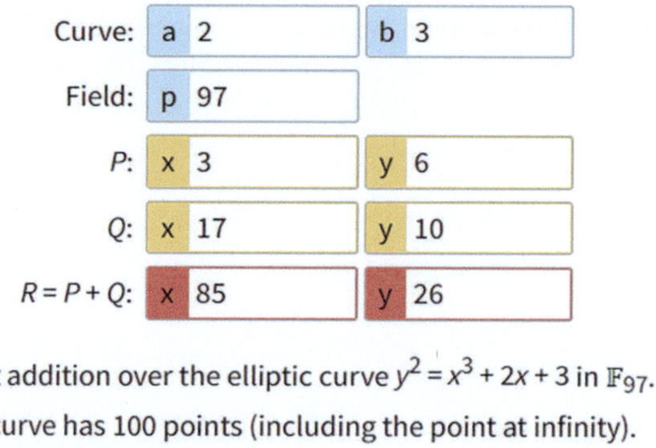

Fig. 6.21 Verification by using a website

In addition, we can easily verify that (85,26) is on the above ECC curve as well.

	A	B	C	D	E	F	G	H
1		x	y	y^2	x^3+2x+3	mod (y^2, 97)	mod(x^3+2x+3)	
2	P	3	6	36	36	36	36	
3	Q	17	10	100	4950	3	3	
4	P+Q	85	26	676	614298	94	94	

Fig. 6.22 MOD for P, Q, and P + Q

6.13 P = k*G Explained

This section is based on the logic discussed in the previous section. Assume that our private key is 10, G = (2, 22), and we have the following three equations.

$$\begin{cases} y^2(mod\ 67) = x^3 + 2x + 3(mod 67) \\ G = (2, 22) \\ k = 10 \end{cases} \tag{6.8}$$

The procedure is given below.

Step 1: Choose a private key, such as 10.
Step 2: To get the public key, we multiply the generator point G = (2, 22) by k = 10. This involves adding elliptic curve points to compute P = 10 times G.

After performing Elliptic curve point multiplication (a series of additions), we get the public key. Suppose the result of this operation is: Public Key: P=(13,22).

Since the procedure is tedious when we conduct a calculation ourselves manually, we have two methods to get our results. For Method 1, we can use the website at https://andrea.corbellini.name/ecc/interactive/modk-mul.html. The result is shown below.

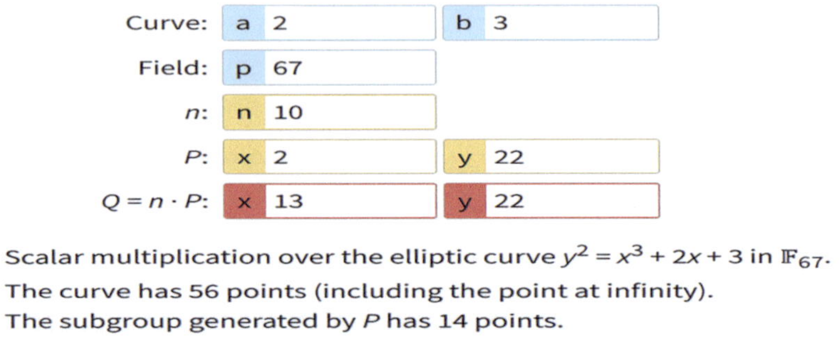

Fig. 6.23 The result by using a website (Q = n*p)

The second way is to use our hidden function, `.Gxk()` (see Appendix D for this example).

6.14 Ethereum's Secp256k1 Explained

Ethereum uses the elliptic curve '`secp256k1`' for its cryptographic operations, primarily in generating public and private keys. This elliptic curve is defined over a finite field, making it a part of the Elliptic Curve Cryptography (ECC) family, known for its high security with smaller key sizes. The curve's equation is given as ($y^2 = x^3 + 7$). The term '`secp256k1`' reflects its parameters: "`secp`" stands for "Standards for Efficient Cryptography," "`256`" denotes the bit length of the field size (a 256-bit prime number), and "`k1`" indicates a specific curve form known for its efficiency. Using this curve, Ethereum can ensure the secure and efficient creation of public–private key pairs for signing and validating transactions.

One key advantage of `secp256k1` is its resistance to certain cryptographic attacks, such as those targeting the discrete logarithm problem. This strength is essential in Ethereum's blockchain, where users sign transactions with their private keys, and anyone with access to the public key can verify the signature without knowing the private key. This curve is also used by Bitcoin, making it a popular choice in the broader cryptocurrency ecosystem. Its adoption ensures interoperability and ease of integration between various platforms and cryptographic libraries, bolstering Ethereum's decentralized environment's overall security and reliability.

6.15 GX, GY, and P for Secp256k1

Ethereum `secp256k1` uses the Elliptic curve, defined by the following equation:

$$y^2 = x^3 + 7$$

The (`x,y`) values for generator point (`G`) for this curve and `p` (a prime) are given below.

```
Gx=5506626302227734366957871889516853432625060345377759417550
0187360389 116729240
Gy=3267051002075881697808308513050704318447127338065924327593
8904335757337482424
p=1157920892373161954235709850086879078532699846656405640394575 84007908834671663
```

The above p-value is equivalent to the following value.

$$p = 2^{256} - 2^{32} - 977 \tag{6.9}$$

To confirm that the above (`Gx`, `Gy`) are on the Elliptic Curve with the prime mentioned above, readers must use one of our hidden functions called `.onECC()`. The reason is that those values are way too big for Excel to handle. We need to install an R package called '`gmp`' to use this function. To install it, just copy and paste the following line to your R Console or RStudio.

```
install.packages("gmp")
```

To check whether the above `Gx` and `Gy` are on the ECC curve, we launch the function by typing `.onECC()`. There are five choices, as shown below.

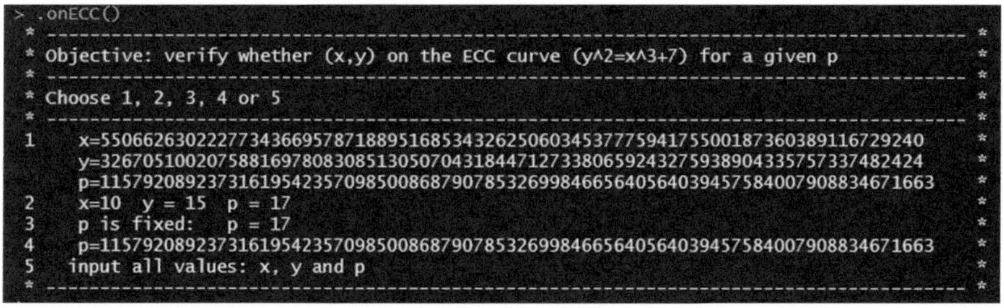

Fig. 6.24 Verifying whether (x,y) on the ECC curve (.onECC)

We will see the following results after choosing 1 and hitting the Enter key.

```
1
 * ------------------------------------------------------------------------ *
 *  Result:                                                                  *
 *    Left side  (y^2 mod p)    : 32748224938747404814623910738487752935528512903530129802856995983256684603122
 *    Right side (x^3 + 7 mod p): 32748224938747404814623910738487752935528512903530129802856995983256684603122
The point (Gx, Gy) is on the elliptic curve.
 * ------------------------------------------------------------------------ *
```

Fig. 6.25 The result of one run

6.16 Our `.BigNumbreCalculation` Function

When the values of `x`, `y`, or `p` (prime) are big, Excel cannot handle them. Because of this, we generated a hidden function called `.bigNumberCalculation()`, abbreviated as `.bigN()`. Type its name, and we will see the following two examples.

```
> .bigN
function(){
"Objective: solve the issue with big nubmers


Example 1># x^3 +7 (mod p)
        x=55066263022277343669578718895168534326250603453777594175500187360389116729240
        p=115792089237316195423570985008687907853269984665640564039457584007908834671663
        -----  result ------------------------------------------
        32748224938747404814623910738487752935528512903530129802856995983256684603122

Example 2># y^2 (mod p)
          y=32670510020758816978083085130507043184471273380659243275938904335757337482424
          p=115792089237316195423570985008687907853269984665640564039457584007908834671663
         -----  result ------------------------------------------
         32748224938747404814623910738487752935528512903530129802856995983256684603122
```

Fig. 6.26 The help of the Big Number function (.bigN)

The above two examples verify that the left-hand side is the same as the right-hand side with very big `x`, `y`, and `p` values. The function requires two packages. After launching R, you can copy and paste the following two lines to your R console.

```
install.packages("gmp")
install.packages("clipr").
```

6.17 K = k*G: K = 1

This section is optional.

In this section, we look at the formula that a public key is derived from a private key.

$$K = k * G,$$

where `k` is the private key (a randomly generated integer), and `G` is the generator point of the curve (as defined above). `K` is a public key, resulting from multiplying the private key `k` with the generator point G using elliptic curve point multiplication. We will see the most straightforward formula when `k` takes a value 1. In hexadecimal form. The Ethereum generator (`Gx, Gy`) is in a hexadecimal format:

```
Gx=0x79BE667EF9DCBBAC55A06295CE870B07029BFCDB2DCE28D959F2815B1
6F81798
Gy=0x483ADA7726A3C4655DA4FBFC0E1108A8FD17B448A68554199C47D0
8FFB10D4B8
```

When the private key is all zeros except the last digit (000...01) `"000000000000000000000000000000000000000000000000000000000000000001"`, this is equivalent to multiplying the generator point GGG by 1:

$$\mathrm{K} = \mathrm{k\,G} = 1\,\mathrm{G} = \mathrm{G}$$

In other words, the resulting public key is just the generator point `G` itself. We can manually calculate a public `k`. Computing the public key manually using the elliptic curve arithmetic (point addition and point doubling) is theoretically possible but practically very complex and time-consuming without a library like ecdsa. It involves multiple steps of elliptic curve point operations.

Example Output Analysis: for the private key `"0000000000000000000000000000000000000000000000000000000000000001"`, the generated public key should match the coordinates of the generator point *G*:

Public Key (hex):

```
79be667ef9dcbbac55a06295ce870b07029bfcdb2dce28d959f2815b16f817
98
483ada7726a3c4655da4fbfc0e1108a8fd17b448a68554199c47d08ffb1
0d4b8
```

X-coordinate (first 64 characters):

```
79be667ef9dcbbac55a06295ce870b07029bfcdb2dce28d959f2815b16f817
98
```

Y-coordinate (last 64 characters):

```
483ada7726a3c4655da4fbfc0e1108a8fd17b448a68554199c47d08ffb10d4
b8
```

The compressed format adds a prefix (0 × 02 or 0 × 03) depending on the parity of the Y-coordinate: Compressed Public Key (hex):

```
0279be667ef9dcbbac55a06295ce870b07029bfcdb2dce28d959f2815b16f8
1798
```

6.18 Why Is ECC Secure?

Security comes from the fact that even though it's easy to compute `P = k × G`, it's tough to reverse the process and determine `k` given only `P` and `G`. This is the foundation of ECC's security and why it's used to generate public and private keys. Here are three points. First, the private key is a random number. Second, the public key is a point on the elliptic curve derived by multiplying the private key with the generator point. Third, the process is secure because of the difficulty in solving the ECDLP, which protects the private key even if the public key is known.

6.19 QR Code for a Given Public Key

At https://allprivatekeys.com/mnemonic-code-converter, we can find QR codes in addition to both public and private keys. The first way to generate a QR code is to visit the website at https://www.qr-code-generator.com/. The top part is shown below.

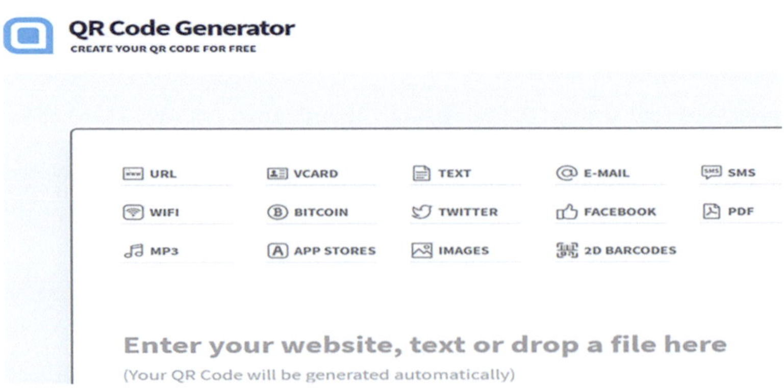

Fig. 6.27 The QR code generator using a website

Assume that our public key is `xpub6CcevYbyANYfkfNgwjCeGyeXq89SuEfm63FE7T`
We simply copy and paste it there.

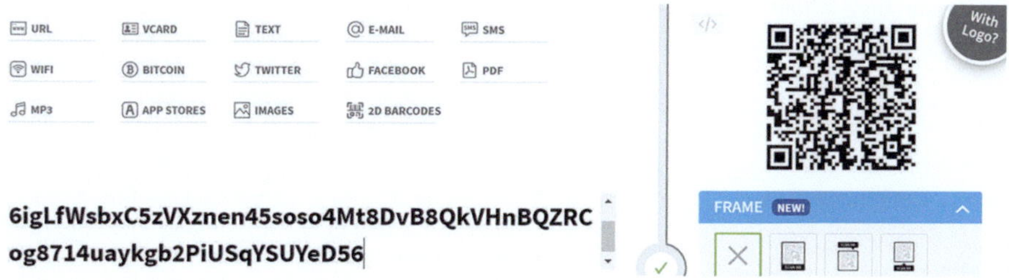

Fig. 6.28 One result by using the website

The second method is to generate those QR codes ourselves. The essential R package is "`qrcode`". We can install the package by issuing the following line of R code.

```
install.packages("qrcode").
```

One example is shown below.

```
.qrcode ().
Input a public key below.
```

```
xpub6CcevYbyANYfkfNgwjCeGyeXq89SuEfm63FE7Tx6igLfWsbxC5zVXznen4
5soso4Mt 8DvB8QkVHnBQZRCog8714uaykgb2PiUSqYSUYeD56
```

The related QR code is shown below.

Fig. 6.29 The image of a QR code

A QR code (generated using a public key) can be used in various applications, particularly cryptocurrency, secure communication, and authentication. Table 6.2 summarizes the usage of a QR code based on a public key.

QR codes provide a convenient and efficient way to share public keys, enabling secure and easy interactions in various scenarios, from financial transactions to secure messaging and identity verification. The ease of scanning a QR code makes it an ideal method for transferring sensitive information in a user-friendly and error-free manner.

Table 6.2 Usage of a QR code based on a public key

Purpose	Explanation
Cryptocurrency Wallet Addresses	A QR code containing a cryptocurrency public key (or wallet address) can be scanned to receive funds. Users can quickly display the QR code on their devices or print documents to receive payments. Others can scan the code to send cryptocurrency to the associated wallet address, simplifying the transaction process
Secure Communication	QR codes can be used to share public keys for secure messaging applications. Users can initiate encrypted communication by scanning a QR code containing a public key. This ensures that messages are encrypted with the recipient's public key, maintaining confidentiality
Digital Identity Verification	QR codes can store public keys for digital identity, acting as a digital signature. When a public key is embedded in a QR code, it can be used to verify the authenticity of a document, user, or: transaction. For example, a digital ID card might contain a QR code with a public key to authenticate the cardholder's identity
Two-factor authentication (2FA)	QR codes can generate one-time passwords (OTPs) in 2FA setups. During the setup of 2FA, a QR code containing a public key or shared secret is scanned by an authentication app (like Google Authenticator or Authy). This allows the app to generate time-based OTPs that users must enter alongside their regular password
Secure File Sharing	QR codes can facilitate the sharing of public keys for encrypted file transfers. Users can share their public keys via QR codes to allow others to encrypt files meant for them. Only the intended recipient with the corresponding private key can decrypt and access the file
Access Control and Smart Contracts	Public keys encoded in QR codes can be used for access control in smart contracts or IoT devices. A QR code with a public key can be scanned to grant or verify access to a system or device. In blockchain-based applications, smart contracts can validate the ownership or authorization by matching the scanned public key with stored credentials
VCard Information:	QR codes can include public keys as part of a vCard (virtual contact card) for secure contact sharing. Scanning the QR code automatically adds the contact information and the public key to the user's address book, facilitating secure communication from the start

6.20 Extracting Contents from a QR Code

Sometimes, we need an operation to extract the contents from a QR code. For example, at https://qrcoderaptor.com/, we will see the following image (the second choice).

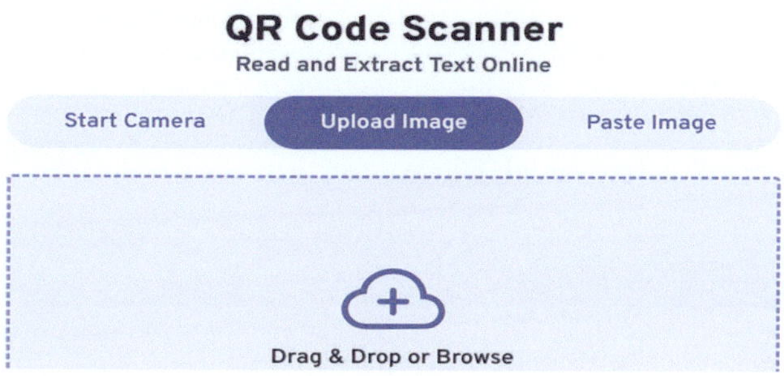

Fig. 6.30 Extracting the contents from a QR code: QR code Scanner

Assume that we have the following QR code sitting on our device.

Fig. 6.31 The image of a QR code as an input

After loading the following image, we will see the following result.

↓ QR Code Result ↓

-----BEGIN PUBLIC KEY----- MIIBIjANBgkqhkiG9w0BAQEFAAOCAQ8A MIIBCgKCAQEA2aJ4IU9sMRTreubTHMjz wYyavHI2/0NItneoNS0owQr3Sqp r2v0MajymNSLTV2ccbUu6jW0LBFyACnILd7XH IaLIp510A0GS2ZnAnGte9Z HE4PIfTJ0x5IfBGUE2Phwz+xc2TujSDSIBAesSmvqd x0kSGiY4AKnKZWu1 wGZ3SBKhwKsDzLZwXKR5QPuOmrYXuUmbUC2iTofckyiM4TyI g3KCnsPO zW0W2rzOSBIWrGZrIHsO4xQt8yWOjfEtnkDGZd1DGpeLzIqaBLI9m7pb ZDI cJZ4OPgg6VM+Hb4PkzSNxtccgLcUfZXrpZW3zT5IgvZ09Jsj/5s8wkRxFkI Vu aQIDAQAB -----END PUBLIC KEY-----

Copy

Fig. 6.32 The contents of the above QR code (a public key)

6.21 Our Hidden Functions

We have generated a few functions to help our readers/students understand those concepts better and simplify operations. Those functions are listed in the following table.

```
> .sf(6)
CHAPTER                                    NAME                 SHORTCUT
      6 install.packages('gmp')
      6 install.packages('clipr')
      6 install.packages('qrcode')
      6 install.packages('openssl')
      6 --------------------------------
      6 .primeNumbers                         .prime
      6 .isPrime
      6 .eccPlot
      6 .onECC
      6 .P_plus_Q                             # R=P+Q
      6 .Gxk                                  # R=G*k (k times)
      6 .bigNumberCalculation                 .bigN     # need 'gmp'
      6 .qrcode                                         # need 'qrcode'
      6 .encodeWithPublicKey                  .en7      # need 'openssl'
      6 .decodeWithPriateKey                  .de7      # need 'openssl'
>
```

Fig. 6.33 A list of hidden functions related to Chapter 6

6.22 From a Private Key to an Address

This section is optional.

Before we know it, we can derive a public key from a private key. In addition, an account address is part of a public key. After launching Ganache, we can click the key on the right-hand side.

Fig. 6.34 The image of the Ganache platform

One example is shown below.

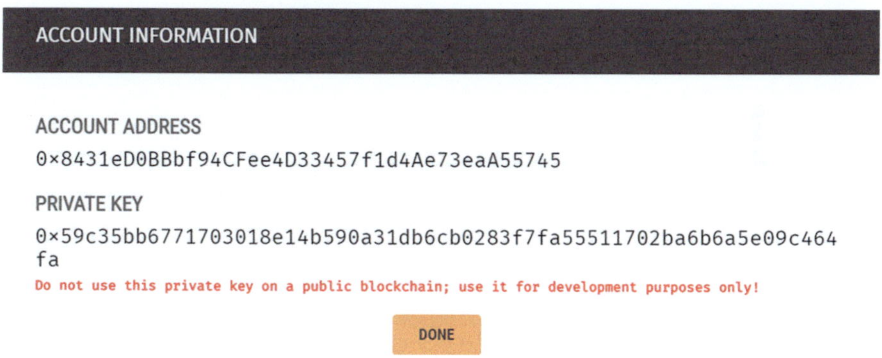

Fig. 6.35 A private key

We have the account address and a private key from the above image. By running the Python program in Appendix E, we can verify that we can get the corresponding account address by inputting the above private key.

Appendix A: Issue the Following Line of R Code for Week 6

```
source("http://datayyy.com/i2ft/week6.txt")
```

```
*------------------------------------------------------------------------*
* Introduction to FinTech using Excel                 by Dr. Yan 2025     *
*        (in an R-assisted learning environment)                          *
*------------------------------------------------------------------------*
*  .c1  Introduction and Excel Basics            .c16 R basics(optional)  *
*  .c2  Blockchain 1: (Numbers & alphanumeric)   .c17 Macro    (optional) *
*  .c3             2: (ASCII and Sha256)         .c18 VBA      (optional) *
*  .c4  Ledger and distributed ledger                                     *
*  .c5  Cryptography   1: and public/private keys                         *
*  .c6                 2: Advanced                                        *
* -----------------------------------------------------------------------*
* >.c6       # go to chapter  6                                           *
* >.uu       # go to utility submenu                                      *
* >.ft       # back to this menu                                          *
*------------------------------------------------------------------------*
```

Fig. 6.36 The menu for Week 6

Appendix B: Issue .chapter6 or .c6 to Get the Contents of Chapter 6

```
> .c6
function(i=0){
"i  Chapter 6: Advanced cryptography (optional)
 -  ------------------------------      --  -----------------------
 1  Introduction                        21  Public and private keys
 2  Prime number                        22     : package 'openssl'
 3     : examples:                      23       Method 1: generate viewable keys
 4     : links                          24       Method 2: generate binary keys
 5     : 2 packages' installations      25    : .encodeWithPublicKey(), Encode with a public key
 6     : .prime()   function            26    : .decodeWithPrivateKey(),Decode with a private key
 7     : .isPrime() function            27    :from a private key to a pubic key
 8  Excel mod() function                28    : public key to account address
 9       several examples               29    :.bigNumberCalculation()
10  Elliptic Curve                      30  QR code
11     : trapdoor function              31    : usages
12     : one example                    32    : advantages
13     : all pairs (x,y)  Excel         33    : install.packages('qrcode')
14     : .eccPlot()                     34    : our .qrcode() function
15     : ..onECC()                      35    :
16     : .P_plus_Q()                    36 Appendix C: private to a public keys (Python)
17     : .GxK()                         37 Appendix D: private key to an address (Python)
18              : example 1             38 Question
19  Videos                              39
20  Links                               40 our hidden functions

Example #1:>.c6    # see the above list
Example #2:>.c6()  # the same as above
Example #3:>.c6(1) # see the 1st explanation
```

Fig. 6.37 The contents of Chapter 6

Appendix C: Optional: from a Private Key to a Public Key (Python Program)

```
from ecdsa import SigningKey, SECP256k1
# Example private key (in hexadecimal format)
p= "0000000000000000000000000000000000000000000000000000000000
000001"
# length is 64
p_bytes = bytes.fromhex(p) # Convert the private key to bytes
# Generate the signing key using the secp256k1 curve
signing_key = SigningKey.from_string(p_bytes, curve=SECP256k1)
verifying_key = signing_key.verifying_key # Generate the verifying
key (which is the public key)
public_key_bytes = verifying_key.to_string() # public key in
uncompressed format (64 bytes)
public_key_hex = public_key_bytes.hex()
print("Public Key (hex):")
print(public_key_hex)
#79be667ef9dcbbac55a06295ce870b07029bfcdb2dce28d959f2815b1
6f81798483ada7726a3c4655da4fbfc0e1108a8fd17b448a68554199c47d0
8ffb10d4b8
len(public_key_hex) # Out[49]: 128
# Optional: Get the public key in compressed format (33 bytes)
compressed_public_key = b"\x02" + public_key_bytes[:32] if pub-
lic_key_bytes[32] % 2 == 0 else b"\x03" + public_key_bytes[:32
]
compressed_public_key_hex = compressed_public_key.hex()
print(" --- Compressed public key in hex -------------")
print(compressed_public_key_hex)
#0279be667ef9dcbbac55a06295ce870b07029bfcdb2dce28d959f2815b1
6f81798
# length is 66
```

Appendix D: Our Hidden `.Gxk()` Function

Type `.Gxk()` will launch this function, as shown below.

```
> .Gxk()
 * -------------------------------------------------------------- *
 * Objective: R=Q*k = Q + Q + Q + Q  + ... Q  (k times)           *
 *            y^2 (mod p) = x^3+ax+b (mod p)                      *
 * -------------------------------------------------------------- *
 * Step 1: input a and b     such as  2 3                         *
1: 2 3
3:
Read 2 items
```

Fig. 6.38 The.GxK function

The above image shows values `a` and `b`, when entering `67` as `p`, `Q` for `2,22` and `k` as 10.

```
 * -------------------------------------------------------------- *
 * Step 2: input p (prime) such as 67                             *
67
 * -------------------------------------------------------------- *
 * Step 3: input Q pint  such as 2 22                             *
1: 2 22
3:
Read 2 items
 * -------------------------------------------------------------- *
 * Step 4: input k such as 10 (number of repeat)                  *
10
```

Fig. 6.39 Steps 2 and 3

The result is shown below.

```
i= 1 P= 2 22
i= 2 P= 35 1
i= 3 P= 52 22
i= 4 P= 13 45
i= 5 P= 1 41
i= 6 P= 23 42
i= 7 P= 66 0
i= 8 P= 23 25
i= 9 P= 1 26
i= 10 P= 13 22
>
```

Fig. 6.40 The final result

Appendix E: (Optional) from a Private Key to an Address (Python Program)

Fig. 6.41 The image of a private key

```
import hashlib
from Crypto.Hash import keccak
from ecdsa import SigningKey, SECP256k1
# Copy a private key from Ganache
private_key_hex = "59c35bb6771703018e14b590a31db6cb0283f7fa555
11702ba6b6a5e09c464fa"
private_key_bytes = bytes.fromhex(private_key_hex) # Convert to
bytes
# Generate signing and verifying (public) key
signing_key = SigningKey.from_string(private_key_bytes,
curve=SECP256k1)
verifying_key = signing_key.verifying_key
public_key_bytes = verifying_key.to_string() # This gives the
uncompressed 64-byte public key
public_key_hex = public_key_bytes.hex() # Convert to hexadecimal
format
print(public_key_hex)
keccak_hash = keccak.new(digest_bits=256) # last 40 bytes of the
Keccak-256 hash
keccak_hash.update(bytes.fromhex(public_key_hex))
public_key_hash = keccak_hash.hexdigest()
ethereum_address = "0x" + public_key_hash[-40:] # Ethereum address
(last 20 bytes of the hash)
print("Ethereum Address:", ethereum_address)
```

```
#4cfb67e0e22f916bf193be52f25562d923052570e5c3bb2d52ae647848e5
dd61979aa60dff6c901728fa5c7d9093e3eb29ae9bf7dd28575713cca85cf6
04feeb
Ethereum Address: 0x8431ed0bbbf94cfee4d33457f1d4ae73eaa55745
```

Exercises

Note that * indicates difficult ones.

6.1 What is the R package needed to generate a QR code?
6.2 What are the usages for a QR code for a public key?
6.3 At https://allprivatekeys.com/mnemonic-code-converter, generate a pair of public and private keys, then generate a QR code for the public key you got.
6.4 Why is it impossible to use brute force to decode a message using a public key?
6.5* Complete the Excel file for Enigma with more than one letter (Hint: use the Macro in Appendix C).
6.6* Generate public and private keys to code the following message.
"`Jone Deo borrowed $500 from Mary on 9/6/2024`".
6.7 In this chapter, we use `y^2=x^3−x+1` to generate the following graph using Excel. On the left-hand ssside, there is just one dot when y is close to zero. Modify the data set to make a few more dots at the left end.

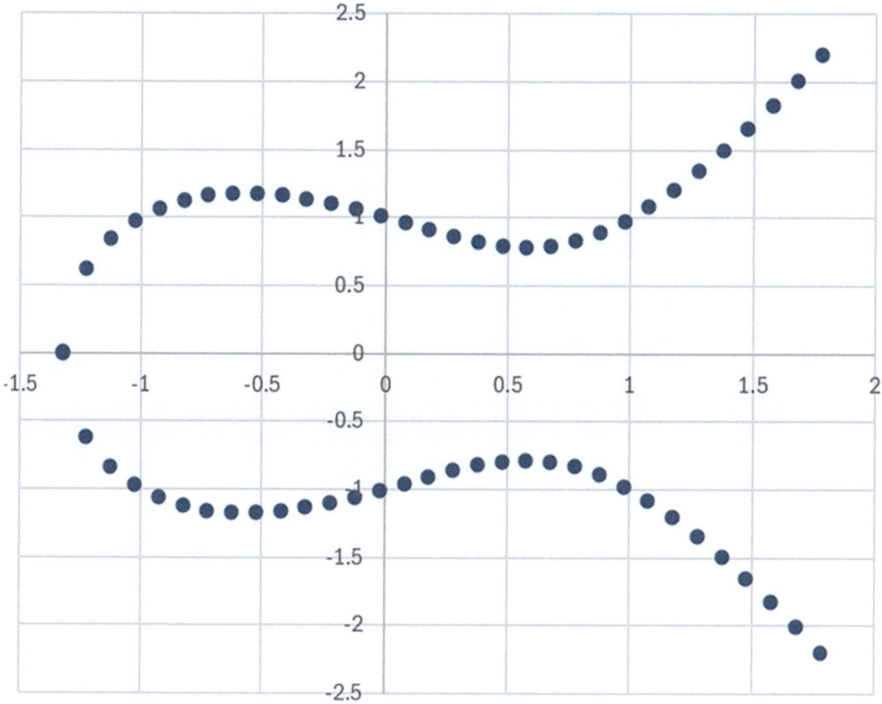

Fig. 6.42 The image of data points on the ECC curve

6.8 Explain the equation of an elliptic curve used in cryptography. What does each parameter in the equation ($y^2 = x^3 + ax + b$) represent?
6.9 Describe the significance of the `secp256k1` curve in Ethereum and Bitcoin. Why is it a preferred choice for these cryptocurrencies?
6.11 How does generating a public key from a private key work in ECC? Why is it computationally infeasible to reverse this process?
6.12 Explain the discrete logarithm problem in the context of ECC. How does this problem contribute to the security of elliptic curve cryptography?
6.13 What is the significance of the base point (generator point) in ECC? How is it used in generating keys?
6.14 Discuss the role of private and public keys in an ECC-based cryptographic system. How are these keys used in encryption and digital signatures?
6.15 Given a private key, how would you generate the corresponding public key using the equation of an elliptic curve? Describe the steps involved.**
6.16 What are the key challenges involved in implementing ECC algorithms in practice? How do these challenges affect security?
6.17 When plotting an elliptic curve graph in Excel, what specific features or properties of the curve are most important to observe?
6.18 Use Excel and explain how you would create a spreadsheet to graph the elliptic curve (`y^2 = x^3 + 7`). What formulas would you use?

6.19 Describe the process of performing point addition on an elliptic curve. How can this be represented graphically in Excel?

6.20 In ECC, what does the term "scalar multiplication" mean? How is this operation used to derive the public key from the private key?

6.21 If the equation of an elliptic curve is (`y^2 = x^3−4x + 1`), identify the valid points on this curve for a given finite field size. How can you verify these points?

6.22 Given a private key value of 12345 and using the base point (`G` = (2, 22)), calculate the corresponding public key using scalar multiplication. Assume a small finite field for simplification.

6.23 Suppose you encounter a scenario where the elliptic curve graph shows multiple intersecting points at a given x-coordinate. Explain why this might happen and how to interpret these points in cryptographic applications.

6.24 Discuss the potential vulnerabilities of ECC. What cryptographic attacks could potentially compromise ECC systems, and how can these be mitigated?

6.25 How can errors in generating or storing private keys compromise the security of an ECC-based system? Provide examples of potential risks.

6.26 How does the choice of different parameters (e.g., coefficients `a` and `b`, the prime field size) affect the elliptic curve's shape and security? Provide an example of how changing these parameters might alter the ECC graph in Excel.

6.27 For the following ECC curve and P(6,7) and Q(21,6):

$$y^2(mod\,97) = x^3 + 4x + 3(mod\,97)$$

Verify whether P and Q are on the curve. If they do, use two methods to calculate P+Q.

6.28* Verify the following account number from its given private key.

Fig. 6.43 The image of a private key

6.29 Calculate the P value (P=G*k) with the following information:

$$\begin{cases} y^2(mod\,97) = x^3 + 4x + 20(mod\,97) \\ G = (44, 423) \\ k = 200 \end{cases}$$

6.30* If you know Python, please verify the following address, given the private key.

```
ACCOUNT ADDRESS
0x95426f18FCF7b61b6F48e20eAF1E1368CA54e86C
PRIVATE KEY
0x9158ca1929776f635e28f33a487b5b80c2d913082911eb0d95f024
520da76617
Do not use this private key on a public blockchain; use it for
development purposes only!
```

References

Cornell, English Letter Frequency (based on a sample of 40,000 words). https://pi.math.cornell.edu/~mec/2003-2004/cryptography/subs/frequencies.html

Dumas, A. (1844). Count of Monte Cristo. http://gutenberg.org/files/1184/1184-0.txt

ECC formulae. https://www.cs.purdue.edu/homes/ssw/cs655/ec.pdf

Elliptic Curve point addition (Fp). https://andrea.corbellini.name/ecc/interactive/modk-add.html

Elliptic Curve scalar multiplication ($_p$). https://andrea.corbellini.name/ecc/interactive/modk-mul.html

Gubser, M. (2016). Asymmetric cryptography—Elliptic curve cryptography. https://www.noser.com/techblog/asymmetric-cryptography-elliptic-curve-cryptography/

Lepcha, M. (2023). What is SHA-256? https://www.techopedia.com/definition/sha-256

Mnemonic word list. https://raw.githubusercontent.com/bitcoin/bips/master/bip-0039/english.txt

OpenSSL. https://www.openssl.org/, R package, Toolkit for Encryption, Signatures and Certificates Based on OpenSSL, https://archive.linux.duke.edu/cran/web/packages/openssl/openssl.pdf

Prime Numbers—Definition, Chart, Prime Numbers 1 to 1000, Examples, https://byjus.com/maths/prime-numbers/

Prime Number Lists. https://www.mathsisfun.com/numbers/prime-number-lists.html

QR code generator. https://www.qr-code-generator.com/

https://library.fiveable.me/key-terms/algebraic-geometry/elliptic-curve-discrete-logarithm-problem

RapidTables, Decimal to Hexadecimal converter. https://www.rapidtables.com/convert/number/decimal-to-hex.html

Cryptocurrency and Ganache 7

First, we discuss some basic concepts, such as what cryptocurrencies are, the benefits of using a cryptocurrency, what types of cryptocurrencies exist, and the potential risks. Hands-on experience is critical when studying cryptocurrency. Based on this, we will explain Ganache. We can find the server on this simulation platform, use a mnemonic phrase, 10 account addresses, and their balances, conduct transactions in terms of WEI (smallest unit of ETH, unit for Ethereum), and look for the transaction records and blocks. In this chapter, the following topics will be covered:

- Introduction to cryptocurrencies and their types
- Stablecoin, Bitcoin, Ethereum, Tether and Ripple
- What is Ganache
- Exploring Ganache: server address, Mnemonic, public and private keys, accounting balances
- Is my computer connected to the Ganache?
- Checking account addresses and account balances
- Unit conversion
- Conducting transactions and checking the results.

Supplementary Information The online version contains supplementary material available at https://doi.org/10.1007/978-3-031-89779-5_7.

Y. Yan, *Introduction to FinTech using Excel*, Springer Texts in Business and Economics, https://doi.org/10.1007/978-3-031-89779-5_7

7.1 Cryptocurrencies

Cryptocurrency is a decentralized digital currency that investors can buy and sell on the blockchain. Unlike physical cash, such as banknotes or coins, cryptocurrencies exist digitally and can be accessed using computers and other electronic devices. No government or financial institution issues a decentralized currency. Instead of being controlled by a single entity, a cryptocurrency's blockchain operates through a decentralized network of computers worldwide. Individuals with advanced technical and coding skills can create their cryptocurrency. The absence of a central authority can enhance cryptocurrency security. David Donovan, executive vice president at Publicis Sapient, explains, "It's hack-proof because there isn't a single point of failure."

7.2 How Does Cryptocurrency Work?

Cryptocurrencies operate on blockchain technology, a decentralized ledger that records all transactions across a network of computers. Each transaction is grouped into blocks and added to a chain in a linear, chronological order. This process ensures that the transaction history is transparent and secure. The decentralized nature of the blockchain means that no single entity controls the entire network, reducing the risk of fraud and manipulation.

At the heart of cryptocurrencies are cryptographic algorithms that secure transactions and control the creation of new units. These algorithms use complex mathematical problems that network participants solve, often called miners, who validate transactions and add them to the blockchain. This process, known as mining, ensures the ledger's integrity and maintains the cryptocurrency's decentralized nature.

7.3 Benefits of Cryptocurrency

One of cryptocurrency's primary benefits is its ability to facilitate fast, low-cost transactions, especially across international borders. Traditional financial systems often involve intermediaries, which can slow down the process and increase transaction fees. Cryptocurrencies eliminate the need for these intermediaries, allowing for more efficient and cost-effective transfers of value.

Additionally, cryptocurrencies offer enhanced privacy and security. Transactions made with cryptocurrencies do not require personal information, which can help protect users from identity theft. Cryptographic techniques ensure that transactions are secure and digital assets are less susceptible to hacking than traditional financial systems.

7.4 Risks/Challenges of Cryptocurrency

Despite their advantages, cryptocurrencies also come with various risks and challenges. One significant concern is the volatility of cryptocurrency prices. Unlike traditional currencies that are relatively stable, cryptocurrencies can experience dramatic fluctuations in value within short periods. This volatility makes them a risky investment option and can deter their use as a reliable medium of exchange.

Regulatory uncertainty is another challenge facing cryptocurrencies. Different countries have varying regulations, ranging from acceptance and integration into the financial system to outright bans. The lack of a standardized regulatory framework can create confusion and pose legal risks for users and businesses dealing with cryptocurrencies. Furthermore, the anonymity associated with cryptocurrency transactions has raised concerns about their potential use in illegal activities, such as money laundering and terrorism financing.

7.5 Digital Wallets

Individuals need a digital wallet, a software application that stores private and public keys to use cryptocurrencies. These keys are essential for sending and receiving cryptocurrencies, as they authenticate ownership and authorize transactions. Different types of wallets exist, including hardware, software, and online wallets, each offering varying levels of security and convenience.

Hardware wallets are physical devices that store private keys offline, making them highly secure against hacking attempts. Software wallets, which can be installed on a computer or smartphone, offer more convenience but may be vulnerable to malware attacks. Online wallets are hosted on the cloud and are accessible from any internet-connected device, providing ease of access but posing a higher risk of security breaches.

7.6 DeFi and the Future of Cryptocurrency

Decentralized Finance, or DeFi, is an emerging sector within the cryptocurrency space that aims to recreate traditional financial services using decentralized blockchain technology. DeFi platforms offer a range of services, including lending, borrowing, and trading, without the need for intermediaries like banks. Using smart contracts, DeFi eliminates the need for trust and gives users more control over their financial assets.

The future of cryptocurrency is closely tied to the development of DeFi and other innovative applications of blockchain technology. As more people adopt cryptocurrencies and explore their potential, we may see a shift in how financial services are provided and accessed. However, the growth of DeFi also brings challenges, such as the need for robust security measures and regulatory frameworks to protect users and ensure the financial system's stability.

7.7 Types of Cryptocurrencies

Cryptocurrencies come in various forms, each serving different purposes and offering unique features. The most well-known type is Bitcoin, the first cryptocurrency created as a decentralized digital currency to function as an alternative to traditional fiat currencies. Bitcoin operates on a peer-to-peer network and uses a proof-of-work consensus mechanism to validate transactions and secure the network. Its primary appeal lies in its decentralized nature, limited supply, and potential to serve as a store of value or "digital gold."

Beyond Bitcoin, there are altcoins, which refer to any cryptocurrency other than Bitcoin. Altcoins include many digital currencies, such as Ethereum, Ripple (XRP), Litecoin, etc. Ethereum is notable for introducing the concept of smart contracts, which are self-executing contracts with the terms of the agreement directly written into code. This innovation has enabled the development of decentralized applications (dApps) and opened the door to various new use cases beyond simple transactions. Other altcoins, like Ripple, focus on providing fast, low-cost, cross-border payment solutions, highlighting the diverse applications of different cryptocurrencies.

7.8 What Is a Stablecoin?

Stablecoins are a type of cryptocurrency designed to minimize price volatility by pegging their value to a stable asset, such as a fiat currency like the U.S. dollar or commodities like gold. This pegging mechanism helps maintain a stable value, making stablecoins an attractive option for those who seek the benefits of digital currencies without the extreme price fluctuations typically associated with other cryptocurrencies. Examples of popular stablecoins include Tether (USDT), USD Coin (USDC), and Dai (DAI), each of which is pegged to the U.S. dollar at a 1:1 ratio.

Stablecoins play a crucial role in the cryptocurrency ecosystem by providing a stable medium of exchange, a unit of account, and a store of value. They are commonly used on cryptocurrency exchanges to facilitate trading, as they allow traders to move quickly in and out of positions without the need to convert to fiat currency. Moreover, stablecoins are increasingly being utilized in the emerging field of decentralized finance (DeFi) for lending, borrowing, and yield farming, offering users a stable and efficient means of participating in the crypto economy.

7.9 Bitcoin

Bitcoin, created by an anonymous person or group known as Satoshi Nakamoto, was the first cryptocurrency introduced in 2008. It is a decentralized digital currency that allows peer-to-peer transactions over the Internet without needing a central authority or intermediary like a bank. Bitcoin operates on a blockchain, a distributed ledger that records all transactions across a network of computers, ensuring transparency and security. Its limited supply of 21 million coins makes Bitcoin a deflationary asset, often compared to digital gold. Bitcoin's primary use case is as a store of value and medium of exchange, and it has gained widespread recognition as a hedge against inflation and traditional financial market uncertainties.

7.10 Ethereum

Ethereum, launched in 2015 by Vitalik Buterin and a team of co-founders, is more than just a cryptocurrency; it's a decentralized platform that enables developers to build and deploy smart contracts and decentralized applications (dApps). Unlike Bitcoin, which primarily focuses on being a digital currency, Ethereum's blockchain is programmable, meaning developers can create applications that run on the blockchain, executing automatically without intermediaries. The native cryptocurrency of the Ethereum platform is Ether (ETH), which is used to power transactions and computational services on the network. Ethereum's flexibility and innovation have made it a foundational technology for decentralized finance (DeFi), non-fungible tokens (NFTs), and other blockchain-based solutions.

The concept of smart contracts is difficult to explain, and related implementations are associated with a new programming language called Solidity. We postponed the related discussion quite late in the course (book) in Chapter 15: Smart Contracts using Ethereum.

7.11 Tether

Tether (USDT) is a type of cryptocurrency known as a stablecoin, designed to maintain a stable value by being pegged to a fiat currency, typically the US dollar. Each Tether token represents one US dollar, providing a digital alternative to traditional currencies. Tether was introduced to offer the stability of fiat currencies while retaining the benefits of cryptocurrencies, such as fast transactions and blockchain transparency. This stability makes Tether a popular choice for traders and investors who want to avoid the volatility often associated with other cryptocurrencies like Bitcoin or Ethereum.

The value of Tether is supported by reserves that include traditional currency, cash equivalents, and other assets. Tether Limited, the company behind USDT, claims that each Tether token is backed by reserves held in its accounts, although this has been a subject of scrutiny and controversy. Despite these concerns, Tether remains one of the most widely used stablecoins in the market. It plays a significant role in cryptocurrency exchanges by providing a stable medium of exchange and acting as a bridge between traditional and digital currencies.

7.12 Ripple

Ripple is a real-time gross settlement system, currency exchange, and remittance network developed by Ripple Labs Inc., a U.S.-based technology company. Unlike many other cryptocurrencies, Ripple is designed to facilitate international payments and cross-border transfers between financial institutions. It achieves this by using a consensus ledger and its native cryptocurrency, XRP, to streamline transactions, making them faster and more cost-effective. Ripple's main appeal is its ability to process payments in seconds, unlike traditional banking systems, which can take days.

XRP, Ripple's cryptocurrency, serves as a bridge currency for financial institutions, allowing them to transfer money across borders without relying on traditional foreign exchange markets. Ripple's network uses a unique consensus protocol rather than the proof-of-work system standard in cryptocurrencies like Bitcoin. This allows transactions to be validated quickly and with minimal energy consumption. Ripple has partnered with many banks and payment providers, making it one of the most widely adopted digital assets and blockchain technology platforms.

7.13 Sources of Information

CoinMarketCap (https://coinmarketcap.com) is one of the most widely used websites for cryptocurrency market data. It provides real-time data on thousands of cryptocurrencies, including their market capitalization, price, trading volume, and circulating supply. Users can view detailed information about each cryptocurrency, including charts and historical prices.

CoinGecko (https://www.coingecko.com) is another popular platform that offers comprehensive data on cryptocurrencies. It provides market capitalization, price, volume, and other critical metrics for various digital assets. CoinGecko also includes features like developer activity, community engagement, and more.

CryptoCompare (https://www.cryptocompare.com) offers various cryptocurrency data, including market capitalization, price data, and trading volumes. It also provides tools for comparing cryptocurrencies and tracking portfolio performance and offers detailed reviews of exchanges and wallets.

7.14 What Is Ganache?

Ganache is a popular cryptocurrency and blockchain development tool for Ethereum-based projects. It acts as a personal blockchain, enabling developers to create, test, and deploy smart contracts in a controlled environment. By simulating the behavior of the Ethereum network, Ganache allows developers to manage accounts, inspect blockchain data, and mine blocks without the need to connect to the leading Ethereum network. This helps streamline the development process, making identifying and fixing issues easier before deploying to a live environment.

One of Ganache's key features is its ability to provide instant feedback on transactions and contract interactions, essential for efficient debugging. Developers can use Ganache to experiment with different scenarios, perform stress testing, and ensure their smart contracts behave as expected. Ganache simplifies the complex tasks associated with blockchain development by offering a user-friendly interface and detailed logs, making it an invaluable tool for beginners and experienced cryptocurrency developers.

For this book/course, we use Ganache to illustrate some basic concepts, such as server (for connection), mnemonic, public and private keys, account addresses, account balance (in ETH), conducting a fake transaction, checking transaction Hash, Block, and others.

7.15 Ganache Installation

You can download and install this excellent software at https://www.trufflesuite.com/ganache. After launching it, the following image will appear.

Fig. 7.1 The Ganache platform

For this course, click "QUICKSTART" and see the following image.

Fig. 7.2 The top part of the Ganache platform

To save space, only two accounts are shown above. After launching Ganache, you are presented with several key features essential for blockchain development and testing. The following Table 7.1 summarizes those features.

These features make Ganache an indispensable tool for developers working with Ethereum-based projects, providing a safe and controlled environment to experiment and build blockchain applications. In this case, the PRC server is HTTP://127.0.0.1:7545, and the MNEMONIC Phrase is: `file tip cabbage evolve clutch hold foam tourist come wedding fog rough`. After clicking the first key image, we will have the following picture.

Table 7.1 Most essential features of the Ganache platform

Feature	Explanation
Mnemonic Phrase	Ganache provides a mnemonic phrase, a sequence of 12 or 24 words used to generate multiple private keys and addresses deterministically. This feature is handy for recovering accounts or creating multiple accounts that are easy to manage. The mnemonic ensures that even if you lose access to your private keys, you can regenerate them using the same mnemonic
Accounts	Ganache automatically generates a list of accounts, each with its address and private key. These accounts are pre-funded with a set amount of Ether (ETH) to facilitate testing transactions without requiring real ETH. Each account is associated with a private key, which is crucial for signing transactions and proving ownership of the account's assets
Private Keys	Each account in Ganache has a corresponding private key. The private key is critical in cryptocurrency transactions, allowing users to sign transactions and access their funds. In Ganache, these private keys are easily accessible, making it simple for developers to simulate transactions and interactions with the blockchain
RPC Server	Ganache runs a local RPC (Remote Procedure Call) server that simulates the Ethereum blockchain. This server allows you to interact with your local blockchain using standard web3 libraries and tools, making it possible to deploy smart contracts, send transactions, and query blockchain data as you would on a real Ethereum network. This feature is essential for testing and debugging before deploying on a live network

Fig. 7.3 A private key

Corresponding to the Account address of 0 × `3038b0000CC118A5D06dA9488a284a3788cc93DE`, its private key is `6f1fef45d85a722766ed6d1f81394be26a6bbfa36dd4953c5033a1143a975011`.

For different accounts, there are other private keys. It is worth noting that the account address is not the public key but is derived from it. The relationship between an Ethereum account address, public key, and private key can be explained as follows:

1. Private Key: This is a randomly generated 256-bit number, which is kept secret. It is used to sign transactions and prove ownership of the funds in your account.
2. Public Key: The public key is mathematically derived from the private key using Elliptic Curve Cryptography (specifically, the secp256k1 curve). It is then used to generate the account address.
3. Account Address: The Ethereum account address is derived from the public key by taking the last 20 bytes (40 hexadecimal characters) of the Keccak-256 hash of the public key. This address is used to identify an account on the Ethereum network.

In the example, the private key 6f1fef45d85a722766ed6d1f81394be26a6bbfa36dd4953c5033a1143a975011 would be used to generate a public key, which is then hashed to create the account address 0 × 3038b0000CC118A5D06dA9488a284a3788cc93DE.

7.16 Search Hidden Functions

We have generated a few functions to help our readers/students understand those concepts better and simplify operations. To find their names and usages, we use a function called `.searchHiddenFunctions()` with an input of 7.

```
> .searchHiddenFunctions(7)
 CHAPTER                          NAME                 SHORTCUT
       7  install Ganache
       7  install.packages('httr')
       7  install.packagess('jsonlite')
       7  install.packages('gmp')
       7 .isConnected2ganache           .is  # need 3 packages
       7 .accountAddresses              .ad  # need 3 packages
       7 .accountBalances               .ab  # need 3 packages
       7 .transferWEI                   .tw  # need 3 packages
       7 .latestTransaction             .lt  # need 3 packages
       7 .latestBlock                   .lb  # need 3 packages
>
```

Fig. 7.4 The hidden functions related to Chapter 7

In the following few sections, we will explain the usage of those hidden functions.

7.17 Packages Needed

The above-mentioned hidden functions related to Ganache need a few R packages. The function to install R packages is `install.packages()`. You can copy and paste the following three lines to your R console.

```
install.packages("httr")
install.packages("jsonlite")
install.packages("gmp")
```

For this course, you need to install each package just once.

7.18 Is My Computer Connected to Ganache?

First, we should check whether our computer (or R functions) is connected to the Ganache platform. The function's name is `.isConnectedGanache()`, and its shortcut is `.connected()`.

```
> .connected()

 Is your R connected with the Ganache?
  [1] "no"
  Check whether you have launched Ganache yet.
> |
```

Fig. 7.5 Checking whether functions connected with Ganache (.connected)

Now, after launching Ganache, we recheck it, as shown below.

```
> .connected()

 Is your R connected with the Ganache?
  [1] "yes"
>
>
```

Fig. 7.6 The result when connected

7.19 Account Addresses

The second hidden function can be used to check the account's addresses, as shown below.

```
> .accountAddresses()
     Account                                    Address
1   account1 0x3330d8e920fc9bc1220fc81f31923a52900ea6b1
2   account2 0x387eb2f8c3cf9b4d6713329d5970a00d522ff5fc
3   account3 0x4ddd213ab4c165172e0042c2c479f04c310c3c7c
4   account4 0x0162a86c95256325814e070d6e576ac62f09fb68
5   account5 0x71e9b7fa9828543bbf22546c5f8abfcd6e5c295f
6   account6 0x5c9e781f741a6f0d01069852a883045e3ef9f0df
7   account7 0xf4fac6289fffd0f35f1821eca32376d89d609c7c
8   account8 0x8d244f29e700ee5781c457ba49b79e9102a0dfed
9   account9 0xc1e5e071b9d80a3d4e4849e00e361ab740bfb552
10 account10 0xb8bf0d8106733ea1f9922a674f4f35eeb9655100
>
```

Fig. 7.7 Checking account addresses

Note that you will get ten entirely different account addresses.

Table 7.2 Unit conversion

Unit Name	Wei Value	Number of Wei	Power
Wei (wei)	1 wei	1	1
Kwei (babbage)	1e3 wei	1,000	3
Mwei (lovelace)	1e6 wei	1,000,000	6
Gwei (shannon)	1e9 wei	1,000,000,000	9
Twei (szabo)	1e12 wei	1,000,000,000,000	12
Pwei (finney)	1e15 wei	1,000,000,000,000,000	15
Ether (buterin)	1e18 wei	1,000,000,000,000,000,000	18

7.20 Checking Account Balances

The function related to checking account balances is `.accountBalances()`. Since we haven't conducted any transactions, the initial balances for all the accounts are 100 ETH.

```
> .accountBalances()
Initial balances:
0x3330d8e920fc9bc1220fc81f31923a52900ea6b1 : 100 ETH
0x387eb2f8c3cf9b4d6713329d5970a00d522ff5fc : 100 ETH
0x4ddd213ab4c165172e0042c2c479f04c310c3c7c : 100 ETH
0x0162a86c95256325814e070d6e576ac62f09fb68 : 100 ETH
0x71e9b7fa9828543bbf22546c5f8abfcd6e5c295f : 100 ETH
0x5c9e781f741a6f0d01069852a883045e3ef9f0df : 100 ETH
0xf4fac6289fffd0f35f1821eca32376d89d609c7c : 100 ETH
0x8d244f29e700ee5781c457ba49b79e9102a0dfed : 100 ETH
0xc1e5e071b9d80a3d4e4849e00e361ab740bfb552 : 100 ETH
0xb8bf0d8106733ea1f9922a674f4f35eeb9655100 : 100 ETH
>
```

Fig. 7.8 Checking account balances

7.21 Unit Conversion

After launching the Ganache platform, the unit reported ETH. However, we usually transfer WEI, the smallest unit of Ethereum cryptocurrency. Their relationships are shown in the following Table 7.2.

The bottom line is that 1ETH is equivalent to 10^18 Wei.

7.22 Transferring Money in WEI

The function used to transfer cryptocurrency in WEI is called. `transerWEI()`. By typing its name, we can find its related usage.

```
> .transferWEI
function(){
"Objective: transfer cryptocurrency in WEI between accounts
     (assume Ganache is available)

Example 1:> .transferWEI()
     Step 1: enter 1, 2, ..., or 10 (for a sender)
     Step 2: enter 1, 2, ..., or 10 (for a receiver)
     Step 3: amount in WEI
Example 2:> .tw() # short-cut
```

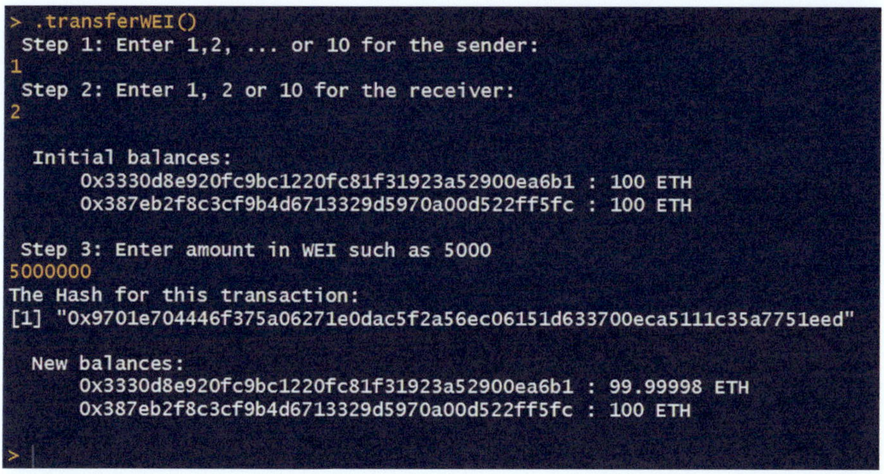

Fig. 7.9 An illustration of one transaction

From the above explanation, we must enter three inputs: the sender's number, the receiver's number, and the amount (in terms of WEI). Below is one transaction.

From the above result, we transfer money from Account #1 to Account #2 in the amount of 5,000,000, i.e., 5 million WEIs. The output includes the Hash of this transaction and it is 0 × `9701e704446f375a06271e0dac5f2a56ec06151d633700eca5111c35a7751eed`.

We can check its length, which is shown below.

```
> a="0x9701e704446f375a06271e0dac5f2a56ec06151d633700eca5111c35
a7751eed"
> nchar(a)
[1] 66
```

Go to Ganache and manually check the transaction by clicking on TRANSACTIONS on the menu bar, as shown below.

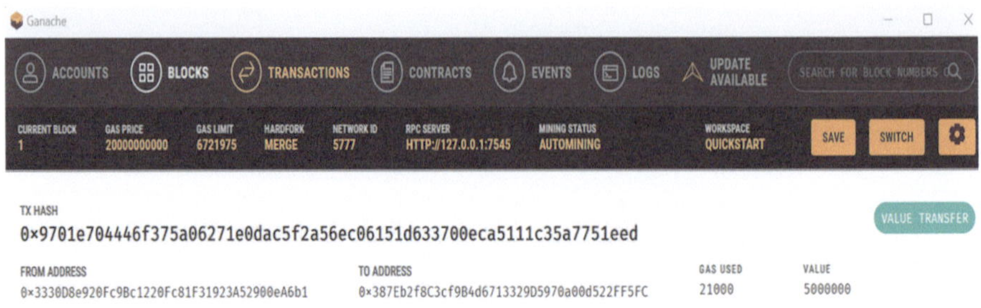

Fig. 7.10 The transaction record from Ganache

The `TX_HASH` is the transaction hash, also known as the transaction ID (TXID) for this transaction. The above image shows 21,000WEI, the GAS USED, and Gas can be viewed as a transaction cost. The value transferred is 5,000,000 (in terms of WEI).

7.23 Checking the Transaction

Alternatively, readers can use our function called `.latestTransaction ()` to get the same information discussed in the previous section, as shown below.

Fig. 7.11 The latest transaction (the.latestTransaction function)

7.24 Block Information

We will have the following image after clicking "BLOCKS" on the menu bar.

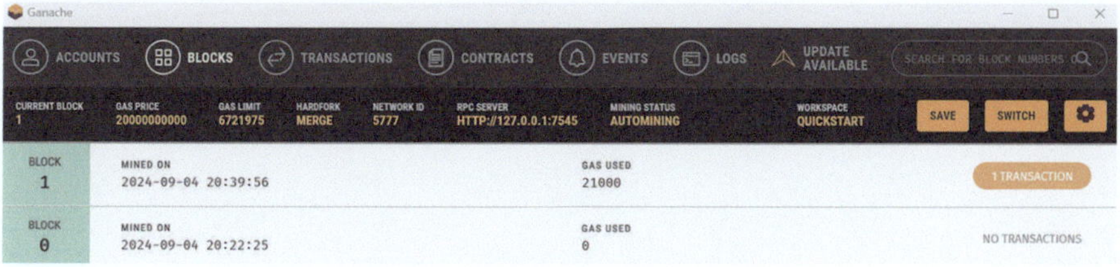

Fig. 7.12 Information from Blocks on the menu bar

We will have the following information by clicking BOX 1 on the left-hand side.

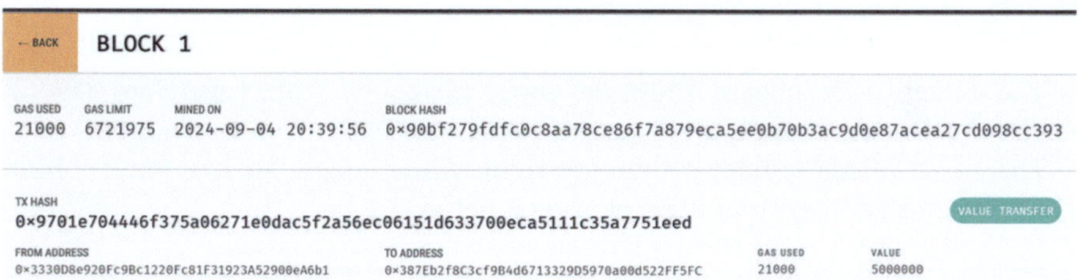

Fig. 7.13 The contents of Block 1

In addition to the information we know already, we have a time stamp: `MINDED ON 2024-09-9 20:39:56, and block hash: 0×90bf279fdfc0c8aa78ce86f7a879eca5ee0b70b3ac9d0e87acea27cd098cc393.`

Since Ganache is used as a simulated platform, the Hashes for both transaction and block are not real. How about in the real world? The following section shows how to use those Hashes to get more information in a real-world situation.

7.25 Searching for Info for a Given Tx_Hash

One website is called Bitcoin Explorer, and the link is at https://blockstream.info/. The following image shows the top part of the website.

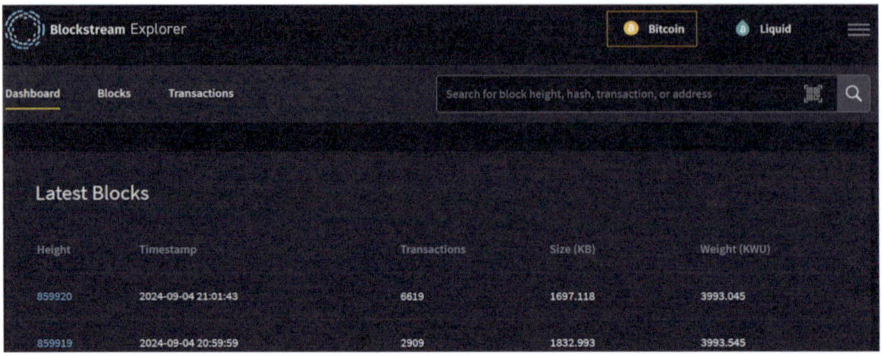

Fig. 7.14 Searching for information (the Blockstream Explorer)

The default is Dashboard. From the above image, we realize there are 859,920 blocks (for Bitcoin) with a time stamp of 2024–09-24 21:02:43.

There is a search window at the top right of the image. We can enter a hash, transaction, or address from here, as shown below.

Fig. 7.15 Searching for block height, hash, transaction, or address

Let's choose Block 859,916. When entering 859,916, we will see the following result (top part only).

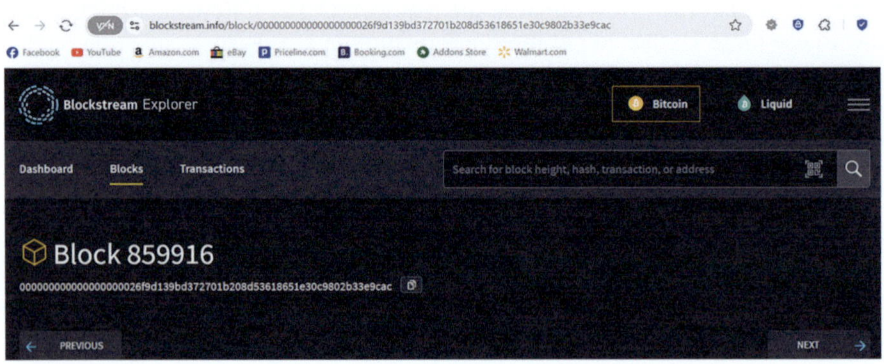

Fig. 7.16 The illustration of Block 859,916

After clicking "PREVIOUS", we will go to Block 859,915, as shown below.

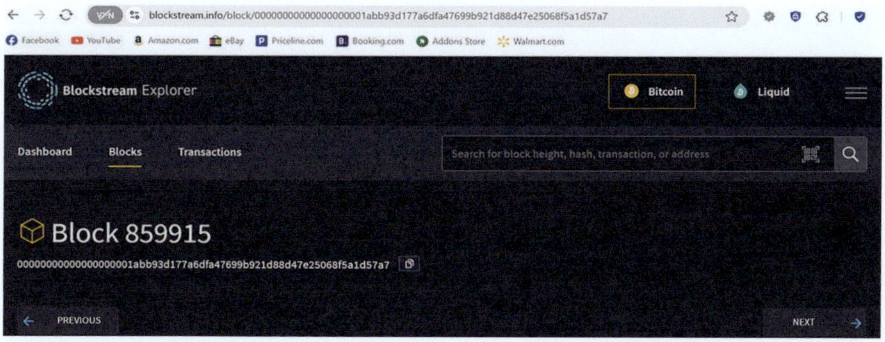

Fig. 7.17 Previous block: Block 859,915

Let's go back to Block 859,916. The following information will be below, under "Previous" and "Next."

Fig. 7.18 Back to Block 859,916

After clicking "DETAIL + ", we will get complete details, as shown below.

Fig. 7.19 The detailed information about this block

If we scroll down the webpage further, we will see specific information related to individual transactions. From the first line shown below, we know that this block contains 7536 transactions, 25 of which are shown below.

Fig. 7.20 Showing 25 out of 7,536 transactions

7.26 Looking into Individual Transactions

From the last image shown in the previous section, the hash of the first transaction is ada46e87ee86f6c251891615a1a13e0ab02beea790f378d0a8647b68960e07a8. After clicking the link, we will get the following result:

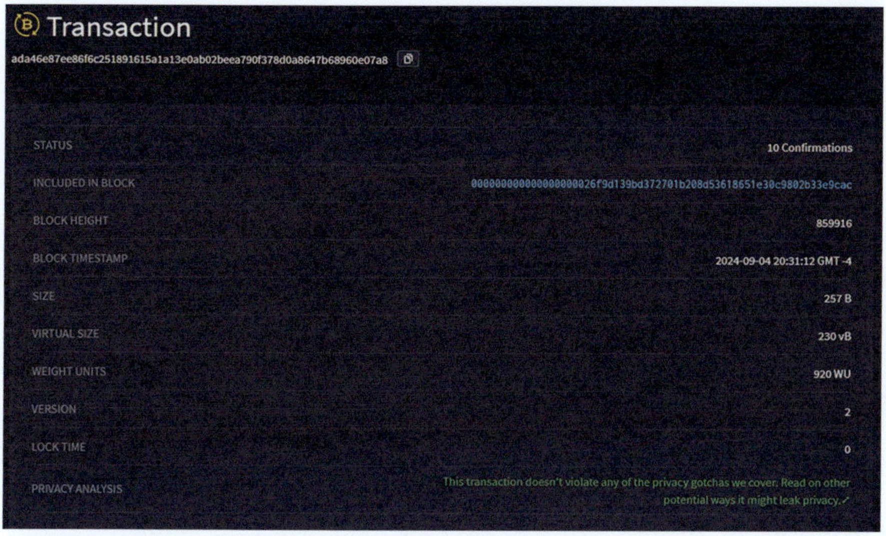

Fig. 7.21 The information about one transaction

Alternatively, we can paste the transaction hash in the search box to get the same webpage, as shown below.

Fig. 7.22 The Hash of this transaction

Appendix A: Issue the Following Line of R Code for Week 7

```
source("http://datayyy.com/i2ft/week7.txt")
```

```
*------------------------------------------------------------------------*
* Introduction to FinTech using Excel                   by Dr. Yan 2025    *
*       (in an R-assisted learning environment)                          *
*------------------------------------------------------------------------*
*  .c1 Introduction & Excel Basics              .c16 R basics(optional) *
*  .c2 Blockchain  1: Numbers/alphanumeric cases .c17 Macro (optional)   *
*  .c3             2: ASCII and Sha256)          .c18 VBA  (optional)    *
*  .c4 Ledger and distributed ledger                                     *
*  .c5  Cryptography   1: and public/private keys                        *
*  .c6                 2: Advanced                                       *
* -----------------------------------------------------------------------*
* >.c6       # go to chapter  6                                          *
* >.uu       # go to utility submenu                                     *
* >.ft       # back to this menu                                         *
*------------------------------------------------------------------------*
```

Fig. 7.23 The menu for Week 7

Appendix B: Typing `.chapter7` or `.c7`, We Will Have the Following Contents Related to Chapter 7

```
> .c7
function(i=0){
"i  Chapter 7: Cryptocurrency          i   Ganache
 -  ------------------------------    --  -----------------------
 1  Introduction                      21  Ganache: what is it?
 2  What is cryptocurrency?           22      : install Ganache
 3  How do cryptocurrencies work?     23      : launch Ganache
 4  Blockchain technology             24      : explore Ganache
 5  Public transactions/pseudonymous  25      : units: ETH, WEI
 6  Consensus: proof of work          26      : mnemonic
 7             : proof of stake       27      : mnemonic to a private key
 8  Types                             28      : account address/public key
 9  What is digital currency?         29      : private keys
10  How to invest                     30 Link Ganache and R: a note
11  Should you invest?                31c     : 3 packages preinstalled?
12  What is a crypto wallet?          32c     : is connected
13  Abstract from the founder         33c     : show accounts
14  blockchain.com                    34c     : show balances
15  Ethereum Blockchain Explorer      35c     : transfer WEI
16  eth converter                     36      : check the BLOCKS
17  the first block                   37      : check the TRANSACTIONS
18  one block was mined on 9/30/2022  38c     : check the latest block
19  Videos                            39c     : check the latest transaction
20  Links                             40  cryptobubbles

Example #1:>.c7    # see the above list
Example #2:>.c7()  # the same as above
Example #3:>.c7(1) # see the 1st explanation
```

Fig. 7.24 The contents of Chapter 7

Exercises

Note that * indicates difficult ones.

7.1 What is cryptocurrency, and how does it differ from traditional forms of currency?
7.2 Discuss the key characteristics that distinguish cryptocurrencies from fiat money.
7.3 Explain the role of blockchain technology in the functioning of cryptocurrencies.
7.4 How does blockchain ensure the security and integrity of transactions?
7.5 What are the main types of cryptocurrencies, and what unique features do they offer?
7.6 Provide examples of different cryptocurrencies and their primary use cases.
7.7 Describe the concept of decentralization in the context of cryptocurrencies. Why is it important?
7.8 What is a cryptocurrency wallet, and what are the different types of wallets available?
7.9 How does decentralization benefit the cryptocurrency ecosystem?
7.10 Discuss the advantages and disadvantages of hardware, software, and online wallets.
7.11 What are stablecoins, and how do they maintain a stable value compared to other cryptocurrencies?
7.12 Explain the mechanisms used to peg stablecoins to stable assets.
7.13 Identify the benefits and risks associated with investing in cryptocurrencies.
7.14 What should investors consider before investing in cryptocurrencies?
7.15 What is mining in the context of cryptocurrencies, and why is it an essential process?
7.16 Describe the mining and its role in validating transactions and securing the network.
7.17 How do smart contracts work, and what do they play in the cryptocurrency ecosystem?
7.18 Discuss the potential impact of cryptocurrency on traditional financial systems.
7.19 How might the widespread adoption of cryptocurrencies change banking and finance?
7.20 What is Ganache, and why is it beneficial for blockchain development?
7.21 Explain how Ganache helps developers in testing and deploying smart contracts.
7.22 How does Ganache simulate a blockchain network, and what are its key features?
7.23 Discuss the tools and capabilities that Ganache offers to developers.
7.24 Describe the process of setting up a personal blockchain using Ganache. What steps are involved in creating and configuring a local blockchain environment?

7.25 What are the benefits of using Ganache to test smart contracts before deploying them to the leading Ethereum network? How does Ganache help identify and resolve potential issues in smart contracts?
7.26 Explain using Ganache to interact with smart contracts and manage accounts. What are the typical use cases for using Ganache in a development workflow?
7.27 What is the importance of mining blocks in Ganache, and how does it differ from mining on the leading Ethereum network? Discuss how block mining is simulated in Ganache and its impact on testing.
7.28 How can Ganache be integrated with other development tools like Truffle or Remix? Provide an overview of how Ganache works with these tools to streamline the development process.
7.29 Developers face some common challenges when using Ganache, and how can they be addressed? Identify potential pitfalls and solutions when working with Ganache.
7.30 Discuss the future potential of tools like Ganache in the evolving blockchain and cryptocurrency development landscape. How might tools like Ganache adapt to new technologies and use cases?

References

Crypto Bubbles. https://cryptobubbles.net/
Crypto market cap. https://coinmarketcap.com/
Erskine, K. (2018). *Data exploration and visualization of the tetherbBlockchain*. https://rpubs.com/keith_erskine/381106
Ganache. https://archive.trufflesuite.com/docs/ganache/
Ganache documents. https://archive.trufflesuite.com/docs/
Crypto Glossary: HODL, Bear, Bullish, and more (msn.com).

Crypto Markets, Risk, Risk-Return Tradeoff

8

Cryptocurrencies have many benefits, including no central authority, speedy transactions, decentralized blockchain, anonymity, and convenience. On the other hand, many risks are involved, such as higher volatility than traditional investments such as stocks and bonds, much higher hacking possibility, and regulatory uncertainty. In this chapter, the following topics will be covered:

- Introduction
- Definition of risks
- Hedging, speculation, and arbitrages
- Total risk (standard deviation of returns), market risk
- How to use Excel to calculate total risk and annualize it
- Tradeoff measures: Sharpe, Treynor, and Sortino ratios
- Market manipulations
- VaR (Value at Risk) for cryptocurrencies
- Unquantifiable risks such as regulatory risk, lawsuit, fraud, and traditional hacking and theft

---

Supplementary Information The online version contains supplementary material available at https://doi.org/10.1007/978-3-031-89779-5_8.

Y. Yan, *Introduction to FinTech using Excel*, Springer Texts in Business and Economics, https://doi.org/10.1007/978-3-031-89779-5_8

8.1 Introduction

Griffin and Amin Shams (2020) study the role of the largest stablecoin, Tether, on Bitcoin and other cryptocurrency prices. They find that purchases with Tether are timed following market downturns and result in sizable increases in Bitcoin prices. The following image shows the flow between various crypto exchanges (Fig. 1: Aggregate flow of Tether between primary addresses).

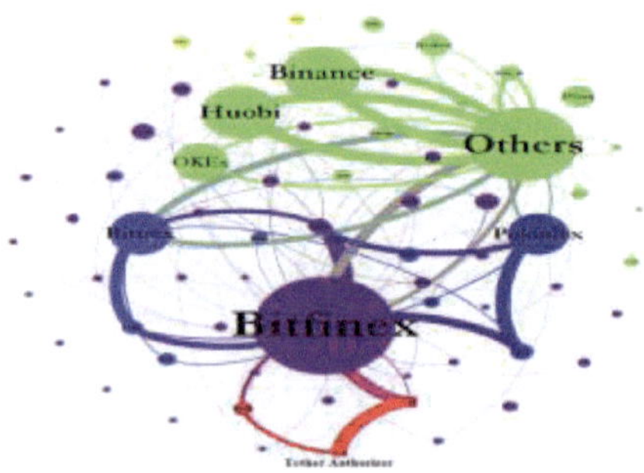

Fig. 8.1 Aggregate flow of Tether between several primary addresses

The thickness of the edges is proportional to the magnitude of the flow between two nodes, and the node size is proportional to aggregate inflow and outflow for each node. Internode flows are excluded. They supply code to replicate their result. Unfortunately, the code is written in Python. Morini (2017) argues that blockchain derivatives are easier to manage and carry less default risk than their traditional equivalent since the consensus settlement of the underlying blockchain and smart contract automation. For the discussion related to Smart Contracts, see Chapter14: Smart Contracts. Liu and Tsyvinski (2021) show that cryptocurrency returns are driven and can be predicted by certain factors, such as momentum and investor attention. Osterrieder (2016) shows that Bitcoin returns do not follow a normal distribution.

8.2 Crypto Market: Overview and Dynamics

At https://cryptobubbles.net/, we can find the returns over one year (2/9/2025). Almost all cryptocurrencies have enjoyed tremendous gains over one year. Some even have over 6,000%!

Fig. 8.2 An image of Crypto bubbles

Crypto markets are decentralized digital marketplaces where cryptocurrencies such as Bitcoin, Ethereum, and thousands of alternative tokens are traded. Unlike traditional financial markets, crypto markets operate 24/7, enabling continuous trading across global exchanges. These markets are facilitated by blockchain technology, which ensures transparent and secure transactions without intermediaries like banks. The crypto ecosystem includes spot trading, derivatives like futures and options, decentralized finance (DeFi) platforms, and non-fungible tokens (NFTs), creating a diverse and dynamic financial landscape.

One unique characteristic of crypto markets is their high volatility. Prices can experience significant swings within hours or even minutes due to factors like regulatory announcements, technological developments, macroeconomic shifts, or speculative behavior. This volatility presents risks and opportunities, attracting traders seeking high returns while deterring risk-averse investors. Liquidity also varies widely across cryptocurrencies, with major coins like Bitcoin and Ethereum enjoying robust liquidity. In contrast, lesser-known tokens may suffer from low trading volumes and high price manipulation risk.

The risk-return tradeoff is a fundamental principle in crypto markets. Higher potential returns often accompany higher risks, including price volatility, regulatory uncertainty, cybersecurity threats, and market manipulation. Crypto assets lack the historical data and stability of traditional investments, making risk assessment particularly challenging. Despite these challenges, the promise of outsized returns continues to attract investors, especially in a low-yield conventional investment environment.

Crypto markets also exhibit unique risks, such as technological vulnerabilities. Hacks, smart contract bugs, and wallet security breaches can result in significant financial losses. Conversely, early adopters of successful projects can see exponential gains. Investors employ strategies like portfolio diversification, technical analysis, and dollar-cost averaging to manage these risks. Understanding the relationship between risk and return is crucial for navigating the complexities of crypto markets, where opportunities and threats coexist.

8.3 A Graph of the Bitcoin Closing Price

At https://coincodex.com/crypto/bitcoin/historical-data/, readers can download historical monthly, daily, and weekly data sets for Bitcoin. The first several lines are shown below.

	A	B	C	D	E	F	G
1	Date	Open	High	Low	Close	Volume	MarketCap
2	7/17/2010	0.05	0.0858	0.05	0.0679	0	220535.68
3	8/1/2010	0.0611	0.071	0.057	0.06	0	239049.69
4	9/1/2010	0.0629	0.0637	0.059	0.0619	0	246746.63
5	10/1/2010	0.062	0.1989	0.0611	0.1925	0	460966.58

Fig. 8.3 The first several lines of Bitcoin data

The ending month is December 2024, as shown below. Note that many rows are hidden for easy illustration.

	A	B	C	D	E	F
1	Date	Price	Open	High	Low	Vol.
2	7/31/2010	0.1	0.1	0.1	0	221.74K
3	8/31/2010	0.1	0.1	0.2	0.1	216.81K
172	9/30/2024	70281.8	63329.9	73569.4	59075.7	2.56M
173	10/31/2024	96405.7	70278.7	99617.4	66834	4.16M
174	11/30/2024	93557.2	96404.7	108244.9	91522.3	4.41M

Fig. 8.4 The data with many hidden rows

We have the following graph with the Close price as the y-axis and the Date as the x-axis.

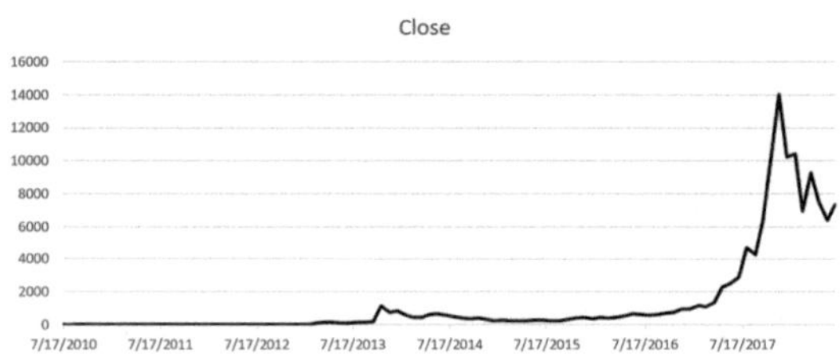

Fig. 8.5 The graphic presentation of Bitcoin price

The graph shows that Bitcoin's price has increased dramatically over 15 years. Later in the chapter, an alternative way to get monthly or daily data will be given.

8.4 Sources of Data

Many platforms provide comprehensive tools and datasets to analyze cryptocurrencies, whether we are studying historical trends, evaluating market sentiment, or tracking real-time prices and liquidity. To access those websites, readers can use our `.searchWebs ()` function, abbreviated as `.sw()`, by using a key phrase of "`crypto data`," as shown below.

```
> .sw("crypto data")
 ID       NAME                                         WEBSITE
 690 crypto data https://coinmarketcap.com
 691 crypto data https://www.coingecko.com
 692 crypto data https://glassnode.com
 693 crypto data https://www.cryptocompare.com
 694 crypto data https://messari.io
 695 crypto data https://santiment.net
 696 crypto data https://www.theblock.co
 697 crypto data https://www.kaiko.com
 698 crypto data https://cryptoquant.com
 699 crypto data https://www.tradingview.com
 700 crypto data https://nomics.com
 701 crypto data https://alternative.me/crypto/fearandgreedindex
>
```

Fig. 8.6 Searching for data sources related to crypto

By replacing the key phrase with an ID number, we can go directly to that website. The following table offers some simple explanations for those links (Table 8.1).

In addition, our hidden functions make retrieving some data sets quite efficient; see the related section at the end of this chapter.

8.5 Our Hidden Functions

Many of this chapter's hidden functions relate to retrieving data, so this section was discussed earlier instead of at the end of the chapter. To find out the hidden functions for this chapter, we use the `.searchHiddenFunctions ()` function with an input of 8, as shown below.

```
> .searchHiddenFunctions(8)
 CHAPTER                               NAME                         SHORTCUT
       8 install.packages('quantmod')
       8 --------------------------------
       8 .show_btcMonthly                 # BTC-USD Bitcoin
       8 .show_btcDaily                   # BTC-USD Bitcoin
       8 .show_xrpMonthly                 # XRP-USD
       8 .show_xrpcDaily                  # XRP-USD
       8 .show_coinDaily                  # coinbase
       8 .show_coinMonthly                # coinbase
       8 .show_usdtDaily                  # Tether (USDT)
       8 .show_usdtMonthly                # Techer (USDT)
       8 .anyStockDailyData               .anyd  # need 'quantmod'
       8 .anyStockMonthlyData             .anym  # need 'quantmod'
       8 .merge
       8 .show_ibmDaily
       8 .show_ibmMonthly
       8 .show_sp500daily
       8 .show_sp500monthly
       8 .show_ff3daily
       8 .show_ff3monthly
>
```

Fig. 8.7 The hidden functions related to Chapter 8

For example, the `.show_btcMonthly ()` function will offer the monthly historical data for Bitcoin, as shown below. The default value is $n = 2$, which means the first two lines will be displayed on our screen. A negative integer will ask the program to show the last n lines.

Table 8.1 Sources of data

Name	Website	Note
CoinMarketCap	https://coinmarketcap.com	Data on cryptocurrency prices, market capitalization, trading volumes, and historical data
CoinGecko	https://www.coingecko.com	Tracks cryptocurrency prices, market statistics, developer activity, and community metrics
Glassnode	https://glassnode.com	Offers on-chain data and metrics, including wallet activity, miner behavior, and market sentiment analysis
CryptoCompare	https://www.cryptocompare.com	Provides real-time and historical data on cryptocurrency prices, trading volumes, and exchange activity
Messari	https://messari.io	Offers research, news, and detailed analytics on blockchain projects and crypto markets
Sentiment	https://santiment.net	Focuses on on-chain and social sentiment data, offering insights into crowd psychology and market trends
The Block	https://www.theblock.co	Delivers in-depth research, news, and analytics on blockchain and crypto market trends
Kaiko	https://www.kaiko.com	Provides institutional-grade crypto market data, including trade data, order book snapshots, and historical price feeds
CryptoQuant	https://cryptoquant.com	Specializes in on-chain and exchange-related data, offering insights into market liquidity, miner flows, and stablecoin metrics
TradingView	https://www.tradingview.com	Offers advanced charting tools, crypto price data access, and trading platform integration

(continued)

Table 8.1 (continued)

Name	Website	Note
Nomics	https://nomics.com	Crypto market data, including prices, volumes, and historical performance across exchanges
Crypto Fear & Greed Index	https://alternative.me/crypto/fearandgreedindex	Measures market sentiment using factors like volatility, trading volume, and social media activity to gauge fear or greed levels

```
> .show_btcMonthly()
        Date    Open    High     Low   Close Adj.Close    Volume
1 2014-10-01 387.427 411.698 289.296 338.321   338.321 902994450
2 2014-11-01 338.650 457.093 320.626 378.047   378.047 659733360
> .show_btcMonthly(-2)
          Date     Open     High      Low    Close Adj.Close       Volume
119 2024-08-01 64625.84 65593.24 49121.24 58969.90  58969.90 1.043105e+12
120 2024-09-01 58969.80 66480.70 52598.70 65879.17  65879.17 8.272336e+11
>
```

Fig. 8.8 The monthly data function related to Bitcoin (.show_btcMonthly)

When zero is input, such as `.show_btcMonthly (0)`, the function will export the whole data set to Excel. The first several lines are shown below.

	A	B	C	D	E	F	G
1	Date	Open	High	Low	Close	Adj.Close	Volume
2	10/1/2014	387.427	411.698	289.296	338.321	338.321	9.03E+08
3	11/1/2014	338.65	457.093	320.626	378.047	378.047	6.6E+08
4	12/1/2014	378.249	384.038	304.232	320.193	320.193	5.53E+08
5	1/1/2015	320.435	320.435	171.51	217.464	217.464	1.1E+09

Fig. 8.9 Monthly data to Excel: .show_btcMonthly (0)

The functions starting with `.show` will use the data sets we supplied. The advantage is that they are pretty reliable and easy to use. The disadvantages are that there are only a few stocks, and the data sets might need to be updated to the latest data. To overcome those shortcomings, we have designed two hidden functions called `.anyStockDailyData ()`, abbreviated as `.anyD()`, and `.anyStockMonthlyData()`, abbreviated as `.anyM()`, which are unique since they retrieve data directly from Yahoo!Finance. Those two functions depend on an R package called `quantmod`. To install it, readers can copy and paste the following line to their R console.

`install.packages("quantmod").`

One example is shown below.

```
> .anym()

  Input your ticker here:
ibm

 Launch Excel and paste the data there
  Note that if you see just one column
        highlight it, click on 'Data' ->'Text to Columns'
        choose 'Delimited'-> Comma  -> Finish
>
```

Fig. 8.10 Getting monthly data for a given stock ticker

The disadvantage is that those functions depend on Yahoo! Finance's policy via the related package. If Yahoo!Finance changes the policy; those two functions may not work or require specific modifications.

The following sections will review fundamental concepts: total risk, firm-specific risk, market risk, LPTD (Lower Partial Standard Deviation), Sharpe, Treynor, and Sortino ratios. The last three ratios measure a risk-return trade-off. The functions starting with `.show_` perform the same way with the data sets we generate.

8.6 Total Risk and Firm-Specific Risk

We know many definitions of risks from corporate finance and investment courses. A general model is that a company's total risk has two components: market risk and firm-specific risk.

$$total\ risk = total\ risk + firm - specific\ risk \tag{8.1}$$

In finance, the standard deviation of returns is used to measure total risk, while the beta is used to measure the market. In addition to total and market risks, other definitions of risk include VaR (Value at Risk). For this chapter, we will focus on total risk in terms of calculation and for simplicity. We will also mention other non-quantitative risks, such as hacking, market manipulation, and regulatory risk. The following sections will discuss some risks we could not quantify. Later in the chapter, it is shown that the annualized risk for Bitcoin is 75%, while it is 24% for IBM.

8.7 Hedging, Speculation, and Arbitrage

A hedge is an investment selected to reduce the potential for loss in other investments because its price tends to move in the opposite direction. This strategy works as an insurance policy, offsetting any steep losses in other investments. For example, a company in the US imports certain raw materials from England and promises to pay 5 million pounds in 6 months. The company is facing an exchange risk if the pound appreciates the US dollar again. The company can buy pounds today and deposit them in a foreign bank to accumulate to 5 million in 6 months. The company has a position in the first hand, then takes an opposite position to neutralize the risk.

Speculating is putting money into financial endeavors with a high probability of failure. Speculating seeks abnormal returns from bets that can go one way or another. While speculating is likened to gambling, it is not precisely the same as speculators trying to decide on the direction of their trades. However, the inherent speculative risk involved in the transaction tends to be significantly above average. These traders buy securities knowing they will be held for only a short period before selling. They may frequently move into and out of a position. Arbitrage is buying and selling simultaneously to exploit the price difference between two crypto exchanges.

8.8 Speculative Assets

Speculative assets are financial instruments or investments that people purchase primarily with the expectation of a price increase, allowing them to sell the asset at a profit. These assets are characterized by their high risk and potential for high reward. They rely more on market sentiment, speculation, and future expectations than intrinsic value or fundamental economic factors. The key characteristics of Speculative Assets are summarized in the following table (Table 8.2).

The following table lists a few examples of Speculative Assets (Table 8.3).

Table 8.2 Main characteristics of speculative assets

Character	Explanation
High volatility	The prices of speculative assets tend to fluctuate widely and rapidly, making them attractive for short-term traders looking to capitalize on quick price movements
High risk	Speculative investments carry a significant risk of loss, as their value can be heavily influenced by market psychology, rumors, or macroeconomic events rather than stable, underlying fundamentals
Potential for high returns	While risky, speculative assets can offer substantial returns if the market conditions favorably match the investor's position
No intrinsic value	Many speculative assets may not have a tangible or intrinsic value, and their prices may be primarily driven by investor sentiment and speculative demand

Table 8.3 Examples of speculative assets

Cryptocurrencies	Digital currencies like Bitcoin and Ethereum often experience significant price swings influenced by market speculation, regulatory news, and technological developments
Penny stocks	Low-priced, small-cap stocks that trade at a relatively low price per share are subject to high volatility and speculative trading
Commodities	As investors bet on price movements, certain commodities, such as oil, gold, and silver, can become speculative assets during economic uncertainty or market turmoil
Venture capital investments	Investments in early-stage startups that have high growth potential but also a high chance of failure
Real estate in booming markets:	Properties are purchased with the expectation of rapid appreciation due to trends instead of steady rental income or long-term value

While all investments carry some level of risk, speculative assets are distinct because they are often chosen for their potential to provide quick, significant returns, and they are typically less concerned with long-term growth, income, or stability. In contrast, traditional investments, such as blue-chip stocks, bonds, or real estate intended for rental income, tend to focus more on long-term value, stability, and regular income streams. Investors engaging in speculative activities should be prepared for the possibility of significant losses, given the unpredictable nature of the markets and the inherent risks involved.

8.9 ROI (Return on Investment)

At https://www.blockchain.com/explorer/assets/usdc, we can get the following information in terms of ROI (on 2/9/2025).

ROI	USD (%)	ETH	BTC (%)
6H	–0.00	–0.23	–0.17
1D	–0.00	0.11	0.23
1W	–0.00	9.30	5.48
1M	–0.00	24.72	–1.72
6M	0.01	1.13	–38.96
1Y	–0.03	–4.90	–49.94
3Y	–0.04	11.25	–55.95
5Y	0.20	–89.89	–89.25

There might be some problems with those numbers.

8.10 Annualizing a Standard Deviation

When downloading historical price data, we have three steps to calculate a standard deviation.

Step 1: calculate returns.

Step 2: Calculate the standard deviation

Step 3: annualizing the standard deviation based on the following formulae.

For a monthly frequency, we have the following formula:

$$\sigma_{annual} = \sqrt{12} * \sigma_{monthly} \tag{8.2}$$

For a daily frequency, we have the following formula.

$$\sigma_{annual} = \sqrt{252} * \sigma_{daily} \tag{8.3}$$

In the above formula, 252 is the number of trading days within a year. The market risk can be defined as the slope of the following regression.

$$R_i = R_f + \beta(R_{mkt} - R_t) \tag{8.4}$$

The following regression is better in terms of interpretation.

$$R_i - R_f = \alpha + \beta(R_{mkt} - R_t) \tag{8.5}$$

On the left-hand side, it is the stock's excess returns; the dependent variable is the excess market returns. We compare apples with apples.

8.11 LPSD (Lower Partial Standard Deviation)

When estimating a standard deviation, we use all returns. However, many argue this is incorrect since a positive deviation from the mean should not be treated as harmful as a negative deviation from the mean. Thus, the following definition considers returns less than a benchmark. Assume that we have `n` returns with a benchmark of `Rb`. With losing generosity, we can assume that the first `k` returns are less than the benchmark return given. The following formula calculates LPSD.

$$LPSD = \sqrt{\frac{\sum_{i=1}^{k}(R_i - R_b)^2}{n-1}} whereR_i < R_b \tag{8.6}$$

LPSD will be used by the Sortino ratio discussed in the next section.

8.12 Trade-Off Between Risk and Return

When investing, we should balance risk and return. For a ratio, a general formula is given below.

$$Tradoff = \frac{benefit}{cost} = \frac{return}{risk} \tag{8.7}$$

Based on the above logic, the Sharpe Ratio is defined below.

$$Sharpe\ ratio = \frac{excess\ return}{total\ risk} = \frac{\overline{R} - Rf}{\sigma} \tag{8.8}$$

where $\overline{R}$ is the mean return, `Rf` is the risk-free rate, and σ is the total risk as the standard deviation of returns. Unlike the Sharpe ratio, which uses total risk as the denominator, the Treynor Ratio uses market risk instead. The following formula defines it.

$$Treynor\ ratio = \frac{excess\ return}{market\ risk} = \frac{\overline{R} - Rf}{\beta} \tag{8.9}$$

Sortino Ratio uses LPSD instead of a standard deviation, as shown below.

$$Sortino\ ratio = \frac{excess\ return}{LPSD} = \frac{\overline{R} - Rf}{LPSD} \tag{8.10}$$

8.13 IBM's Total Risk and Sharpe Ratio

As the first step, we download historical IBM's monthly price data. There are generally three ways to get the data.

	A	B	C	D	E	F	G
1	Date	Open	High	Low	Close	Adj.Close	Volume
2	2/1/1962	6.97897	7.15105	6.78139	6.84512	1.42072225	6087720
3	3/1/1962	6.87062	7.08732	6.75908	6.79095	1.40966988	5687625
4	4/1/1962	6.78776	6.78776	5.73614	5.78713	1.20129573	1.4E+07
5	5/1/1962	5.78713	6.24283	4.52518	5.00319	1.03856587	5.2E+07
6	6/1/1962	4.98407	4.98407	3.82409	4.32441	0.89780581	7.2E+07
7	7/1/1962	4.32441	5.01593	4.31485	4.93308	1.02417397	4.3E+07
8	8/1/1962	4.92033	5.28681	4.72275	5.05099	1.04865336	4.3E+07
9	9/1/1962	5.05099	5.11791	4.44232	4.50605	0.9357028	3.5E+07

Fig. 8.11 The several lines of monthly data of IBM

We choose the latest 10 years (from 2014 to 2024) to compare with Bitcoin easily.

	A	B	C	D	E	F	G
1	Date	Open	High	Low	Close	Adj.Close	Volume
2	10/1/2014	181.558	182.495	154.015	157.17	102.216881	152983045
3	11/1/2014	157.027	157.715	152.772	155.038	100.83033	83696316
4	12/1/2014	154.532	157.285	143.881	153.384	100.437462	106256131
5	1/1/2015	154.216	156.128	142.945	146.568	95.9739761	122813059
6	2/1/2015	147.228	157.734	144.847	154.818	101.376503	81229117

Fig. 8.12 The IMB's monthly data starting from 2014

When calculating returns, we should consider how the data set was sorted.

	A	F	H	I	J	K
1	Date	Adj.Close	ret	count	119	
2	10/1/2014	102.216881				
3	11/1/2014	100.83033	-0.01356	mean	0.00873	=AVERAGE(H:H)
4	12/1/2014	100.437462	-0.0039	std	0.06703	=STDEV(H:H)
5	1/1/2015	95.9739761	-0.04444	std_annua	0.23221	=J4*SQRT(12)
6	2/1/2015	101.376503	0.05629	rf	0.01	
7	3/1/2015	101.179863	-0.00194	rf_monthl	0.00083	=J6/12
8	4/1/2015	107.981888	0.06723	Sharpe	0.11783	=(J3-J7)/J4
9	5/1/2015	106.948051	-0.00957			

Fig. 8.13 Return calculation and the number of returns

The annualized standard deviation is 23%. Assume that the annual risk-free rate is 1%. Based on the formula, the Sharpe ratio is 11.78%.

8.14 Bitcoin'S Total Risk and Sharpe Ratio

Since the process is identical to the previous section, only the result is shown below. The period is from 10/1/2014 to 9/1/2024 (10 years). The annualized risk is very high, 75% compared to 23% for IBM.

	A	F	H	I	J	K
1	Date	Adj.Close	ret	count	119	=COUNT(H:H)
2	10/1/2014	338.321		mean_ret	0.06673	=AVERAGE(H:H)
3	11/1/2014	378.047	0.11742	std	0.21675	=STDEV(H:H)
4	12/1/2014	320.193	-0.15303	rf	0.01	
5	1/1/2015	217.464	-0.32083	rf_monthly	0.00083	=J4/12
6	2/1/2015	254.263	0.16922	Sharpe	0.30401	=(J2-J5)/J3
7	3/1/2015	244.224	-0.03948			
8	4/1/2015	236.145	-0.03308	risk_annual	0.75085	=J3*SQRT(12)
9	5/1/2015	230.19	-0.02522			

Fig. 8.14 The calculated Bitcoin's total risk and Sharpe Ratio

8.15 Do Bitcoin'S Returns Follow a Normal Distribution?

Osterrieder (2016) shows that Bitcoin's returns do not follow a normal distribution. This section will test whether Bitcoin's returns follow a normal distribution. The data set is from 2014 to 2024, as shown below.

	A	B	C	D	E	F
1	Date	Open	High	Low	Close	Adj.Close
2	10/1/2014	387.427	411.698	289.296	338.321	338.321
3	11/1/2014	338.65	457.093	320.626	378.047	378.047
118	6/1/2024	67489.6	71907.9	58601.7	62678.3	62678.3
119	7/1/2024	62673.6	69987.5	53717.4	64619.3	64619.3
120	8/1/2024	64625.8	65593.2	49121.2	58969.9	58969.9
121	9/1/2024	58969.8	66480.7	52598.7	65879.2	65879.2
122						

Fig. 8.15 The first and last several observations of Bitcoin monthly data

The procedure is divided into a few steps.

Step 1: Calculate returns, then their mean (`ret_mean`) and standard deviation (`std`).

Step 2: Standardize those returns using the following formula: `ret2=(ret-ret_mean)/std`.

	A	B	C	D	E	F	G
1	Date	Adj.Close	ret			mean	0.06673
2	10/1/2014	338.321		ret2		std	0.21675
3	11/1/2014	378.047	0.11742	0.23388	=(C3-$G$1)/$G$2		
4	12/1/2014	320.193	-0.15303	-1.01389		min	-2.05035
5	1/1/2015	217.464	-0.32083	-1.78805		max	2.90454

Fig. 8.16 Mean, minimum, and maximum of returns

Step 3: Generate a `bin` column from –3 to 3 with an incremental value of 0.25.

Step 4: Click 'Data,' 'Data Analysis', then 'Histogram.' Enter the following information.

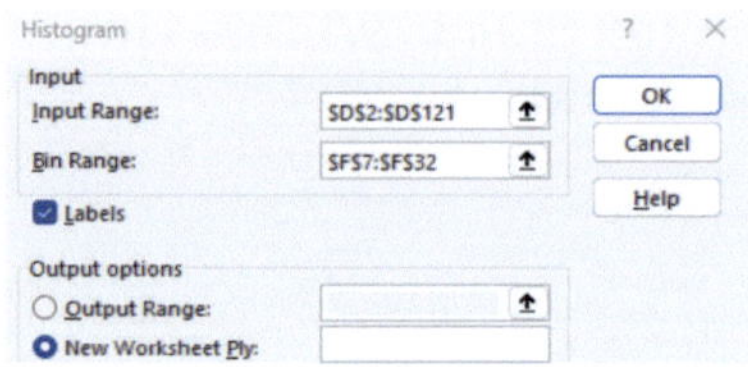

Fig. 8.17 Parameters for Excel histogram functionality

Step 5: Calculate frequency based on a normal distribution.

J9 =(NORMSDIST(H9)-NORMSDIST(H8))*$J$1

	H	I	J	K	L	M
1			119	=count(D:D)		
6						
7	bin	Frequency	freq2	(freq2-freq1)^2/freq2		
8	-3	0				
9	-2.75	0	0.193954	0.193954	=(J9-I9)^2/J9	
10	-2.5	0	0.3843583	0.384358		

Fig. 8.18 Frequency calculation based on a normal distribution

The formula in cell J9 is `=(NORMSDIST(H9)-NORMSDIST(H8))*$J$1` and cell J1 contains the count of bins. The formula in cell K9 is `=(J9-I9)^2/J9` because of the following formula.

$$\chi^2 = \sum_{i=1}^{n} \frac{\left(n_i - n_i^{normal}\right)^2}{n_i^{normal}}, \tag{8.11}$$

where χ^2 is the chi-square statistic, `n` is the number of bins, n_i is the frequency in bin `i`, and n_i^{normal} Is the frequency in bin `i` from a normal distribution. The summation is shown below.

	H	I	J	K	L	M	N
1			119	=COUNT(D:D)			
32	3	1	0.19395	3.349817			
33	More	0			24	=COUNT(K9:K32)	
34			sum	32.67994	=SUM(K9:K32)		
35			chisq	35.17246	=CHISQ.INV.RT(0.05,L33-1)		

Fig. 8.19 Chi-Square statistic and its critical value

Since the summation is 32.7 and less than 35.2, the critical value with a significance level of 5%, we fail to reject the null hypothesis. Our conclusion is that Bitcoin's returns follow a normal distribution.

8.16 Two Ways to Estimate VAR

VaR (Value at Risk) is defined as "the maximum loss for a given confidence level over a fixed period." Below are three examples.

Example #1: Today, I own 5,000 shares of Walmart stocks worth $277,000. With a 99% confidence level, my maximum loss tomorrow is $15,239.

Example #2: Our mutual fund is worth $10m today. With 95% confidence, the maximum loss over the next 3 months is 0.5m.

Example #3: Our bank's value is $350m. Our VaR is $10m, and we are 99% confident that it will increase to $10 m over the next 6 months.

There are many ways to calculate the VaR for a given stock or portfolio. The first method depends on the normality assumption, i.e., we assume that the underlying portfolio's returns follow a normal distribution.

$$VaR = p * (\overline{R} - z * \sigma) \tag{8.12}$$

where p is our position, such as the value of our holding or portfolio value, $\overline{R}$ is the mean return, z is the Z-value (depends on the confidence level), and σ is the standard deviation. When the confidence interval is 99%, z = 2.326, and when it is 95%, z = 1.64. We can apply the following formula to calculate the z value. We have the following formula for a given α (confidence interval).

$$z = abs(= NORMSINV(\alpha)), \tag{8.13}$$

where the `normsinv()` function is the Excel inverse function for standard normal distribution. For example, = `ABS(NORMSINV(0.05))` will give us 1.644853627. Alternatively, Eq. (8.4) can be written in the following way.

$$VaR = p * (\overline{R} + normsinv(alpha) * \sigma) \tag{8.14}$$

What are VaRs when holding \$1 IBM's stocks vs. Bitcoin for one month with a 99% confidence interval? Based on the previous section, we know that monthly mean returns for IBM and Bitcoin are 0.008732236 and 0.066727, respectively. The monthly standard deviations for IBM and Bitcoin are 0.067033786 and 0.216751, respectively. Thus, we have the following two results.

$$VaR(IBM) = 10^6 * (0.008732236 - 1.64 * 0.067033786) = -\$101{,}203$$

$$VaR(Bitcoin) = 10^6 * (0.066727 - 1.64 * 0.216751) = -\$288{,}745$$

The above calculations show that Bitcoin's VaR is almost three times that of IBM for the same time period and confidence interval.

The above approach is based on the normality assumption, i.e., the underlying returns follow a normal distribution. We know that a normal distribution is symmetric. However, many returns have a heavy left tail; in other words, VaR, based on the normality assumption, will underestimate their true risk. The second approach is based on sorting. Assume that we have `n` returns. We sort our returns from lowest to highest. The following formula will give the VaR based on sorting.

$$VaR(sorting) = p * ret(k), \tag{8.15}$$

where $k = int(\alpha * n))$, and `int()` is the Excel integer function. For example, our significance level (α) is 0.05, and `n` is 119. Then `k` = `int(0.05*119)` = 5.

	A	B	C	D	E	F	G
1	Date	Adj.Close	ret	n	119	ret_sorted	
2	10/1/2014	338.321		alpha	0.05		
3	11/1/2014	378.047	0.11742	k	5	-0.3777	1
4	12/1/2014	320.193	-0.153	p	$1,000,000	-0.3641	2
5	1/1/2015	217.464	-0.3208			-0.3536	3
6	2/1/2015	254.263	0.16922			-0.3293	4
7	3/1/2015	244.224	-0.0395	VaR	-320835	-0.3208	5
8	4/1/2015	236.145	-0.0331			-0.278	6
9	5/1/2015	230.19	-0.0252			-0.2513	7

Fig. 8.20 The estimated VaR based on the sorted returns

The formula in cell E is = `E4*F7`, i.e., the position multiplied by the fifth lowest return. Compared with the formula approach (depending on the normality assumption), VaR based on sorting is higher (\$320,835 vs. \$288,745).

8.17 Four Moments and Modified VAR

We used the following formula in the previous section to estimate a VaR (based on the normality assumption).

$$VaR = p * (\overline{R} - z * \sigma)$$

Table 8.4 Four moments and their Excel functions

#	Name	Excel function
1	Mean	= Average()
2	Standard deviation	= stdev()
3	Skewness	= skew()
4	Kurtosis	= kurt()

This formula has two related moments: mean and standard deviation. The following table shows the four moments for returns (Table 8.4).

The third method is Modified VaR, which is defined using the following formula:

$$\begin{cases} MVaR = p * \left(\overline{R} - tt * \sigma\right) \\ z = abs(normsinv(\alpha)) \\ tt = z + \frac{1}{6}\left(z^2 - 1\right)S + \frac{1}{24}\left(z^3 - 3z\right)K - \frac{1}{36}\left(2z^3 - 5z\right)S^2, \end{cases} \tag{8.16}$$

where `P` is the position, R is the mean return (the first moment), σ is the standard deviation (the second moment), S is the skewness of returns (the third moment), and `K` is the kurtosis of returns (the fourth moment). We have a few problems related to the end of the chapter.

8.18 Bitcoin Block 868,419

Let's look at an individual block. We chose Block 868,419 randomly. The website structure is https://www.blockchain.com/explorer/blocks/btc/plus the block number, i.e., https://www.blockchain.com/explorer/blocks/btc/861489. The top part is shown below.

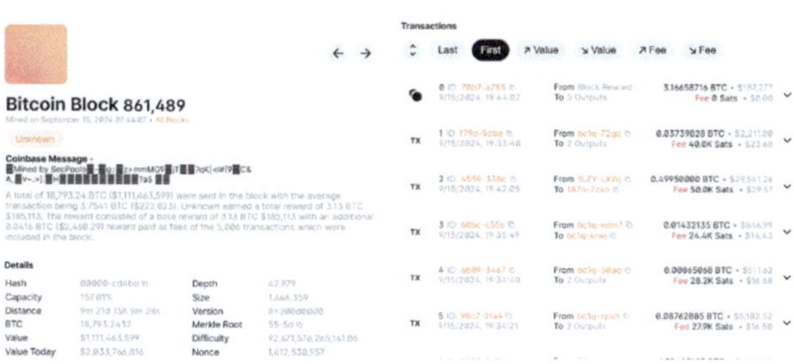

Fig. 8.21 The information related to Bitcoin Block 861,489

By clicking the copy icon beside the Hash, as shown below, we can get the Hash of the block: 00000000000000000002f1b6c71c0bb0c028500e6a57885d3d82a6fc48ecd4bb.

Table 8.5 Details for Block 861,489 (as of 9/15/2024)

Hash	00,000-cd4bb	Depth	12,530
Capacity	157.01%	Size	1,646,359
Distance	29m 54s	Version	0 × 200d0000
BTC	18,793.2432	Merkle Root	55 – 5d
Value	$1,111,463,599	Difficulty	92,671,576,265,161.06
Value today	$1,109,849,072	Nonce	1,612,530,957
Average value	3.7541436676 BTC	Bits	386,075,020
Median value	0.00031856 BTC	Weight	3,993,430 WU
Input value	18,793.28 BTC	Minted	3.13 BTC
Output value	18,796.41 BTC	Reward	3.16658716 BTC
Transactions	5,006	Mined on	Sep 15, 2024, 7:44:07 PM
Witness Tx's	4,895	Height	861,489
Inputs	8,065	Confirmations	3
Outputs	12,153	Fee Range	1–262 sat/byte
Fees	0.04158716 BTC	Average Fee	0.00000831
Fees Kb	0.0000253 BTC	Median Fee	0.00000262
Fees kWU	0.0000104 BTC	Miner	Unknown

Fig. 8.22 The Hash value for this block under "Details"

The information is summarized in the following table. According to the table, 18,793.24 BTC ($1,111,463,599) were sent in the block, with the average transaction being 3.7541 BTC ($222,023). An unknown user earned a total reward of 3.13 BTC ($185,113). The reward consisted of a base reward of 3.13 BTC ($185,113) with an additional 0.0416 BTC ($2,460.29) paid as fees for the 5,006 transactions included in the block (Table 8.5).

8.19 USDC

USDC's price is pegged 1–1 to the US Dollar. The platform maintains this peg through a simple 100% collateralization mechanism. If a user initiates a transaction to buy one USD Coin using fiat currency, that currency is deposited and stored as one U.S. dollar, and the new USDC is minted. On the other hand, if a user were to sell a USD Coin in exchange for fiat currency, then the USDC is "burned" when the fiat money is transferred back to your bank account. In theory, for every 1 USDC token in circulation, there is USD $1 held in collateral. To purchase USDC, a user must first meet the Know Your Customer (KYC) identity requirements. Users can link their bank account and wire transfer in US Dollars following that process. That money is then converted into USDC, and the customer can use an exchange to trade it for other cryptocurrencies. Users can also convert the USDC back into US Dollars, which will be wired back into their bank account.

8.20 Regulatory Risk

Regulatory risk is the possibility that changes in laws and regulations could negatively impact a company's operations, financial health, or strategic direction. It's a type of legal risk that can have many different forms and consequences because the nature of government controls varies across industries and regulators. Here are some examples of regulatory risk. Labor laws: changes to labor laws, such as minimum wage, vacation time, and sick leave, can impact a company's operational costs and employee relations. IT and cybersecurity: the complex rules around how to handle, protect, and disclose information, along with the threat of cyberattacks, increase regulatory risk in these areas.

8.21 Example: XRP Drops 4% Within 24 Hours

Sharma (10/1/2024) noted that XRP's value dropped by 4% in the past 24 h. Two factors may have contributed to this decline. First, Ripple, the company behind XRP, released 1 billion XRP tokens on October 1, 2024. This increase in supply, combined with insufficient demand, can lead to a price drop as market forces adjust. Second, there has been growing speculation about a possible SEC appeal in court. Following a favorable ruling for Ripple in July, the SEC had until October 7 to appeal. Many lawyers anticipate an appeal, given the SEC's recent focus on enforcing regulations against crypto companies.

8.22 Crypto Has a Higher Probability of Hacking

Compared with other assets, we see a much higher probability of hacking in terms of cryptocurrency. Tidy (2021) shows the largest-ever cryptocurrency hacks in the following table (Table 8.6).

8.23 Scandal #1: The FTX Collapse

Have you wondered about the massive crypto debacle of FTX and its wunderkind former CEO Sam Bankman-Fried? NBC News breaks down what happened and why it matters. By Elizabeth Napolitano and Brian Cheung, it's a collapse that some have called crypto's "Lehman moment." The bankruptcy of the crypto giant FTX and the resignation of its founder, Sam Bankman-Fried, has left customers in

Table 8.6 The Largest Cryptocurrency hacks

BitGrail	$146m was hacked from the Italian exchange in 2018. It's estimated that 230,000 BitGrail users lost funds
KuCoin	$281m was stolen by suspected North Korean hackers from this attack on the Seychelles-based exchange in 2020. The company recovered most of the funds and refunded customers
MtGox	$450m of mainly Bitcoin was hacked in 2014, which caused the Japanese exchange to collapse. None of the customers have been reimbursed yet
Coincheck:	$534m was stolen in 2018 from the Japanese exchange. Customers were eventually reimbursed
Poly network	Earlier this month, the Chinese platform was hacked, and $610 m in various coins were stolen. The hacker returned all the funds, and customers have started being reimbursed

limbo and investors writing off what once looked like the next big thing in tech, and it happened in a matter of days. But in the complex crypto world, such a collapse can be hard to parse. Here's the basics of what went down.

How did it become so big? The company, founded in 2019, quickly rose to international prominence through high-profile acquisitions, aggressive marketing strategies, and low trading fees. Competitor platforms include Kraken, Coinbase, and Gemini. Even those unfamiliar with the technology were lured to FTX with promises to park their money in accounts and earn much higher yields than traditional banks. Major venture capital groups also bought in, investing almost $2 billion in the company. Sam Bankman-Fried, FTX's 30-year-old founder, became the face of the company and, to some, crypto at large. Celebrity endorsements and major sports sponsorships made FTX hard to miss.

8.24 The Scandal #2: $1 Billion Fraud

On November 6, 2020, federal agents seized more than $1 billion worth of bitcoins linked to the now-defunct Silk Road website, a criminal marketplace on the dark web. This may have been the Justice Department's largest-ever seizure of cryptocurrency.

According to court documents, the Justice Department said it is moving to have the 69,370 bitcoins—valued at more than $15,000 apiece—forfeited to the government. The bitcoins once belonged to Silk Road's founder, Ross Ulbricht, who was sentenced to life in prison in 2015. Bitcoins were the only currency allowed on Silk Road, which authorities say was used for criminal transactions, including the sale of drugs and guns, as well as money laundering.

8.25 The Scandal #3: Coinbase Lawsuit

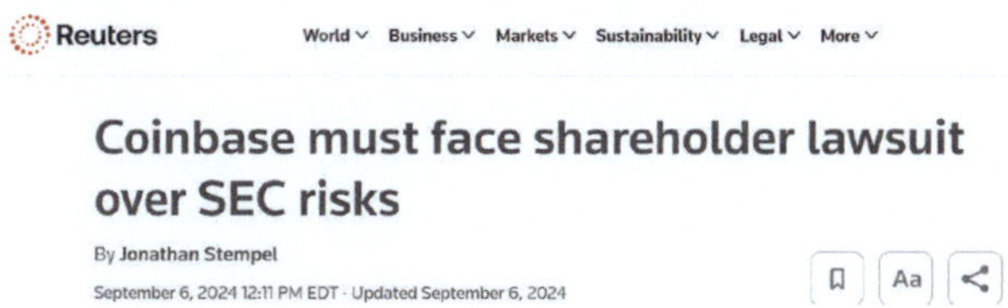
Reuters
World Business Markets Sustainability Legal More

Coinbase must face shareholder lawsuit over SEC risks

By Jonathan Stempel

September 6, 2024 12:11 PM EDT · Updated September 6, 2024

Aa

Fig. 8.23 An image of the Coinbase Lawsuit

(Link: Coinbase must face shareholder lawsuit over SEC risks | Reuters)

Sept 6 (Reuters)—A federal judge rejected Coinbase's (COIN.O) opens new tab bid to dismiss a proposed class action by shareholders who accused the operator of the largest U.S. cryptocurrency exchange of downplaying the likelihood the U.S. Securities and Exchange Commission would sue it. U.S. District Judge Brian Martinotti in Newark, New Jersey, ruled on Thursday, 15 months after the SEC's June 6, 2023, civil lawsuit accusing Coinbase of operating an unregistered securities exchange. Coinbase's share price fell 12% that day.

8.26 Rug Pulls

A rug pull occurs when crypto developers abandon a project but keep the funds raised from investors. Bad actors can list a new token on a decentralized exchange, pair it with a legitimate cryptocurrency, and drum up interest on social media to lure in investors. Once enough money is funneled into their token, the developers scratch the project and run it with investor funds. This scam plagues early investors who think they're getting early access to up-and-coming cryptos when, in reality, they're scammed out of their money.

"If it sounds too good to be true, it probably is," explains Shaun Heng, the VP of Growth & Operations at CoinMarketCap, one of the most frequented websites for tracking crypto prices. "Pay close attention to the websites and third parties involved. Don't rely on comments from anyone on social media, no matter what people are saying or how many positive reviews there are. If you can't find verifiable reviews, the chances of the opportunity being a scam are higher." A quick tip: By sticking to centralized cryptocurrency exchanges, which typically have stricter oversight and regulations, you have a better chance of avoiding illegitimate projects.

8.27 Traditional Hacking and Theft

Crypto markets have unique characteristics relative to other asset markets. However, investors are susceptible to traditional scams like account hacks and identity theft. To trade crypto, investors need a crypto wallet, which can be a digital or physical device. These wallets have keys—both public and private. The former is a public address that allows crypto to be deposited into the wallet, similar to how routing and bank account numbers enable direct deposits. The latter is like the password to an online banking platform. Whoever has access to that password can control the funds within the account.

Just as you wouldn't share your credit card number with a stranger, you should keep your private keys somewhere safe. Fraudsters can use this information to hack accounts and withdraw funds—and they'll employ various tricks to get investors to reveal their private information. Be cautious of crypto phishing emails that may pose as a crypto exchange or wallet provider. The same goes for unsolicited out-of-the-blue promotions from suspicious websites and imposter accounts. Scammers often pretend to be celebrities or affiliates of major companies, promising guaranteed and immediate returns if you act quickly.

To avoid accidentally falling for phishing emails, verify that the sender's email address is valid and/or recognizable. Scammers often use addresses with generic domains and random characters.

8.28 The First Blockchain Antitrust Case

Of all the areas where blockchain has made headlines, antitrust has ranked relatively low. To the extent that there have been disputes or regulatory activity, they have so far revolved around the financial aspects of crypto assets and less so around market distortions, which is antitrust's domain. But where there is money, there is power, and where there is power, there is abuse of power, so it was only a matter of time until an antitrust claim would arise. In December 2018, UnitedCorp, a diversified technology company, sued Bitmain, the largest Bitcoin mining pool, and several other high-profile stakeholders in the first blockchain dispute focused on antitrust (United American Corp. v. Bitmain, Inc. Complaint). The case is complex because of the technical details and the convoluted alleged anticompetitive scheme. But at its core, one finds a familiar claim of conspiracy. Interestingly, the filing attorneys are corporate/financial law experts—not antitrust experts—perhaps indicative that blockchain cases, particularly Bitcoin, continue to be lumped together under financial regulation.

The case is currently pending before the District Court for the Southern District of Florida. It is hard to predict how much the court will engage with the case. In all its boldness, the complaint leaves much to be desired, as it fails to map the facts and legal claims onto the requirements of the allegedly violated Sect. 1 of the Sherman Act. That said, the case opens for the first time a window into how the crypto-economy can malfunction in a way that harms consumers and the industry's competitive dynamics.

Appendix A: Issue the Following Line of R Code for Week 8

```
source ("http://datayyy.com/i2ft/week8.txt")
```

```
*-------------------------------------------------------------------------*
* Introduction to FinTech using Excel                by Dr. Yan 2025      *
*        (in an R-assisted learning environment)                          *
*-------------------------------------------------------------------------*
*  .c1  Introduction and Excel Basics                 .c15 Term Projects    *
*  .c2  Blockchain 1: (Numbers & alphanumeric)        .c16 R basics(optional) *
*  .c3             2: (ASCII and Sha256)              .c17 Macro (optional)  *
*  .c4  Ledger and distributed ledger                 .c18 VBA  (optional)   *
*  .c5  Cryptography    1: and public/private keys                        *
*  .c6                  2: Advanced                                       *
*  .c7  Cryptocurrency and Ganache                                        *
*  .c8                  2: markets and benefit/risk tradeoff              *
*-------------------------------------------------------------------------*
* >.c8       # go to chapter 8                                            *
* >.uu       # go to utility submenu                                      *
* >.ft       # back to this menu                                          *
*-------------------------------------------------------------------------*
>
```

Fig. 8.24 The menu for Week 8

Appendix B: Typing .chapter8 or .c8 Leads to the Following Contents

```
> .chapter8
function(i=0){
"i  Chap 8:Cryptocurrency market  i  Risk, trade-off             i  Explanations
-   ----------------------------  --  --------------------------  --  -------------------------
 1  Introduction                  21  Risk definitions            41  VaR: definition
 2  10 largest cryptocurrencies   22    : total risk              42    : A few simple examples
 3  What is FTX?                  23    : market risk             43    : normal distribution
 4  Scandal: FTX collapse         24  Trade-off: Sharpe ratio etc 44    : density vs. cumulative distribution
 5  Fraud  #1: $1b (2020)         25  Covariance and correlation  45    : Method #1: to calculate VaR (normality)
 6         #2: 2023               26  Impact of correlation       46             :The simplest formula for VaR
 7 Crypto scams                   27  Hedging                     47    : Method #2 to calculate VaR (sorting)
 8    cryptocurrency scams?       28     : perfect hedging        48    : Excel functions for 4 moments
 9 Type 1: market manipulation    29  Speculation                 49    : Method #3: Modified VaR
10      2: Pump-and-dump schemes  30     : example                50   Normality test
11      3: Rug pulls              31  Arbitrage                   51     : critical value for a chisq
12      4: hacking and theft      32     : example                52   sources of data
13      5: ICO scam               33  Getting data: method 1      53  .searchHiddenFunctins(8)
14  LPSD                          34      #2: .show_ibmDaily      54  BTC  : .show_btcMonthly   and .show_btcDaily
15  Regularity risk               35      #3: any stock           55  SP500: .show_sp500monthly
and .show_sp500daily
16   :podcast                     36  Total risk: S&P500          56        .show_ff3Monthlyff3 and show_ff3Daily
17   :1st blockchain antitrust    37     : IBM                    57   .show_ibmMonthly        and .show_ibmDaily
18   : [continued]                38     : BTC                    58   .show_wmtMonthly        and .show_wmtDaily
19  Videos & podcast              39  correlation: S&P500, BTC    59  install.packages('quantmod')
20  Links                         40          : corr(S&P, IBM)    60   .anyStockMonthlyData,
and .anyStockDailyData

Example #1:>.c8    # see the above list
Example #2:>.c8()  # the same as above
Example #3:>.c8(1) # see the 1st explanation
```

Fig. 8.25 The contents of Chapter 8

Exercises

Note that * indicates difficult ones.

8.1 Calculate the standard deviation of daily returns for a given set of cryptocurrency prices over 30 days.
8.2 Using Excel, simulate 100 random cryptocurrency price changes and compute the standard deviation of returns.
8.3 Compare the standard deviation of returns for two cryptocurrencies over six months. Discuss which is riskier and why.
8.4 Given a portfolio of two cryptocurrencies, calculate the portfolio's standard deviation of returns assuming no correlation.
8.5 Explain how standard deviation can be used to understand risk in cryptocurrency investments. Provide numerical examples to support your explanation.
8.6 Calculate the beta of a cryptocurrency relative to a significant stock index using hypothetical monthly return data.
8.7 Interpret a beta of 1.5 for a cryptocurrency. What does it imply about the cryptocurrency's market risk?
8.8 Create an Excel chart showing the relationship between Bitcoin's returns and a stock market index. Use it to estimate the beta visually.
8.9 Compare the beta of two cryptocurrencies. How might their betas influence your investment decisions?
8.10 Explain the significance of a negative beta in the context of cryptocurrencies. Provide a hypothetical example.
8.11 Calculate the Sharpe ratio for a cryptocurrency portfolio given its average return, risk-free rate, and standard deviation.
8.12 For two portfolios, compute the Sharpe ratio and identify which offers a better risk-adjusted return.
8.13 Using Excel, simulate 50 random returns for a cryptocurrency and compute the Sortino ratio assuming a minimum acceptable return of 2%.
8.14 Explain the Treynor ratio and its relevance in assessing cryptocurrency portfolios. Calculate the ratio for a hypothetical portfolio.
8.15 Compare the Sharpe and Sortino ratios for a cryptocurrency with high volatility but positive returns. Which ratio better reflects its risk-adjusted performance?
8.16 A cryptocurrency has an annual return of 20%, a risk-free rate of 5%, and a standard deviation of 30%. Compute the Sharpe ratio and interpret the result.
8.17 A portfolio consists of 60% Bitcoin and 40% Ethereum. Calculate the portfolio's expected return and risk given their returns and risks.
8.18 Assume you have $10,000 to invest in three cryptocurrencies. Allocate your investment to maximize the Sharpe ratio and justify your allocation using Excel.
8.19 Calculate and compare the Treynor ratio for a portfolio with beta values of 1.2, 0.8, and –0.5, given a market return of 10%.

8.20 Use Excel to create a risk-return scatterplot for five cryptocurrencies. Discuss which offers the best risk-return tradeoff.
8.21 Discuss the limitations of using the Sharpe ratio for evaluating cryptocurrency investments.
8.22 How does market risk (beta) differ from total risk (standard deviation) in cryptocurrencies?
8.23 Provide an example where the Sortino ratio offers better insights than the Sharpe ratio for evaluating a cryptocurrency's performance.
8.24 Discuss how the risk-return tradeoff applies to extremely volatile cryptocurrencies like meme coins.
8.25* Osterrieder (2016) shows that the returns of Bitcoin do not follow a normal distribution. However, this chapter shows that the opposite is true. Is there a reason for this discrepancy? You could replicate both periods.
8.26* Using the last 10-year data to conduct a normality test for IBM and XRP. Do their monthly returns follow a normal distribution?
8.27* Using the last 10 years' data to calculate VaR using three methods. Compare and comment on your results.

References

Blockchain assets Ethereum. https://www.blockchain.com/explorer/assets/eth

Blockchain assets USDC. https://www.blockchain.com/explorer/assets/usdc

Blockchain assets BTC. https://www.blockchain.com/explorer/assets/btc

Crypto Bubbles. https://cryptobubbles.net/

Crypto-assets and their risks for financial stability. https://www.esma.europa.eu/sites/default/files/library/esma50-165-2251_crypto_assets_and_financial_stability.pdf

Crypto market cap. https://coinmarketcap.com/

Erskine, K. (2018). Data Exploration and Visualization of the Tether Blockchain. https://rpubs.com/keith_erskine/381106

Fleiss, A., Eom, G., & Tu, E. (2021). Risk Analysis of Cryptocurrency. *International Journal of Cryptocurrency Research.* https://papers.ssrn.com/sol3/papers.cfm?abstract_id=3924387

Griffin, & Shams, A. (2020). Is Bitcoin Really Untethered? *Journal of Finance*, click here for the link.

Liu, Y., & Tsyvinski, A. (2021). *Review of Financial Studies*, Risks and Returns of Cryptocurrency. https://academic.oup.com/rfs/article/34/6/2689/5912024?login=false

Morini, M. (2017). Managing Derivatives on a Blockchain. A Financial Market Professional Implementation.

Osterrieder, J. O. (2016). The Statistics of Bitcoin and Cryptocurrencies. https://papers.ssrn.com/sol3/papers.cfm?abstract_id=2872158

Sharma, S. (2024). XRP drops 4%: Is the SEC preparing to appeal by Oct 7? https://www.msn.com/en-us/money/markets/xrp-drops-4-is-the-sec-preparing-to-appeal-by-oct-7/ar-AA1rvEP2

Stempel, J. (2024). Coinbase must face shareholder lawsuit over SEC risks. https://www.reuters.com/legal/coinbase-must-face-shareholder-lawsuit-over-sec-risks-2024-09-06/

Tidy, J. (2021). The real victims of mass crypto-hacks that keep happening. https://www.bbc.com/news/technology-58331959

9 Blockchain Applications and Simulations

First, we will start with a simple introduction to various applications of blockchain technology, such as finance, accounting, supply chain, and legal. Then, we show how to use Monte Carlo Simulation to generate a set of transactions, such as 2,000 observations. The Merkle Tree methodology is used to 'merge' transactions in a block to generate a final hash (Merkle Root hash). Finally, students learn how to generate their blockchain. In this chapter, the following topics will be covered:

- Various applications of Blockchain Technology
- Introduction to Monte Carlo Simulations
- The concept of a random seed
- Generating 2,000 transactions using Excel
- Merkle Tree Methodology
- Using a website to calculate Merkle Tree root
- Manually check the results
- Our hidden function: `.merkleTree ()`
- Form your blockchain

Supplementary Information The online version contains supplementary material available at https://doi.org/10.1007/978-3-031-89779-5_9.

Y. Yan, *Introduction to FinTech using Excel*, Springer Texts in Business and Economics, https://doi.org/10.1007/978-3-031-89779-5_9

Table 9.1 A list of potential applications of Blockchain

#	Application	#	Application
1	Cryptocurrencies	10	Energy trading
2	Smart contracts	11	Cross-border payments
3	Supply chain management	12	Decentralized social media
4	Healthcare records	13	Decentralized cloud storage
5	Voting systems	14	Insurance
6	Digital identity verification	15	Gaming and NFTs
7	Financial services	16	Humanitarian aid
8	Real estate transactions	17	Tokenization of assets
9	Intellectual property protection		

9.1 Various Applications of Blockchain

There are many applications of blockchain. The following table shows a list. In this chapter, we plan to use Excel and Monte Carlo Simulation to generate some data sets, such as transaction data sets. After that, we will discuss the so-called Merkle Tree method to calculate a block's hashes. After that, we will show you how to link those blocks to form a blockchain. The same methodology can be used for other applications. The following table shows the applications of the basic concepts of Blockchain in various areas. Again, doing a good term project by applying what you have learned is a good idea (Table 9.1).

Each of these applications demonstrates the versatility and potential of blockchain technology to transform various industries and enhance trust, transparency, and efficiency.

9.2 Cryptocurrencies

Blockchain is most famous for powering cryptocurrencies like Bitcoin and Ethereum. It enables decentralized digital currencies by maintaining a transparent and immutable ledger of all transactions without needing a central authority like a bank. This decentralization reduces transaction fees and enhances security. A few cryptos' market caps are shown below (as of 9/24/2024) via https://coinmarketcap.com.

#	Name	Price	1h %	24h %	7d %	Market Cap	Volume(24h)	Circulating Supply
1	BTC	$63,726.88	0.35%	0.43%	4.39%	$1,259,141,327,316	$27,151,957,788	19,758,403 BTC
	Bitcoin						425,318 BTC	
2	ETH	$2,643.23	0.33%	1.24%	11.77%	$318,145,166,107	$16,420,920,642	120,362,208 ETH
	Ethereum						6,198,493 ETH	
3	USDT	$1.00	0.00%	0.01%	0.02%	$119,230,487,618	$53,517,780,673	119,243,573,831 USDT
	Tether						53,520,394,948 USDT	
4	BNB	$608.21	0.19%	0.38%	10.71%	$88,758,005,486	$1,987,212,767	145,933,400 BNB
	BNB						3,262,060 BNB	
5	SOL	$147.18	0.03%	2.38%	10.62%	$68,986,840,390	$2,478,299,891	468,729,465 SOL
	Solana						16,780,388 SOL	
6	USDC	$1.00	0.01%	0.01%	0.01%	$35,938,717,231	$5,828,677,420	35,943,151,753 USDC
	USDC						5,828,039,102 USDC	
7	XRP	$0.59	0.25%	0.11%	0.51%	$33,150,299,641	$938,247,741	56,434,507,880 XRP
	XRP						1,595,504,680 XRP	
8	DOGE	$0.11	0.87%	1.87%	7.15%	$15,952,740,756	$687,010,002	146,092,476,384 DOGE
	Dogecoin						6,275,452,846 DOGE	
9	TON	$5.61	1.56%	0.04%	2.03%	$14,219,189,073	$196,832,345	2,533,299,645 TON
	Toncoin						35,403,149 TON	
10	ADA	$0.38	0.92%	6.35%	13.31%	$13,727,556,303	$311,395,856	35,960,643,044 ADA
	Cardano						812,344,702 ADA	

Fig. 9.1 Information related to a few cryptocurrencies

9.3 Smart Contracts

Smart contracts are self-executing contracts with the terms of the agreement directly written into code. Stored and replicated on a blockchain, they automatically execute and enforce agreements without intermediaries, reducing the risk of fraud and speeding up the process. Platforms like Ethereum popularized this concept.

We can get some information from a few websites. At https://solidity-by-example.org/, interested readers can find many sample programs for smart contracts written in Solidity, as shown below (the top part).

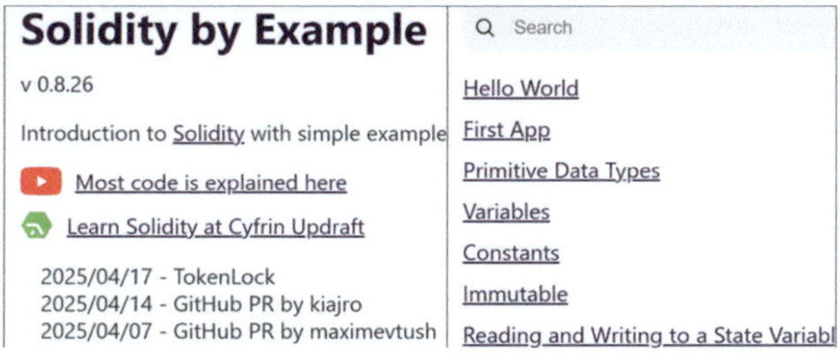

Figs. 9.2 and 9.3 Smart contracts (solidity by example)

9.4 Supply Chain Management

Blockchain technology improves supply chain transparency and traceability by allowing all parties involved to track the movement of goods from production to delivery. It provides an immutable ledger of product details, reduces fraud, improves inventory management, and ensures quality control across global networks. Later in the chapter, we show how to generate 2,000 transactions using a simulation tool in Excel. We can use the following line for the supply chain as our starting point.

```
TX1: 2023-01-02 10:30:45 Warehouse A shipped 120 units of product
XYZ to Store B.
```

After reading the related sections, readers will understand the mean of the above line.

9.5 Healthcare Records

Blockchain provides a secure and tamper-proof system for managing electronic health records (EHRs). Patients and healthcare providers can have real-time access to accurate and up-to-date medical histories while maintaining patient privacy and preventing unauthorized access. The one-line standard is shown below.

```
TX1: 2023-01-02 14:20:30 Dr. Smith prescribed 200mg of Medication
ABC to patient John Doe.
```

9.6 Voting Systems

Blockchain-based voting systems offer a transparent and secure alternative to traditional voting. Each vote can be encrypted, immutably recorded on the blockchain and tracked, ensuring that election results are tamper-proof and reducing the possibility of voter fraud or election rigging.

Later in the chapter, we show that a project could involve signatures using private and public keys. A private key generates a signature attached to a vote, and the voter's corresponding public key can be used to verify their signature. The following line could be used as a standard to generate some simulated records.

```
TX1: 2023-01-02 08:15:10 Jane Doe voted for Candidate X in the Dis-
trict 12 election.
```

9.7 Digital Identity Verification

Blockchain can be used to create secure and immutable digital identities. These blockchain-based IDs give people greater control over their data, making identity verification processes more efficient and safe. It can also prevent identity theft.

Like the Voting systems mentioned above, digital ID validation will be associated with public and private keys. Learners can build a Blockchain using a set of signatures generated using owners' private keys. Again, anyone can verify those signatures by using publicly viable keys (public keys).

9.8 Financial Services

Blockchain enables faster and more secure transactions, cross-border payments, and decentralized finance (DeFi) platforms in banking and finance. Blockchain reduces the need for intermediaries, cutting costs and time for clearing and settlement processes in traditional financial systems. The related one-line standard is given below.

```
TX1: 2023-01-02 15:45:23 Alan applied for a personal loan of $20,00
0 from XYZ Bank.
```

9.9 Real Estate Transactions

Blockchain streamlines real estate transactions by recording property ownership and legal agreements on a transparent and immutable ledger. Smart contracts can automate parts of the buying, selling, or renting processes, eliminating intermediaries and reducing fraud.

9.10 Intellectual Property Protection

Blockchain can protect intellectual property by providing proof of ownership for digital content like music, art, or literature. Artists and creators can securely publish their works on the blockchain, ensuring they receive proper attribution and royalties whenever their content is used.

9.11 Energy Trading

In the energy sector, blockchain facilitates peer-to-peer energy trading. People can trade excess solar or wind energy directly with others using smart contracts without needing energy companies as intermediaries. This decentralized approach promotes energy efficiency and reduces costs.

9.12 Cross-Border Payments

Blockchain technology provides a faster, more affordable way to conduct cross-border payments. Traditional methods can take several days and involve multiple intermediaries, whereas blockchain enables near-instant transactions with minimal fees, enhancing global financial inclusion.

```
TX1: 2023-01-02 17:55:30 Martin sent €500 to Maria in Spain using
SwiftPay.
```

9.13 Decentralized Social Media

Blockchain-based social media platforms offer users greater control over their data, content ownership, and monetization. These platforms aim to reduce censorship, as no single entity can control the network while providing more privacy and security to users.

9.14 Decentralized Cloud Storage

Blockchain enables decentralized cloud storage solutions, where data is stored across a network of computers instead of centralized data centers. Users can securely store, share, and retrieve data while ensuring privacy and protection from data breaches or server failures.

9.15 Insurance

Blockchain transforms the insurance industry by automating claims processing through smart contracts. Once the conditions of an insurance policy are met (e.g., in the case of an accident), the smart contract can automatically trigger the payout, making the process more efficient and reducing fraud.

```
TX1: 2023-01-02 13:22:15 Bob submitted a claim for $1,200 for car
repairs to SafeDrive Insurance.
```

9.16 Gaming and NFTs

In gaming, blockchain enables players to own in-game assets like characters, skins, or weapons as non-fungible tokens (NFTs). These assets can be traded, sold, or used across different games, giving players real ownership and control over their digital assets.

```
TX1: 2023-01-02 20:10:40 Player1 earned 250 XP after defeating the
Dragon Boss in FantasyQuest.
```

9.17 Humanitarian Aid

Blockchain improves the distribution of humanitarian aid by ensuring transparency and accountability in how funds or resources are used. It enables the secure tracking of donations, preventing fraud and ensuring that aid reaches the intended recipients. Again, for this area, we can also apply the concepts of public and private keys and designated signatures for each humanitarian aid package. The aid workers can use their assigned private keys to sign those products, and auditors can use their corresponding public keys to verify their signatures.

9.18 Tokening Assets

Blockchain allows tokenizing real-world assets like stocks, bonds, real estate, or art. These digital tokens represent fractional ownership, making investing in high-value assets easier and increasing liquidity in previously non-liquid markets.

9.19 Project Template #1

Hands-on experience is critical to learning various new concepts or technology. This is especially true for many abstract concepts. After learners and students construct their blockchains, they would understand this concept much better. The objective of such an exercise or term project is that learners and students will:

(1) understand how to generate random numbers and the concept of random seed
(2) how to use `vlookup()`, `int()`, `text(,'mm/dd/yyyy')`, and `concatenate()`
(3) how to generate `n` transactions
(4) how to generate `n` hashes from those `n` transactions
(5) how to group them by using the Merkle Tree method
(6) how to link the current block with the previous one

For example, we can generate 100 transactions and generate 100 hashes (using sha256). Assume we divide them into five blocks (20 transactions each). After applying the Merkle Tree methodology, we have just 5 Merkle Root hashes. As the last step, we link those five blocks.

9.20 Project Template #2

It is similar to Project Template #1 described in the previous section, except we add a signature for each transaction. We are using voting as an example. Assume that we have ten voters and we use two voters as one block.

Step 1: Generate ten random names
Step 2: Generate ten pairs of public and private keys
Step 3: Generate ten voting records
Step 4: Use their private key to generate ten signatures
Step 5: Generate each block's Merkle Tree Root
Step 6: Link those five blocks
Verify those signatures by using their public keys.

9.21 Generating a Column:1 to 2000

In the next section, we will show how to generate 2,000 transactions. One task is to create a column of numbers from 1 to 2 and up to 2,000. Below is the procedure. We assume that the first number starts in cell A1.

Step 1: Enter 1 in cell A1.
Step 2: Go to the Home tab.
Step 3: In the Editing group, click on Fill. Select Series from the dropdown menu.

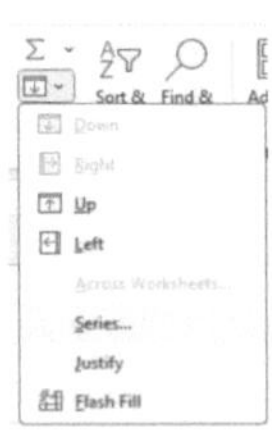

Fig. 9.4 Selecting "Series…"

Step 4: In the Series dialog box, make the following selections:
Series in: Columns, Type: Linear, Step Value: 1, Stop Value: 2000.
Click OK.

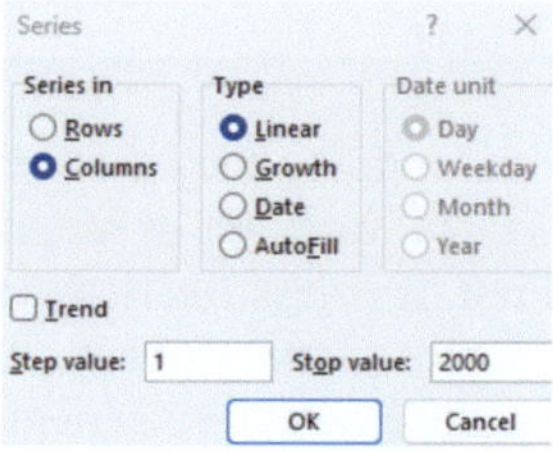

Fig. 9.5 The parameters for "Series in", Type, Step value, and Stop value

9.22 Generating 2,000 Transactions

We will use the next few sections to explain how to generate those simulated transactions. As the first step, we copy the following line to cell A1. This is our standard format. Learners and students will choose another standard for other topics, such as voting systems. The techniques are almost identical.

```
TX1: 2023-01-02 06:58:27 Sue received 0.0006 BTC from Emma.
```

Then, we enter two columns, 1 to 15, and 15 names, and name those two columns as `table` to simplify our notions. Based on the method explained in the previous section, we generate a column from 1 to 2000, as shown below. Note that we hide some rows to make our spreadsheet clean.

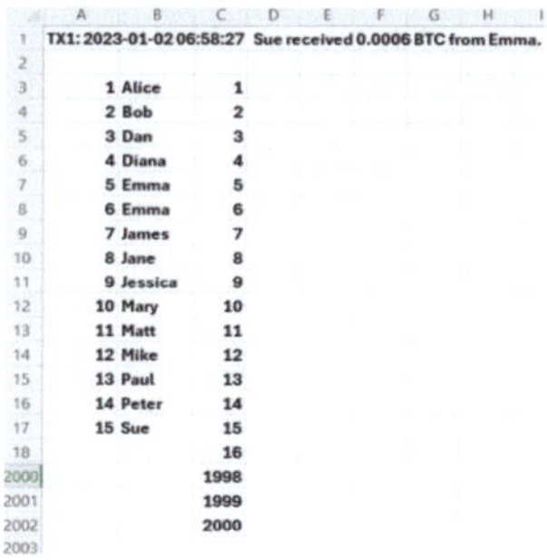

	A	B	C
1	TX1: 2023-01-02 06:58:27 Sue received 0.0006 BTC from Emma.		
2			
3	1	Alice	1
4	2	Bob	2
5	3	Dan	3
6	4	Diana	4
7	5	Emma	5
8	6	Emma	6
9	7	James	7
10	8	Jane	8
11	9	Jessica	9
12	10	Mary	10
13	11	Matt	11
14	12	Mike	12
15	13	Paul	13
16	14	Peter	14
17	15	Sue	15
18			16
2000			1998
2001			1999
2002			2000
2003			

Fig. 9.6 The column with values from 1 to 2,000 (many hidden rows)

9.23 Adding a Few Parts

When demonstrating to students or doing the exercise yourself, it might be a good idea to use the Excel `concat ()` function at an early stage. There are at least two advantages to doing so. First, it is less likely that our formula would not work since there are just a few variables we would link. Second, students would gain more confidence when they see the results. We generate a column of date variables and then combine those three parts: TX, ID number, and date.

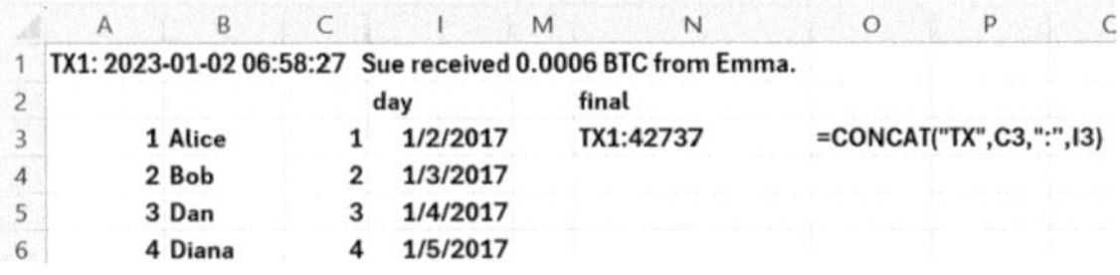

	A	B	C	I	M	N	O	P
1	TX1: 2023-01-02 06:58:27 Sue received 0.0006 BTC from Emma.							
2				day		final		
3		1	Alice	1	1/2/2017	TX1:42737	=CONCAT("TX",C3,":",I3)	
4		2	Bob	2	1/3/2017			
5		3	Dan	3	1/4/2017			
6		4	Diana	4	1/5/2017			

Fig. 9.7 Adding "TX1:" and date (the date format is not correct)

However, one issue is that the result shows an integer 42,737 instead of 1/2/2017. We can generate a designed date using the Excel `text()` function.

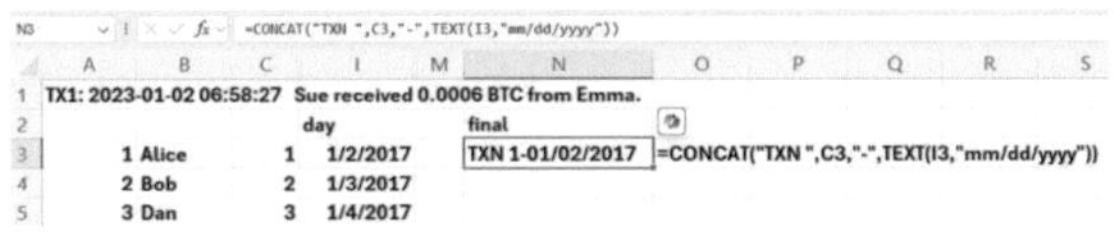

=CONCAT("TXN ",C3,"-",TEXT(I3,"mm/dd/yyyy"))

	A	B	C	I	M	N	O
1	TX1: 2023-01-02 06:58:27 Sue received 0.0006 BTC from Emma.						
2				day		final	
3		1	Alice	1	1/2/2017	TXN 1-01/02/2017	=CONCAT("TXN ",C3,"-",TEXT(I3,"mm/dd/yyyy"))
4		2	Bob	2	1/3/2017		
5		3	Dan	3	1/4/2017		

Fig. 9.8 Making a correct format for the date variable

Then, we can copy the formula to the whole column.

9.24 Adding H:M:S and Name1

To add more columns between the date and final columns, we can insert the columns `h`, `m`, and `s` (for hour, minute, and second).

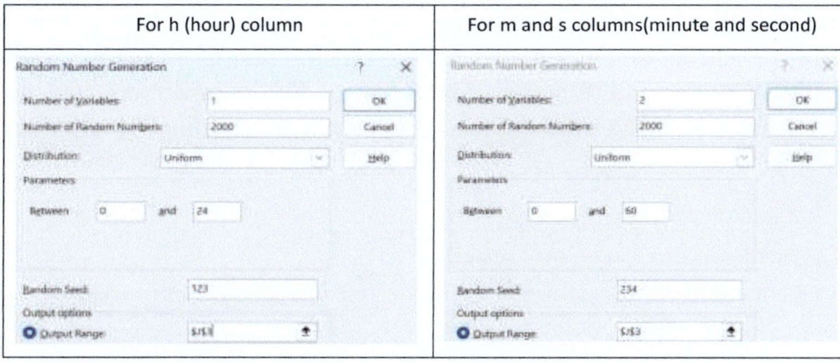

Figs. 9.9 and 9.10 Random number generation for hour, minute, and second

The random seed for Hour is 123, and the random seed for m and s columns is 234. To make our notation look better, we name a cell 'space', which contains just two spaces. The top few lines are shown below.

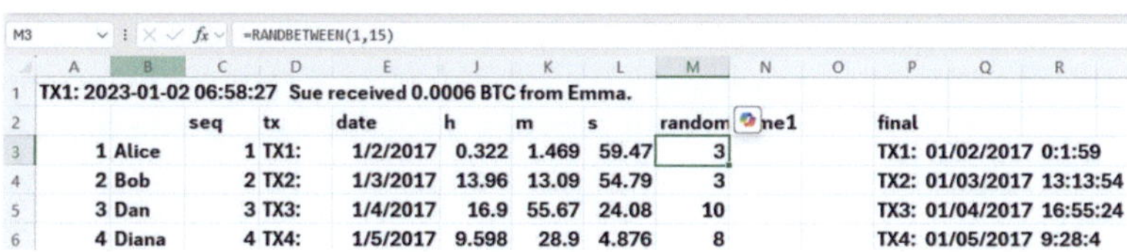

M3 =RANDBETWEEN(1,15)

	A	B	C	D	E	J	K	L	M	N	O	P	Q	R
1	TX1: 2023-01-02 06:58:27 Sue received 0.0006 BTC from Emma.													
2			seq	tx	date	h	m	s	random	name1		final		
3	1	Alice	1	TX1:	1/2/2017	0.322	1.469	59.47	3			TX1: 01/02/2017 0:1:59		
4	2	Bob	2	TX2:	1/3/2017	13.96	13.09	54.79	3			TX2: 01/03/2017 13:13:54		
5	3	Dan	3	TX3:	1/4/2017	16.9	55.67	24.08	10			TX3: 01/04/2017 16:55:24		
6	4	Diana	4	TX4:	1/5/2017	9.598	28.9	4.876	8			TX4: 01/05/2017 9:28:4		

Fig. 9.11 The combination of "TX1:", date, hour, minute, and second

9.25 Adding Name1 and Amount

To choose a set of random numbers between 1 and 15 (for 15 names), we can use the Excel `randbetween(1,15)`. There are two shortcomings to using this function. First, when changing anything subsequently, this set of numbers will change. Second, generating the same set of random numbers isn't easy. We can use the copy as a value to deal with the first issue of personal exercise. However, there is no good way to deal with the second one.

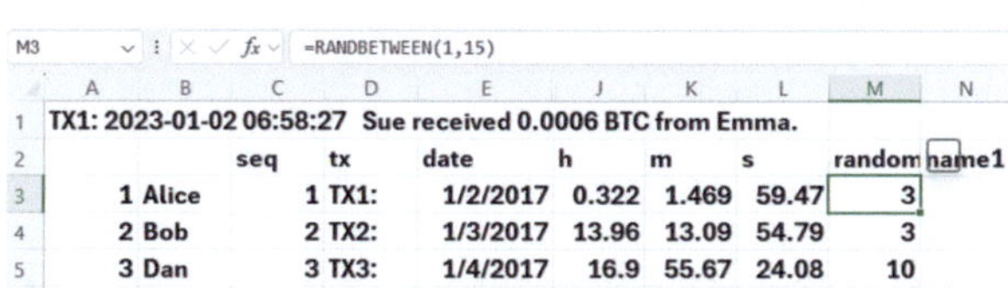

M3 =RANDBETWEEN(1,15)

	A	B	C	D	E	J	K	L	M	N
1	TX1: 2023-01-02 06:58:27 Sue received 0.0006 BTC from Emma.									
2			seq	tx	date	h	m	s	random	name1
3	1	Alice	1	TX1:	1/2/2017	0.322	1.469	59.47	3	
4	2	Bob	2	TX2:	1/3/2017	13.96	13.09	54.79	3	
5	3	Dan	3	TX3:	1/4/2017	16.9	55.67	24.08	10	
6	4	Diana	4	TX4:	1/5/2017	9.598	28.9	4.876	8	

Fig. 9.12 Excel RANDOMBETWEEN(1,15) for 15 names

Because of this, we still use "Random number generations". The parameters for the Uniform Distribution are 1 to 16, and the random seed is 345. To find a name, we use the `vlookup ()` function. Since the random numbers are not integers, we apply the Excel `int()` function to convert them. The final column includes name1.

N3 =VLOOKUP(M3,table,2)

	A	B	C	D	E	J	K	L	M	N	O	P
1	TX1: 2023-01-02 06:58:27 Sue received 0.0006 BTC from Emma.											
2			seq	tx	date	h	m	s	random	name1		final
3	1	Alice		1	TX1:	1/2/2017	0.322	1.469	59.47	1.53311	Alice	TX1: 01/02/2017 0:1:59 Alice
4	2	Bob		2	TX2:	1/3/2017	13.96	13.09	54.79	7.012909	James	TX2: 01/03/2017 13:13:54 James
5	3	Dan		3	TX3:	1/4/2017	16.9	55.67	24.08	11.98346	Matt	TX3: 01/04/2017 16:55:24 Matt
6	4	Diana		4	TX4:	1/5/2017	9.598	28.9	4.876	7.2979	James	TX4: 01/05/2017 9:28:4 James
7	5	Emma		5	TX5:	1/6/2017	23.7	13.8	1.809	14.01874	Peter	TX5: 01/06/2017 23:13:1 Peter
8	6	Emma		6	TX6:	1/7/2017	2.391	7.345	10.33	11.54308	Matt	TX6: 01/07/2017 2:7:10 Matt

Fig. 9.13 Searching for the first name by using Excel VLOOKUP

9.26 Adding Actions

For an action taken by any individual, we generate the following two columns in 4 rows and name them "actions." Again, readers and students can add more actions here.

S	T
1	sent
2	received
3	expected
4	would spend

Fig. 9.14 Four types of actions

For the action column, we generated a random column with parameters of (1, 5) for a uniform distribution, and the random seed is 456. The amount column contains a set of random numbers. The parameters for the uniform distribution are 0.0001 and 0.01, and the random seed is 567.

	A	B	C	E	I	J	K	L	M	N	O	S	T
1	TX1: 2023-01-02 06:58:27 Sue received 0.0006 BTC from Emma.											0	sent
2			seq	date	random	name1	random2	action	amount	5 digits	final	1	received
3	1	Alice	1	1/2/2017	1.49776	Alice	0.15379	sent	0.00067	0.00067	TX1: 01/02/2017 0:1:59 Alice sent 0.00067BTC	2	expected
4	2	Bob	2	1/3/2017	6.61205	Emma	2.67489	expected	0.00228	0.00228	TX2: 01/03/2017 13:13:54 Emma expected 0.0(	3	would spend
5	3	Dan	3	1/4/2017	11.2512	Jessica	0.81254	sent	0.00763	0.00763	TX3: 01/04/2017 16:55:24 Jessica sent 0.00763BTC		
6	4	Diana	4	1/5/2017	6.97137	Emma	3.1015	would spend	0.00459	0.00459	TX4: 01/05/2017 9:28:4 Emma would spend 0.00459BTC		
7	5	Emma	5	1/6/2017	13.1508	Jessica	2.66653	expected	0.00751	0.00751	TX5: 01/06/2017 23:13:1 Jessica expected 0.00	expected	from
8	6	Emma	6	1/7/2017	10.8402	Jessica	0.0147	sent	0.00313	0.00313	TX6: 01/07/2017 2:7:10 Jessica sent 0.00313BT	received	from

Fig. 9.15 A random amount

The formula in cell S4 is = `CONCAT("TX",C3,":",TEXT(I3,"mm/dd/yyyy"),space,INT(J3),":",INT(K3),":",INT(L3),space,N3,space BTC").`

The Excel `round()` function was applied to clarify the amount.

9.27 The Final Column

When using 'send', we should use 'to', while for 'received' we expect 'from'. For this reason, we generated the following set of values.

V	W
sent	to
received	from
expected	from
would spend	previously received from

Fig. 9.16 Four types of directions (column W)

As the first step, we need to sort it out. After that, we name it '`fromTo`'.

expected	from
received	from
sent	to
would spend	previously received from

Fig. 9.17 The sorted result

Our result is shown below.

	A	B	E	K	L	O	P	Q
1	TX1: 2023-01-02 06:58:27 Sue received 0.0006 BTC from Emma.							
2			date	random	action	toFrom	name2	final
3	1	Alice	1/2/2017	0.15379	sent	to	Dan	TX1: 01/02/2017 0:1:59 Alice sent 0.00067BTC to Dan.
4	2	Bob	1/3/2017	2.67489	expected	from	Jane	TX2: 01/03/2017 13:13:54 Emma expected 0.00228BTC from Jane.
5	3	Dan	1/4/2017	0.81254	sent	to	Matt	TX3: 01/04/2017 16:55:24 Matt sent 0.00763BTC to Matt.
6	4	Diana	1/5/2017	3.1015	would spe	previous r	Jane	TX4: 01/05/2017 9:28:4 Emma would spend 0.00459BTC previous received from Jane
7	5	Emma	1/6/2017	2.66653	expected	from	Matt	TX5: 01/06/2017 23:13:1 Matt expected 0.00751BTC from Matt.
8	6	Emma	1/7/2017	0.0147	sent	to	Matt	TX6: 01/07/2017 2:7:10 Mary sent 0.00313BTC to Matt.
9	7	James	1/8/2017	1.87514	received	from	Dan	TX7: 01/08/2017 22:7:10 Alice received 0.0012BTC from Dan.
10	8	Jane	1/9/2017	0.82261	sent	to	Emma	TX8: 01/09/2017 23:6:17 Dan sent 0.0034BTC to Emma.
11	9	Jessica	1/10/2017	0.3117	sent	to	Emma	TX9: 01/10/2017 7:46:22 Dan sent 0.00036BTC to Emma.
12	10	Mary	1/11/2017	1.2461	received	from	Emma	TX10: 01/11/2017 20:9:26 Dan received 0.00556BTC from Emma.

Fig. 9.18 The final result

For name2, the formula is = `VLOOKUP(INT(M3) + 2,table,2)`.The final column has the following formula in cell U3.

```
=CONCAT("TX",C3,":",TEXT(I3,"mm/dd/yyyy"),space,INT(J3
),":",INT(K3),
":",INT(L3),space,N3,space,P3,space,ROUND(Q3,6),"
BTC",space,R3,space,T3,".")
```

9.28 Bitcoin'S Block vs. Transaction

Before discussing Merkle Tree in the next few sections, we will show the incentive to discuss and explain the topic. At https://blockstream.info/, we will see the following image (as of 2/13/2027 19:25).

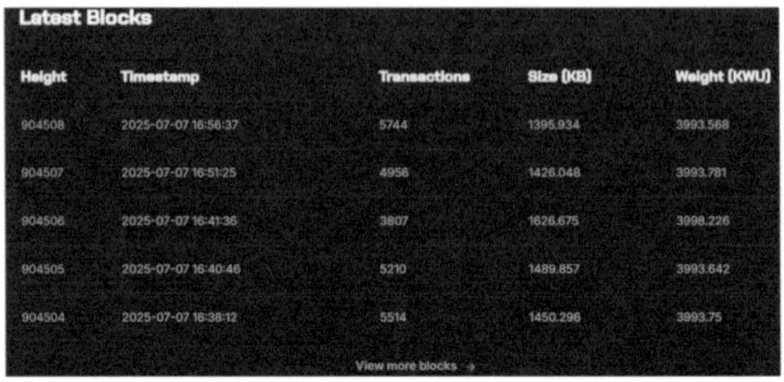

Latest Blocks

Height	Timestamp	Transactions	Size (KB)	Weight (KWU)
904508	2025-07-07 16:56:37	5744	1395.934	3993.568
904507	2025-07-07 16:51:25	4956	1426.048	3993.781
904506	2025-07-07 16:41:36	3807	1626.675	3998.226
904505	2025-07-07 16:40:46	5210	1489.857	3993.642
904504	2025-07-07 16:38:12	5514	1450.296	3993.75

View more blocks →

Fig. 9.19 The latest Blocks

The latest block is block 883,654, which has 1,492 transactions. One simple question is how to get a block's hash using so many transactions. The Merkle Tree is the solution.

9.29 The Merkle Tree

The Merkle Tree A data structure in which hashed data is used to create another hash representing the data in a file. This structure makes it easy for computers to compare information because it only takes a few milliseconds to generate hashes from the information and verify that the results are identical. Below is its logic. Assume that we have no transactions and plan to form a block.

Step 1: Input n transactions.

Step 2: Generate related sha256 hashes

Step 3: if n is an odd number, we repeat the last hash. For example, for five hashes, we have:

h_1, h_2, h_3, h_4, h_5, h_5.

Step 4: We generate a new hash for each pair of hashes. For example, from h_1 and h_2, we have h_12, and from h_3 and h_4, we have h_34, and so on.

Step 4: Now, we end up with n2=n/2 number of hashes. Again, if n2 is an odd number, we repeat the last hash.

Step 5: Repeat Steps 3 and 4 until we end up with just one hash.

The following graph shows the process based on eight transactions.

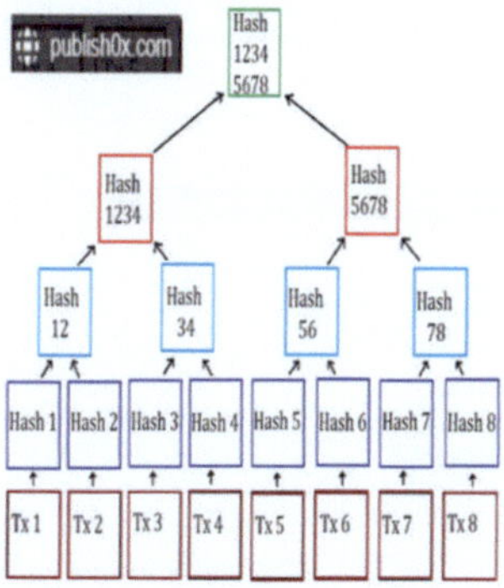

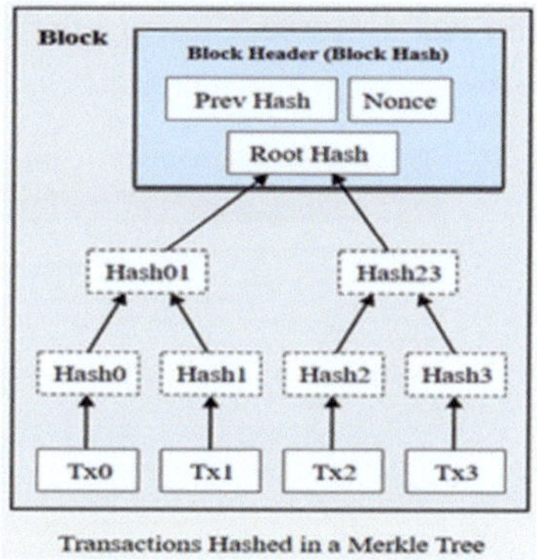

Figs. 9.20 and 9.21 Two illustrations of Merkle Trees

The image on the left above is from publish0x.com, and the image on the right is from Nakamoto (2008).

9.30 Case Sensitivity

When generating a 256hash, the input text is case-sensitive—for example, using 'John Doe' and JOHN DOE as examples. At https://passwords-generator.org/sha256-hash-generator, we will get the following different hashes.

```
John Doe
6CEA57C2FB6CBC2A40411135005760F241FFFC3E5E67AB99882726431037F9
08
JOHN DOE
2B37E5E537EE6F8FAD661E19E090B27CD0CFD2923077D8F56A68772316F3A4
B9
```

The website has a button allowing users to get a lower- or upper-case hash, as shown below.

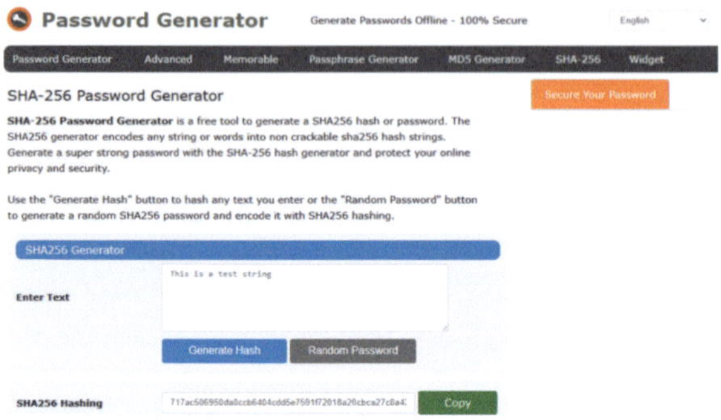

Fig. 9.22 Case sensitive for a given phrase

This is usually fine for text input. However, when combining two hashes to generate a new one, like the Merkle Tree, we must know that inputting lower-case or upper-case hashes will lead to different results.

9.31 A Set of Sample Transactions

To facilitate our discussion and illustration, we will use the following transactions. For example, we will use two and four transactions to calculate our Merkle Root and verify the results using a website. The set is given below.

```
TX1: 2014-01-02 06:08:14    Sue expects 0.2327 ETH from Emma.
TX2: 2014-01-03 18:24:39    Mike receives 0.0221 BTC from Peter.
TX3: 2014-01-06 09:24:24    Matt sends 0.0266 BTC to Matt.
TX4: 2014-01-07 20:21:46    Mike receives 0.3359 ETH from Sue.
TX5: 2014-01-08 21:08:06    James receives 0.0650 BTC from Emma.
TX6: 2014-01-09 01:08:25    Mary receives 0.2986 ETH from Emma.
TX7: 2014-01-10 12:13:58    Jane spends 0.0375 BTC previously
received from Diana.
TX8: 2014-01-13 20:27:52    Dan expects 0.0413 BTC from James.
TX9: 2014-01-14 12:15:52    Dan receives 0.0355 BTC from Bob.
TX10: 2014-01-15 10:50:10    Peter spends 0.2119 ETH previously
received from Mary.
```

Later in the chapter, we will show how to use one of our hidden functions to get the above data set.

9.32 Only Two Transactions

The simplest will be just one transaction. Then, the Merle Root will be the hash of this transaction. Thus, we start with two transactions. We copy the first two transactions, as shown below.

```
TX1:  2014-01-02 06:08:14    Sue expects 0.2327 ETH from Emma.
TX2:  2014-01-03 18:24:39    Mike receives 0.0221 BTC from Peter.
```

The first way is to use the website we discussed intensively in Chapter 3: Blockchain 2 ASCII and sha256, https://passwordsgenerator.net/sha256-hash-generator/.

```
EEC45A93C5D80844DAB52A6A92C88F96A878C16136128F72B1844713255B9
A90
5870E85827362181A1D8AD75292144E449758090C49F7162A69667B75689
1CD1
```

Based on the Merkle Tree Methodology, we combine them.

```
EEC45A93C5D80844DAB52A6A92C88F96A878C16136128F72B1844
713255B9A905870E85827362181A1D8AD75292144E449758090C49F
7162A69667B756891CD1
```

When trying again at the above website, we get the Merkle root (value), as shown below.

```
D38FCC3BCFED4A2B9D2CBAFA2064AB0F3DF8C1DE1072622F7CABA9B0F5CD3
009
```

Later in the chapter, we show that one of the hidden functions, `.merkleTree()`, can also be used to verify this result. Since the above website's default setting is upper-case, we deliberately designed this function to use upper-case intermediate hashes. The function `.merkleTreeLowCase()` will use lower-case intermediate hashes.

9.33 Three Transactions

For this example, we will use our `.merkleTree()` function to get the Merkle Root, then use the same website and the `.combine2hashes()` function to verify. The three transactions are given below.

```
TX1:  2014-01-02 06:08:14    Sue expects 0.2327 ETH from Emma.
TX2:  2014-01-03 18:24:39    Mike receives 0.0221 BTC from Peter.
TX3:  2014-01-06 09:24:24    Matt sends 0.0266 BTC to Matt.
```

The shortcut of the `.merkleTree ()` is `.mtree()`. We will get the following result after typing `.mtree()` and hitting the Enter key.

```
* ------------------------------------------------------------- *
* Objective: generate a Merkle Tree (Root) *
*       Copy your transactions, then hit the Enter key *
* ------------------------------------------------------------- *
* Launch a text editor/Excel and paste your hashes there *
*    Then hit the Enter Key to continue *
Round #: 1 and n= 4
EEC45A93C5D80844DAB52A6A92C88F96A878C16136128F72B1844713255B9
A90
5870E85827362181A1D8AD75292144E449758090C49F7162A69667B75689
1CD1
D2DCE95351600DF7E761E868BDF7481E26F8E54B26B3400063AFE398D67E4
C1D
D2DCE95351600DF7E761E868BDF7481E26F8E54B26B3400063AFE398D67E4
C1D
Round #: 2 and n= 2
D38FCC3BCFED4A2B9D2CBAFA2064AB0F3DF8C1DE1072622F7CABA9B0F5CD3
009
F05876143356B65A25D0CB5E55599D719F21F44D55D996EB79672D970
DBCDA47  *  ---------------------------------------------------
-------- *
Merkle Root:
7C95CD7A8173467778D2631744AAE58704B90627940E0D73CF9D2E70856CC3
98
* ------------------------------------------------------------- *
```

9.34 .merkleTreeBothCases ()

The function `.merkleTree ()` automatically converts all hashes to uppercase, consistent with the website's default setting. A new function `.merkleTreeBothCases ()` also converts both cases. Our input will be from the following three transactions.

```
TX4: 2024-02-06 20:34:02  Dan receives 0.0621 ETH from Emma.
TX5: 2024-02-07 21:23:15  Alice receives 0.0794 BTC from Diana.
TX6: 2024-02-08 01:26:57  Sue sends 0.0391 BTC to Bob.
```

To start the function, we can use its shortcut `.mtree2()`.

```
> .mtree2()

  * ------------------------------------------------------------ *
  *  Objective: generate a Merkle Tree (Root)                    *
  *              Copy your transactions, then hit the Enter key  *

  * How do you treat your hashes?                                *
  *   1       upper-case letters                                 *
  *   2       lower-case letters                                 *
1
  * ------------------------------------------------------------ *
  * Launch a text editor/Excel and paste your hashes there       *
  *     Then hit the Enter Key to continue
```

Fig. 9.23 The hidden Merkel Tree function #2 (.mtree2)

The result is shown below.

```
 Round #: 1  and n= 4
6023AF59B812567CE947DADEDFCEF8911756EFE0B4AA4398A753817C22BE085E
37DA70ED821E51983BA4E27FBC273872A47F494CB8230EEAB8E598DCEF676DF4
1BF67BE5169BA0520B8BDA39211D95DA66592FF742CC0C04727361D4F6BCFED3
1BF67BE5169BA0520B8BDA39211D95DA66592FF742CC0C04727361D4F6BCFED3

 Round #: 2  and n= 2
130121DED8EA9F85FE4B4F69C4835B3DF2DF3FABD7491DE44E2AE8155A48DD99
1CAD444C55684555299631D378E2DFE5CCAFF2CF4D8F9BFCE39314264A764767

 * ---------------------------------------------------------- *
 *  Your merkle Root:                                         *
C1E4331C466373E87949AAF3E09F9A5475CAE625C10C2B1218A8E366AE48D0ED
 * ---------------------------------------------------------- *
```

Fig. 9.24 Rounds #1 and #2 and final Merkle Root

This result is equivalent to the result generated by `.merkleTree ()` or `.mtree()`. On the other hand, if you choose 2 (lowercase), the result is shown below.

```
 Round #: 1  and n= 4
6023af59b812567ce947dadedfcef8911756efe0b4aa4398a753817c22be085e
37da70ed821e51983ba4e27fbc273872a47f494cb8230eeab8e598dcef676df4
1bf67be5169ba0520b8bda39211d95da66592ff742cc0c04727361d4f6bcfed3
1bf67be5169ba0520b8bda39211d95da66592ff742cc0c04727361d4f6bcfed3

 Round #: 2  and n= 2
1b0485e557cfc62757da3a138a36f479a21aa575f48fdfd046ea9b905833b1ec
8586e2772650e09672de1e14e3ef10cf5496498c85e1a15ec27303235a43b6f1

 * ---------------------------------------------------------- *
 *  Your merkle Root:                                         *
c97e7739c2769c7329f680ce875ca974699832888972470613 9a46f54963962a
 * ---------------------------------------------------------- *
```

Fig. 9.25 The result for lower case

9.35 Our Hidden Functions

There are two ways to discover this chapter's hidden functions. The first is to type.chapter9 or.`c9` (see Appendix 2 for more details). The second is to use the.`searchHiddenFunctions ()` function, as shown below.

```
> .searchHiddenFunctions(9)
 CHAPTER                              NAME                              SHORTCUT
       9 install.packages('digest')
       9 install.packages('dplyr')
       9 install.packages('stringr')
       9 -------------------------------
       9 .fakeLedger                     .fl   # need 'dplyr'
       9 .fakeTransactions               .ftr  # need 'stringr' and 'dplyr'
       9 .fakeHashes                     .fh
       9 .howManyRoundKerleTree          .round
       9 .combine2hashes                 .c2h    # need 'digest'
       9 .combine2hashes2                .c2h2   # need 'digest'
       9 .merkleTree                     .mtree  # need 'digest'
       9 .merkleTreeBothCases            .mtree2 # need 'digest'
       9 .merkleTreeHashAsInput          .mtree3 # need 'digest'
>
```

Fig. 9.26 The hidden functions related to Chapter 9

9.36 Our .howManyRoundkerleTree () Function

One function calculates how many rounds the underlying function will run. For a simple value such as 8, we can calculate it ourselves: 8, 4, 2, and 1. For 100 transactions, we will have 100, 50, 26 (25 + 1), 14 (13 + 1), 8 (7 + 1), 4, 2, and 1. The shortcut function for this function is.`round()`. A few examples are shown below.

```
> .round()
*-------------------------------------------------- *
*  Objective: calculate how many rounds needed to    *
*             get the Merkle Root (Merkle Tree)      *
*-------------------------------------------------- *
*  Input an integer such as 500                      *
*                 number of transactions)            *
8
 Input n= 8
*-------------------------------------------------- *
Round # 1 , n= 8
Round # 2 , n= 4
Round # 3 , n= 2
*-------------------------------------------------- *
```

Fig. 9.27 Estimating how many rounds for a given set of transactions

The second example is to input an integer directly, as shown below.

9.37 Our .fakeHashes () Function

This function will generate a set of fake hashes. Those hashes can be used by.`merkleTree3hashAsInput ()`, discussed in the next section, shown below.

```
> .fakeHashes()
 * ------------------------------------------------- *
 *  Objective: generate n fake 64-character hashes   *
 * ------------------------------------------------- *
 *  1) Enter the number of hashes to generate:       *
10
 * 2) Enter a random seed if you prefer, otherwise   *
 *    just hit the Enter Key                         *
123
 *  Generated hashes:                                *
ee2d2915a43d589af42a8b88c279698d23d0a64bef9c68896ab464af581c47be
c108a854e8e9bef3d5a7556ef051013c45e28358fd8627fdbe8ddf2dcf62659e
4472919b195eb3d0dd527d2de706a6ce695def6a945f7f46a3bdbc28659861fc
273e6307dd38f75af372c33b509a3a867d4c1acd587bf93ccd4f6c0779871c48
669cb97e569a08cc2945caa8396869f3c788846dd5a099090c9a46b498351dec
0f48328d013904487684c19e56c8f04cbe474e631c00101c70e2114eb8c9c599
5bfff23aa2c62ef1e628c6ded83159b8bcca6c4a02b140ebd2d81e52281f0597
9f9c353c3d8f7690e17296a0b12cced25d9f4310fb0b4b11be245ff9e2a2d070
fa37bc997b6103a84ab714c15998a65fb2a7fad637b2d75369fa7df398523883
e354076ebe4d5eef27e9463fbdf8aa2dc96c18d53edd51177a486267a9406573
 * ------------------------------------------------- *
 * Launch your text editor and paste hashes there.   *
 * ------------------------------------------------- *
```

Fig. 9.28 Generating fake Hashes function (.fakeHashes)

The random seed generates the same set of hashes. The shortcut to the above function is `.fh()`.

9.38 Our `.merkleTreeHashAsInut()` Function

The input data to our hidden function `.merkleTree ()` are transactions. By design, those transactions are one-line records. However, readers and students might have irregular inputs, such as multiple-line text. In those cases, users can generate their hash first by using a website or our hidden functions. In other words, before running our Merle Tree function, our inputs are hashes instead of a set of transactions. For this purpose, we generated a function `.merkleTreeHashAsInput()`. Assume that we have the following three hashes.

```
ee2d2915a43d589af42a8b88c279698d23d0a64bef9c68896ab464af581c4
7be
c108a854e8e9bef3d5a7556ef051013c45e28358fd8627fdbe8ddf2dcf626
59e
4472919b195eb3d0dd527d2de706a6ce695def6a945f7f46a3bdbc2865986
1fc
```

We have the following result after typing `.merkleTreeHashAsInput()` and then hitting the Enter Key. For the upper-case or lower-case, 1 is chosen, i.e., for an upper-case scenario.

```
> .merkleTreeHashAsInput()

 * ------------------------------------------------------------ *
 *  Objective: generate a Merkle Tree (Root)                    *
 *              Copy your hashes, then hit the Enter key        *
 *              Note: not transaction data !!!!!                *

 * How do you treat your hashes?                                *
 *   1       upper-case letters                                 *
 *   2       lower-case letters                                 *
1
```

Fig. 9.29 The Merkle Tree Function using Hashes as inputs (.merkleTreeHashAsInput)

The result is shown below.

```
 Round #: 1  and n= 4
EE2D2915A43D589AF42A8B88C279698D23D0A64BEF9C68896AB464AF581C47BE
C108A854E8E9BEF3D5A7556EF051013C45E28358FD8627FDBE8DDF2DCF62659E
4472919B195EB3D0DD527D2DE706A6CE695DEF6A945F7F46A3BDBC28659861FC
4472919B195EB3D0DD527D2DE706A6CE695DEF6A945F7F46A3BDBC28659861FC

 Round #: 2  and n= 2
4C957DA124A25462F40EB4B93DAC8F0F6AEE151406E3CEB7639E787EF3D0FBB7
409F062ADFE9200DD95254BE8066EF5A163C1CF7DB0AAA689A1F85E20C1C5EC3

 * ------------------------------------------------------------ *
 *   Your Merkle Root is given below:                           *
BA1CEC981278B83FBC34D7CCE1A6CE8C7C49F4CF84F3A073DAFB489580517DA3
 * ------------------------------------------------------------ *
```

Fig. 9.30 Rounds #1 and #2 and Merkel Root (4 Hashes as inputs)

On the other hand, if the lowercase is chosen for the same input, the result is shown below.

```
 Round #: 1  and n= 4
ee2d2915a43d589af42a8b88c279698d23d0a64bef9c68896ab464af581c47be
c108a854e8e9bef3d5a7556ef051013c45e28358fd8627fdbe8ddf2dcf62659e
4472919b195eb3d0dd527d2de706a6ce695def6a945f7f46a3bdbc28659861fc
4472919b195eb3d0dd527d2de706a6ce695def6a945f7f46a3bdbc28659861fc

 Round #: 2  and n= 2
ba0d1b32552f3eb0d3196a1ab60db5806ffff20573c639b9a1adff927816d8ae
735ca4ecee1fec1dbd972c0e67c2d0f398ab3f67c9a0cae3e862e2ebf074dc83

 * ------------------------------------------------------------ *
 *   Your Merkle Root is given below:                           *
9272ca81e586f6a8d6357be3461e8f783422e4dc0e7e590bb9b329ba64e07564
 * ------------------------------------------------------------ *
```

Fig. 9.31 Lower case as inputs

9.39 Our `.fakeTransactions()` Function

As discussed earlier in the chapter, generating your transactions using Excel is a good exercise. One apparent reason is that learners or students can develop their own data sets, such as voting data, using the same methodology. On the other hand, to generate fake transaction data, we have a hidden function, the `.fakeTransactions()` function, as shown below.

```
> .fakeTransactions()

 * ---------------------------------------------------------- *
 * Objective: generate transactions for a Merkle Tree         *
 * ---------------------------------------------------------- *
 *    1) Input a starting date, such as 1/2/2024              *
2/1/2024
 *    2)  Input the number of days, such as 200               *
200
 *    3) Input a random seed such as 123 for reproducibility *
 *       If you don't want a seed, hit the Enter-key.         *
123
 * The first few observations are shown below.

TX1: 2024-02-01 06:58:27   Sue spends 0.0006 BTC previously received from Emma.
TX2: 2024-02-02 18:08:21   Diana receives 0.0260 BTC from Jane.
TX3: 2024-02-05 09:53:07   James expects 0.0642 BTC from Mary.
TX4: 2024-02-06 20:34:02   Dan receives 0.0621 ETH from Emma.
TX5: 2024-02-07 21:23:15   Alice receives 0.0794 BTC from Diana.
TX6: 2024-02-08 01:26:57   Sue sends 0.0391 BTC to Bob.
TX7: 2024-02-09 12:41:28   Emma receives 0.2556 ETH from Emma.
TX8: 2024-02-12 20:04:28   Sue expects 0.0083 BTC from Mary.
TX9: 2024-02-13 12:20:44   Sue spends 0.3345 ETH previously received from Alice.
TX10: 2024-02-14 10:40:39   Sue expects 0.2405 ETH from Mike.
TX11: 2024-02-15 22:18:02   Matt sends 0.2852 ETH to Dan.
TX12: 2024-02-16 10:49:41   Mike spends 0.0892 BTC previously received from Diana.

 *  Launch Excel and paste those transactions there.          *
 * ---------------------------------------------------------- *
>
```

Fig. 9.32 Generating fake Transaction function (.fakeTransaction)

9.40 Our. combin2hashes () Function

This function is used to verify the result by combining two hashes. The shortcut is. c2h.

```
> .c2h()

 * ------------------------------------------------------------ *
 *  Objective: generate a new hash by combining two             *
 *  Step 1:  input the first hash                               *
192bf9ea50cbf23423a734a59ca515fb108e86b6b980b69a40f5fb398249e15e
 *  Step 2:  input the 2nd hash                                 *
9d8eaadf76b14eb426bd98a37450e6cd0826fbcd6c8120f173bf4b31263acd3c
 *  you final hash is given below:                              *
2e7b01aace3f90e71b6d986f053ff01a2d44a80b31fe803fe13286a3e36d8720
 * ------------------------------------------------------------ *
```

Fig. 9.33 The hidden function to combine two Hashes (.c2h)

9.41 Our.Combin2hashes2() Function

This is similar to the above function. The only difference is that we don't have to input each hash separately. Instead, we copy two hashes. The shortcut is.c2h2.

```
> .c2h2()
 * ------------------------------------------------------------- *
 *  Objective: generate a new hash by copying two hashes          *
 *             copy two hashes from your clipboard or Excel       *

 * ------------------------------------------------------------- *
 *   Your inputted hashes are:                                    *
192bf9ea50cbf23423a734a59ca515fb108e86b6b980b69a40f5fb398249e15e
9d8eaadf76b14eb426bd98a37450e6cd0826fbcd6c8120f173bf4b31263acd3c
 * ------------------------------------------------------------- *
 *  you combined hash is given below:                             *
2e7b01aace3f90e71b6d986f053ff01a2d44a80b31fe803fe13286a3e36d8720
 * ------------------------------------------------------------- *
```

Fig. 9.34 An illustration of the hidden .c2h2 function

9.42 Conclusion

After reading this chapter, learners/students are expected to generate their blockchains. Assume that you have some 20 irregular transactions or emails or voting results. And you plan to build up a 5-block blockchain.

Step 1: Generate 20 hashes for those 20 data sets.

Step 2: Apply one of our Merkle Tree functions.

Step 3: Link those five blocks.

For those steps, the website https://passwordsgenerator.net/sha256-hash-generator/ can convert inputs to hashes and generate a Merkle Tree root. Alternatively, our related hidden functions can be used. For example, we can generate an Excel file with five blocks. One of the sample spreadsheets is shown below.

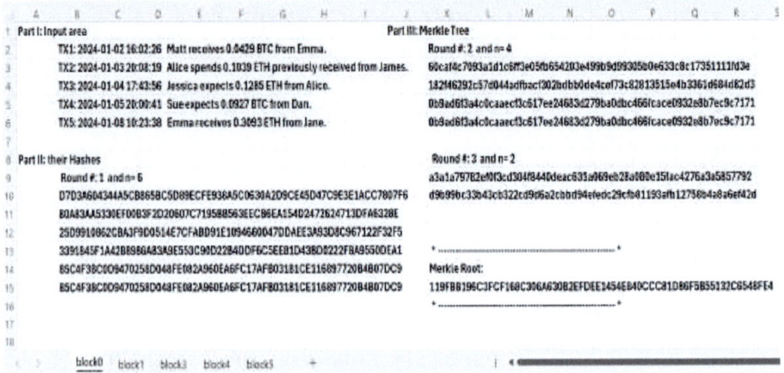

Fig. 9.35 The conclusion

Only block0 is shown, and this can be treated as a template. Users can modify the input areas using their data. The rest is copied from the result of running a Merkle Tree function. Since this is the Genesis Block, it has no previous hash to link with. For the next block, readers/students must find a way to link to the last hash or Merle Root.

Appendix A: Issue the Following Line of R Code for Week 9

```
source("http://datayyy.com/i2ft/week9.txt")
```

```
*---------------------------------------------------------------------*
* Introduction to FinTech using Excel                by Dr. Yan 2025   *
*        (in an R-assisted learning environment)                       *
*---------------------------------------------------------------------*
*   .c1  Introduction and Excel Basics              .c15 Term Projects *
*   .c2  Blockchain 1: (Numbers & alphanumeric)     .c16 R basics(optional) *
*   .c3              2: (ASCII and Sha256)          .c17 Macro (optional) *
*   .c4  Ledger and distributed ledger              .c18 VBA  (optional) *
*   .c5  Cryptography   1: and public/private keys                    *
*   .c6                 2: Advanced                                   *
*   .c7  Cryptocurrency and Ganache                                   *
*   .c8                 2: markets, risk, risk/return tradeoff        *
*   .c9  Blockchain's Applications with Simulations                   *
*---------------------------------------------------------------------*
* >.c9       # go to chapter 9                                        *
* >.uu        # go to utility submenu                                 *
* >.ft        # back to this menu                                     *
*---------------------------------------------------------------------*
```

Fig. 9.36 The menu for Week 9

Appendix B: Typing `.chapter9` or `.c9`, we will have the following contents related to Chapter 9.

```
> .chapter9
function(i=0){
"i  Chap 9: Blockchain apps  &      i   Simulations                   i   Hidden functions
 -  -------------------------      --  -----------------------       --  -------------------
 1  Introduction                   21  Project template #1           41 .searchHiddenFunctions(9)
 2   :#1  cryptocurrencies         22                   #2           42 .fakeLedger              .fl
 3   :#2  Smart Contracts          23  What is simulation?           43 .fakeTransactions        .ftr
 4   :#3  Supply Chain             24     : random numbers           44 .fakeHashes              .fh
 5   :#4  Healthcare Records       25     : Excel rand() function    45 .howManyRound4merkleTree(), .round()
 6   :#5  Voting Systems           26     : Data Analysis not available 46 .merkleTree           .mtr
 7   :#6  Identity Verification    27     : random seed              47 .combine2hashes          .c2h
 8   :#7  Financial Services       28     : from a uniform, normal   48 .combine2hashes2         .c2h2
 9   :#8  Real Estate Transactions 29  Data: fake ledger             49  2024 Election simulator
10   :#9  Intellectual Property    30     : sample transactions      50  MIT election data
11   :10 Energy Trading            31     :        : Excel procedure 51  census: voting data
12   :11 Cross-Border Payments     32     : sample voting data       52  Merkle tree proof
13   :12 Decentralized Social Media 33    :        : Excel procedure
14   :13 Decentralized Cloud Storage 34   : fake hashes
15   :14 Insurance                 35  Merkle tree
16   :15 Gaming and NFTs           36     : logic
17   :16 Humanitarian Aid          37     : logic for 10 transactions
18   :17 Tokenization of Assets    38     : 1,2, and 5 transactions
19    Videos                       39     : image of 8 transactions
40    Links                        40     : .merkleTree() function

Example #1:>.c9    # see the above list
Example #2:>.c9()  # the same as above
Example #3:>.c9(1) # see the 1st explanation
```

Fig. 9.37 The contents of Chapter 9

Exercises

Note that * indicates difficult ones.

9.1 What is the usage of a random seed?

9.2 What is a Merkle Root, and how is it used in blockchain technology?
Explain the role of the Merkle Root in ensuring data integrity in blockchain.

9.3 Describe how a Merkle Tree is constructed. What are the components involved in this process? Discuss the structure of Merkle Trees, including leaves, non-leaf nodes, and the root.

9.4 How does the Merkle Root contribute to the security and efficiency of blockchain networks? Analyze the security benefits of the Merkle Root in preventing data tampering.

9.5 Why are Merkle Trees considered more efficient for verifying transactions than storing entire data blocks? Discuss the advantages of using Merkle Trees for transaction verification in blockchains.

9.6 How does the Merkle Root facilitate validating a specific transaction in a block without downloading the entire blockchain? Explain how a light client can use the Merkle Proof to validate a transaction.

9.7 Can you simulate creating a Merkle Root using a small set of transactions? Walk through each step. Provide a step-by-step explanation of generating a Merkle Root from a set of transactions.

9.8 How do block headers use Merkle Roots to verify the integrity of blockchain data? Describe the relationship between block headers and the Merkle Root.

9.9 Compare Merkle Trees with other data structures used to ensure data integrity in blockchain. Explore the differences between Merkle Trees and alternative data integrity structures like Patricia trees or hash chains.

9.10 What are some potential challenges or limitations of using Merkle Trees in large-scale blockchain applications? Discuss scalability, performance, and complexity issues in Merkle Tree-based systems.

9.11 What role does hashing play in generating a Merkle Root? Explain how hash functions are used to combine transactions into the Merkle Tree.

9.12 At https://passwordsgenerator.net/sha256-hash-generator/, can we get a lower-case hash?

9.13 Does combining two hashes matter if we use upper or lower cases?

9.14 Using the website at https://passwordsgenerator.net/sha256-hash-generator/, what is their Merkle Root for the following three transactions?

```
TX8: 2024-02-12 20:04:28 Sue expects 0.0083 BTC from Mary.
TX9: 2024-02-13 12:2:4 Sue spent 0.0043 ETH received from
Alice.
TX10: 2024-02-14 10:40:39 Sue expects 0.2405 ETH from Mike.
```

9.15 Redo the above question using our hidden function called `.sha256()`.

9.16 Redo again by using our `.merkleTree ()` function.

9.17 What are the differences between two functions associated with the Merkle Tree calculation: `.merkleTree ()` and `.merkleTreeBothCases ()`?

9.18 Give five sentences and generate five hashes using a hidden function called `.sha256()`.

9.19 Is it case-sensitive when using the website https://passwordsgenerator.net/sha256-hash-generator/ to generate a hash?

9.20 For the following five hashes, generate their Merkle Root.

```
5879dbba04af2f3f97de30c510d43a0f72754864ae8ae3ef010cc5e1
ec167c29
43a2936ac1902f78df9a20294ba8d86c8015abf58776a7c3d71c1d662
340e570
989f46b7618f67cc94c93ecd2cd5a380a59fe4baf9c22e3cb481b7
9aecb5a31b
508d1777dda12911d582b27dc67d7102da2428e6c0eda27e5c8fb689
76ba9e15
508bb822e9d5d17b906255049f9e8f2223f0bd2e2d5adce4aba8b1d2
90cc0d20
```

9.21 Using the function `.merkleTree ()`, input a list of 5 transactions. What is the Merkle Root generated from your data? Explain the steps the function takes to compute the Merkle Root. Students will run the function and analyze how the transactions are hashed and combined into a Merkle Tree.

9.22 Run `.merkleTreeBothCases ()` using a set of 6 transactions. Compare the Merkle Root when using padding (if the transaction count is odd) and without padding. How does the Merkle Root differ between the two cases?

9.23 With the function `.merkleTreeHashAsInput()`, input pre-hashed transactions instead of raw data. Compare the Merkle Root generated from pre-hashed data to the root generated by `.merkleTree ()` for the same raw transactions. What differences, if any, do you observe?

9.24 Create a simulation where ten transactions are input for `.merkleTree ()`. Now, remove one transaction and re-run the function. How does the change in the transaction list impact the Merkle Root? Explain the implications of this change for blockchain security. This tests their understanding of how altering transaction data affects the integrity of the Merkle Tree.

9.25 Generate a Merkle Tree using `.merkleTree ()` and then manually calculate the Merkle Root for the same set of transactions step-by-step. Compare your manual result with the function's output. Are the results consistent? If not, identify where the discrepancy occurs.

9.26* Generate a set of records related to Health Care. Generate a blockchain by applying the methodology discussed in this chapter.

```
TX1: 2023-01-02 14:20:30 Dr. Smith prescribed 200mg of Medi-
cation ABC to patient John Doe.
```

9.27* Generate a set of records related to Finance. Generate a blockchain by applying the methodology discussed in this chapter. For example, you can download 20 companies' balance sheets and income statements as input.

9.28* Generate a set of records related to Supply Chain. Apply the methodology discussed in this chapter to create a blockchain.

```
X1: 2023-01-02 10:30:45 Warehouse A shipped 120 units of product XYZ to Store B.
```

9.29* Using Excel, generate 20 records using the following line as your starting point.

```
TX1: 2023-01-02 15:45:23 Alan applied for a personal loan of
$20,000 from XYZ Bank.
```

Then, divide them into five blocks (four records for each block), generate a block hash, and link them to form a blockchain.

References

Crypto Bubbles. Retrieved from https://cryptobubbles.net/
Coinmarketcap, Cryptocurrency Prices, Charts And Market Capitalizations | CoinMarketCap. Retrieved from https://coinmarketcap.com/
Erskine, K. (2018). Data Exploration and Visualization of the Tether Blockchain. Retrieved from https://rpubs.com/keith_erskine/381106
Nakamoto, S. (2008). Retrieved from https://nakamotoinstitute.org/library/bitcoin/
SHA256 Hash Generator. Retrieved from https://passwordsgenerator.net/sha256-hash-generator/

Unsupervised Learning Using Excel 10

Unsupervised Learning finds a hidden structure in unlabeled and unstructured data. First, we explain the definitions of "labeled" and unstructured data. Then, we will show two ways to use Excel to generate a 3-centroid random data set. After that, we show how to use K-means to generate k clusters for a given data set. The Elbow method finds an optimal k, the number of centers/clusters. The grocery data set is introduced and used for the association analysis. Unstructured data might have too many dimensions, so PCA (Principal Component Analysis) can be introduced to reduce the dimensions of relative multi-dimensional data. In this chapter, the following topics will be covered:

- Unsupervised learning vs. supervised learning
- What is labeled data?
- Structured vs. unstructured data
- Type I: Clustering analysis
- Excel: generate 3-centroid random numbers
- K-means methodology
- Elbow method for an optimal k
- Type II: Association rule and the groceries data set
- Type III: PCA (Principal Component Analysis)
- Our hidden functions

Supplementary Information The online version contains supplementary material available at https://doi.org/10.1007/978-3-031-89779-5_10.

Y. Yan, *Introduction to FinTech using Excel*, Springer Texts in Business and Economics, https://doi.org/10.1007/978-3-031-89779-5_10

10.1 What is Unsupervised Learning?

Unsupervised Learning finds hidden structures in unlabeled and unstructured data. On the other hand, supervised learning is used to analyze structured data using statistical techniques. Unsupervised learning is a type of machine learning in which the algorithm learns patterns from unlabeled data. For labeled data sets, we use linear regression as an illustration. Assume we have the following regression.

$$y = \alpha + \beta_1 x_1 + \beta_2 x_2 + \beta_3 x_3, \tag{10.1}$$

where `y` is the dependent variable, and `x1`, `x2`, `x3` are the dependent variables. We can estimate alpha and three betas with data related to `y`, `x1`, `x2`, and `x3`. Here, `y` is the so-called labeled data variable. On the other hand, without the y-dependent variable, we still can classify our data sets into groups based on `x1`, `x2`, and `x3`.

10.2 Structured vs. Unstructured Data

Data can be loosely classified into two categories: structured and unstructured. Structured data refers to data that is organized in a highly predictable and predefined manner, typically arranged in rows and columns within a relational database or spreadsheet. Examples of structured data include financial records, customer information, transactional data, sensor readings, and inventory databases. Structured data is characterized by its uniformity, consistency, and well-defined schema, facilitating efficient data storage, retrieval, and analysis.

Unstructured data, on the other hand, refers to data that needs a predefined data model or organizational structure, making it more challenging to analyze using traditional methods. It comes in various formats and needs to fit neatly into rows and columns like structured data. It includes text documents, emails, social media posts, images, videos, audio recordings, web pages, and sensor data streams. Unstructured data is characterized by its variability, complexity, and lack of uniformity, presenting unique data analysis and interpretation challenges.

10.3 Three Categories

Unsupervised learning can be divided into three categories: clustering analysis, association, and dimension reduction. Below is a summary of each category.

(1) Clustering Analysis: Clustering is a technique for grouping similar data points based on their features without predefined labels. The goal is to identify patterns or structures in the data by grouping similar objects while keeping groups or clusters as distinct as possible. Popular clustering methods include K-means, hierarchical clustering, and DBSCAN. These techniques are widely used in customer segmentation, image analysis, and anomaly detection.

(2) Association: Association focuses on finding relationships or rules between variables in large datasets. One of the most common applications is market basket analysis, which identifies patterns in customer purchasing behavior (e.g., if a customer buys bread, they are likely also to buy butter). Association rules mining techniques like Apriori and FP-Growth generate rules that highlight strong correlations between items. This approach is used in recommendation systems, retail, and fraud detection.
(3) Dimension Reduction: Dimension reduction techniques aim to reduce the number of variables or features in a dataset while preserving its essential structure. This is useful for handling high-dimensional data, reducing noise, and improving the efficiency of machine-learning models. Popular methods include Principal Component Analysis (PCA) and t-SNE (t-distributed Stochastic Neighbor Embedding). Dimension reduction helps in visualization, compressing data, and improving the performance of algorithms by eliminating redundant or irrelevant features.

10.4 The Concept of Clustering

Clustering is a fundamental task in unsupervised learning. The goal is to partition a dataset into groups, or clusters, of data points similar to each other while being dissimilar to data points in other clusters. Unlike supervised learning, clustering does not rely on labeled data, meaning no predefined categories or class labels exist. Instead, clustering algorithms identify patterns and structures in the data based solely on the intrinsic properties of the data itself.

The objective of clustering is to find natural groupings or clusters within the data, assuming that data points within the same cluster are more closely related than those in different clusters. Clustering algorithms typically operate by iteratively assigning data points to clusters based on specific criteria, such as proximity or similarity measures, and updating cluster centroids or boundaries until convergence. Standard clustering algorithms include K-means, hierarchical clustering, DBSCAN, and Gaussian mixture models. Clustering finds diverse applications across various domains, including customer segmentation, image segmentation, anomaly detection, and recommendation systems, helping to uncover hidden patterns and structures within complex datasets.

10.5 Definition of Centroid

In k-means analysis (discussed later in the chapter) and other similar analyses, the centroid is the central point of a cluster. It represents the mean (average) position of all the data points within that cluster. The centroid is used to define the location of the cluster in the data space, and during the k-means algorithm, data points are assigned to the cluster with the nearest centroid. At each iteration of k-means, the centroids are recalculated based on the updated assignment of data points, and the process continues until the centroids stabilize (i.e., no further changes in the cluster assignments or the positions of the centroids). In essence, the centroid is the point that minimizes the total distance between itself and all other points in its cluster.

10.6 Excel: 3-Centroid Random Dataset

Later in the chapter, we will show how to use real-world data to detect clusters. In the meantime, we will use simulated data to test our models, such as testing the optimal number of clusters. Because of this, readers and students should learn how to generate those data sets in the first place. Assume we have three centroids. There are two approaches: manually and using a Macro.

To generate a 3-centroid random dataset in Excel, we can break down the process into several steps and provide two methods: a manual approach using Excel formulas and an automated approach using a Macro. The goal is to create random data points around three predefined centroids.

Step 1: Generate the following data set and name it a '`table`' variable.

table

	A	B	C
1	Centroid	x0	y0
2	1	5	5
3	2	15	15
4	3	25	25

Fig. 10.1 Defining x and y values for three centroids

Step 2: Assume we are interested in 30 `x` and `y` data pairs. Create a column of 30 random numbers from a uniform distribution. The top part of the result is below (30 by 2 with a random seed of 123).

	A	B	C	D	E
1	ID	3-centroid		random (seed 123)	
2	1	5	5	0.013428144	0.581469161
3	2	15	15	0.704214606	0.399914548
4	3	25	25	0.987670522	0.099642933
5				0.938413648	0.997283853
6				0.297860652	0.85647145

Fig. 10.2 30 sets of random numbers with a seed of 123

Step 3: Generate a column with values of 1,2,3 for three centroids. The first ten observations belong to Centroid 1, the second ten to Centroid 2, and the last 10 to Centroid 3.

	A	B	C	D	E	F
1	ID	3-centroid		random (seed 123)		centroid
2	1	5	5	0.013428144	0.581469161	1
3	2	15	15	0.704214606	0.399914548	1
4	3	25	25	0.987670522	0.099642933	1
5				0.938413648	0.997283853	1
6				0.297860652	0.85647145	1
7				0.62346263	0.022888882	1

Fig. 10.3 Generating column F

Step 4: Generate the x and y columns.

G2 fx =VLOOKUP(F2,table,2)+(D2-0.4)*4

	A	B	C	D	E	F	G	H	I	J	K
1	ID	3-centroid		random (seed 123)		centroid	x	y	=VLOOKUP(F2,table,2)+(D2-0.4)*4		
2	1	5	5	0.013428144	0.581469161	1	3.453713	5.325877	=VLOOKUP(F2,table,3)+(E2-0.5)*4		
3	2	15	15	0.704214606	0.399914548	1	6.216858	4.599658			
4	3	25	25	0.987670522	0.099642933	1	7.350682	3.398572			
5				0.938413648	0.997283853	1	7.153655	6.989135			
6				0.297860652	0.85647145	1	4.591443	6.425886			

Fig. 10.4 Generating x and y columns (columns G and H)

The formula in cell G2 (under the `x` label) is = `vlookup(E2,table) + (D2 - 0.5) * 4`. This will create a random number within ±2 of the centroid's X-coordinate. The formula for the Y-coordinate in H2 is = `vlookup(E2,table) + (E2-0.5) * 4`. This will create a random number within ±2 of the centroid's Y-coordinate. The following is the graphic presentation of those three clusters.

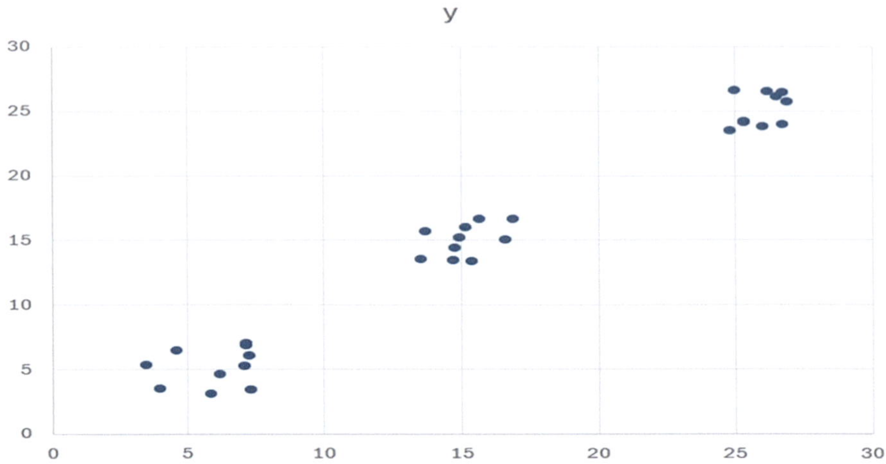

Fig. 10.5 A graphic presentation of three sets of data

In the above graphic presentation, we can see three distinct clusters. This is because the initial settings of the three centroids are different. In the following section, we show the results when they are close to each other.

10.7 Excel 3-Centroid Random Dataset (II)

This section is almost identical to the previous section, except we add two choices: (1) the initial locations of the three centroids and (2) the level of variation within each centroid. Those two factors are strongly correlated. To start, let's fix the variables within ± 2. If the distances between centroids are pretty large, such as 10, 20, or 30, we would see three distinct groups in terms of their scatter graph. However, when their distances decrease, those three groups will tangle with each other. The same logic applies when fixing the distances but increasing the level of variables. In the following example, we keep the variation level the same (see cell B5) but reduce the distances between those three centroids.

	A	B	C
1	centroid	x0	y0
2	1	5	5
3	2	9	9
4	3	12	12
5	variation	4	

Fig. 10.6 Excel 3 sets of x 0 and y 0 plus a variation

The following image shows a few related formulae. Please pay attention to the formulae used in G2 and H2 since both use $B$5, considering the change in the level of variation within each centroid.

	A	B	C	D	E	F	G	H	I	J	K	L
1	centroid	x0	y0	random (seed 123)		centroid	x	y	=VLOOKUP(F2,table,2)+(D2-0.5)*$B$5			
2	1	5	5	0.013428144	0.581469161	1	3.053713	5.325877	=VLOOKUP(F2,table,3)+(E2-0.5)*$B$5			
3	2	9	9	0.704214606	0.399914548	1	5.816858	4.599658				
4	3	12	12	0.987670522	0.099642933	1	6.950682	3.398572				
5	variation	4		0.938413648	0.997283853	1	6.753655	6.989135				
6				0.297860652	0.85647145	1	4.191443	6.425886				
7				0.62346263	0.022888882	1	5.493851	3.091556				
8				0.136722922	0.117893002	1	3.546892	3.471572				

Fig. 10.7 The table using Excel VLOOKUP

Since many observations will be mixed up at the borders, we will use color to illustrate them. Usually, so many #NA's are observed.

	A	B	C	F	G	H	M	N	O	P	Q	R
1	centroid	x0	y0	centroid	x	y	<-F2	Centroid1	Centroid2	Centroid3		
2	1	5	5	1	3.053713	5.325877		5.325877	#N/A	#N/A	=IF(F2=$A$4,H2,NA())	
3	2	9	9	1	5.816858	4.599658		4.599658	#N/A	#N/A		
4	3	12	12	1	6.950682	3.398572		3.398572	#N/A	#N/A		
5	variation	4		1	6.753655	6.989135		6.989135	#N/A	#N/A		
6				1	4.191443	6.425886		6.425886	#N/A	#N/A		
7				1	5.493851	3.091556		3.091556	#N/A	#N/A		
8				1	3.546892	3.471572		3.471572	#N/A	#N/A		
9				1	6.714591	5.268868		5.268868	#N/A	#N/A		
10				1	6.754753	6.856929		6.856929	#N/A	#N/A		
11				1	6.853511	6.006684		6.006684	#N/A	#N/A		
12				2	8.960387	7.33375		#N/A	7.33375	#N/A		
13				2	7.085818	7.484146		#N/A	7.484146	#N/A		
14				2	8.511643	9.205267		#N/A	9.205267	#N/A		

Fig. 10.8 Grouping with #NA

We generate three columns called "Centroid1", "Centroid2", and "Centroid3". The formulae in N2, O2, and P2 are `= if(F2 = $A$2,H2,NA ())`, `= if(O2 = $A$3,H2,na(),` `= if(F2 = $A$4, H2, NA())`, respectively. To draw the following graphs, we highlight column G (x column), hold the Control Key, and then highlight columns N:P (i.e., Centroid1 to Centroid3).

G	H	M	N	O	P
x	y	<- F2	Centroid1	Centroid2	Centroid3
3.053713	5.325877		5.325877	#N/A	#N/A
5.816858	4.599658		4.599658	#N/A	#N/A
6.950682	3.398572		3.398572	#N/A	#N/A
6.753655	6.989135		6.989135	#N/A	#N/A
4.191443	6.425886		6.425886	#N/A	#N/A
5.493851	3.091556		3.091556	#N/A	#N/A
3.546892	3.471572		3.471572	#N/A	#N/A
6.714591	5.268868		5.268868	#N/A	#N/A
6.754753	6.856929		6.856929	#N/A	#N/A
6.853511	6.006684		6.006684	#N/A	#N/A
8.960387	7.33375		#N/A	7.33375	#N/A

Fig. 10.9 Grouping into three centroids

After that, choose Insert, "Recommended Charts," then the appropriate chart; see the following graph.

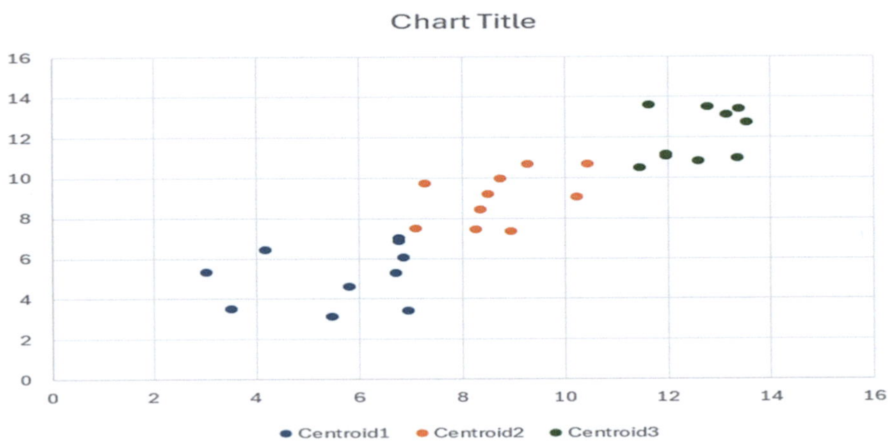

Fig. 10.10 A graphic presentation of three groups

10.8 Excel 3-Centroid Data Set (III): Macro

From the above two sections, readers have learned how to generate a set of random numbers with three centroids. The procedure is clear, and readers will thoroughly understand the underlying logic. However, it is tedious and easy to make mistakes. Readers and students will try the procedure mentioned above at least once. It is also an excellent in-class exercise for instructors. Since those data sets will be used to test the K-means method, generating them quickly is a good idea. We can achieve this quite conveniently by using an Excel Macro. The procedure is given below.

Step 1: Click "Developer" on the Excel menu bar, then Macro.

Step 2: Enter any name, such as `tt`, then click "Create".

Fig. 10.11 Any name for a Macro's name

After clicking "Create", the following result will pop up.

Fig. 10.12 An illustration of a Macro called tt

Step 3: Copy the Macro shown in Appendix C and replace the empty Macro with the new one. The top part is shown below.

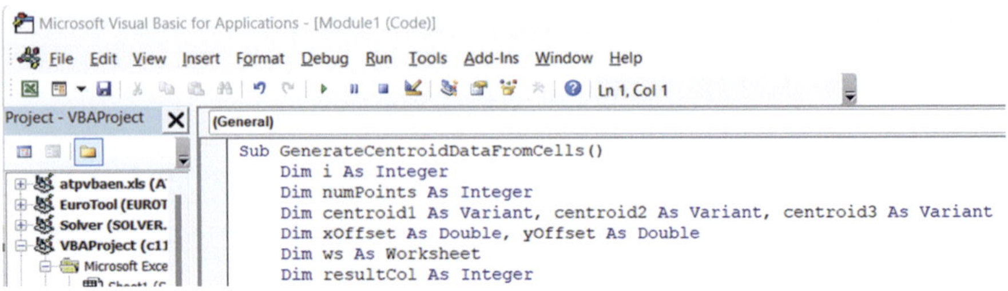

Fig. 10.13 Replacing "tt" with a new one

Step 4: Click "File", then "Close and Return to Macro Excel", as shown below.

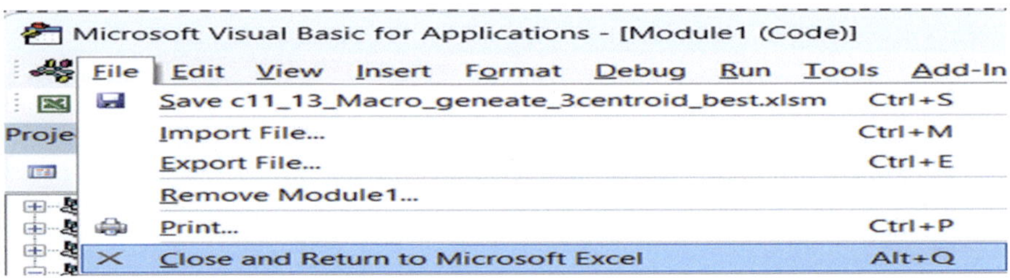

Fig. 10.14 Going back to Excel

Before running this Macro, we enter the following values. As before, A1:B3 are three pairs of x and y values for three centroids. The value in A4 indicates the number of random values for each centroid. In this case, the total observations will be 1,500 (500*3).

	A	B
1	5	5
2	15	15
3	25	25
4	500	

Fig. 10.15 Three pairs of x and y values

To run the Macro, we click "Developer" and "Macro," then choose the correct Macro Name and click "RUN." The final result is shown below. Note that many rows are hidden.

	A	B	C	D	E
1	5	5	X	Y	Centroid
2	15	15	6.296521	3.613047	1
3	25	25	6.17299	4.714597	1
4	500		5.17547	3.28577	1
5			3.226111	6.341368	1
1498			25.69901	26.74541	3
1499			24.75636	25.02308	3
1500			24.07424	23.11681	3
1501			26.15097	26.31288	3

Fig. 10.16 The result of running a related Macro

10.9 Graphic Representation of Clustering

The K-means algorithm partitions data into k clusters based on similarity. It iteratively assigns data points to the nearest cluster centroid and updates the centroids until convergence. Applications include customer segmentation, anomaly detection, and image segmentation. A visual representation can be a more effective way to show the effect. For this purpose, we have generated a few hidden functions. We wrote a function `.clusterPlot ()` that takes two inputs: a random seed (for reproduction purposes) and the number of centers. Note that the underlying random numbers are designed for three centroids.

```
>.clusterPlot().
* ------------------------------------------- *
* Step 1: input a random seed
123
3
* Step 2: input the number of centers
* ------------------------------------------- *
```

The related graph is shown below.

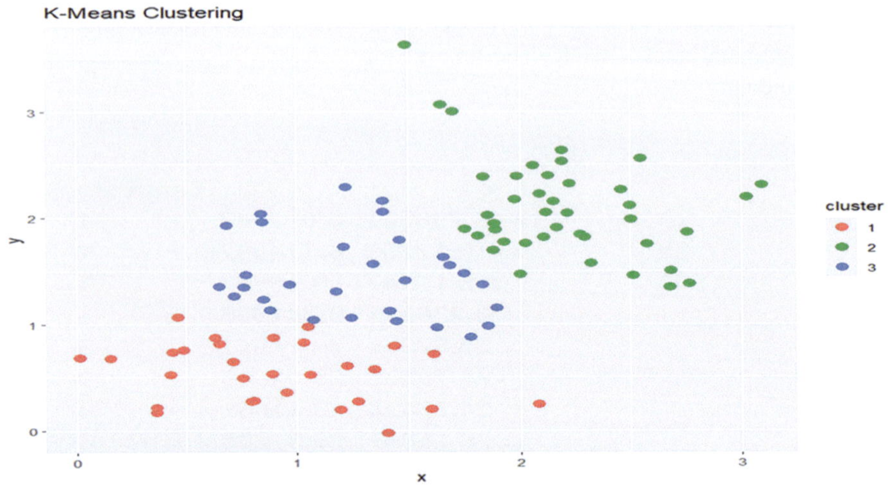

Fig. 10.17 A graphic presentation of three groups of data

10.10 The `.nCentroidsData ()` Function

This chapter shows that we can use Excel to generate a set of values based on a given number of centroids, such as 3, 4, or 5. However, the process is quite tedious, and it is difficult for a potential instructor to do an in-class exercise. Because of this, we generated the `.nCentroidsData ()` function, which takes a few input values. Its usage is demonstrated below.

```
> .nCentroidsData()
   * ------------------------------------------------ *
   * Objective: generate a simulated data set with    *
   *            n such as 2,3,4,5 centroids           *
   * ------------------------------------------------ *
   * Step 1: input a random seed                      *
123
   * Step 2: input the number of centroids (2,3,4,5)  *
3
Enter x1,y1,x2,y2, ...
  such as 1 1 5 5 10 10
1: 1 1 5 5 10 10
7:
Read 6 items
   * Step 3: input the std, such as 0.5, 1, etc.      *
0.5
   * Step 4: input the number of observations         *
50
   * ------------------------------------------------ *
   *  Launch Excel and pate the data there            *
   * ------------------------------------------------ *
> |
```

Fig. 10.18 Generating data for n centroids (.nCentroidsData)

Later in the chapter, we will use this method to get our data sets. Since a random seed of 123 is used, interested readers can replicate our result. The first few observations are shown below.

	A	B
1	x	y
2	0.719762	1.126659
3	0.884911	0.985727
4	1.779354	0.978565
5	1.035254	1.684301
6	1.064644	0.887115
7	1.857532	1.758235
8	1.230458	0.225624
9	0.367469	1.292307

Fig. 10.19 Generated results with x and y columns

10.11 K-Means Methodology

K-means is a popular unsupervised learning algorithm used for clustering, which aims to partition a dataset into K distinct, non-overlapping groups or clusters. The algorithm randomly chooses K initial cluster centers, called centroids, or by some method. K-means aims to minimize the sum of squared distances between each data point and the nearest centroid, thus grouping similar data points.

The process involves iterating between two steps: assignment and update. Each data point is assigned to the nearest centroid based on Euclidean distance in the assignment step. In the update step, the centroids are recalculated as the mean of all points in each cluster. These steps are repeated until the centroids no longer change significantly, indicating convergence. The result is a set of K clusters that attempt to minimize the within-cluster variance, making K-means an effective and computationally efficient method for discovering underlying patterns in data. However, the choice of K and the initial placement of centroids can affect the result.

10.12 K-Means by Using Excel

We aim to group our input data sets into `n` categories by minimizing the total distance. The procedure is given below. Assume that we try three centroids.

Step 1: Input the data.

Step 2: Randomly set some arbitrary values for the three centers.

Step 3: Calculate the three distances.

Step 4: Choose the shortest distance.

Step 5: Calculate the summation of step 4.

Step 6: Minimize the summation by changing the three sets of points (x,y).

Step 7: Calculate the means of those three centers and replace the starting values with those three means until they converge.

Step 8: Minimize the within variance for a given target (means `x` and `y`).

Below, we will show how to get our results. The data set is from`.nCentroidsData ()` with the following parameter values: seed = 123, number of centroids =3, standard deviation =0.5, x 1,y1, x2,y2, x3,y3 = (1 1 5 5 10 10). In cells A1:B3, we enter some arbitrary values, shown below.

	A	B	C	D
1	1	1	x	y
2	2	2	0.719762	1.126659
3	3	3	0.884911	0.985727
4			1.779354	0.978565
5			1.035254	1.684301

Fig. 10.20 Three centroids with x and y columns

Then, from those three centers, we calculate the three differences. The minimum will be in column H. In E2, the formula is = `SQRT((C2-x1_)^2 + (D2-y1_)^2)` since we name A1 as x1_ and B1 as y1_ to simplify the notations.

F2 =SQRT((D2-x1_)^2+(E2-y1_)^2)

	A	B	C	D	E	F	G	H
1	center	center_x	center_y	x	y	distance1	distance2	distance3
2	1	1	1	0.719762	1.126659	0.307532	1.549753	2.951083
3	2	2	2	0.884911	0.985727	0.11597	1.507373	2.92077
4	3	3	3	1.779354	0.978565	0.779649	1.044995	2.361393
50				1.389983	0.88215	0.4074	1.273464	2.660347
51				0.958315	0.48679	0.514901	1.837094	3.238009
52				4.644797	5.393869	5.708821	4.302708	2.904474
101				4.356485	4.40726	4.782825	3.368668	1.954592
102				11.09941	9.812199	13.40346	11.9929	10.58331
148				9.949513	10.93343	13.37037	11.9583	10.5468
149				9.32008	9.324549	11.76953	10.35532	8.941103
150				9.667615	10.01049	12.50266	11.08875	9.674921
151				10.24273	10.62496	13.34421	11.93032	10.51652

Fig. 10.21 Distance calculation

Using the Excel min() function, the H column will be the shortest of those three distances, as shown below. Column J contains the group ID.

I2 =MIN(F2:H2)

	A	B	C	D	E	F	G	H	I	J	K
1	center	center_x	center_y	x	y	distance1	distance2	distance3		Group ID	
2	1	1	1	0.719762	1.126659	0.307532	1.549753	2.951083	0.307532	1	=IF(I2=F2,1,IF(I2=G2,2,3))
3	2	2	2	0.884911	0.985727	0.11597	1.507373	2.92077	0.11597	1	
4	3	3	3	1.779354	0.978565	0.779649	1.044995	2.361393	0.779649	1	
50				1.389983	0.88215	0.4074	1.273464	2.660347	0.4074	1	
51				0.958315	0.48679	0.514901	1.837094	3.238009	0.514901	1	
52				4.644797	5.393869	5.708821	4.302708	2.904474	2.904474	3	
101				4.356485	4.40726	4.782825	3.368668	1.954592	1.954592	3	
102				11.09941	9.812199	13.40346	11.9929	10.58331	10.58331	3	
148				9.949513	10.93343	13.37037	11.9583	10.5468	10.5468	3	
149				9.32008	9.324549	11.76953	10.35532	8.941103	8.941103	3	
150				9.667615	10.01049	12.50266	11.08875	9.674921	9.674921	3	
151				10.24273	10.62496	13.34421	11.93032	10.51652	10.51652	3	
152											

Fig. 10.22 Classification based on the minimum distance

Then, the summation of the H column is calculated, shown below.

	A	B	C	D	E	F	G	H	I	J
1	center	center_x	center_y	x	y	distance1	distance2	distance3		Group ID
2	1	1	1	0.719762	1.126659	0.307532	1.549753	2.951083	0.307532	1
3	2	2	2	0.884911	0.985727	0.11597	1.507373	2.92077	0.11597	1
4	3	3	3	1.779354	0.978565	0.779649	1.044995	2.361393	0.779649	1
50				1.389983	0.88215	0.4074	1.273464	2.660347	0.4074	1
51				0.958315	0.48679	0.514901	1.837094	3.238009	0.514901	1
52				4.644797	5.393869	5.708821	4.302708	2.904474	2.904474	3
101				4.356485	4.40726	4.782825	3.368668	1.954592	1.954592	3
102				11.09941	9.812199	13.40346	11.9929	10.58331	10.58331	3
148				9.949513	10.93343	13.37037	11.9583	10.5468	10.5468	3
149				9.32008	9.324549	11.76953	10.35532	8.941103	8.941103	3
150				9.667615	10.01049	12.50266	11.08875	9.674921	9.674921	3
151				10.24273	10.62496	13.34421	11.93032	10.51652	10.51652	3
152										
153									667.2763	

Fig. 10.23 Adding group ID

As the final step, we will use Excel `solver ()` to minimize the summation by changing A1:B3.

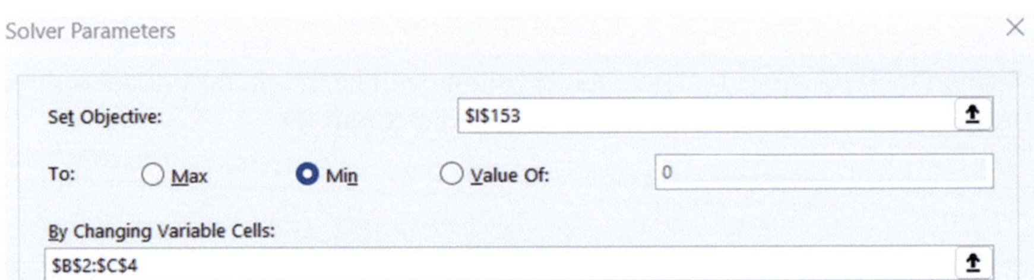

Fig. 10.24 Excel SOLVER functionality

The result is shown below.

	A	B	C	D	E	F	G	H	I	J
1	center	center_x	center_y	x	y	distance1	distance2	distance3		Group ID
2	1	1.002015	1.060798	0.719762	1.126659	0.289835	5.670336	12.85164	0.289835	1
3	2	4.861573	4.999398	0.884911	0.985727	0.1391	5.65008	12.83393	0.1391	1
4	3	9.907752	10.11251	1.779354	0.978565	0.781677	5.066279	12.22701	0.781677	1
50				1.389983	0.88215	0.427123	5.385506	12.55994	0.427123	1

Fig. 10.25 The result

Next, we calculate the means of `x` and `y` for each center, as shown below in M2:N4.

	A	B	C	D	E	F	G	H	I	J	L	M	N	O	P	Q	R
1	center	center_x	center_y	x	y	distance1	distance2	distance3		Group ID		mean x	mean y				
2	1	1.002015	1.060798	0.719762	1.126659	0.289835	5.670336	12.85164	0.289835	1	1	1.017202	1.073204134	=AVERAGEIF($J$2:$J$151,"="&$L2,E$2:E$151)			
3	2	4.861573	4.999398	0.884911	0.985727	0.1391	5.65008	12.83393	0.1391	1	2	4.87305	5.019403419				
4	3	9.907752	10.11251	1.779354	0.978565	0.781677	5.066279	12.22701	0.781677	1	3	9.99574	10.12472538				
50				1.389983	0.88215	0.427123	5.385506	12.55994	0.427123	1		=AVERAGEIF($J$2:$J$151,"="&$L4,D$2:D$151)					
51				0.958315	0.48679	0.575669	5.966495	13.14332	0.575669	1							

Fig. 10.26 Mean calculation

The initial values B2:C4 are different from M2:N4. We replace B2:C4 values with M2:N4 until they converge, i.e., they are identical.

	A	B	C	F	G	H	I	J	K	L	M	N	O	P	Q
1	center	center_x	center_y	distance1	distance2	distance3		Group ID		mean x	mean y				
2	1	1.017202	1.073204	0.302205	5.692386	12.92319	0.302205	1	1	1.017202	1.073204134	=AVERAGEIF($J$2:$J$151,"="&$K2,E$2:E$151)			
3	2	4.87305	5.019403	0.158597	5.672371	12.90459	0.158597	1	2	4.87305	5.019403419				
4	3	9.99574	10.12473	0.768006	5.089138	12.29476	0.768006	1	3	9.99574	10.12472538				
50				0.418888	5.4082	12.62871	0.418888	1		=AVERAGEIF($J$2:$J$151,"="&$K4,D$2:D$151)					

Fig. 10.27 The result

For the next step, we will minimize the within variance of the distance by fixing the average x and y. The following image shows the initial within-center variances and our targets.

	A	B	C	D	E	F	G	H	I	J	K	L	M
1	center	center_x	center_y	x	y	distance1	distance2	distance3		Group ID		mean x	mean y
2	1	1.017202	1.073204	0.719762	1.126659257	0.302205	5.692386	12.92319	0.302205	1	1	1.017202	1.073204134
3	2	4.87305	5.019403	0.884911	0.985726622	0.158597	5.672371	12.90459	0.158597	1	2	4.87305	5.019403419
4	3	9.99574	10.12473	1.779354	0.978564771	0.768006	5.089138	12.29476	0.768006	1	3	9.99574	10.12472538
50				1.389983	0.88214982	0.418888	5.4082	12.62871	0.418888	1		=AVERAGEIF($J$2:$J$151,"=	
51				0.958315	0.48678955	0.589364	5.989135	13.2123	0.589364	1			
52				4.644797	5.393869424	5.641595	0.438548	7.14238	0.438548	2		target	
101				4.356485	4.407259958	4.718765	0.800974	8.030604	0.800974	2		1.017202	1.073204134
102				11.09941	9.812198564	13.34245	7.857378	1.147062	1.147062	3		4.87305	5.019403419
148				9.949513	10.93342592	13.30452	7.793981	0.810021	0.810021	3		9.99574	10.12472538
149				9.32008	9.324548657	11.70566	6.189536	1.047282	1.047282	3			
150				9.667615	10.01049179	12.43804	6.920897	0.347441	0.347441	3			
151				10.24273	10.62495729	13.27955	7.762454	0.557885	0.557885	3			
152													
153					=VAR(F2:F151)	25.34067	8.190559	25.06289					

Fig. 10.28 Initial within-center variances and our targets

Again, we will apply the Excel `solver ()` function thrice. The settings for the first center is shown below. The extra ones are two constraints by limiting the averages are the same as our targets.

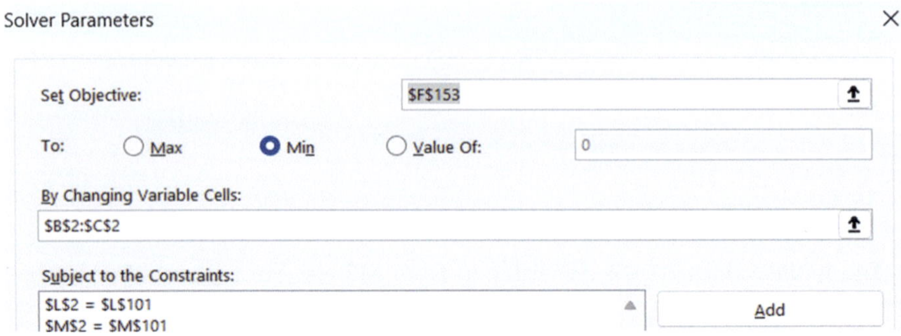

Fig. 10.29 The Excel SOLVER functionality

The result is shown below.

	A	B	C	D	E	F	G	H	I	J	K	L	M
1	center	center_x	center_y	x	y	distance1	distance2	distance3		Group ID		mean x	mean y
2	1	3.403763	3.818652	0.719762	1.126659257	3.801406	5.692373	8.323845	3.801406	1	1	1.017202	1.073204134
3	2	4.872802	5.019649	0.884911	0.985726622	3.790789	5.672372	8.207967	3.790789	1	2	4.87305	5.019403419
4	3	8.695382	3.50907	1.779354	0.978564771	3.271819	5.089182	7.364435	3.271819	1	3	9.99574	10.12472538
50				1.389983	0.88214982	3.560668	5.408228	7.763348	3.560668	1			
51				0.958315	0.48678955	4.132979	5.989158	8.306406	4.132979	1			
52				4.644797	5.393869424	2.005362	0.43821	4.467629	0.43821	2		target	
01				4.356485	4.407259958	1.119883	0.801001	4.430889	0.801001	2		1.017202	1.073204134
02				11.09941	9.812198564	9.754256	7.857425	6.746018	6.746018	3		4.87305	5.019403419
48				9.949513	10.93342592	9.667825	7.793956	7.529536	7.529536	3		9.99574	10.12472538
49				9.32008	9.324548657	8.081937	6.189543	5.848935	5.848935	3			
50				9.667615	10.01049179	8.807652	6.920892	6.573715	6.573715	3			
51				10.24273	10.62495729	9.648692	7.762449	7.28218	7.28218	3			
52													
53					=VAR(F2:F151)	9.670184	8.190552	2.916157					

Fig. 10.30 The final result

10.13 The `.kmeans ()` Function

Using Excel, as described in the previous section, will help our readers and students understand the K-means better. However, applying the procedure described in the previous section is quite cumbersome. In addition, there are so many steps involved that making mistakes is easy. For this purpose, we generated a function `.kmeans ()` that is quite easy to use.

```
> .kmeans()
 * ------------------------------------------------ *
 * Objective: apply the K-means methodology          *
 *            1) copy data                           *
 *            2) enter n (number of proposed centers) *
 * ------------------------------------------------ *
 * Step 1: copy the data set                         *
 * ------------------------------------------------ *

 * Step 2: input n (number of proposed centers)      *
 * ------------------------------------------------ *
3
 * ------------------------------------------------ *
 * K-Mean centers:                                  *
          x         y
1  9.733356 10.274106
2 10.462200  9.859161
3  2.945126  3.046304
 * ------------------------------------------------ *
 * Cluster:                                         *
  [1] 3 3 3 3 3 3 3 3 3 3 3 3 3 3 3 3 3 3 3 3 3 3 3 3 3 3 3 3 3
 [30] 3 3 3 3 3 3 3 3 3 3 3 3 3 3 3 3 3 3 3 3 3 3 3 3 3 3 3 3 3
 [59] 3 3 3 3 3 3 3 3 3 3 3 3 3 3 3 3 3 3 3 3 3 3 3 3 3 3 3 3 3
 [88] 3 3 3 3 3 3 3 3 3 3 3 3 3 2 2 1 2 1 1 1 1 2 2 2 2 2 1 1 2
[117] 1 2 1 1 1 1 2 2 1 2 1 1 2 1 2 1 1 1 1 1 1 1 2 1 1 1 2 1 1
[146] 2 1 1 1 1
 * ------------------------------------------------ *
 * Winthin SS (Sum of Errors)                       *
[1]   7.371432   6.440733 804.152749
 * ------------------------------------------------ *
 * Total SS (Sum of Errors)                         *
[1] 4153.242
 * ------------------------------------------------ *
 *  The proportion of the total variance explained  *
[1] 0.8030539
 * ------------------------------------------------ *
```

Fig. 10.31 An illustration of the.kmean function

This final ratio can be considered the R^2 when running a linear regression.

```
> a=7.371432+6.440733+804.152749
> total= 4153.242
> (total-a)/total
[1] 0.8030539
```

10.14 IRIS Data Set

This is one of the earliest datasets used in literature on classification methods and is widely used in statistics and machine learning. The data set contains 3 classes of 50 instances each, where each class refers to a type of iris plant. One class is linearly separable from the other 2; the latter are not linearly separable from each other. The iris data set is famous for machine learning. It is a labeled data set. However, it can be used for unsupervised learning as well. For this data set, we have generated a function `.show_iris ()`. By typing the function's name, we will know its objective and how to use it.

```
> .show_iris
function(n=2){
" Objective: show the Iris data
       n  : n > 0 for the first n obs (default is 2)
            n < 0 for the last  n obs
            n = 0 for all observations

 Example 1> .show_iris()
          sepal_length sepal_width petal_length petal_width        class
        1          5.1         3.5          1.4         0.2 Iris-setosa
        2          4.9         3.0          1.4         0.2 Iris-setosa

Example 2>.show_iris(-3)
          sepal_length sepal_width petal_length petal_width           class
      148          6.5         3.0          5.2         2.0 Iris-virginica
      149          6.2         3.4          5.4         2.3 Iris-virginica
      150          5.9         3.0          5.1         1.8 Iris-virginica

 Example 3>.show_iris(0)
          Launch Excel and paste
```

Fig. 10.32 Showing the Iris data function (.show_iris)

10.15 K-Means for Iris Data Set

For this case, readers can use our hidden function called `.kmeans ()`, shown below.

```
> .kmeans()
 * ------------------------------------------------ *
 * Objective: apply the K-means methodology         *
 *            1) copy data                          *
 *            2) enter n (number of proposed centers) *
 * ------------------------------------------------ *
 * Step 1: copy the data set                        *
 * ------------------------------------------------ *

 * Step 2: input n (number of proposed centers)     *
 * ------------------------------------------------ *
3
 * ------------------------------------------------ *
 * K-Mean centers:                                  *
  sepal_length sepal_width petal_length petal_width
1     6.850000    3.073684     5.742105    2.071053
2     5.006000    3.418000     1.464000    0.244000
3     5.901613    2.748387     4.393548    1.433871
 * ------------------------------------------------ *
 * Within SS (Sum of Errors)                        *
[1] 23.87947 15.24040 39.82097
 * ------------------------------------------------ *
 * Total SS (Sum of Errors)                         *
[1] 680.8244
 * ------------------------------------------------ *
 *  The proportion of the total variance explained  *
[1] 0.8840511
 * ------------------------------------------------ *
```

Fig. 10.33 K-means using the Iris data set

The proportion of variables explained by those three centers is 88.41%. The difference between the total sum of errors and the summation of the within-group sum of errors divided by the total sum of errors is shown below.

```
> a=23.87947+15.24040+39.82097
> total= 680.8244
> (total-a)/total
[1] 0.8840511
```

10.16 Optimal K: Elbow Method

The elbow method is a heuristic technique used to determine the optimal number of clusters, ‘k’, in unsupervised learning algorithms such as K-means clustering. The process involves plotting the within-cluster sum of squares (WCSS) or distortion as a function of the number of clusters. As the number of clusters increases, the

WCSS typically decreases because each data point is closer to its respective cluster centroid.

However, beyond a certain point, adding more clusters does not significantly reduce the WCSS, resulting in a diminishing rate of improvement. The optimal number of clusters, 'k', is identified at the "elbow" point on the plot, where the rate of decrease in WCSS sharply decreases, indicating that additional clusters do not explain much more variance in the data.

The elbow method provides a simple yet effective way to choose an appropriate value for 'k' in clustering algorithms, balancing model complexity and explanatory power.

10.17 Elbow Method Illustration

We have generated a function called `.elbowPlot ()` to show the so-called Elbow Method. The graph is shown below.

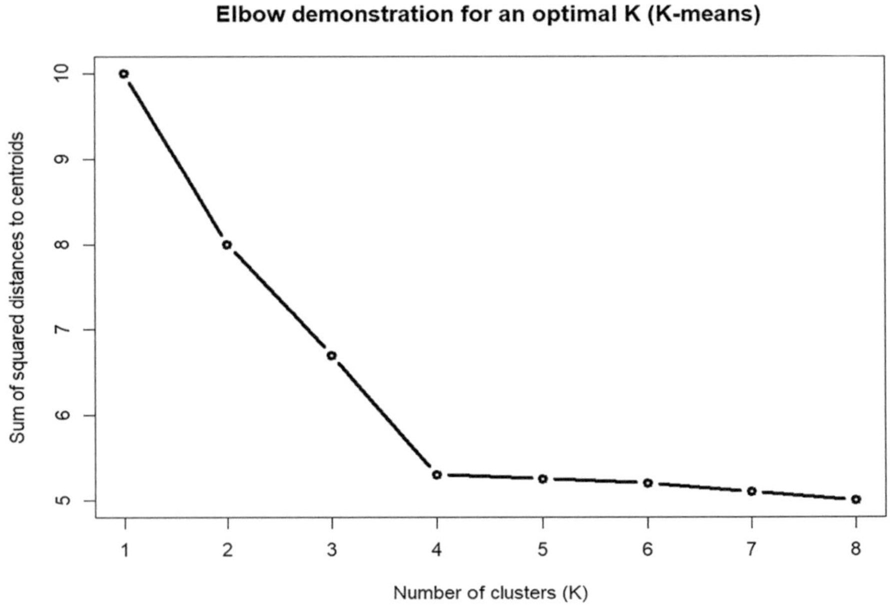

Fig. 10.34 The Elbow method to choose an optimal k

10.18 Type II: Association

Association in unsupervised learning focuses on finding patterns or relationships between variables within a dataset without any predefined categories or labels. This method is often used to discover how certain items or features co-occur, forming associations or rules that help understand underlying structures in the data. One of the most well-known applications of association is market basket analysis, where retailers analyze customer purchase patterns to identify which products are frequently bought together.

The output of association algorithms typically comes in the form of 'association rules, such as "if item A is purchased, then item B is likely to be purchased," which can be utilized for strategic decisions like product placement, promotions, and cross-selling.

A common algorithm used in association analysis is the 'Apriori algorithm', which identifies frequent item sets in a dataset and generates association rules based on them. Each rule has two key metrics: 'support' and 'confidence'. Support measures how frequently the rule applies in the dataset, while confidence indicates how often the rule holds true. For example, in a retail dataset, a rule might be "80% of customers who buy bread also buy butter," where the support is the percentage of total transactions that include both items, and the confidence is the probability that butter will be bought given that bread is purchased. Association analysis provides valuable insights for understanding item relationships and making data-driven decisions. The Support and Confidence formulas are given below.

$$support(Milk) = \frac{n(Milk)}{n(Total)}, \tag{10.2}$$

$$Confidence(Milk \rightarrow Bread) = \frac{n(Milk\ and\ Bread)}{n(Milk)}, \tag{10.3}$$

where `n(Milk)` of transactions including Milk, `n(Milk and Bread)` is the number of transactions including both items.

10.19 The Concept of Lift

In the context of association rule learning (a key concept in unsupervised learning), lift is a measure used to evaluate the strength of a rule, comparing the observed support for the rule to the expected support assuming that the rule's antecedent and consequent are independent. The lift of an association rule $A \rightarrow B$ is defined as.

$$A \rightarrow B = \frac{support(A \cap B)}{Support(A) * support(B)}, \tag{10.4}$$

where Support of $(A \cap B)$ is the proportion of transactions where both A and B appear together. Support(A) is the proportion of transactions where A appears, and Support(B) is the proportion where B appears. Lift measures how much more likely the items A and B are to occur together than if they were independent.

If Lift > 1: A and B are positively correlated (i.e., often occur together).

If Lift = 1: A and B are independent.

If Lift < 1: A and B are negatively correlated (i.e., the presence of one reduces the likelihood of the other).

Let's look at one example. The support values are:

$$support(milk) = \frac{200}{1000} = 0.2$$

$$support(bread) = \frac{150}{1000} = 0.15$$

$$support(milk \cap bread) = \frac{50}{1000} = 0.05$$

Now, we can calculate the lift for the rule Milk - > Bread:

$$Lift(milk \rightarrow bread) = \frac{0.05}{0.2 * 0.15} = 1.67$$

Since the lift is greater than 1, it suggests that customers who buy milk are more likely to also buy bread, compared to customers chosen at random.

10.20 Excel: Simulating a Dataset

We can absolutely use Excel to generate a dataset for association analysis using random number generation. This process involves creating a mock dataset that simulates customer transactions (or any other event-driven data), and then you can apply basic Excel functions to calculate association metrics like "support" and "confidence.". The steps are given below. We can simulate a transactional dataset with items like "Bread," "Milk,", "Butter," and "Eggs". Let's generate just 10 rows for those two items.

Step 1: Create a column for transaction plus a 10 by 4 set of random numbers (drawn from a uniform distribution with a random seed of 123).

	A	B	C	D	E
1					prob. To buy ->
2	transactioni	random nubmers (seed 123)			
3	1	0.013428144	0.58147	0.704215	0.399914548
4	2	0.987670522	0.09964	0.938414	0.997283853
5	3	0.297860652	0.85647	0.623463	0.022888882
6	4	0.136722922	0.11789	0.928648	0.567217017
7	5	0.938688314	0.96423	0.963378	0.751670888
8	6	0.490096744	0.08344	0.021455	0.121036409
9	7	0.377910703	0.55132	0.866482	0.91256447
10	8	0.807000946	0.50371	0.339183	0.358195746
11	9	0.318033387	0.10807	0.068697	0.676717429
12	10	0.43714713	0.73971	0.568224	0.910916471

Fig. 10.35 A set of random numbers with 123 as a random seed

Step 2: Based on the assigned probability to buy, we generate 1 (buy) and 0 (not to buy) as shown below.

F3 fx =IF(B4<F$1,1,0)

	A	B	C	D	E	F	G	H	I
1					prob. To buy ->	0.7	0.6	0.4	0.6
2	transactioni	random nubmers (seed 123)				Bread	Milk	Butter	Eggs
3	1	0.013428144	0.58147	0.704215	0.399914548	0	1	0	0
4	2	0.987670522	0.09964	0.938414	0.997283853	1	0	0	1
5	3	0.297860652	0.85647	0.623463	0.022888882	1	1	0	1
6	4	0.136722922	0.11789	0.928648	0.567217017	0	0	0	0
7	5	0.938688314	0.96423	0.963378	0.751670888	1	1	1	1
8	6	0.490096744	0.08344	0.021455	0.121036409	1	1	0	0
9	7	0.377910703	0.55132	0.866482	0.91256447	0	1	1	1
10	8	0.807000946	0.50371	0.339183	0.358195746	1	1	1	0
11	9	0.318033387	0.10807	0.068697	0.676717429	1	0	0	0
12	10	0.43714713	0.73971	0.568224	0.910916471				

Fig. 10.36 Classifying data into four groups based on probability to buy

The formula in cell F3 is = `if(B4 < F$1,1,0)`.

Step 4: Calculate support for those 4 items. The formula in K3 is `=SUM(F3:F11)/COUNT($A$3:$A$11)`.

K3 fx =SUM(F3:F11)/COUNT($A$3:$A$11)

	A	B	C	D	E	F	G	H	I	J	K	L	M	N
1					prob. Tc	0.7	0.6	0.4	0.6		------------------- support			
2	transactioni	random nubmers (seed 123)				Bread	Milk	Butter	Eggs		Bread	Milk	Butter	Eggs
3	1	0.01	0.58	0.70	0.40	0	1	0	0		0.666666667	0.666667	0.333333	0.444444
4	2	0.99	0.10	0.94	1.00	1	0	0	1					
5	3	0.30	0.86	0.62	0.02	1	1	0	1		=SUM(F3:F11)/COUNT($A$3:$A$11)			
6	4	0.14	0.12	0.93	0.57	0	0	0	0					
7	5	0.94	0.96	0.96	0.75	1	1	1	1					
8	6	0.49	0.08	0.02	0.12	1	1	0	0					
9	7	0.38	0.55	0.87	0.91	0	1	1	1					
10	8	0.81	0.50	0.34	0.36	1	1	1	0					
11	9	0.32	0.11	0.07	0.68	1	0	0	0					
12	10	0.44	0.74	0.57	0.91									

Fig. 10.37 Calculating the measure of "Support"

Using Excel in this way, we can simulate real-world association rule mining and guide users through a clear, hands-on exercise in generating and analyzing patterns within transactional data.

10.21 The Grocery Data Set

Market Basket Analysis is one of the key techniques used by large retailers to uncover associations between items. It works by looking for combinations of items that occur together frequently in transactions. To put it another way, it allows retailers to identify relationships between the items that people buy. Association Rules are widely used to analyze retail baskets or transaction data and are intended to identify strong rules discovered in transaction data using measures of interests, based on the concept of strong rules. The data set is downloadable at Kaggle. The first several observations are shown below. In total, there are 38,765 observations.

```
Member_number,Date,itemDescription
1808,21-07-2015,tropical fruit
2552,05-01-2015,whole milk
2300,19-09-2015,pip fruit
1187,12-12-2015,other vegetables
3037,01-02-2015,whole milk
4941,14-02-2015,rolls/buns
4501,08-05-2015,other vegetables
3803,23-12-2015,pot plants
2762,20-03-2015,whole milk
4119,12-02-2015,tropical fruit
1340,24-02-2015,citrus fruit
2193,14-04-2015,beef
1997,21-07-2015,frankfurter
4546,03-09-2015,chicken
4736,21-07-2015,butter
1959,30-03-2015,fruit/vegetable juice
```

Fig. 10.38 The first several lines of the Grocery data set

There are three columns: `Member_number`, `Date` and `ItemDescription`. Since the initial structure of the data is confusing, let's sort the data by the first two columns.

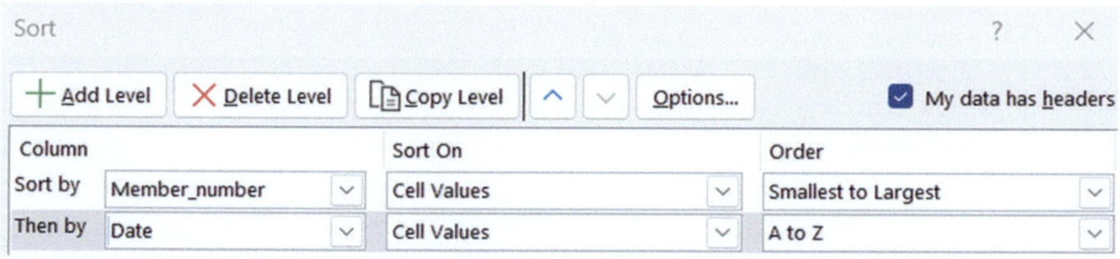

Fig. 10.39 Sorting the data sets by two variables

After sorting, the first several observations are shown below.

	A	B	C	D
1	Member_numb	Date	itemDescription	
2	1000	15-03-2015	sausage	
3	1000	15-03-2015	whole milk	
4	1000	15-03-2015	semi-finished bread	
5	1000	15-03-2015	yogurt	
6	1000	24-06-2014	whole milk	
7	1000	24-06-2014	pastry	
8	1000	24-06-2014	salty snack	
9	1000	24-07-2015	canned beer	
10	1000	24-07-2015	misc. beverages	
11	1000	25-11-2015	sausage	
12	1000	25-11-2015	hygiene articles	
13	1000	27-05-2015	soda	
14	1000	27-05-2015	pickled vegetables	
15	1001	7/2/2014	sausage	
16	1001	7/2/2014	whole milk	
17	1001	7/2/2014	rolls/buns	
18	1001	12/12/2014	whole milk	
19	1001	12/12/2014	soda	
20	1001	2/5/2015	frankfurter	

Fig. 10.40 The data set after sorting

Now, the structure of the data set is clear. The first four observations (A2:C5) belong to the first transaction and A6:C8 are for the second transaction. For the date column (B), we have two date formats. However, this inconsistency will not have any impact on our further analysis since we will not look at time series. For the next step, we combine Columns A and B.

D2 fx =CONCAT(A2,"_",B2)

	A	B	C	D	E	F
1	Member_numb	Date	itemDescription	transaction		
2	1000	15-03-2015	sausage	1000_15-03-2015	=CONCAT(A2,"_",B2)	
3	1000	15-03-2015	whole milk	1000_15-03-2015		
4	1000	15-03-2015	semi-finished bread	1000_15-03-2015		
5	1000	15-03-2015	yogurt	1000_15-03-2015		
6	1000	24-06-2014	whole milk	1000_24-06-2014		

Fig. 10.41 Combination of the Member number and the date

To make our spreadsheet clear, we copy Columns C and D to a new spreadsheet as values. Now, they become A and B columns in our new spreadsheet.

	A	B	C
1	transaction	itemDescription	
2	1000_15-03-2015	sausage	
3	1000_15-03-2015	whole milk	
4	1000_15-03-2015	semi-finished bread	
5	1000_15-03-2015	yogurt	
6	1000_24-06-2014	whole milk	

Fig. 10.42 Showing Item Description

Now, we can use the Excel Pivot Table to count the number of transactions and unique items. Highlight Column A, then click on "Insert" and 'PivotTable", as shown below.

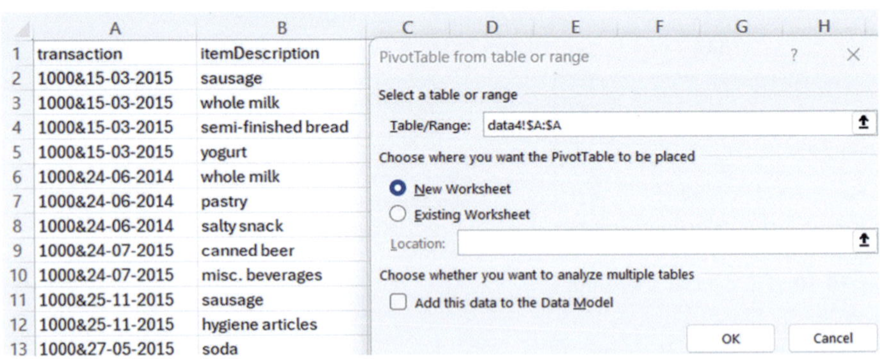

Fig. 10.43 Using the Excel pivot table

For the Pivot Table, we grab the only item to both Rows and Values, shown below in the left image.

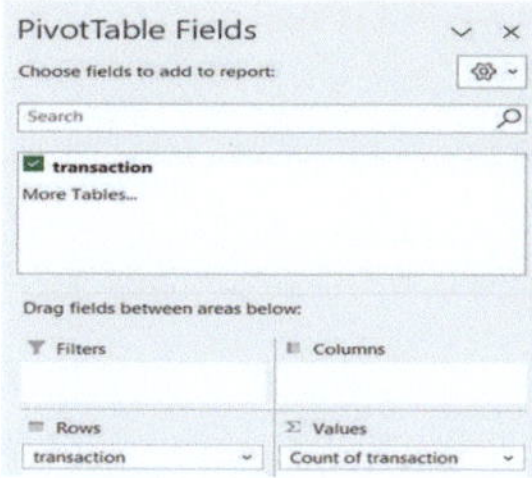

3	Row Labels	Count of transaction
4	1000&15-03-2015	4
5	1000&24-06-2014	3
6	1000&24-07-2015	2
7	1000&25-11-2015	2
8	1000&27-05-2015	2
9	1001&14-04-2015	2
10	1001&20-01-2015	3
11	1001&41822	3
12	1001&41985	2

14961	4999&24-01-2015	6
14962	4999&26-12-2015	2
14963	4999&41886	2
14964	5000&16-11-2014	2
14965	5000&41885	2
14966	5000&42279	3
14967	(blank)	
14968	Grand Total	38765

Figs. 10.44, 10.45 and 10.46 Using pivotable, the top and bottom of the result

In total, we have 38,765 transactions (see the above image on the right). Similarly, we can get the unique number of transactions and their frequency by using the Excel Pivot Table functionality. The result is shown below.

	A	B	C	D	E	F
1	Row Labels	Count of itemDescription		Row Labels	Count of itemDescription	
2	abrasive cleaner	22		Grand Total	38765	
3	artif. sweetener	29		whole milk	2502	
4	baby cosmetics	3		other vegetables	1898	
5	bags	4		rolls/buns	1716	
6	baking powder	122		soda	1514	
7	bathroom cleaner	17		yogurt	1334	
8	beef	516		root vegetables	1071	
9	berries	327		tropical fruit	1032	
10	beverages	251		bottled water	933	
11	bottled beer	687		sausage	924	
12	bottled water	933		citrus fruit	812	
13	brandy	38		pastry	785	
14	brown bread	571		pip fruit	744	

Fig. 10.47 The frequencies of various items

Columns A and B are the output from running Excel Pivot Table. Note that Columns D and E are sorted by frequency. From columns D and E, we know that "whole milk" and "Soda" are number 1 and number 4 most frequency purchased groceries. In the next section, we will continue to explore this data set further to explain the concept of association. An alternative way to get the data is to use our function called `.show_groceriesData ()`, shown below.

```
> .show_groceriesData
function(n=2){
" Objective: show the IBM daily data
        n   : n > 0 for the first n obs (default is 2)
              n < 0 for the last  n obs
              n = 0 for all observations

 Example 1 > .show_groceriesData()
              Member_number        Date itemDescription
          1            1808 21-07-2015  tropical fruit
          2            2552 05-01-2015      whole milk

 Example 2>.show_groceriesData(-3)
              Member_number        Date        itemDescription
      38763            1097 16-04-2014               cake bar
      38764            1510 03-12-2014 fruit/vegetable juice
      38765            1521 26-12-2014               cat food

 Example 3:>.show_groceriesData(0)
                Windows users: launch Excel and paste
```

Fig. 10.48 An easy way to get the data (.show_groceriesData)

After typing `.show_groceriesData (0)`, we can paste the complete data set to Excel.

10.22 Our `.grocery ()` Function

To help readers and students generate a data set for further analysis, we have written a hidden function called `.grocery ()`. The original data set has 38,765 observations, 14,963 unique transactions (unique member number and date), and 167 unique grocery items. The structure of the desired output is shown below.

Transaction	whole.milk	other.vegetables	rolls.buns	soda	yogurt
1000_15-03-2015	1	0	0	0	1
1000_24-06-2014	1	0	0	0	0
1000_27-05-2015	0	0	0	1	0
1001_07-02-2014	1	0	1	0	0
1001_12-12-2014	1	0	0	1	0
1001_20-01-2015	0	0	0	1	0
1002_09-02-2014	0	1	0	0	0
1002_26-04-2014	1	0	0	0	0

Fig. 10.49 The top few lines of the data set

The image above shows the first several lines with 5 most frequently purchased items. The top 20 items are shown below.

```
                  Item Freq
1           whole milk 2502
2     other vegetables 1898
3           rolls/buns 1716
4                 soda 1514
5               yogurt 1334
6      root vegetables 1071
7       tropical fruit 1032
8        bottled water  933
9              sausage  924
10        citrus fruit  812
11              pastry  785
12           pip fruit  744
13       shopping bags  731
14         canned beer  717
15        bottled beer  687
16 whipped/sour cream   662
17          newspapers  596
18         frankfurter  580
19         brown bread  571
20      domestic eggs   566
```

Fig. 10.50 Top 20 most frequently purchased items

To use the function, type `.grocery ()`, as shown below. The first two steps are shown below.

```
> .grocery()
 * ---------------------------------------------------------- *
 * Objective: explore the Groceries Data Set                  *
 * ---------------------------------------------------------- *
 *  Step 1: want to view the first and last three lines?      *
 *  1      yes                                                *
 *  2      no                                                 *
2
 * ---------------------------------------------------------- *
 *  Step 2: combine the first and second items                *
 *         see the first 3 lines below.                       *
 * ---------------------------------------------------------- *
       Transacton                  Item
1 1000_15-03-2015               sausage
2 1000_15-03-2015            whole milk
3 1000_15-03-2015 semi-finished bread
 * ---------------------------------------------------------- *
```

Fig. 10.51 The first two steps of the.grocery function

Then, we will see the number of unique transactions, the first three lines, and the top ten frequently purchased items.

```
 * ------------------------------------------------------- *
 *  Step 3: Generate unique transactions                   *
 *          do you want to print the first 3 lines?        *
 *  1       yes                                            *
 *  2       no                                             *
1
 The number of unique transactions is 14963
1000_15-03-2015
1000_24-06-2014
1000_24-07-2015
 * ------------------------------------------------------- *
 * ------------------------------------------------------- *
 *  Step 4: Calculate the frequency table for items      *
 *          Input the number of top items                *
10
                Item Freq
1         whole milk 2502
2   other vegetables 1898
3         rolls/buns 1716
4               soda 1514
5             yogurt 1334
6    root vegetables 1071
7     tropical fruit 1032
8      bottled water  933
9            sausage  924
10      citrus fruit  812
 * ------------------------------------------------------- *
```

Fig. 10.52 Steps 3 and 4 of the function

As the last step, we input the number of desired data items, such as 10 or 20.

```
 * ------------------------------------------------------- *
 *  Step 5: Generate an output with the following format *
 *          assume that you choose 9 items                 *
 *    ID, whole milk,other vegetables, ..., item9          *
 *          1    ,   0            , ...,    1              *
 * ------------------------------------------------------- *
 *       input the number of items:                        *
5
 * Launch Excel and paste it there for further analysis
```

Fig. 10.53 The number of desired items

After pasting the above data set to Excel, you might see just one line, as shown below.

A1 | f_x | Transaction,whole.milk,other.vegetables,rolls.buns,soda,yogurt

	A	B	C	D	E	F	G	H	I	J
1	Transaction,whole.milk,other.vegetables,rolls.buns,soda,yogurt									
2	1000_15-03-2015,1,0,0,0,1									
3	1000_24-06-2014,1,0,0,0,0									
4	1000_27-05-2015,0,0,0,1,0									
5	1001_07-02-2014,1,0,1,0,0									
6	1001_12-12-2014,1,0,0,1,0									

Fig. 10.54 Copying transactions data to Excel

Highlight this column, click 'Data' on the menu bar, then 'Text to Columns…', and 'Delimited. Choose a comma as the delimiter, as shown below.

	A	B	C	D	E	F
1	Transaction	whole.milk	other.vegetables	rolls.buns	soda	yogurt
2	1000_15-03-2015	1	0	0	0	1
3	1000_24-06-2014	1	0	0	0	0
4	1000_27-05-2015	0	0	0	1	0
5	1001_07-02-2014	1	0	1	0	0
6	1001_12-12-2014	1	0	0	1	0
7	1001_20-01-2015	0	0	0	1	0
8	1002_09-02-2014	0	1	0	0	0
9	1002_26-04-2014	1	0	0	0	0
10	1003_10-02-2015	0	0	1	0	0

Fig. 10.55 Separating them into several columns

10.23 Association: Groceries Data Set

We calculate a few statistics based on the previous section's output. The support will be the summation, and the confidence of A leading to B will be the frequency of buying both A and B divided by the number of purchasing A. Let's look at whole milk, soda, and yogurt.

G2 | f_x | =IF(SUM(B2,E2)=2,1,0)

	A	B	E	F	G	H
1	Transaction	whole.milk	soda	yogurt	whole.milk and soda	whole.milk and yogurt
2	1000_15-03-2015	1	0	1	0	1
3	1000_24-06-2014	1	0	0	0	0
4	1000_27-05-2015	0	1	0	0	0
5	1001_07-02-2014	1	0	0	0	0
6	1001_12-12-2014	1	1	0	1	0
7	1001_20-01-2015	0	1	0	0	0

Fig. 10.56 Association

The result is shown below. The support for each item is the summation. The association between Whole Milk and Soda is = `SUM(G:G)/K2`, where column G is when both items were purchased simultaneously. The confidence that Whole Milk leads to Soda is 7.36%.

	A	B	E	F	G	H	I	J	K	L	M	N	O
1	Transaction	whole.milk	soda	yogurt	whole.milk and soda	whole.milk and yogurt			whole.milk	other.vege	rolls.buns	soda	yogurt
2	1000_15-03-2015	1	0	1	0	1		support	2363	1827	1646	1453	1285
3	1000_24-06-2014	1	0	0	0	0							
4	1000_27-05-2015	0	1	0	0	0							
5	1001_07-02-2014	1	0	0	0	0		confidence	whole.milk -> soda		0.073635	=SUM(G:G)/K2	
6	1001_12-12-2014	1	1	0	1	0			whole.mild -> yogurt		0.070673	=SUM(H:H)/K2	
7	1001_20-01-2015	0	1	0	0	0			soda -> whole milk		0.119752	=SUM(G:G)/N2	
8	1002_09-02-2014	0	0	0	0	0			yogurt -> whole milk		0.129961	=SUM(H:H)/O2	

Fig. 10.57 The result

10.24 Principal Component Analysis (PCA)

Principal Component Analysis (PCA) is a technique used to reduce the complexity of large datasets by transforming a set of numerous variables into a smaller set of summary indices, known as principal components. These new components capture most of the essential information from the original variables. Importantly, principal components are new, uncorrelated variables formed as linear combinations of the original data points.

PCA is beneficial for simplifying large data tables. When faced with vast amounts of data, identifying key variables and uncovering patterns can be challenging. By reducing the dimensionality of the data, PCA makes it easier to visualize, analyze, and detect meaningful patterns within your dataset.

10.25 Excel Matrix Multiplication

Assume we have a matrix multiplication A * B. The dimensions of those two matrices are A(n,k) and B(m,n), i.e., the number of columns of A (the first matrix) should be the same as the number of rows of B (the second column). The dimension of the product is C(n,m).

$$c_{i,j} = \sum_{1}^{k} a_{i,p} b_{p,j} \tag{10.5}$$

Let's look at one example below.

G2 | {=MMULT(A2:C4,E2:E4)}

	A	B	C	D	E	F	G	H
1	A (3 by 3)				B (3 by 1)		C (3 by 1)	
2	1	2	3		1		14	
3	4	5	6		2		32	
4	8	9	2		3		32	

Fig. 10.58 An example of Excel matrix multiplication

Matrix A is 3 by 3 and Vector B is 3 by 1. Their matrix multiplication is 3 by 1. The Excel function used is `MMULT(A,B)`. The last step after typing the function is to hit the Ctrl-shift-Enter keys at the same time. For example, in G2, the value is (1,2,3) vs. (1,2,3), i.e. 1*1 + 2*2 + 3*8 = 1 + 4 + 9 = 14.,

10.26 Eigen Values and Eigen Vectors

This example is borrowed from Make Simple (2021). Let's look at the following matrix multiplication. Matrix A's dimensions are 3 by 3, and Vector B's dimensions are 3 by 1. The formula in G2:G4 is = `mmult(A2:C4,E2:E4)`.

	A	B	C	D	E	F	G
1	Matrix A				Vector B		Vector C
2	3	4	-2		1		3
3	1	4	-1		1		3
4	2	6	-1		2		6

Fig. 10.59 The Excel MMULT function for matrix multiplication

Comparing vectors B and C, we will find that Vector C is the same as multiplying vector B by 3, as shown below.

			eigen vector	lambda				
3	4	-2	1		1		3
1	4	-1	1	3*	1	=>	3
2	6	-1	2		2		6

Fig. 10.60 Eigen vector and Eigen value (lambda)

Vector B is called an eigenvector, and 3 is the eigenvalue. The eigenvector and eigenvalue (λ) derivation is beyond the scope of this book. In the next section, our hidden function will calculate those two values for us.

10.27 Our Hidden.eigen () Function

We generated a hidden function called.eigen () to help readers and students easily obtain eigenvectors and eigenvalues. Below is one example.

```
> .eigen()
 * ----------------------------------------------------------------- *
 * Objective: generrate eigen vectors and values                     *
 * ----------------------------------------------------------------- *
 *  Copy yoru matrix then hit the Enter Key                          *
 *    one example is hown below.                                     *
 * ----------------------------------------------------------------- *
3 4 -2
1 4  1
2 6 -1

 * ----------------------------------------------------------------- *
 *  Your input is shown below.                                       *
 * ----------------------------------------------------------------- *
  V1 V2 V3
1  3  4 -2
2  1  4  1
3  2  6 -1
 * ----------------------------------------------------------------- *
 *  Eigen values are shown below.                                    *
 * ----------------------------------------------------------------- *
$values
[1]  5.750535  1.690016 -1.440552

 *  Eigen vectors are shown below.                                    *
$vectors
           [,1]       [,2]       [,3]
[1,] -0.4106298 -0.9283907  0.5752012
[2,] -0.6177066  0.3564930 -0.2489475
[3,] -0.6706875  0.1048977  0.7792103
```

Fig. 10.61 The hidden function to calculate Eigen vectors (.eigen)

Using Excel, we can easily verify those values.

10.28 our.PcaExamples () Function

Again, to help our readers and students learn his course more easily, we have generated a hidden function called.pcaExamples (). By typing the function's name, we will see one example. The top part is shown below.

```
> .pcaExamples
function(){
"Objective: show a few examples
 Example >.pcae()
         * ------------------------------------------------------------- *
         *  Objective: show a few examples                               *
         * ------------------------------------------------------------- *
         *  1           iris                                             *
         *  2           cars                                             *
         *  3           USArrests                                        *
         *  4           wine                                             *
         *  5           attitude                                         *
         *  Esc to exit                                                  *
         * ------------------------------------------------------------- *
         *  Enter your choice                                            *
    1
```

Fig. 10.62 The function shows PCA model (.pcaExample)

The choice is `1` as shown in the above image.

```
   * ------------------------------------------------------------- *
   *  The first and last 3 lines are shown below.                  *
   * ------------------------------------------------------------- *
    Sepal.Length Sepal.Width Petal.Length Petal.Width Species
  1          5.1         3.5          1.4         0.2  setosa
  2          4.9         3.0          1.4         0.2  setosa
  3          4.7         3.2          1.3         0.2  setosa
    Sepal.Length Sepal.Width Petal.Length Petal.Width   Species
148          6.5         3.0          5.2         2.0 virginica
149          6.2         3.4          5.4         2.3 virginica
150          5.9         3.0          5.1         1.8 virginica
  * ------------------------------------------------------------- *
  * PCA result are given below.                                   *
  * ------------------------------------------------------------- *
  Importance of components:
                            PC1    PC2     PC3     PC4
  Standard deviation     1.7084 0.9560 0.38309 0.14393
  Proportion of Variance 0.7296 0.2285 0.03669 0.00518
  Cumulative Proportion  0.7296 0.9581 0.99482 1.00000
  * ------------------------------------------------------------- *
```

Fig. 10.63 The PCA example using the Iris data set

PC1 stands for Principal Component 1. If we use just one component, the explanation power is 73%. On the other hand, if we use two components, the power will be 99.49%.

10.29 PCA Example Using Excel

Below is one example of PCA using Excel. Let's assume you have a dataset of 5 observations (rows) and 3 variables (columns) representing features like `X1`, `X2`, and `X3`, as shown below.

```
2.5    2.4    3.5
0.5    0.7    1
2.2    2.9    3.1
1.9    2.2    2.9
3.1    3    4.1
```

Let's copy the above data set to Excel.

Step 1. Standardize the Data (Z-Score Normalization): PCA requires the data to be standardized (centered and scaled) so that all variables are on the same scale. This removes the bias due to differing units or ranges.

$$z = \frac{x - \overline{x}}{\sigma} \tag{10.6}$$

We can apply the Excel `standardize()` function, as shown below.

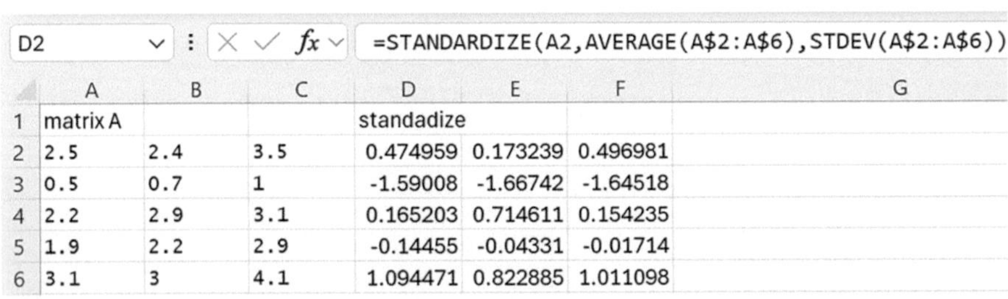

D2 =STANDARDIZE(A2,AVERAGE(A$2:A$6),STDEV(A$2:A$6))

	A	B	C	D	E	F	G
1	matrix A			standadize			
2	2.5	2.4	3.5	0.474959	0.173239	0.496981	
3	0.5	0.7	1	-1.59008	-1.66742	-1.64518	
4	2.2	2.9	3.1	0.165203	0.714611	0.154235	
5	1.9	2.2	2.9	-0.14455	-0.04331	-0.01714	
6	3.1	3	4.1	1.094471	0.822885	1.011098	

Fig. 10.64 The Excel STANDARDIZE function

Step 2: Apply our hidden called.`eigen ()` to get the eigenvalues and eigenvectors.

```
 * ---------------------------------------------------------------- *
 *  Your input is shown below.                                      *
 * ---------------------------------------------------------------- *
   V1  V2  V3
1 2.5 2.4 3.5
2 0.5 0.7 1.0
3 2.2 2.9 3.1
4 1.9 2.2 2.9
5 3.1 3.0 4.1
 * ---------------------------------------------------------------- *
 *  Eigen values are shown below.                                   *
 * ---------------------------------------------------------------- *
$values
[1] 3.0627053 0.3995216 0.1933801

 *  Eigen vectors are shown below.                                  *
$vectors
          [,1]       [,2]       [,3]
[1,] 0.5775990  0.4027175  0.7100690
[2,] 0.4637403 -0.8777274  0.1205801
[3,] 0.6718067  0.2596406 -0.6937308
```

Fig. 10.65 Using the.eigen function

Copy those values to Excel.

Step 3: Our principal components will be the product of the standardized data and the eigenmatrix, as shown below.

L2 fx {=MMULT(D2:F6,H2:J4)}

	D	E	F	G	H	I	J	K	L	M	N
1	standadize				Eigen vector				PC1	PC2	PC3
2	0.474959	0.173239	0.496981		0.577599	0.402718	0.710069		0.688549	0.168254	0.013372
3	-1.59008	-1.66742	-1.64518		0.46374	-0.87773	0.12058		-2.79692	0.396036	-0.18882
4	0.165203	0.714611	0.154235		0.671807	0.259641	-0.69373		0.530431	-0.52066	0.096476
5	-0.14455	-0.04331	-0.01714						-0.11509	-0.02465	-0.09598
6	1.094471	0.822885	1.011098		Eigen values				1.693033	-0.01898	0.174944
7					3.0627053	0.3995216	0.1933801				

Fig. 10.66 Matrix multiplication using the Excel MMULT function

Later in the chapter, we will show a hidden function to get the above result.

10.30 Hidden Functions for This Chapter

The function called `.searchHiddenFunctions ()` can be used to discover this chapter's related functions.

```
> .searchHiddenFunctions(10)
  CHAPTER                          NAME                     SHORTCUT
       10 install.packages('ggplot2')
       10 .clusterPlot                 .cPlot    # need 'ggplot2'
       10 .generateNcentroidsData      .nCentroidsData
       10 .elbowPlot
       10 .show_iris
       10 .show_groceriesData
       10 .grocery
       10 .kmeans
       10 .eigen
       10 .pcaExamples                 .pcae
       10 .pca
```

Fig. 10.67 The hidden functions related to Chapter 10

Appendix A: After launching R, issue one of the following lines of R code.

```
source("http://datayyy.com/i2ft/week10.txt")
```

```
source("http://datayyy.com/i2ft/week10.txt")
```

```
*---------------------------------------------------------------------*
* Introduction to FinTech using Excel                 by Dr. Yan 2025   *
*       (in an R-assisted learning environment)                       *
*---------------------------------------------------------------------*
*  .c1  Introduction and Excel Basics            .c15 Term Projects     *
*  .c2  Blockchain 1: (Numbers & alphanumeric)   .c16 R basics(optional) *
*  .c3             2: (ASCII and Sha256)         .c17 Macro (optional)   *
*  .c4  Ledger and distributed ledger            .c18 VBA  (optional)    *
*  .c5  Cryptography    1: and public/private keys                     *
*  .c6                  2: Advanced                                    *
*  .c7  Cryptocurrency and Ganache                                     *
*  .c8                  2: markets, risk, risk/return tradeoff         *
*  .c9  Blockchain's Applications with Simulations                     *
*---------------------------------------------------------------------*
* .c10  Machine Learning in finance 1: Unsupervised Learning           *
* .c11                              2: Supervised Learning: regressions *
* .c16  Term projects                                                  *
* --------------------------------------------------------------------*
* >.c11       # go to chapter 11                                       *
* >.uu        # go to utility submenu                                  *
* >.ft        # back to this menu                                      *
*---------------------------------------------------------------------*
```

Fig. 10.68 The menu for Week 10

Appendix B: For Chapter 10, just type `.chapter10`, shown below.

```
> .c10()
function(i=0){
"i  Chapter 10: unsupervised Learning   i  Explanation                       i  Our hidden functions
 -  ----------------------------------  -- -------------------------------- --  -----------------------
 1  Supervised / unsupervised learning  21 Type II: Association             41  install.packages('ggplot2')
 2  structured / unstructured data      22        : support and confidence  42  .clusterPlot()
 3  Unsupervised learning               23        : Example                 43  .generateNcentroidsData(
 4         : 3 categories               24        : Groceries Data Set      44  .elbowPlot()
 5  Type I: Concept of cluster          25        : .show_grocediesData()   45  .show_iris()
 6          : Centroid                  26        : .grocery()              46  .kmeans()
 7           Excel 1: generate 3-centroid 27      :                         47  .show_groceriesData()
 8                 2: two choices       28 Type III : PCA                   48  .grocery()
 9                 3: a Macro           29    : Excel matrix multiplication 49  .eigen()
10                   : how to run a Macro 30  : Eigen vectors and values    50  .pcaExamples()
11             .nCentroidsData() function 31  : Excel eigen value/vector    51  .pca()
12        : K-means methodology         32    : .eigen() hidden function    52  .mmult()
13        :  Excel to get 3 centers     33    : iris data set
14        : .kmeans hidden function     34    : cars data set
15        : optional k                  35    : USArrests data set
16        : .elbow() function           35    : wine
17        : K-means interactive         36    : attitude
18        : K-means interactive         38    : .pcaExamples()
19  Videos                              39    : .pca() function
20  Links                               40    : .mmult() mimic Excel function

Example 1>.c10     # find out the list
Example 2>.c10()   # find out the list
Example 3>.c10(1)  # see the first explanation
```

Fig. 10.69 The contents of Chapter 10

Appendix C: Excel Macro to generate a 3-centroid random data set

```
Sub GenerateCentroidDataFromCells()
  Dim i As Integer
  Dim numPoints As Integer
  Dim centroid1 As Variant, centroid2 As Variant, centroid3 As Vari-
ant
  Dim xOffset As Double, yOffset As Double
  Dim ws As Worksheet
  Dim resultCol As Integer
  ' Set the worksheet to the current active sheet
  Set ws = ActiveSheet
  ' Read the number of points to generate from cell A4
  numPoints = ws.Cells(4, 1).Value
  ' Read centroids from cells A1:C3 (students enter these values)
  centroid1=Array(ws.Cells(1,1).Value,ws.Cells(1,2).Value)
'X1,Y1from A1:B1
```

```
  centroid2 = Array(ws.Cells(2, 1).Value, ws.Cells(2, 2).Value) '
X2, Y2 from A2:B2
  centroid3 = Array(ws.Cells(3, 1).Value, ws.Cells(3, 2).Value) '
X3, Y3 from A3:B3
  ' Set the start column for results (either column C or D)
  resultCol = 3 ' Column C = 3, Column D = 4 (adjust as needed)
  ' Clear previous generated data (but keep A1:B3)
  ws.Range(ws.Cells(1, resultCol), ws.Cells(1 + 3 * numPoints,
resultCol + 2)).ClearContents
  ' Place headers for the generated data in the result columns
  ws.Cells(1, resultCol).Value = "X"
  ws.Cells(1, resultCol + 1).Value = "Y"
  ws.Cells(1, resultCol + 2).Value = "Centroid"
  ' Generate data for Centroid 1
  For i = 1 To numPoints
    xOffset = (Rnd - 0.5) * 4
    yOffset = (Rnd - 0.5) * 4
    ws.Cells(i + 1, resultCol).Value = centroid1(0) + xOffset
    ws.Cells(i + 1, resultCol + 1).Value = centroid1(1) + yOffset
    ws.Cells(i + 1, resultCol + 2).Value = "1"
  Next i
  ' Generate data for Centroid 2
  For i = 1 To numPoints
    xOffset = (Rnd - 0.5) * 4
    yOffset = (Rnd - 0.5) * 4
    ws.Cells(i+numPoints+1,resultCol).Value  =  centroid2(0)  +
xOffset
    ws.Cells(i+numPoints+1,resultCol+1).Value=centroid2(1)    +
yOffset
    ws.Cells(i+numPoints+1,resultCol+2).Value="2"
  Next i
  ' Generate data for Centroid 3
  For i = 1 To numPoints
    xOffset = (Rnd - 0.5) * 4
    yOffset = (Rnd - 0.5) * 4
    ws.Cells(i+2*numPoints+1,resultCol).Value = centroid3(0) +
xOffset
    ws.Cells(i+2*numPoints+1,resultCol+1).Value     =     cen-
troid3(1)+yOffset
    ws.Cells(i + 2 * numPoints + 1, resultCol + 2).Value = "3"
  Next i
  MsgBox "Data Generated!"
End Sub
```

Exercises

10.1 What does 'labeled data' mean?
10.2 What is unsupervised learning?
10.3 Define clustering analysis. How is it used in unsupervised learning?
10.4 How do we use Excel to generate 400 random values with 4 centroids?
10.5 What is the role of distance metrics (e.g., Euclidean distance) in clustering analysis?
10.6 Why is normalizing or scaling the data important before applying clustering algorithms?
10.7 How do you interpret cluster centroids in a K-means clustering model?
10.8 How would you perform K-means clustering using Excel? Outline the steps.
10.9 Use Excel formulas to calculate the Euclidean distance between two data points.
10.10 After clustering, how can you use Excel charts to visualize the results of K-means clustering?
10.11 Explain how you can use conditional formatting in Excel to highlight clusters in your dataset.
10.12 Describe how to use the Solver add-in in Excel to optimize the clustering solution.
10.13 How would you determine the optimal number of clusters in K-means using Excel?
10.14 Explain how to use a dendrogram to visualize the hierarchical clustering results in Excel.
10.15 What is the "elbow method," and how can it be applied using Excel to find the right number of clusters?
10.16 What is association analysis in the context of unsupervised learning?
10.17 Define support, confidence, and lift in the context of association rule mining.
10.18 What are the key differences between clustering analysis and association rule mining?
10.19 How can Excel be used to manually calculate support, confidence, and lift for association rules?
10.20 How would you use PivotTables in Excel to analyze large datasets for frequent items?
10.21 Describe how you can perform basic market basket analysis using Excel.
10.22 How can Excel's `COUNTIF()` and `SUMIF()` functions be used to calculate support for item sets?
10.23 How can Excel charts be used to visualize frequent item sets and association rules?
10.24 How would you use Excel's Data Analysis ToolPak to assist with association rule mining?
10.25 How can the lift ratio be interpreted when evaluating the strength of an association rule?

10.26 What are the limitations of using Excel for large-scale association rule mining?
10.27 What is Principal Component Analysis (PCA), and how does it differ from clustering and association analysis?
10.28 Why is PCA considered a dimensionality reduction technique?
10.29 What are eigenvalues and eigenvectors, and how are they relevant in PCA?
10.30 How does PCA deal with correlated variables in a dataset?
10.31 Explain the process of transforming original variables into principal components.
10.32 How do you interpret the variance explained by the principal components in a PCA model?
10.33 What are some common applications of PCA in data analysis?
10.34 Describe the steps to perform PCA manually using Excel. What formulas are involved?
10.35 How can you use Excel to calculate the covariance matrix for a dataset as part of the PCA process?
10.36 Explain how you would extract eigenvalues and eigenvectors from the covariance matrix using Excel.
10.37 Describe how to scale and center the data before applying PCA in Excel.
10.38 How can you visualize principal components and the data projection onto them using Excel charts?
10.39 How do we use the hidden function to generate 400 random values for 4 centroids?
10.40* Get the Fama-French 3-factor time series and conduct a PCA analysis. What percentage of the variations can be explained if just for one factor (PC1)? At https://mba.tuck.dartmouth.edu/pages/faculty/ken.french/data_library.html, you can download the monthly 3-factor time series data.
10.41 Use the Excel 'Random Generation function ' to generate a 100 by 10 (number of rows and number of columns) data set, shown below.

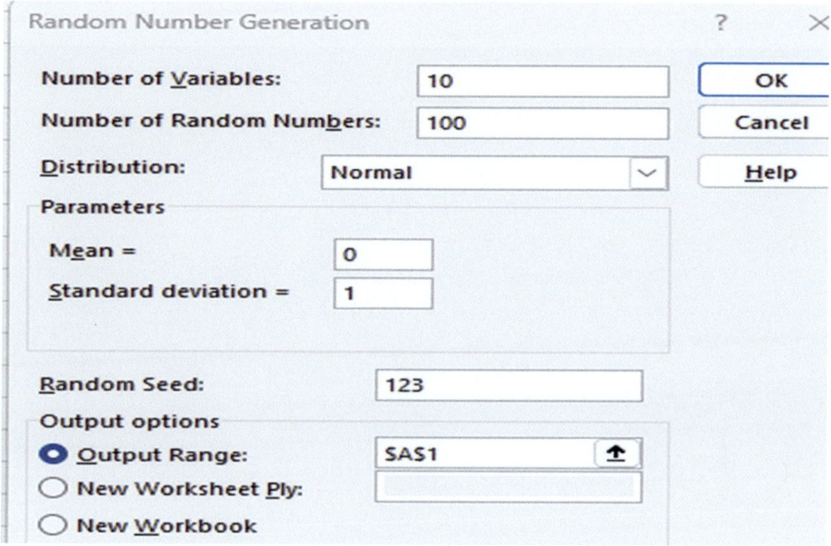

Fig. 10.70 The Excel Random Number Generation functionality

Conduct a PCA analysis. What are the eigenvalues and eigenvectors? How many principal components would you recommend if the percentages explained are 80 and 90%?

References

Banoula, M. (2023). K-means Clustering Algorithm: Applications, Types, & How Does It Work? https://www.simplilearn.com/tutorials/machine-learning-tutorial/k-means-clustering-algorithm

Kaggle Grocery data set. https://www.kaggle.com/datasets/heeraldedhia/groceries-dataset?resource=download

K-Means Clustering Simulation. https://user.ceng.metu.edu.tr/~akifakkus/courses/ceng574/k-means/

Kmeans interactive. https://commons.wikimedia.org/wiki/File:K-means_convergence.gif

Kurama, V., & Jessica Powers. (2022). Unsupervised Learning with Python: A Beginner's Guide. https://builtin.com/data-science/unsupervised-learning-python

Machine Learning (in Finance). https://corporatefinanceinstitute.com/resources/data-science/machine-learning-in-finance/

Make Simple. (2020). Principal Component Analysis (PCA): Understand it by manual calculation on Excel. Retrieved form https://www.youtube.com/watch?v=eAcYYH9pKQ4

Excel and Python code. retrieved form https://github.com/TiongSun/PCA_manual_calculation

Mis Helper. (2021). How to Calculate the Confidence, Support, and Lift of Association Rules. https://www.mishelper.com/data-mining/association-rules/metrics/

NumXL. (2013). PCA tutorial in Excel (youtube.com). https://www.youtube.com/watch?v=WCigXTRVH78

UCI Machine Learning Repository. https://archive.ics.uci.edu/

UCI Iris data set. https://archive.ics.uci.edu/dataset/53/iris

Supervised Learning (I) Using Excel: Classifications

11

Supervised Learning could be grouped into two categories: Classification and Regressions. This chapter is about the former, and the next is about the latter. We arrange this chapter immediately following Chapter 10: Unsupervised Learning since many concepts are similar, such as classification vs. clustering and using the K-means method. In addition, readers and students can reinforce what they learned in the previous chapter. In this chapter, the following topics will be covered:

- What is supervised learning?
- Difference between classification and clustering
- Data preparation, such as coding categorical variables
- Excel for Iris Example
- K-means methodology
- Accuracy, precision, recall, and F1
- A quick explanation of the confusion matrix
- Our hidden functions

11.1 What Is Supervised Learning?

In this chapter, we will explore machine learning techniques that leverage labeled data to train models for tasks such as classification and clustering. Supervised learning involves training algorithms on a dataset where the input-output pairs are

---

Supplementary Information The online version contains supplementary material available at https://doi.org/10.1007/978-3-031-89779-5_11.

Y. Yan, *Introduction to FinTech using Excel*, Springer Texts in Business and Economics, https://doi.org/10.1007/978-3-031-89779-5_11

known, allowing the model to learn patterns and make predictions or classifications based on unseen data. This chapter focuses on classification techniques, which aim to categorize data into predefined classes, and clustering methods like k-means, where the objective is to group data points based on similarities without any prior labels for the groups.

While traditional regression models fall under supervised learning, this chapter avoids explicit regression analysis to concentrate on discrete and unsupervised classification methods. We can simulate and understand key concepts in classification and clustering through Excel's built-in functions and features, such as pivot tables, conditional formatting, and simple macros.

11.2 Classification vs. Clustering

Classification and clustering are two distinct approaches in machine learning that serve different purposes in analyzing data. In classification, the goal is to assign data points to predefined categories or classes based on input features. The algorithm is trained on labeled data, meaning that the corresponding output class is known for each input. For example, in a classification task, you might predict whether an email is "spam" or "not spam" based on its content and other attributes. In supervised learning, classification models use this labeled data to learn patterns and make predictions on new, unseen data. Standard algorithms include decision trees, support vector machines, and k-nearest neighbors.

On the other hand, clustering is an unsupervised learning technique where the algorithm groups similar data points together without prior knowledge of the group labels. Clustering aims to find structure in the data by identifying inherent groupings or patterns. For instance, a k-means algorithm might cluster customers based on purchasing behavior, grouping them into segments like "frequent shoppers" or "occasional buyers." Unlike classification, clustering doesn't require labeled data, and the number of clusters (or groupings) is typically determined in advance or inferred during the process. While classification is used to predict specific outcomes, clustering is used primarily to uncover hidden patterns and relationships in the data.

11.3 Data Preparation for Classification

Data preparation is crucial in any classification task, as the input data's quality and structure directly impact the model's performance. In this stage, raw data is cleaned, transformed, and organized to ensure the classification algorithm can adequately analyze it. Essential tasks include handling missing values, dealing with outliers, and converting categorical variables into numerical formats (e.g., by using label encoding or one-hot encoding). Feature selection or engineering may also be necessary to identify which variables are most relevant for the classification task, reducing noise and improving model accuracy. For example, in a dataset predicting customer churn, features such as "last purchase date" or "number of customer service calls" might be more important than less informative fields like "customer ID."

Normalization or standardization is another critical aspect of data preparation, especially when the features have different scales. For instance, if one feature represents income in thousands while another represents age in years, the model might give undue importance to income due to its larger values. Scaling these features to a standard range ensures that no single feature dominates the classification process. Data preparation also involves splitting the dataset into training and test sets, ensuring that the model is trained on a portion of the data and evaluated on unseen data to prevent overfitting.

Example 1 is how to handle missing values. In a dataset containing employee information (e.g., age, department, salary), missing values in the "salary" column could lead to inaccurate predictions. A common approach would be to impute these missing values by replacing them with the mean or median salary for the relevant department.

Example 2 is to encode categorical variables. If we are classifying emails as "spam" or "not spam," an essential feature could be the "email provider" (e.g., Gmail, Yahoo). Since this is a categorical variable, you need to convert it into a numerical form, such as assigning 1 to Gmail and 2 to Yahoo or using one-hot encoding to create separate binary columns for each provider.

11.4 What Is the KNN Algorithm?

The k-nearest neighbors (KNN) algorithm is a nonparametric, supervised learning method that classifies or predicts a data point's category based on its proximity to other points. It's one of the simplest and most widely used classifiers in machine learning. Although KNN can be applied to both regression and classification tasks, it is most often used for classification, relying on the assumption that similar data points are located near each other.

In classification tasks, the algorithm assigns a class label through a "majority vote," meaning the most common label among neighboring points is selected. While the correct term is "plurality voting" (since a true majority vote requires over 50%, usually relevant for two categories), "majority vote" is more commonly used. For scenarios with multiple categories, such as four, the decision might only require a vote share of more than 25% rather than a full majority.

11.5 K-Means vs. KNN

We discussed the K-means methodology in the previous chapter. Despite being popular algorithms in machine learning, k-means and k-nearest neighbors (k-NN) have significant differences. They serve different purposes and work in distinct ways. Table 11.1 summarizes the breakdown of their fundamental differences.

Table 11.1 Summary table for the differences between K-means and Knn

Feature	k-Means	k-NN
Learning Type	Unsupervised (Clustering)	Supervised (Classification)
Purpose	Group data into clusters based on similarity	Classify new data based on known labels
Label Requirement	No labeled data is required	Requires labeled data for training
Output	Cluster assignments	Class prediction for new data
How it Works	Iterative refinement of centroids and clusters	Distance-based voting for nearest neighbors
Applications	Market segmentation, document clustering	Image recognition, medical diagnosis
Efficiency	More efficient but dependent on iterations	It can be slow with large datasets

Difference #1: Purpose in Classification vs. Clustering

K-NN is a supervised learning algorithm used primarily for classification (and sometimes for regression). It relies on labeled data to classify new data points based on their proximity to known data points. Given a test point, k-NN looks for the closest k-labeled points (neighbors) in the training set and assigns the majority class among those neighbors to the test point.

K-Means is an unsupervised learning algorithm used for clustering. It groups unlabeled data points into *k* clusters based on their similarity, typically measured by distance. In k-means, the algorithm partitions the data into k clusters where each data point belongs to the cluster with the nearest mean value, or centroid. K-Means doesn't require labeled data and aims to discover patterns in the data by grouping similar points.

Difference #2: Training and testing samples

As a supervised learning algorithm, k-NN requires a training dataset that is already labeled. The goal is to classify new data points based on existing categories, and the labels guide the decision-making process during classification.

K-Means: k-Means is an unsupervised learning algorithm for unlabeled data. Its goal is not to predict labels but to find natural groupings or clusters within the data based on similarities.

Difference #3: How They Work

k-NN: When classifying a new data point, compute the distance (often Euclidean distance) from the test point to every point in the training set. Identify the *k* nearest neighbors to the test point. Assign the label based on the majority vote from these nearest neighbors.

K-Means works iteratively to partition data into *k* clusters: Initialize by selecting *k* random centroids. Assign each data point to the nearest centroid, forming k clusters. Recalculate the centroids of the clusters based on the data points assigned to them. Repeat the process (reassign points and recompute centroids) until the cluster assignments no longer change or a maximum number of iterations is reached.

Difference #4: Outcome

K-NN: The outcome of k-NN is a classification for each test point. For example, a flower from the Iris dataset might be classified as "Setosa" based on the species of its nearest neighbors.

K-Means: The outcome of k-means is a set of clusters. Each data point is assigned to one of the `k` clusters based on similarity, but no explicit "label" is associated with these clusters. Instead, they represent groupings found by the algorithm.

Difference #5. Training Process

Like many machine learning algorithms, K-NN does not have a traditional "training phase." Instead, it stores the entire training dataset, and classification is done at the time of prediction by comparing the test data point to all training data points.

K-Means has a clear training phase, where it iteratively refines the cluster centroids based on the input data. This process continues until convergence (no change in cluster assignments) or the maximum number of iterations is reached.

Difference #6: Efficiency

k-NN can be computationally expensive when classifying new points because it has to compute the distance between the test point and all training points for each prediction. For large datasets, this can be slow.

K-Means is typically more efficient for clustering large datasets, as it relies on updating centroids rather than comparing all points to each other. However, the number of iterations and the choice of `k` can affect the efficiency.

Difference #7: Applications

k-NN is commonly used for tasks such as image recognition, handwriting detection, and medical diagnosis, where similarity-based classification is essential.

K-Means is used in market segmentation, image compression, document clustering, and anomaly detection, where the goal is to discover underlying patterns or natural groupings.

K-NN is a supervised classification algorithm that predicts new data classes based on similarity to known labeled data. K-means, on the other hand, is an unsupervised clustering algorithm that organizes data into clusters based on similarity without any prior labels.

11.6 Using Excel to Classify Iris Data

Using Excel to build and test a classification model with the Iris dataset involves some manual steps. While Excel doesn't have built-in machine learning functions, we can simulate the process using rudimentary methods, such as k-nearest neighbors (k-NN) or simple decision rules based on the data. In this approach, we'll randomly split the data into a training set (75%) and a test set (25%), then classify the test data using an essential distance measure, like the Euclidean distance, to find the nearest neighbors.

Step 1: Input the Iris data, generate a random number column, and choose a trading sample. The formula in cell G2 is =if(F2>1-0.75,1,0).

G2 fx =IF(F2>1-0.75,1,0)

	A	B	C	D	E	F	G
1	sepal_leng	sepal_widt	petal_lengt	petal_width	class	random seed 12	taining
2	5.1	3.5	1.4	0.2	Iris-setosa	0.002349925	0
3	4.9	3	1.4	0.2	Iris-setosa	0.171758171	0
4	4.7	3.2	1.3	0.2	Iris-setosa	0.190191351	0
5	4.6	3.1	1.5	0.2	Iris-setosa	0.886623737	1
6	5	3.6	1.4	0.2	Iris-setosa	0.047547838	0
7	5.4	3.9	1.7	0.4	Iris-setosa	0.798059023	1
8	4.6	3.4	1.4	0.3	Iris-setosa	0.395123142	1

Fig. 11.1 The first several lines of the Iris data set

Step 2: Calculate the mean values for those three categories. The function is cell I3 is =AVERAGEIFS(A:A,$E:$E,"="&$H4,$G:$G,"=1"). There are two conditions: the first being "Iris-setosa" and the second being those values belonging to the training sample data set, i.e., column G is 1.

I4 fx =AVERAGEIFS(A:A,$E:$E,"="&$H4,$G:$G,"=1")

	A	B	C	D	E	F	G	H	I	J	K	L
1	sepal_leng	sepal_widt	petal_leng	petal_width	class	random seed 12	taining					
2	5.1	3.5	1.4	0.2	Iris-setosa	0.002349925	0					
3	4.9	3	1.4	0.2	Iris-setosa	0.171758171	0		sepal_leng	sepal_widt	petal_leng	petal_width
4	4.7	3.2	1.3	0.2	Iris-setosa	0.190191351	0	Iris-setosa	5.046875	3.440625	1.503125	0.259375
5	4.6	3.1	1.5	0.2	Iris-setosa	0.886623737	1	Iris-versicolor	5.962857	2.802857	4.28	1.32
6	5	3.6	1.4	0.2	Iris-setosa	0.047547838	0	Iris-virginica	6.516667	2.952778	5.494444	2.022222
7	5.4	3.9	1.7	0.4	Iris-setosa	0.798059023	1					
8	4.6	3.4	1.4	0.3	Iris-setosa	0.395123142	1					

Fig. 11.2 Estimating means

Step 3: We calculate three distances from those three centers for the testing sample. In cell I2, the formula is =IF($G2=0,SQRT(($A2−$O$4)^2 + ($B2−$P$4)^2 + ($C2−$Q$4)^2 + ($D2−$R$4)^2),""), as shown below.

H2 fx =IF($G2=0,SQRT(($A2-$O$4)^2+($B2-$P$4)^2+($C2-$Q$4)^2+($D2-$R$4)^2),"")

	E	F	G	H	I	J	K	N	O	P	Q	R
1	class	randon	taining	distance1	distance2	distance3	min					
2	Iris-setosa	0.00	0	0.143205	3.283189	4.731951578	0.1432055					
3	Iris-setosa	0.17	0	0.479461	3.273733	4.764536723	0.479461		sepal_leng	sepal_widt	petal_leng	petal_width
4	Iris-setosa	0.19	0	0.472237	3.447801	4.926992453	0.472237	Iris-setosa	5.046875	3.440625	1.503125	0.259375
5	Iris-setosa	0.89	1					Iris-versicolor	5.962857	2.802857	4.28	1.32
6	Iris-setosa	0.05	0	0.204347	3.333366	4.775368417	0.2043473	Iris-virginica	6.516667	2.952778	5.494444	2.022222
7	Iris-setosa	0.80	1									

Fig. 11.3 Distance calculation

In cell I2, the formula is = IF($G2 = 0,SQRT(($A2−$O$5)^2 + ($B2−$P$5)^2 + ($C2−$Q$5)^2 + ($D2−$R$5)^2),"") and in cell J2, the formula is = IF($G2 = 0,SQRT(($A2−$O$6)^2 + ($B2−$P$6)^2 + ($C2−$Q$6)^2 + ($D2−$R$6)^2),""). The minimum values of three distances are in column K.

Step 4: We will classify the test sample. As shown below, we classify the observations used for testing based on the shortest distance.

L2 fx =IF(G2=0,IF(K2=H2,$N$4,IF(K2=I2,$N$5,$N$6)),"")

	E	G	H	I	J	K	L	M	N	O	P	Q	R
1	class	taining	distance1	distance2	distance3	min	class2	correct					
2	Iris-setosa	0	0.143205	3.283189	4.731951578	0.1432055	Iris-setosa	1	=IF(G2=0,IF(E2=L2,1,0),"")				
3	Iris-setosa	0	0.479461	3.273733	4.764536723	0.479461	Iris-setosa	1		sepal_leng	sepal_widt	petal_leng	petal_width
4	Iris-setosa	0	0.472237	3.447801	4.926992453	0.472237	Iris-setosa	1	Iris-setosa	5.046875	3.440625	1.503125	0.259375
5	Iris-setosa	1							Iris-versicolor	5.962857	2.802857	4.28	1.32
6	Iris-setosa	0	0.204347	3.333366	4.775368417	0.2043473	Iris-setosa	1	Iris-virginica	6.516667	2.952778	5.494444	2.022222
7	Iris-setosa	1											

Fig. 11.4 Classification based on the shortest distance

Class 2 will be our classification for the testing data set. In cell L2, the formula will be =IF(G2=0,IF(K2=H2,$N$4,IF(K2=I2,$N$5,$N$6)),"").

Step 5: If the new classification is the same as the original one, then number 1 will be assigned; otherwise, it will be a zero.

The result shows that the accuracy is 93.6%, the number of correct classifications divided by the sample size of the testing sample.

11.7 Accuracy, Precision, Recall, and F1

Below are the definitions of accuracy, precision, recall, and F1. First, look at a matrix (2 by 2) related to the actual and predicted results (Table 11.2).

In the above matrix, TP is True Positive, FN is False Negative, FP is for False Positive, and TN is for True Negative. The definition of accuracy is defined below.

$$Accuracty = \frac{TP + TN}{allobs.} = \frac{TP + TN}{TP + FP + FN + TN} \tag{11.1}$$

Accuracy is the number of all correctly predicted values divided by all the values. The precision is defined below.

$$Precision = \frac{TP}{TP + FP} \tag{11.2}$$

Precision is related to the first column in the above table. It can be viewed as the percentage we predicted correct for all positive cases. For example, there are 10 cases of cancer. If we predicted 4 cases correctly, then the precision is 4/(4 + 6) = 0.4. The recall formula is given below.

$$Recall \frac{TP}{TP + FN} \tag{11.3}$$

The first row in the above table is associated with the recall. F1 shows the balance between Precision and Recall.

$$F1 = \frac{Precision * Recall}{mean(Precision, Recall)} = \frac{Precision * Recall}{\frac{Precision+Recall}{2}} = \frac{2 * Precision * Recall}{Precision + Recall} \tag{11.4}$$

Table 11.2 A matrix for actual and predicted outcomes

		Actual result	
Forecasted		T (True)	F (False)
	T (True)	TP	FN
	F (False)	FP	TN

11.8 Our Hidden .knnExamples () Function

To help readers and students learn classification better, we have generated a function called `.knnExamles()` that uses a few famous data sets, such as Iris, Cars, USArrest, wine, and attitude. This function depends on two packages. Copying and pasting the following two lines to your R console will install them.

```
install.packages('caret')
install.packages('class')
```

Below, we show how to use this function to get results for the iris data set. Typing the function name launches it.

```
> .knnExamples()
 * ---------------------------------------------------------------- *
 *  Objective: a few examples for Knn (K Nearest Neighbors)          *
 * ---------------------------------------------------------------- *
 *   Hit the Enter Key to continue                                   *

 * ---------------------------------------------------------------- *
 * Step 1: choose a data set                                         *
 * ---------------------------------------------------------------- *
 *  1          iris                                                  *
 *  2          cars                                                  *
 *  3          USArrests                                             *
 *  4          wine                                                  *
 *  5          attitude                                              *
 *  Esc to exit                                                      *
 * ---------------------------------------------------------------- *
 *  Enter your choice                                                *
1
```

Fig. 11.5 Showing example using Knn (.knnExamples)

For Step 1, we choose a data set. If we choose 1, the iris data set will be used. The next choice will be a random seed.

```
 * ---------------------------------------------------------------- *
 * Step 2: enter a random seed such as 123                           *
 * ---------------------------------------------------------------- *
 *  Enter your choice                                                *
123
```

Fig. 11.6 Step 2: Choose a random seed

If interested readers want the same result, choose 123 as your random seed.

```
* ---------------------------------------------------------------- *
* Step 3: enter a value such as 0.75 to deviding the original     *
*         into trading and testing sample (75% vs. 25%)          *
* ---------------------------------------------------------------- *
*  Enter your choice                                              *
0.75
```

Fig. 11.7 Step 3: Dividing the data set into training and test samples

Based on the above input, 75% of the data set will be used as a training sample, while the rest will be used to test the model. The result is shown below. The top part is from the confusion matrix.

```
Confusion Matrix and Statistics

            Reference
Prediction   setosa versicolor virginica
  setosa         49          0         0
  versicolor      0         48         6
  virginica       0          2        44

Overall Statistics

               Accuracy : 0.9463
                 95% CI : (0.8969, 0.9765)
    No Information Rate : 0.3356
    P-Value [Acc > NIR] : < 2.2e-16

                  Kappa : 0.9195

 Mcnemar's Test P-Value : NA

Statistics by Class:

                     Class: setosa Class: versicolor Class: virginica
Sensitivity                 1.0000            0.9600           0.8800
Specificity                 1.0000            0.9394           0.9798
Pos Pred Value              1.0000            0.8889           0.9565
Neg Pred Value              1.0000            0.9789           0.9417
Prevalence                  0.3289            0.3356           0.3356
Detection Rate              0.3289            0.3221           0.2953
Detection Prevalence        0.3289            0.3624           0.3087
Balanced Accuracy           1.0000            0.9497           0.9299
```

Fig. 11.8 Confusion matrix and test statistics

The last part is related to Accuracy, Precision, Recall, and F1.

```
* ---------------------------------------------------------------- *
*  Knn Model Performance:                                          *
* ---------------------------------------------------------------- *
*      Accuracy:  0.9463087
*      Precision:  1 0.8888889 0.9565217
*      Recall:  1 0.96 0.88
*      F1 Score:  1 0.9230769 0.9166667
* ---------------------------------------------------------------- *
>
```

Fig. 11.9 The model performance

The Precision for the last two are 44/(44 + 6) = 0.88 and 48/(48 + 2) = 0.96.

11.9 Confusion Matrix

A confusion matrix evaluates the performance of a machine learning model. Learn how to interpret it to assess your model's accuracy. Below is one example.

```
> print(confusionMatrix)
Confusion Matrix and Statistics

            Reference
Prediction   setosa versicolor virginica
  setosa         49          0         0
  versicolor      0         48         6
  virginica       0          2        44

Overall Statistics

               Accuracy : 0.9463
                 95% CI : (0.8969, 0.9765)
    No Information Rate : 0.3356
    P-Value [Acc > NIR] : < 2.2e-16

                  Kappa : 0.9195

 Mcnemar's Test P-Value : NA

Statistics by Class:

                     Class: setosa Class: versicolor Class: virginica
Sensitivity                 1.0000            0.9600           0.8800
Specificity                 1.0000            0.9394           0.9798
Pos Pred Value              1.0000            0.8889           0.9565
Neg Pred Value              1.0000            0.9789           0.9417
Prevalence                  0.3289            0.3356           0.3356
Detection Rate              0.3289            0.3221           0.2953
Detection Prevalence        0.3289            0.3624           0.3087
Balanced Accuracy           1.0000            0.9497           0.9299
>
```

Fig. 11.10 One sample of Confusion Matrix

The confusion matrix describes the performance of a classification model on the Iris dataset across three classes: `setosa`, `versicolor`, and `virginia`. It provides a detailed breakdown of predictions versus actual values.

Setosa was perfectly classified, with all 49 predictions being correct. Versicolor had some misclassifications: 48 were correctly predicted, but 6 were wrongly predicted as virginica. Virginica had 44 correct predictions, but 2 instances were misclassified as versicolor.

Overall Performance: Accuracy is 94.63%, i.e., the model correctly predicted 94.63% of the observations. Kappa is 0.9195; the model has a strong agreement beyond chance. For a 95% confidence interval, the true accuracy of the model is likely between 89.69% and 97.65%. The P-value is <2.2e-16, indicating that the model performs significantly better than random guessing. For Class-Level Performance:

Class #1. Setosa: Sensitivity (Recall): 1.00 (The model correctly identified all setosa samples.) Specificity: 1.00 (No other species were incorrectly classified as setosa.) Precision (Positive Predictive Value): 1.00 (All predictions for setosa were correct.)
Class #2 Versicolor: Sensitivity: 0.96 (96% of the actual versicolor samples were correctly identified.) Specificity is 0.94 (Only a tiny portion of non-versicolor were misclassified as versicolor.) Precision is 0.89 (89% of the predictions for versicolor were correct.)
Class #3. Virginica: Sensitivity: 0.88 (88% of the actual virginica samples were correctly identified.) Specificity is 0.98 (Very few non-virginica samples were misclassified as virginica.) Precision is 0.96 (96% of the predictions for virginica were correct.)

The model performs exceptionally well for setosa, with perfect classification (no misclassifications). There is some slight confusion between versicolor and virginica, with some virginica samples being predicted as versicolor and vice versa. Overall, the model demonstrates high accuracy and robust performance across all metrics, indicating that it is well-suited for this classification task.

11.10 Our.`knn ()` Hidden Function

To help readers and students understand the K-NN method better, we generated a function called `.knn ()`. For this function, we need to install two packages. Just copy and paste the following two lines to your R console.

```
install.packages('caret')
 install.packages('class')
```

Typing the function name will show its usage plus one example. Since the function will ask to copy a data set from a clipboard or Excel, we can use the `.show_iris (0)`, as shown below.

```
>.show_iris (0)
Windows users: launch Excel and paste
```

The above command assures that the data set is copied to a clipboard. We issue the following command.

```
> .knn()
 * ------------------------------------------------------------- *
 *  Objective: run knn with your data                            *
 * ------------------------------------------------------------- *
 * Step 1: copy your Excel data  set, then hit the Enter Key     *
 * ------------------------------------------------------------- *
```

Fig. 11.11 The function applying the Knn methodology (the .knn hidden function)

After hitting the Enter Key, the underlying function asks whether there is a header for your input data set. Since we know that the iris data set has a header, we answer 1.

```
 * ------------------------------------------------------------- *
 * Step 2: Does your data set have a header?                     *
 * ------------------------------------------------------------- *
 *  1          yes                                                *
 *  2          no                                                 *
1
 * ------------------------------------------------------------- *
 *  The first 3 observations are shown below.                    *
 * ------------------------------------------------------------- *
sepal_length sepal_width petal_length petal_width       class
         5.1         3.5          1.4         0.2 Iris-setosa
         4.9         3.0          1.4         0.2 Iris-setosa
         4.7         3.2          1.3         0.2 Iris-setosa
```

Fig. 11.12 Step 2: whether the data has a header line

Next, we use the underlying function which column will be used as our target. Based on the above few lines, we know that column 5, under `Class`, will be the classification.

```
 * ------------------------------------------------------------- *
 * Step 3: Which column is your classfication (classes)?         *
 * ------------------------------------------------------------- *
5
```

Fig. 11.13 Step 3: Specifying which column is used for classification

The random seed is for reproduction. Assume that we choose 123. The training and test data set partitions are 75% and 25%, respectively.

```
* ------------------------------------------------------------ *
* Step 4: enter a random seed such as 123                      *
* ------------------------------------------------------------ *
*  Enter your choice                                           *
123
* ------------------------------------------------------------ *
* Step 5: What is the proportion, such as 0.75, of your        *
*         data will be used as training data                   *
* ------------------------------------------------------------ *
*  Enter your choice                                           *
0.75
* ------------------------------------------------------------ *
* Step 6:Input k value such as 3                               *
3
```

Fig. 11.14 Steps 4 to 6

The result is shown below.

```
Confusion Matrix and Statistics

                 Reference
Prediction        Iris-setosa Iris-versicolor Iris-virginica
  Iris-setosa              12               0              0
  Iris-versicolor           0              14              3
  Iris-virginica            0               0             10

Overall Statistics

               Accuracy : 0.9231
                 95% CI : (0.7913, 0.9838)
    No Information Rate : 0.359
    P-Value [Acc > NIR] : 2.419e-13

                  Kappa : 0.884

 Mcnemar's Test P-Value : NA
```

Fig. 11.15 The confusion matrix

11.11 Our.KnnPredict () Hidden Function

This function is quite similar to our hidden function called .knn (), except we add one more step to predict classification for a given set of x values, as shown below.

```
 * ---------------------------------------------------------------- *
 * Step 7: input your x values                                      *
 *         e.g., for Iris                                           *
4.9 3.0 1.4 0.2
 * ---------------------------------------------------------------- *
1: 4.9 3.0 1.4 0.2
5:
Read 4 items
 * ---------------------------------------------------------------- *
 * Our prediction for x = 4.9 3 1.4 0.2  is:
[1] Iris-setosa
Levels: Iris-setosa Iris-versicolor Iris-virginica
 * ---------------------------------------------------------------- *
```

Fig. 11.16 Step 7: Prediction with a set of inputs

11.12 Decision Tree: Supervised Learning

The Decision Tree method is a widely used technique in supervised learning. It helps model decisions and their possible consequences by breaking down data into smaller subsets based on conditions. It is beneficial for both classification and regression tasks. In a decision tree, each internal node represents a decision based on a feature or attribute, and each branch corresponds to the outcome of that decision. The leaves represent the final classifications or outcomes. The model recursively splits the data at each node, trying to maximize some measure of "purity," such as information gain (via entropy) or the Gini index, until the data in each leaf is homogenous or meets a stopping criterion.

One of the key strengths of decision trees is their simplicity and interpretability. They are easy to visualize and explain, making them particularly useful when transparency is important. Decision trees can capture complex, non-linear relationships in data and perform well with numerical and categorical data. However, they can be prone to overfitting, especially when the tree becomes too deep, leading to a model that fits the training data too closely and fails to generalize well to new data. Techniques like pruning or setting a maximum depth can help mitigate this issue and improve the model's performance.

11.13 The Hitters Data Set

The Hitters data set contains major league baseball data from the 1986 and 1987 seasons. To access the data easily, we have written a hidden function called `.show_hitters()`, which is shown below.

```
> .show_hitters()
           Name AtBat Hits HmRun Runs RBI Walks Years CAtBat CHits CHmRun CRuns CRBI CWalks
1 Andy Allanson   293   66     1   30  29    14     1    293    66      1    30   29     14
2    Alan Ashby   315   81     7   24  38    39    14   3449   835     69   321  414    375
  League Division PutOuts Assists Errors Salary NewLeague
1      A        E     446      33     20     NA         A
2      N        W     632      43     10    475         N
> .show_hitters(-3)
              Name AtBat Hits HmRun Runs RBI Walks Years CAtBat CHits CHmRun CRuns CRBI CWalks
320 Wayne Tolleson   475  126     3   61  43    52     6   1700   433      7   217   93    146
321  Willie Upshaw   573  144     9   85  60    78     8   3198   857     97   470  420    332
322  Willie Wilson   631  170     9   77  44    31    11   4908  1457     30   775  357    249
    League Division PutOuts Assists Errors Salary NewLeague
320      A        W      37     113      7    385         A
321      A        E    1314     131     12    960         A
322      A        W     408       4      3   1000         A
> .show_hitters(0)
 Windows users: launch Excel and paste
```

Fig. 11.17 The first several lines of the Hitters data set

For more detailed information, interested readers can search at https://rdrr.io/cran/ISLR/man/Hitters.html. For the Decision Tree method, we use just three variables: salary, years, and HmRun (the number of home runs). After copying to Excel and deleting unnecessary columns, several observations of those three columns are shown below.

	A	B	C
1	HmRun	Years	Salary
2	1	1	NA
3	7	14	475
4	18	3	480
5	20	11	500
6	10	2	91.5
7	4	11	750

Fig. 11.18 Three variables: number of home runs, number of years, and salary

After adding an ID column, we sort the data set by Salary. We sort the data by ID after deleting those observations with NA, as shown below. In total, we have 163 valid observations. Note that some rows are hidden.

	A	B	C	D
1	ID	HmRun	Years	Salary
2	2	7	14	475
3	3	18	3	480
4	4	20	11	500
260	318	7	5	700
261	319	5	12	875
262	320	3	6	385
263	321	9	8	960
264	322	9	11	1000
265				

Fig. 11.19 Adding an ID column

11.14 Decision Tree Using the Hitters Data

We can simulate a simplified process version through manual steps to explore a Decision Tree using Excel with our dataset. The goal of a decision tree is to split data into groups that help explain the target variable, which in your case is Salary.

Step 1: Sort the data by one of the predictors, such as HmRun or Years.
Step 2: Choose a HmRun variable to split the data.
Step 3: Calculate the means of two groups
Step 5: Compute the Residual Sum of Squares (RSS): For each group, calculate the sum of squared differences from the mean salary to measure its homogeneity.
Step 6: Test other splits.
Step 7: Choose the best split that minimizes the total RSS for the groups.
Step 8: We can try splitting the data based on Years instead of HmRun and repeat the above process.

Assume that we plan to split our data set by the midpoint, i.e., 20 (40 + 0)/2.

	A	B	C	D	G	H	I	J
1	ID	HmRun	Years	Salary		Split by HmRun		
2	2	7	14	475		max	40	=MAX(B:B)
3	3	18	3	480		min	0	=MIN(B:B)
4	4	20	11	500		midPoint	20	=AVERAGE(I2:I3)
5	5	10	2	91.5				

Fig. 11.20 Max, min, and average based on the number of home runs

We calculate the averages of those two groups, shown below.

	B	C	D	H	I	J
1	HmRun	Years	Salary	Split by HmRun		
2	7	14	475	max	40	=MAX(B:B)
3	18	3	480	min	0	=MIN(B:B)
4	20	11	500	midPoint	20	=AVERAGE(I2:I3)
5	10	2	91.5			
6	4	11	750	count1	218	=COUNTIF(B:B,"<="&I4)
7	1	2	70	count2	45	=COUNTIF(B:B,">"&I4)
8	0	3	100			
9	6	2	75	mean1	482.1361	=AVERAGEIFS(D:D,B:B,"<="&$I$4)
10	17	13	1100	mean2	796.5076	=AVERAGEIFS(D:D,B:B,">"&$I$4)

Fig. 11.21 Calculating the meanings of those two groups

The formula in cell I9 is =`AVERAGEIFS(D:D,B:B,"<="&$I$4)` and the formula in cell I10 is =`AVERAGEIFS(D:D,B:B,">"&$I$4)`. We calculate the deviation squared for the next steps, as shown below.

E2 `=IF($B2<=$I$4,($D2-$I$9)^2,"")`

	B	C	D	E	F	G
1	HmRun	Years	Salary	Group1< 20	group >20	
2	7	14	475	50.92		=IF($B2>$I$4,($D2-$I$10)^2,"")
3	18	3	480	4.56		
4	20	11	500	319.12		
5	10	2	91.5	152596.55		
6	4	11	750	71751.08		
7	1	2	70	169856.15		
8	0	3	100	146027.99		
9	6	2	75	165759.79		
10	17	13	1100	381755.81		
11	21	10	517.143		78044.55	

Fig. 11.22 Calculating squared deviations

The formula in cell E2 (the first deviation squared for Group 1) is = `IF($B2 <= $I$4,($D2-$I$9)^2,"")` and the formula in cell F2 (the first deviation squared for Group 2) is = `IF($B2 > $I$4,($D2-$I$10)^2,"")`. After that, we calculate the squared of the summation of those squared deviations divided by `n-1`, as shown below.

I12 | fx =SQRT(SUM(E:E)/(COUNT(E:E)-1))

	B	C	D	E	F	H	I	J	K	L
1	HmRun	Years	Salary	Group1< 20	group >20	Split by HmRun				
2	7	14	475	50.92		max	40	=MAX(B:B)		
3	18	3	480	4.56		min	0	=MIN(B:B)		
4	20	11	500	319.12		midPoint	20	=AVERAGE(I2:I3)		
5	10	2	91.5	152596.55						
6	4	11	750	71751.08		count1	218	=COUNTIF(B:B,"<="&I4)		
7	1	2	70	169856.15		count2	45	=COUNTIF(B:B,">"&I4)		
8	0	3	100	146027.99						
9	6	2	75	165759.79		mean1	482.1361	=AVERAGEIFS(D:D,B:B,"<="&$I$4)		
10	17	13	1100	381755.81		mean2	796.5076	=AVERAGEIFS(D:D,B:B,">"&$I$4)		
11	21	10	517.143		78044.55					
12	4	9	512.5	921.97		RSS1	408.5178	=SQRT(SUM(E:E)/(COUNT(E:E)-1))		
13	13	4	550	4605.51		RSS2	552.2331	=SQRT(SUM(F:F)/(COUNT(F:F)-1))		
14	0	6	700	47464.68		total	960.7509	=SUM(I12:I13)		

Fig. 11.23 Squared summation

Since the cut-off point is a choice variable, we can change it to get another set of values, as shown below, when the cut-off point is 10 instead of 20.

	B	C	D	E	F	H	I	J	K	L
1	HmRun	Years	Salary	Group1< 20	group >20	Split by HmRun				
2	7	14	475	3560.38		max	40	=MAX(B:B)		
3	18	3	480		42605.80	min	0	=MIN(B:B)		
4	20	11	500		34749.33	choose	10			
5	10	2	91.5	104866.55						
6	4	11	750	112003.30		count1	146	=COUNTIF(B:B,"<="&I4)		
7	1	2	70	119253.54		count2	117	=COUNTIF(B:B,">"&I4)		
8	0	3	100	99433.67						
9	6	2	75	115825.23		mean1	415.3311	=AVERAGEIFS(D:D,B:B,"<="&$I$4)		
10	17	13	1100		171055.25	mean2	686.4117	=AVERAGEIFS(D:D,B:B,">"&$I$4)		
11	21	10	517.143		28651.90					
12	4	9	512.5	9441.80		RSS1	360.5157	=SQRT(SUM(E:E)/(COUNT(E:E)-1))		
13	13	4	550		18608.16	RSS2	506.0015	=SQRT(SUM(F:F)/(COUNT(F:F)-1))		
14	0	6	700	81036.41		total	866.5173	=SUM(I12:I13)		

Fig. 11.24 The result with a different cut-off point

We can do the same thing for Years instead of HmRun (the number of home runs); see one of the end-of-chapter problems.

11.15 Decision Tree: Graph

The following graph for the decision tree is based on the Hitter data set. Again, only three variables are used: `salary`, `HmRun`, and `years`. The decision tree is for the relationships between salary, number of years, and number of home runs. The graph is given below. Based on the Bobbitt (2022) program, we generated a hidden function called `.hittersPlot()`. To use the function, readers need to install three packages.

```
install.packages('ISLR')
install.packages('rpart')
install.packages('rpart.plot')
```

To generate the plot (graph), type `.hittersDecisionTreePlot()`, as shown below.

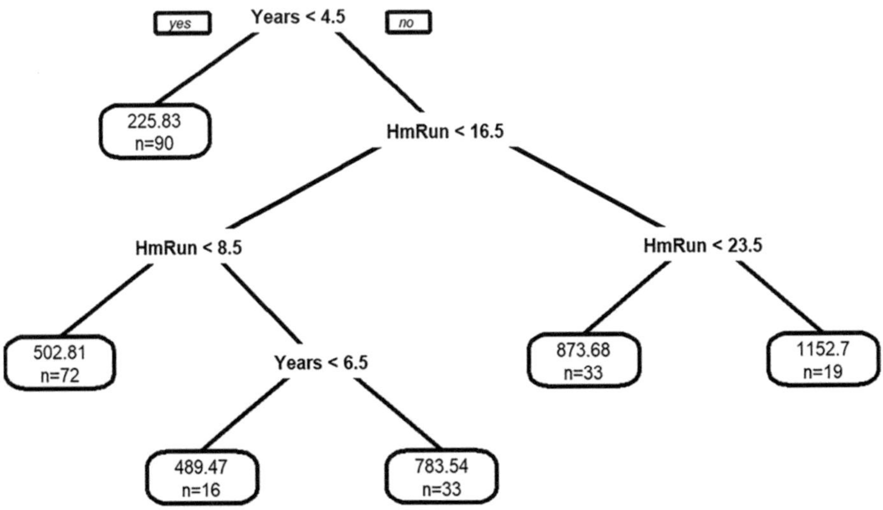

Fig. 11.25 A graphic presentation of a decision tree

From the above tree, we see six terminals. If the number of years is less than 5, the salary will be $226 k. If the Home Run is larger than 24, the annual salary will be $1,153,000, i.e., over $1 million annually.

11.16 The Titanic Data Set

There are several data sets for Titanic. We have generated a hidden function called `.show_titanic()`.

	A	B	C	D	E	F	G	H
1	Passenger	Survived	Pclass	Sex	Age	SibSp	Parch	Fare
2	1	0	3	male	22	1	0	7.25
3	2	1	1	female	38	1	0	71.2833
4	3	1	3	female	26	0	0	7.925
5	4	1	1	female	35	1	0	53.1
6	5	0	3	male	35	0	0	8.05
7	6	0	3	male	NA	0	0	8.4583
8	7	0	1	male	54	0	0	51.8625

Fig. 11.26 Several lines of the Titanic data set

11.17 Decision Tree: Titanic Data

We have generated a hidden function called `.decisionTree_titanic()`, abbreviated as `.dtTitanic()`. After typing `.dtTitanic()`, we will see the following image.

```
> .dtTitanic()
 * ------------------------------------------------------- *
 * Objective: draw a fancy decision tree for               *
 *            using the Titanic data set                   *
 * ------------------------------------------------------- *
 *    Hit the enter key to continue
```

Fig. 11.27 The Decision Tree model using the Titanic data set (.dtTitanic)

After hitting the enter key, we will have two choices.

```
 * ---------------------------------------------------------- *
 *    Do you want to print the first 3 lines?                 *
 * ---------------------------------------------------------- *
 *   1   for yes                                              *
 *   2   for yes                                              *
1
  PassengerId Survived Pclass    Sex Age SibSp Parch    Fare
1           1        0      3   male  22     1     0  7.2500
2           2        1      1 female  38     1     0 71.2833
3           3        1      3 female  26     0     0  7.9250
 * ---------------------------------------------------------- *
 *   input a random seed, such as 123                         *
 * ---------------------------------------------------------- *
234
```

Fig. 11.28 Printing a few lines

The fancy Decision Tree image is shown below.

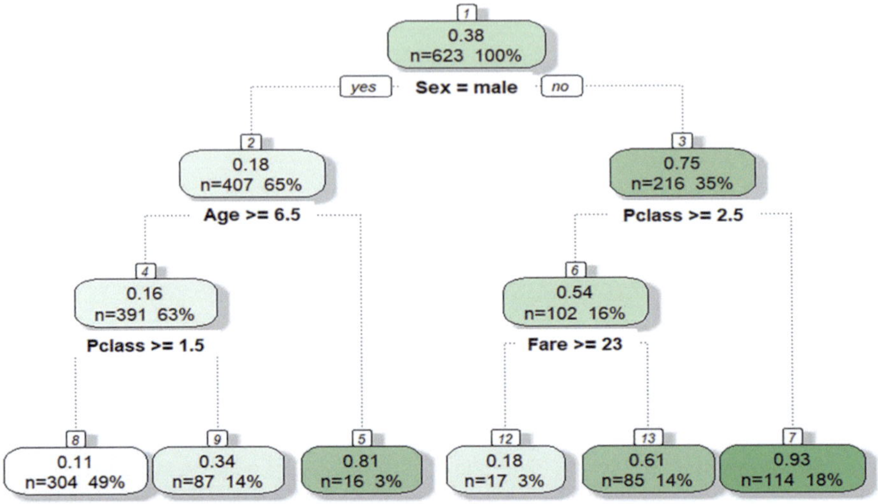

Fig. 11.29 Decision Tree based on the Titanic data set

The first question is whether the package is male. There are 407 YESs at 65 percent, while the number of NOs is 216 at 35 percent. Other nodes can be interpreted in the same way. The summation of the bottom row should be 100%, i.e., $0.49 + 0.14 + 0.03 + 0.03 + 0.14 + 0.18 = 1.01$ (0.01 is a rounding error).

11.18 Logistic Regression

Logistic regression is a widely used supervised learning technique for classification problems where the outcome variable is categorical, typically binary. Unlike linear regression, which predicts continuous values, logistic regression predicts the probability that a given input belongs to a particular category. It is beneficial when the response variable takes values like 0 or 1, representing two distinct classes. The model uses a sigmoid function (the logistic function) to map predicted values to probabilities between 0 and 1, making it ideal for binary classification. Logistic regression models the log odds (or logit) of the outcome as a linear combination of input features, enabling a straightforward interpretation of how each predictor affects the probability of a specific class.

One of the critical advantages of logistic regression is its simplicity and interpretability. Logistic regression can reveal how input feature changes affect an outcome's probability by calculating the odds ratios. Although logistic regression can be extended to multiclass problems through one-vs-rest or softmax regression, its foundational binary classification framework makes it a powerful tool for email spam detection, medical diagnosis, and customer churn prediction. Despite its name, logistic regression is, at its core, a classification method and can be extended to nonlinear problems by introducing polynomials or interaction terms.

11.19 Logistic Regression: Math

The fundamental equations in Logistic Regression are given below. The Sigmoid function is shown below.

$$f(z) = \frac{1}{1+e^{-z}} = \frac{e^z}{1+e^z}, \tag{11.5}$$

where z $= \beta_0 + \beta_0 x_1 + \beta_0 x_1 + \ldots + \beta_n x_n$. The probability prediction formula when the dependent variable y is 1 is shown below.

$$P(y=1|X) = \frac{1}{1+e^{-(\beta_0+\beta_0 x_1+\beta_0 x_1+\ldots+\beta_n x_n)}} \tag{11.6}$$

The log-odds ratio is given below.

$$\log\left(\frac{P(y=1|X}{P(y=0|X}\right) = \beta_0 + \beta_0 x_1 + \beta_0 x_1 + \ldots + \beta_n x_n \tag{11.7}$$

11.20 The Sigmoid Function Graph

With Excel, we can draw a graph for the sigmoid function. The range is from -10 to 10, with an incremental value of 10. The first several observations are shown below.

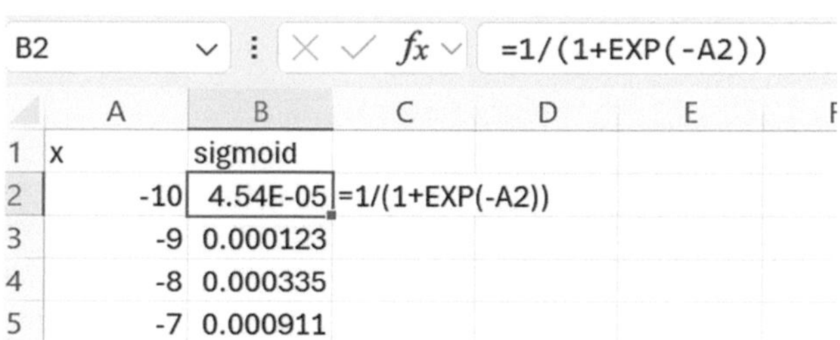
B2 =1/(1+EXP(-A2))

	A	B	C	D	E	F
1	x	sigmoid				
2	-10	4.54E-05	=1/(1+EXP(-A2))			
3	-9	0.000123				
4	-8	0.000335				
5	-7	0.000911				

Fig. 11.30 The Sigmoid function

The formula in cell B2 is =1/(1+EXP(-A2)). The final graph is shown below.

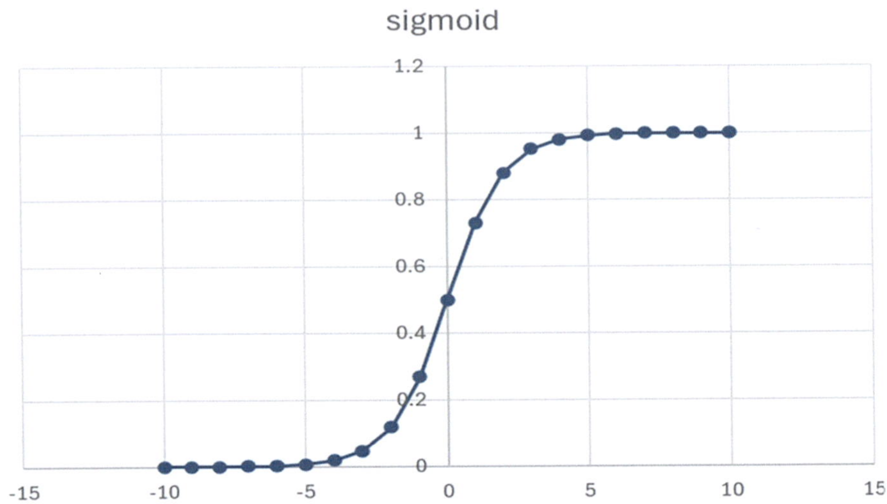

Fig. 11.31 A graphic presentation of the Sigmoid function

11.21 The Heart Disease Data Set

The Heart Disease data set will be used to run a logistic regression. The first step is to download the data at https://raw.githubusercontent.com/rikhuijzer/heart-disease-dataset/refs/heads/main/heart-disease-dataset.csv. The top few lines are shown below.

```
age,sex,chest_pain_type,resting_bp_s,cholesterol,fasting_blood_sugar,resting_ecg,max_heart_rate,exercise_angina,oldpeak,st_slope,target
40.0,1.0,2.0,140.0,289.0,0.0,0.0,172.0,0.0,0.0,1.0,0.0
49.0,0.0,3.0,160.0,180.0,0.0,0.0,156.0,0.0,1.0,2.0,1.0
37.0,1.0,2.0,130.0,283.0,0.0,1.0,98.0,0.0,0.0,1.0,0.0
48.0,0.0,4.0,138.0,214.0,0.0,0.0,108.0,1.0,1.5,2.0,1.0
54.0,1.0,3.0,150.0,195.0,0.0,0.0,122.0,0.0,0.0,1.0,0.0
39.0,1.0,3.0,120.0,339.0,0.0,0.0,170.0,0.0,0.0,1.0,0.0
```

Fig. 11.32 Several lines of the Heart Disease data set

The second way to get the data set is to use our hidden function called `.show_heartDisease()`, shown below.

```
> .show_heartDisease()
  age sex chest_pain_type resting_bp_s cholesterol fasting_blood_sugar resting_ecg max_heart_rate
1  40   1               2          140         289                   0           0            172
2  49   0               3          160         180                   0           0            156
  exercise_angina oldpeak st_slope target
1               0       0        1      0
2               0       1        2      1
> .show_heartDisease(-2)
     age sex chest_pain_type resting_bp_s cholesterol fasting_blood_sugar resting_ecg max_heart_rate
1189  57   0               2          130         236                   0           2            174
1190  38   1               3          138         175                   0           0            173
     exercise_angina oldpeak st_slope target
1189               0       0        2      1
1190               0       0        1      0
> .show_heartDisease(0)
 Windows users: launch Excel and paste
```

Fig. 11.33 An easy way to obtain the data (.show_heartDisease)

11.22 Excel: Run a Logistic Regression

The top few lines in Excel are shown below.

	A	B	C	D	E	F	G	H	I	J	K	L
1	age	sex	chest_pair	resting_bp	cholesterc	fasting_blc	resting_ec	max_heart	exercise_a	oldpeak	st_slope	target
2	40	1	2	140	289	0	0	172	0	0	1	0
3	49	0	3	160	180	0	0	156	0	1	2	1
4	37	1	2	130	283	0	1	98	0	0	1	0
5	48	0	4	138	214	0	0	108	1	1.5	2	1
6	54	1	3	150	195	0	0	122	0	0	1	0
7	39	1	3	120	339	0	0	170	0	0	1	0
8	45	0	2	130	237	0	0	170	0	0	1	0
9	54	1	2	110	208	0	0	142	0	0	1	0

Fig. 11.34 Data to Excel

We have 12 columns, 11 variables (which can be treated as independent variables), and one target (which can be treated as dependent variables).

Step 1: We insert two rows at the top. The second row is for beta values with a set of random values.

	A	B	C	D	E	F	G	H	I	J	K	L	M
1	beta0												
2	0	0	0	0	0	0	0	0	0	0	0	0	
3		age	sex	chest_pair	resting_bp	cholesterc	fasting_blc	resting_ec	max_heart	exercise_a	oldpeak	st_slope	target
4		40	1	2	140	289	0	0	172	0	0	1	0
5		49	0	3	160	180	0	0	156	0	1	2	1
6		37	1	2	130	283	0	1	98	0	0	1	0
7		48	0	4	138	214	0	0	108	1	1.5	2	1
8		54	1	3	150	195	0	0	122	0	0	1	0

Fig. 11.35 Adding two rows on top

Step 2: Apply equation (11.7). To make the presentation better, some columns are hidden. The formula in cell N4 is =

log($A$2+SUMPRODUCT($B$2:$L$2,B4:L4)). Note that we use the Excel `sumproduct()` function.

O4 =$A$2+SUMPRODUCT($B$2:$L$2,B4:L4)

	A	B	C	J	K	L	M	O
1	beta0							
2	0	0	0	0	0	0		
3		age	sex	exercise_a	oldpeak	st_slope	target	logit
4		40	1	0	0	1	0	0.00
5		49	0	0	1	2	1	0.00
6		37	1	0	0	1	0	0.00
7		48	0	1	1.5	2	1	0.00

Fig. 11.36 Applying the Excel SUMPRODUCT function

Step 3: Calculate the odds; the formula in cell P4 is = exp(O4).

P4 =EXP(O4)

	A	B	C	J	K	L	M	O	P
1	beta0								
2	0	0	0	0	0	0			
3		age	sex	exercise_a	oldpeak	st_slope	target	logit	odds
4		40	1	0	0	1	0	0.00	1
5		49	0	0	1	2	1	0.00	1
6		37	1	0	0	1	0	0.00	1

Fig. 11.37 Applying the Excel EXP function

Step 4: Calculate the probability.

Q4 =P4/(1+P4)

	A	B	C	J	K	L	M	O	P	Q
1	beta0									
2	0	0	0	0	0	0				
3		age	sex	exercise_a	oldpeak	st_slope	target	logit	odds	prob
4		40	1	0	0	1	0	0.00	1	0.5
5		49	0	0	1	2	1	0.00	1	0.5
6		37	1	0	0	1	0	0.00	1	0.5
7		48	0	1	1.5	2	1	0.00	1	0.5

Fig. 11.38 Calculating the probability

Step 5: We calculate the correct probability prediction using the proper classification.

R4 =IF(M4=1,Q4,1-Q4)

	A	B	M	O	P	Q	R
1	beta0						1.9152E-174
2	0	0					
3		age	target	logit	odds	prob	correct match
4		40	0	0.00	1	0.5	0.5
5		49	1	0.00	1	0.5	0.5
6		37	0	0.00	1	0.5	0.5
7		48	1	0.00	1	0.5	0.5

Fig. 11.39 The correct probability prediction

In the above image, we use the known classification, i.e., column M under target.

Step 6: Calculate the log of the correct-matched probability. The formula in cell S4 is log(R4).

S4 =LOG(R4)

	A	B	M	O	P	Q	R	S
1	beta0						1.9152E-174	=1/EXP(40
2	0	0						
3		age	target	logit	odds	prob	correct match	log(p)
4		40	0	0.00	1	0.5	0.5	-0.30103
5		49	1	0.00	1	0.5	0.5	-0.30103
6		37	0	0.00	1	0.5	0.5	-0.30103
7		48	1	0.00	1	0.5	0.5	-0.30103
8		54	0	0.00	1	0.5	0.5	-0.30103

Fig. 11.40 Applying the Excel LOG function

Step 7: The log-matched probabilities will be summed in cell T4.

T4 =SUM(S:S)

	A	B	M	O	P	Q	R	S	T
1	beta0						1.9152E-174	=1/EXP(40	0.5
2	0	0							
3		age	target	logit	odds	prob	correct match	log(p)	
4		40	0	0.00	1	0.5	0.5	-0.30103	-358.226
5		49	1	0.00	1	0.5	0.5	-0.30103	
6		37	0	0.00	1	0.5	0.5	-0.30103	
7		48	1	0.00	1	0.5	0.5	-0.30103	

Fig. 11.41 Calculating summation

Step 8: By applying the Excel solver (), we maximize the summation in cell T4 by changing the beta values, i.e., A2:L2.

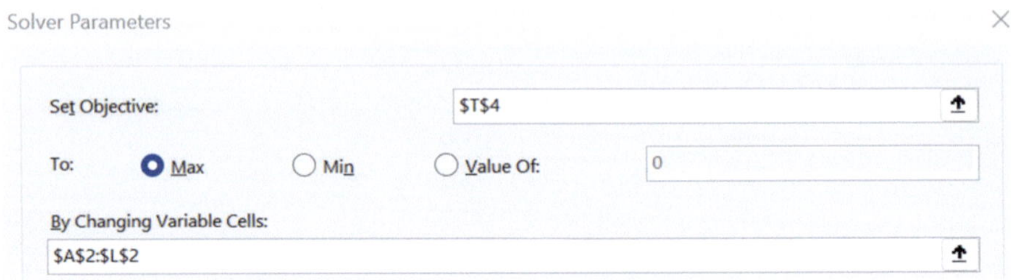

Fig. 11.42 Applying the Excel SOLVER functionality

After clicking 'Solve,' we will have the following beta values.

	A	B	C	D	E	F	G	H	I	J	K	L
1	beta0											
2	-6.2284	0.017661	1.425807	0.787754	0.007046	-0.00246	0.824235	0.119927	-0.0112	1.030466	0.377315	1.234428

Fig. 11.43 The result of beta values

Step 9: In cell N1, we enter 0.5 for our cut-off point, i.e., when the probability is higher than this value: is so 1, 0 otherwise.

N4 fx =IF(Q4>$N$1,1,0)

	H	I	J	K	L	M	N
1							0.5
2	.119927	-0.0112	1.030466	0.377315	1.234428		
3	sting_ec	max_heart	exercise_a	oldpeak	st_slope	target	predicted
4	0	172	0	0	1	0	0
5	0	156	0	1	2	1	0
6	1	98	0	0	1	0	0
7	0	108	1	1.5	2	1	1
8	0	122	0	0	1	0	0
9	0	170	0	0	1	0	0

Fig. 11.44 Using 0.5 as a cutoff point

Step 10: Generate a confusion matrix and calculate accuracy, precision, recall, and F1 parameters; see below.

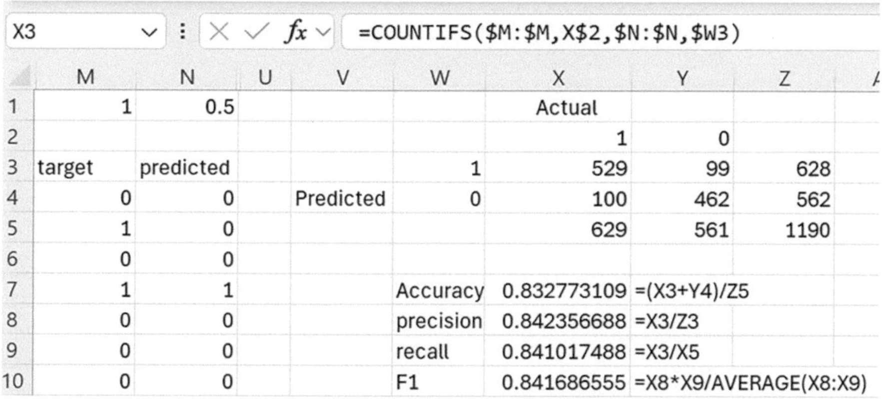

X3 =COUNTIFS($M:$M,X$2,$N:$N,$W3)

	M	N	U	V	W	X	Y	Z
1	1	0.5				Actual		
2						1	0	
3	target	predicted			1	529	99	628
4	0	0		Predicted	0	100	462	562
5	1	0				629	561	1190
6	0	0						
7	1	1			Accuracy	0.832773109	=(X3+Y4)/Z5	
8	0	0			precision	0.842356688	=X3/Z3	
9	0	0			recall	0.841017488	=X3/X5	
10	0	0			F1	0.841686555	=X8*X9/AVERAGE(X8:X9)	

Fig. 11.45 Generating a confusion matrix

The formula in cell X3 is = `COUNTIFS($M:$M,X$2,$N:$N,$W3)`. We must use appropriate dollar signs before we copy the formula to the rest of the confusion matrix. Our logistic regression is 83% accurate.

11.23 Our Hidden Functions

We can use the function.searchHiddenFuntions(), abbreviated as.sf () for the hidden functions related to this chapter.

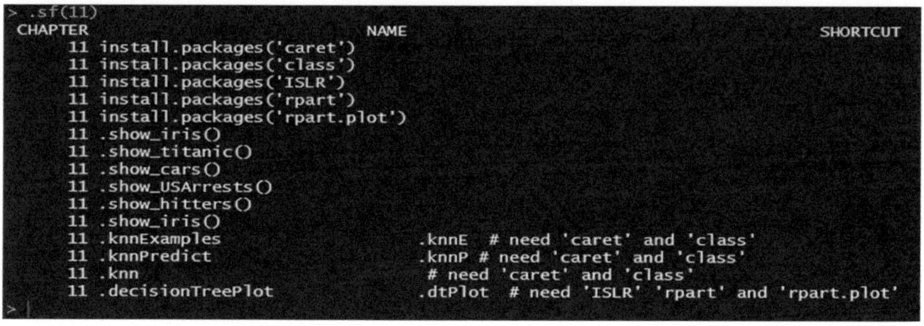

```
> .sf(11)
CHAPTER                    NAME                                    SHORTCUT
     11 install.packages('caret')
     11 install.packages('class')
     11 install.packages('ISLR')
     11 install.packages('rpart')
     11 install.packages('rpart.plot')
     11 .show_iris()
     11 .show_titanic()
     11 .show_cars()
     11 .show_USArrests()
     11 .show_hitters()
     11 .show_iris()
     11 .knnExamples          .knnE  # need 'caret' and 'class'
     11 .knnPredict           .knnP # need 'caret' and 'class'
     11 .knn                   # need 'caret' and 'class'
     11 .decisionTreePlot     .dtPlot  # need 'ISLR' 'rpart' and 'rpart.plot'
>
```

Fig. 11.46 Hidden functions related to Chapter 11

Appendix A: After Launching R, Issue One of the Following Lines of R Code

```
source("http://datayyy.com/i2ft/week11.txt")
```

```
*---------------------------------------------------------------------*
* Introduction to FinTech using Excel               by Dr. Yan 2025    *
*       (in an R-assisted learning environment)                        *
*---------------------------------------------------------------------*
*   .c1   Introduction and Excel Basics            .c16  Term projects  *
*   .c2   Blockchain 1: (Numbers & alphanumeric)   .c17 R basics(optional) *
*   .c3              2: (ASCII and Sha256)         .c18 Macro   (optional) *
*   .c4   Ledger and distributed ledger            .c19 VBA     (optional) *
*   .c5   Cryptography   1: and public/private keys                    *
*   .c6                  2: Advanced                                   *
*   .c7   Cryptocurrency and Ganache                                   *
*   .c8                  2: markets, risk, risk/return tradeoff        *
*   .c9   Blockchain's Applications with Simulations                   *
*---------------------------------------------------------------------*
* .c10  Machine Learning  in Fin 1: Unsupervised Learning              *
* .c11                             2: Supervised Learning: classifications *
* --------------------------------------------------------------------*
* >.c11       # go to chapter 11                                       *
* >.uu        # go to utility submenu                                  *
* >.ft        # back to this menu                                      *
*---------------------------------------------------------------------*
```

Fig. 11.47 The menu for Week 11

Appendix B: For Chapter 11, Just Type `.chapter11`, Shown Below

```
> .chapter11
function(i=0){
"i  C11: Supervised learning: Classifications
 -  ----------------------------            --  ---------------------
 1  Supervised vs unsupervised              21  Links of some useful data sets
 2  Main categories                         22  Confusion matrix: Accuracy
 3  Classifications vs clustering           23                  : Precision
 4  data preparation                        24                  : recall
 5  What is Knn?                            25                  : F1
 6  k-means/knn: difference Purpose         26  data: overdraw
 7    #2: Training/testing samples          27  Our hidden .knnExamples() function
 8    #3: How do they word                  28     : .knn()
 9    #4: Output                            29     : .knnPredict()
10    #5: Training process                  30  Decision tree
11    #6: Efficiency                        31     : hitters data set
12    #7: Applications                      32     : using Excel
13  iris data set                           33     : graph
14       .show_iris() function              34     : .hittersDecisionTreePlot()
15  Excel classification Iris data          35 Logistic regression
16  confusion matrix                        36     :   formulae
17      example 1                           37     : heart disease data set
18      example 2                           38     : Titanic data set
19  Videos                                  39 categorical to numerical    :
20  Links                                   40 House price prediction

 Example #1>.c11      # find out the list
 Example #2>.c11()    # the same as the above
 Example #3>.c11(1)  # see the first explanation
```

Fig. 11.48 The contents of Chapter 11

Exercises

11.1 State the critical difference between classification and regression in supervised learning.
11.2 What are the primary steps involved in a classification task using Excel?
11.3 Explain how K-Nearest Neighbors (KNN) works for classification tasks.
11.4 What is the role of the decision boundary in classification models?
11.5 What are training and testing data, and why are they essential in supervised learning?
11.6 What is the significance of the confusion matrix in evaluating a classification model?
11.7 Use a Pivot Table in Excel to categorize data from the Iris dataset into classes. What are the most common classes?
11.8 Classify the following Iris dataset manually using a Pivot Table in Excel. What are the results for each class? Example data: Sepal.Length = 5.1, Sepal.Width = 3.5, Petal.Length = 1.4, Petal.Width = 0.2.
11.9 Using Excel's COUNTIF() function, classify data into two categories based on a numeric threshold.
11.10 Construct a Pivot Table to classify loan applicants based on their income level and approval status.
11.11 For a given dataset, use the IF() function to create a rule that classifies records based on a criterion (e.g., age > 30).
11.12 How would you use Excel's VLOOKUP() function to help classify data based on predefined classes?
11.13 Use COUNTIF() to calculate the accuracy of a classification model in Excel. Provide an example.
11.14 Use the AVERAGEIF() function to calculate the mean of a dataset for one specific class. How does this help in understanding the class characteristics?
11.15 Using Excel, simulate a small classification dataset (10 rows). Classify it using a combination of IF() and VLOOKUP() functions.
11.16 Given a confusion matrix for a classification task in Excel, calculate the following: Accuracy, Precision, Recall, and F1 Score.
11.17 Interpret the following confusion matrix generated in Excel and explain how you would improve the classification model:
   - Actual Positive: 50, Predicted Positive: 45
   - Actual Negative: 50, Predicted Negative: 40
11.18 Calculate the Precision and Recall of a classification model using Excel formulas based on provided classification results.
11.19 Manually implement the K-Nearest Neighbors (KNN) algorithm in Excel for a simple classification task using a small dataset (e.g., ten samples). Explain your steps.
11.20 What Excel formulas/functions can be used to measure the distance between two data points for a KNN algorithm?

11.21 Using Euclidean distance as a metric, classify new data points in a given dataset in Excel. How would you assign the class?

11.22 A company has three types of products (A, B, and C). Use Excel to classify the product based on sales and customer feedback data. Outline the steps.

11.23 How would you handle missing values in a classification dataset using Excel?

11.24 Given a large dataset, explain how you can efficiently classify and visualize the results using Pivot Tables and charts in Excel.

11.25 What is supervised learning?

11.26 What does 'labeled data' mean?

11.27 What are the differences between supervised and unsupervised learning?

11.28 How do we use Excel to generate 400 random values with four centroids?

11.29 How do we use the hidden function to generate 400 random values for four centroids?

11.30* To get the Hitters data set, use `.show_hitters(0)`. Calculate the decision tree using the Years variable instead of the HmRun (the number of Home Runs) discussed in this chapter.

11.31* To get the Hitters data set, use `.show_hitters(0)`. Calculate the decision tree using the HmRun (the number of Home Runs) discussed in this chapter. Then, find the optimal cut-off point using the Excel solver () function.

11.32 Given the logistic regression model $P(y = 1|X) = \frac{1}{1+e^{-(2+0.5x_1-0.7x_2)}}$, answer the following questions:

(1) Calculate the predicted probability $P(y = 1|x_1 = 2, x_2 = 3)$.

(2) If the predicted probability is more significant than 0.5, which class does the model predict?

11.33 In a logistic regression model for predicting where a loan application will be approved (y=1) for approval, y=0 for rejection), the fitted model is:

$$\log\left(\frac{P(y = 1)}{P(y = 0}\right) = -1.5 + 0.8x_1 - 0.3x_2$$

where x_1 represents the applicant's credit score, and x_2 represents the amount of existing debt.

11.34 You are given a dataset where logistic regression is used to classify whether a customer will churn (1) or stay (0). The dataset has 1000 observations, and after fitting a logistic regression model, you obtain the confusion matrix below:

	Actual: Churn(1)	Actual: No churn(0)
Predicted: Churn(1)	450	50
Predicted: No churn(0)	100	400

(1) Calculate the model's accuracy, precision, recall, and F1 score.

(2) Based on these metrics, evaluate the performance of the model.

11.35 Consider a logistic regression model predicting whether an email is spam (1) or not spam (0). For a specific test set, the following probabilities are predicted:

Email 1: P(spam) =0.9 and actual y=1
Email 2: P(spam) =0.2 and actual y=0
Email 3: P(spam) =0.6 and actual y=1

Using the log-loss function, calculate the overall log-loss for this test set.

11.36 Why is feature scaling important in logistic regression when using certain optimization techniques like gradient descent? How would the model be affected if features are on vastly different scales?

References

Banoula, M. (2023). *K-means clustering algorithm: Applications, types, & how does it work?* https://www.simplilearn.com/tutorials/machine-learning-tutorial/k-means-clustering-algorithm

Bobbitt, Z. (2022). *How to plot a decision tree in R (with example).* https://www.statology.org/plot-decision-tree-in-r/

Hitter data set. https://rdrr.io/cran/ISLR/man/Hitters.html

IBM, What is the k-nearest neighbors (KNN) algorithm?. https://www.ibm.com/topics/knn

Kurama, V., & Powers, J. (2022). *Unsupervised learning with Python: A beginner's guide.* https://builtin.com/data-science/unsupervised-learning-python

Machine Learning (in Finance). https://corporatefinanceinstitute.com/resources/data-science/machine-learning-in-finance/

Parag's Web, Hitters data set. https://pmagunia.com/dataset/r-dataset-package-islr-hitters#:~:text=The%20Hitters%20data%20set%20is%20found%20in%20the,load%20the%20data%20into%20a%20variable%20called%20Hitters.

UCI Machine Learning Repository. https://archive.ics.uci.edu/

UCI Iris data set. https://archive.ics.uci.edu/dataset/53/iris

Supervised Learning (II): Regressions 12

This is the second part of "Supervised Learning: Regressions". There is a good chance that most readers and students have learned this part already. It might be a good idea for those readers to go through this chapter quickly or skip it to save time. We start with the simple ones: linear regressions, such as one-factor linear regressions, multi-variable regressions, collinearity, dummy variables for categorical variables, and linear models for non-linear variables. In addition, we will use several examples for Logistic Regressions. In this chapter, the following topics will be covered.

- What is linear regression?
- CAPM (Capital Asset Pricing Model): one-factor linear model
- Multivariate linear regression: Fama–French 3-factor model
- Collinearity and how to solve it
- Generate correlated random numbers
- Dummy variables for categorical variables
- Linear regressions for non-linear variables
- Logistic regression: review
- Our hidden functions

Supplementary Information The online version contains supplementary material available at https://doi.org/10.1007/978-3-031-89779-5_12.

Y. Yan, *Introduction to FinTech using Excel*, Springer Texts in Business and Economics, https://doi.org/10.1007/978-3-031-89779-5_12

12.1 Introduction

In this chapter, readers will delve deeper into regression analysis, one of the foundational techniques in supervised learning. It starts with a comprehensive look at the linear model: a straightforward yet powerful approach to understanding relationships between predictors and an outcome. Following this, logistic regression will be revisited to illustrate how it differs from linear regression and is uniquely suited for binary classification problems, such as predicting the probability of a default on a loan.

The Capital Asset Pricing Model (CAPM) is introduced to bridge machine learning with financial applications, shedding light on how expected returns can be predicted using risk factors. Building on this, the Fama–French 3-Factor Model will be covered, offering a more robust framework by considering size and value factors alongside the market risk factor to explain asset returns better.

12.2 Linear Regression

Linear regression has the following form: Here, we assume that there are n independent variables and one dependent variable.

$$y = \alpha + \beta_1 x_1 + \beta_2 x_2 + + \ldots \beta_n x_n, \tag{12.1}$$

They are called linear because their graphs will be straight lines. This property is more apparent with just one independent variable. Assume that we have just one independent variable.

$$y = \alpha + \beta x \tag{12.2}$$

The α will be the intercept, and the β will be the slope. We will have the following graph if the α is 5 and the β is 2.

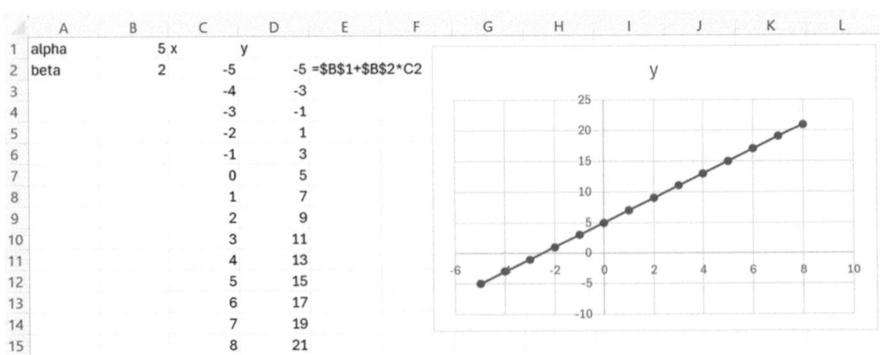

Fig. 12.1 A graphic presentation of a linear regression

Another way to classify a linear regression is that the powers of those independent variables are 1.

12.3 Covariance and Correlation

Assume that we have two sets of variables: x and y. The covariance is defined below:

$$\sigma_{x,\,y} = \frac{\sum_{i=1}^{n}(x_i - \overline{x})(y_i - \overline{y})}{n-1}, \tag{12.3}$$

where $\sigma_{x,\,y}$ is the covariance between x and y, $\overline{x}$ ($\overline{y}$) is the mean of x (y). The following equation gives the correlation between x and y.

$$\rho_{x,\,y} = \frac{\sigma_{x,y}}{\sigma_x \sigma_y}. \tag{12.4}$$

where σ_x (σ_y) is the standard deviation of x (y). The range of correlation between -1 and 1. In terms of co-movement, the correlation is a better measure than covariance. For example, if the covariance is positive, we only know that two stocks are moving in the same direction. If the correlation between stocks A and B is 0.9, and the correlation between A and C is 0.8, we can claim that stock A is more strongly correlated with B than C. However, we could not compare the covariances between A, B, and C.

12.4 Correlation: Air Quality Data Set

There are two ways to get the data. The first is at http://datayyy.com/i2ft/data/air quality.csv. Alternatively, we can use the `.show_airquality()` function.

```
> .show_airquality(0)
Windows users: launch Excel and paste
```

The top part is shown below.

	A	B	C	D	E	F
1	Ozone	Solar.R	Wind	Temp	Month	Day
2	41	190	7.4	67	5	1
3	36	118	8	72	5	2
4	12	149	12.6	74	5	3
5	18	313	11.5	62	5	4
6	NA	NA	14.3	56	5	5
7	28	NA	14.9	66	5	6
8	23	299	8.6	65	5	7

Fig. 12.2 The first several lines of the airQuality data set

As the first step, we have to clean the data since many NAs exist in the raw data set, as shown above. The number of observations in the raw data is 153, and there are 111 for clean data. The result of the correlations between several independent variables and Ozone is shown below.

G5 f_x =CORREL($A:$A,B:B)

	A	B	C	D	E	F	G	H	I	J	K
1	Ozone	Solar.R	Wind	Temp	Month	Day	111	=COUNT(A:A)			
2	41	190	7.4	67	5	1					
3	36	118	8	72	5	2	corr(Ozone and other)				
4	12	149	12.6	74	5	3	Solar.R	Wind	Temp	Month	Day
5	18	313	11.5	62	5	4	0.348342	-0.6125	0.698541	0.142885	-0.00519
6	23	299	8.6	65	5	7					

Fig. 12.3 Calculating correlation between Ozone and other variables

The result shows that `both Solar. R and Temp` (temperature) positively correlate with the Ozone level. In addition, temperature is more strongly correlated with the Ozone level. The correlation between Ozone level and Wind Speed is negative. The last two correlations (Monthly and Day with the Ozone level) are meaningless. For this, we have designed one of the end-chapter problems.

12.5 Correlations: Stocks and S&P500

The S&P500 is a market index: the market cap is weighted based on the 500 most extensive stocks in the USA. It is common sense that most stocks would follow when the market goes up. In a sense, most stock returns will positively correlate with the market index. Let's download a few stocks to see their correlations with the S&P500. For the data issues, interested readers can download them at https://finance.yahoo.com.

	A	B	C	D	E	F	G	H	I	J	K	L
1	Date	IBM_Adj.Close		Date	SP500Adj.Close		Date	WMT_Adj.Close		DATE	AAPL_ADJ.CLOSE	
2	2/1/1962	1.420722		1/1/1985	179.63		9/1/1972	0.010295		1/1/1985	0.101327	
3	3/1/1962	1.40967		2/1/1985	181.18		10/1/1972	0.0114		2/1/1985	0.086477	
4	4/1/1962	1.201296		3/1/1985	180.66		11/1/1972	0.0114		3/1/1985	0.077305	
5	5/1/1962	1.038566		4/1/1985	179.83		12/1/1972	0.012195		4/1/1985	0.074248	
6	6/1/1962	0.897806		5/1/1985	189.55		1/1/1973	0.010472		5/1/1985	0.060709	

Fig. 12.4 The annual data for several stocks and S&P500

In the first step, we merge those data sets by date. For the second step, we calculate returns for those stocks and the S&P500 index, as shown below.

F3 fx =B3/B2-1

	A	B	C	D	E	F	G	H	I
1	DATE	IBM_ADJ.CLOS	SP500ADJ.C	WMT_ADJ.	AAPL_ADJ.CLOS	IBM_ret	sp500ret	wmt_ret	aapl_ret
2	1/1/1985	11.5026722	179.63	0.282114	0.101327				
3	1/1/1986	13.21679497	211.78	0.400522	0.0808	0.14902	0.178979	0.41972	-0.20258
4	1/1/1987	11.59296799	274.07999	0.606925	0.193919	-0.12286	0.294173	0.515332	1.399988
5	1/1/1988	10.43545246	257.07001	0.687965	0.291457	-0.09985	-0.06206	0.133526	0.502983
6	1/1/1989	12.59659672	297.47	0.852735	0.267374	0.207096	0.157156	0.239503	-0.08263
7	1/1/1990	9.921445847	329.07999	1.082949	0.243178	-0.21237	0.106263	0.269972	-0.09049

Fig. 12.5 Return calculations for both individual stocks and S&P500

The correlation calculations are shown below.

(4 fx =CORREL($F:$F,F:F)

F	G	H	I	J	K	L	M	N	O	P
IBM_ret	sp500ret	wmt_ret	aapl_ret							
0.14902	0.178979	0.41972	-0.20258		IBM	sp500	WMT	AAPL		
-0.12286	0.294173	0.515332	1.399988	IBM	1	0.64304	0.4915	0.331212	=CORREL($F:$F,I:I)	
-0.09985	-0.06206	0.133526	0.502983	SP500	0.64304	1	0.658219	0.464141	=CORREL(I:I,$G:$G)	
0.207096	0.157156	0.239503	-0.08263	WMT	0.4915	0.658219	1	0.384827	=CORREL(I:I,$H:$H)	
-0.21237	0.106263	0.269972	-0.09049	AAPL	0.331212	0.464141	0.384827	1	=CORREL(I:I,$I:$I)	
0.345663	0.045126	0.5563	0.652629							

Fig. 12.6 The correlation matrix by using the Excel CORREL function

The above result shows that Walmart strongly correlates with the S&P500 index compared with IBM and Apple. The same is true for Apple stock.

12.6 CAPM (Capital Asset Pricing Model)

The CAPM (Capital Asset Pricing Model) theory was developed in the 1960s. It is quite popular among academics and practitioners due to its simplicity and usefulness. CAPM can be viewed as a one-factor model. Multiple factor models will be discussed in the next chapter. Within this model, beta (β) reflects the market risk of an underlying security, while its volatility (standard deviation of returns) reflects the total risk. CAPM can be used to estimate the cost of equity, the price a firm must pay if it issues equity as its source of capital. The basic logic behind CAPM is that individual stock returns (R_i) are linearly correlated with a single risk factor, i.e., a stock market index. The basic CAPM formula has the following form:

$$R_{i,t} - R_{f,t} = \alpha + \beta\left(R_{m,t} - R_{f,t}\right) + \varepsilon_t, \tag{12.5}$$

where $R_{i,t}$ is the return on stock i at time t, $R_{f,t}$ is the risk-free rate at time t, and $R_{m,t}$ is the market return (such as the S&P500) at time t. Usually, we run the above linear regression to estimate the beta. Alternatively, we have the following formula to calculate beta:

$$\beta_i = \frac{cov(R_i, R_m)}{var(R_m)} = \frac{\rho_{(R_i,R_m)*\sigma_i}}{\sigma_m}, \tag{12.6}$$

here $cov(R_i, R_m)$ is the covariance between an individual stock's returns and the market returns, $\rho(R_i, R_m)$ is the corresponding correlation, σ_i is the standard deviation of the stock's returns and σ_m is the standard deviation of market returns. It is important to note that the correlation and market risk's beta are positively correlated in the above equation. Following the above example, we could estimate β by applying the above equation.

12.7 Getting Stocks' Data

We need data on individual stocks and market indexes to calculate market risk, which is defined as the beta or the slope of a linear regression. For example, we need its historical data to calculate IBM's market risk. The first way is to download IBM's historical monthly data at Yahoo!Finance. Go to https://finance.yahoo.com, enter 'IBM', click 'Historical Data' on the left, choose the appropriate period, monthly, and then download.

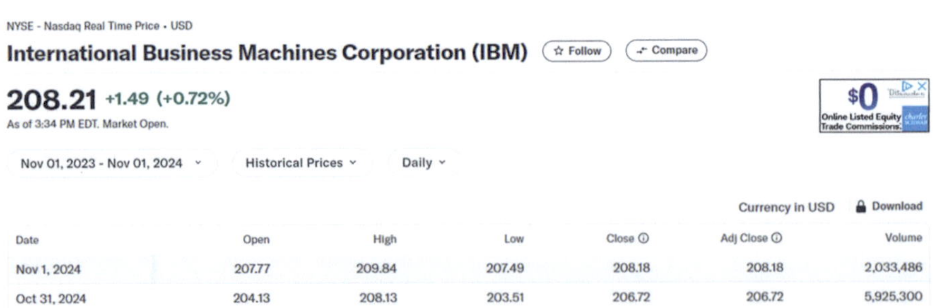

Fig. 12.7 The IBM's data from Yahoo!Finance

The second way is to use our `.show_ibmMonthly()` function.

```
> .show_ibmMonthly(0)
Windows users: launch Excel and paste
```

The first several lines are shown below.

	A	B	C	D	E	F	G
1	Date	Open	High	Low	Close	Adj.Close	Volume
2	2/1/1962	6.978967	7.151052	6.781389	6.845124	1.420722	6087720
3	3/1/1962	6.870618	7.087317	6.759082	6.79095	1.40967	5687625
4	4/1/1962	6.787763	6.787763	5.736138	5.787126	1.201296	13516935
5	5/1/1962	5.787126	6.24283	4.525175	5.003187	1.038566	51659325

Fig. 12.8 The first several lines of IBM monthly data

For a market index, we can use S&P500. When downloading the S&P500 data from Yahoo!Finance, its ticker is `^GSPC`. Alternatively, our `.show_sp500monthly()` function can be used.

```
> .show_sp500monthly(0)
Windows users: launch Excel and paste
```

The first several lines are shown below.

J	K	L	M	N	O	P
Date	Open	High	Low	Close	Adj.Close	Volume
1/1/1985	167.2	180.27	163.36	179.63	179.63	2.67E+09
2/1/1985	179.63	183.95	177.75	181.18	181.18	2.19E+09
3/1/1985	181.18	183.89	176.53	180.66	180.66	2.15E+09
4/1/1985	180.66	183.61	177.86	179.83	179.83	1.98E+09

Fig. 12.9 The several lines of S&P500 monthly data

The following section will use those two data sets to calculate IBM's beta.

12.8 Two Ways to Calculate IBM's Beta

Assume that we plan to use 5-year data from 2019 to 2023. We matched the two data sets in the previous section and calculated their returns.

E3 =B3/B2-1

	A	B	C	D	E	F	G
1	Date	Adj.Close	Date	Adj.Close	ibm_ret	sp500_ret	
2	12/1/2018	82.82565	12/1/2018	2506.85			
3	1/1/2019	97.94512	1/1/2019	2704.1	0.182546	0.078684	=D3/D2-1
4	2/1/2019	100.6484	2/1/2019	2784.49	0.0276	0.029729	
5	3/1/2019	104.0104	3/1/2019	2834.4	0.033403	0.017924	
60	10/1/2023	139.1161	10/1/2023	4193.8	0.030934	-0.02198	
61	11/1/2023	152.5045	11/1/2023	4567.8	0.096239	0.089179	
62	12/1/2023	159.0879	12/1/2023	4769.83	0.043169	0.044229	

Fig. 12.10 The merged IBM and SP500 data set

The first approach assumes any set of `beta0` and `beta1`, such as 0.5 and 1. Based on the CAPM, we calculate the expected returns for IBM. Then, we calculate squared error terms, i.e., $(y_i - \hat{y}_i)^2$, where y_i is the true value and $\hat{y}_i$ is the estimated value for its value. We aim to minimize the summation of those squared errors by changing `beta0` and `beta1`. The annual risk-free rate is 0.1. The starting `beta0` and `beta1` are arbitrarily set as 0.2 and 1. We name cell L1 as beta0, L2 as beta1, and L3 as `rf_monthly`.

K	L	M
beta0	0.5	
beta1	1	
annual Rf	0.01	
monthly Rf	0.000833	=L3/12

Fig. 12.11 Assigning random values for beta0 and beta1

Based on the CAPM formula, we calculate `y_hat`, shown below.

G3 =beta0+beta1*(F3-rf_monthly)

	A	B	C	D	E	F	G	H	I
1	Date	Adj.Close	Date	Adj.Close	ibm_ret	sp500_ret			
2	12/1/2018	82.82565	12/1/2018	2506.85			y_hat	(y-y_hat)^2	
3	1/1/2019	97.94512	1/1/2019	2704.1	0.182546	0.078684	0.5779	0.1563	=(E3-G3)^2
4	2/1/2019	100.6484	2/1/2019	2784.49	0.0276	0.029729	0.5289	0.2513	
5	3/1/2019	104.0104	3/1/2019	2834.4	0.033403	0.017924	0.5171	0.2340	
60	10/1/2023	139.1161	10/1/2023	4193.8	0.030934	-0.02198	0.4772	0.1991	
61	11/1/2023	152.5045	11/1/2023	4567.8	0.096239	0.089179	0.5883	0.2422	
62	12/1/2023	159.0879	12/1/2023	4769.83	0.043169	0.044229	0.5434	0.2502	
63							sum->	15.0919	=SUM(H3:H62)

Fig. 12.12 Calculating predicted value and squared error terms

As the last step, we use the Excel `solver ()` function to minimize the summation of those squared error terms (in cell H63) by changing beta0 and beta1 (L1:L2).

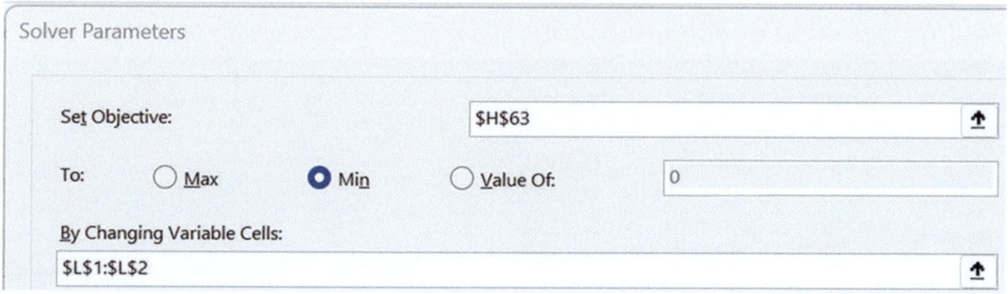

Fig. 12.13 Settings for the Excel SOLVER functionality

After clicking on 'Solve', we will get the following `beta0` and `beta1`.

H63 =SUM(H3:H62)

	A	B	C	D	E	F	G	H	I	J	K	L	M
1	Date	Adj.Close	Date	Adj.Close	ibm_ret	sp500_ret					beta0	0.004867	
2	12/1/2018	82.82565	12/1/2018	2506.85			y_hat	(y-y_hat)^2			beta1	0.745121	
3	1/1/2019	97.94512	1/1/2019	2704.1	0.182546	0.078684	0.0629	0.0143	=(E3-G3)^2	=beta0+beta1*(F3-rf_monthly)	annual Rf	0.01	
4	2/1/2019	100.6484	2/1/2019	2784.49	0.0276	0.029729	0.0264	0.0000			monthly Rf	0.000833	=L3/12
5	3/1/2019	104.0104	3/1/2019	2834.4	0.033403	0.017924	0.0176	0.0002					
60	10/1/2023	139.1161	10/1/2023	4193.8	0.030934	-0.02198	-0.0121	0.0019					
61	11/1/2023	152.5045	11/1/2023	4567.8	0.096239	0.089179	0.0707	0.0007					
62	12/1/2023	159.0879	12/1/2023	4769.83	0.043169	0.044229	0.0372	0.0000					
63							sum->	0.1990	=SUM(H3:H62)				

Fig. 12.14 The result of running Excel SOLVER

IBM's market risk is 0.75, which is less risky than the average stock (the average is 1). Although this method offers a good understanding of the underlying logic, we seldom use it since other methods provide more information, such as the T-value and P-values of our intercept and slope. The second method uses the Excel `LINEST(y's,x's)`, as shown below.

E3 =LINEST(A3:A62,C3:C62)

	A	B	C	D	E	F
1		sp500_ret				
2	ibm_ret		sp500-rf			
3	0.182546	0.078684	0.077851		0.745121	0.004867
4	0.0276	0.029729	0.028896			
5	0.033403	0.017924	0.017091			
58	0.01838	-0.01772	-0.01855			
59	-0.03348	-0.04872	-0.04955			
60	0.030934	-0.02198	-0.02281			
61	0.096239	0.089179	0.088346			
62	0.043169	0.044229	0.043396			

Fig. 12.15 Method 2: Using the Excel LINEST function

The above output shows `alpha` (intercept) and `beta` (the slope). This method can quickly obtain values. However, Method 3, discussed in the next section, is much better.

12.9 3rd Way to Calculate IBM's Beta

The third way is to run a linear regression. The following image shows our starting data. In addition, both returns for IBM and the market are calculated accordingly.

G3 =F3-$I$2

	A	B	C	D	E	F	G	H	I
1	Date	Adj.Close	Date	Adj.Close		sp500_ret			0.01
2	12/1/2018	82.82565	12/1/2018	2506.85	ibm_ret		sp500-rf		0.000833
3	1/1/2019	97.94512	1/1/2019	2704.1	0.182546	0.078684	0.077851	=F3-$I$2	
4	2/1/2019	100.6484	2/1/2019	2784.49	0.0276	0.029729	0.028896		
5	3/1/2019	104.0104	3/1/2019	2834.4	0.033403	0.017924	0.017091		
6	4/1/2019	103.3986	4/1/2019	2945.83	-0.00588	0.039313	0.03848		
7	5/1/2019	93.60938	5/1/2019	2752.06	-0.09467	-0.06578	-0.06661		

Fig. 12.16 The starting data set

Click "Data" on the menu bar, "Data Analysis," and "Regression," then enter the following information.

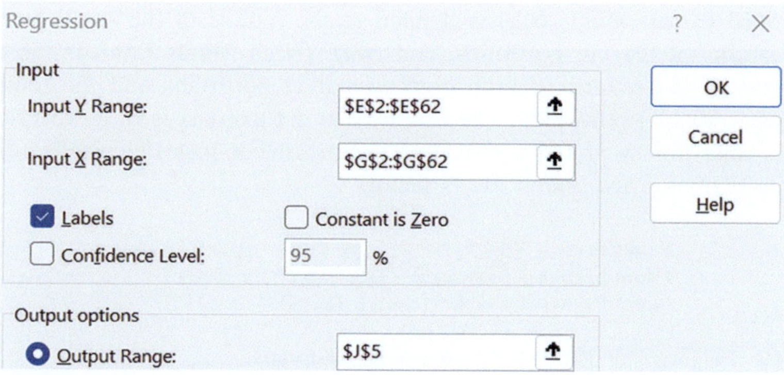

Fig. 12.17 Settings for Excel REGRESSION functionality

The result is shown below.

SUMMARY OUTPUT

Regression Statistics	
Multiple R	0.565473
R Square	0.31976
Adjusted R	0.308032
Standard E	0.058579
Observatic	60

ANOVA

	df	*SS*	*MS*	*F*	*gnificance F*
Regressior	1	0.093557	0.093557	27.26405	2.51E-06
Residual	58	0.199029	0.003432		
Total	59	0.292586			

	Coefficients	*tandard Errc*	*t Stat*	*P-value*	*Lower 95%*	*Upper 95%*	*ower 95.0%*	*pper 95.0%*
Intercept	0.004867	0.007734	0.629271	0.531643	-0.01061	0.020349	-0.01061	0.020349
sp500-rf	0.745121	0.142702	5.221499	2.51E-06	0.459471	1.030771	0.459471	1.030771

Fig. 12.18 The result after running the regression

The above image will provide more information. For example, the slope `(beta)` is statistically different from zero, but this is not true for the intercept. The R2 is 32%, and the adjusted R2 is 31%. For multivariable linear regression, the adjusted R2 will be used to compare the performance of linear regression with different numbers of independent variables.

12.10 Fama–French 3-Factor Data

The famous Fama–French 3-factor model is formulated and given below.

$$R_i = R_f + \beta_{mkt}\left(R_m - R_f\right) + \beta_{SMB} * SMB + \beta_{HML} * HML. \tag{12.7}$$

where *SMB* (Small Minus Big) is defined as the returns of the small portfolios minus returns of the big portfolios, and *HML* (High Minus Low) is the difference between the returns of high book-to-market portfolios and the returns of low book-to-market portfolios. The first way to get the data is to go to Professor French's data library at https://mba.tuck.dartmouth.edu/pages/faculty/ken.french/data_library.html. Then search for "3 factors".

Fama/French 3 Factors TXT CSV Details Historical Archives
Fama/French 3 Factors [Weekly] TXT CSV Details
Fama/French 3 Factors [Daily] TXT CSV Details

Fig. 12.19 The image for downloading Fama–French 3 factors

The first several lines of the monthly data are shown below.

```
File    Edit    View

This file was created by CMPT_ME_BEME_RETS using the 202409 CRSP database.
The 1-month TBill rate data until 202405 are from Ibbotson Associates. Starting from 202406,
Month Treasury Bill Index.

,Mkt-RF,SMB,HML,RF
192607,    2.96,   -2.56,   -2.43,    0.22
192608,    2.64,   -1.17,    3.82,    0.25
192609,    0.36,   -1.40,    0.13,    0.23
192610.   -3.24.   -0.09.    0.70.    0.32
```

Fig. 12.20 The raw Fama–French 3-factor monthly data

The second way to get the data is using our hidden function, `.show_ff3monthly()`.

```
> .show_ff3monthly()
        DATE MKT_RF     SMB     HML     RF
1 1926-07-01 0.0296 -0.0256 -0.0243 0.0022
2 1926-08-01 0.0264 -0.0117  0.0382 0.0025
> .show_ff3monthly(0)
 Windows users: launch Excel and paste
```

Fig. 12.21 An easy way to get the Fama–French 3-factor monthly data

The first several lines are shown below.

	A	B	C	D	E
1	DATE	MKT_RF	SMB	HML	RF
2	7/1/1926	0.0296	-0.0256	-0.0243	0.0022
3	8/1/1926	0.0264	-0.0117	0.0382	0.0025
4	9/1/1926	0.0036	-0.014	0.0013	0.0023
5	10/1/1926	-0.0324	-9.00E-04	0.007	0.0032

Fig. 12.22 The first several lines of Fama–French 3-factor monthly data

If you download the data from Professor French's data library, all the values should be divided by 100. On the other hand, if you use the data from the above-hidden functions, you don't need to divide them by 100.

12.11 The Fama–French 3-Factor Model

Let's run a Fama-Frech 3-factor model using IBM's monthly data. Then, we compare its performance with CAPM (a single-factor model). Again, there are two ways to get the data. For the first method, interested readers can go to https://finance.yahoo.com to download IBM's monthly data and Professor French's data library to download their monthly data. Alternatively, readers can use our functions `.show_ibmMonthly()` and `.show_ff3monthly()`, as shown below.

C3 fx =B3/B2-1

	A	B	C	D	E	F	G	H
1	Date	IBM_Adj.Cl	ret	DATE	MKT_RF	SMB	HML	RF
2	2/1/1962	1.420722		7/1/1926	0.0296	-0.0256	-0.0243	0.0022
3	3/1/1962	1.40967	-0.0077794	8/1/1926	0.0264	-0.0117	0.0382	0.0025
4	4/1/1962	1.201296	-0.1478177	9/1/1926	0.0036	-0.014	0.0013	0.0023
5	5/1/1962	1.038566	-0.1354619	10/1/1926	-0.0324	-9.00E-04	0.007	0.0032

Fig. 12.23 IBM return calculation plus the Fama-French 3-factor time series

In the first step, we calculate IBM's monthly returns. Then, we merge those two data sets. The first several lines are shown below.

	A	B	C	D	E	F	G
1	DATE	IBM_ADJ.CLOS	RET	MKT_RF	SMB	HML	RF
2	1/1/1963	1.121887326	0.086539	0.0493	0.0308	0.0221	0.0025
3	1/1/1964	1.436306715	0.069033	0.0224	-0.0011	0.0148	0.003
4	1/1/1965	1.487232566	0.095237	0.0354	0.027	0.0012	0.0028
5	1/1/1966	1.646789193	-0.00601	0.0072	0.0384	0.0356	0.0038

Fig. 12.24 Merging stock returns and Fama–French 3-factors

Assume we use the last 5 years' data from 2019 to 2023, shown below.

	A	B	C	D	E	F	G	H
1	DATE	IBM_ADJ.CLOS	RET	MKT_RF	SMB	HML	RF	ret-rf
2	1/1/2019	97.94512177	0.182546	0.084	0.0288	-0.0045	0.0021	0.180446
3	2/1/2019	100.6484146	0.0276	0.034	0.0206	-0.0271	0.0018	0.0258
56	7/1/2023	137.0959778	0.077498	0.0321	0.0205	0.0411	0.0045	0.072998
57	8/1/2023	139.615799	0.01838	-0.0239	-0.032	-0.0108	0.0045	0.01388
58	9/1/2023	134.941864	-0.03348	-0.0524	-0.0249	0.0145	0.0043	-0.03778
59	10/1/2023	139.1161194	0.030934	-0.0318	-0.0388	0.0019	0.0047	0.026234
60	11/1/2023	152.5045013	0.096239	0.0883	-3.00E-04	0.0166	0.0044	0.091839
61	12/1/2023	159.0879364	0.043169	0.0487	0.0636	0.0492	0.0043	0.038869
62								

Fig. 12.25 Getting just five-year data

The top part of the regression is shown below.

SUMMARY OUTPUT

Regression Statistics	
Multiple R	0.631434
R Square	0.398708
Adjusted R	0.366496
Standard E	0.05598
Observatic	60

ANOVA

	df	*SS*	*MS*	*F*	*gnificance F*
Regressior	3	0.116364	0.038788	12.37762	2.55E-06
Residual	56	0.175489	0.003134		
Total	59	0.291853			

Fig. 12.26 The top 2 parts of running the Fama–French 3-factor model

The adjusted R2 is 36.6%. Using the same data set for a one-factor model will give us an adjusted R^2 of 28%. Thus, the Fama–French 3-factor model is better than CAPM. The last part is shown below.

	Coefficients	*tandard Erro*	*t Stat*	*P-value*	*Lower 95%*	*Upper 95%*	*ower 95.0%*	*pper 95.0%*
Intercept	0.002918	0.007424	0.393042	0.695781	-0.01195	0.017791	-0.01195	0.017791
MKT_RF	0.742726	0.139103	5.339378	1.75E-06	0.464068	1.021383	0.464068	1.021383
SMB	-0.44413	0.265185	-1.67478	0.099554	-0.97536	0.087103	-0.97536	0.087103
HML	0.41649	0.155043	2.686285	0.009492	0.105901	0.72708	0.105901	0.72708

Fig. 12.27 The bottom part of running the Fama–French 3-factor model

From the output, we know that MKT_RF and HML are statistically significant at the 1% significance level, and the SMB (Small Minus Big) is statistically significant at the 10% significance level.

12.12 Air Quality Regression

The `airquality` data can be used for linear regression.

```
> .show_airquality(0)
Windows users: launch Excel and paste
```

The top part is shown below.

	A	B	C	D	E	F
1	Ozone	Solar.R	Wind	Temp	Month	Day
2	41	190	7.4	67	5	1
3	36	118	8	72	5	2
4	12	149	12.6	74	5	3
5	18	313	11.5	62	5	4
6	NA	NA	14.3	56	5	5
7	28	NA	14.9	66	5	6
8	23	299	8.6	65	5	7

Fig. 12.28 The first several lines of the airQuality data

For the data set, we find many NA and missing code. Thus, we want to remove those observations. The first method has the following steps:

Step 1: Identify which columns contain NAs.
Step 2: Sort the first column with NAs, then remove those observations.
Step 3: Repeat Step 2 for other columns.

This will be one of the end-chapter questions. The second method is to apply our`.drop_na ()` function mentioned at the end of the chapter. The data set has 153 observations. After removing observations containing NAs, it has 111 observations. The first several lines of the clean data set are shown below.

	A	B	C	D	E	F
1	Ozone	Solar.R	Wind	Temp	Month	Day
2	41	190	7.4	67	5	1
3	36	118	8	72	5	2
4	12	149	12.6	74	5	3
5	18	313	11.5	62	5	4
6	23	299	8.6	65	5	7
7	19	99	13.8	59	5	8

Fig. 12.29 The data set after removing NAs

Let's run a linear regression with column A (Ozone level) as y and columns B:D as x (Solar Radiation, Wind Speed, and Temperature). The settings are shown below.

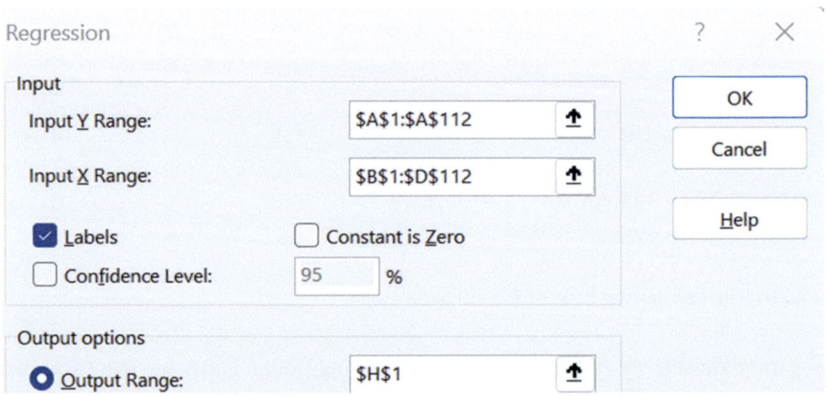

Fig. 12.30 Settings of the linear regression

The result is shown below.

Regression Statistics	
Multiple R	0.778392
R Square	0.605895
Adjusted R	0.594845
Standard E	21.18075
Observatic	111

ANOVA

	df	SS	MS	F	gnificance F
Regressior	3	73799.12	24599.71	54.83366	1.51E-21
Residual	107	48002.79	448.6242		
Total	110	121801.9			

	Coefficients	andard Errc	t Stat	P-value	Lower 95%	Upper 95%	ower 95.0%	pper 95.0%
Intercept	-64.3421	23.05472	-2.79084	0.006227	-110.045	-18.6388	-110.045	-18.6388
Solar.R	0.059821	0.023186	2.579979	0.011237	0.013856	0.105785	0.013856	0.105785
Wind	-3.33359	0.654407	-5.09406	1.52E-06	-4.63088	-2.03631	-4.63088	-2.03631
Temp	1.652093	0.25353	6.516366	2.42E-09	1.1495	2.154686	1.1495	2.154686

Fig. 12.31 The result of running a linear regression

From the output, we know that the quality of the model is very good since the adjusted R^2 is 59%. All three independent variables are statistically different from zero with the following P-values (0.01,0, and 0). Solar Radiation and temperature impacts are positive, i.e., the higher their values, the higher (worse) the Ozone level. Two variables are not considered. There are seven unique values for the month: 5,6,7,8 and 9.

12.13 Adding Categorical Variables

In this section, we convert the column month into several categorical variables. Since there are 5 values (5, 6, 7, 8, and 9), we need just 4 dummy variables: `d_june, d_july, d_aug, and d_sept`, as shown below. The formula in G2 is = `IF($E2 = 6,1,0)`.

G2 =IF($E2=6,1,0)

	A	B	C	D	E	F	G	H	I	J	K
1	Ozone	Solar.R	Wind	Temp	Month	Day	d_june	d_july	d_aug	d_sept	
2	41	190	7.4	67	5	1	0	0	0	0	=IF($E2=9,1,0)
3	36	118	8	72	5	2	0	0	0	0	
25	37	279	7.4	76	5	31	0	0	0	0	
26	29	127	9.7	82	6	7	1	0	0	0	
33	12	120	11.5	73	6	19	1	0	0	0	
34	13	137	10.3	76	6	20	1	0	0	0	
35	135	269	4.1	84	7	1	0	1	0	0	
36	49	248	9.2	85	7	2	0	1	0	0	

Fig. 12.32 Adding and converting categorical variables

The data set used to run a new regression is shown below.

	A	B	C	D	E	F	G
1	SUMMARY OUTPUT						
2							
3	*Regression Statistics*						
4	Multiple R	0.798036					
5	R Square	0.636861					
6	Adjusted R	0.612182					
7	Standard E	20.72262					
8	Observatic	111					
9							
10	ANOVA						
11		*df*	*SS*	*MS*	*F*	*gnificance F*	
12	Regressior	7	77570.93	11081.56	25.80546	4.57E-20	
13	Residual	103	44230.98	429.427			
14	Total	110	121801.9				

Fig. 12.33 The top two parts after running a linear regression

The bottom part of the relation associated with those dummy variables is shown below. From the output, we know that only September is significant at the 5% level.

15									
16		*Coefficients*	*andard Err*	*t Stat*	*P-value*	*Lower 95%*	*Upper 95%*	*ower 95.0%*	*pper 95.0%*
17	Intercept	-74.2348	26.10184	-2.84405	0.005374	-126.002	-22.468	-126.002	-22.468
18	Solar.R	0.05222	0.023667	2.206472	0.029572	0.005283	0.099158	0.005283	0.099158
19	Wind	-3.10872	0.660086	-4.70957	7.78E-06	-4.41785	-1.79959	-4.41785	-1.79959
20	Temp	1.875111	0.340727	5.503266	2.74E-07	1.199359	2.550862	1.199359	2.550862
21	d_june	-14.759	9.122687	-1.61783	0.108758	-32.8516	3.333745	-32.8516	3.333745
22	d_july	-8.74861	7.829061	-1.11745	0.2664	-24.2757	6.778482	-24.2757	6.778482
23	d_aug	-4.19654	8.146928	-0.51511	0.607582	-20.354	11.96098	-20.354	11.96098
24	d_sept	-15.9673	6.655607	-2.39907	0.018234	-29.1671	-2.76746	-29.1671	-2.76746

Fig. 12.34 The bottom part after running a linear regression

12.14 Correlated Random Numbers

Assume we plan to generate a two-time series with a correlation of 0.85. Below is the procedure. Step 1: we generate two time series (A and B) with zero correlations: x_1^A, x_1^A, …, x_n^A and x_1^B, x_1^B, …, x_n^B. Step 2: Apply the following formula.

Assume that we want a correlation coefficient of ρ.

$$\begin{cases} y_i^A = x_i^A \\ y_i^B = \rho x_i^A + x_i^B\sqrt{1-\rho^2} \end{cases} \tag{12.8}$$

Let's look at a simple example. After launching Excel, we choose "Data", "Data Analysis", and Random Number Generation, then select the following parameters.

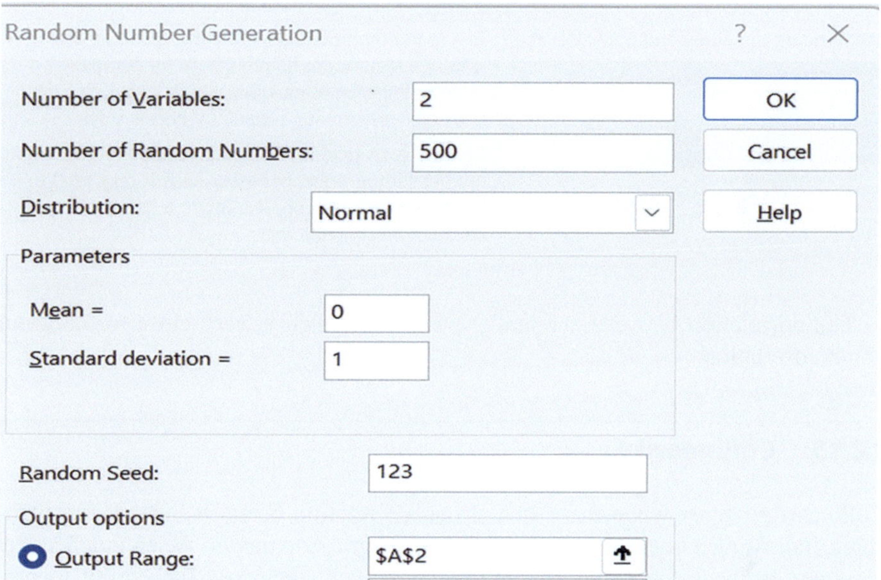

Fig. 12.35 The settings for Random Number Generation

Assume we want to get two sets of random numbers, 5000 each, drawn from a normal distribution (with 0 and 1 as mean and standard deviation, respectively) with a set correlation of 0.85.

	A	B	C	D	E	F	G
1	x1	x2	y1	y2	0.85		
2	-2.2136	0.205654	-2.2136	-1.77323	=A2*$E$1+B2*SQRT(1-$E$1^2)		
3	0.536561	-0.25357	0.536561	0.322501			
4	2.246707	-1.28359	2.246707	1.233529	0.864447	=CORREL(C:C,D:D)	
5	1.541594	2.780216	1.541594	2.774924			
99	1.354801	0.205263	1.354801	1.25971			
499	0.562629	0.537533	0.562629	0.761398			
500	-0.8817	0.923426	-0.8817	-0.263			
501	0.759551	0.037915	0.759551	0.665591			
502							

Fig. 12.36 Generating two correlated sets of random numbers

Table 12.1 Examples of collinearity

Height and Weight	In a model predicting health outcomes, height and weight could be included as independent variables, but they are often correlated, especially within specific population groups
Education Level and Income	If a model includes education level and income to predict job satisfaction, these two variables may be correlated because higher education levels often correspond to higher incomes
Advertising Spending and Sales Revenue	In a marketing model, advertising spending and sales revenue might be predictors for company growth, but they often show a high correlation, as increased advertising frequently boosts sales
House Age and Condition	In real estate models, house age and condition might predict selling price, but older houses may tend to be in poorer condition, leading to a correlation between these predictors

The correlation between `y1` and `y2` is 0.86, which is very close to 0.85, our target correlation.

12.15 Collinearity

Collinearity occurs when there is a strong correlation between independent variables, indicating a linear relationship within a regression model. When independent variables in the same model are highly correlated, they lose the ability to predict the dependent variable independently. This overlap means they account for the same portion of the variance in the dependent variable, which lowers their statistical significance. Below are a few examples shown in a Table 12.1.

12.16 Steps to Address Collinearity

Below is the procedure for dealing with collinearity.

Step 1: Calculate correlation coefficients or use variance inflation factors (VIFs) to quantify the extent of correlation. A VIF above 5 or 10 is generally a sign of multicollinearity.
Step 2A: Remove one of the Correlated Variables: If two variables are highly correlated and provide similar information, consider removing one from the model.
Step 2B: Combine the Variables: If it makes sense theoretically, you can create a composite variable. For example, instead of including height and weight separately, you could use Body Mass Index (BMI), which combines both.

Step 2C: Use Principal Component Analysis (PCA): PCA is a dimensionality reduction technique that transforms correlated variables into a set of uncorrelated components, which can be used as predictors.
Step 2D: Use Regularization Methods: Techniques like ridge regression (L2 regularization) can help reduce the impact of collinearity by penalizing significant coefficients, allowing the model to stabilize despite having correlated variables.

By following these steps, you can reduce or eliminate the adverse effects of collinearity in your regression model.

12.17 Variance Inflation Factors (VIFs)

Assume that we have `n` independent variables. Then, we choose one independent variable as the dependent variable and run a linear regression against the test of independent variables, i.e., `n-1` independent variables. The formula for its VIF is given below:

$$VIF_i = \frac{1}{1 - R_i^2}, i = 1, 2, \ldots, n, \tag{12.9}$$

where R_i^2 Is the R-squared value from the linear regression when the ith independent variable is used as `y` (dependent variable). The above equation shows that a VIF of 1 represents no multicollinearity, and higher values indicate a sign of multicollinearity. For a critical VIF value, Choueiry (2023) offers the following Table 12.2.

The Fama–French 3-factor time series is used to test their VIFs. The last five years' data are shown below.

Table 12.2 Threshold for VIF

Threshold	Reference
> 10 is problematic	Vittinghoff E et. Al (2005)
> 5 or > 10 is problematic	James G et al. (2017)
> 5 is cause for concern and > 10 indicates a severe problem	Menard S. (2001)
≥ 2.5 considerable collinearity	Johnston R et al. (2018)

	A	B	C	D	E
1	DATE	MKT_RF	SMB	HML	RF
2	8/1/2019	-0.0258	-0.0239	-0.0479	0.0016
3	9/1/2019	0.0143	-0.0097	0.0677	0.0018
59	5/1/2024	0.0434	0.0078	-0.0166	0.0044
60	6/1/2024	0.0277	-0.0306	-0.0331	0.0041
61	7/1/2024	0.0124	0.0684	0.057	0.0045

Fig. 12.37 Several lines from the Fama–French 3-factor time series

When using MKT_RF (Market return minus risk-free rate) as y and SMB and HML as x, we have the following result: The R2 is 0.088535. The corresponding VIF is 1.10. According to the above table, we can claim that there is no collinearity.

65	*Regression Statistics*			
66	Multiple R	0.297548		
67	R Square	0.088535	1.097135	=1/(1-B67)
68	Adjusted R Squa	0.056554		
69	Standard Error	0.052509		
70	Observations	60		

Fig. 12.38 Estimating VIF using MKT-RF as y and SML and HML as x

The following two graphs show SMB and HML used as y, respectively. Their corresponding VIFs are 1.11 and 1.01. Thus, none of them show any sign of collinearity.

Regression Statistics		
Multiple R	0.311524	
R Square	0.097047	1.10747775
Adjusted R	0.065365	
Standard E	0.029912	
Observatic	60	

Regression Statistics		
Multiple R	0.107255	
R Square	0.011504	1.011637
Adjusted R	-0.02318	
Standard E	0.048512	
Observatic	60	

Fig. 12.39 and 12.40 Estimating VIFs using SML and HML as y, respectively

12.18 Polynomial Regression

Polynomial regression is a form of regression analysis in which the relationship between the independent variable x and the dependent variable y is modeled as an n nth-degree polynomial. While linear regression fits a straight line to data, polynomial regression can fit more complex curves, making it helpful in capturing non-linear patterns. The polynomial regression equation looks like this:

$$y = \beta_0 + \beta_1 x + \beta_2 x^2 + \ldots + \beta_n x^n + \tag{12.10}$$

Here, β_0, β_1, …,β_n are the coefficients to be estimated, and ϵ is the error term. The degree of the polynomial (n) determines the model's flexibility. A higher degree can fit more complex patterns but may also lead to overfitting, where the model captures noise rather than the underlying trend.

12.19 Linear Models for Non-Linear Variables

Let's look at the following model. There is only one independent variable, but the power of the second term is 2.

$$y = \alpha + \beta_1 x + \beta_2 x^2, \tag{12.11}$$

This is not a linear model. However, as shown below, the above model can be converted to a linear model with a simple substitution.

$$y = \alpha + \beta_1 x_1 + \beta_2 x_2 \tag{12.12}$$

Here, $x_1 = x$ and $x_2 = x^2$. For example, for stock returns, we can test whether excess market returns can influence individual stocks' returns linearly and non-linearly. If the coefficient of the second term is zero, then we can claim that a market excess return can only include the individual stock's return linearly. Suppose we have a dataset with values of x (e.g., years of experience) and y (e.g., salary).

	A	B
1	Experience (Years)	Salary ($)
2	1	30,000
3	2	35,000
4	3	37,000
5	4	45,000
6	5	52,000
7	6	58,000

Fig. 12.41 The several lines of Experience and Salary variables

For a linear model, we have the following result.

D	E	F	G	H	I	J	K	L
SUMMARY OUTPUT								
Regression Statistics								
Multiple R	0.988615							
R Square	0.97736							
Adjusted R	0.9717							
Standard E	1810.025							
Observatic	6							
ANOVA								
	df	*SS*	*MS*	*F*	*gnificance F*			
Regressior	1	5.66E+08	5.66E+08	172.6788	0.000194			
Residual	4	13104762	3276190					
Total	5	5.79E+08						
	Coefficients	*andard Err*	*t Stat*	*P-value*	*Lower 95%*	*Upper 95%*	*ower 95.0%*	*pper 95.0%*
Intercept	22933.33	1685.042	13.60995	0.000169	18254.91	27611.76	18254.91	27611.76
Experience	5685.714	432.6787	13.14073	0.000194	4484.406	6887.023	4484.406	6887.023

Fig. 12.42 The result with years as the independent variable

Based on the p-values, both the intercept and slope are statistically significant. For a quadratic model, i.e., the highest power is 2. We have the following inputs for a quadratic model.

C2 | fx | =B2^2

	A	B	C
1	Salary ($)	Experience (Years)	year^2
2	30,000	1	1
3	35,000	2	4
4	37,000	3	9
5	45,000	4	16
6	52,000	5	25
7	58,000	6	36

Fig. 12.43 Adding squared year as the second independent variable

The result is shown below.

E	F	G	H	I	J	K	L	M
SUMMARY OUTPUT								
Regression Statistics								
Multiple R	0.995095							
R Square	0.990214							
Adjusted R	0.983691							
Standard E	1374.08							
Observatic	6							
ANOVA								
	df	*SS*	*MS*	*F*	*gnificance F*			
Regressior	2	5.73E+08	2.87E+08	151.785	0.000968			
Residual	3	5664286	1888095					
Total	5	5.79E+08						
	Coefficients	*andard Err*	*t Stat*	*P-value*	*Lower 95%*	*Upper 95%*	*ower 95.0%*	*pper 95.0%*
Intercept	27100	2458.029	11.0251	0.001598	19277.46	34922.54	19277.46	34922.54
Experience	2560.714	1608.109	1.592376	0.209544	-2557.01	7678.436	-2557.01	7678.436
year^2	446.4286	224.8866	1.985128	0.141351	-269.261	1162.118	-269.261	1162.118

Fig. 12.44 The result with 2 independent variables (year and squared year)

Even though the adjusted R^2 is better than a linear model (98% vs. 97%), both $\beta1$ and $\beta2$ are statistically not different from zero. Their p-values are 0.21 and 0.14, respectively.

12.20 Logistic Regression

The previous chapter discussed this topic in detail using Excel. In addition to Excel, we introduce a hidden function called `.logisticRegression()`, abbreviated as `.lg()`. Assume that we have the following data set called `default`.

	A	B	C	D
1	default	student	balance	income
2	No	No	729.5265	44361.63
3	No	Yes	817.1804	12106.13
4	No	No	1073.549	31767.14
5	No	No	529.2506	35704.49

Fig. 12.45 Several lines of the Student Default data set

To initiate the program, type `.lg()`, as shown below.

```
* ------------------------------------------------------ *
* Objective: run a logistic regression                  *
* ------------------------------------------------------ *
* Step 1: Copy your data then hit the Enter Key         *

* ---The first several lines are shown below --------- *
default student    balance    income
     No      No   729.5265 44361.63
     No     Yes   817.1804 12106.13
     No      No 1073.5492 31767.14
```

Fig. 12.46 The first step of a hidden function for logistic regression

The first column will be our target; see the next step. Column 2 is a categorical variable; see below for Step 3.

```
  * ----------------------------------------------------- *
  * Step 2: which column is your target (y), such as 1   *
  * ----------------------------------------------------- *
1
  * ----------------------------------------------------- *
  * Step 3: Which columns are categorical variables      *
  *         except the target column                     *
  * ----------------------------------------------------- *
  *         such as 1 2 3                                *
  *         0 for nothing                                *
  * ----------------------------------------------------- *
1: 2
2:
Read 1 item
```

Fig. 12.47 Steps 2 and 3 for the.lg hidden function

Steps 4 and 5 are related to giving a random seed and the proportion for the training sample.

```
  * ----------------------------------------------------- *
  * Step 4: Enter a random seed, such as 123             *
123
  * ----------------------------------------------------- *
  * Step 5: Eenter a value for training such as 0.7      *
0.7
```

Fig. 12.48 Steps 4 and 5 for the hidden.lg function

The model's output uses the training data set, as shown below.

```
Call:
glm(formula = aa, family = "binomial", data = train)

Coefficients:
                 Estimate     Std. Error z value                Pr(>|z|)
(Intercept) -11.055360943    0.603950232 -18.305 <0.0000000000000002 ***
studentYes   -0.729562678    0.290994996  -2.507              0.0122 *
balance       0.005940425    0.000288345  20.602 <0.0000000000000002 ***
income       -0.000002305    0.000010026  -0.230              0.8182
---
Signif. codes:  0 '***' 0.001 '**' 0.01 '*' 0.05 '.' 0.1 ' ' 1

(Dispersion parameter for binomial family taken to be 1)

    Null deviance: 2013.1  on 7047  degrees of freedom
Residual deviance: 1042.5  on 7044  degrees of freedom
AIC: 1050.5

Number of Fisher Scoring iterations: 8
```

Fig. 12.49 The result of running the hidden function (.lg)

The last step is to find the quality of the model. Below, the conventional value of 0.5 is used.

```
 * ---------------------------------------------------- *
 * Step 6: Generating predictions and confusion matrix  *
 * ---------------------------------------------------- *
 *    Enter a cut-off point such as 0.5                 *
0.5
```

Fig. 12.50 Step 6: Entering a cutoff point

The final result is shown below.

```
 * ---------------------------------------------------- *
         Actual
Predicted   No  Yes
      No  2838   80
      Yes    9   25
 * ---------------------------------------------------- *
 *  Coufusion matrix:                                   *
 * ---------------------------------------------------- *
Accuracy: 0.9699
Sensitivity (True Positive Rate): 0.2381
Specificity (True Negative Rate): 0.9968
 * ---------------------------------------------------- *
```

Fig. 12.51 The performance and confusion matrix

12.21 Our Hidden Functions

For hidden functions related to this chapter, we can use the function `.searchHiddenFuntions()`, abbreviated as `.sf ()`.

```
> .sf(12)
 CHAPTER                          NAME                                  SHORTCUT
      12 install.packages('clipr')
      12 install.packages('tydyr')
      12 .show_airquality()
      12 .show_ibmMonthly()
      12 .show_ff3monthly()
      12 .merge2datasets()          .merge # need 'clipr'
      12 .drop_na()                 # need both 'clipr' and 'tidyr'
>
```

Fig. 12.52 The hidden functions related to Chapter 12

Appendix A: After Launching R, Issue One of the Following Lines of R Code

```
source("http://datayyy.com/i2ft/week12.txt")
```

```
*------------------------------------------------------------------------*
* Introduction to FinTech using Excel                  by Dr. Yan 2025   *
*       (in an R-assisted learning environment)                          *
*------------------------------------------------------------------------*
*  .c1  Introduction and Excel Basics           .c15 Term Projects       *
*  .c2  Blockchain 1: (Numbers & alphanumeric)  .c16 R basics(optional)  *
*  .c3           2: (ASCII and Sha256)          .c17 Macro (optional)    *
*  .c4  Ledger and distributed ledger           .c18 VBA  (optional)     *
*  .c5  Cryptography   1: and public/private keys                        *
*  .c6                 2: Advanced                                       *
*  .c7  Cryptocurrency and Ganache                                       *
*  .c8                 2: markets, risk, risk/return tradeoff            *
*  .c9  Blockchain's Applications with Simulations                       *
*------------------------------------------------------------------------*
* .c10  Machine Learning in finance 1: Unsupervised Learning             *
* .c11                              2: Supervised Learning: regressions  *
* .c12                                           : classifications       *
* -----------------------------------------------------------------------*
* >.c12      # go to chapter 12                                          *
* >.uu       # go to utility submenu                                     *
* >.ft       # back to this menu                                         *
*------------------------------------------------------------------------*
```

Fig. 12.53 The menu for Week 12

Appendix B: For Chapter 12, just Type `.chapter12`, Shown Below

```
> .chapter12
function(i=0){
"i  C12: Supervised learning (regressions)
 -  ------------------------           --  ---------------------
 1  Supervised vs unsupervised         21  Polynomial model example
 2  Main categories                    22      Example 2
 3  Regression types                   23  Covariance vs. correlation
 4  10 examples for predictions        24  correlated 2 random numbers
 5  total risk vs. market risk         25  Collinearity
 6  Linear model: definition           26     : How to correct
 7           : graphs                  27     : VIF (Variance inflation factor)
 8           : 3 ways to run           28     : cut-off points
 9           : CAPM                    29     : Fama-French 3-factor VIF calculation
10           : CAPM for IBM            30     : another example
11           :       output            31 Categorical variable
12  Fama-French 3-factor               32   a dummy variable
13      : download a zip file          33    n categorical variables
14      : csv/Pickle data set          34  Logistic regression (review)
15      : IBM 3-factor model           35       : formula
16      :        output                36       : example
17 Linear models 4 nonlinear var       37  our function .logisticRegression()
18 Polynomial model                    38      Example #1
19  Videos                             39      Example #2
20  Links                              40c     Example #3

 Example #1>.c12       # find out the list
 Example #2>.c12()     # the same as the above
 Example #3>.c12(1)  # see the first explanation
```

Fig. 12.54 The contents of Chapter 12

Exercises

12.1 What is a linear model?

12.2 What are the characteristics of a linear model?

12.3 What is the definition of beta?

12.4 What type of risk does a beta try to measure?

12.5 What is the definition of market risk?

12.6 What are the usages of the CAPM?

12.7 What is the correlation between market indices? For example, you can download price data for the S&P500 (its Yahoo ticker is "^GSPC") and the Dow Jones Industrial Average ("^DJI") over the last 10 years. Then, estimate their returns and calculate the corresponding correlation. Comment on your result.

12.8 What is the correlation between IBM stock returns and DELL's from 2006 to 2010?

12.9 Retrieve the `airquality` data set using the following command.

```
> .show_airquality(0)
Windows users: launch Excel and paste
```

The first several observations are shown below.

	A	B	C	D	E	F
1	Ozone	Solar.R	Wind	Temp	Month	Day
2	41	190	7.4	67	5	1
3	36	118	8	72	5	2
4	12	149	12.6	74	5	3
5	18	313	11.5	62	5	4
6	NA	NA	14.3	56	5	5
7	28	NA	14.9	66	5	6
8	23	299	8.6	65	5	7

Fig. 12.55 The several lines of the airQuality data

Import the data in Excel and remove all the NAs.

12.10 Describe in your own words what regression analysis is and explain the difference between simple and multiple regression models.

12.11 Use the LINEST function in Excel to conduct a simple linear regression analysis for a given dataset. Interpret the output values.

12.12 Multivariate Regression: Set up a multivariate regression model in Excel with at least three independent variables. Explain the purpose of each variable.

12.13 Evaluate Multivariate Models: Interpret the results of a multivariate regression model. Discuss which variables are significant and why.

12.14 Explain what collinearity is and why it is problematic in regression analysis. How can you identify collinearity in a dataset using Excel?

12.15 Calculate the Variance Inflation Factor (VIF) in Excel to assess collinearity for each predictor in a multivariate regression model. Identify any variable with a high VIF and suggest ways to address it.

12.16 Generate Random Correlations: Generate two sets of random numbers in Excel with a specified level of correlation (e.g., 0.8). Describe the steps you took to create these correlated variables.

12.17 Explore Correlation Impact: Investigate how increasing or decreasing correlation between two independent variables impacts the coefficients in a regression model.

12.18 Use Excel to calculate the expected return of an asset using the CAPM formula. Assume you have risk-free rate, beta, and market return data.

12.19 CAPM Interpretation: Interpret the results of the CAPM model. How does the asset's risk (beta) influence its expected return?

12.20 Explain the purpose of the Fama-French 3-factor model and the role of each factor: market, size, and value.

12.21 Use the Fama-French 3-factor model (Market, SMB, HML) and run a regression in Excel to estimate a stock's sensitivity to each factor. Interpret the coefficients.

12.22 Describe when logistic regression is more suitable than linear regression. Provide an example of a scenario where logistic regression would be appropriate.

12.23 Set up a logistic regression model in Excel to classify data into two categories. Use Excel's Solver to optimize the model and interpret the results.

12.24 Describe how you would transform non-linear variables (e.g., log transformation, polynomial terms) in Excel to fit them into a linear regression model.

12.25 Create a scatter plot of a non-linear dataset in Excel and experiment with transformations (e.g., square root, square) to find a suitable linear relationship.

12.26 Convert a categorical variable (e.g., region: North, South, East, West) into dummy variables in Excel. Explain the process and the resulting variables.

12.27 Run a regression model in Excel that includes continuous and dummy variables. Interpret the coefficients for the dummy variables.

12.28 Use a multivariate regression model in Excel to predict monthly sales based on advertising spend, season, and competitor pricing. Discuss any assumptions made.

12.29 Use a dataset with variables like square feet (footage), number of bedrooms, and location, and build a regression model to predict housing prices. Explain which variables have the most substantial impact on price.

12.30 Evaluate R-Squared and Adjusted R-Squared: Explain the difference between R-squared and adjusted R-squared. Using Excel, compare these metrics for a regression model and interpret what they suggest about the model's fit.

12.31 What is VIF? What is a good cutoff value for whether the independent variables have a collinearity?

12.32 Add an interaction term between two variables in a regression model and interpret the impact on the outcome.

12.33 Using the air quality data set, we can calculate the correlations between several variables and the Ozone level, as shown below.

G5 fx =CORREL($A:$A,B:B)

	A	B	C	D	E	F	G	H	I	J	K
1	Ozone	Solar.R	Wind	Temp	Month	Day	111	=COUNT(A:A)			
2	41	190	7.4	67	5	1					
3	36	118	8	72	5	2	corr(Ozone and other)				
4	12	149	12.6	74	5	3	Solar.R	Wind	Temp	Month	Day
5	18	313	11.5	62	5	4	0.348342	-0.6125	0.698541	0.142885	-0.00519
6	23	299	8.6	65	5	7					

Fig. 12.56 Applying the Excel CORREL function

Why are the last two correlations (between the Month and the Ozone level and between the Day and the Ozone level) meaningless?

12.34 * Use our hidden function called `.logisticRegression()` and the `quality` data set to run the Logistic Regression.

12.35 In the chapter, we calculate the VIFs using the latest five-years data (8/1/2019 to 7/1/2024) of the Fama-French 3-factor time series. Reproduce the same result. Then, the results will be compared with the data from the first five years (1926 to 1930) of the time series. Comment on your result.

12.36 Use the data set called `airquality` to calculate their VIFs and comment on your result. Two ways to get the data: (1) http://datayyy.com/i2ft/data/airquality.csv; (2) issue the following line.

```
> .show_airquality(0)
Windows users: launch Excel and paste
```

References

Air now gov, Ozone and Your Health, EPA-456/F-09–001, Air Quality Index. https://www.airnow.gov/sites/default/files/2020-02/ozone-c.pdf

Choueiry, G. (2023). What is an Acceptable Value for VIF? (With References), https://quantifyinghealth.com/vif-threshold/

French's Data Library. https://mba.tuck.dartmouth.edu/pages/faculty/ken.french/data_library.html

Frost, J. (2020). Variance Inflation Factors (VIFs). https://statisticsbyjim.com/regression/variance-inflation-factors/

James, G., Witten, D., Hastie, T., & Tibshirani, R. (2017). *An introduction to statistical learning: With applications* (1st ed.). Corr. 7th printing 2017 edition. Springer.

Johnston, R., Jones, K., & Manley, D. (2018). Confounding and collinearity in regression analysis: A cautionary tale and an alternative procedure, illustrated by studies of British voting behavior. *Quality & Quantity, 52*(4), 1957–1976. https://doi.org/10.1007/s11135-017-0584-6

Menard, S. (2001). *Applied logistic regression analysis* (2nd ed.). Sage Publications.

UCI Machine Learning Repository. https://archive.ics.uci.edu/

UCI Iris data set. https://archive.ics.uci.edu/dataset/53/iris

Vittinghoff, E. (2005). *Regression methods in biostatistics: Linear, logistic, survival, and repeated measures models*. Springer.

13 Neural Networks Using Excel and Our Hidden Functions

The concept of Neural Networks is quite new and difficult to understand. This is especially true for most business school students. Because of this, we first explain a neural network's basic concepts and graphs. Then, we will use Excel to build up the simplest Neural Network (one layer and one neuron) using the famous Iris data set. After understanding the basic operations using Excel, we will show our hidden functions such as `.showNN()`, `.showNN_iris()`, `.showNN_iris2()`, and `.nn()`. In the function names, `NN` (`nn`) stands for Neural Network. In this chapter, the following topics will be covered:

- What are Neural Networks?
- Basic concepts related to Neural Networks
- Normalization of input variables
- Procedure of building a neural network
- Using Excel to build a neural network: iris dataset
- Using Excel to build neural networks: default data set
- One-layer one-neuron: `.showNN() and.showNN_iris()`
- One-layer two-neuron: `.showNN_iris2()` and `.showNN_default()`
- A general function: `.nn()`

Supplementary Information The online version contains supplementary material available at https://doi.org/10.1007/978-3-031-89779-5_13.

Y. Yan, *Introduction to FinTech using Excel*, Springer Texts in Business and Economics, https://doi.org/10.1007/978-3-031-89779-5_13

13.1 Introduction to Neural Networks

Neural networks, also known as artificial neural networks (ANN), are a class of machine-learning algorithms inspired by the human brain. Neural networks are designed to recognize patterns and make predictions by learning from data through a process called training. We will discuss how neural networks function as interconnected layers of "neurons," each performing mathematical computations. Although neural networks are typically implemented using advanced programming languages, this chapter will demonstrate how they can be built and understood using Excel, making the concept more accessible to beginners.

13.2 Layers vs. Neurons

In a neural network, layers and neurons are the fundamental building blocks, each playing a distinct role in processing and learning from data. The following image shows two hidden layers with four neurons each. In addition, we will have two inputs and just one output.

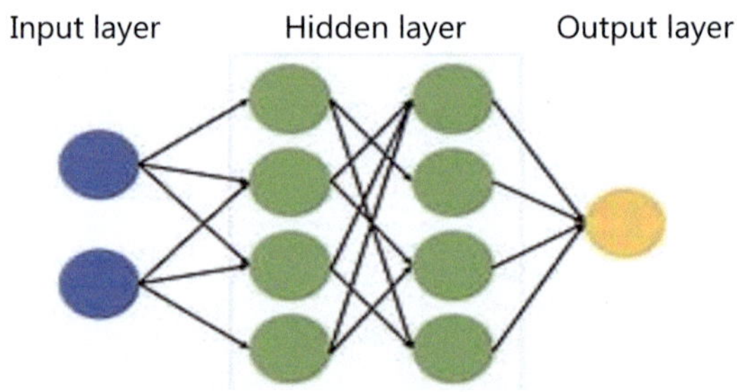

Fig. 13.1 Three layers: input, hidden, and output layers

A layer is a collection of neurons grouped, working collaboratively to perform a specific level of transformation on the data as it flows through the network. Layers are organized sequentially, each feeding its output to the next. The input layer receives raw data, hidden layers transform the data, and the output layer provides the final prediction or classification. Layers determine the neural network's architecture and impact its ability to model complex relationships.

Neurons, on the other hand, are the individual computational units within each layer. They receive inputs, apply weights and biases, process them through an activation function, and pass the output forward. Each neuron in a layer captures specific patterns or features, and together, neurons in hidden layers form a more complex representation of the data. The number of neurons in each layer and their connections influence the network's learning capacity and flexibility. While layers dictate the structure and flow of data, neurons perform the granular calculations within each layer.

13.3 Basic Concepts

This section introduces essential concepts such as neurons (nodes), weights, biases, and activation functions. We will also explain the roles of input, hidden, and output layers and the significance of forward propagation and backpropagation for training a network. By breaking down these complex terms into more straightforward ideas, readers will develop a strong foundation that will make it easier to follow the subsequent Excel-based tutorials. The following graph is from edge-ai-vision.com. From a given set of inputs, they go through three hidden layers. Those outputs will go to the final output. Our task is to find the weights and related functions for each step.

Below is one of the most straightforward outputs: two input variables and one hidden layer with one neuron. Later in the chapter, we will explain how to use the following output to predict a binary classification.

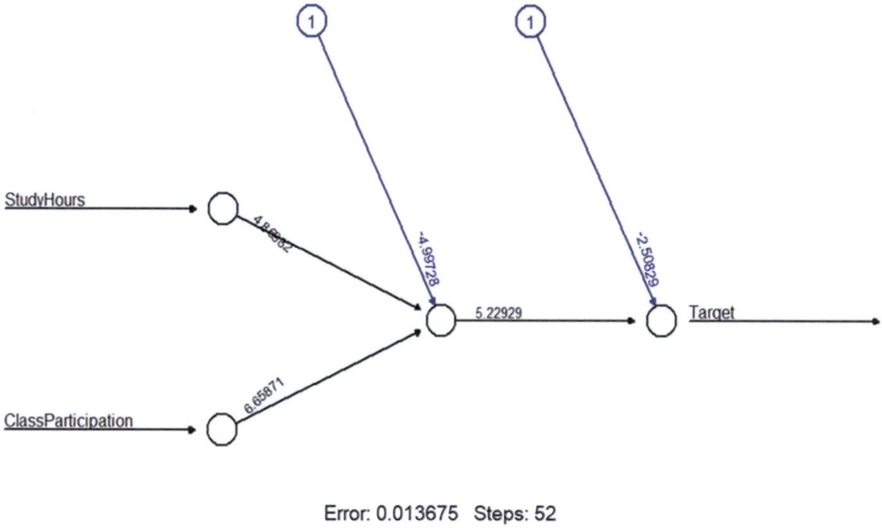

Fig. 13.2 The structure of one output

13.4 Review the Sigmoid Function

This function was discussed in one of the previous chapters. Assume that we have n input variables ($x_1, x_2, \ldots, x_n$), and the estimated parameters are $\beta_0, \beta_1, \ldots,$ and β_n. The Sigmoid function is given below.

$$f(x) = \frac{1}{1+e^{-z}} = \frac{1}{1+e^{-(\beta_0+\beta_1 x_1+\beta_2 x_2+\ldots+\beta_n x_n)}}, \tag{13.1}$$

where $z = \beta_0 + \beta_1 x_1 + \beta_2 x_2 + \ldots + \beta_n x_n$. Most of the time, the underlying program will estimate those beta values. The graph is shown below.

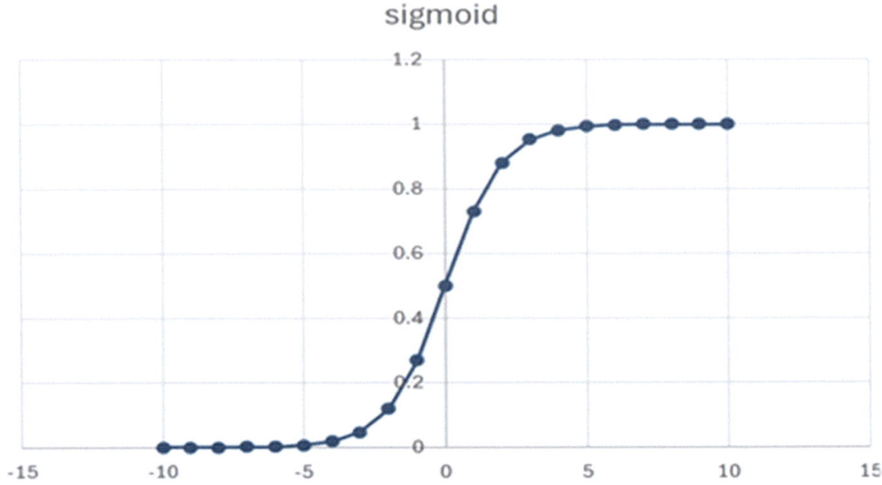

Fig. 13.3 A graphic presentation of the Sigmoid function

We could set up a benchmark probability for a binary forecasting value. If `f(x)` is greater than this benchmark probability, the classification will be 1; otherwise, it will be 0. For two given values of z, we have the following result.

	A	B	C	D
1	2.5	0.924142	=1/((1+EXP(-A1)))	
2	-1.4	0.197816	=1/((1+EXP(-A2)))	

Fig. 13.4 The Excel exponential function (EXP)

On the other hand, we have the following results for a set of 3 inputs plus four estimated parameters. Note that the Excel `sumproduct()` function is applied.

	A	B	C	D	E	F	G	H	I	J	K
1	x1	x2	x3	intecept+sumproduct					sigmoid		
2	2	3	5	-2.94	=$A$7+SUMPRODUCT(A2:C2,$B$7:$D$7)				0.050211	=1/(1+EXP(-D2))	
3	-1	4	4	-5.37	=$A$7+SUMPRODUCT(A3:C3,$B$7:$D$7)				0.004633	=1/(1+EXP(-D3))	
4	3	-2	2.5	4.035	=$A$7+SUMPRODUCT(A4:C4,$B$7:$D$7)				0.982622	=1/(1+EXP(-D4))	
5											
6	beta0	beta1	beta2	beta3							
7	0.01	0.3	-1.4	0.13							

Fig. 13.5 The Excel SUMPRODUCT function

The derivative of a sigmoid function, f (x), is the function's slope at any point, indicating the change rate of the function's output concerning its input. The derivative can be calculated by using the chain rule of calculus. The formula for the derivative is given below.

$$f'(x) = f(x) * [1 - f(x)] \tag{13.2}$$

Later in the chapter, we will use this formula. The derivative at cell B3 is shown below.

	A	B	C	D
1	x	sigmoid		
2	0.5	0.62245933	=1/(1+EXP(-A2))	
3	derivative->	0.23500371	=B2*(1-B2)	

Fig. 13.6 The derivative of the Sigmoid function

We can manually prove it since the derivative is the limit of $\Delta y/\Delta x$, as $\frac{\Delta y}{\Delta x} \to 0$ We can assume a tiny value and then calculate both values, i.e., [f(x + tiny)-f(x)]/ tiny, as shown below.

	A	B	C	D
1	x	sigmoid		
2	0.5	0.622459331	=1/(1+EXP(-A2))	
3	derivative->	0.235003712	=B2*(1-B2)	
4	tiny	sigmoid2		
5	0.000001	0.622459566	=1/(1+EXP(-A7))	
6	x2	0.235003683	=(B5-B2)/A5	
7	0.500001	=A2+A5		

Fig. 13.7 The second way to calculate the derivative using a tiny value

13.5 Activation Function

An activation function in a neural network is a mathematical function applied to a neuron's output to introduce non-linearity, enabling the network to learn complex patterns in data. Without activation functions, the entire network would behave like a single linear model, regardless of depth, limiting its ability to capture intricate relationships. By transforming the weighted sum of a neuron's inputs, activation functions allow the network to model non-linear phenomena, making it suitable for tasks like image recognition, language processing, and other forms of complex data interpretation.

The following flow chart is for one layer with just one neuron. Assume that we have three inputs. We calculate a weighted summation and then apply the Sigmoid function (as an Activation function) to get an output (y).

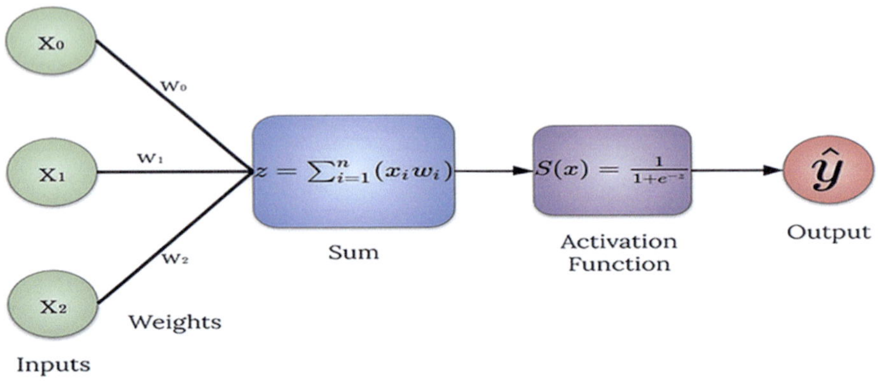

Fig. 13.8 The flow chart for one neuron

There are various activation functions, each with unique properties and use cases. Some common ones include the Sigmoid, which maps outputs between 0 and 1 and is often used in binary classification; the hyperbolic tangent (tanh), which outputs between −1 and 1 and tends to work well in hidden layers; and the Rectified Linear Unit (ReLU), a popular choice for hidden layers because of its simplicity and effectiveness in mitigating issues like vanishing gradients. Each activation function is critical in determining the neural network's learning dynamics and overall performance. This chapter will simplify our task using the Sigmoid function reviewed in the previous section.

13.6 Types of Classification

Classification in neural networks involves categorizing input data into classes or categories. The type of classification problem depends on the nature and number of classes. The Table 13.1 summarizes a few common types of classification and their typical activation functions.

The sigmoid activation function is commonly used in the output layer for binary classification. Sigmoid maps output values between 0 and 1, which makes it suitable for predicting probabilities of two classes. The final prediction is often based on a threshold (usually 0.5), where values above the threshold are assigned to one class, and those below are assigned to the other. A softmax activation function is used in the output layer for Multi-Class Classification. Softmax outputs a probability distribution over all classes, with the highest probability indicating the predicted class. This approach works well because softmax ensures that all probabilities sum

Table 13.1 Types of classification using neural networks

Type	Explanation	Activation
Binary classification	This is the simplest form, where the model classifies inputs into one of two classes, such as spam vs. not spam or true vs. false	Sigmoid
Multi-class classification	the model assigns an input to one of multiple possible classes, such as predicting the digit in an image from 0 to 9	softmax
Multi-label classification	Unlike multi-class classification, where each input belongs to only one class, multi-label classification allows an input to be associated with multiple classes. For example, in image tagging, a picture could simultaneously be tagged as "beach," "sunset," and "vacation."	Sigmoid
Ordinal classification	In ordinal classification, classes have a natural order, such as movie ratings from 1 to 5 stars	Softmax or sigmoid

to 1, making it suitable for mutually exclusive classes. In the Multi-Label Classification case, the sigmoid activation function is applied independently to each output node, yielding a probability for each class. Each probability can then be used to determine whether or not a specific label applies to the input.

For Ordinal Classification, although the network may still use softmax or sigmoid functions, additional methods are sometimes needed to account for the ordinal nature of the classes, as neither function inherently captures class order. Each activation function choice aligns with the problem type and helps the network effectively process and categorize the input data according to its specific classification structure.

This chapter will focus on binary classification using a Sigmoid function as our activation function. This focus will simplify the whole process. In addition, after understanding some basic concepts, procedures, and examples, readers and students can easily expand their learning if they are interested in other classifications.

13.7 Normalization

Normalization helps the network learn more effectively, and readers will learn how to use Excel's functions, such as MIN and MAX, to achieve this. Below, let's use a straightforward example: just 4 rows of data sets with two variables (study hours and class participation). The Pass/Fail is a dummy variable with 1 = pass and zero fail. The normalized values are given in columns D and E.

D2 =(A2-MIN(A:A))/(MAX(A:A)-MIN(A:A))

	A	B	C	D	E	F	G	H
1	studyHours	ClassParticipation	Pass/Fail	normalized_hours	normalized_class			
2	5	3	1	0.57143	0.75000	=(B2-MIN(B:B))/(MAX(B:B)-MIN(B:B))		
3	2	1	0	0.14286	0.25000			
4	8	4	1	1.00000	1.00000			
5	1	0	0	0.00000	0.00000			
6								

Fig. 13.9 One example of normalization

For example, in cell D2, the formula is = `(A2-MIN(A:A))/(MAX(A:A)-MIN(A:A))`.

13.8 Categorical Values to Numerical Values

Later in the chapter, we will introduce a general function called `.nn()`, which accepts any data input. However, it has a requirement: all columns should be numerical variables except for class (classification) columns.

	A	B	C	D
1	default	student	balance	income
2	No	No	729.526495	44361.625
3	No	Yes	817.180407	12106.135
4	No	No	1073.54916	31767.139
5	No	No	529.250605	35704.494
6	No	No	785.655883	38463.496

Fig. 13.10 Several lines of the default data

Column B is a categorical variable. Assume we will code Yes as 1 and No as 0; see the following result. The formula in cell F2 is = `IF(B2 = "No",0,1)`.

F2 =IF(B2="No",0,1)

	A	B	C	D	E	F	G	H
1	default	student	balance	income	default	student	balance	income
2	No	No	729.5265	44361.63	No	0	729.5265	44361.63
3	No	Yes	817.1804	12106.13	No	1	817.1804	12106.13
4	No	No	1073.549	31767.14	No	0	1073.549	31767.14
5	No	No	529.2506	35704.49	No	0	529.2506	35704.49
6	No	No	785.6559	38463.5	No	0	785.6559	38463.5
7	No	Yes	919.5885	7491.559	No	1	919.5885	7491.559

Fig. 13.11 Categorical variables to numerical ones

When calling the `.nn()` function, we should copy columns F:H as our input data set instead of the original data columns (A:C).

13.9 Two Types of Approaches

In this chapter, we will discuss two approaches: using Excel only; and using both Excel and our hidden functions. For the first approach, learners could understand the fundamental logic behind Neural Networks. However, it is challenging to generate a good result. The second approach is quite general, i.e., we can apply it to almost all the data sets, any number of layers, and neurons. The downside is that there are black boxes with our hidden functions in addition to downloading some R packages. We will start with the first approach since their concepts are easy to understand, even if the procedure is tedious and has a less accurate result. After understanding the logic, we will introduce our second approach, mixing Excel and hidden functions.

13.10 Example #1: Using Excel for Neural Networks

This is approach #1: use Excel only. The data set is the famous Iris data. There are two ways to get the data. For Method I, readers can download it at the UCI Machine Learning Depository (link; https://archive.ics.uci.edu/dataset/53/iris). The second way is to use our hidden function called `.show_iris ()`, as shown below.

```
> .show_titanic(0)
Windows users: launch Excel and paste
```

In practice, users divide the data set into training and test samples. The training sample is used to build up a model, while the test sample is used to verify the quality of the model. In this exercise, we estimate our model by using all 150 observations. The first several lines are given below.

	A	B	C	D	E
1	sepal_length	sepal_width	petal_length	petal_width	class
2	5.1	3.5	1.4	0.2	Iris-setosa
3	4.9	3	1.4	0.2	Iris-setosa
4	4.7	3.2	1.3	0.2	Iris-setosa
5	4.6	3.1	1.5	0.2	Iris-setosa

Fig. 13.12 The several lines of the Iris data

To make our calculations more accessible, we use a binary classification: when the class is "Iris-setosa," the output is 1; otherwise, it is 0, as shown below.

F2 =IF(E2=$E$2,1,0)

	A	B	C	D	E	F
1	sepal_length	sepal_width	petal_length	petal_width	class	true_output
2	5.1	3.5	1.4	0.2	Iris-setosa	1
3	4.9	3	1.4	0.2	Iris-setosa	1
4	4.7	3.2	1.3	0.2	Iris-setosa	1
5	4.6	3.1	1.5	0.2	Iris-setosa	1

Fig. 13.13 Generating a "true_output" column

The formula in cell F2 is = `IF(E2 = $E$2,1,0)`. Those three categories sort the original data. To make it more interesting, we add a column of random numbers and then sort the data by this column of random numbers. The random seed is 234.

	A	B	C	D	E	F	G
1	sepal_length	sepal_width	petal_length	petal_width	class	true_outpu	seed234
2	5.1	3.5	1.4	0.2	Iris-setosa	1	0.024476
3	4.9	3	1.4	0.2	Iris-setosa	1	0.99118
4	4.7	3.2	1.3	0.2	Iris-setosa	1	0.218207
5	4.6	3.1	1.5	0.2	Iris-setosa	1	0.913236
6	5	3.6	1.4	0.2	Iris-setosa	1	0.927793
7	5.4	3.9	1.7	0.4	Iris-setosa	1	0.401257

Fig. 13.14 Generating a column of random numbers (seed 123)

After sorting by this column of random numbers, we have the following working data.

	A	B	C	D	E	F	G
1							
2	sepal_length	sepal_width	petal_length	petal_width	class	class	seed234
3	6.6	2.9	4.6	1.3	Iris-versicoloı	0	0.0121
4	5	3	1.6	0.2	Iris-setosa	1	0.0124
5	6	3	4.8	1.8	Iris-virginica	0	0.0148
6	5.1	3.5	1.4	0.2	Iris-setosa	1	0.0245
7	4.9	3.1	1.5	0.1	Iris-setosa	1	0.0302

Fig. 13.15 The data after sorting

For column F, we can check the change of weights since we have both 0 and 1. We generate four weight columns and assign random weights for the first row. For example, we assign 0.1, 0.2, 0.3, and 0.4 for those two initial weights.

H3 | fx | 0.1

	A	B	C	D	F	H	I	J	K
1						------ weights	------------------------		
2	sepal_length	sepal_width	petal_length	petal_width	class	w1	w2	w3	w4
3	6.6	2.9	4.6	1.3	0	0.100	0.200	0.300	0.400
4	5	3	1.6	0.2	1				
5	6	3	4.8	1.8	0				
6	5.1	3.5	1.4	0.2	1				

Fig. 13.16 Assigning a random set of w1, w2, w3, and w4

For the next step, we calculate bias and (estimate output) by applying the Sigmoid function. The formula in cell L3 is = `SUMPRODUCT(A3:D3,H3:K3)`. This is × `1*w1 +` × `2*w2 +` × `3*w3 +` × `4*w4`. We can manually calculate the result: `6.6*0.1 + 2.9*0.2 + 4.6*0.3 + 1.3*0.4 = 3.14`. For cell M3, the formula is = `1/(1 + EXP(-L3))`. To verify, we have = `1/(1 + EXP(-3.14)) = 0.9585129`.

L3 | fx | =SUMPRODUCT(A3:D3,H3:K3)

	A	B	C	D	F	H	I	J	K	L	M	N
1						------ weights	----------------------			sumproc	sigmoid	
2	sepal_length	sepal_width	petal_length	petal_width	class	w1	w2	w3	w4	bias	output	
3	6.6	2.9	4.6	1.3	0	0.100	0.200	0.300	0.400	3.140	0.959	=1/(1+EXP(-L3)
4	5	3	1.6	0.2	1							
5	6	3	4.8	1.8	0							
6	5.1	3.5	1.4	0.2	1							
7	4.9	3.1	1.5	0.1	1							

Fig. 13.17 Applying the Excel SUMPRODUCT function

A huge error exists when comparing 0.959 in cell M3 with 0 in cell F3. We add four columns called weight adjustments to adjust our initial random weights. In cell N3, the formula is = `($F3-$M3)*A3*$M3*(1-$M3)`. The formula's logic is error * inputX * sigmoid curve gradian(output). For N3, this is (true_output - output) * × 1 *output*(1-output).

N3 | fx | =($F3-$M3)*A3*$M3*(1-$M3)

	A	B	C	D	F	H	I	J	K	L	M	N	O	P	Q
1						------ weights	------------------------			sumprodu	sigmoid	------ weight adjustment	------------------		
2	sepal_le	sepal_w	petal_le	petal_wi	class	w1	w2	w3	w4	bias	output	w1adj	w2adj	w3adj	w4adj
3	6.6	2.9	4.6	1.3	0	0.100	0.200	0.300	0.400	3.140	0.959	-0.252			
4	5	3	1.6	0.2	1	-0.152									
5	6	3	4.8	1.8	0	-0.152									

Fig. 13.18 Calculating Sigmoid by applying SUMPRODUCT

The dollar signs in the formula are intended to copy to another three weight adjustment cells. For the second weight for `w1`, we use the old one plus the corresponding adjustment. The formula in cell H4 is = `H3 + N3`. This is true for the second `w2`, `w3`, and `w4`, as shown below.

H4 | fx | =H3+N3

	H	I	J	K	L	M	N	O	P	Q
1	------ weights ------------------------				sumproc	sigmoid	- weight adjustments ----------------------			
2	w1	w2	w3	w4	bias	output	w1adj	w2adj	w3adj	w4adj
3	0.100	0.200	0.300	0.400	3.140	0.959	-0.252	-0.111	-0.175	-0.050
4	-0.152	-0.052	0.189	0.225						
5	-0.152									

Fig. 13.19 Weight adjusted (e.g., cell H4 formula = H3 + N3)

The result after we add those functions is shown below. Rows 9 to 142 are hidden to make our presentation easy to understand.

	A	B	C	D	F	H	I	J	K	L	M	N	O	P	Q
1						------ weights ------------------------				sumproc	sigmoid	- weight adjustments --------------------			
2	sepal_le	sepal_w	petal_le	petal_w	class	w1	w2	w3	w4	bias	output	w1adj	w2adj	w3adj	w4adj
3	6.6	2.9	4.6	1.3	0	0.100	0.200	0.300	0.400	3.140	0.959	-0.252	-0.111	-0.175	-0.050
4	5	3	1.6	0.2	1	-0.152	0.089	0.125	0.350	-0.220	0.445	0.685	0.411	0.219	0.027
5	6	3	4.8	1.8	0	0.534	0.501	0.344	0.378	7.034	0.999	-0.005	-0.003	-0.004	-0.002
6	5.1	3.5	1.4	0.2	1	0.528	0.498	0.340	0.376	4.988	0.993	0.000	0.000	0.000	0.000
7	4.9	3.1	1.5	0.1	1	0.529	0.498	0.340	0.376	4.681	0.991	0.000	0.000	0.000	0.000
8	6.1	2.8	4	1.3	0	0.529	0.498	0.340	0.376	6.470	0.998	-0.009	-0.004	-0.006	-0.002
143	7.2	3	5.8	1.6	0	0.176	1.343	-1.708	-0.492	-5.397	0.005	0.000	0.000	0.000	0.000
144	7.6	3	6.6	2.1	0	0.176	1.343	-1.708	-0.492	-6.941	0.001	0.000	0.000	0.000	0.000
145	5	3.5	1.3	0.3	1	0.176	1.343	-1.708	-0.492	3.212	0.961	0.007	0.005	0.002	0.000
146	6.5	3	5.5	1.8	0	0.183	1.348	-1.706	-0.492	-5.035	0.006	0.000	0.000	0.000	0.000
147	5.6	3	4.1	1.3	0	0.183	1.348	-1.707	-0.492	-2.568	0.071	-0.026	-0.014	-0.019	-0.006
148	6	2.2	4	1	0	0.157	1.334	-1.726	-0.498	-3.528	0.029	-0.005	-0.002	-0.003	-0.001
149	4.9	3	1.4	0.2	1	0.152	1.332	-1.729	-0.499	2.220	0.902	0.042	0.026	0.012	0.002
150	5.5	2.6	4.4	1.2	0	0.194	1.358	-1.717	-0.497	-3.552	0.028	-0.004	-0.002	-0.003	-0.001
151	5.7	2.8	4.5	1.3	0	0.190	1.356	-1.720	-0.498	-3.508	0.029	-0.005	-0.002	-0.004	-0.001
152	4.4	3.2	1.3	0.2	1	0.185	1.354	-1.724	-0.499	2.807	0.943	0.013	0.010	0.004	0.001
153															

Fig. 13.20 The data set with many hidden rows

If we pay attention to columns F and M for the last several rows, we can find that the model correctly classifies those observations. For example, the true classification for the last five rows is (0, 1, 0, 0, 1), and the estimated outputs are (0.029, 0.902, 0.028, 0.03, and 0.943).

13.11 Training vs. Test Samples

Researchers usually divide the data set into two parts for neural networks: the training and test data sets. The division is usually 75% and 25% test. Thus, readers and students should learn to use Excel to divide a given data set into two parts. The following exercise will use a default data set with 10,000 observations. There are two ways to get the data. Method I downloads the data at http://datayyy.com/i2ft/data/default.csv while Method II issues the following line of code.

```
> .show_default(0)
Windows users: launch Excel and paste
```

The first several lines are shown below.

	A	B	C	D
1	default	student	balance	income
2	No	No	729.526495	44361.6251
3	No	Yes	817.180407	12106.1347
4	No	No	1073.54916	31767.1389
5	No	No	529.250605	35704.4939
6	No	No	785.655883	38463.4959

Fig. 13.21 The several rows of the Student Default data set

First, we generate a column called ID from 1 to the last. This column is optional, and we will explain the underlying logic.

G2   fx =IF(F2>1-$H$1,"train","test")

	A	B	C	D	E	F	G	H	I	J
1	default	student	balance	income	ID	random12	train_test	0.75		
2	No	No	729.526495	44361.6251	1	0.013428	test	=IF(F2>1-$H$1,"train","test")		
3	No	Yes	817.180407	12106.1347	2	0.581469	train			
4	No	No	1073.54916	31767.1389	3	0.704215	train			
5	No	No	529.250605	35704.4939	4	0.399915	train			
6	No	No	785.655883	38463.4959	5	0.987671	train			
7	No	Yes	919.58853	7491.55857	6	0.099643	test			
9996	No	Yes	172.412987	14955.9417	9995	0.568529	train			
9997	No	No	711.55502	52992.3789	9996	0.320383	train			
9998	No	No	757.962918	19660.7218	9997	0.721244	train			
9999	No	No	845.411989	58636.157	9998	0.308634	train			
10000	No	No	1569.00905	36669.1124	9999	0.398755	train			
10001	No	Yes	200.922183	16862.9523	10000	0.404798	train			

Fig. 13.22 Generating an ID column and dividing into training and testing samples

The random seed used is 123. The function in cell G2 is = `IF(F2 > 1-$H$1,"train","test")`. In other words, for any random numbers larger than 0.25, the observations will be classified as trading observations. The next step will be sorting the data by column G and copying those two sets. The ID column will be used when sorting those two data sets.

7512	No	No	711.55502	52992.3789	9996	0.320383	train	train
7513	No	No	757.962918	19660.7218	9997	0.721244	train	train
7514	No	No	845.411989	58636.157	9998	0.308634	train	train
7515	No	No	1569.00905	36669.1124	9999	0.398755	train	train
7516	No	Yes	200.922183	16862.9523	10000	0.404798	train	train
7517	No	No	729.526495	44361.6251	1	0.013428	test	test
7518	No	Yes	919.58853	7491.55857	6	0.099643	test	test
7519	No	Yes	1220.58375	13268.5622	12	0.022889	test	test
7520	No	No	237.045114	28251.6953	13	0.136723	test	test
7521	No	No	606.742343	44994.5558	14	0.117893	test	test

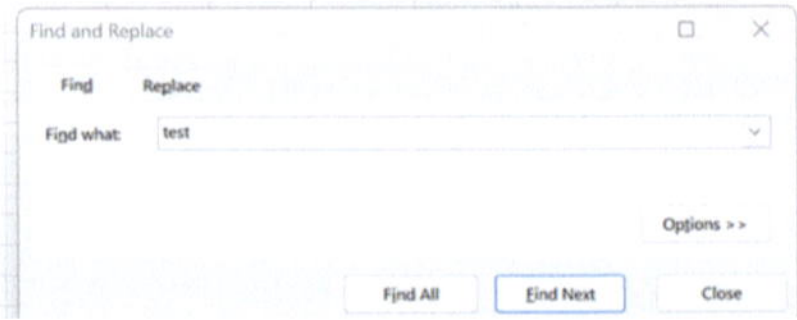

Fig. 13.23 Sorting the data set to separate two groups

The first several lines of the training data set are shown below. With IDs, we can easily manually compare this data set with the original one. However, we must delete this ID and random number columns when using this data set.

	A	B	C	D	E	F	G	H
1	default	student	balance	income	ID	random12	train_test	train_test
2	No	Yes	817.180407	12106.1347	2	0.581469	train	train
3	No	No	1073.54916	31767.1389	3	0.704215	train	train
4	No	No	529.250605	35704.4939	4	0.399915	train	train
5	No	No	785.655883	38463.4959	5	0.987671	train	train
6	No	No	825.513331	24905.2266	7	0.938414	train	train
7	No	Yes	808.667504	17600.4513	8	0.997284	train	train
8	No	No	1161.05785	37468.5293	9	0.297861	train	train

Fig. 13.24 The several lines of the training data set

The first several lines of the test sample are shown below.

	A	B	C	D	E	F	G	H
1	default	student	balance	income	ID	random12	train_test	train_test
2	No	No	729.5265	44361.63	1	0.013428	test	test
3	No	Yes	919.5885	7491.559	6	0.099643	test	test
4	No	Yes	1220.584	13268.56	12	0.022889	test	test
5	No	No	237.0451	28251.7	13	0.136723	test	test
6	No	No	606.7423	44994.56	14	0.117893	test	test

Fig. 13.25 The several lines of the testing data set

13.12 Rules: A One-Layer One-Neuron Neural Networks

From this section onwards, we will discuss our hidden functions. Again, we start from the simplest neural networks with just one layer and one neuron. Assume that we have n variables (x_1, x_2, …, x_n) with a binary output of or 0, i.e., our classification. Several rules are given below.

Rule #1: After running a certain program, we end up with `n+3` estimated parameters.
Rule #2: We apply the Sigmoid function from the input to the hidden layer by using `n+1` estimated parameters.
Rule #3: We apply the Sigmoid function the second time from the hidden layer by using 2 estimated parameters.

Now, let `n` = 2, i.e., have just two input variables with one hidden layer. Assume after running a certain program, we end up with just 5 estimates: $\beta_{0,}^{\rightarrow h}$, $\beta_1^{\rightarrow h}$, $\beta_2^{\rightarrow h}$, $\beta_0^{\rightarrow o}$. and $\beta_{1,}^{\rightarrow h}$. $\beta_{0,}^{\rightarrow h}$ ($\beta_{0,}^{\rightarrow o}$) is the first coefficient (a constant) from our input to the hidden layer (from the hidden layer to the output). Since we have 2 input variables, the number of estimated parameters will be 3 (2 + 1). Since there is just one value from the input variables to the hidden layer, the estimated parameters will be 2 (1 + 1).

$$h = \frac{1}{1 + e^{-\left(\beta_0 + \beta_1 x_1^{\rightarrow h} + \beta_2 x_2^{\rightarrow h}\right)}} \tag{13.3}$$

The final output, the probability of the observation belonging to the hypothesis category, is given below.

$$\mathrm{p} = \frac{1}{1 + e^{-\left(\beta_0^{\rightarrow o} + \beta_1^{\rightarrow 0} h\right)}} \tag{13.4}$$

In the next few sections, we will show how to get the results.

13.13 Procedure for Building a Neural Networks

For this section, we offer a general procedure for building up a neural network. We assume that we have two input variables with one layer of the simplest neural network. To make the procedure easy to carry out, our hidden function called `.nn()` or other names, such as `.showNN(),.showNN_iris()` and `.showNN_iris2()`, will be used.

Step 1: Input the data
Step 2: Normalize the data, such as $x^{new} = \left(x^{old} - min\right)/(max - min))$.
Step 3: run our .nn() function to get the result.
The output has two sets of values:
Input to the neuron: $\beta_0^1, \beta_1^1 and \beta_2^1$.
Neuron to the output: $\beta_0^2, and \beta_1^2$.
Step 4: Get the values from the standard inputs to the neuron
$aa = \beta_0^1 + \beta_1^1 x_1^{std} + \beta_2^1 x_2^{std}$, then $y = \frac{1}{1+e^{-aa}}$
Step 5: From the neuron to the output: $bb = \beta_0^2 + \beta_1^2 y$, then $z = \frac{1}{1+e^{-bb}}$
Step 6: From the neuron to the output: if z > 0.5, the output is 1, otherwise it is 0.

13.14 One-Layer One-Neuron #1: Pass or Fail

We use a straightforward data set with 4 observations and 2 variables. The first variable is the number of hours students spend preparing for an exam, and the second variable is the evaluation of class participation. The raw data occupies cells A1: C5, and the normalized values are in cells D1: E4.

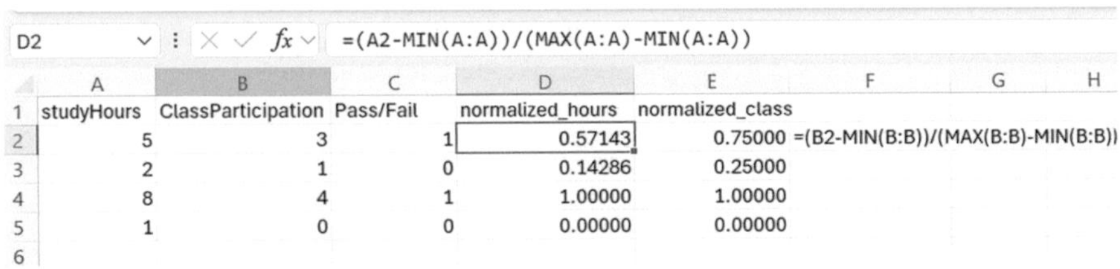
D2 =(A2-MIN(A:A))/(MAX(A:A)-MIN(A:A))

	A	B	C	D	E	F	G	H
1	studyHours	ClassParticipation	Pass/Fail	normalized_hours	normalized_class			
2	5	3	1	0.57143	0.75000	=(B2-MIN(B:B))/(MAX(B:B)-MIN(B:B))		
3	2	1	0	0.14286	0.25000			
4	8	4	1	1.00000	1.00000			
5	1	0	0	0.00000	0.00000			
6								

Fig. 13.26 Normalization

We use the data set above for the function called .showNN(). There are two choice variables: the number of layers (neuron) and a random seed. The second one is for reproduction purposes. After running this function by choosing 1 as the number of hidden layers and 123 as the random seed, we will get the following matrix.

```
error                              0.01367510
reached.threshold                  0.00875548
steps                              52.00000000
Intercept.to.1layhid1              -4.99727565
StudyHours.to.1layhid1             4.86982251
ClassParticipation.to.1layhid1     6.65870831
Intercept.to.Target                -2.50829161
1layhid1.to.Target                 5.22928774
```

Let's look at the first normalized two values: 0.57143 (number of studying hours) and 0.75 (class participation). Let's calculate the h value:

aa = -4.99727565 + 4.86982251*0.57143 + 6.65870831*0.75 = 2.779518

h = 1/(1 + exp(−aa) = 1/(1 + exp(−2.779518)) = 0.9415589

From the hidden layer to the output, we have.

bb = -2.50829161 + 5.22928774*0.9415589 = 2.415391

h = 1/(1 + exp(−bb) = 1/(1 + exp(−2.415391)) = 0.9179934

The probability of the first student passing the exam is very high. If the cutoff point is 0.5, then the classification value for this student will be 1.

13.15 Our Hidden .ShowNN() Function

This function depends on the R package called ‘neuralnet’. Copy and paste the following line to your R console to install it.

```
install.packages("neuralnet").
```

This function is based on the above data set with just 4 observations with 2 variables. By typing .showNN(), we will see the following image.

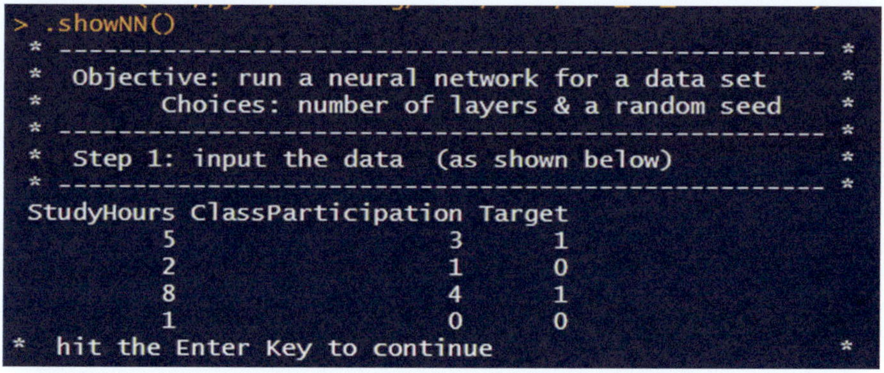

Fig. 13.27 Step 1 of the Neural Network function (.showNN)

The next image shows the original data and normalized data.

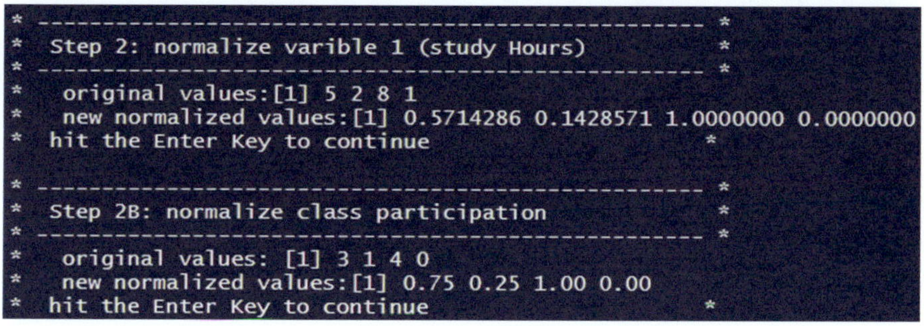

Fig. 13.28 Step 2 of the hidden Neural Network function (.showNN)

For the following two inputs are 1 (the number of hidden layers) and 123 (a random seed), we have:

```
input the number of hidden layers, such as 2
* ------------------------------------------------- *
1
* ------------------------------------------------- *
input a random seed, such as 123
* ------------------------------------------------- *
123
```

Fig. 13.29 Entering the number of hidden layers and random seed

The final output is shown below. The matrix below was used in the previous section.

```
                                        [,1]
error                             0.01367510
reached.threshold                 0.00875548
steps                            52.00000000
Intercept.to.1layhid1            -4.99727565
StudyHours.to.1layhid1            4.86982251
ClassParticipation.to.1layhid1    6.65870831
Intercept.to.Target              -2.50829161
1layhid1.to.Target                5.22928774
[1] "Predicted Values (Pass = 1, Fail = 0):"
     [,1]
[1,]    1
[2,]    0
[3,]    1
[4,]    0
[1] "Accuracy: 100 %"
```

Fig. 13.30 The final output

The graph is shown below.

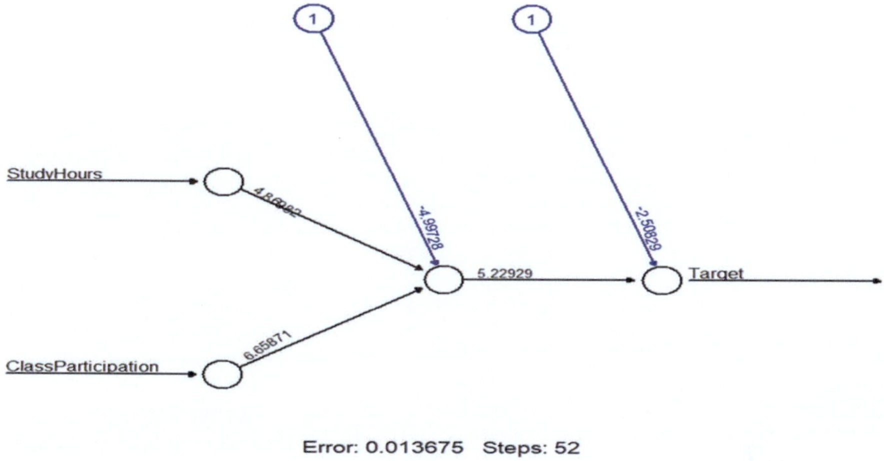

Fig. 13.31 A graphic presentation of the output

The two estimated parameters associated with Study Hours and Class Participation are apparent. The coefficient from the input to the hidden layer is –4.99727, accompanying the slide line. The second slide line is for the intercept from the hidden layer to the output.

13.16 One-Layer One-Neuron #2: Iris Data Set

Based on the famous iris data set, we have generated a function called `.showNN_iris()`. This function classifies a species using just two input variables: petal length and petal width. After typing `.showNN_iris()`, we will start the process.

```
> .showNN_iris()
 * ---------------------------------------------------------------- *
 *   Objective: show Neural Network using the IRIS data               *
 *              using Petal.Length and Petal.Width                    *
 * ---------------------------------------------------------------- *
 *   Do you want to print the first two lines?                        *
 * ---------------------------------------------------------------- *
1    yes
2    no
1
  Sepal.Length Sepal.Width Petal.Length Petal.Width Species
1          5.1         3.5          1.4         0.2  setosa
2          4.9         3.0          1.4         0.2  setosa
 * ---------------------------------------------------------------- *
 *   Enter a random seed for reproduction, such as 123               *
 * ---------------------------------------------------------------- *
```

Fig. 13.32 An illustrational Neural Network using the Iris data set

The following few inputs are a random seed for reproduction, which species to classify, and the number of layers, as shown below.

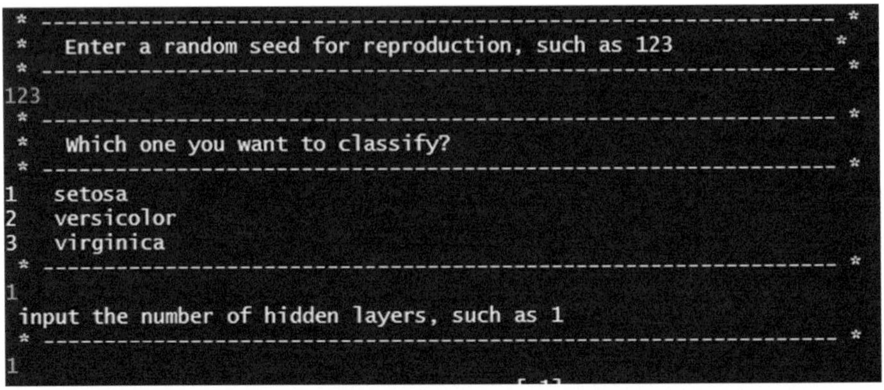

Fig. 13.33 Entering a random seed and which item to be classified

The output (matrix) is shown below.

```
                                      [,1]
error                               0.014652129
reached.threshold                   0.009314983
steps                              92.000000000
Intercept.to.1layhid1              -5.002629887
Petal.Length.to.1layhid1            8.338222511
Petal.Width.to.1layhid1            10.127108314
Intercept.to.Species == "setosa"    4.198225511
1layhid1.to.Species == "setosa"    -8.970712265
```

The corresponding graph is shown below.

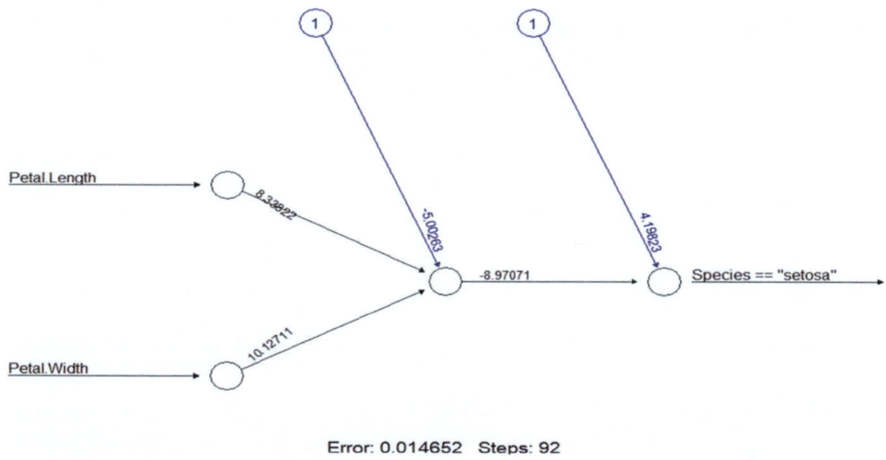

Fig. 13.34 A graphic presentation of the output

After running `.showNN_iris()` function with a seed value of 123 and one layer, we can paste the results to Excel.

	A	B	C	D	E	F
1		V1			max	min
2	error	0.014652129		Sepal.Length	7.9	4.3
3	reached.threshold	0.009314983		Sepal.Width	4.4	2
4	steps	92		Petal.Length	6.9	1
5	Intercept.to.1layhid1	-5.002629887		Petal.Width	2.5	0.1
6	Petal.Length.to.1layhid1	8.338222511				
7	Petal.Width.to.1layhid1	10.12710831				
8	Intercept.to.Species == "setosa"	4.198225511				
9	1layhid1.to.Species == "setosa"	-8.970712265				

Fig. 13.35 Copying the output to Excel

Let's use the first several lines of the data set to test whether they belong to '`Iris-setosa`' or not.

J7 fx =(J2-$F$4)/($E$4-$F$4)

	D	E	F	G	H	I	J	K	L	M
1		max	min		sepal_length	sepal_width	petal_length	petal_width	class	
2	Sepal.Length	7.9	4.3		5.1	3.5	1.4	0.2	Iris-setosa	
3	Sepal.Width	4.4	2		4.9	3	1.4	0.2	Iris-setosa	
4	Petal.Length	6.9	1		4.7	3.2	1.3	0.2	Iris-setosa	
5	Petal.Width	2.5	0.1		4.6	3.1	1.5	0.2	Iris-setosa	
6										
7							0.06779661	-0.13559322	=(K2-$F$4)/($E$4-$F$4)	

Fig. 13.36 Several observations for testing purposes

As the first step, we normalize those two variables. The formula in cell J7 is = `(J2-$F$4)/($E$4-$F$4)` and the formula in cell K7 is = `(K2-$F$4)/($E$4-$F$4)`.

	B	C	I	J	K	L	M
1	V1		sepa	petal_length	petal_width	class	
2	0.014652129		3.5	1.4	0.2	Iris-setosa	
3	0.009314983		3	1.4	0.2	Iris-setosa	
4	92		3.2	1.3	0.2	Iris-setosa	
5	-5.002629887		3.1	1.5	0.2	Iris-setosa	
6	8.338222511						
7	10.12710831			0.06779661	-0.13559322	=(K2-$F$4)/($E$4-$F$4)	
8	4.198225511						
9	-8.970712265	to the neuron		-5.81049389	=B5+J7*B6+K7*B7		
10		Sigmoid		0.002987	=1/(1+EXP(-J9))		
11		to the output		4.17142998	=B8+B9*J10		
12		Sigmoid		0.98480429	=1/(1+EXP(-J11))		
13				Setosa	=IF(J12>0.5,"Setosa","No")		

Fig. 13.37 Classifying one observation

There are two steps: (1) from the normalized inputs to the hidden layer and (2) from the hidden layer to the final putout. In cell J9 the formula is = `B5 + J7*B6 + K7*B7` and the formula in cell J10 is = `1/(1 + EXP(-J9))`, i.e., applying the Sigmoid function. After that, in cell J11, the formula is = `B8 + B9*J10` and in cell J12, the formula is = `1/(1 + EXP(-J11))`. Since the final value is 98%, i.e., it has a 98% chance of being '`Iris-setosa`'.

13.17 A One-Layer Two-Neuron Neural Networks: Iris Data

The structure of a two-hidden layer case is more complex than that of just one hidden layer. The following graph shows the relationship between inputs, two hidden layers, and the output. In this case, we still use just two input variables.

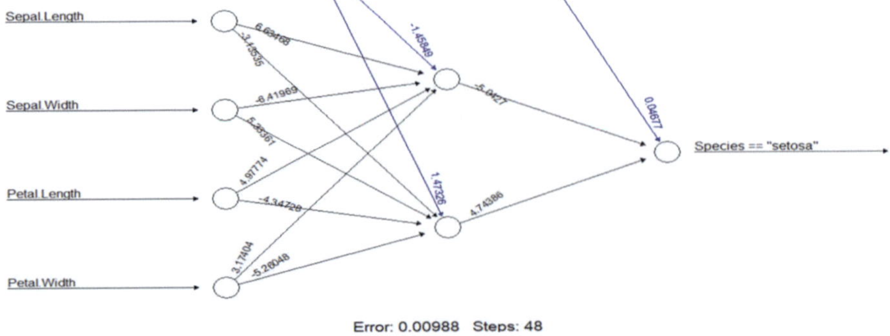

Fig. 13.38 A graphic presentation of one-hidden layer with two neurons

We can figure out how many parameters and their relationship with the above graph. Since we have four input variables, we need five parameters to calculate the hidden layer (neuron) value. This is also true for the upper layer (neuron). Thus, we have 10 (5*2) parameters. With 2 values, we need another three parameters to get the final output. Therefore, the total number is 13, as shown below. The following are the two outputs from running `.showNN_iris2()` with a random seed of 333.

	A	B	C	D	E	F
1		V1			max	min
2	error	0.009879887		Sepal.Length	7.9	4.3
3	reached.threshold	0.009092754		Sepal.Width	4.4	2
4	steps	48		Petal.Length	6.9	1
5	Intercept.to.1layhid1	-1.45849495		Petal.Width	2.5	0.1
6	Sepal.Length.to.1layhid1	6.634680993				
7	Sepal.Width.to.1layhid1	-6.419689792			13 =COUNT(B5:B17)	
8	Petal.Length.to.1layhid1	4.977738971				
9	Petal.Width.to.1layhid1	3.174039404				
10	Intercept.to.1layhid2	1.473261381				
11	Sepal.Length.to.1layhid2	-3.135346118				
12	Sepal.Width.to.1layhid2	5.333607737				
13	Petal.Length.to.1layhid2	-4.347282539				
14	Petal.Width.to.1layhid2	-5.260482479				
15	Intercept.to.Species == "setosa	0.046767602				
16	1layhid1.to.Species == "setosa'	-5.042703616				
17	1layhid2.to.Species == "setosa'	4.743861619				

Fig. 13.39 The final result

13.18 Our Hidden `.nn ()` Function

This is a more general function since it gets data from a user's Excel file or clipboard. After typing `.nn()`, you will see the following image. For the first step, we copy a data set from Excel and then hit the Enter Key.

```
* ------------------------------------------------------------ *
*   Objective: run a Neural Network with a given data set       *
* ------------------------------------------------------------ *
*  Step 1: copy your data then hit the enter key                *
* ------------------------------------------------------------ *
```

Fig. 13.40 Step 1 of the hidden function called .nn

Assume that we have the following data set. Columns A: D are the original data set. Since we plan to use student, balance, and income as our input x variables to explain whether a person will default, we have to assign students a numerical value.

	A	B	C	D	E	F	G	H
1	default	student	balance	income	default	student	balance	income
2	No	No	729.5265	44361.62507	No	0	729.5265	44361.63
3	No	Yes	817.1804	12106.1347	No	1	817.1804	12106.13
4	No	No	1073.549	31767.13895	No	0	1073.549	31767.14
5	No	No	529.2506	35704.49394	No	0	529.2506	35704.49
6	No	No	785.6559	38463.49588	No	0	785.6559	38463.5
7	No	Yes	919.5885	7491.558572	No	1	919.5885	7491.559

Fig. 13.41 The several lines of the student default data set

After copying data from columns E to H, we hit the Enter Key. Two more questions are shown below. Since the answer is yes for the second question, we will see three observations (compare them with values from E2:H4) in the above Excel image.

```
*   Step 1B: Does your data set include a header?                              *
*    1          yes                                                            *
*    2          no                                                             *
1
*    Step 1C: Do you want to print the first three lines?                      *
* ---------------------------------------------------------------------------- *
1    yes
2    no
1
 default student    balance    income
      No        0  729.5265 44361.63
      No        1  817.1804 12106.13
      No        0 1073.5492 31767.14
```

Fig. 13.42 Steps 1B and 1C of the hidden function

For Step 2, we will tell the underlying software which column will be used as our target. Since the first column shows whether a person defaults or not, we choose 1.

```
* ---------------------------------------------------------------------------- *
*    Step 2: Which column is your target (class, default, etc.)                *
* ---------------------------------------------------------------------------- *
1
* ---------------------------------------------------------------------------- *
*    Paste the max and min values for several variables to Excel              *
*         then hit the Enter Key to continue                                   *
* ---------------------------------------------------------------------------- *
```

Fig. 13.43 Step 2 of the hidden function

The max and min values pasted to Excel are shown below.

J	K	L
	max	min
student	1	0
balance	2654.323	0
income	73554.23	771.9677

Fig. 13.44 The maximums and minimums of three variables

After getting the output matrix for a given data set, we will use those maximum and minimum values to normalize our input values. The formula will be `x_new = (x_old-min)/(max-min)`. By printing a few lines, users can easily verify the accuracy of normalization.

```
* ------------------------------------------------------------------------ *
*   Do you want to print 3 lines of the normalized observations          *
* ------------------------------------------------------------------------ *
1     yes
2     no
1
* ------------------------------------------------------------------------ *
default student    balance    income
     No        0 0.2748447 0.5989049
     No        1 0.3078678 0.1557270
     No        0 0.4044532 0.4258616
```

Fig. 13.45 Printed three lines

The next two questions are for a random seed and the number of hidden layers. For the random seed, we use 123 and enter 1 for just one hidden layer.

```
* ------------------------------------------------------------------------ *
*   Step 3: Enter a random seed for reproduction, such as 123            *
* ------------------------------------------------------------------------ *
123
Step 4: input the number of hidden layers, such as 1 or 2               *
* ------------------------------------------------------------------------ *
1
```

Fig. 13.46 Steps 3 and 4: a random seed and number of hidden layers

The following image shows the output matrix, which can be copied to our Excel.

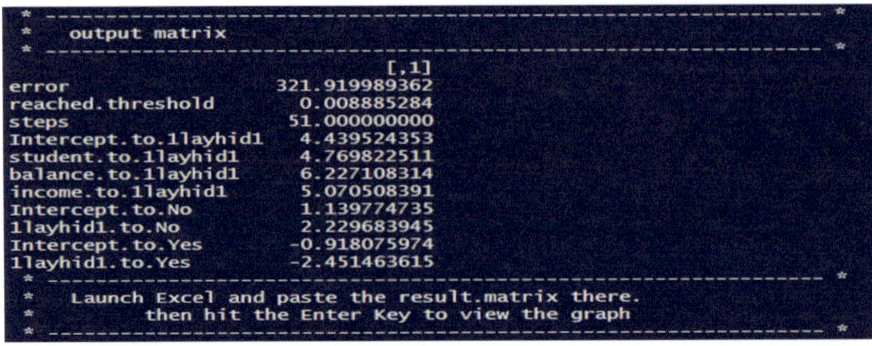

```
* ---------------------------------------------------------------- *
*   output matrix
* ---------------------------------------------------------------- *
                                       [,1]
error                         321.919989362
reached.threshold               0.008885284
steps                          51.000000000
Intercept.to.1layhid1           4.439524353
student.to.1layhid1             4.769822511
balance.to.1layhid1             6.227108314
income.to.1layhid1              5.070508391
Intercept.to.No                 1.139774735
1layhid1.to.No                  2.229683945
Intercept.to.Yes               -0.918075974
1layhid1.to.Yes                -2.451463615
* ---------------------------------------------------------------- *
*   Launch Excel and paste the result.matrix there.
*           then hit the Enter Key to view the graph
* ---------------------------------------------------------------- *
```

Fig. 13.47 Copying the output matrix to Excel

The corresponding image is shown below. Please pay attention to the number of output nodes. We have two instead of one.

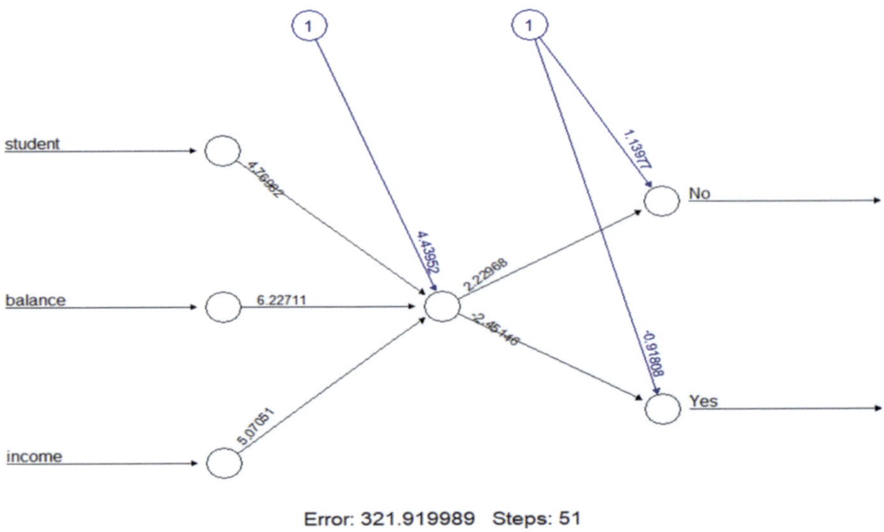

Fig. 13.48 A graphic presentation of the final result

13.19 The Impact of a Dummy Variable

This section is closely associated with the previous section. The only difference in input is that we have 1 or 0 for the default column instead of yes and no.

	A	B	C	D	E	F	G	H
1	default	student	balance	income	default	student	balance	income
2	No	No	729.5265	44361.62507	0	0	729.5265	44361.63
3	No	Yes	817.1804	12106.1347	1	1	817.1804	12106.13
4	No	No	1073.549	31767.13895	0	0	1073.549	31767.14
5	No	No	529.2506	35704.49394	0	0	529.2506	35704.49
6	No	No	785.6559	38463.49588	0	0	785.6559	38463.5
7	No	Yes	919.5885	7491.558572	1	1	919.5885	7491.559
8	No	No	825.5133	24905.22658	0	0	825.5133	24905.23

Fig. 13.49 Several lines of the student default data set

The graph is shown below. Now, we have just one output instead of two.

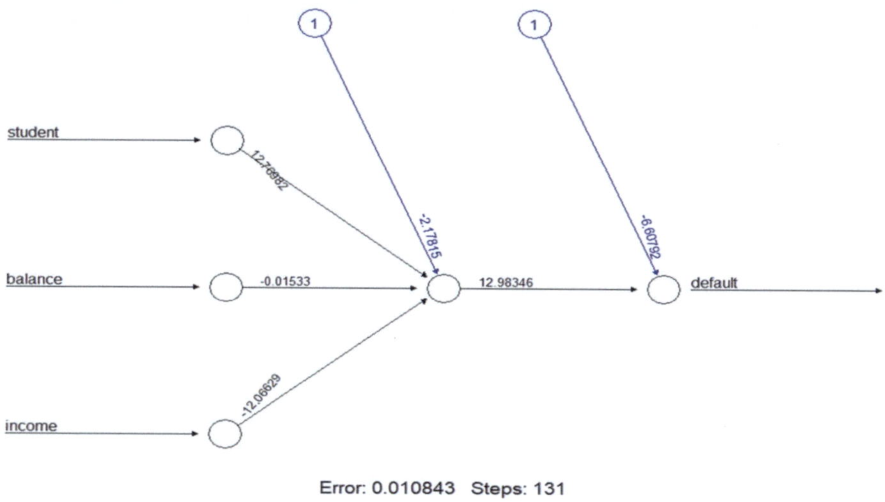

Fig. 13.50 A graphic presentation of the final output

The corresponding output matrix is shown below.

```
 * ------------------------------------------------------------- *
 *   output matrix
 * ------------------------------------------------------------- *
                                    [,1]
error                        0.010842501
reached.threshold            0.008605222
steps                      131.000000000
Intercept.to.1layhid1       -2.178148108
student.to.1layhid1         12.769822511
balance.to.1layhid1         -0.015333490
income.to.1layhid1         -12.066291609
Intercept.to.default        -6.607917343
1layhid1.to.default         12.983464987
```

Fig. 13.51 The output matrix

If using the iris data with one hidden layer and a random seed of 123, we will get the following image. To save space, the related output matrix is not presented here.

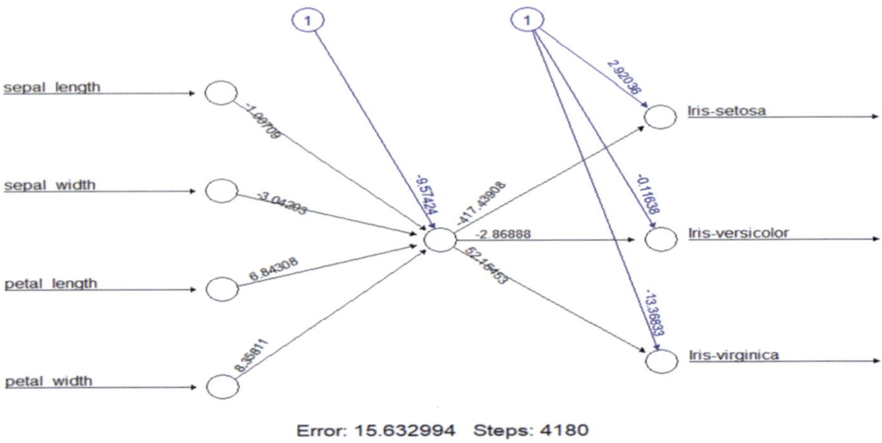

Fig. 13.52 A graphic presentation of the output

13.20 Our Hidden Functions

For the hidden functions related to this chapter, we can use the function `.searchHiddenFuntions()`, abbreviated as `.sf()`.

```
> .sf(13)
 CHAPTER                              NAME            SHORTCUT
      13 install.packages('neuralnet')
      13 .show_irs()                         # data set
      13 .show_default()                     # data set
      13 .show_heartDisease()                # data set
      13 .show_titanic()                     # data set
      13 .showNN()                           # need 'neuralnet
      13 .showNN_iris()                      # need 'neuralnet
      13 .showNN_iris2()                     # need 'neuralnet
      13 .nn()                               # need 'neuralnet
>
```

Fig. 13.53 The hidden functions related to Chapter 13

Appendix A: After launching R, issue one of the following lines of R code

```
source("http://datayyy.com/i2ft/week13.txt")
.chapter13
```

```
> .chapter13
function(i=0){
" i  Chapter 13: Neural Network using Excel      i  data sets/hidden functions
  -  -------------------------------------      --  ----------------------
  1  What is a neural network?                  21   data: .show_iris
  2  Basic concepts                             22        : .show_default
  3  Review of sigmoid function                 23        : .show_hitters
  4  Rules                                      24        : .show_heartDisease
  5        : one example                        25  function: .showNN_iris
  6  Normalization
  7  Procedure
  8  Categorical values to numeric ones
  9  One-layer case #1: Pass or fail
 10      : result
 11      : result
 12  One-layer case #2: iris
 13      .show_iris2
 14  Two-layer
 15      .shownn()
 16      .show_iris2()
 17  .nn() function: pass/fail
 18       : pass/fail
 19  Videos
 20  Links

 Example #1:>.c13    # see the above list
 Example #2:>.c13()  # see the above list
 Example #3:>.c13(1) # see the 1st explanation
```

Fig. 13.54 The contents of Chapter 13 [note: the above image is a updated one]

Exercises

13.1 What is a Neural Network?

13.2 What is the definition of a hidden layer?

13.3 Are there any differences between a neuron and a hidden layer?

13.4 What is the definition of a Sigmoid function?

13.5 Briefly explain a neural network and describe its essential components: neurons, weights, biases, and activation functions.

13.6 Explain the advantages and limitations of using Excel for neural network computations.

13.7 Matrix Multiplication for Neural Networks: Use Excel to calculate the dot product of two matrices, representing weights and inputs for a simple neural network layer.

13.8 Demonstrate Excel data normalization by transforming data points into values between 0 and 1 using min-max scaling.

13.9 Create a binary classification model in Excel that predicts pass/fail outcomes based on test scores and previous academic data.

13.10 Write an Excel formula to implement the sigmoid activation function. Apply it to a range of input values and interpret the output.

13.11 Use Excel to calculate the mean squared error (MSE) for a neural network's predictions and actual values.

13.12 Using Excel, demonstrate how to split a dataset into training and testing sets by sampling 80% of the data for training and the rest for testing.

13.13 Use Excel's `RAND()` function to initialize random weights for a simple neural network and discuss why initialization is essential.

13.14 Given a confusion matrix for a binary classification model, calculate accuracy, precision, recall, and F1 score using Excel formulas.

13.15 Test various learning rates and activation functions on a sample dataset in Excel and analyze how these changes affect model accuracy.

13.16 Demonstrate how feature scaling affects a neural network's performance in Excel by comparing results with and without scaled input data.

13.17 This chapter shows how to use Excel to build a one-layer, one-neuron Neural Network. The first several lines of observations are given below. What happens if we don't randomize the data set and use the original data set directly?

F2 fx =IF(E2=$E$2,1,0)

	A	B	C	D	E	F
1	sepal_length	sepal_width	petal_length	petal_width	class	true_output
2	5.1	3.5	1.4	0.2	Iris-setosa	1
3	4.9	3	1.4	0.2	Iris-setosa	1
4	4.7	3.2	1.3	0.2	Iris-setosa	1
5	4.6	3.1	1.5	0.2	Iris-setosa	1

Fig. 13.55 Several lines of the Iris data set

13.18 Based on the following output, answer a few questions

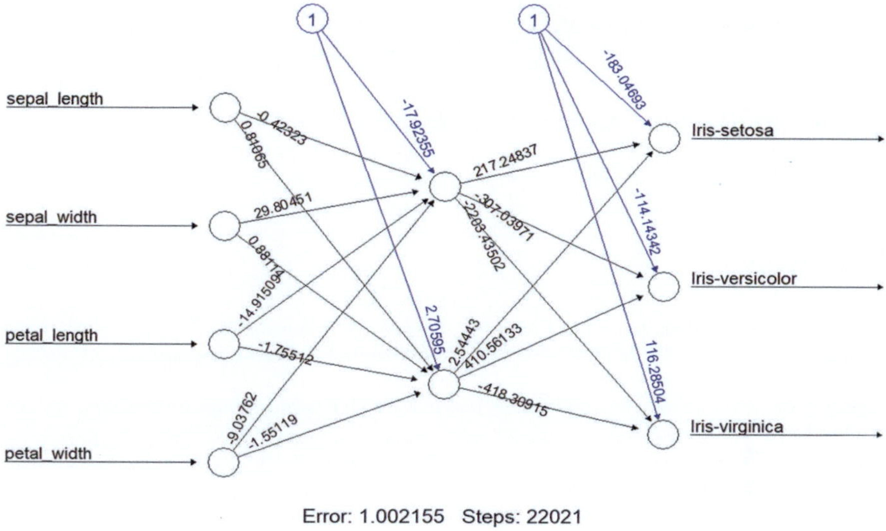

Fig. 13.56 A graphic presentation of an output

a. How many layers and neurons exist?
b. How many input variables exist?
c. Classify the following data.
sepal_length sepal_width petal_length petal_width

6.7	3.0	5.2	2.3
6.3	2.5	5.0	1.9
6.5	3.0	5.2	2.0.

13.19 * This chapter uses Excel to build a Neural Network. The formula used is $w_1x_1 + w_2x_2 + \ldots + w_nx_n$. This is the same as $\beta_1x_1 + \beta_2x_2 + \ldots + \beta_nx_n$. However, for all our hidden functions, the formula used is beta sub 0 plus beta sub 1, x sub 1 plus beta sub 2, x sub 2 plus is $\beta_0+\beta_1x_1+\beta_2x_2++\beta_nx_n$.. In this sense, the latter adds an intercept. Explain why we can (or cannot) add an intercept for the approach using Excel. [Hint: you can redo the same exercise to see if you could add a constant term.]

13.20 Divide the Iris data set into training and test samples. Then,

1. Use Excel to build up a Neural Network.
2. Use the test data to measure your model's performance.
3. Generate a confusion matrix, and
4. Calculate accuracy, precision, recall, and F1.

13.21 Repeat the above exercise using our hidden function, `.nn()`.

13.22 Use Excel to build a Neural Network using the default data set. There are two ways to get the data. Method I: download the default data set at http://datayyy.com/i2ft/data/default.csv, and Method II: Issue the following line.

```
> .show_default(0)
Windows users: launch Excel and paste
```

13.23 Repeat the Above Exercise Using Our Hidden Function, `.Nn()`.

References

Banoula, Mayank, 2023, K-means Clustering Algorithm: Applications, Types, & How Does It Work? https://www.simplilearn.com/tutorials/machine-learning-tutorial/k-means-clustering-algorithm

Bobbitt, Zach, 2022, How to Plot a Decision Tree in R (With Example), https://www.statology.org/plot-decision-tree-in-r/

Clark, Drew. 2020, Neural Network in Excel Example, https://www.mynextemployee.com/post/neural-network-in-excel-example

Hitter data set, https://rdrr.io/cran/ISLR/man/Hitters.html

IBM, What is the k-nearest neighbors (KNN) algorithm?, https://www.ibm.com/topics/knn

Kurama, Vihar, and Jessica Powers, 2022, Unsupervised Learning with Python: A Beginner's Guide,https://builtin.com/data-science/unsupervised-learning-python

Machine Learning (in Finance), https://corporatefinanceinstitute.com/resources/data-science/machine-learning-in-finance/

Parag's Web, Hitters data set, https://pmagunia.com/dataset/r-dataset-package-islr-hitters#:~:text=The%20Hitters%20data%20set%20is%20found%20in%20the,load%20the%20data%20into%20a%20variable%20called%20Hitters.

Penick, HJ, 2023, Neural Net in Excel, https://getneuralnet.com/neural-net-in-excel/

UCI Machine Learning Repository, https://archive.ics.uci.edu/

UCI Iris data set, https://archive.ics.uci.edu/dataset/53/iris

Yen, Leon, 2024, Building a Neural Network in Excel: A 6-Step How-To Guide. https://www.datamation.com/big-data/neural-network-in-excel/

14 Smart Contracts

Knowledge related to smart contracts is vitally important to understanding FinTech. The primary reason is that various smart contracts carry out many dApp (Deep Applications) in Finance. To have a good grasp of smart contracts, hands-on experience is vital. Unfortunately, readers or students must understand a programming language called Solidity when writing a smart contract (in terms of the Ethereum blockchain). Teaching a programming language is beyond the scope of this course/book. In this chapter, the following topics will be covered:

- Definition of smart contracts and their five metaphors
- Properties of smart contracts
- MetaMask and Remix
- Smart contract: Hello World!
- Smart contract: money transfer
- Verified smart contract
- More on Solidity

Note that the second half of the chapter would be optional to have a tradeoff since it discusses how to copy and paste smart contracts written in Solidity.

14.1 Definition of a Smart Contract

A smart contract can be viewed as a self-executing agreement with the terms of the agreement directly written into code. When conditions are met, the contract automatically executes and enforces the terms. According to Ethereum, "Smart contracts are the fundamental building blocks of Ethereum's application layer. They are computer programs stored on the blockchain that follow 'if this then

Y. Yan, *Introduction to FinTech using Excel*, Springer Texts in Business and Economics, https://doi.org/10.1007/978-3-031-89779-5_14

that' logic and are guaranteed to execute according to the rules defined by its code, which cannot be changed once created."

14.2 Metaphor #1: A Vending Machine

A smart contract can be compared to a vending machine, where specific inputs always lead to predetermined outcomes.

Step 1: You choose the item you want.
Step 2: The machine shows the price of the item.
Step 3: You pay the required amount.
Step 4: The vending machine checks if you've paid the correct amount.
Step 5: Once verified, the machine releases the item.

The machine will only dispense the product if all conditions are satisfied. Nothing is dispensed if you don't choose a product or provide enough money. Similarly, smart contracts are carried out automatically when all the required conditions are met.

14.3 Metaphor #2: Go Fund Me

Here is the second way to describe a smart contract. Imagine a so-called Go-fund-me organization that serves as an intermediary. Anyone with a good reason can launch a Go-fund-me project with a target amount. The organization will keep the money until the target is reached. If the target is reached, the intermediary will give the money to the person or organization that launched the project. Otherwise, the funds will be returned to the donors.

14.4 Metaphor #3: A Music Concert

Assume that an organizer wants to have a music event. Because of the cost, they worry about selling enough tickets to cover the cost. Now, there is a trusted organization that keeps an escrow account for selling the tickers. If the amount reaches the target sales, they pass the money to the music organizer, and the organizer starts the music. If not, the trusted party will return the funds to the ticker buyers after deducting a small amount as the service fee.

14.5 Metaphor #4: A Rental Lockbox

Imagine renting a vacation home that uses a digital lockbox for the keys. The lockbox operates like a smart contract.

Step 1: You book the rental and pay the required amount online.
Step 2: The system verifies the payment and automatically sends you a unique code to unlock the box at the property.
Step 3: When you arrive, you enter the code, and the lockbox opens, giving you access to the keys.
Step 4: The code expires once the rental period ends, and you can no longer access the lockbox.

Like in a smart contract, once all the conditions (payment, rental period) are met, the contract executes automatically without needing a third-party intermediary.

14.6 Metaphor #5: An Escrow Account

An escrow account acts like a smart contract in a home purchase transaction.

Step 1: The buyer agrees to purchase a home and deposits the agreed-upon amount into an escrow account.
Step 2: Once all the legal documents are signed, the seller agrees to transfer the property to the buyer.
Step 3: The escrow service ensures that the buyer's funds and the seller's documents are in order before the transaction is finalized.
Step 4: Once all conditions are met, the escrow service releases the money to the seller and transfers ownership of the property to the buyer.

In this scenario, the escrow service guarantees neither party can back out without meeting their obligations, just like a smart contract automates and ensures that both sides follow predefined terms.

14.7 The Properties of Smart Contracts

Table 14.1 lists a few fundamental properties of a smart contract.

In the following few sections, we will explain some of those properties.

Table 14.1 Main properties of a smart contract

#	Explanation
1	Automatic executed
2	Decentralized and transparent
3	Predictable outcomes
4	Smart contracts have no private key
5	A smart contract can receive a transfer

14.8 Automatic Execution

The key advantage of a smart contract is that it runs clear, predefined code automatically when certain conditions are satisfied. There's no need for human involvement to interpret or negotiate the outcome, eliminating the requirement for trusted intermediaries.

For instance, you could create a smart contract to hold money in escrow for a child, which allows them to access the funds only after a specific date. If they attempt to withdraw the money before that time, the contract won't execute. Another example could be a contract that automatically transfers a digital car title to you when you complete payment to the dealer.

14.9 Predictable Outcomes

Traditional contracts can be unclear because they depend on humans to interpret and enforce them. This can lead to differing interpretations, such as two judges arriving at different conclusions, resulting in inconsistent decisions and unequal outcomes. Smart contracts eliminate this uncertainty. They operate strictly according to the terms written in their code, ensuring they consistently produce the same result under identical conditions.

14.10 Platforms and Languages Used

There are several crypto-related blockchains where smart contracts can be run. However, the languages used might be different. In addition, some cryptos depend on others' blockchains to run their smart contracts (Table 14.2).

Table 14.2 Blockchains, Languages where smart contracts can be run

Crypto	Platform	Language
Ethereum	Remix, https://remix.ethereum.org	Solidity
Solana	Solana Playground	Rust, C, and C++
Avalanche	https://subnets.avax.network/c-chain	EVM, Solidity
Cardano	Plutus Playground	Haskell
Polkadot	Parity Substrate	Rust, WebAssembly
Binance	Binance Chain	Solidity, Vyper
Tezos	SmartPy	Michelson, SmartPy
Algorand	Algorand Developer Portal	Python, Reach, TEAL
Fantom	Fantom Opera	Solidity
EOS	EOSIO	C++

Avalanche has three chains: C-Chain, P-Chain, and X-Chain. The C-Chain is the default smart contract blockchain on Avalanche and enables the creation of any EVM-compatible applications and assets. The Contract Chain (C-Chain) runs on an Ethereum Virtual Machine and is used to deploy smart contracts and connect to dApps.

14.11 MetaMask

MetaMask is a popular software cryptocurrency wallet primarily used to interact with the Ethereum blockchain. It functions as a browser extension or mobile app that enables users to manage their Ethereum-based assets, such as Ether (ETH) and ERC-20 tokens, and connect to decentralized applications (dApps). MetaMask provides users a secure interface to send, receive, and store digital currencies while offering features like private key management, seed phrase recovery, and transaction signing. Its user-friendly interface makes it one of the most accessible entry points for newcomers to decentralized finance (DeFi).

In addition to wallet functionality, MetaMask enables users to interact with smart contracts and decentralized applications. By connecting to dApps, users can perform various blockchain-based activities, such as decentralized trading, yield farming, and NFT transactions, without relying on a centralized intermediary. MetaMask allows users to switch between different Ethereum-compatible networks, such as the Binance Smart Chain or Polygon, and it supports test networks like Rinkeby, which is helpful for developers testing blockchain applications.

14.12 Installation of MetaMask

The procedure to Install MetaMask on a PC (Windows) is given below.

Step 1: Open your web browser. Launch Google Chrome, Firefox, or Microsoft Edge (MetaMask works best with these browsers).
Step 2: Visit the MetaMask website: Go to the official MetaMask website at https://metamask.io.
Step 3: Download the MetaMask extension: Click on the "Download" button, and you will be redirected to the appropriate extension page for your browser (Chrome Web Store for Chrome or Firefox Add-ons for Firefox).
Step 4: Install the extension: Click on "Add to Chrome" (or the equivalent button for your browser), then confirm by clicking "Add Extension." The MetaMask extension will be added to your browser.
Step 5: Launch MetaMask: After installation, you will see the MetaMask fox icon in your browser toolbar. Click on it to open MetaMask.

Step 6: Set up your wallet: You will be prompted to either create a new wallet or import an existing one. If creating a new wallet, follow the prompts to set up a password and securely store your recovery seed phrase (a backup for your account).
Step 7: Start using MetaMask: Once set up, you can use MetaMask to manage Ethereum assets, connect to decentralized applications (dApps), and more.

The procedure to Install MetaMask on a Mac is shown below.

Step 1: Open your preferred browser: Launch Safari, Google Chrome, or Firefox (MetaMask is most compatible with Chrome and Firefox).
Step 2: Navigate to the MetaMask website: Go to https://metamask.io to ensure you download from the official source.
Step 3: Download the MetaMask extension. Click on the "Download" button. Depending on your browser, you'll be directed to the Chrome Web Store, Firefox Add-ons, or another appropriate platform to install the extension.
Step 4: Install the MetaMask extension: Select "Add to Chrome" or "Add to Firefox" (depending on your browser). Confirm the installation by selecting "Add Extension." Once the installation is complete, the MetaMask icon will appear in the browser toolbar.
Step 5: Open MetaMask: Click on the fox icon in the browser toolbar to open MetaMask.
Step 6: Create or import a wallet: If you're a new user, select the "Create a Wallet" option and follow the steps to set up a strong password and save your recovery seed phrase. For existing users, choose the "Import Wallet" option to restore your wallet using the seed phrase.
Step 7: Start managing your crypto assets. After setup, you can use MetaMask to manage Ethereum, connect to dApps, or participate in DeFi activities.

14.13 Illustration of MetaMask

Windows users can click the Extension icon and then MetaMask, as shown below.

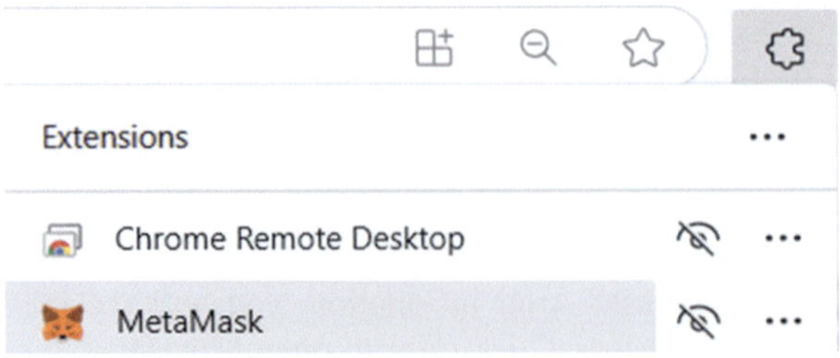

Fig. 14.1 Microsoft extension then MetaMask

After clicking the Fox icon, we must make a new wallet or input an existing one.

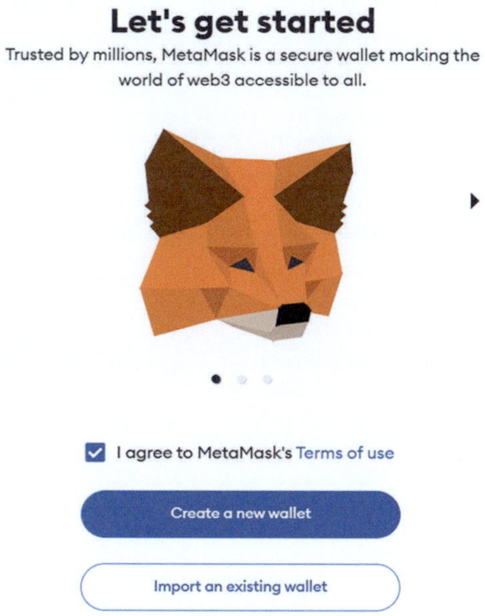

Fig. 14.2 The image of MetaMask

The following image shows that the user has to input 12 recovery words.

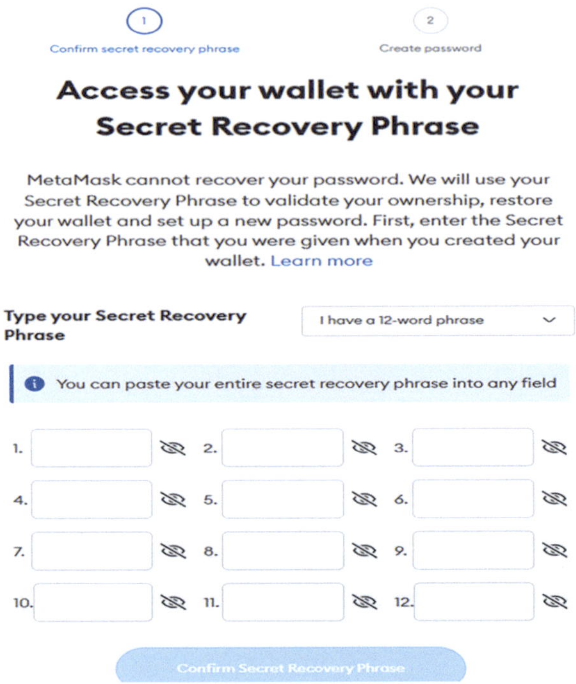

Fig. 14.3 Accessing your wallet

After inputting those 12 words correctly, we will have the following image. Thus, it is essential to keep your initial 12 words in a safe place.

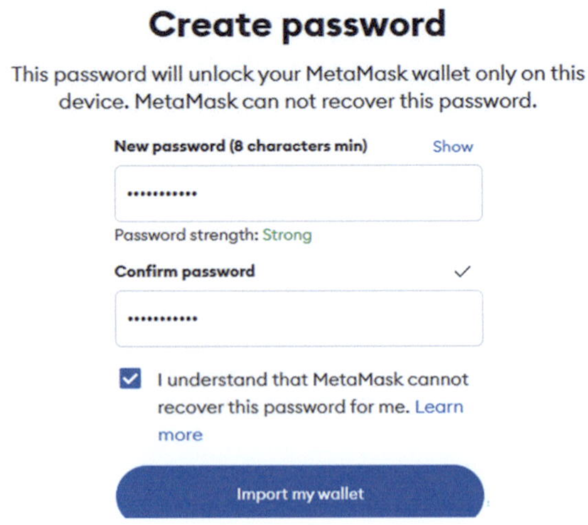

Fig. 14.4 Creating a password

14.14 Remix: Smart Contracts' Platform

The remix offered by Ethereum is the platform to run a smart contract.

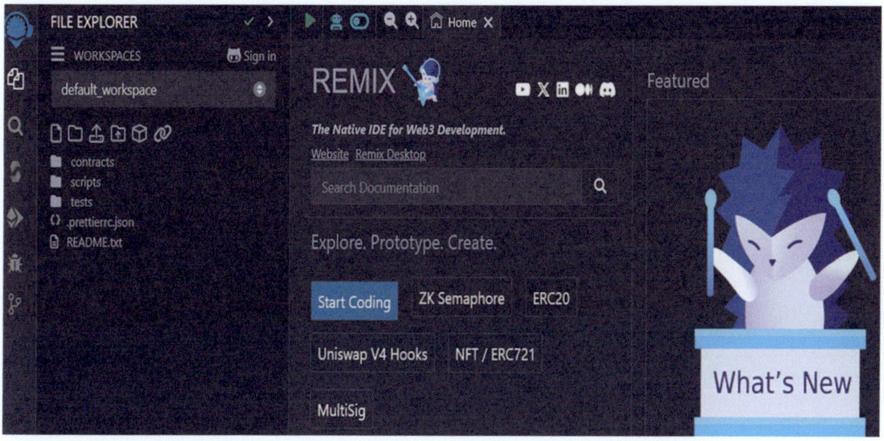

Fig. 14.5 The Remix platform

14.15 The First Example

Below, let's show you how to run a straightforward smart contract. The procedure is given below.

Step 1: Go to https://remix.ethereum.org.

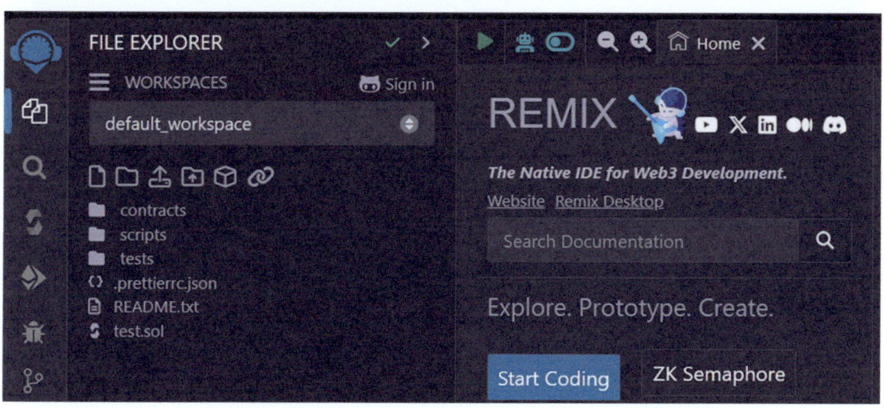

Fig. 14.6 The Remix platform

Step 2: Click the first icon, 'Create a New file.'
Copy and paste the following program.

```
// SPDX-License-Identifier: MIT
// compiler version must be greater than or equal to 0.8.26 and less
than 0.9.0
pragma solidity ^0.8.26;
contract HelloWorld {
string public greet = "Hello World!";
}
```

Source code: https://solidity-by-example.org/hello-world/

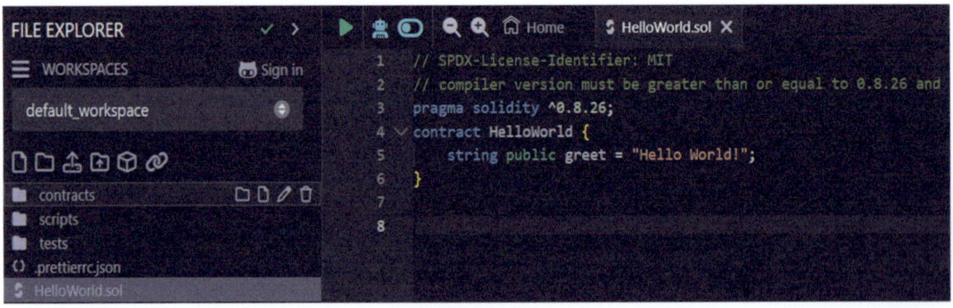

Fig. 14.7 Copying the code to the Remix platform

Step 3: Click the icon on the left to compile the HelloWorld program, as shown below.

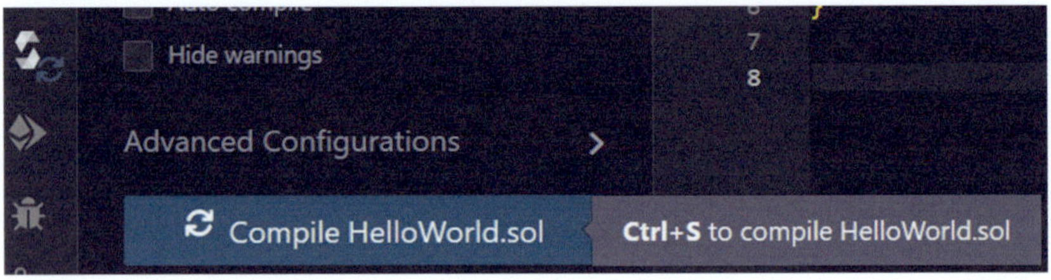

Fig. 14.8 Compiling the program

We will see a green tick if there is no error after compiling.

Fig. 14.9 No error message (a green tick on the left)

Step 4: Click the icon for 'Deploy & run transaction."

Fig. 14.10 "Deploy & run transactions"

The following settings will appear:

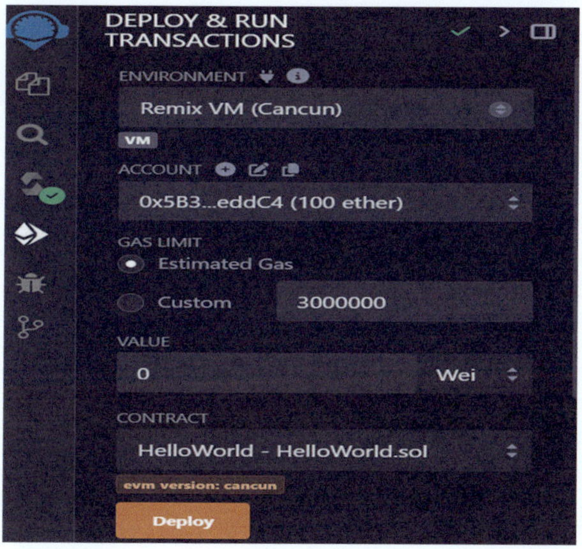

Fig. 14.11 The result after "Deploy & run transactions"

Note that we have “`Remix VM (Cancun)`” under ENVIRONMENT. Cancun is the current fork of Ethereum. Make sure that `HelloWorld-HelloWorld.sol` under CONTRACT is chosen. Now, we can click the ‘Deploy’ icon.

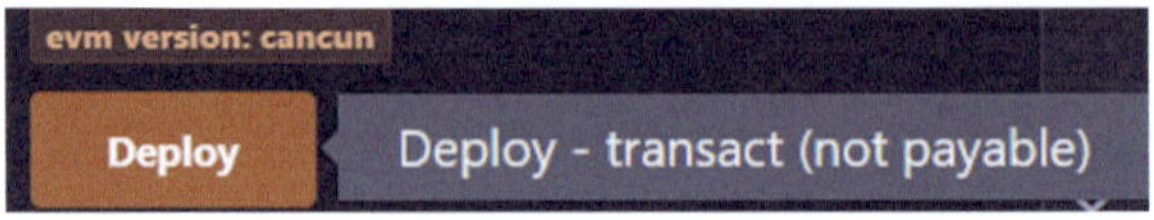

Fig. 14.12 The Deploy icon

If there is no bug, we will see the following entry.

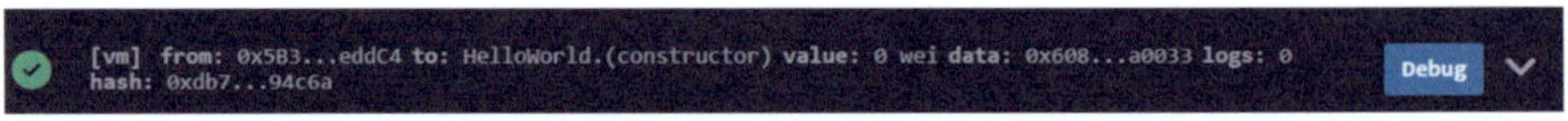

Fig. 14.13 No bug (a green tick on the left)

From the far right of the above image, we click the arrow pointing down; we will see the following information.

```
status  0x1 Transaction mined and execution succeed
transaction hash        0xdb7480d9fd32ebbea12423a9a6b3234f1c3619d36c66cf8b32fba2d453494c6a
block hash              0x7df23d599f00ecd4eaf2fe30aa240029289512d894a870b27428f28100d0d140
block number            1
contract address        0xd9145CCE52D386f254917e481eB44e9943F39138
from                    0x5B38Da6a701c568545dCfcB03FcB875f56beddC4
to      HelloWorld.(constructor)
gas                     227143 gas
transaction cost        197515 gas
execution cost          123915 gas
```

Fig. 14.14 The status

Based on the above information, the transaction is successfully executed with both hashes for transaction and block.

14.16 Debugger

We will get more information after clicking the ‘debug’ blue icon, as shown below.

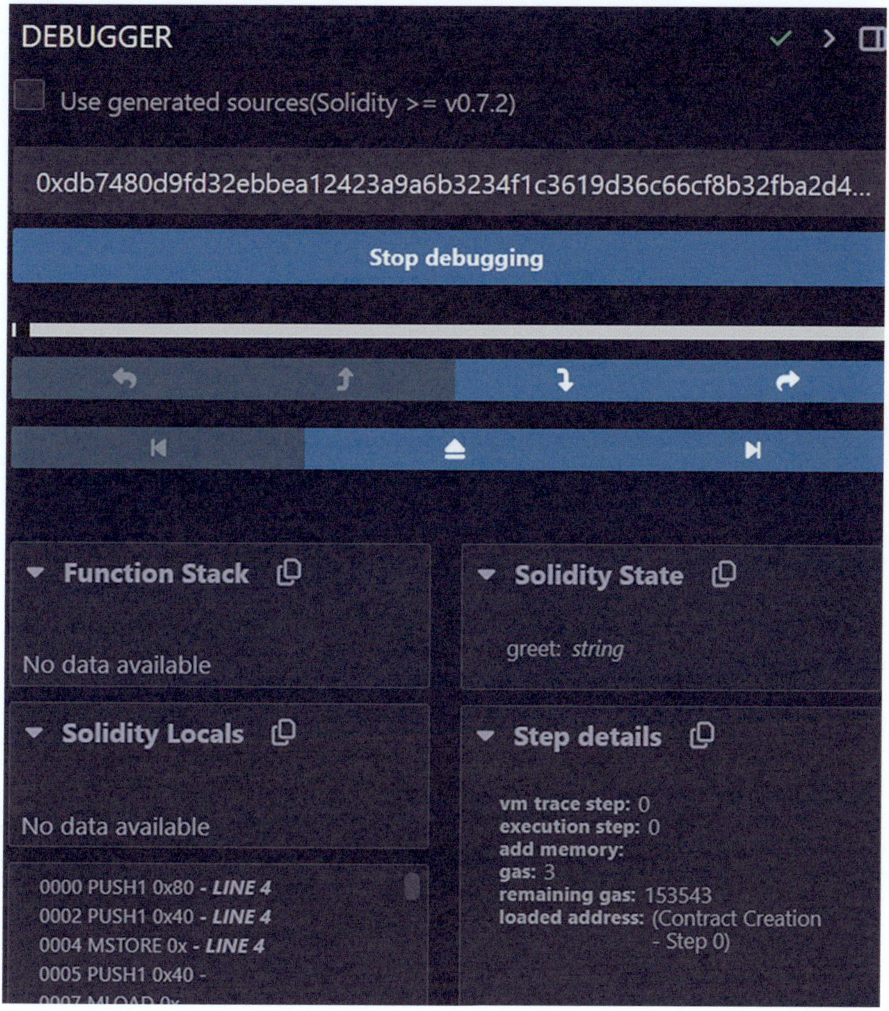

Fig. 14.15 The image of a Debugger

The first hash is for this transaction.

14.17 Contracts Verified

After clicking 'Stop Debug,' we will get the following message: When Debugging with a transaction hash, if the contract is verified, Remix will try to fetch the source code from Sourcify or Etherscan. Put in your Etherscan API key in the Remix settings. For supported networks, please see the Sourcify docs and https://etherscan.io/contractsVerified.

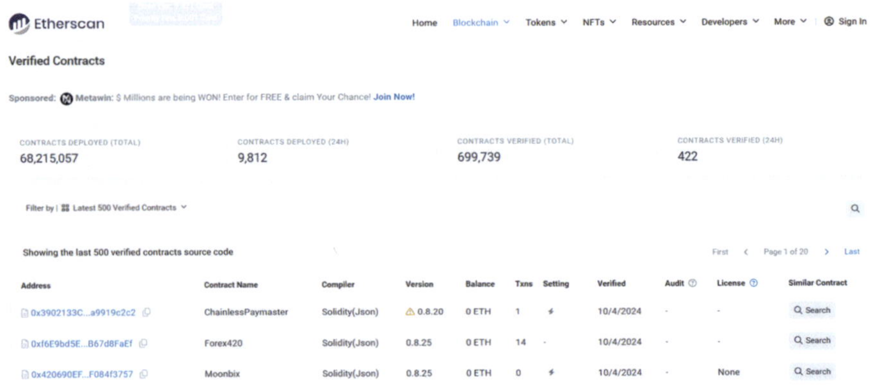

Fig. 14.16 Contract verification

14.18 Solidity Examples

At https://solidity-by-example.org/, we can find many examples of smart contracts. The first part is shown below.

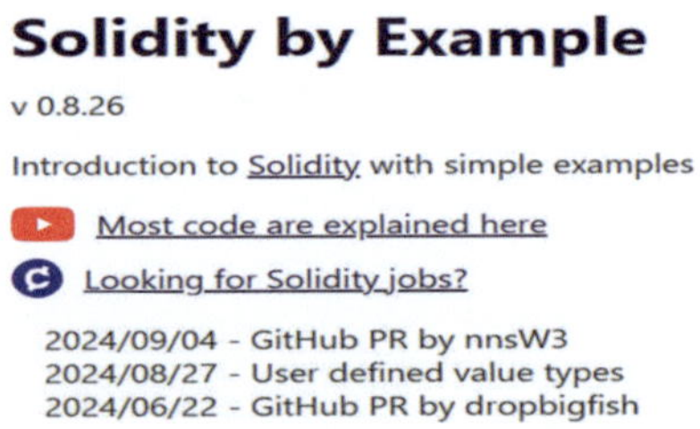

Fig. 14.17 Solidity by Example

The first several programs written in Solidity are shown below.

Fig. 14.18 Several examples

By clicking an individual program, we can see its code and even run it by launching Remix.

14.19 Linking Remix with MetaMask

To link Remix with MetaMask, follow the following procedure:

Step 1: Launch both the Remix IDE (https://remix.ethereum.org/) and MetaMask

Step 2: Go to the Deploy & Run Transactions tab on the left in Remix, as shown below.

Fig. 14.19 The Image of "Deploy & run transactions"

Step 3: Under Environment, choose "Injected Provider- MetaMask," shown below.

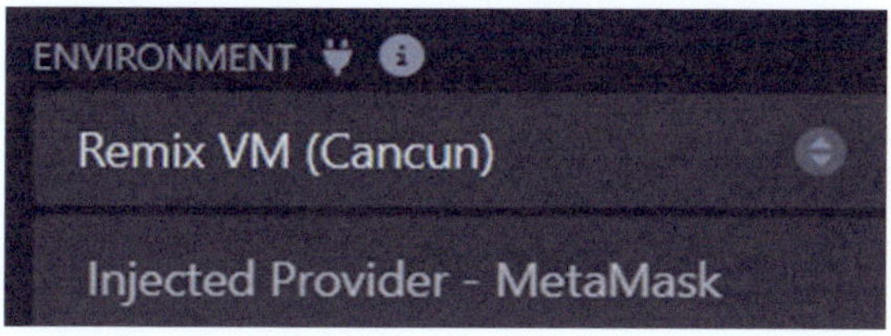

Fig. 14.20 "Injected Provider-MetaMask"

In Chapter 7: Cryptocurrency and Ganache, we learn about Ganache's primary usage. Remix (Ethereum IDE) can be connected to Ganache. Thus, we can deploy our Solidity smart contracts on a local blockchain instead of a public Ethereum network, making testing faster and cheaper. Below is the procedure.

Step 1: Launch both Ganache and Remix IDE (https://remix.ethereum.org/).

Step 2: Go to the Deploy & Run Transactions tab on the left in Remix, as shown below.

Fig. 14.21 Deploy & run transactions

Step 3: Under Environment, choose “Injected Provider -MetaMask,” as shown below.

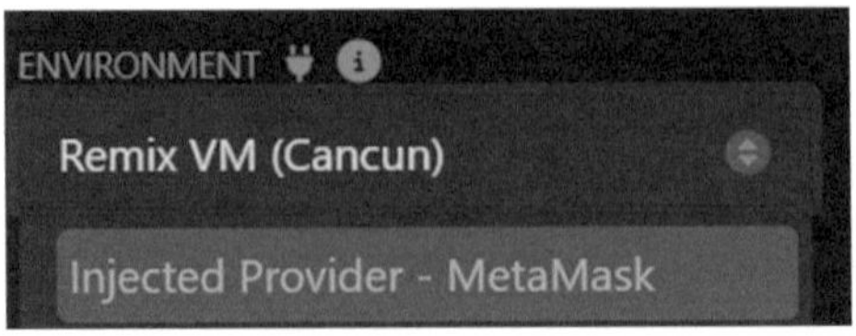

Fig. 14.22 “Injected Provider-MetaMask”

14.20 ERC20

ERC20 is a technical standard for creating and issuing smart contracts on the Ethereum blockchain, particularly for fungible tokens. It defines a standard set of rules that all Ethereum tokens following this standard must implement, including how tokens are transferred, balances are tracked, and ownership is managed. This ensures that ERC20 tokens are compatible with various wallets and exchanges.

Appendix A: Issue the Following Line of R Code for Week 15

source (“http://datayyy.com/i2ft/week15.tx)

```
*------------------------------------------------------------------------*
* Introduction to FinTech using Excel                        2025         *
*         (in an R-assisted learning environment)                         *
*------------------------------------------------------------------------*
*  .c1  Introduction and Excel Basics            .c16 R basics(optional)  *
*  .c2  Blockchain 1: (Numbers & alphanumeric)   .c17 Macro (optional)    *
*  .c3             2: (ASCII and Sha256)         .c18 VBA  (optional)     *
*  .c4  Ledger and distributed ledger                                     *
*  .c5  Cryptography   1: and public/private keys                         *
*  .c6                 2: Advanced                                        *
*  .c7  Cryptocurrency and Ganache                                        *
*  .c8                 2: markets, risk, risk/return tradeoff             *
*  .c9  Blockchain's Applications with Simulations                        *
*------------------------------------------------------------------------*
* .c10  Machine Learning in finance 1: Supervised Learning                *
* .c11                              2: Unsupervised Learning              *
* .c12                              3: Neural Network                     *
* .c13  Robo-Advisor and automated trading                                *
* .c14  Smart Contracts (the 2nd part could be optional)                  *
* .c15  Term projects                                                     *
* -----------------------------------------------------------------------*
* >.c15      # go to chapter 15                                           *
* >.uu       # go to utility submenu                                      *
* >.ft       # back to this menu                                          *
*------------------------------------------------------------------------*
```

Fig. 14.23 The menu for Week 15

Appendix B: Typing `.chapter14` to See the Contents Related to Chapter 14.

```
> .chapter14
function(i=0){
"i Chapter 14:Smart Contracts   i  Simple Solidity              i  Explanation
- ---------------------------   -- --------------------        -- ----------------------
1  Smart contracts              21 pragma (1st line)            41 Constructor
2  Metaphor: Vending machine    22 uint256                      42    : error 1
3           : go fund me        23 Remix live                   43    : error 2
4           : music event       24 Public variable              44 code #1: run without installation
5           : Rental box        25 Readme for Remix             45 explanation for
6           : escrow account    26 Comment lines                46 code #2: Storage
7 MetaMask                      27 Visibility Quantifiers       47 code #3: buy order
8   : Installation              28 Visibility example           48 Code  #4:    myContract
9 Solidity                      29 Solidity cheat sheets        49 Code #5:  CustomerAccount
10   EX 1: 'Hello World!'       30 GitHub's location 4 Solidity 50          : CustomerAccount 2
11        : verified            31 Remix online/starting point  51 Code #6: contract Owner
12 Alice &  Bob's conversations 32 Solidity examples            52 Enforcing Contract Terms
13        : code                33 Warning: SPDX license        53 Code #7: Owner
14        : Procedure           34 Version: pragma              54 Code #8: Ballot
15  Main features and documents 35 Hello World!                 55 safeMath
16  install Solidity on Windows 36 Contract: count              56 Implement Ether Management Functions
17  Procedure/One short video   37 IfElse                       57 Voter
18  solidity types              38 variable                     58 myToken
19  Videos                      39 Gas optimization             59 Underflow and overflow
20  Links                       40 Try/catch                    60 Using Python for smart contracts

 Example #1> .c14    # see the above list
 Example #2> .c14()  # the same as above
 Example #3> .c14(1) # see the 1st explanation
```

Fig. 14.24 The contents of Chapter 14

Exercises

Note that * indicates difficult ones.

14.1 Explain a smart contract and define how it differs from traditional contracts.

14.2 List and briefly describe three critical characteristics of a smart contract.

14.3 How does a blockchain facilitate the functioning of smart contracts? Provide a basic explanation.

14.4 Explain how smart contracts benefit from decentralization and transparency in blockchain networks.

14.5 Discuss the role of automation in smart contracts and provide an example of how it reduces manual intervention.

14.6 Explain what immutability means in the context of smart contracts and how it impacts contract execution.

14.7 Describe how smart contracts self-execute when predefined conditions are met. Provide an example.

14.8 List and briefly explain two practical use cases of smart contracts outside cryptocurrencies.

14.9 What are some limitations of smart contracts in the current technological landscape?

14.10 Compare traditional contracts with smart contracts regarding enforcement, execution, and cost.
14.11 How does removing third-party intermediaries in smart contracts affect transaction costs (Human Involvement)?
14.12 Do smart contracts have legal standing in most countries? Briefly discuss the challenges around legal recognition.
14.13 Identify the essential components of a smart contract, such as conditions, actions, and stakeholders.
14.14 Describe how a smart contract gets triggered and what its actions are once activated.
14.15 How is data stored and retrieved within smart contracts on the blockchain?
14.16 Design a basic smart contract scenario for a rental agreement, listing the parties involved, conditions, and outcomes.
14.17 Outline a primary use case of a smart contract for processing insurance claims. What conditions must be met for the contract to be executed?
14.18 Explain how a smart contract can be used in a crowdfunding campaign, ensuring funds are released only when the funding goal is reached.
14.19 Why is Ethereum considered the most popular platform for smart contracts? (without going deep into Solidity).
14.20 Ether as Gas: Explain the role of "gas" in executing a smart contract on the Ethereum blockchain.
14.21 How does the complexity of a smart contract affect transaction costs on a blockchain like Ethereum?
14.22 Discuss the risks associated with coding errors or vulnerabilities in smart contracts. Provide an example of a historical event where this caused issues.
14.23 Briefly describe a real-world example of a smart contract hack or failure. What could have been done differently to prevent it?
14.24 What industries are most likely to benefit from the widespread adoption of smart contracts? Provide two examples.
14.25 How do smart contracts fit into the broader FinTech ecosystem? Discuss the potential impact on financial services like lending or asset management.
14.26 What is MetaMask? What is its usage?
14.27 Can we use MetaMask to send or receive cryptocurrency?
14.28 Are there any cost implications when using MetaMask?
14.29 Can we link MetaMask with Remix?
14.30* At https://solidity-by-example.org, try the "Reading and Writing to a State Variable" sample program. Alternatively, try the link at https://solidity-by-example.org/state-variables/.
14.32* At https://solidity-by-example.org/hacks/denial-of-service/, try the Solidity function called "Denial of Service."

References

Avalanche, how do I manage the smart contract, https://support.avax.network/en/articles/6333375-explorer-how-do-i-manage-smart-contracts
Ethereum (ETH) Blockchain Explorer, https://etherscan.io
Ethereum Remix platform, https://remix.ethereum.org/
Ethereum, Introduction to Smark Contract, https://ethereum.org/en/smart-contracts/
Etherscan smart contracts search, https://etherscan.io/searchcontract
Solana smart contracts search, https://solana.com/docs/core/programs
Solidity by example ORG, https://solidity-by-example.org/
Szabo, Nick Szabo,1996, Smart Contracts: Building Blocks for Digital Markets, https://www.fon.hum.uva.nl/rob/Courses/InformationInSpeech/CDROM/Literature/LOTwinterschool2006/szabo.best.vwh.net/smart_contracts_2.html
How to write and deploy your first smart contract (freecodecamp.org). https://www.freecodecamp.org/news/how-to-write-and-deploy-your-first-smart-contract-341d5e2ffb35/
What is A Smart Contract? | Smart Contracts Tutorial | Smart Contracts in Blockchain | Simplilearn (youtube.com). https://www.youtube.com/watch?v=_J6G5g-nKg0&t=1s

Term Projects 15

To save space, most of this chapter will be accessible only online (see Appendices A and B for how to access it). Doing a term project is a good idea to check the knowledge of FinTech-related concepts and skills. The printed version of this chapter includes just a few sections, such as the Introduction, the Format of a Term Project, and the Basic Requirements. A list of potential projects is available online (see Appendix B).

15.1 Introduction

A term project is an invaluable opportunity to consolidate and apply the knowledge from a one-semester course like Introduction to FinTech using Excel. This hands-on activity allows students to synthesize concepts such as blockchain, cryptocurrency, encryption, and ledger systems in practical scenarios. By working on a project, students deepen their understanding of Excel functionalities and enhance their ability to use these tools for solving real-world FinTech problems. Whether creating financial models, simulating blockchain transactions, or analyzing cryptocurrency trends, the project bridges the gap between theoretical learning and industry-relevant applications, ensuring students leave the course with a tangible skill set.

Moreover, a term project fosters critical thinking, creativity, and collaboration, which are essential for succeeding in the rapidly evolving FinTech landscape. As students tackle challenges and implement solutions, they gain confidence in their ability to address complex problems independently. The project also serves as a portfolio piece, demonstrating their expertise to potential employers or academic programs. Ultimately, it transforms abstract concepts into actionable insights,

Y. Yan, *Introduction to FinTech using Excel*, Springer Texts in Business and Economics, https://doi.org/10.1007/978-3-031-89779-5_15

ensuring that the knowledge acquired during the course translates into meaningful professional growth.

15.2 The Basic Format for a Term Project

A term project could be a group project. If taking a course, students can form a small group with a maximum of 3. This structure is better since students can discuss related issues to improve their skills by learning from other students. In addition to a written report, a group presentation will help the whole class for the following reasons. First, students learn how to convey their ideas more effectively. Second, students can be exposed to other topics. Third, students' comments on others' topics could also earn them credit. For a list of potential term-project topics, please see Appendix B. To avoid duplications, choosing a topic will be on a first-come and first-served basis.

Appendix A: Issue the Following Line of R Code

```
source("http://datayyy.com/i2ft/week15.txt")
```

```
*----------------------------------------------------------------------*
* Introduction to FinTech using Excel               by Dr. Yan 2025   *
*      (in an R-assisted learning environment)                         *
*----------------------------------------------------------------------*
*   .c1  Introduction and Excel Basics                                 *
*   .c2  Blockchain 1: (Numbers & alphanumeric)                        *
*   .c3             2: (ASCII and Sha256)                              *
*   .c4  Ledger and distributed ledger                                 *
*   .c5  Cryptography    1: and public/private keys                    *
*   .c6                  2: Advanced                                   *
*   .c7  Cryptocurrency and Ganache                                    *
*   .c8                  2: markets, risk, risk/return tradeoff        *
*   .c9  Blockchain's Applications with Simulations                    *
*----------------------------------------------------------------------*
* .c10   Machine Learning  in Fin 1: Unsupervised Learning             *
* .c11                            2: Supervised Learning: classifications *
* .c12                                        : classifications        *
* .c13                            3: Neural Network/deep learning      *
* .c14   Smart Contracts                                               *
*----------------------------------------------------------------------*
* .c15   Term projects                                                 *
* .c16   R basics     (optional)                                       *
* .c17   Excel Macro (optional)                                        *
* .c18   Excel VBA    (optional)                                       *
*----------------------------------------------------------------------*
* >.c15       # go to chapter 15                                       *
* >.uu        # go to utility submenu                                  *
* >.ft        # back to this menu                                      *
*----------------------------------------------------------------------*
```

Fig. 15.1 The menu for Week 15

Appendix B: For a List of Projects, We Type .chapter15

```
> .chapter15
function(i=0){
"i  Chapter 15: Term Projects       i  Projects
 -  ----------------------------   --  ----------------------------
 1  Requirements                   21  Unsupervised learning 1
 2  'Data analysis' not available  22     :2
 3  'VBA' is not available         23     :3
 4  Blockchain: template 1         24     :4
 5             : template 2        25     :5
 6     :3 transaction data         26 Supervised learning
 7     :4                          27     : Retirement calculator
 8     :5                          28     : CAPM, FF3, FFC4, or FF5?
 9     :6                          29     : Test of the January Effect
10     :7                          30     : Bankruptcy prediction: Z-score
11  Public/private keys            31  Neural Network 1
12     :2                          32     :2
13     :3                          33     :3
14     :4                          34     :4
15  Signature 1                    35     :5
16     :2                          36 Smart contract 1
17     :3                          37     :2
18     :4                          38     :3
19  Videos                         39     :4
20  Links                          40  Topics taken already (updated on mm/dd/yyyy)

 Example 1:>.c15      # see the above list
 Example 2:>.c15()    # see the above list
 Example 3:>.c15(1)   # see the first explanation
```

Fig. 15.2 The contents of Chapter 15

R Installation and Basics

16

This chapter is optional. Like the previous chapter, most of this chapter will be accessible only online (see Appendix A for how to access it). Excel is the computational tool for this book (course). However, Excel is far from enough. Because of this, we have designed an "R-assisted Learning Environment." In other words, readers, students, and potential instructors must know just two lines of R code (discussed in Sect. 16.2). Even for those two lines, learners can adopt a Copy-and-Paste strategy. This chapter teaches the basic R-related concepts and techniques, such as assigning values to a new variable, whether R is case-sensitive, how to use the embedded R functions, and how to find help for a given function.

16.1 R Installation

We must install R software before accessing our rich materials beyond the printed book. To install R, we have the following steps:

Step 1: Go to http://r-project.org/
Step 2: Click "CRAN" on the left.
Step 3: Choose a server nearby.
Step 4: Choose the appropriate type, such as Windows or Mac.
Step 5: Download.

The above software is R Console, which is simple. Alternatively, learners can download and use RStudio, which is used more frequently by more experienced R programmers, at https://www.rstudio.com/products/rstudio/download/. For this book, R Console, i.e., the first method, is good enough.

Y. Yan, *Introduction to FinTech using Excel*, Springer Texts in Business and Economics, https://doi.org/10.1007/978-3-031-89779-5_16

16.2 Two Lines of R Code

The first line of R code activates the functions we have written. For example, we issue the following line to get the first week's materials.

```
source("http://datayyy.com/i2ft/week1.txt")
```

For other weeks, we replace 1 with another integer. The second line is to install an R package. For example, we issue the following line to install the `qrcode` R package.

```
install.packages("qrcode")
```

Appendix A: To Access the Materials Related to Chapter 16, We Issue the Following Lines

```
source("http://datayyy.com/i2ft/week15.txt")
.chapter16
```

```
> .chapter16
function(i=0){
" i  Chapter 16: R basics (optional)            i  Value Assignment and simple Functions
  -  -----------------------------------       --  -------------------------------------
  1  Download and install R                    21  Assignment without defining it
  2  Launch/quit R, one line for this course   22  Three ways to assign a value
  3  Comment line and comment paragraph        23  Upper and down arrow keys
  4  3 ways to assign a value/values           24  One benefit of -> assignment
  5  Use the up and down arrow keys            25  String variable
  6  R is case sensitive                       26  typeof() function
  7  Normal operations: +, -, /, ^ (power)     27  x<-c(1,10)
  8  listing function ls()                     28  .nLetterFunctions
  9  remove a variable or several variables    29  scan() function
 10  remove all variables                      30  x=1:100
 11  use meaningful variable names             31  seq() function
 12  current working directory                 32  read.table('clipboard')
 13  head() and tail() functions               33  help(read.table)
 14  mean() and sd()                           34  readline() function
 15  put several commands on one line          35  mean() and sd() functions
 16  The simplest function                     36  other embedded functions
 17  use .nLetterFunctions()                   37  Precision of R
 18  use the help()  function                  38  .Machine
 19  Videos
 20  Links

  Example #1:>.c16    # see the above list
  Example #2:>.c16()  # same as the above
  Example #3:>.c16(1) # see the first explanation
```

Fig. 16.1 The contents of chapter 16

Excel Macros 17

Like the previous chapter, this one is optional and can only be accessed online (see Appendices A and B for how to access it). This chapter will briefly explain the Excel Macro language and how to use the so-called copy-and-paste method to use others' Macros. A good strategy is recommended when using others' Macros. A few simple examples are used as an illustration.

17.1 Introduction

The Excel Macro is a valuable tool for using Excel. However, teaching the Macro language is beyond the scope of this book. On the other hand, learning a programming language such as R is a much better investment than learning the Macro language. Students/readers can use the copy-and-paste method to choose the appropriate Macro among our close to 50 Macros. In addition, we will show how to use record users' own Macro.

17.2 If "Developer" Is Not Available

If "Developer" is unavailable on your menu bar, we will do the following steps to activate it.

Step 1: Click 'File'.
Step 2: Click 'Options'.
Step 3: Click 'Customize Ribbon'.
Step 4: Activate 'developer' and click 'OK'.

Y. Yan, *Introduction to FinTech using Excel*, Springer Texts in Business and Economics, https://doi.org/10.1007/978-3-031-89779-5_17

17.3 Copy-and-Paste a Macro

Below, we show how to copy a Macro to clean your Excel spreadsheet from A1 to N50. After cleaning the range, the cursor will return to cell A1. The Marco is shown below.

```
Sub clean()
    Range("A1:N50"). Select
    Selection.Delete Shift:=xlToLeft
    Range("A1"). Select
End Sub
```

The procedure is given below.

Step 1: Copy the above the Macro.
Step 2: Click "Developer", then "Macros".
Step 3: Enter `tt` as the name .
Step 4: Click "Create." (You will see the following three lines.)

```
Sub tt()
End Sub
```

Step 5: Replace the above three lines with your copied Macro.
Step 6: Click "File" then "Close and Return to Microsoft Excel."

To run the Macro, we click "Developer,", "Macros," then choose a proper Macro and click "Run," as shown below.

Fig. 17.1 The image of a Macro

17.4 A Strategy to Work with Others' Macros

This book offers a limited number of Macros. Thus, searching online using a keyword to find an appropriate Macro is fantastic. However, users may find specific error messages. Our recommendation is 'Don't try to debug others' Macros. Just abandon it and try to find another useable Macro. This will save users tons of effort and time.

17.5 Recording Your Macro

One simple but beneficial technique is to record your own Macro. Assume that we want to generate a Macro to clean our spreadsheet. After that, move our cursor to cell A1. The procedure is shown below.

Step 1: Click "Developer," then "Record Macro," as shown below.

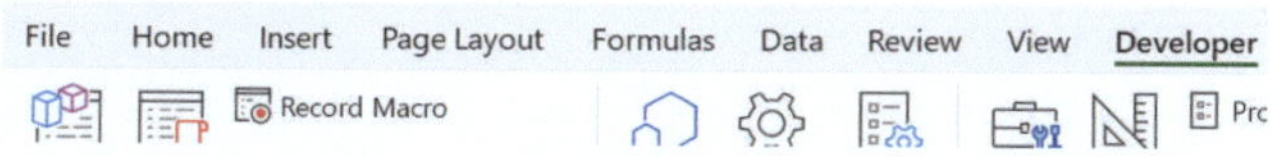

Fig. 17.2 The location of "Developer" on the Excel menu bar

Step 2: Give a name or use the default one. Enter a shortcut key, shown below.

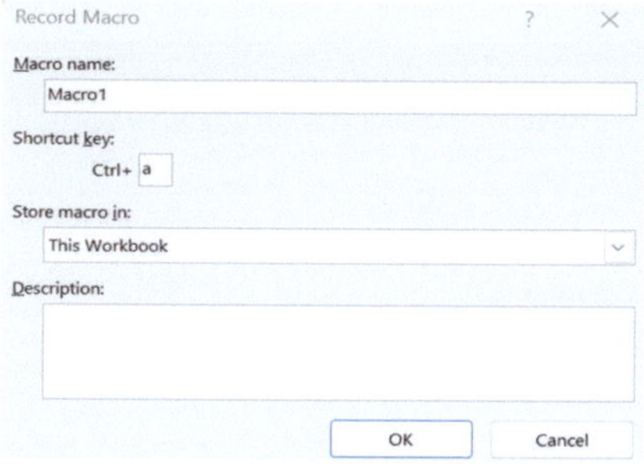

Fig. 17.3 Entering a Macro name and ctrl-a

Step 3: Choose an area and delete everything. After that, move your cursor to A1.
Step 4: Click 'Stop Recording'.

There are two ways to run this Macro. The first method is to click "Developer," "Macro," choose the name, and click "Run." The second method uses two keys, "Ctrl-A," to run it.

Appendix A: We Issue Two Lines to Access Chapter 17's Materials

```
source("http://datayyy.com/i2ft/week15.txt")
.chapter17
```

```
> .chapter17
function(i=0){
"i  Chapter 17: Simple Macros   i   Explanation                           i   Introduction to FinTech
 -  -------------------------   --  ----------------------------------    --  ----------------
 1  Developer not available     21  Macro 4 cleaning                      41  increase H4'value by 1
 2  Record the simplest Macro   22  Macro 4 hiding   columns              42  calculate letter frequencies
 3  How to run a Marco?         23  Macro 4 unhiding columns              43  Rotate Rotor #1
 4  How to edit a macro         24  Macro 4 hiding   rows
 5  A simple macro              25  Macro 4 unhiding rows
 6  Recording short-cut: Ctrl-a 26  Macro 4 creating a pie
 7  Assign a shortcut key       27  Macro 4 adding 10
 8  Message box: Hello World!   28  Macro 4 copying from one cell to another
 9  Copy others macros          29  Macro 4 copying to the current cell
10  Ctrl-d to clean             30  Macro 4 generating five 9
11  Ctrl-h to hide              31  Macro 4 generating 1,3, 5, ...,
12  Ctrl-u to unhide            32  Macro 4 double loops
13  Extension should be *.xlsm  33  Macro 4 assigning z to (x,y): x,y,z in A1,A2,A3
14  Link a button to a Macro    34  Macro 4 printing a multiple-line message box
15  call Macros from a Macro    35  Macro 4 printing your instruction
16  If left cell empty-> Done   36  Macro 4 (input box and save to A1)
17  Move 1 cell to the right    37  Macro 4 deleting the range of A1:Z100
18  Move down/up/right/left     38  Macro 4 unhide 1st column/1st row
19  A set of one-line commands  39  Macro 4 add_a row_column (Binomial tree option model)
20  Links                       40  Macro 4 clean (Binomial tree option model)

 Example #1:>.c17    # see the above list
 Example #2:>.c17()  # the same as the above
 Example #3:>.c17(1) # see the 1st explanation
```

Fig. 17.4 The contents of Chapter 17

Excel VBA

18

Like the previous two chapters, this one is optional and can only be accessed online (see Appendices A and B for how to access it). This chapter will briefly explain Excel VBA (Visual Basic Applications) and how to use the so-called copy-and-paste method to use others' VBA. A few examples are used as an illustration.

18.1 Introduction

Excel VBA (Visual Basic Applications) is quite a valuable tool for using Excel. However, teaching VBA is beyond the scope of this book. On the other hand, learning a programming language such as R is a much better investment than learning VBA. Students/readers can use the copy-and-paste method to choose the appropriate VBAs among our close to 50 VBAs students can use them. When an error occurs, users will adopt the same strategy as when dealing with Excel Macros: dump the VBA without trying to debug it and then search for an executable one.

18.2 Copy-and-Paste a Simple VBA

The `effect()` function can be used for Excel to calculate the EAR (Effective Annual Rate). Students might wonder why a function called `EAR()` does not exist in the first place. We can use the following VBA to achieve this.

Supplementary Information The online version contains supplementary material available at https://doi.org/10.1007/978-3-031-89779-5_18.

Y. Yan, *Introduction to FinTech using Excel*, Springer Texts in Business and Economics, https://doi.org/10.1007/978-3-031-89779-5_18

```
Function EAR(APR,npery) As Variant
  EAR=(1+APR/npery)^npery-1
End Function
Function EARhelp() As String
  EARhelp = "usage: =EAR(APR,compounding_freq)"
End Function
```

The second function is a help function that shows related help. Below is the procedure for copying and pasting the above VBAs.

Step 1: Copy the above two VBA
Step 2: From Excel, click 'Developer' on the menu bar, "VBA", "Insert", then click "Module"
Step 3: Paste the above VBAs, as shown below.

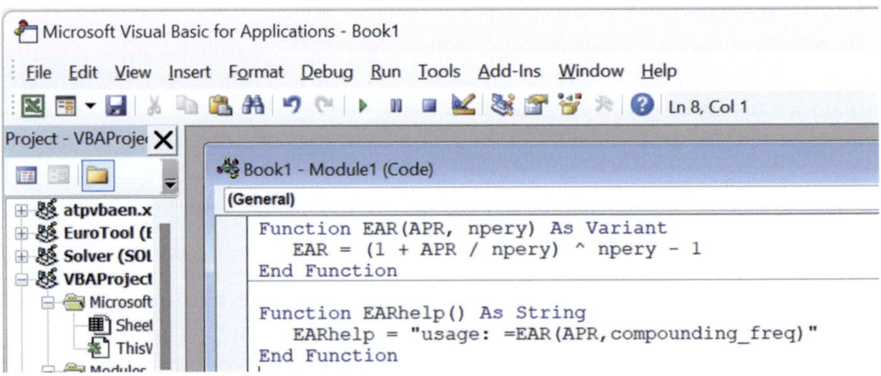

Fig. 18.1 The image of a VBA Module

Step 4: Click "File", then "Close and Return to Microsoft Excel."
Now, we can use both functions; see below.

	A	B	C	D	E	F
1		usage: =EAR(APR,compounding_freq)				=EARhelp()
2		0.1025				=EAR(0.1,2)

Fig. 18.2 The EAR VBA example

The second example is more advantageous since Excel has no equivalent function! The Excel `effect()` offers an Effective Annual Rate plus a compounding frequency for a given annual rate. How about the Effective Quarterly Rate and Effective Weekly Rate? The following VBA would achieve this.

```
Function EFFECTyan (APR1 As Variant, n1 As Integer, n2 As Integer)
As Variant
' author yuxing.yan date: 2/4/2013
  Dim i, n, roduct As String
  If n1 > 365 And n2 > 365 Then
    EFFECTyan = APR1
  ElseIf n1 > 365 And n2 < 365 Then
    EFFECTyan = Exp(APR1) ^ (1 / n2) - 1
  ElseIf n1 < 365 And n2 > 365 Then
    EFFECTyan = n1 * Log(1 + APR1 / n1)
  Else
    EFFECTyan = (1 + APR1 / n1) ^ (n1 / n2) - 1
  End If
End Function
Function effectYanHelp() As String
effectYanHelp= "usage: =effectYan(APR1,n1,n2)"
End Function
```

Several examples are shown below.

	A	B	C	D	E	F
1		usage: =effectYan(APR1,n1,n2)			=EffectYanHelp()	
2		0.0247			=EffectYan(0.1,2,4)	
3		0.1025			=EffectYan(0.1,2,1)	
4		0.00826			=EffectYan(0.1,4,12)	

Fig. 18.3 The EffectYan VBA example

Appendix A: To Access the Materials Related to Chapter 18, We Issue the Following Two Lines

```
source("http://datayyy.com/i2ft/week15.txt")
.chapter18
```

```
> .chapter18
function(i=0){
" i  Chapter 18: Simple VBAs                         i   Descriptin                   i   Description
 -  ------------------------------------------       --  -------------------          --  ------------
  1 VBA If 'Developer' is not available              26 VBA 4 finding duplicates (2)      51 VBA 4 Sortino ratio
  2 VBA How to copy-and-paste other's VBA?           27 VBA 4 freqGivenNumber             52 VBA 4 todayPrice()
  3 VBA After you copy and paste other's VBA         28 VBA 4 fvGrowingAnnuity            53 VBA 4 varGivenProb
  4 VBA 4 APR2APR                                    29 VBA 4 fvNoSign() function
  5 VBA 4 APR2effect                                 30 VBA 4 generating a var-cov matrix
  6 VBA 4 Black-Scholes-Merton call option           31 VBA 4 geomeanYan() geomean 4 ret
  7 VBA 4 Black-Scholes-Merton put (no dividend)     32 VBA 4 Linear reg: T,R,E
  8 VBA 4 Black pricing European options on futures  33 VBA 4 Linear reg:T,R,E
  9 VBA 4 bond bond price                            34 VBA 4 links
 10 VBA 4 bond convexity                             35 VBA 4 LPSD
 11 VBA 4 Bond duration                              36 VBA 4 meanGivenProb
 12 VBA 4 Cholesky decomposition                     37 VBA 4 Modified duration
 13 VBA 4 converting 23.23 to words                  38 VBA 4 noRepeats
 14 VBA 4 converting miles to km                     39 VBA 4 npvTrue()/npvYan() functions
 15 VBA 4 doubling an input value                    40 VBA 4 others
 16 VBA 4 downloading several years' fin statements  41 VBA 4 payback period
 17 VBA 4 durationYan                                42 VBA 4 pGivenT_1sided()
 18 VBA 4 DW test (Durin-Watson autocorrelation test) 43 VBA 4 pGivenT2sided()
 19 VBA 4 EAR (Effective Annual Rate)                44 VBA 4 pv of growing perpeturity
 20 VBA 4 effective rate conversion: EFFECTyan()     45 VBA 4 pvGrowingAnnuity
 21 VBA 4 estimating a correlation matrix            46 VBA 4 pvNoSign() fucntion
 22 VBA 4 estimating mean                            47 VBA 4 pvPerpetuity
 23 VBA 4 estimating the area                        48 VBA 4 removing errors
 24 VBA 4 financial statements (2)                   49 VBA 4 secondHighestValue
 25 VBA 4 finding duplicates                         50 VBA 4 showFormula() function

  Example #1:>.c18       # find out the above list
  Example #2:>.c18()     # the same as the above
  Example #3:>.c18(1)    # see the first explanation
```

Fig. 18.4 The contents of Chapter 18

Index

Y. Yan, *Introduction to FinTech using Excel*, Springer Texts in Business and Economics, https://doi.org/10.1007/978-3-031-89779-5

MIX
Papier aus verantwortungsvollen Quellen
Paper from responsible sources
FSC® C105338

If you have any concerns about our products,
you can contact us on
ProductSafety@springernature.com

In case Publisher is established outside the EU,
the EU authorized representative is:
Springer Nature Customer Service Center GmbH
Europaplatz 3, 69115 Heidelberg, Germany

Printed by Libri Plureos GmbH
in Hamburg, Germany